Reading Disorders

VARIETIES AND TREATMENTS

This is a volume in

PERSPECTIVES IN
NEUROLINGUISTICS, NEUROPSYCHOLOGY,
    AND PSYCHOLINGUISTICS

A Series of Monographs and Treatises

A complete list of titles in this series appears at the end of this volume.

Reading Disorders

VARIETIES AND TREATMENTS

Edited by

R. N. MALATESHA

School of Education
Oregon State University
Corvallis, Oregon

P. G. AARON

Department of Educational Psychology
Indiana State University
Terre Haute, Indiana

With a Foreword by
O. L. ZANGWILL

ACADEMIC PRESS 1982
A Subsidiary of Harcourt Brace Jovanovich, Publishers

New York   London
Paris   San Diego   San Francisco   São Paulo   Sydney   Tokyo   Toronto

ACADEMIC PRESS, INC.
111 Fifth Avenue, New York, New York 10003

United Kingdom Edition published by
ACADEMIC PRESS, INC. (LONDON) LTD.
24/28 Oval Road, London NW1   7DX

Library of Congress Cataloging in Publication Data
Main entry under title:

Reading disorders.

   (Perspectives in neurolinguistics, neuropsychology,
and psycholinguistics)
   Includes bibliographies and index.
   1. Dyslexia.   2. Alexia.   3. Reading disability.
I. Malatesha, R. N.   II. Aaron, P. G.   III. Series.
RC394.W6R4   616.85'53   82-4039
ISBN 0-12-466320-6   AACR2

PRINTED IN THE UNITED STATES OF AMERICA

82 83 84 85   9 8 7 6 5 4 3 2 1

To Bill Kern, Frank Jerse, David Turney, and Chuck Stamps
Who, in the final analysis, were responsible for it.

Contents

Part One.   Developmental Dyslexia

Section One.   Neuropsychological Aspects

Chapter One
The Neuropsychology of Developmental Dyslexia

P. G. AARON

Chapter Two
Clinical Subtypes of Developmental Dyslexia:
Resolution of an Irresolute Problem

R. N. MALATESHA and DEBORAH R. DOUGAN

Chapter Three
Typology of Developmental Dyslexia:
Evidence for Its Construct Validity

JOSEPH H. ROSENTHAL, ELENA BODER, and ENOCH CALLAWAY

Chapter Four
Component Processes in Reading Disabilities: Neuropsychological
Investigation of Distinct Reading Subskill Deficits

H. GERRY TAYLOR, JACK M. FLETCHER, and PAUL SATZ

Section Two.   Cognitive Aspects

Chapter Five
Cognitive Models of Reading: Implications for Assessment
and Treatment of Reading Disability

ROBERT CALFEE

Chapter Six
Reading Disorders and Information-Processing Disorders

J. RISPENS

Chapter Seven
The Role of Selective Attention in Reading Disability

MARCEL KINSBOURNE

Section Three.   Biological Aspects

Chapter Eight
The Neurobiology of Developmental Reading Disorders

FRANCIS J. PIROZZOLO and EDWARD C. HANSCH

Part Two.   Acquired Alexia

Part Three.   Treatment

Chapter Seventeen
Dyslexia in Adolescents

CARL L. KLINE

Chapter Eighteen
The Orton–Gillingham Approach to Remediation in
Developmental Dyslexia

ALICE ANSARA

Chapter Nineteen
Services for College Dyslexics

BARBARA K. CORDONI

Chapter Twenty
Differential Treatment of Reading Disability
of Diverse Etiologies

P. G. AARON, SONDRA L. GRANTHAM,
and NANCY CAMPBELL

Chapter Twenty-One
Psychotropic Drugs in the Treatment of Reading Disorders

MICHAEL G. AMAN

Chapter Twenty-Two
Adult Outcome of Reading Disorders

OTFRIED SPREEN

Contributors

Numbers in parentheses indicate the pages on which the authors' contributions begin.

P. G. AARON, Ph.D. (5, 449), Department of Educational Psychology, Indiana State University, Terre Haute, Indiana 47809

MICHAEL G. AMAN, Ph.D. (453), Department of Psychiatry, School of Medicine, University of Auckland, Auckland, New Zealand

ALICE ANSARA[1] (409), Bulletin of The Orton Society, Towson, Maryland 21204

ELENA BODER, M.D. (93), Department of Pediatrics (Pediatric Neurology), School of Medicine, University of California, Los Angeles, Los Angeles, California 90042

ROBERT CALFEE, Ph.D. (151), School of Education, Stanford University, Stanford, California 94305

ENOCH CALLAWAY, M.D. (93), Langley Porter Neuropsychiatric Institute, University of California Medical Center, San Francisco, California 94143

NANCY D. CAMPBELL, M.A. (449), Community Services Division, Hamilton Center Inc., Terre Haute, Indiana 47804

BARBARA K. CORDONI, Ed.D. (435), Department of Special Education, Southern Illinois University, Carbondale, Illinois 62901

ANTONIO R. DAMASIO, M.D. (305), Division of Behavioral Neurology, University of Iowa, College of Medicine, Iowa City, Iowa 52242

J. C. DeFRIES, Ph.D. (255), Institute for Behavioral Genetics, University of Colorado, Boulder, Colorado 80309

SADIE N. DECKER, Ph.D. (255), Institute for Behavioral Genetics, University of Colorado, Boulder, Colorado 80309

[1]Deceased.

DEBORAH R. DOUGAN, M.A. (69), Program in Educational Neuroscience, School of Education, Oregon State University, Corvallis, Oregon 97331

HERMAN T. EPSTEIN, Ph.D. (293), Department of Biology, Brandeis University, Waltham, Massachusetts 02254

JAMES R. EVANS, Ph.D. (371), Department of Psychology, University of South Carolina, Columbia, South Carolina 29208

JACK M. FLETCHER, Ph.D. (121), Neuropsychology Research, Texas Research Institute of Mental Sciences, Texas Medical Center, Houston, Texas 77030

SONDRA L. GRANTHAM, M.A. (449), University School, Indiana State University, Terre Haute, Indiana 47809

EDWARD C. HANSCH, Ph.D. (215), Department of Psychology, University of Minnesota, Minneapolis, Minnesota 55455

KENNETH M. HEILMAN, M.D. (315), Department of Neurology, J. Hillis Miller Health Center, University of Florida, College of Medicine, Gainesville, Florida 32610

JOHN R. HUGHES, M.D., Ph.D., D.M. (Oxon) (233), Department of Neurology, University of Illinois Medical Center, Chicago, Illinois 60612

MARCEL KINSBOURNE, M.D. (199), Behavioral Neurology Department, Eunice Kennedy Shriver Center, 200 Trapelo Road, Waltham, Massachusetts 02254

CARL L. KLINE, M.D., F.R.C.P. (389), Department of Psychology, Faculty of Medicine, University of British Columbia, Vancouver, British Columbia, V52 1K1 Canada

HELGARD KREMIN, Ph.D. (341), Unité de Recherches, Neurophysiologique et Neurolinguistiques de l' INSERM, Laboratoire de Pathologie du Language de l'E.H.E.S.S., École Pratique des Hautes Études, E.R.A. No. 274 au C. N. R. S., Paris, France

R. N. MALATESHA, Ph.D. (69), Program in Educational Foundations and Reading, School of Education, Oregon State University, Corvallis, Oregon 97331

FRANCIS J. PIROZZOLO, Ph.D. (215), Department of Neurology, Baylor College of Medicine, Texas Medical Center, Houston, Texas 77030

J. RISPENS, Ph.D. (177), Rijksuniversiteit Groningen, Instituut voor Orthopedagogiek, 9712 GA Groningen, The Netherlands

JOSPEH H. ROSENTHAL, M.D., Ph.D. (93), Learning Disabilities Clinic, Department of Pediatrics, Kaiser-Permanente Medical Center, Oakland, California 94611

LESLIE J. ROTHI, Ph.D. (315), Veterans Administration Medical Center, Gainesville, Florida 32610

PAUL SATZ, Ph.D. (121), Director of Research, Camarillo State Hospital, Camarillo, California 93010

OTFRIED SPREEN, Ph.D. (473), Department of Psychology, University of Victoria, Victoria, British Columbia, V8W 2Y2, Canada

H. GERRY TAYLOR, Ph.D. (121), Department of Pediatrics, Child Development Unit, Children's Hospital of Pittsburgh, 125 DeSota Street, Pittsburgh, Pennsylvania 15213

NILS R. VARNEY, Ph.D. (305), Veterans Administration Medical Center and Department of Neurology, University of Iowa College of Medicine, Iowa City, Iowa 52242

MARYANNE WOLF, Ph.D. (281), Eliot-Pearson Department of Child Study, Tufts University, Medford, Massachusetts 02155

This volume is devoted to reading disabilities, more especially the difficulties in learning to read which are not uncommon among schoolchildren of good intelligence who are entirely free from emotional problems and certainly do not lack adequate educational opportunity. Such difficulties, which are nowadays referred to as *specific or developmental dyslexia*, were first recognized toward the end of the last century by Morgan, Hinshelwood, and others and were termed "congenital word-blindness" in view of their superficial similarity to the acquired dyslexias in adults resulting from cortical lesions involving the posterior portions of the left cerebral hemisphere. Indeed "congenital word-blindness" was regarded by Hinshelwood as due to maldevelopment of those areas of the cortex, in particular the angular gyrus, which he believed to store the images of words and which he thought were essential to reading. More important, perhaps, was the observation by Hinshelwood, Stephenson, and others that "congenital word-blindness" not uncommonly runs in families. Stephenson reported a striking instance of six cases in three generations of the same family. This familial tendency to backwardness in reading, not uncommonly associated with related handicaps in the acquisition of skills—linguistic, and on occasion motor—has been repeatedly described in recent years as a common, though by no means necessary, condition of reading disability in schoolchildren. At the same time, it undoubtedly suggests a genetic influence in the causation of the disorder.

Although "congenital word-blindness" aroused some interest among doctors in the earlier decades of this century, it was some time before it attracted the attention of psychologists, many of whom were at first deeply skeptical of its existence. A notable exception, however, was Lucy G. Fildes, who in 1921 published a noteworthy paper in the neurological journal *Brain*. This was an experimental study of 26 subjects diagnosed as cases of "congenital word-blindness," though in fact many of them were also mentally subnormal. Moreover, Fildes found no relation whatsoever between IQ as measured by the Terman Scale and reading performance: Indeed, one of the two poorest readers in her group was reported to be of superior intelligence. It might therefore seem that Fildes was the first to establish the relative independence of intelligence and reading attainment in backward children.

The somewhat informal experiments reported by Fildes were mainly concerned with the adequacy of form and pattern discrimination, short-term memory, and associative learning. Her results indicated that whereas visual form and pattern perception were essentially normal, there was definite weakness in verbal short-term memory and, more significantly, in associative learning, either visual, verbal, or both. While stressing that nothing in her experimental results indicated the existence of a "visual word-center," she evidently regarded the condition as essentially a learning disability. Few people today would disagree with her conclusion.

Despite Fildes's skepticism regarding "word-blindness," the term continued to be used by pediatricians and others well into the 1920s. Indeed, it featured in the title of Orton's famous paper, "Word-blindness in Schoolchildren" published in 1926, although he abandoned it in his later writings. As is widely recognized today, Orton's work led not only to reading difficulties in children being approached along essentially neurological lines but also to a novel conception of their causation in terms of laterality and cerebral dominance, which for many years exerted considerable influence upon psychologists and teachers. It also led to new lines of research, not only on handedness and its possible relationship to the origin of reading disorders but also on stuttering and related impediments of oral fluency. From a practical point of view, Orton did much to stress the need for the remedial treatment of backwardness in reading and devised several methods which still have their advocates today.

At the same time, Orton's conception of developmental dyslexia as a congenital neurological syndrome has been recognized as having many shortcomings. In the first place, his theory of "strephosymbolia" was bound up with a concept of mirror-representation of words in the nondominant cerebral hemisphere, which even in its more sophisticated recent formulations by Noble and by Corballis and Beale is unlikely to convince hard-headed neuroscientists. In any case, there can be no doubt that Orton grossly overrated both the incidence and the significance of reversal errors in the reading and writing of dyslexic subjects and although they undoubtedly occur, and sometimes persist until a relatively late age, it is most improbable that they possess any outstanding importance. In the second place, it has now become apparent that left or mixed handedness, or discrepant lateral preferences as between hand, foot, and eye, though by no means uncommon in dyslexic subjects or in their families, are neither a necessary nor a sufficient condition of severe backwardness in reading. While there is much to be said for Orton's attempt to explain reading, writing, and speech problems within the framework of developmental neurology, it seems unlikely that a fully satisfactory explanation will be formulated solely in terms of functional lateralization and anomalies of cerebral dominance.

Possibly because of these shortcomings, the impact of Orton's work on psychology has been a good deal less productive than might have been anticipated. Although it did inspire a certain amount of experimental research in the 1920s and 1930s on handedness and shift of handedness in relation to both stuttering and the problem of dyslexia, much of this work was on a comparatively small scale and paid scant attention to the very varied constitution of the groups of backward readers chosen to study. Whereas some may have been truly congenital dyslexics in Orton's sense, many were merely backward or disadvantaged readers who performed poorly on reading attainment tests. Among educational psychologists, especially, there was little understanding of the genetic and neurological issues involved in recalcitrant disorders of reading or of the possible relations between reading skill and the lateralization of cortical function. It is only in quite recent years that developments in neuropsychology have brought a new perspective into research on educational disabilities and an awareness of the limitations of large-scale studies of heterogeneous groups of backward readers of diverse history, background, and composition.

On the positive side, neuropsychology has brought about a realization that the concept of cerebral lateralization of function goes far beyond its traditional links with handedness and the cerebral representation of speech. This advance owes much to the increasing opportunities open to psychologists since the end of World War II to work with neurological patients and to explore in depth the differential effects of unilateral lesions of the major and minor hemispheres. Not unrelated to this is the widespread interest aroused by the developments of new techniques of radical surgery, in particular hemispherectomy and commissurotomy, and the brilliant experimental studies of Roger Sperry and his colleagues on the effects of hemisphere disconnection in healthy human subjects. At present, it is true, these techniques have very real limitations, and interpretation of their findings is often controversial. Nonetheless, they have opened the way to a fresh understanding of the functions of the cerebral hemispheres, whether considered in relative isolation or in their total integrative capacity.

It must not be forgotten, too, that these advances in neuropsychological technique are closely bound up with new approaches to the theoretical treatment of general psychological issues. Nowhere is this more apparent than in contemporary approaches to the psychology of human intellectual functions, in particular, language and communication. In this field, particularly, we are witnessing a virtual revolution brought about by the coalescence of ideas in human information processing, cognitive psychology, and artificial intelligence. Model making, particularly of the brain, is today a flourishing trade and while it runs the risk of producing models too remote from biological reality to cohere with prevailing modes of thought in the neurosciences, it nonetheless serves an essential purpose in generating fresh experiment and thereby catalyzing scientific advance.

The editors of this volume have organized their voluminous material in three major parts, varying widely in length, style, and coverage. The first, and by far the longest part, is devoted to developmental dyslexia and comprises three sections, covering general neuropsychological aspects, cognitive aspects, and biological issues, respectively. Although there is inevitably some overlap, the many contributors on the whole succeed well in focusing on areas of the subject in which they possess special experience, and they have evidently been encouraged to develop their own points of view. The length of this part of the book, although it might seem excessive in relation to the two succeeding parts, may be amply justified in terms of the interest which developmental reading and writing problems nowadays attract and their obvious educational and social significance.

The second part, consisting of only three chapters, provides an account of reading difficulties that may present in adults who have sustained circumscribed brain lesions. While these alexias, as they are known in clinical neurology, are usually associated with aphasia and often also with agraphia, they may occasionally present in relatively "pure" form without significant impairment in other aspects of language or communication. Their inclusion here testifies to the editors' good sense in reminding us that the study of developmental dyslexia had its origins in what Macdonald Critchley has called the "aphasiological context" and its implication that, in the long run, both developmental and acquired dyslexia will find explanation within a common neuropsychological framework. At the same time, it is a pity that no author was found to produce an authoritative contribution on acquired dyslexia in children.

The last part deals with remedial education in dyslexia, with special reference to its implications in children of normal or superior intelligence. Although a great deal of useful work is presented and summarized, it is still only too apparent that remedial methods are still for the most part empirical and await a fully scientific rationale before they can hope to attain general acceptance. More stringent validation of existing methods of helping dyslexic children is badly needed and the occupational and social implications of this disability are well worth more detailed study.

The editors deserve warm commendation on their success in assembling a book displaying wide knowledge and diverse specialist accomplishment. It will be of value not only to clinical and educational psychologists who have to deal with dyslexic children in the course of their duties but also to medical men anxious to keep abreast of developments in our understanding of the causes of special disabilities and how they may best be handled. Neuroscientists, too, may find some of the chapters—in particular those dealing with such topics as minimal brain damage, cerebral lateralization, or the contribution of electroencephalography—of interest in relation to disorders of language. Finally, educators will find this volume a virtual encyclopedia of reading disorders, which should equip them admirably to find their way through the bewildering and controversial issues posed by backwardness in reading. The two editors and their many contributors deserve our respect and gratitude.

O. L. *Zangwill*, F.R.S.
THE PSYCHOLOGICAL LABORATORY
UNIVERSITY OF CAMBRIDGE

Preface

In the preface to his 1917 book, *Congenital Word-blindness,* Hinshelwood wrote, "I have devoted considerable space to the subject of acquired word-blindness, without an adequate knowledge of which, in my opinion, congenital word-blindness cannot be properly understood." A great deal of information regarding the psychological and biological aspects of acquired alexia and developmental dyslexia has been accumulated since that time, and the present book represents an effort to bring some of this knowledge together. Since the time of Dejerine, it has been recognized that alexia is not a homogeneous clinical entity but is made up of clinical subtypes. The heterogeneous nature of dyslexia, however, has only recently been suspected, and while being vigorously promoted by some authorities, it is only grudgingly accepted by others and even overtly rejected by a few. In this book, almost every chapter dealing with dyslexia furnishes evidence that supports the view that developmental dyslexia is heterogeneous in nature. It is highly likely that failure to recognize the variegated nature of dyslexia will blunt the acuity of diagnostic procedures and diminish the effectiveness of treatment efforts.

An aspect of the study of dyslexia that has lagged far behind others is research into the relative efficacy of the different methods of reading remediation. One of the aims of this book is to focus attention on different remediation procedures and to bring research regarding treatment methods of dyslexia into the mainstream of scientific study.

Reading Disorders: Varieties and Treatments is divided into three parts: Developmental Dyslexia, Acquired Alexia, and Treatment Procedures. Part I deals with three distinct aspects of dyslexia: neuropsychological, cognitive, and biological. The three chapters on alexia that appear in Part II provide the reader with a succinct view of the acquired disability as well as an opportunity to compare subtypes of alexia with those of dys-

lexia. Chapters in Part III present descriptions of a wide variety of remedial techniques that range from classroom instruction to drug treatment
of developmental reading disabilities. The possible outcomes of such
treatment approaches are also discussed in these chapters.

Contributors to this volume are recognized experts in the field they
have chosen to write about, and we thank them for their splendid accomplishments. The work and effort involved in editing this volume was
shared equally by the two of us. The credit for creating the chapters
which make up the book, of course, goes to our contributors.

Reading Disorders
VARIETIES AND TREATMENTS

Part One

Developmental Dyslexia

Section One
Neuropsychological Aspects

Chapter One

The Neuropsychology of Developmental Dyslexia

P. G. AARON

INTRODUCTION

Dyslexia, as the term is used in this chapter, refers to an inability of children of normal intelligence to acquire reading skills appropriate for their age. Such a developmental deficit occurs in spite of the usual efforts on the part of the teacher and the learner. Descriptive labels such as "specific reading retardation" (Yule & Rutter, 1976), "specific

5

reading disability," "developmental dyslexia" (Rabinovitch, 1968), and "unexpected reading failure" (Symmes & Rapoport, 1972) are all considered to be equivalent terms. In contrast, the term *alexia* is used in this chapter to refer to the loss of reading ability which results from brain injury in a literate individual.

Dyslexia, as a clinical entity, has been recognized and investigated since the latter part of the last century. The paradoxical inability of some children of normal and occasionally superior intelligence to master the rudiments of reading intrigued physicians and educators who came in contact with them. These investigators tended to consider the etiology and nature of dyslexia in terms of their own professional backgrounds, medical practitioners often preferring an anatomical explanation and educators resorting to a functional analysis of the problem. Many characteristics of the dyslexic syndrome such as the preponderance of boys over girls, the genetic predisposition, and a possible association with language deficit, were, however, noted by these investigators, if only in passing. After a period of relative quiescence, there has been, during the past 2 decades, a resurgence of investigative work in dyslexia, partly due to the fact that "learning disability" has emerged as a legitimate field of inquiry. Research in dyslexia has therefore been pursued with enormous vigor and persistence by experts with diverse professional backgrounds—pediatric neurologists, reading specialists, and cognitive psychologists. This, of course, has resulted in a plethora of data, but disappointingly, as Benton (1980) has pointed out: "The mass of information has not proved to be as useful as one would have anticipated [partly due to the fact that] it is very difficult to integrate the observations into a coherent body of knowledge [p. 21]."

One of the reasons for this failure to develop a well-integrated theory of dyslexia is the artificial barrier that seems to exist between the different professional specialities. Thus, many neurologists are generally not very well acquainted with standardized tests of reading or specific methods of teaching reading, and few specialists who operate in an educational setting pay any attention to biological or neurological aspects of reading disabilities. They are at times even suspicious of terms such as dyslexia. Such lack of communication between the different professional subgroups has resulted in the development of theories and opinions that are rather narrow and limited in scope. Fortunately, there are increasing signs that these barriers are being broken down, and we can look forward with optimism to a future of greater interdisciplinary cooperation and understanding.

This chapter is an attempt to present a coherent view of the nature and etiology of dyslexia by drawing together information available in such diverse fields as neurology, reading instruction, cognitive psychology, and linguistics. This goal is accomplished with the aid of a hypothesis—the imbalance hypothesis—which is used as a paradigm to mold together into an integrated form research findings from the various fields. This chapter is divided into three major sections: a presentation of the imbalance hypothesis, a description of experiments that support the hypothesis, and an evaluation of the power of the imbalance hypothesis to explain certain known facts about dyslexia.

Underlying this exposition is the belief that the "single cause–single symptom" explanation of dyslexia is a simplistic notion which should be discarded forthwith and that dyslexia represents instead a group of disorders, each constituent subgroup having its own unique set of symptom characteristics. A logical starting point for presenting these viewpoints would be an examination of the reading process itself.

THE READING PROCESS

Operationally, it is convenient to consider the process involved in the reading of connected prose as consisting of two stages: encoding and comprehension (see Calfee, Chapter 5 of this volume). The encoding stage is further assumed to have two components, namely the simultaneous processing of a word and the sequential processing of certain units within a word or a sentence.

The second stage in reading involves the construction of ideas, which is accomplished by combining units of information made available by the process of encoding. The term *comprehension* is used to denote this process. The reader's linguistic competence, knowledge of syntax and semantics, and stock of concepts all play a role in comprehension. In this sense, it is very similar to "sentence meaning," which is described by Caramazza and Berndt (1978) in the following manner: "Lexical meanings can be considered to have fixed representations but sentence meanings are novel, complex representations constructed by combining the meanings of single lexical items [p. 910]." This chapter is concerned mainly with the first stage of reading process: encoding. It should be noted that the term *encoding* as used here has a broader connotation than the mere conversion of letters into their corresponding phonemes.

As noted earlier, the encoding operation has two components, one involving the simultaneous process, the other the sequential process. The simultaneous process is an analog operation involving the parallel processing of salient features within a word, resulting in a direct conversion of the visual form of the word. The sequential operation, on the other hand, involves a conversion of letters into their corresponding phonetic equivalents, at least in the beginning reader. Some alexic patients may also depend on sequential operation, as may skilled readers encountering new or difficult words (Baddeley, 1979). Experimental evidence exists, however, to show that reading comprehension can take place in the absence of such a phonetic conversion of letters. In the skilled reader, the sequential operation, therefore, most likely involves the serial processing of words or other functional linguistic units within a sentence as a rehearsal strategy in the short term memory stage. Such a sequential operation is necessary to maintain the syntactic order of words within a sentence and is, therefore, aided by the reader's syntactic and linguistic competency. In the skilled reader, these two operations—simultaneous and sequential processing of information—might appear to be fused and inseparable, but in fact, they are carried out simultaneously but independently. This statement could be supported by experimental findings. For instance, data obtained by Meyer, Schvaneveldt, and Ruddy (1974) in a word–nonword discrimination task are compatible with the dual model of lexical access. Baron and Treiman (1980), on the basis of their own work and those of others, conclude that in reading, parallel use of multiple paths will be the rule rather than the exception. Bradshaw (1975), after reviewing pertinent literature, concluded that "even the most radical parallel model of word perception in reading demands that serial processing commence at some stage, whether it is the word, phrase, or sentence [p. 124]." An additional source of evidence is the reading errors committed by disabled readers, both dyslexic and alexic. The possibility that these errors could be dichotomized indicates that one or the other process is underutilized by these readers. For instance, several reports describe certain alexic symptoms that imply a breakdown of the sequential process in reading (Patterson, 1978; Coltheart, 1980a; Marcel, 1980). Patients displaying such symptoms could read concrete nouns but could not read aloud nonsense words, and they encountered greater difficulty in reading abstract nouns and function words than in reading concrete nouns. The paralexic errors committed by these patients bear little or no phonological resemblance to the printed words. A second group of patients reportedly does not make such semantic errors, but fails to recognize words readily and seems to depend more on the phonetic aspects of the word than on its meaning (Marshall & Newcombe, 1973). Among other things, this group of alexic patients seems to be deficient in the ability to process the word simultaneously as an analog. These observations have led investigators to propose that two pathways are involved in reading—a grapheme–phoneme route and a direct grapheme–lexical route (Sasanuma, 1980).

Clinical studies of neurological patients indicate that impairment of the putative phonological route results in a failure to read grammatical function words, abstract nouns, and unknown words (Shallice & Warrington, 1975; Marcel & Patterson, 1978) and obstruction of access to the lexical store results in word recognition defects, even though these words may be pronounced correctly (Marcel, 1980). Efficient reading is impaired under both these conditions, and the patients produce characteristically different errors. It is reasonable, therefore, to assume that normal reading requires the integrity of these two functional systems (see Coltheart, 1980c, p. 197, for a dissident opinion). Children, particularly those with reading problems, are also known to make similar errors while reading, and several studies indicate that such errors are not accidental or random, and that for this reason, they provide insight into the nature of the reading process (Goodman, 1969). The major types of reading errors made by dyslexic children are discussed later in this chapter.

THE IMBALANCE HYPOTHESIS

The encoding operation, which is part of the normal reading process, is believed to involve two information-processing strategies—simultaneous and sequential. The parallel processing of certain letters within a word involves the simultaneous operation, whereas the serial processing of letters within a word (in the beginning reader) or morphemic units within a sentence (in the skilled reader) involves the sequential operation. It has to be noted that sequential operations can occur at two different levels either as a letter-by-letter processing of a word in the beginning or the neurologically impaired reader or as a word-by-word processing of a sentence in the skilled reader. It is further proposed that skilled reading involves the concurrent deployment of both simultaneous and sequential processing of stimuli and that an underutilization of one process or the other is likely to impair efficient reading. Such inefficient use of one strategy inevitably goes hand-in-hand with an overdependence on the other. As the resulting imbalance can be in the direction of either one of the two processes, we can expect two subtypes of reading disorders. In addition, the observation that some children can demonstrate fluent oral reading yet fail to comprehend what they have read suggests that there also exists a third type of reading disorder—comprehension dyslexia. This form of dyslexia is attributed to some deficit at the second stage of reading. The proposition that an imbalance of information-processing strategies gives rise to dyslexia is hereafter referred to as the *imbalance hypothesis*. This hypothesis is not a de novo proposition; similar views, in rudimentary forms, have been expressed in the past (Bakker, Teunissen, & Bosch, 1976; Kerschner, 1977; Witelson, 1977; Aaron, 1978).

Before examining the imbalance hypothesis, it is necessary to give evidence that both the simultaneous and sequential processes are involved in skilled reading. In this chapter, the term *skilled reading* contrasts both with *beginning reading*, wherein the learner simply translates the printed word into its auditory equivalent first and then attempts to get the meaning form the pronounced word, and with *speed reading*, wherein the reading material usually is of a nontechnical nature and is, therefore, not dense in meaning and content. Any individual who reads at a level and speed that is commensurate with his grade or class level is considered to be a *skilled reader*. Most college-level material involves skilled reading but not necessarily speed reading.

*Evidence for the Involvement of the
Simultaneous Process in Reading*

A considerable amount of evidence exists to show that the skilled reader processes a word or a few morphemes simultaneously as a single unit. The belief that it is words and not the letters of the alphabet that constitute the basic unit of reading goes back to the last century when Cattell (1886) showed that single words were recognized as quickly as single letters. The fact that the entire script of a language could be written in the form of logograms also strengthens the notion of the simultaneous processing of verbal stimuli. In fact, the belief that the skilled reader reads words directly for meaning and not letters is the basis for teaching the beginning reader sight vocabulary even before the letters of the alphabet.

The finding that response time for recognition of nonwords (which are processed serially, letter by letter) is longer than it is for words (Wheeler, 1970; Aderman & Smith, 1971) also lends support to the view that words are processed in a simultaneous fashion.

The issue whether the word is processed serially or simultaneously has been studied by a number of investigators. The consensus appears to be that even though a word is processed all at once, the operation is accomplished by processing a number of letters within the word in a parallel fashion during a single fixation of the eye. A study by Massaro and Klitzke (1977) showed that in a reaction-time experiment subjects took longer to react correctly when the stimulus and target words were similar (*mate–mete*) than when they were dissimilar (*mate–glad*). This led the investigators to conclude that words are identified by processing the letters that comprise the word. Letters within a word, however, are processed in a parallel, simultaneous fashion, since a letter within a word is identified more quickly than when the letter is presented alone—a phenomenon that cannot be accounted for by serial processing of letters. The extraction and parallel processing of letters in a word has also been demonstrated by Adams (1979), who found that the increase in accuracy of report of tachistoscopically presented words, pseudowords, and nonwords was negatively accelerated across increasing effective response time.

Evidence for the Involvement of the Sequential Process in Reading

Perhaps the most vigorous statements of support for sequential processes in reading come from Gough and his associates (Gough, 1972; Gough & Cosky, 1977; Gough & Hillinger, 1980). According to them, the reader "plods through the sentence, letter by letter, word by word" (Gough, 1972, p. 354). This statement has been modified somewhat to say that selected attributes of the word are processed serially (Gough & Hillinger, 1980) and that such selected attributes are not necessarily individual letters but could be some distinctive feature of the letters. These attributes, nevertheless, have to be processed serially. Reading, then, proceeds by recognizing "the letters of the printed words and their order and by segmenting the spoken word into its constitutional phonemes" (Gough & Hillinger, 1980). These investigators support their views by citing experiments which show that recognition time for tachistoscopically presented stimuli increases as a function of word length. Such findings are taken to indicate that the number of letters in a word is an important variable in word recognition. Gough and Hillinger also argue that processing individual words as single perceptual units alone cannot account for fluent reading of English, since an average reader of the Chinese language (in which every word has to be processed as a single logogram) can master no more than 2000 logograms, whereas a skilled reader of English can recognize and read as many as 50,000 words.

Massaro (1975) has argued that some of these experiments reported by Gough do not really demonstrate that letter recognition is a serial

process since in these studies subjects were asked to make oral responses rather than to identify the correct stimulus by means of recognition tasks. In addition, Massaro quotes a number of studies that
fail to support a left-to-right serial recognition of letters in skilled reading. It appears, therefore, that serial processing of letters within a word
has to be limited to special cases, such as beginning readers and alexic
patients, and to conditions wherein the skilled reader encounters difficulties in reading. For instance, Shankweiler and Liberman (1972)
found medial segments in the word to be among those misread often
by children. If phonetic recoding is taken as an indication of serial
processing, then the findings of Liberman and her associates (1980)
provide support for the use of such an operation by the beginning
reader. Furthermore, some studies have concluded that, at least in early
grades, the relationship between a knowledge of phonetics and reading
achievement remains positive and substantial (Gibson & Levin, 1975,
p. 150, 197). Several investigators (Marshall & Newcombe, 1973; Hécaen
& Kremin, 1977) also have reported alexic patients who could not read
words but could, nevertheless, read the component letters of the word.
It is not illogical, therefore, to conclude, that, under certain circumstances, sequential processing of phonetic or morphemic elements or
a combination of both constitutes an important component in reading.
It has to be pointed out, however, that evidence for phonemic recoding
in skilled readers has been obtained by Conrad (1964), Baddeley (1966),
Kleiman (1975), and Tzeng, Hung, and Wang (1977). At any rate, it is
reasonable to expect, in the skilled reader, the rehearsal process which
extends the life of morphemes at the short-term memory stage and
maintains their serial order within the phrase to involve sequential
operation. Poor sequential processing ability is, therefore, closely associated with poor syntactic ability and is an impediment to efficient
reading. Consequently, the reader is made to rely heavily on simultaneous visual information-processing strategies. Such excessive dependence on orthographic features often leads to characteristic errors
of reading such as omission or substitution of inflections and other
errors of syntax.

*Evidence for the Involvement of Both Simultaneous
and Sequential Processes in Reading*

EVIDENCE FROM COGNITIVE PSYCHOLOGY

This brief review indicates that experimental evidence and arguments
could be marshaled in support of involvement of both simultaneous

and sequential operations in reading. Even though the two viewpoints might appear to be contradictory, simultaneous and serial processing operations need not be mutually exclusive insofar as reading is concerned. It is quite conceivable that these two operations could be carried out concurrently as parallel processes (Meyer, Schvaneveldt, & Ruddy, 1974, Baron & Treiman, 1980). In fact, skilled and accurate reading may require the proper utilization of both these processes, such a feat of information processing being entirely within the capability of the human brain. After all, we have two cerebral hemispheres.

A number of studies support the possibility of these two processes being simultaneously involved in the processing of complex information. Studies carried out under analog and name-matching paradigms (Posner, 1969) support the existence of two modes of stimulus identification, both possibly operating in parallel rather than in tandem. Das, Kirby, and Jarman, in their interesting book *Simultaneous and Successive Cognitive Processes* (1979), quote a number of studies that underscore the importance of the two processes. According to these authors:

> Simultaneous integration refers to the synthesis of separate elements into groups, these groups often taking on spatial overtones. The essential nature of this sort of processing is that any portion of the result is at once surveyable. . . . Successive information processing [called sequential processing in this chapter] refers to processing information in a serial order. . . . In successive processing the system is not totally surveyable at any point in time [pp. 49, 50].

One of the studies reported by Das *et al.* involved the administration of a battery of tests to a group of 104 fourth-grade boys. When the Gates–MacGinitie vocabulary and reading scores of these children were correlated with factors obtained from the "simultaneous–successive" battery scores, impressives loading on reading scores were obtained. These investigators concluded that "complex performance such as reading achievement are dependent upon both modes of processing [p. 80]." A more direct investigation of the nature of reading ability was carried out by Leong within the framework of a simultaneous–successive processing paradigm (Das *et al.*, 1979). The subjects were 58 boys who were retarded in reading and a matched group of normal readers. A 10-test battery was administered to the two groups, and a principal-component analysis yielded three factors, simultaneous and successive factors being two among them. The factor structure of the two groups was similar, even though the performance of the poor readers in the tests was lower than that of normal readers. Leong concluded that both simultaneous and successive processing are necessary for reading competence.

Paivio's (1977) imagery system—in which elementary images are organized into higher order structures so that the informational output of the system has a synchronous or spatial character—and the verbal system—in which linguistic units are organized into higher order sequential structures—are very similar to the simultaneous and sequential processes described here. When these processes are applied to reading behavior, it is proposed that a word is processed both as an imagery and as an acoustic stimulus.

EVIDENCE FROM NEUROPSYCHOLOGY

It would be tempting to relate the simultaneous and sequential processes to the right and left cerebral hemispheres respectively, even though Das *et al.* (1979) prefer to view them in terms of a "front to back" model by ascribing simultaneous processing to cortical zones in the temporal–parietal–occipital regions and sequential processing to the frontotemporal regions of both hemispheres. Such a view may not be entirely without clinical support. For example, Benson, Brown, and Tomlinson (1971) studied a number of alexic patients and found that some could read letters much better than words whereas others could read words better than letters. Similar observations have been made by Hécaen and Kremin (1976). The lesions responsible for the two types of deficits were located in the dominant hemisphere of a majority of these patients, although in different regions. It should, however, be pointed out that right hemisphere lesions are also known to affect reading ability (Hirose, Kin, & Murakami, 1977; Kinsbourne & Warrington, 1962; Patterson & Zangwill, 1967). At any rate, the Benson, Brown, and Tomlinson study shows that word identification and letter naming are dissociable processes, probably related to simultaneous and sequential operations.

Difficulties encountered by aphasic–alexic patients in the processing of a sequence of words is also reproted by Benson (1977). A study by Albert (1972) also found that many patients with left hemisphere disturbance could comprehend (by reading) single-language items correctly but experienced inordinate difficulty maintaining multiple-language items in the correct sequence. Problems in understanding written as well as spoken material dependent upon a specific verbal sequence were notable in patients with left frontal disorder.

Experimental evidence for relating the two processing strategies to the two hemispheres is quite impressive (Levy & Sperry, 1968; Nebes, 1974). That hemispheric specialization of functions is a complex phenomenon that is influenced by a number of variables—such as type of stimuli used, the type of response required, and delay in response involved—has been pointed out in a review by Madden and Nebes (1980). There also exists ample evidence to show that the right hemisphere possesses linguistic ability, although of a circumscribed nature (Zaidel, 1976; Searleman, 1977; Bub & Whitaker, 1980). As a result, the initial notion that the left hemisphere is verbal and the right hemisphere is nonverbal has been considerably modified to accommodate a more function-oriented description of the differences between the hemispheres. Consequently, a more dynamic role could be assigned to the right hemisphere than the one with which it has been credited until now.

Of great relevance to the hypothesis are the findings that the right hemisphere is more competent in recognizing concrete nouns than in recognizing abstract nouns (Ellis & Shepherd, 1974; Hines, 1977) and that the right hemisphere is better in operations that involve analog matching than it is in operations that require name matching (Cohen, 1972; Geffen, Bradshaw, & Nettleton, 1972). Reading errors committed by brain-injured adults also indicate a right hemisphere role in reading. Coltheart (1980c, p. 330) has reviewed some of these studies carried out with alexic patients who commit semantic errors and misread or fail to read function words and inflexions. He favors the view that there may exist a right hemisphere lexicon which can play a part in reading but points out that the right hemisphere is poor in syntactic ability and has difficulty in handling function words and inflections as its lexical store of abstract words is rather barren. Unless the idea of left hemisphere inhibition is invoked, there is no compelling reason to believe that the right hemisphere lays dormant until a lesion sustained by the left hemisphere arouses it into the act of reading. Most probably, it had been making such a contribution to reading all along. Furthermore, an organic lesion does not seem to be required to bring the "right hemisphere-type" of reading to surface. Many dyslexic children and young adults commit reading errors that are strikingly similar to those committed by these alexic patients (Aaron, Baker, & Hickox, in press). The reading errors of these dyslexic children and adults, with apparently normal brains, reveal agrammatic errors, as well as omission and substitution of function words and inflexions. This suggests a probable, perhaps even a dominant, right hemisphere role in the reading behavior of some individuals.

Evidence for a combined contribution by the two hemispheres in reading is available from a study by Pirozzolo and Rayner (1977). On the basis of tachistoscopic presentation of verbal stimuli to normal readers, these investigators concluded that word identification is a multistage process, with visual feature analysis of the word carried out by the right hemisphere and identification and naming carried out by the left hemisphere. They go on to say that it is quite possible that the gross featural information which is nonsemantic in nature may be utilized by the right hemisphere whereas more discrete information from the foveal region may be utilized by the left hemisphere. Rayner and Bertera (1979) also found that parafoveal vision provided gross types of information about the word and, therefore, was useful in reading.

Tangential evidence in support of the dual process in reading comes from observations of reading-disabled children. It has been reported (Johnson & Myklebust, 1967) that some children could not analyze a word into its parts or synthesize sounds into words, whereas others could analyze or synthesize a word but had poor visual memory for words. Subjective reports by blind subjects show that maximum efficiency in reading Braille is achieved when fingers of both hands are used simultaneously (Smith, 1929). Although this may be because the right hand serves as a guide to the left, it is possible that optimal reading efficiency is achieved when information is sent simultaneously to both hemispheres.

In summary, cognitive as well as neuropsychological studies suggest that reading involves both an ability to process verbal information sequentially and an ability to process verbal stimuli simultaneously as visual gestalts. It also appears that the two cerebral hemispheres can carry out these two forms of information-processing strategies independently. What is crucial for the imbalance hypothesis is the demonstration that these two processes are independent of each other and are essential for skilled reading. Proof of hemispheric specialization of these two processes will strengthen the imbalance hypothesis, but the integrity of the hypothesis does not rest upon a proof of such a functional specialization of the two hemispheres.

EXPERIMENTAL SUPPORT FOR THE IMBALANCE HYPOTHESIS

Five different studies which utilize a variety of investigative procedures and subjects will be discussed. Findings of these studies are interpreted as evidence supportive of the imbalance hypothesis.

Study 1

In the first study (Aaron, 1978), the strategy used for testing the validity of the imbalance hypothesis was to classify dyslexic children into two categories, "sequential-deficient" and "simultaneous-deficient," and to determine if these deficiencies reflected a corresponding imbalance in information-processing strategies. Classification of dyslexic children into sequential-deficient and simultaneous-deficient groups was accomplished with the aid of Boder's diagnostic screening procedure (Boder, 1973). This procedure involves administering a word-reading inventory of graded difficulty and, on the basis of the subjects' performance, asking them to write from dictation five words from among those read without hesitation (sight vocabulary) and five words from among those read with difficulty (unknown vocabulary). According to Boder (also see Rosenthal, Boder, & Callaway, this volume), children who are poor in remembering the sequential order of elements within a word depend on the overall word image for spelling. Consequently, such children omit, reverse, or displace letters within a word; in the writing to dictation task they may make bizarre mistakes, writing *koo* for 'book' or *faete* for 'father.' On the other hand, children who have poor simultaneous-processing ability depend heavily on sequential auditory memory and tend to write words the way they sound rather than the way they look, for example, *tebl* for 'table' or *maek* for 'make', (Figures 1.1 and 1.2 show the spelling errors committed by children with each of the two kinds of deficits.)

Boder's diagnostic screening test was administered to a group of 46 reading disabled children from grades 2, 3, and 4. As determined by the primary mental ability test of intelligence, these children had a

Figure 1.1. Spelling of a child with sequential-processing deficit. (Note the reversal of the name.)

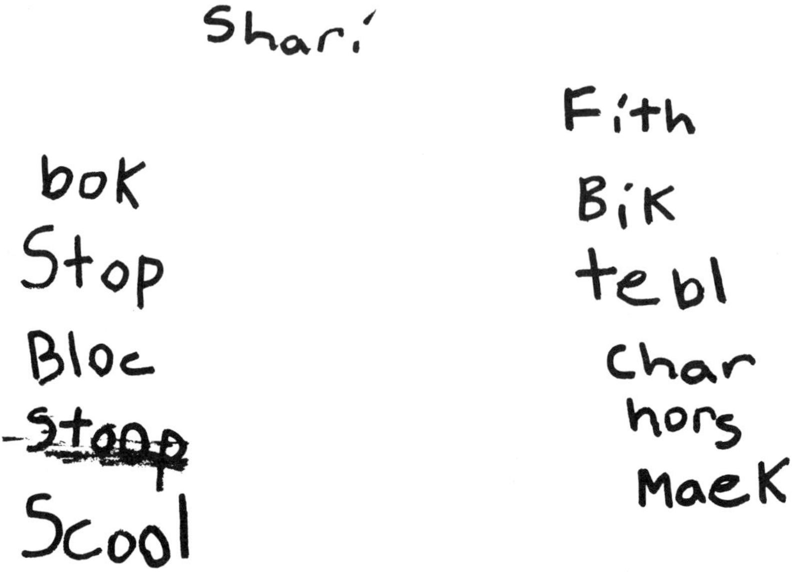

Shari'

Fith

bok   Bik

Stop   tebl

Bloc   Char

-Stonp   hors

Scool   MaeK

Figure 1.2. Spelling of a child with simultaneous-processing deficit.

mean IQ of 94.2, were free from any noticeable psychological or neurological impairments, and were reading at least one grade below expectation (Gates–McGinitie Reading Test). Following the specific procedures recommended by Boder, the subjects were classified into the two subgroups on the basis of the nature of their spelling errors. After this initial screening, an attempt was made to match each child in one group with another child from the other group on the basis of chronological age, mental age, and sex. Such a matching resulted in 14 pairs of subjects. Another matched group of 14 normal readers was also selected to serve as the control group.

Four tests were administered to all the three groups. A Kodak Carousel projector with a rear-view screen and timer was used for Tests 1, 3, and 4.

1. MEMORY FOR FACES

A set of 25 photographs of men and women taken from a college yearbook was made into photographic slides. The photographs were selected with care to eliminate any readily distinguishable feature such as moustache, hair style, or dress. Each of the 25 slides was shown to each subject on a rear-view screen for 5 sec. The intertrial interval was about 1 sec. After the exposure of all the 25 slides, a multiple choice test, in which three similar looking faces appeared simultaneously with each original picture, was administered. The subject had to identify correctly the face he had seen before. As human faces cannot be readily verbalized, it was expected that those children who were simultaneous-deficient would correctly identify significantly fewer photographs than the other groups.

2. WISC DIGIT SPAN

This test of auditory sequential memory was administered to all children, and the memory for the sequence of both forward and backward digits was noted. As this task tests the ability to process information sequentially, it was expected that the simultaneous-deficient children would obtain higher scores than the other reading-disabled group.

3. REPRODUCTION OF PAIRED-LETTER STIMULI

In this task, 16 paired-letter stimuli were used. The construction of these stimuli involved placing two letters such as *d* and *b* close to each other with a very fine dividing line between them and photographing them in order to make projection slides. When projected, the stimuli appeared to have almost no space between the letters. During testing, each stimulus was projected on the screen for a period of 2 sec and the subject was asked to reproduce on a piece of paper what he had seen.

These stimuli were designed in such a way that each stimulus could be reproduced as a letter and its reversed form or as a single visual gestalt. For example, the stimuli db and HH could be processed analytically and sequentially as *d* and *b* and *H* and *H* or as single visual gestalts:

db   HH

It was assumed that the written response would adequately reflect the information-processing strategy of the subject and that the sequential-deficient child would process them as a single gestalt whereas the simultaneous-deficient child would process them as two discrete letters.

4. REPRODUCTION OF INDIVIDUAL LETTERS AND SHAPES

Individual letters and unfamiliar geometrical shapes were also photographed and made into slides. Sixteen such slides were prepared and each slide was exposed under two different recall conditions. Under immediate recall, the stimulus was exposed for .5 sec and the subject was asked to reproduce immediately on a piece of paper what he had seen. The next stimulus appeared on the screen soon after the subject had finished writing. Under delayed recall, the same set of slides, rearranged in a different order, was exposed for .5 sec. Immediately following the presentation of each stimulus the experimenter read aloud a series of three digits (if the stimulus was a letter) or three letters (if the stimulus was a shape) and the subject was asked to repeat it. This interpolated task took approximately 5 sec. Following this delay, the subject was asked to reproduce on a sheet of paper what he had seen on the screen. When the subject had finished writing, the next stimulus appeared on the screen.

The task was aimed to study the tendency of some young children to reverse or rotate letters when they write. It is known that human beings generally process pictures and shapes without regard to their left–right orientation along the horizontal axis (Standing, Conezio, & Haber, 1970). Consequently, it was expected that sequential-deficient children who process the stimulus as a picture, very much like a gestalt, would disregard the left–right orientation and produce more reversals than children who were adept at sequential processing. The purpose of administering the task under two different recall conditions was to see if reversal was primarily a perceptual or memory phenomenon.

Four important findings emerged:

1. The sequential-deficient group identified significantly more faces than did the simultaneous-deficient group ($p < .02$). The performance of the former group in this task was not significantly different from that of the control group.

2. The simultaneous-deficient group recalled more sequence of digits than the sequential-deficient group did ($p < .10$). The number of digits recalled by the sequential-deficient group was also lower than that of the control group ($p < .001$).

3. The sequential-deficient group also reproduced significantly more fused letters (Figures 1.3 and 1.4) than did the other two groups. ($p < .02$).

4. The sequential-deficient group reversed more letters and shapes than the other groups did under delayed recall ($p < .02$). Under immediate recall, there was no significant difference in reversals among the three groups which seems to indicate that letter reversal is primarily a long-term memory storage–retrieval problem. Several studies show that adult humans can recognize a picture or a geometrical shape as familiar even if it is the left–right mirror image of the one seen before and that they cannot tell if it is the original or not (Bartlett, 1932; Standing, Conezio, & Haber, 1970; Rock, 1973). Thus, right–left direction along the horizontal axis is not a crucial feature in the processing of such visual gestalts. In the present study,

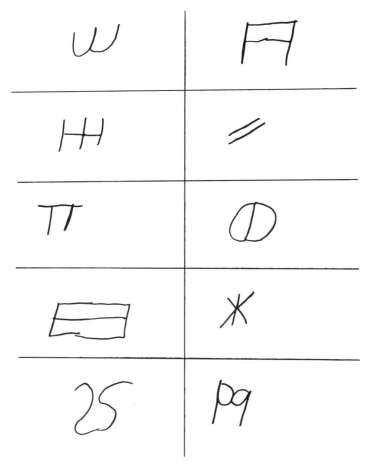

Figure 1.3. Reproduction of paired letters by a child deficient in sequential-processing ability.

significantly more letters were reversed by some children who had superior memory for faces, indicating that they tend to process letters as though they are pictures rather than as phonetic units.

These results indicate that dyslexic children deficient in one information-processing strategy are normal in the other strategy and that normal readers do not have such an imbalance.

Study 2

If deficient sequential ability causes dyslexia in some children and deficient simultaneous ability impedes reading ability in other children,

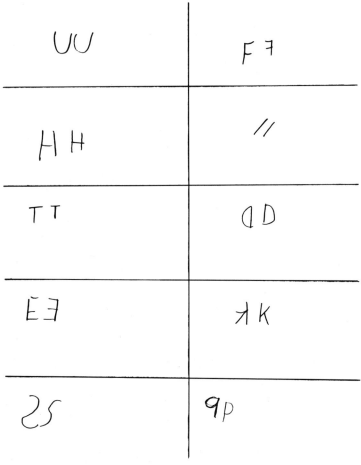

Figure 1.4. Reproduction of paired letters by a child deficient in simultaneous-processing ability.

and if comprehension deficits are responsible for reading disability in yet another group of children, then it is logical to expect that when a battery of tests that assesses these abilities is given, dyslexic children belonging to the three different subtypes should display performance profiles that are different from each other. In addition, one would also expect a wide degree of "within subject" variation of test performance: That is, the child with a sequential processing disability would be expected to perform poorly on tests of sequential ability, but show average or above average performance in tests of simultaneous abilities as well as in tests of comprehension; the child with a simultaneous processing disability would show an entirely different profile. In contrast, children who have normal reading ability and children whose reading disability could be attributed to subnormal mental capacity would not show such wide fluctuations in their performance; they would tend to perform more or less uniformly on all the tests.

To recapitulate, when a battery of tests is given, a typical sequential-deficient dyslexic subject would, according to the imbalance hypothesis, do poorly only in tests of sequential ability and do reasonably well in all other tests; a simultaneous-deficient subject would show an opposite test performance profile; and a subject with a comprehension deficit would be poor in tests of comprehension but would show no deficit in tests of sequential or simultaneous operations. On the basis of such a logic, theoretical models of test score profiles could be generated for each dyslexic subtype.

This proposition was put to test by administering a battery of tests to 24 third- and fourth-grade children (15 boys and 9 girls) drawn from a larger group attending special classes for children with learning and behavior problems. Of these 24 children, 19 were reading at about two grade levels below expectation and the remaining 5 were reading at grade level but had behavioral problems. These 5 children were used as a control group and are referred to as the "normal IQ–normal reading" group. Out of the 19 reading-disabled children, 15 had average or above average IQ scores (Henmon–Nelson Test of Mental Ability) and were therefore considered genuine cases of dyslexia. The remaining 4 reading-disabled children had IQs below 90 which could, perhaps, explain their reading deficiencies. These 4 children were treated as a second control group and are referred to as the "low IQ–poor reading" group.

A large battery of tests, which included, among others, two tests each of comprehension, language ability, sequential and simultaneous information processing abilities, was administered to all 24 children.[1] The tests were

1. Reading Comprehension subtest from Durrell Analysis of Reading Difficulty (Durrell, 1955)

[1] The Northwestern syntax screening test has norms for children up to 7 years and 11 months and the token test has norms for children up to 12 years. The WISC digit span is reported to have a high loading on successive information processing ability (Das, Kirby, & Jarman, 1979). The memory for sequences subtest is a standardized instrument which requires the subject to arrange a series of pictures in the same sequence as uttered by the examiner. The test therefore includes both auditory and visual modalities. The memory for faces test is a revised form of the one used in Study 1. In the revised form, 42 photographs are mounted in an album and each is shown to the subject for a period of 5 sec.

2. Listening Comprehension, Oral Reading, and Spelling subtests
   from Durrell
3. Token Test (Noll, 1970)
4. Northwestern Syntax Screening Test (NSST; Lee, 1969)
5. Digit Span (WISC-R)
6. Memory for Sequences subtest (Goldman, Fristoe, & Woodcock,
   1974)
7. Sight Vocabulary subtest (Durrell, 1955)
8. Memory for Faces Test (Aaron, unpublished).

Each child's performance on each of the tests was classified as below
or above average in terms of the age appropriate norms.

Theoretical distribution of scores that could be obtained on these
eight tests by a typical dyslexic child belonging to each of the three
subtypes (sequential, simultaneous, and comprehension deficient) were
generated using three separate differential diagnostic grids. These are
shown in Tables 1.1, 1.2, and 1.3.

Each of the eight items shown in the grid is scored as plus or minus,
depending upon whether the criterion is satisfied or not. For example,
the first item in Table 1.1 reads "listening comprehension—no deficit."
As it is believed that dyslexic children with a sequential information-
processing deficit do not have any appreciable degree of deficit in
comprehending spoken utterances that are syntactically simple, the first
column in Table 1.1 is marked plus. As the child with a simultaneous

Table 1.1

Theoretical Performance Profile of a Typical Child with Sequential Information-Processing Deficit

	Sequential processes	Simultaneous processes	Comprehension
Listening comprehension— no deficit	+	+	−
Reading comprehension—not below oral reading level	+	+	−
Token test—below average	+	−	+
NSST—below average	+	−	+
Digit span—below average	+	−	−
Memory for sequences— below average	+	−	−
Sight vocabulary— above average	+	−	+
Memory for faces— above average	+	−	+
	8	2	4

Table 1.2
Theoretical Performance Profile of a Typical Child with Simultaneous Information-Processing Deficit

	Sequential processes	Simultaneous processes	Comprehension
Listening comprehension— no deficit	+	+	−
Reading comprehension— not below oral reading level	+	+	−
Token test—above average	−	+	−
NSST—above average	−	+	−
Digit span—above average	−	+	+
Memory for sequences— above average	−	+	+
Sight vocabulary— below average	−	+	−
Memory for faces— below average	−	+	−
	2	8	2

information-processing deficit is also believed not to have such a comprehension deficit, the second column is also given a plus sign. In other words, adequate comprehension of spoken sentences is a characteristic that is shared by these two subtypes of dyslexics. In contrast, reading-disabled children with a comprehension deficit are known to have difficulty in the proper understanding of oral language and, therefore,

Table 1.3
Theoretical Performance Profile of a Typical Child with Comprehension Deficit

	Sequential processes	Simultaneous processes	Comprehension
Listening comprehension— deficit present	−	−	+
Reading comprehension— below oral reading level	−	−	+
Token test—below average	+	−	+
NSST—below average	+	−	+
Digit span—above average	−	+	+
Memory for sequences— above average	−	+	+
Sight vocabulary— above average	+	−	+
Memory for faces— above average	+	−	+
	4	2	8

the third column is given a minus sign. All the eight items in Table 1.1 are worded in such a way that a typical child with a sequential deficit will obtain a profile of 8–2–4. That is, such a child, in terms of his test performance, will share two symptoms with the child with a simultaneous deficit, and four symptoms with the child with a comprehension deficit. The wording of some of the eight criteria could be changed in such a way that a dyslexic child with typical simultaneous processing deficiency would score a maximum of eight points. His profile would be 2–8–2 (Table 1.2). Similar manipulations would generate the profile for a typical child with comprehension deficits which would be 4–2–8 (Table 1.3). These three profiles are the expected or theoretical distribution of test scores for the three typical dyslexic subtypes.

The next step was to actually administer the eight tests to all children, interpret the scores in terms of being above or below the test mean, and assign plus or minus signs according to the criteria shown in the diagnostic grid, and thus obtain a test performance profile for each subject. This provided the observed distribution of test scores for each child. Subsequently, each such observed profile was tested for statistical fit ($\chi^2 = p < .05$) with each of the three typical theoretical distributions. The theoretical profile that matched the child's obtained profile was considered to be indicative of the child's information-processing deficit. For example, if a dyslexic child's observed distribution of scores did not deviate significantly ($\chi^2 = p < .05$) from the 8–2–4 profile, then that child was considered to have a sequential processing deficit, but not a simultaneous processing or comprehension deficit. If the observed profile did not match any one of the three theoretical profiles, it was regarded as "unclassified."

The χ^2 values obtained according to this procedure showed that the observed profiles of 11 of the 15 dyslexic children matched one or another of the three theoretical profiles (Figure 1.5), whereas none of the profiles of the 5 normal-IQ–normal readers and only 1 of the 4 profiles of the low-IQ–poor readers matched any of these three theoretical profiles (Figure 1.6). Of the 11 dyslexic children whose profiles conformed to any one of the theoretical types, 3 matched the sequential-deficient profile, 2 matched the simultaneous-deficient pattern, and 6 matched the comprehension-deficient profile. The remaining 4 dyslexic children were unclassified.

In addition to the administration of these tests, the subjects' reading of passages from Durrell's test was taped and later analyzed for reading errors. Investigators differ in the types of errors they look for and in the interpretation of their significance; in the present context, such

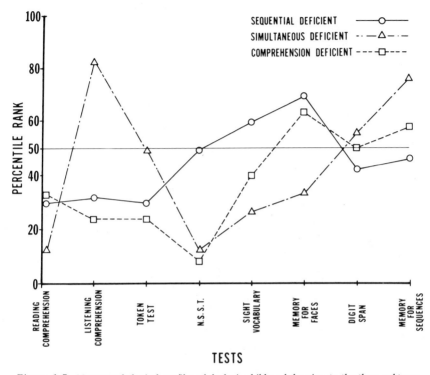

Figure 1.5. *Neuropsychological profiles of dyslexic children belonging to the three subtypes.*

errors were interpreted within a neurolinguistic framework. The types of reading errors committed by the three groups of dyslexics will be described first and their neuropsychological significance will be discussed subsequently.

THE SEQUENTIAL-DEFICIENT GROUP

Reading error analysis of the three children (two boys and one girl) who were deficient in sequential information-processing strategies showed that they frequently omitted, substituted, or added words—more often function words than content words. Such errors invariably resulted in agrammatic sentences. Two out of three children also tended to omit inflexions and seldom corrected the resulting agrammatic sentences. The following sample is illustrative of their reading errors.

Text: In 1807, Robert Fulton took the first long trip in a steam boat.
M.M.:   *In 1807, Robert Fulton took the first long trip in__ steam boat.*
Text: This was faster than   a steam boat had ever gone before.
M.M.:   *This was **fast__ that and** a steam boat had ever gone before.*

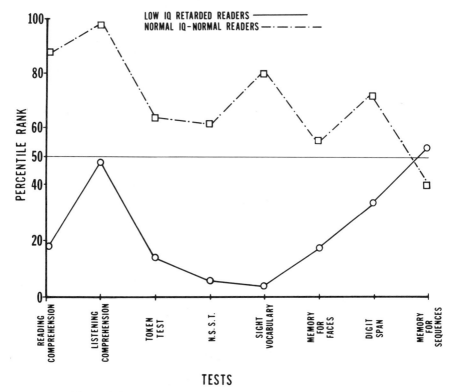

Figure 1.6. *Neuropsychological profiles of normal and low-IQ readers.*

Text: They [fishermen] were afraid its noise and splashing would drive
M.M.:   *They*   *were afraid* *it* *noise and* **splash__** *would drive*
Text: away all the fish.
M.M.:   **all** *away all ___ fish.*

The simultaneous-deficient group. The reading of the two children (both boys) placed in this group revealed few·syntactic or semantic errors. Reading errors were mainly limited to misreading of unknown words. Frequently, each boy resorted to letter-by-letter decoding, but even then was not able to pronounce the word correctly. They also showed a tendency to substitute known words for unknown words. These substitutions, being meaningful, did not affect the syntactical integrity of the sentences. When misreading did affect the syntactical integrity of the sentences, the subjects hastened to read the sentence again and correct the grammatical error. The following are some of the sentences that contained reading errors, reproduced verbatim.

Text: In 1807, Robert Fulton took the first long trip in a   steamboat.
A.L.: *In 1807, Robert Fulton took the first long trip in **the** steamboat.*
Text: He went   one hundred and fifty miles up the Hudson river.
A.L.: *He **wanted** . . . **went** one hundred and fifty miles up the Hudson river.*
Text: Late   in the summer a man started   to build a house.
S.C.: *L..a..t..e in the summer a man   s..t..u..d   to build a house.*
Text: Then he built the floor and the cellar steps himself.
S.C.: *Then he **put**   the floor and the   ___   **sides** himself.*
Text: He told the boys next door, that they might   use it.
S.C.: *He told the boys next door, that **the midnight** ... **they might**   use it.*

THE COMPREHENSION-DEFICIENT GROUP

Analysis of reading errors showed that children in this group (five girls and one boy) did not pay much attention to word meaning. Their reading errors included many instances of word substitutions, and such misreadings often resulted in meaningless sentences. Occasionally, neologisms were produced. Even though these children did not seem to encounter particular difficulties in pronouncing new words, they produced many sentences with altered meanings. Self-corrections were rarely observed in this group. Here is a sample of their reading.

Text: In 1807, Robert Fulton took the first long trip in a steam boat.
N.H.: *In 1807, Robert Fulton took the first long trip in a steam boat.*
Text: He went one hundred and fifty miles.
N.H.: *He went one **hour**   and fifty **minutes.***
Text: Crowds   gathered on both banks of the river.
N.H.: ***According** gathered on both **bridge** of the river.*
Text: They were afraid   that its noise and splashing would drive away all the fish.
M.G.: *They were **afraind** that its noise and **splarting** would drive away all the fish.*

It would appear from the foregoing analysis that the sequential-deficient group experienced difficulty with function words, inflexions, and other syntactical aspects of language. As these children were able to read the root of the word and often left the inflexion out, they seem to rely on their sight vocabulary and disregard the phonetic elements of the word. This was particularly evident when they encountered unknown words which they could not pronounce and for which they proceeded to substitute known words. When such a substitution could not be readily accomplished, these children gave up their attempt to pronounce the word altogether.

The simultaneous-deficient group showed an almost opposite pattern of deficits and strengths. They were able to phonetically decode many new words and were able to correct grammatically incorrect sentences.

Their numerous word substitutions, however, indicated that they were deficient in sight vocabulary. This would suggest that they were poor in analog matching of words with their images, and were overly dependent on serial feature analysis of words.

The comprehension-deficient group did not find decoding, as such, a serious impediment in their reading; their phonetic skills as well as their stock of sight vocabulary could be considered adequate. The major problem this group experienced was with the semantic aspect of the sentence, as was shown by their construction of semantically inappropriate sentences and their production of neologisms. As their performance in the sequential and simultaneous tests was within normal limits, this group may be considered to be quite distinct from the other two.

Both psychological tests and reading error analysis indicate that many dyslexic children show an imbalance in the strategies they utilize in reading written sentences. Data presented in Figure 1.5 also show that children in each of the three subgroups performed well above average in some tests and very poorly in some other tests, suggesting serious imbalances in the information-processing strategies employed by these children. Also note the similarity between these profiles and the ones obtained by DeFries and Decker (this volume).

Study 3

The two studies discussed so far used groups of children to examine the validity of the imbalance hypothesis. Because the nomothetic approach tends to obscure individual differences, we will turn our attention to case studies which, although they do not permit a generalization over larger populations, nevertheless provide an opportunity for an in-depth examination of intraindividual imbalances in information-processing strategies.

The existence of serious imbalances in the cognitive abilities of dyslexic children had been noticed and reported at the turn of the century by pioneers of research in dyslexia. The phenomenon that a child intelligent in every respect could not be taught to read puzzled both teachers and parents and made dyslexia a clinical entity worthy of investigation. Hinshelwood (1917), for example, describes in great detail five case histories of dyslexic children who could read no more than a few very common two- or three-letter words in spite of their many years of schooling. However, all five children, without a single exception, were described as having "auditory memory" that ranged from very good to excellent.

In a study of two dyslexic college students we also found striking imbalance of cognitive abilities. A complete description of this investigation is given elsewhere (Aaron, Baxter, & Lucenti, 1980), and only information relevant to the imbalance hypothesis will be presented here.

CASE 1

S.H., a 21-year-old right-handed male, has had severe reading difficulty since childhood. He appeared to be physically healthy and revealed no signs of neurological or aphasic problems. Childhood history was free from traumatic accidents or serious illnesses even though there was a family history of reading disability. In the university he is considered as a handicapped student and receives privileges such as financial support to hire a "reader," normally extended to blind students. The Ishihara test revealed normal color vision and the ophthalmologist found no visual field defects. His oral communicative language was free of any noticeable impairments.

CASE 2

D.B., a healthy 22-year-old left-handed male student, has experienced difficulty with printed material, especially in the comprehension of it. Both parents were reportedly well educated and normal. No motor deficit or clumsiness was apparent, and childhood history was uneventful. According to his own report, he can read rapidly but has difficulty in figuring out, as well as remembering, what he has just read. He has tried to overcome this difficulty by writing down what he thinks to be important and then trying to remember visually as much as he can. No language defect was evident in normal conversation during the course of the investigation.

The following tests were administered to the two subjects over a period of 3 months:

1. Wechsler's Adult Intelligence Scale (WAIS).
2. The Aphasia Test (Goodglass & Kaplan, 1972).
3. Stanford Diagnostic Reading Test.
4. Word reading, writing, pronouncing, and copying task. Forty words were selected from a set of 60 words used by Kinsbourne and Warrington (1962) to study the paralexic errors made by patients with cerebral lesions. Subjects were required to perform the following tasks during different sessions: read each word, write to dictation, pronounce the word when the examiner spelled it orally, and copy it. Words used ranged from familiar

three-letter words such as *sit* and *egg* to uncommon words such as *plausible* and *sarcastic*.

5. Sentence Repetition Test (Newcombe & Marshall, 1967). This consists of a list of 20 sentences, some of which are syntactically incorrect. Subjects were required to repeat each sentence after it had been read by the examiner.

6. Comprehension of connected prose. Paragraphs from the Stanford Diagnostic Reading Test were read to the subject, who was then required to write a summary of each paragraph.

7. Token Test (DeRenzi & Vignolo, 1962).

8. Picture interpretation. Pictures (telegraph boy; birthday party; and wash day from Stanford–Binet, 1937, 1963) portraying complex scenes were shown to the subjects who were asked to describe them.

9. Spatial Relations and Abstract Reasoning subtests from the Differential Aptitude Tests (Bennett, Seashore, & Wesman, 1973). The Spatial Relations subtest is a nonverbal instrument which measures the ability to visualize a constructed object from a picture of a pattern. It tests the ability to imagine how an object would appear if rotated in various ways. The abstract reasoning test measures nonverbal reasoning ability by requiring subjects to discover the principle governing the change in a series of abstract figures.

10. Memory for faces test. This is a nonverbal test of memory for visual gestalt developed locally in our laboratory. This is a revised form of the memory for faces test (see Note 1).

The quantitative aspects of the test results are shown in Tables 1.4 and 1.5. As could be expected, both subjects were retarded in reading. On the Stanford Diagnostic Reading Test, S.H. obtained a grade equiv-

Table 1.4
WAIS Subtest Scaled Scores of the Two Dyslexic Subjects

	S.H.	D.B.		S.H.	D.B.
Full-scale IQ	116	99			
Verbal IQ	115	99	Performance IQ	114	100
Information	8	11	Picture completion	13	11
Comprehension	12	10	Picture arrangement	11	11
Arithmetic	10	8	Block design	12	12
Similarities	14	9	Object assembly	14	9
Digit span	17	11	Digit–symbol	10	8
Vocabulary	11	9			

Table 1.5
Summary of Scores Obtained in Some Selected Tests by the Two Dyslexic Subjects[a]

Tests	S.H.	D.B.
Stanford Diagnostic Reading Test		
Reading rate (grade equivalent)	3.0	10.6
Comprehension (grade equivalent)	4.7	9.6
Token Test	99.0	5.0
Benton's Visual Retention Test		
Immediate reproduction	99.0	10.0
Delayed reproduction	99.0	10.0
Differential Aptitude Tests		
Space relations	99.0	31.0
Abstract reasoning	75.0	34.0
Memory for faces test	5.0	99.0

[a] Scores are in percentile ranks except reading; percentile ranks for Benton's Visual Retention Test and the Token Test are approximations.

alent of 3.0 and 4.7 for reading rate and comprehension, respectively; the corresponding scores for D.B. were 10.6 and 9.6. The subjects had no visual field defects or hearing deficits; both could repeat sentences correctly, and their copying of words was free from errors. Scores obtained in the WAIS show the subjects to be in the average and above average range of intelligence with no significant discrepancy between their verbal and performance IQs. When the subtest scaled scores are examined, however, some interesting differences emerge. S.H. has below average score in information with strikingly superior score in digit span. D.B., on the contrary, was poor in arithmetic and digit symbol with no noticeably superior score in any of the subtests. In the aphasia test, S.H.'s performance fell within normal limits except in writing and color naming. In reading, as well as in writing to dictation, S.H. performed poorly; his reading rate was inferior to his level of comprehension. The beginnings and endings of words were almost always read correctly with the substitution errors being limited to the middle part of the word, indicating that he was not able to perceive the entire word (e.g., *single* for 'seige', *advancing* for 'advising', and *sound* for 'should'). In picture interpretation (Test 8) S.H. paid attention to details, proceeded in a random fashion, and finally arrived at the major theme of the story. He produced all the Benton figures without error. In the facial recognition test (Test 11) his score was equivalent to the 5th percentile, which is the poorest performance we have seen in our laboratory. In contrast, he solved all 60 problems in the spatial relations test (Test 10), a performance that places him in the 99th percentile. Considering the fact that the average postgraduate student can attain only the 70th percentile rank, this is a remarkable feat. In the abstract reasoning test he obtained a score equivalent to the 75th percentile. In writing to dictation, he had a tendency to write words the way they sound (e.g., *shod* for 'should', *wais* for 'was').

In summary, S.H. encountered difficulty in simultaneous processing of complex stimuli such as faces, whole words, and pictures, but seemed to have an overcompensating sequential ability as indicated by his excellent memory for digits. His phonetic spelling indicates that he relies on such a strategy for processing information.

D.B., in contrast, performed normally on all subtests of writing, oral reading, and color identification. Compared to S.H., however, he did poorly in tests of verbal agility, animal naming, and finger identification. Of interest were the paraphasic errors he committed in the word recognition test. He made few mistakes in the decoding aspect of reading, pronouncing, and copying. Unlike S.H., the reading rate of D.B. was consistently superior to his level of comprehension. In writing to dictation, however, he made many errors of letter omission, substitution, and reversals (e.g., *expodes* for 'explodes', *percieved* for 'perceived', and *nessecary* for 'necessary'). In the Comprehension Test (Test 6) his performance showed deficiency in understanding the central idea contained in each paragraph. Deficits were also seen in his performance on the Token Test. D.B. described the pictures normally by reporting the central theme first. In the reproduction of Benton figures (Test 9) he committed many errors which were primarily due to improper sequential placement of the figures within each set. On the memory for faces test (Test 11) he obtained a perfect score of 42, which places him in the 99th percentile. This is the best performance we have come across in our laboratory. In summary, D.B. was deficient in reading comprehension, recalling names from memory, arithmetic calculation, finger identification, and WAIS digit symbol. In contrast, his better-than-average performance in WAIS block design and his superior memory for faces indicate an underlying excellent simultaneous-processing ability. His nonphonetic spelling pattern and reading errors reveal that he tends to make use of such a strategy in spelling and reading.

These two subjects, therefore, seem to be representative cases of two different subtypes of dyslexia, and their performances on the various tests lend credibility to the imbalance hypothesis by revealing the "within subject" imbalances in information-processing strategies.

Study 4

The next piece of supporting evidence for the imbalance hypothesis is presented in the form of what may best be described as a psycho-

historical case study. It is an analysis of the assets and of certain weaknesses of Leonardo da Vinci, who is considered by many to be the
universal genius of the fifteenth century.

Richter (1890/1979, p. XIV), who closely analyzed a good part of
Leonardo's writings, reported that he made use of an orthography
peculiar to himself and had an unusual way of spelling. Reti (1974, p.
60), as well as Clark (1959, p. 64), noted that Leonardo wrote haphaz-
ardly, spelling arbitrarily, and skipping words and phrases. According
to Vasari (Bax, 1932, p. 136), his earliest biographer, Leonardo wrote
backward, in rude characters, and with his left hand. Probably due to
the uncritical writings of some authors, the belief that Leonardo wrote
most of his material in mirror-reversed form in order to protect his
writing from indicting scrutiny has gained wide acceptance and become
deeply entrenched in the public mind. The erroneous nature of such
a belief, however, was recognized during the latter part of the last
century by Richter (1890/1970, p. 8) who presented convincing arguments to show that Leonardo in fact did not intend to conceal his
writings. In support of his view, Richter quotes passages from Leonardo's notebooks indicating that he wished to publish his writings and
that he desired sincerely that they should be known and read. Furthermore, even his earliest notes, written at the age of 21 when Leonardo could not have anticipated any papal recriminations or royal sanc-
tions, were written backward. In addition to his inconsistent style of
writing, it is also reported that Leonardo experienced discomfort with
the spoken language and encountered difficulty in speaking fluently
as a result of his limited vocabulary (Stites, Stites, & Castiglioni, 1970,
p. 364).

Although his errors were not numerous, Leonardo did make mistakes in arithmetic computation. For example, in one of his diary entries,
he adds up 25, 2, 16, 6, and 1 and arrives at the figure of 48 (Reti,
1974, p. 58). While dealing with one of the geometric problems, Leonardo, after inscribing a section of a hexagon in a circle, proceeds to
divide the area outside the hexagon into a certain number of submultiple
portions. Then he goes on to make a table with two columns, one with
numbers 1–50, the other with the product of each number in column
one multiplied by 6. In the construction of such a multiplication table
of 6, he makes a simple error by entering 104 as the product of 6 ×
34. He continues this mistake with all the subsequent figures and ultimately arrives at the last multiplication, 50 × 6. Leonardo enters the
answer as 200 (Reti, 1974, p. 77).

At least three instances of syntactical errors committed by Leonardo
have been documented from his diary entries. He records Caterina's
(his mother?) arrival by writing "On the 16th of July Caterina came on

the 16th of July, 1493 [Eissler, 1961, p. 331]." Two separate but identical entries of his father's death read "On July 9, 1504, Wednesday at 7 o'clock died Ser Piere da Vinci, notary of the palace of the Podesta, my father, at 7 o'clock. He was 80 years old, and left ten sons and two daughters [Schapiro, 1955 p. 8; Richter, 1950, p. 344]." In addition to the repetition of the phrase 7 o'clock, other errors have been detected. The day of death was Tuesday and not Wednesday as Leonardo had written, his father's age was 78 instead of 80 years, and it is possible that the number of children is incorrect (Schapiro, 1955). It is significant that all these errors involve numbers or other elements of information that are sequential in nature.

Leonardo himself was aware of his limitations with regard to his reading. Phrases such as "not being a literary man" and "I having no literary skill" are frequently found in his writings. These statements, although they are liable to be interpreted as referring to his lack of formal education, could also be construed as a confession of his poor reading skill. In what may be considered as a self-portrait, Leonardo describes the painter as follows:

> He is well dressed . . . he wears the clothes he likes . . . and his house is full of delightful paintings and is spotlessly clean. He is often accompanied by music and by men who read from a variety of beautiful works, and he can *listen* to these with great pleasure [Ludwig, 1909; italics mine].

Why should other men read to the artist? Is it because he is engaged in painting, or is it because he could not read well?

Stites, Stites, and Castiglioni (1970) pose the question of why Leonardo did not become a notary, following the tradition of his father and his stepbrother. They conclude that the reason was that the statutes of the Guild of Lawyers and Notaries rejected from membership all illegitimate sons. Although such an explanation is probably true, it is also known that in Italian Renaissance society, although illegitimacy generally carried a stain of some sort, men could be made to overlook it by the force of power and place or by means of money and a dispensation (Martines, 1968, p. 28). There exists a possibility that Leonardo found it difficult to cope with the medieval grammar school curriculum which, in addition to the quadrivium, was heavily loaded with reading and memorization of Latin language and literature.

Although Leonardo seems to have had these putative weaknesses, he possessed extraordinary assets as well. One of Leonardo's greatest assets was his ability to deal with three-dimensional space. As Wallace (1966, p. 152) puts it, "few masters have approached Leonardo's ability to create three-dimensional effects by graphic means." His sketches, paintings, and drawings bear mute witness to this extraordinary skill. For example, some of his sketches of the Madonna and child are compositions in a two-point perspective in which the room where Madonna sits is set at an angle to the viewer's plane of sight. According to Stites *et al.* (1970, p. 63), such a composition is a daring innovation not found in other Italian paintings of that era. Leonardo's painting of the *Madonna and Child with St. Anne* (Anne Matterza) provides further evidence of superior spatial visualization. Portraying the personal relationship among the three figures (St. Anne, Mary, and the Christ Child) without violating the importance attributed to them by religious tradition had posed a tremendous problem in composition for all artists who had attempted this theme. Some artists like Hans Fries and Hans Holbein tried to solve the problem by making Anne sit beside Mary and placing the child between them. In such an arrangement, however, the figures become static and lose a good deal of dynamism. Others, such as Jakob Cornelisz and Petrus Christus, placed the Christ Child on the lap of Mary who, in turn, was held by Anne. Such a composition results in progressively smaller figures with St. Anne becoming the most pervading and dominant person, a contradiction of religious convention. Leonardo seems to have solved the problem of the hierarchy of religious importance without sacrificing dynamism through a gestalt-like fusion of figures in the form of the "pyramidal arrangement." Many critics consider this as a significant contribution (Eissler, 1961, p. 47). Such a fusion of figures is also strikingly apparent in the *Last Supper*, in which the disciples are portrayed in groups of three. Attempts to separate the figures of John from Judas and those of James and Thomas would not be any easier than separating Mary from Anne. One may, therefore, conclude that it was Leonardo's cognitive style of perceiving and imaging in terms of visual gestalts that facilitated such creations.

The celebrated *Mona Lisa* has been subjected to several interpretations, including a psychoanalytic interpretation by Freud (1964), who attributes the enigmatic quality of the painting to Leonardo's childhood experiences and other personality conflicts. It is quite possible, however, that the model for Mona Lisa did indeed possess a strange and compelling personality, the fleeting manifestation of which, as it swept across her face, was captured and preserved for posterity by the photographic mind of Leonardo. Indeed, Stites *et al.* (1970, p. 329) present rather convincing evidence to show that Mona Lisa was actually the remarkable Isabelle d' Este, daughter of the Duke and Duchess of Ferrara and the wife of the Marquis Genzaga of Mantua, and not the wife of the Florentine merchant Giocondo as is commonly believed.

Isabella is reported to have had a complicated personality and, as Cartwright (1932, p. 83) reports, she was described by one of her admirers as the greatest woman in the world. It is not surprising, therefore that such a unique model together with Leonardo's unusual talent—freezing action in a photograph-like fashion and transferring it to the canvas with impressive veracity (as revealed by his sketches of the battle of Anghiari)—should result in the *Mona Lisa*.

In addition to art, Leonardo's skill in the areas of applied engineering, geometry, and music could be viewed as evidence of his superior simultaneous information-processing ability. Leonardo's manuscripts from 1496 through 1499 devote a great deal more space to geometry than to any other subject matter. This is an indication of his preoccupation with that field during those years. In fact, while copying Euclid's theorems, Leonardo did not transcribe the Latin text word for word but often translated and recorded the theorems in an unusual form: a series of drawings. For him, drawing was another form of expression, a medium in which he excelled. Leonardo was also much occupied with music, and it appears that he was not only an excellent performer on the lyre but also an instructor.

Spatial ability is known to correlate better with geometry than with arithmetics (Barakat, 1951; Smith, 1960), and it is also believed that "the ability to recognize and to execute and above all, to create a melodic pattern is a spatial ability not unlike the visual detection of an embedded figure or the mental rotation of a geometrical form [Harris, 1978, p. 425]." Conversely, a proclivity to commit syntactical errors in language and a deficit in sequential ability seem to go hand in hand. Based on the observation of alexic patients with lesions in the frontal areas of the cortex, Benson (1977) concluded that several functions essential for reading, such as the ability to maintain the sequence of verbal information and the ability to interpret grammatical structures, deteriorate with frontal pathological conditions. This finding suggests a close relationship between syntactical ability and sequential information-processing ability.

These principles, when applied to Leonardo, would suggest that he had a striking imbalance in his cognitive abilities with a remarkably well-developed simultaneous information-processing skill and an associated weak sequential ability.

It has been hinted in earlier sections of the chapter that such an imbalance may be related to a form of cerebral organization that is different from the usual. Do we have any evidence that is suggestive of an unusual form of cerebral organization in the case of Leonardo?

Vasari's biographical account of Leonardo indicates that he was not right-handed. Evidence for the possibility that he was mixed-handed or ambidexterous comes from several other observations. A record made by the secretary of Cardinal Louis of Aragon regarding a 1517 visit to Amboise makes reference to a stroke suffered by Leonardo and describes him as "the most excellent painter of our time from who [sic] one could not expect any more good work since he is subject to a certain paralysis of the *right* hand [Stites *et al.*, 1970, p. 379; italics mine]." If Leonardo used his left hand exclusively for painting, paralysis of the right hand should have had no effect on his artistic work. Either Leonardo used both hands equally well or the cardinal's secretary was mistaken in his observation. Furthermore, Leonardo's letters to Machiavelli and Cardinal Ippolite d' Este show that he could write from left to right, in the conventional manner, probably with his right hand (as the direction of the strokes indicates) and do so with ease and clarity, as these letters reveal no signs of belabored writing in the form of misformed or distorted characters (Stites *et al.*, 1970, p. 320). The observation that Leonardo's paralysis was limited to the right side of the body indicates that the lesion resulting from the stroke was localized in his left hemisphere. The absence of any remarks by the secretary regarding any speech impairment suggests that language in Leonardo was localized either in his right hemisphere or was diffusely represented in both hemispheres.[2] Because the evidence indicates that Leonardo was ambidexterous rather than consistently left-handed, one is led to the conclusion that his cerebral organization could be considered diffuse. Such a form of organization frequently is associated with deficiencies in linguistic skills and arithmetic calculation and with superior abilities in spatial visualization and other space-related tasks. Support for such a conclusion is provided by a number of studies. Corballis and Beale (1976), after citing some of these studies, conclude that

> There may be a category of individuals who inherit not left-handedness *per se*, but the absence of any consistent predisposition to be left or right-handed. Because of random influences during development, some of these individuals will be left-handed, some right-handed, and many will display mixed preferences. We shall suggest . . . that these "bilateral" individuals may show some specific deficits in reading, writing, or in telling left from right, but they may compensate by showing *superior*

[2] The additional remark by the Cardinal's secretary that "although Leonardo can no longer paint with his former sweetness, he can still draw and teach others [Stites *et al.*, 1970, p. 379]" indicates that Leonardo's linguistic ability was not seriously impaired and, in all probability, remained totally unaffected.

ability on other cognitive skills. Since some proportion of these individuals will be left-handers, this could explain why left-handers sometimes excell on certain tasks. Among those we have termed "bilateral" left-handers, it appears that there is a more diffuse representation of language within as well as between hemispheres. It is conceivable that this allows for greater powers of integration [p. 109].

Thus, Leonardo's errors in writing, language, and computation can be viewed as manifestations of a weakness in sequential processing ability, while his great achievements in art and science can be seen as the result of an overcompensating simultaneous processing ability.

Leonardo's uneven cognitive profile should by no means be considered an oddity. Difficulties in reading, spelling, and arithmetic have characterized many men of eminence who distinguished themselves in areas that require holistic–gestalt imaging. Thomas Alva Edison reportedly never learned how to spell, and, up to the time of his manhood, his grammar and syntax were appalling (Thompson, 1971). By his own admission Einstein had poor memory for words (Hoffman, 1972). However, Einstein excelled in geometry from early childhood and, even at an early age, was able to confirm the Pythagorean theorem by simple visualization of the triangle (Patten, 1973). His unusual form of thinking, which was primarily nonverbal and spatial, was responsible for freeing Einstein from the conventional mode of verbally mediated thinking that probably hindered the imagination of other physicists.

Study 5

It is sometimes claimed that the high incidence of reading failure in English language could partly be due to the "irregularity" of English spelling and the unpredictable nature of the grapheme–phoneme correspondence (Hall, 1961). Even though the grapheme–phoneme relationship in English may be more regular than suspected (Carroll, 1964), the fact that every letter of the alphabet does not have a single invariant sound associated with it may be a factor that makes it difficult for some children to learn to read. This may be particularly true of simultaneous-deficient children who may be overly dependent on the sequential features of the written word. This may also explain the frequently made observation that a basically logographic script such as Chinese is hard to learn to read (Downing, 1973, p. 193),[3] since such a script does not

---

[3] Some authors have pointed out that learning to read the Chinese logogram is not entirely dependent upon rote memory alone. The number of strokes in each logogram and the constituent radical and phonetic elements of each character are said to facilitate "feature analysis" of the logogram, thus bringing it closer to the alphabetic script, such as English, than is usually suspected (see C. K. Leong, 1973).

lend itself readily to sequential analysis. At least one experimental study (Kline & Lee, 1972) found that about 13% of the Canadian–Chinese children had difficulty learning to read Chinese, whereas only 9% of the children with a similar background had difficulty in learning to read English. The conflicting conclusion (Rozin, Poritsky, & Sotsky, 1971; Harrigan, 1976) that logograms were in fact far easier to learn to read than English words, for some poor readers whose mother tongue was English, may be due to a possibility that only a few logograms had to be learned. Yet, if a purely logographic script is difficult to read for some children, then it follows from the imbalance hypothesis that a purely alphabetic script should be difficult for some other children. As it is proposed that both simultaneous and sequential processes are involved in fluent reading, children who are deficient in sequential processing ability should encounter difficulty in learning to read an alphabetic script that has a very high degree of letter–sound correspondence.

Recently, an investigation of limited scope was carried out with readers of such a script. Forty children whose mother tongue was Tamil were asked to read passages printed both in Tamil and English, and their performance was taped, transcribed, and analyzed. Tamil is one of the four principal Dravidian languages spoken by more than 30 million people in Southern India, parts of Ceylon, Malaysia, and a few other places in the world. With the exception of classical Sanskrit, Tamil has the oldest written literature in India, with some stone inscriptions dating back to the third century B.C. Contemporary writing is in cursive form and is believed to be a modified version of Brahmi script. It is a highly inflected language, with grammatical categories such as tense, number, and case represented in the form of suffixes. The root of the word, therefore, always occurs at the beginning of the word. Furthermore, it is an agglutinative or synthetic language in the sense that separate formal units of meanings are often incorporated in a single word. For example,

vasi $\longrightarrow$ 'read'
avan $\longrightarrow$ 'he'
vasikiravan (*vasi* + *ki* + *avan*) $\longrightarrow$ 'he who reads'
ukku $\longrightarrow$ 'to'
vasikiravanukku (*vasi* + *ki* + *avan* + *ukku*) $\longrightarrow$ 'to him who reads'.

The Tamil script is almost entirely alphabetical, with each character representing one phoneme only. Because the phoneme–grapheme correspondence is nearly perfect with each character representing a single sound, every written word in Tamil could be read by sounding out its component letters. Consequently, although poor sight vocabulary can slow down one's rate of reading, it cannot bring one to a standstill, as it easily can in the case of English-language material. This, of course, is because unlike Tamil, many English words cannot be read by sounding out the constituent letters of the word. Such a letter-by-letter decoding of Tamil words is possible for the reader who possesses sufficient skill in sequential processing of information. What about the child who does not possess adequate sequential skills? It may be expected that such a child is likely to use simultaneous processing strategies in reading Tamil words by relying heavily on his sight vocabulary. Such an excessive reliance on sight vocabulary is likely to result in the omission of suffixes and inflexions while reading. The preponderance of such syntactic errors committed by sequentially deficient children was noted in the previous study. The first prediction of this study, therefore, was that even a script with a very high degree of grapheme–phoneme correspondence would create difficulty in accurate reading for some children, such difficulty manifesting itself essentially in the form of syntactic errors. The second prediction was based on the assumption that these children would follow essentially the same strategy in reading English and would therefore, again commit many syntactic errors. Consequently, a high degree of correlation could be expected between the number of syntactic errors committed by these children while reading each language.

Forty boys attending grades 8–10 were investigated. Their native language was Tamil, and all had been attending school since they were 5 years old. Almost from the first grade, these children were promoted from one grade to another only if they had demonstrated competence in the different school subjects by passing examinations. There is therefore reason to believe that all the subjects who participated in the study had at least average intelligence. No tests of reading or intelligence have been standardized on children in this part of India. Formal instruction in the English language starts at the fifth grade, and English is taught at least 5 hours each week. The alphabet is introduced first, and the method of reading instruction is essentially phonetic.

These 40 boys were asked to read a long passage of about five paragraphs from their Tamil textbook. The passage chosen was from a chapter that had not yet been taught at school. Subsequently, each child was asked to read three passages (of the same level) from Durrell's reading test (Durrell, 1955). All the eighth-grade boys were started with Durrell's level 2, ninth-grade boys with level 3, and tenth-grade boys with level 4. As each child read passages from both languages, his performance was taped; it was later transcribed, and reading errors were analyzed.

The reading error analysis showed that very few errors of mispronunciation were committed in the reading of Tamil. Mispronunciation of words, literal decoding of words, and omission of words, however, were common in the reading of English. Of great significance were the reading errors that resulted in agrammatism. Such errors were committed in both languages and were mainly caused by omission and substitution of suffixes in Tamil and by omission and substitution of entire words in English. Because many of these errors involved simple English words such as *went, play, car, there,* and *put,* such errors may be interpreted to have been caused by phonetic decoding difficulties rather than by a lack of familiarity with the words. It has to be remembered that even the youngest reader had received at least 3 years of instruction in English. The product moment correlation coefficient obtained between the mean number of agrammatic errors committed in English and the mean number of similar errors committed in Tamil was .92. This impressive correlation between errors in both languages suggests that the mechanisms responsible for the production of agrammatic errors in reading may be the same in both languages.

Because no standardized reading tests are available in the Tamil language, it is extremely difficult to determine with precision how many children actually were reading disabled. A rather crude method was used to compute the probable percentage of children who could be considered as dyslexic. Yule and Rutter (1976) have pointed out that on theoretical grounds, the distribution of discrepancies between predicted and actual attainment in reading should be normal. If an excess of several underachievers is found, this would suggest that severe underachievement or specific reading retardation constitutes a qualitatively different category. Following this logic, the frequency distribution of agrammatic reading errors committed by the subjects in both languages was computed. The results are graphically shown in Figure 1.7. The mean number of agrammatic errors was 5.50 (*SD* 4.56) and 6.45 (*SD* 5.01) for Tamil and English, respectively. Four boys in Tamil and five boys in English accounted for more than 24% of the total errors. In the graph, these boys were responsible for the upswing of the curves. It is also informative to note that the five boys who committed the highest number of errors in reading English also committed the highest number of errors in Tamil. On the basis of these data, it may be concluded that about 10% of these children are disabled readers,

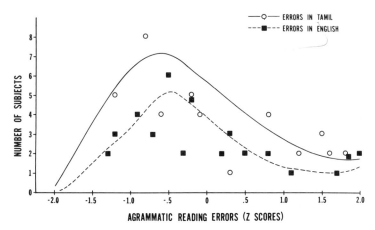

Figure 1.7. Distribution of agrammatic reading errors committed in two different languages.

in both languages. This figure is in agreement with that of Oommen (1973) who estimated that 5–10% of Tamil-speaking children are disabled in reading their native script. These poor readers seem to represent a population qualitatively different from the rest.

Considering the preliminary nature of the study, much significance cannot be attached to these findings. Nevertheless, the notion that a phonetically regular script will drastically minimize reading difficulty does not find support in this study. These retarded readers can decode phonetically most of the words in Tamil, but they commit an extraordinarily great number of agrammatic errors while reading connected prose. More importantly, the two predictions made earlier, namely, that a certain number of children would be found to be poor readers even in a phonetically regular language and that there would be a good deal of similarity between children's performances in Tamil and English, appear to have gained confirmation from the present study. These observations could be readily accommodated within the imbalance hypothesis which holds that subjects deficient in sequential processing ability tend to be overdependent on sight vocabulary and consequently ignore suffixes and inflexions.

The frequently made statement that reading disability is rarely found in some languages may be based on superficial observation wherein all but the severe "word blind" cases go unnoticed. Even simple reading tests may not be able to detect the syntactic deficiencies of some readers. Specialized diagnostic procedures such as reading error analysis should be able to detect subtle deficiencies and show that the prevalence of reading defects is indeed much higher in these languages than suspected.

Summary and Comments on the Five Studies

Despite the differences among them in terms of subjects and methodology used, these five studies each provide information that is supportive of the imbalance hypothesis. The first study showed that sequential- and simultaneous-deficient children exhibit different sets of symptom characteristics. The second study which also investigated children revealed that three separate subtypes of dyslexia could be identified and that these groups are isolable on the basis of their test performance, each subtype having its own unique cognitive profile. The third and fourth studies which utilized the case study approach clearly demonstrated intraindividual imbalances in cognitive abilities. Finally, the last study indicated that reading a highly "regular" phonetic script does not totally eliminate reading difficulties encountered by readers of that script and that such a script does present a problem for a group of children who may be deficient in sequential information-processing ability.

An analysis of the spelling patterns and the reading errors committed by the different dyslexic subgroups further indicates that such errors are not random manifestations but are indications that alternate strategies are being used by these readers. Consequently, dyslexia could be considered as the product of *both* a deficit and the utilization of alternative cognitive strategies (see Heilman & Rothi, this volume, for such a possibility in alexia). This is what the imbalance hypothesis proposes.

THE IMBALANCE HYPOTHESIS AND SOME KNOWN CHARACTERISTICS OF DYSLEXIA

Having examined the imbalance hypothesis in the light of some psychological investigations, we will now consider the adequacy of the hypothesis in explaining some of the reasonably well-established findings regarding dyslexia. There are at least four rather well-documented observations, namely, (*a*) a substantial difference in the sex ratio among dyslexics, (*b*) a greater tendency for reversal writing of letters and words among dyslexic children than among normals, (*c*) an almost constant association between reading disability and defective spelling, and (*d*) the "rarity" of dyslexia in some languages such as Japanese. I will discuss each of these in turn and then examine the relationship between hemispheric specialization and dyslexia.

Sex Difference and Dyslexia

The unequal sex ratio in the epidemiology of many diseases with an excess representation of males as compared to females has been well documented (see Taylor & Ounsted, 1972). Reading disability is no exception to this general observation. In order for the imbalance hypothesis to account for the excessive representation of males among dyslexics, it has to be shown that more male brains are prone to excessive imbalances in information-processing strategies than female brains. A number of studies that have examined sex differences in information-processing strategies within the framework of lateralization of cerebral functions suggest that differences of lateralization between the sexes do exist. Levy (1980), for example, cites a number of studies of normal subjects which show that females exhibit smaller and less consistent hemispheric asymmetries on both nonverbal and verbal tests thus suggesting greater bilateralization of functions in females than in males. A study by Witelson (1976) in which 200 normal boys and girls between the ages of 6 and 13 years were investigated with reference to spatial ability showed that boys performed in a manner consistent with right hemisphere specialization whereas girls did not show such a clear-cut differentiation of functions, thus indicating bilateral representation of spatial ability. A review of dichotic studies by Harshman and Remington (Harris, 1978, p. 471) suggests the possibility that language ability, like spatial ability, may also be strongly lateralized in males. A large-scale study by Lake and Bryden (1976) also indicated a greater right ear superiority for spoken digits in males than in females.

Some clinical studies also support the possibility of an uneven lateralization of functions in the male brain and a more or less uniform distribution of functions between the two hemispheres in the female brain. McGlone and Kertesz (1973), for instance, found that a left hemisphere lesion is likely to affect both language and spatial functions in females, whereas in males the deficit is predominantly limited to language function. McGlone (1977) also reports that left hemisphere lesions resulted in three times more men than women being classified as aphasic. In another study, Sherman (1974) concluded that a left temporal lobectomy affected spatial performance to a much greater extent in females than in males.

Taken together, these studies suggest a stronger lateralization of cognitive abilities in males than in females, and the evidence is particularly convincing for spatial ability. It is possible that such a clear-cut distribution of cognitive abilities in the male may provide a potential condition for excessive dependence on the function that is represented in one of the two hemispheres. Conversely, it may be assumed that in the female brain these functions are relatively uniformly distributed between the two hemispheres and, as a result, the female is able to utilize both simultaneous and sequential functions to more or less an equal degree.

We will examine the feasibility of such an explanation with reference to spatial ability, for which differences between the sexes have been well documented, and see how an uneven distribution of abilities may affect the reading process. Maccoby and Jacklin (1974), in their review of research on sex differences, conclude that male superiority on visual spatial tasks is fairly consistently found in adolescence and adulthood even though not in childhood. The male advantage on tests of spatial ability, according to them, increases through the high school years. In a survey which focused specifically on differences in spatial ability between sexes, Harris (1978) also concluded that "the fact of the male's superior spatial ability is not in dispute; but the explanation is [p. 406]."

That constitutional factors are major determinants of spatial ability is demonstrated by at least three studies (Stafford, 1961; Hartlage, 1970; Bock & Kolakowski, 1973). Bock and Kolakowski studied 167 families and concluded that spatial ability is in part determined by a recessive sex-linked gene. These investigators, however, leave open the possibility of hormonal and environmental factors playing a role in the expressivity of the gene. According to the sex-linked recessive gene model, 25% of the girls could be expected to score above the male mean score, thus producing a 2:1 ratio in favor of males since nearly 50% of the males will score above that mean.

According to the imbalance hypothesis, a relatively superior spatial ability in conjunction with a poor sequential ability is likely to facilitate an excessive dependence on simultaneous processing strategies in reading. Such a reliance on simultaneous processing strategies is likely to lead to a heavy dependence on sight vocabulary and a corresponding neglect of phonetic and other sequential features of the written word. As seen earlier, this may lead to agrammatic errors such as omission and substitution of inflexions and grammatical function words as well as to a nonphonetic pattern of spelling errors. As the ratio of males to females who perform above average in tests of spatial ability is about 2 : 1, other things being equal, we can expect twice as many boys as girls to be overly dependent upon simultaneous strategies. In other words, in a large group of randomly selected children, one can expect twice as many boys as girls to commit agrammatical errors in reading. This is the ratio obtained in the study described earlier (Experiment 2). Also, in an as yet unpublished study (Aaron, Baker, & Hickox) which involved college dyslexics, a similar ratio (4 men and 2 women) was obtained. Admittedly, the number of subjects in both studies is too small to permit any firm conclusions; however, a definite trend is noticeable. These studies also showed that among the dyslexics impaired at the decoding level, those with a sequential processing deficiency constituted the larger of the two subgroups.

If a script such as English, the reading of which calls for a combination of both sequential and simultaneous processes, lends itself more readily to a bilateral distribution of cognitive abilities such as the one found in girls, then relatively pure scripts such as the logographic and purely alphabetic scripts should present greater difficulties for females than males. A study by Kline and Lee (1972) provides partial support for such an expectation. These investigators studied 277 Canadian–Chinese children living in Canada and found that 21% of boys had problems in reading English only and 24% in reading Chinese only. Among girls, the corresponding figures were 5 and 10%. Even though more boys than girls were retarded in English, roughly the same number of boys were retarded in Chinese also. In the case of girls, however, twice as many had trouble with Chinese as in English. The study by Rozin, Poritsky, and Sotsky (1971) which showed that dyslexic children could learn to read far more easily with the aid of Chinese characters than the English alphabets had six boys and only two girls as subjects.

A higher number of male dyslexics is also found to be deficient in the simultaneous processing ability. Not only our studies of dyslexics, but also investigations of "word blind" children (who are apparently deficient in simultaneous processing ability) show a preponderance of males (cf. Hinshelwood, 1917). In order to account for the excessive number of males in the simultaneous-deficient category of dyslexia, the imbalance hypothesis would have to postulate that this many males are also superior to females in sequential information-processing ability. Even though Hinshelwood (1917) was much impressed with the auditory memory of these dyslexics, we do not have adequate experimental data to support such a contention. The imbalance hypothesis, therefore, has to be considered as providing only partial explanation of the sex differences observed in reading disorders.

Reversals in Writing and Dyslexia

As early as 1928, Orton noted that a striking tendency to reverse letters and even whole words while reading and a greater tendency to produce mirror writing were among the features common to dyslexic children. Orton was quick to point out that these children did not have any visual defect and, interestingly, went on to note "indeed the boy with the very severe degree of reading disability . . . was able to make a score on the Healy Pictorial Test that was equalled only by the record of superior adults [1928, pp. 1096–1097]." The term "strephosymbolia" indicates the importance Orton gave to such errors of distortion committed frequently by reading-disabled children. A more than usual amount of reversal and rotation errors in the reading and writings of dyslexic children has also been reported by other investigators (Saunders, 1962; Tjossem, Hansen, & Ripley, 1962; Eisenberg, 1966). In a factor analytic study, Lyle (1969) found that letter and sequence reversals in reading and letter reversals in writing characterized one of the two factors with the highest loading on reading behavior. The second factor Lyle extracted was described as a verbal factor with loadings on WISC arithmetic, information, coding, and digit span subtests. Lyle concluded that all types of reversals were associated with reading retardation.

A more direct investigation of reversal errors, particularly in reading, was undertaken by Liberman and her associates (1971). They studied the occurrence of reversals in reading in an entire school population of second-graders and concluded that letter confusions and reversals of sequence in dyslexics were not ubiquitous phenomena as commonly believed but occurred with appreciable frequency only among the children in the lowest third of the class. Even within the group of poor readers, only some reversed to a significant extent. Yet another study (Fischer, Liberman, & Shankweiler, 1978) showed that reversals in reading represented only a small proportion of the total number of reading errors. These observations probably apply to reversals in writing as well.

Thus, although frequent reference to reversals by investigators of dyslexic children suggests that letter and word reversals in writing are committed more often by dyslexic children than by normal readers, certain studies indicate both that not all poor readers make reversal errors and that even those who do will not systematically reverse everything they write but are inconsistent in their errors. These two generalizations are crucial to the imbalance hypothesis, as it will be argued that not all dyslexics but only one subgroup commit reversal errors in writing and that they do so on a random basis.

Simultaneous information-processing ability is described variously as spatial, synchronous, gestalt-like, and analogous. All these imply that such a process is not distributed over time and does not involve extraction of features by starting at one end and proceeding serially till the other end of the stimulus is reached. Consequently, the left-to-right orientation or any other direction relevant feature of the stimulus is unimportant when a stimulus is processed in a simultaneous fashion. Several studies show that adult humans can recognize a picture or a geometrical shape as familiar, even if it is the left–right mirror image of the one seen before and they cannot tell whether it is the original or not (Bartlett, 1932; Standing *et al.*, 1970; Rock, 1973). It appears, then, that stimuli which could be described as spatial or gestalt are processed without regard to their orientation along the horizontal axis. One can argue, therefore, that subjects who process letters and words as though they are gestalts would also tend to disregard the directional feature of such stimuli. Such a neglect could result in reversals, particularly when such stimuli have to be reproduced from memory. Subjects who process such stimuli sequentially, however, are not likely to commit such orientation errors as they tend to process the stimuli serially from one end to the other. Even the simultaneous-dependent subgroup of dyslexics is likely to reverse only on a random basis as they merely disregard the directional features of the stimulus. They will not, therefore, systematically reverse all the words and letters. Further, inversions and other forms of rotations will seldom occur in their writings.

On the basis of this explanation, two predictions could be made: (*a*) more boys than girls will show reversal errors in their writing, as there are more boys than girls with superior spatial ability; (*b*) among dyslexics, those who are deficient in sequential processing ability, and therefore dependent upon simultaneous processes, will commit a higher number of orientation errors than the dyslexics who have adequate sequential skills.

One of the very few studies (Davidson, 1935) that investigated reversal tendencies in children required kindergarten and first-grade children to look at a letter (such as *b, d, q, p, n, h*) and select from among an array of four letters the one that looked exactly like the stimulus letter. The four-letter multiple choice included, in addition to the standard stimulus, three other visually confusable letters. Davidson found that significantly more first-grade boys than girls made confusion errors (*b* for *d, q* for *p*, etc.). There was no sex difference among kindergarten children. One of the studies mentioned earlier (Aaron, 1978) found that among dyslexic children an ability to remember faces, a tendency to produce nonphonetic spelling errors, and the tendency to reverse write tachistoscopically presented letters were all significantly associated. These children with poor sequential but adequate simultaneous abilities reversed more letters than did control groups and dyslexics who were deficient in simultaneous processing ability. Reversal writing tendency was significantly greater when a 5-sec delay was interposed between the tachistoscopic presentation and writing than when reproduction followed tachistoscopic exposure immediately. This finding, as well as the results of an earlier investigation (Aaron & Malatesha, 1974), indicates that the reversal tendency may not be attributable to a mechanism associated with short-term memory but to some process involving long-term memory. Leonardo's tendency to write in mirror-reversal form could also be attributed to his relatively superior simultaneous processing ability.

Thus, the imbalance hypothesis could explain the frequent occurrence of reversal errors in the writing of dyslexic children by attributing such errors to a tendency of these children to process letters and words simultaneously as though they are gestalts or visual images and not as a string of individual phonetic units. Attributing reversal errors in writing to superior spatial or simultaneous information-processing ability will be in direct conflict with the traditional view that such errors arise as a result of weak visuospatial ability.

Spelling Errors and Dyslexia

The relationship between reading disability and spelling disorders is well established. In a review Malmquist (1958) estimated the correlation coefficient between reading and spelling errors to range from .5 to .8. It is my observation that even though poor spellers may not be poor readers, all poor readers are poor spellers. Any theory of dyslexia, therefore, should account for the excessive amount of spelling errors committed by the dyslexic subject.

Barron (1980), who studied 24 sixth-grade children of normal reading ability and 24 children with poor reading ability, concluded that good readers use both phonological and visual–orthographic strategies in spelling, whereas poor readers use only one of these two strategies. This and similar observations (Nelson, 1980) suggest the possibility that, just as in reading, there are two routes involved in spelling, namely, a phonemic–graphemic route which operates by translating the phonemic elements of the word into their graphemic equivalents, and a direct semantic–graphemic route. Boder's (1973) classification of spelling errors is based on a similar logic, even though she does not place her diagnostic procedure within a linguistic framework.

As mentioned earlier, the child whose sequential processing ability is poor, most probably, depends on the visual gestalt of the word for spelling it. Such a child ignores the sequential order of elements within the word and consequently omits, displaces, and reverses letters within the word. This frequently results in bizarre, nonphonetic spelling. On the contrary, the child who is poor in simultaneous processing ability is likely to depend on the sequential phonetic elements of the word and spells the word the way it sounds. In a way, such a child "regularizes" the spelling of words. These two strategies, therefore, result in two different patterns of misspelling. There is some evidence from clinical neurology to support the possibility that these two strategies of spelling could be related to the two cerebral hemispheres. Luria (1973), for example, reports that aphasic patients with lesions of the left hemisphere who were unable to write a word by dictation could, nevertheless, execute automatized functions such as writing their own signatures. According to Simernitskaya (1974), when patients with right hemisphere lesions who have lost their ability to write automatically and rapidly, were asked to write slowly, in a letter-by-letter fashion, they could write with a minimum number of errors. Simernitskaya concludes that lesions of the left hemisphere result in a breakdown of the coding of sounds into phonemes whereas right hemisphere lesions affect the organization of automated processes.

Available experimental data support a possible association between the two types of spelling patterns and the two types of information-processing strategies. In the study that was described earlier (Aaron, 1978), there emerged relatively strong positive associations between a serial processing ability for digits and phonetic spelling errors on the one hand and an ability to remember faces and nonphonetic spelling errors on the other. In two other studies—one involving 17 dyslexic college students (Aaron, Baker, & Hickox, in press) and another involving 15 elementary school children (described earlier in this chapter)—among the sequential-deficient subjects 4 out of 6 college students and 2 out of 3 children committed predominantly nonphonetic spelling errors. Among the simultaneous-deficient subjects, 3 out of 4 college students were found to be phonetic spellers, and 1 of the 2 children also committed predominantly phonetic errors in spelling.

In spite of the small number of subjects studied, these results suggest that there is a tendency for dyslexic individuals to depend exclusively on one of the two information-processing strategies for spelling. The imbalance hypothesis, therefore, could provide an explanation for the poor spelling of dyslexics and for the two major spelling error patterns into which the majority of dyslexic spelling mistakes fall.

Incidence Variability of Dyslexia in Different Languages

Cross-national differences in teaching methods, age at which reading instruction is begun, and testing procedures render direct comparisons of the extent of reading disabilities in different languages very difficult. Some broad conclusions, nevertheless, can be reached by analyzing data from those comparative studies available. One such general finding is that the incidence of dyslexia varies a great deal from language to language. The lowest incidence of dyslexia is reported for Japanese (Makita, 1968) and one of the highest for English (Critchley, 1970, p. 96). Other languages seem to fall somewhere in between these two extremities. According to one estimate, about 10% of the first-graders in France fail to learn to read French well (Ruthman, 1973). In German-speaking countries, a somewhat lower figure of 5% is reported (Klassen, 1972).

When a superficial comparison of the scripts of different languages and the degree of difficulty in learning to read them is made, a rough relationship between the phonetic regularity of the script and the incidence of dyslexia emerges. Nevertheless, it turns out that the lowest frequency of reading disability is associated with neither the strictly alphabetic nor the purely logographic script, but rather with the script that combines alphabetic and logographic elements. As was mentioned earlier, an investigation indicated that Tamil, which has a very high degree of phoneme–grapheme correspondence, presents difficulties for nearly 10% of the children who study it. This figure is corroborated by Oommen (1973) who thinks that anywhere from 5 to 10% of Tamil-speaking schoolchildren may have poor reading abilities. At the other extreme, the Chinese language uses a highly morphemic script written in the form of logograms; and, as seen earlier, nearly 24% of the boys and 10% of the girls are reported to have difficulty learning to read the Chinese script (Kline & Lee, 1972). According to Goody (1968), the Chinese script is an enormous impediment to literacy in that country, and only a small and specially trained professional group in the total society can master the nearly 50,000 logograms to be learned. In contrast to these two widely different forms of scripts, written Japanese, which is a combination of alphabets and logograms, has the least recorded incidence of dyslexia (Makita, 1968; Sakamoto & Makita, 1973). Makita, on the basis of his survey, reports that less than 1% of the population has reading disorders, and as a matter of fact, dyslexia is a rare phenomenon in Japan. In order to explain such a low incidence of dyslexia, the imbalance hypothesis would have to advance a tentative explanation that the Japanese script somehow minimizes the difficulties encountered by both the sequential deficient and the simultaneous deficient information processor. This would mean that the Japanese script represents a judicious blend of both sequential and simultaneous stimuli so that potential dyslexics of both subtypes encounter a minimum amount of difficulty. Evaluation of such a proposition requires an examination of the Japanese script.

As Sakamoto and Makita (1973) describe it, four separate symbol systems—*hiragana, Katakana, kanji,* and *roma-ji*—can be found in Japanese. Hiragana and Katakana are more or less like English lower case and upper case letters and are phonetic symbols, each character representing a syllable. These two, from an information-processing perspective, could therefore be considered to belong to a single system, the kana system. There are 92 kana characters in use and almost all grammatical morphemes and function words are written in kana. Kanji characters are logograms borrowed from the Chinese language. Each logogram represents a semantic unit. Kanji characters are used mainly to represent nouns, verbs, and adjectives and constitute about 25–30% of written words in a sentence. Therefore, kanji constitutes the second major system of script. Roma-ji is the romanized Japanese alphabet and is rarely used in print.

The first script to which the beginning reader is exposed is the alphabetic kana which, to a large extent, is phonetically regular. Each kana character is pronounced one way only, no matter what word it is part of. All books of the beginning readers are written in the kana script. From then on, a transition is slowly made to the final form of script, which is a combination of kana and kanji characters. Such a transition is accomplished by replacing a few kana characters at a time with the corresponding kanji character. The kana script and the kanji symbol that replaced it have no visual resemblance to each other, so that no unlearning of kana is involved. In other words, the kana script is not like the English letter which assumes different phonetic values when it is embedded in words. The child who has to read the words *America* and *all* has to learn two different sound values for the letter *a*, both of which are different from the way it was pronounced when the alphabet was learned. For an English-speaking child reading these two words means suppressing the original phoneme associated with the character *a*. The immutable symbol–sound relationship may be one of the reasons for the low incidence of dyslexia in the Japanese language.

As we saw, the beginning instruction is entirely in the kana phonetic script. Consequently, children poor in sequential processing ability may have some difficulty with this phonetic processing. These children, nevertheless, could decode the words, albeit at a slow rate, in a letter-by-letter fashion. In fact, some studies point out that children find it more difficult to learn to read kana than kanji characters (Sakamoto & Makita, 1973). According to Sakamato and Makita, 58% of 4-year-old children and 83% of 5-year-old children can read all kana symbols. (Probably, if an effort is made, an equal percentage of English-speaking children can also be taught to read all the letters of the English alphabet. But, unfortunately, they will have to considerably modify their original letter–sound learning when the same letters are encountered in the context of words or when blending them into syllables becomes a necessity.) Introducing the kana script at early stages of learning to read, however, does not detain the sequential-deficient child for too long, as kanji soon comes to the rescue. Consequently, even though these children may not become excellent readers, they nevertheless can read. They can plod through the kana script in a letter-by-letter fashion, and then with kanji they are quite comfortable. The simultaneous-deficient reader, on the other hand, may encounter difficulties with kanji. But the total number of kanji characters in actual use does not exceed 3000, and only about 2000 kanji characters are to be learned by children before the end of high school. Furthermore, an average sentence contains only about 25–35% of its words in the form of kanji characters. Some of these could, of course, be guessed correctly by making use of semantic and contextual cues.

Yet another factor that may be responsible for the low incidence of reading difficulty in Japanese may be the way kana and kanji characters are embedded within a sentence. The kana letters and kanji ideograms come in a prescribed sequence in a sentence. Reading a sentence in Japanese may first involve sequential processing of some kana alphabets, then the simultaneous processing of the kanji logogram, and then probably a few kana characters, and so on. The reader of Japanese script is probably not required to use both sequential and simultaneous processes concurrently in order to encode a word. In this respect, the reading of the English script is different: Many words require the sequential processing of some crucial letters in a word as well as the simultaneous processing of the overall word form, both operations being carried out more or less simultaneously.

According to the imbalance hypothesis, then, the kana and kanji scripts are processed differently and separately, the former in a sequential and the latter in a simultaneous fashion. Clinical and experimental studies support such a view. For example, a tachistoscopic study by Sasanuma, Itoh, Mori, and Kobayashi (1977) found a right visual field superiority for kana nonsense words and another study by Hatta (1977), which used actual words, showed a superior left visual field superiority for kanji words. A number of clinical studies which investigated neurological patients also revealed a dissociation in the reading of kanji and kana scripts (Sasanuma & Fujimura, 1971; Sasanuma, 1974; Yamadori, 1975). Additional evidence for the differential processing of the two types of Japanese scripts by the two cerebral hemispheres has been provided by Sasanuma (1975) and Sasanuma and Monoi (1975). This view is well articulated by Coltheart (1980b), who says that "in Japanese readers, the right hemisphere is better at processing kanji characters than kana characters; the left hemisphere shows the reverse specialization [p. 350]." Summarizing some of these research findings, Sasanuma (1980) concluded that kana and kanji processings include different cognitive strategies with a phonological (grapheme–phoneme) processing for kana and a direct visual (grapheme–meaning) processing for kanji characters.

If a neuropsychologist were asked to devise an ideal script that would minimize the incidence of dyslexia, he would proceed to do so on the logic that such a script should minimize the difficulties that would be experienced by potential readers deficient in sequential and simultaneous processing abilities. Such a script would be a compromise between the alphabetic and morphemic scripts and would, in all probability, resemble Japanese.

Finally, the possibility that the Japanese brain itself is differently organized cannot be left out of consideration. At least one writer has claimed this to be the case (Sibatani, 1980). Such an idea would merit serious consideration if it is shown that in Japanese children who learn English as a second language the incidence of disability in reading English is also very low.

Hemispheric Specialization and Dyslexia

The split brain studies of the 1960s gave a boost to the generally held belief that in a majority of human beings the left hemisphere is verbal and the right hemisphere is spatial. Research carried out during the past 20 years or so has shown, however, that the right hemisphere also has some linguistic capability (Zaidel, 1976; Searleman, 1977). Views about cerebral specialization have been accordingly modified to accommodate these new findings. As Madden and Nebes (1980) have suggested, in the light of available information, it may be more accurate to consider the two hemispheres as differing from each other in the strategies of their operation rather than in the type of information they handle. When viewed in this manner, the left hemisphere could be considered as a sequential processor and the right hemisphere as a simultaneous processor.

The possible relationship between hemispheric specialization and reading disability has been an attractive area for research since the time of Orton, who was the first investigator to speculate on such a relationship (Orton, 1928). The introduction of techniques such as dichotic listening and tachistoscopic presentation of visual stimuli has made possible the experimental investigation of this and similar hypotheses. However, the result has been to dampen the earlier optimism, as the numerous dichotic listening and tachistoscopic studies that have been carried out with the intent of identifying the etiology of reading disability have failed to produce unequivocal results. Satz (1976) reviewed 19 studies, of which 15 had used the dichotic listening task and 4 the visual half field task. He concluded that these studies shed little light on the relationship between cerebral dominance and reading disability, mainly because many factors such as age of the subjects and the methodology and type of test stimuli used confound the data. A review by Naylor (1980) reached essentially a similar conclusion.

Although many factors may contribute to a lack of consensus among these experimental findings, one of the major reasons for the lack of consensus may be the failure to recognize the heterogeneity of dyslexia. A failure to separate the clinical subtypes on some a priori basis usually leads to the pooling of data of all the subjects. As the strengths and weaknesses of the two major subtypes of dyslexias are almost complementary to each other, lumping of the data is likely to wipe out the mean differences between dyslexic children and normal readers. If this is true, then treating the subtypes separately should produce more meaningful results. Has this actually happened?

A few studies have either separated the subtypes on some basis before testing or have investigated only one subgroup of disabled readers. In general, the outcome of these studies appears to be different from that of studies that did not undertake such a procedure (see Malatesha & Dougan, this volume). Witelson (1976) studied 85 dyslexic boys who had a significantly higher performance IQ than verbal IQ. On the basis of their performance in tactual, tachistoscopic, and dichotic listening tests, she concluded that dyslexic boys have bilateral representation of spatial functions and that dyslexics tend to use spatial–holistic strategies more than normals do. Pirozzolo and Rayner (1979) investigated 18 dyslexic children and a group of matched controls on a tachistoscopic task. These subjects could be considered to belong to one of the two dyslexic subgroups as they all had low verbal IQs. It was found that the disabled readers' right hemisphere was superior to the left hemisphere in the perception of words. In addition, the proportion of words presented to the left visual field and correctly identified was higher for the dyslexics than it was for the normals. Kershner (1977) selected disabled readers on the basis of their scores on the Gates–MacGinitie reading comprehension test. Consequently, these subjects could be considered as a special subgroup of dyslexics. Kershner found that the dyslexic children obtained a significantly higher score than a control group of gifted children when visual stimuli were presented bilaterally. This and other findings led him to conclude that the reading-impaired child may be employing a right hemisphere coding strategy for reading. Another study that investigated two dyslexic subgroups is reported by Pirozzolo (1979). The dyslexic children were classified into two subgroups, visual–spatial and auditory–linguistic dyslexics, on the basis of criteria such as verbal–performance IQs, extent of difficulty in phonological aspects of reading, and presence of letter and word reversals. Tachistoscopic studies showed that auditory dyslexics showed no lateral asymmetry for word recognition and that visual dyslexics showed better word recognition in the right than left visual field but were worse than the auditory dyslexics in parafoveal recognition of words. Finally, a study specifically aimed to test the "heterogeneity hypothesis" was undertaken by Keefe and Swinney (1979). These investigators administered dichotic listening and tachistoscopic tasks to groups of reading-disabled and normal readers. Even though they did not subdivide the dyslexic group on any a priori basis, it was found that when mean scores alone were compared, the dyslexic children showed a right ear superiority and a left visual field superiority just like the controls. However, when the lateralization scores were plotted, the graph showed a bimodal distribution of dyslexic subjects and a unimodal distribution of controls. The investigators concluded that such a bimodal distribution indicates that there is one subgroup of dyslexics with a left hemispheric deficit and another subgroup with a right hemispheric deficit.

These few studies which investigated the subgroups separately suggest that lateralization of functions in the cerebral hemispheres of dyslexics differs from that of normal readers, even though they fail to agree on the precise nature of such differences. In contrast, a substantial number of studies reviewed by Satz (1976) and Naylor (1980) failed to find any difference between the control and experimental groups.

Somewhat persuasive evidence for associating the two dyslexic subtypes with the functions of the two cerebral hemispheres comes from clinical investigations of alexic patients. Coltheart (1980b), hypothesizing that deep dyslexia might reflect right hemispheric reading, describes the characteristics of reading executed by the right hemisphere in the following terms: "The right hemisphere is unable to convert print into its phonological representation; it has selective difficulty in processing abstract words; and it is susceptible to semantic errors [p. 350]." Andreevsky and Seron (1975) report that the deep dyslexic could not read aloud conjunctions, prepositions, and inflexions of words. Saffran, Bogyo, Schwartz, and Marin (1980) make similar observations. In general, errors committed by alexic patients indicate that the following symptoms characterize right hemisphere reading: (a) ineffective utilization of phonological features of the word; (b) difficulty in reading aloud grammatical function words and inflexions; (c) little or no difficulty in reading concrete nouns, verbs, and adjectives; and (d) a tendency to commit semantic errors.

The reading errors committed by children deficient in sequential processing ability described in this chapter show a striking resemblance to these right hemisphere reading symptoms of alexic patients. These sequential-deficient children also tended to omit function words and inflexions while reading, and their spelling pattern revealed a failure to take into account the phonological features of the word. A group of college students studied (Aaron, Baker, and Hickox, in press) also committed such reading and spelling errors. A few subjects also showed a tendency to commit semantic errors (e.g., *wait a moment* → "wait a minute"). But the number of such semantic errors was too few to attach much significance to. It should also be mentioned that children who were classified as simultaneous deficient made reading and spelling errors that are reminiscent of those committed by the surface dyslexics (Marshall & Newcombe, 1973), whose reading is largely influenced by the phonetic features of the target word.

Thus it appears that a case for a link between the two subtypes of dyslexia and the functions of the two cerebral hemispheres could be made.

CONCLUSIONS

The imbalance hypothesis seems to explain several facts known about dyslexia such as the predominance of males, variability in incidence of dyslexia from language to language, associated poor spelling ability, and the excessive amount of reversals in the writings of dyslexic children. In addition, the clumsiness and poor coordination of movements often reported for some dyslexic children (Mattis, French, & Rapin,

1975) could also be explained if purposeful motor activity is considered as basically a sequential operation involving a series of movements.

The possibility that other factors, both environmental and psychological, could contribute to developmental dyslexia is fully recognized. Among the psychological factors, language deficit should be given major consideration as many reading-disabled children are reported to be deficient in language skills (Vellutino, 1979). To consider language deficit as an associated factor of dyslexia would not conflict with the imbalance hypothesis as such a view could be accommodated quite readily within the hypothesis. Language deficit would be considered as a symptom just as reading disability is. It is quite possible that language deficit of at least one form may be the result of an inability to deal effectively with sequentially presented information.

Nevertheless, inadequate linguistic ability alone cannot account for all the types of reading disabilities. We have seen a number of dyslexic college students who are intelligent, articulate, and have excellent auditory memory; but some of them could not read anything more than common three- or four-letter words. In addition, a language-processing deficit theory cannot easily explain the almost universal spelling problems of dyslexics; nor could it satisfactorily explain the observed differences in the incidence of dyslexia in different languages. Obviously, something more than language is involved. Similarly, specific deficits such as poor short-term memory or inefficient iconic storage also cannot account for the distinct types of spelling error patterns of dyslexic subjects, or for the sex differences that are so well documented. As a matter of fact, some dyslexics have superior auditory memory and some others have excellent memory for faces.

It appears that experimental findings which support differing viewpoints are like pieces in a jigsaw puzzle. A viable theory of dyslexia will emerge when all these pieces are put together in their proper places.

A NEW DEFINITION OF DYSLEXIA

Existing definitions of dyslexia have been subjected to harsh criticisms (cf. Yule & Rutter, 1976, p. 26). In an article devoted to the issue of the definition of dyslexia, Eisenberg, almost with a prophetic vision, compared the problem of defining dyslexia to that encountered in defining thalassemia (Eisenberg, 1978). According to Eisenberg, attempts to define thalassemia began with the abstraction of a Platonic type based on clinical features that led to the isolation of a group of "classical" cases which provided the basis for laboratory research. In turn, research enabled the disease to be redefined in terms of its pathogenesis . . . the gain in precision also led to a recognition of the molecular heterogenity of what appeared to be a clinical entity [p. 32].

Anyone familiar with the history of the study of dyslexia can sense an evolutionary parallel between thalassemia and dyslexia. Application of a medical paradigm such as the one eventually used in defining thalassemia leads one to the following definition of dyslexia:

A group of disorders of information processing strategies, resulting in inefficent or improper encoding or comprehension of written language. Such a defect of information-processing ability is caused primarily by an underutilization of either the sequential or the simultaneous strategy and a compensatory dependency on the other. The disorder can be broadly classified into encoding and comprehension deficits, and the former could be further subdivided into two distinct subtypes.

REFERENCES

Aaron, P. G. (1978) Dyslexia, an imbalance in cerebral information processing strategies. *Perceptual and Motor Skills, 47,* 699–706.

Aaron, P. G., Baker, C., & Hickox, G. L. In search of the third dyslexia. *Neuropsychologia* (In press).

Aaron, P. G., Baxter, C. F., & Lucenti, J. (1980) Developmental dyslexia and acquired alexia: Two sides of the same coin? *Brain and Language 11,* 1–11.

Aaron, P. G., & Malatesha, R. N. (1974) Discrimination of mirror image stimuli in children. *Neuropsychologia, 12,* 549–551.

Adams, M. J. (1979) Models of word recognition. *Cognitive Psychology, 11,* 133–176.

Aderman, D., & Smith, E. E. (1971) Expectancy as a determinant of functional units in perceptual recognition. *Cognitive Psychology, 2,* 117–129.

Albert, M. L. (1972) Auditory sequencing and left cerebral dominance for language. *Neuropsychologia, 10,* 245–254.

Andreewsky, E., & Seron, X. (1975) Implicit processing of grammatical rules in a case of agrammatism. *Cortex, 11,* 379–390.

Baddeley, A. D. (1966) Short-term memory for word sequences as a function of acoustic, semantic, and formal similarity. *Quarterly Journal of Experimental Psychology, 18,* 362–365.

Baddeley, A. D. (1979) Working memory and reading. In P. A. Kolers, M. E. Wrolstad, & H. Bouma (Eds.), *Processing of visible language.* New York: Plenum Press. Pp. 355–370.

Bakker, D. J., Teunissen, J., & Bosch, J. (1976) Development of laterality—Reading patterns. In R. M. Knights & D. J. Bakker (Eds.), *Neuropsychology of learning disorders: Theoretical approaches.* Baltimore: University Park Press.

Barakat, M. K. (1951) A factorial study of mathematical abilities. *British Journal of Psychology* (Statistics), *4,* 137–156.

Baron, J., & Treiman, R. (1980) Use of orthography in reading and learning to read. In

J. F. Kavanagh & R. L. Venezky (Eds.), *Orthography, reading, and dyslexia*. Baltimore: University Park Press. Pp. 171–189.

Barron, R. W. (1980) Visual and phonological strategies in reading and spelling. In U. Frith (Ed.), *Cognitive processes in spelling*. New York: Academic Press.

Bartlett, R. C. (1932) *Remembering: A study in experimental and social psychology*. Cambridge: Cambridge University Press.

Bax, C. (1932) *Leonardo da Vinci*. Edinburgh: Peter Davies Ltd.

Bennett, G. K., Seashore, H. G., & Wesman, A. G. (1973) *Differential Aptitude Tests*. New York: The Psychological Corp.

Benson, D. F. (1977) The third alexia. *Archives of Neurology, 34*, 327–331.

Benson, D. F., Brown, J., & Tomlinson, E. B. (1971) Varieties of alexia. *Neurology, 21*, 951–957.

Benton, A. L. (1963) *The revised visual retention test*. New York: The Psychological Corp.

Benton, A. L. (1980) Dyslexia: Evolution of a concept. *Bulletin of the Orton Society, 30*, 10–26.

Bock, R. D., & Kolakowski, D. (1973) Further evidence of sex-linked major gene influence on human spatial visualizing ability. *American Journal of Human Genetics, 25*, 1–14.

Boder, E. (1973) Developmental dyslexia: A diagnostic approach based on three typical reading spelling patterns. *Developmental Medicine and Child Neurology, 15*, 663–687.

Bradshaw, J. L. (1975) Three interrelated problems in reading: A review. *Memory and Cognition, 3*, 123–134.

Bub, D., & Whitaker, H. A. (1980) Language and verbal processes. In M. C. Wittrock (Ed.), *The brain and psychology*, New York: Academic Press.

Caramazza A., & Berndt, R. S. (1978) Semantic and syntactic processes in aphasia: A review of the literature. *Psychological Bulletin, 85*, 898–918.

Carroll, J. B. (1964) The analysis of reading instruction: Perspectives from psychology and linguistics. In E. Hilgard (Ed.), *Theories of learning and instruction*. Sixty-third yearbook of the National Society for the Study of Education. Chicago: University of Chicago Press. Pp. 336–353.

Cartwright, J. (1932) *Isabelle d' Este*. London: John Murray.

Clark, K. (1959) *Leonardo da Vinci: An account of his development as an artist*. Baltimore: Penguin.

Cattell, J. M. (1886) The time it takes to see and name objects. *Mind, 11*, 63–65.

Cohen, G. (1972) Hemispheric differences in a letter classification task. *Perception and Psychophysics, 11*, 139–142.

Coltheart, M. (1980a) Deep dyslexia: A review of the syndrome. In M. Coltheart, K. Patterson, & J. C. Marshall (Eds.), *Deep dyslexia*. London: Routledge & Kegan Paul.

Coltheart, M. (1980b) Deep dyslexia: A right-hemisphere hypothesis. In M. Coltheart, K. Patterson, & J. C. Marshall (Eds.), *Deep dyslexia*. London: Routledge & Kegan Paul.

Coltheart, M. (1980c) Reading, phonological recoding, and deep dyslexia. In M. Coltheart, K. Patterson, & J. C. Marshall (Eds.), *Deep dyslexia*. London: Routledge & Kegan Paul.

Conrad, R. (1964) Acoustic confusion in immediate memory. *British Journal of Psychology, 55*, 75–84.

Corballis, M. C. & Beale, I. L. (1976) *The psychology of left and right*. Hillsdale, N.J.: Lawrence Erlbaum.

Critchley, M. (1970) *The dyslexic child*. London: William Heinemann.

Das, J. P., Kirby, J. R., & Jarman, R. F. (1979) *Simultaneous and successive cognitive processes*. New York: Academic Press.

Davidson, H. P. (1935) A study of the confusing letters b, d, p, and q. *Journal of Genetic Psychology, 47*, 458–467.

DeRenzi, E., & Vignolo, L. A. (1962) The token test: A sensitive test to detect receptive disturbances in aphasics. *Brain, 85,* 665–678.

Durrell, D. D. (1955) *Durrell analysis of reading difficulty.* New York: Harcourt, Brace, & Jovanovich.

Eisenberg, L. (1966) The epidemiology of reading retardation and a program for preventive intervention. In J. Moeny (Ed.), *The disabled reader.* Baltimore: Johns Hopkins University Press.

Eisenberg, L. (1978) Definitions of dyslexia: Their consequences for research and policy. In A. L. Benton & D. Pearl (Eds.), *Dyslexia: An appraisal of current knowledge.* New York: Oxford University Press.

Eissler, K. R. (1961) *Leonardo da Vinci: Psychoanalytic notes of the enigma.* New York: International Universities Press.

Ellis, H. D., & Shepherd, J. W. (1974) Recognition of abstract and concrete words presented in left and right visual fields. *Journal of Experimental Psychology, 103,* 1035–1036.

Fisher, W. F., Liberman, I. Y., & Shankweiler, D. (1978) Reading reversals and developmental dyslexia: A further study. *Cortex, 14,* 496–510.

Freud, S. (1964) *Leonardo da Vinci and a memory of his childhood.* New York: W. W. Norton.

Geffen, G. Bradshaw, J. L., & Nettleton, N. C. (1972) Hemispheric asymmetry: Verbal and spatial encoding of visual stimuli. *Journal of Experimental Psychology, 95,* 25–31.

Gibson, E. J., & Levin, H. (1975) *The psychology of reading.* Cambridge, Mass.: MIT Press.

Goldman, R., Fristoe, M., & Woodcock, R. W. (1974) *Auditory memory test.* Circle Pines, Minn.: American Guidance Service.

Goodglass, H., & Kaplan, E. (1972) *The assessment of aphasia and related disorders.* Philadelphia: Lea & Febiger.

Goodman, K. G. (1969) Analysis of oral reading miscues: Applied psycholinguistics. *Reading Research Quarterly, 5,* 9–30.

Goody, J. *Literacy in traditional societies.* (1968) London: Cambridge University Press.

Gough, P. B. (1972) One second reading. In J. F. Kavanah & I. G. Mattingly (Eds.), *Language by ear and by eye.* Cambridge, Mass.: MIT Press.

Gough, P. B., & Cosky, M. J. (1977) One second reading again. In N. J. Castellan, D. B. Pisoni, & G. R. Potts (Eds.), *Cognitive theory* (Vol. 2). Hillsdale, N.J.: Lawrence Erlbaum.

Gough, B. P., & Hillinger, L. M. (1980) Learning to read: An unnatural act. *Bulletin of the Orton Society, 30,* 179–196.

Hall, R. A. (1961) Sound and spelling in English. New York, Chilton.

Harrigan, J. E. (1976) Initial reading instruction: Phonemes, syllables, or ideographs. *Journal of Learning Disabilities, 9,* 21–30.

Harris, L. J. (1978) Sex differences in spatial ability: Possible environmental, genetic, and neurological factors. In M. Kinsbourne (Ed.), *Asymmetrical function of the brain.* London: Cambridge University Press.

Harshman, R. A., & Remington, R. (1978) Sex, language, and the brain. Mimeographed publication.

Hartlage, L. C. (1970) Sex-linked inheritance of spatial ability. *Perceptual and Motor Skills, 31,* 610.

Hatta, T. (1977) Recognition of Japanese Kanji in the left and right visual fields. *Neuropsychologia, 15,* 685–688.

Hécaen, H., & Kremin, H. (1977) Reading disorders resulting from left hemisphere lesions: Aphasic and pure alexia. In H. Whitaker & H. A. Whitaker (Eds.), *Studies in Neurolinguistics* (Vol. 2). New York: Academic Press.

Hines, D. (1977) Differences in tachistoscopic recognition between abstract and concrete words as a function of visual half-field and frequency. *Cortex, 13,* 66–73.

Hinshelwood, J. (1917) *Congenital word-blindness.* London: H. K. Lewis.

Hirose, G., Kin, T., & Murakami, E. (1977) Alexia without agraphia associated with right occipital lesion. *Journal of Neurology, Neurosurgery, and Psychiatry, 40,* 225–227.

Hoffman, B. (1972) *Albert Einstein, creator and rebel.* New York: Viking Press.

Johnson, D. J., & Myklebust, H. R. (1967) *Learning disabilities—Educational principles and practices.* New York: Grune & Stratton.

Keefe, B., & Swinney, D. (1979) On the relationship of hemispheric specialization and developmental dyslexia. *Cortex, 15,* 471–481.

Kershner, J. R. (1977) Cerebral dominance in disabled readers, good readers, and gifted children: Search for a valid model. *Child Development, 48,* 61–67.

Kinsbourne, M. & Warrington, E. K. (1962) A variety of reading disability associated with right hemisphere lesions. *Journal of Neurology, Neurosurgery, and Psychiatry, 25,* 339–344.

Klassen, E. (1972) *The syndrome of specific dyslexia.* Baltimore: University Park Press.

Kleiman, G. M. (1975) Speech recoding in reading. *Journal of Verbal Learning and Verbal Behavior, 24,* 323–339.

Kline, C. L., & Lee, N. (1972) A transcultural study of dyslexia: Analysis of language disabilities in 277 Chinese children simultaneously learning to read and write in English and Chinese. *Journal of Special Education, 6,* 9–26.

Kolers, P. A., & Katzman, M. T. (1966) Naming sequentially presented letters and words. *Language and Speech, 9,* 84–95.

Lake, D. A., & Bryden, M. P. (1976) Handedness and sex differences in hemispheric asymmetry. *Brain and Language, 8,* 266–282.

Lee, L. (1969) *Northwestern Syntax Screening Test.* Evanston, Ill.: Northwestern University.

Leong, C. K. (1973) Chapter 18. In J. Downing (Ed.), Comparative reading: Cross national studies of behavior and processes in reading and writing. New York: Macmillan.

Levy, A. J., & Sperry, R. W. (1968) Differential perceptual capacities in major and minor hemispheres. *Proceedings of the National Academy of Sciences, 61,* 1151 (abstract).

Levy, J. (1980) Cerebral asymmetry and the psychology of man. In M. C. Wittrock (Ed.), *The brain and psychology.* New York: Academic Press.

Liberman, I. Y., Shankweiler, D., Orlando, C., Harris, K. S., & Berti, F. B. (1971) Letter confusion and reversals of sequence in the beginning reader: Implications for Orton's theory of developmental dyslexia. *Cortex, 7,* 127–142.

Liberman, I. Y., Liberman, A. M., Mattingly, I., & Shankweiler, D. (1980) Orthography and the beginning reader. In J. F. Kavanagh & R. L. Venezky (Eds.), *Orthography, reading, and dyslexia,* Baltimore: University Park Press. Pp. 137–153.

Ludwig, M. (1909) *Traktat von der Malerei* (2nd ed.). (German translation of Leonardo da Vinci's *Trattato della pictura.*) Jena: 1909.

Luria, A. R. (1973) *The working brain.* London: Penguin.

Lyle, J. G. (1969) Reading retardation and reversal tencency, a factorial study. *Child Development, 40,* 833–843.

Maccoby, E. M., & Jacklin, C. N. (1974) *The psychology of sex differences.* Stanford: Stanford University Press.

Madden, D. J., & Nebes, R. D. (1980) Visual perception and memory. In M. C. Wittrock (Ed.), *The brain and psychology.* New York: Academic Press.

Makita, K. (1968) The rarity of reading disability in Japanese children. *American Journal of Orthopsychiatry, 38,* 599–614.

Malmquist, E. (1958) *Factors related to reading disabilities in the first grade of the elementary school.* Stockholm: Almquist & Wiksell.

Marcel, A. J., & Patterson, E. K. (1978) Word recognition and production: Reciprocity in clinical and normal studies. In J. Requin (Ed.), *Attention and performance* (Vol. 7). Hillsdale, N.J.: Lawrence Erlbaum.

Marcel, T. (1980) Surface dyslexia and beginning reading: A revised hypothesis of the pronunciation of print and its impairments. In M. Coltheart, K. Patterson, & J. C. Marshall (Eds.), *Deep dyslexia*. London: Routledge, & Kegan Paul.

Marshall, J. C., & Newcombe, F. (1973) Patterns of paralexia. *Journal of Psycholinguistic Research, 2,* 175–199.

Marshall, J. C., & Newcombe, F. (1980) The conceptual status of deep dyslexia: An historical perspective. In M. Coltheart, K. Patterson, & J. C. Marshall (Eds.), *Deep dyslexia*. London: Routledge & Kegan Paul.

Martines, L. (1968) *Lawyers and statecraft in renaissance Florence.* Princeton, N.J.: Princeton University Press.

Massaro, D. W. (1975). Primary and secondary recognition in reading. In D. W. Massaro (Ed.), *Understanding language,* New York: Academic Press.

Massaro, D. W., & Klitzke, D. (1977) Letters are functional in word identification. *Memory and Cognition, 5,* 292–298.

Mattis, S., French, J. H., & Rapin, I. (1975) Dyslexia in children and young adults: Three independent neuropsychological syndromes. *Developmental Medicine and Child Neurology, 17,* 150–163.

McGlone, J. (1977) Sex differences in the cerebral organization of visual function in patients with unilateral brain lesions. *Brain, 100,* 775–793.

McGlone, J., & Kertesz, A. (1973) Sex differences in cerebral processing of visuo-spatial tasks. *Cortex, 9,* 313–320.

Meyer, D. E., Schvaneveldt, R. W., & Ruddy, M. G. (1974) Functions of graphemic and phonemic codes in visual word-recognition. *Memory and Cognition, 2,* 309–321.

Naylor, H. (1980) Reading disability and lateral asymmetry: An information processing analysis. *Psychological Bulletin, 87,* 531–545.

Nebes, R. D. (1974) Dominance of the minor hemisphere in commissurotomized man for the perception of part–whole relationships. In M. Kinsbourne & L. W. Smith (Eds.), *Hemispheric disconnection and cerebral function.* Springfield, Ill.: Charles C. Thomas.

Nelson, H. E. (1980) Analysis of spelling errors in normal and dyslexic children. In U. Frith (Ed.), *Cognitive processes in spelling.* New York: Academic Press.

Newcombe, F., & Marshall, J. C. (1967) Immediate recall of sentences by subjects with unilateral cerebral lesions. *Neuropsychologia, 5,* 329–334.

Noll, J. D. (1970) *The use of the token test with children.* Paper presented at the annual convention of the American Speech and Hearing Association, New York, 1970.

Oommen, C. Reading in India. In J. Downing (Ed.), *Comparative reading: Cross national studies of behavior and processes in reading and writing.* New York: MacMillan, 1973.

Orton, S. T. (1928) Specific reading disability—Strephosymbolia. *Journal of the American Medical Association, 90,* 1095–1099.

Paivio, A. (1977) Images, proposition, and knowledge. In J. M. Nicholos (Ed.), *Images, perception, and knowledge.* Dordrecht, Holland: D. Reidel.

Patten, B. (1973) Visually mediated thinking: A report of the case of Albert Einstein. *Journal of Learning Disabilities, 6,* 15–20.

Patterson, A., & Zangwill, O. L. (1944) Disorders of visual space perception associated with lesions of the right cerebral hemisphere. *Brain, 67,* 331–358.

Patterson, K. (1978) Phonemic dyslexia: Errors of meaning and the meaning of errors. *Quarterly Journal of Experimental Psychology, 30,* 587–601.

Pirozzolo, F. J. (1979) *The neuropsychology of developmental reading disorders*. New York: Praeger.

Pirozzolo, F. J., & Rayner, K. (1977) Hemispheric specialization in reading and word recognition. *Brain and Language, 4,* 248–261.

Pirozzolo, F. J., & Rayner, K. (1979) Cerebral organization and reading disability. *Neuropsychologia, 17,* 485–491.

Posner, M. (1969) Abstraction and the process of recognition. In G. H. Bower & J. T. Spence (Eds.), *The psychology of learning and motivation* (Vol. 3). New York: Academic Press.

Rabinovitch, R. D. (1968) Reading problems in children: Definitions and classifications. In A. H. Keeney & V. T. Keeney (Eds.), *Dyslexia*. St. Louis: C. V. Mosby Co.

Rayner, K., & Bertera, H. J. (1979) Reading without a fovea. *Science, 296,* 468–469.

Reti, L. (1974) *The unknown Leonardo*. New York: McGraw-Hill.

Richter, J. P. (1890) *The notebooks of Leonardo da Vinci*. (Republished by Dover Publications, New York, 1970.)

Rock, I. (1973) *Orientation and form*. New York: Academic Press.

Rozin, P., Poritsky, S., & Sotsky, R. (1971) American children with reading problems can easily learn to read English represented by Chinese characters. *Science, 171,* 1264–1267.

Ruthman, P. (1973) Reading in France. In J. Downing (Ed.), *Reading: Cross national studies of behavior and processes in reading and writing*. New York: Mcmillan.

Saffran, E. M., Bogyo, L. C., Schwartz, M., & Marin, O. (1980) Does deep dyslexia reflect right-hemisphere reading? In M. Coltheart, K. Patterson, & J. C. Marshall (Eds.), *Deep dyslexia*. London: Routledge & Kegan Paul.

Sakamoto, T., & Makita, K. (1973) Reading in Japan. In J. Downing (Ed.), *Reading: Cross national studies of behavior and processes in reading and writing*. New York: Macmillan.

Sasanuma, S. (1974) Kanji versus kana processing in alexia with transient agraphia: A case report. *Cortex, 10,* 89–97.

Sasanuma, S. (1975) Kana and kanji processing in Japanese aphasics. *Brain and Language, 2,* 369–383.

Sasanuma, S. (1980) Acquired dyslexia in Japanese: Clinical features and underlying mechanisms. In M. Coltheart, K. Paterson, & J. C. Marshall (Eds.), *Deep dyslexia*. London: Routledge & Kegan Paul.

Sasanuma, S., Itoh, M., Mori, K., & Kobayashi, Y. (1977) Tachistoscopic recognition of kana and kanji words. *Neuropsychologia, 15,* 547–553.

Sasanuma, S., & Fujimura, O. (1971) Selective impairment of phonetic and nonphonetic transcription of words in aspasic patients. *Cortex, 7,* 1–18.

Sasanuma, S., & Monoi, H. (1975) The syndrome of Gogi (word meaning) aphasia: Selective impairment of kanji processing. *Neurology, 25,* 627–632.

Satz, P. (1976) Cerebral dominance and reading disability: An old problem revisited. In R. M. Knights & D. J. Bakker (Eds.), *The neuropsychology of learning disorders: Theoretical approaches*. Baltimore: University Park Press.

Saunders, R. E. (1962) Dyslexia: Its phenomenology. In J. Money (Eds.), *Reading disability*. Baltimore: Johns Hopkins University Press.

Schapiro, M. (1955–1956) Two slips of Leonardo and a slip of Freud. *Psychoanalysis, 2,* 6–12.

Searleman, A. (1977) A review of right hemispheric linguistic capabilities. *Psychological Bulletin, 84,* 503–528.

Shallice, T., & Warrington, E. K. (1975) Word recognition in a phonemic dyslexic patient. *Quarterly Journal of Experimental Psychology, 27,* 187–199.

Shankweiler, D., & Liberman, I. Y. (1972) Misreading: A search for causes. In J. F. Kavanagh & I. G. Mattingly (Eds.), *Language by ear and by eye.* Cambridge, Mass.: MIT Press.

Sherman, J. A. (1974) Field articulation, sex, spatial visualization, dependency, practice, laterality of the brain, and birth order. *Perceptual and Motor Skills, 38,* 1223–1235.

Sibatani, A. (1980) The Japanese brain. *Science 80, 1,* 22–26.

Simernitskaya, E. G. (1974) On two forms of writing defect following local brain lesions. In S. J. Dimond & G. J. Beaumont (Eds.), *Hemispheric function in the human brain.* New York: Wiley, 1974.

Smith, I. M. (1960) The validity of tests of spatial ability as predictors of success on technical courses. *British Journal of Educational Psychology, 30,* 138–145.

Smith, M. J. (1929) Which hand is the eye of the blind? *Genetic Psychology Monographs, 5,* 209–252.

Stafford, R. E. (1961) Sex differences in spatial visualization as evidence of sex-linked inheritance. *Perceptual and Motor Skills. 13,* 428.

Standing, L., Conezio, J., & Haber, R. N. (1970) Perception and memory for pictures: Single-trial learning of 2500 visual stimuli. *Psychonomic Science, 19,* 73–74.

Stites, R., Stites, E., & Castiglioni, P. (1970) *The sublimations of Leonardo da Vinci.* Washington, D.C.: Smithsonian Institute Press.

Symmes, S. J., & Rapoport, L. J. (1972) Unexpected reading failure. *American Journal of Orthopsychiatry, 42,* 82–91.

Taylor, D. C., & Ounsted, C. (1972) The nature of gender differences explored through ontogenetic analysis of sex ratios in disease. In C. Ounsted & D. C. Taylor (Eds.), *Gender differences: Their ontogeny and significance.* London: Churchill & Livingstone.

Thompson, L. (1971) Language disabilities in men of eminence. *Journal of Learning Disabilities, 4,* 34–35.

Tjossem, T., Hansen, T., & Ripley, H. (1962) An investigation of reading difficulty in young children. *American Journal of Psychiatry, 118,* 1104–1113.

Tzeng, O. J., Hung, D. L., & Wang, W. S. (1977) Speech recoding in reading Chinese characters. *Journal of Experimental Psychology: Human Learning and Memory, 3,* 621–630.

Vellutino, F. R. (1979) *Dyslexia, theory and research.* Cambridge, Mass.: MIT Press.

Wallace, R. (1966) *The world of Leonardo.* New York: Time Inc.

Wheeler, D. D. (1970) Process in word recognition. *Cognitive Psychology, 1,* 59–85.

Witelson, S. (1976) Sex and the single hemisphere: Specialization of the right hemisphere for spatial processing. *Science, 193,* 425–427.

Witelson, S. (1977) Developmental dyslexia: Two right hemispheres and none left? *Science, 195,* 309–311.

Yamadori, A. (1975) Ideogram reading in alexia. *Brain, 98,* 231–238.

Yule, W., & Rutter, M. (1976) The epidemiology and social implications of specific reading retardation. In R. Knights & D. J. Bakker (Eds.), *The neuropsychology of learning disorders: Theoretical approaches.* Baltimore: University Park Press.

Zaidel, E. (1976) Auditory vocabulary of the right hemisphere following brain bisection of hemidecortication. *Cortex, 12,* 191–211.

Chapter Two

Clinical Subtypes of Developmental Dyslexia: Resolution of an Irresolute Problem[1]

R. N. MALATESHA
DEBORAH R. DOUGAN

INTRODUCTION

Anecdotal reports of loss of once-acquired reading ability as a result of brain damage go as far back as A.D. 30 (Benton, 1964). Clinical investigation of alexia, however, was not taken up until the latter part of the nineteenth century when sporadic reports began to appear in the literature and culminated in two definitive anatomopathological studies by Dejerine (cf. Benson & Geschwind, 1969). Interestingly, the nature of developmental reading disability also began to receive clinical attention at about the same time when Morgan in 1896 described a case of a 14-year-old boy who had great difficulty in reading and writing despite normal intelligence. Morgan attributed this problem to a possible underdevelopment of the left angular gyrus. Following Morgan's

[1] This research was supported by a grant from Oregon State University, Corvallis, Oregon. The authors wish to thank Cheryl Williamson and Pat Champion for their help in collecting the data; Paul Satz for providing the dichotic listening tape; and P. G. Aaron for reading the original draft of this chapter.

69

presentation of the above case, Hinshelwood (1917) defined congenital word blindness, as he called the disorder, as a "congenital defect occurring in children with otherwise normal undamaged brains, characterized by a disability in learning to read so great that it is manifestly due to a pathological condition and where the attempts to teach the child by ordinary methods have completely failed [p. 40]." Several terms such as "dyslexia," "strephosymbolia," "specific reading retardation," and "unexpected reading failure" have been used to describe developmental reading disability. According to the World Federation of Neurology, children with specific developmental dyslexia are those who fail to acquire normal reading proficiency despite conventional instruction, sociocultural opportunity, average intelligence, and freedom from gross sensory, emotional, or neurological handicap (Critchley, 1970). This is the definition used in the present study to describe dyslexia, even though terms such as "specific developmental dyslexia" and "reading disability" are used interchangeably.

The study of the nature of dyslexia has received much impetus in the United States since Orton (1937) suggested that faulty or incomplete cerebral dominance might be responsible for reading disability. Numerous researchers over the years have tried to disentangle the nature of dyslexia, and much time and effort have been expended to help the nearly 15% of schoolchildren who are considered reading disabled (Kline & Lee, 1972). Still, the question, Why can't children read? is not satisfactorily answered. As Aaron (1980) noted, "reading has remained one of the least understood and most elusive of all psychological processes, and reading research continues to abound with contradictions and controversies [p. 116]."

One major controversy in the field involves the question of the nature of dyslexia—whether it is a unitary phenomenon or represents a group of disorders. Attempts to describe dyslexia in terms of a unitary cause have historical roots that could be traced all the way back to Morgan (1896) and Hinshelwood (1917), who proposed a neuroanatomical basis for this disorder. Orton (1937) recognized only one form of dyslexia— that which could arise as a result of improper cerebral lateralization. Later on, Kephart (1960), Cruikshank (1968), and others who viewed reading disorder as a form of learning disability attributed the deficit to poor perceptual–motor integration. Hermann (1959) agreed with an emphasis on visual–spatial dysfunction, but suggested that this dysfunction also had a genetic predisposition. Taking a different approach, Bender (1958) explained dyslexia in terms of a maturational lag. Such unitary views of dyslexia are summarized in Table 2.1.

Table 2.1
Etiological Factors Used in Viewing Dyslexia as a Unitary Syndrome

I. Cerebral dominance hypothesis	IV. Genetic trait
1. Orton (1937)	1. Hermann (1959)
II. Maturational lag of cerebral organization	V. Language deficiency
1. Bender (1958)	1. Vellutino (1979)
2. Delacato (1959)	VI. Deficits of the parietal region
3. Smith & Carrigan (1959)	1. Jorm (1979a)
III. Perceptual-motor deficiency	
1. Drew (1956)	
2. Kephart (1960)	
3. Cruikshank (1968)	
4. Frostig & Maslow (1973)	

In this chapter, we propose that one of the reasons for the continued disagreement among researchers as to the nature and etiology of dyslexia is the failure to recognize the possibility that dyslexia actually is a group of disorders and not a single isolated syndrome. Even though in recent years the heterogeneity of dyslexia has been recognized by several researchers, others have ignored and even denied such a possibility. For example, Vellutino (1979) considers some form of verbal deficit as the most important cause of reading disability and has criticized studies that have attributed dyslexia to other factors. Another researcher (Jorm, 1979b) has argued that because at present time there is no satisfactory evidence to support the notion of subtypes, it is better to adopt the more parsimonious view that developmental dyslexia is a unitary syndrome.

One of the aims of this chapter is to show that, contrary to statements such as these, there does indeed exist an impressive amount of data that render the notion of heterogeneity of dyslexia a tenable proposition. A majority of the studies that support the notion of heterogeneity of dyslexia were based on clinical observations, and, consequently, there is wide variation in the estimates of the number of subtypes of dyslexia. These estimates have ranged from two to six. Furthermore, deliberate attempts to investigate the number and nature of clinical subtypes are of relatively recent vintage and thus few in number (e.g., Boder, 1973; Mattis, French, & Rapin, 1975; Doehring & Hoshko, 1977). Some of these studies are reviewed in a later section of this chapter.

Material presented in this chapter is organized under the following topics: the need to recognize clinical subtypes of dyslexia, research supporting the notion of subtypes, conflicts among research findings and their resolution, and clincial subtypes of dyslexia and remediation.

THE NEED FOR RECOGNITION OF CLINICAL
SUBTYPES OF DYSLEXIA

Classification of disease entities into subgroups sharpens the diagnostic procedure, improves accuracy of diagnosis, and, most clearly, enhances the efficacy of treatment. This is a well-established observation in the field of medicine wherein diagnosis and treatment constitute the two most important functions of the practitioner. Even neurological disorders such as cerebral palsy (Denhoff, 1976) and epileptic seizures (Gastaut, 1970) are known to be composed of rather clearly identifiable clinical subtypes with recognizable symptom characteristics. Similarly, psychiatry has recognized the need for the isolation of subtypes, the classification being based either on symptomatology (catatonic schizophrenia, mania, etc.) or on the developmental course of the disorders (process and reactive schizophrenia). Experience shows that different subtypes of mental illness respond differently to different forms of treatment. Perhaps an example closer to the issue under discussion (i.e., heterogeneity of dyslexia) is aphasia, which has been subjected to several forms of classification, usually on the basis of symptom characteristics and the anatomical location of the lesion that caused the deficit.

If the advantages of classification enjoyed by fields such as medicine, psychiatry, and neurology can also be claimed for dyslexia, we can expect greater precision in diagnosis as well as better results from remedial treatments since efforts could be made to match different dyslexic typologies with different treatment methods. Furthermore, failure to delineate the different subtypes invariably leaves the investigator with a broad spectrum of symptoms to handle, the mushy nature of which frequently leads to statements such as "no matter what tests are given, the dyslexic performs poorly," or "dyslexia, as a clinical entity does not exist."

A similar explanation could be advanced to account for the bland outcome of the numerous research studies which often fail to come up with any consistent differences between normal and disabled readers. Such an outcome is not totally unexpected as dyslexic subtypes appear to display strengths and weaknesses complementary to each other which, when combined, tend to cancel each other out. Studies of lateralization of cerebral function carried out with reference to reading disability constitute an example of such a situation. The following observation by Kinsbourne and Hiscock (1978) is very pertinent in this context: "Heterogeneity within groups may completely mask important differences between two groups. Since learning disabled children and normal controls do not seem to differ in any consistent manner on lateralization measures, the matter of classification must be examined closely [p. 177]." This statement is true of most other research studies in reading disability as well. For instance, a majority of studies that deal with dyslexic children treat reading as a monolithic process and fail to specify what aspect of reading these children are retarded in— whether decoding, sight reading, or comprehension. It is not surprising, then, that failure to isolate the subgroups of retarded readers and treat them separately has yielded paltry dividends in terms of clear-cut experimental findings.

REVIEW OF RESEARCH SUPPORTING THE EXISTENCE OF SUBTYPES

Charcot (Freud, 1953), as early as 1896, proposed that two types of learners exist—the visile and audile. Visile learners supposedly learned language predominantly through visual modalities, whereas audible learners were thought to approach language through auditory channels. A number of investigators have recognized such a possibility in the case of dyslexia also and have divided dyslexics into visual and auditory types. Still others have dichotomized dyslexia in terms of cerebral organization, language, or brain impairments. Such a general classificatory scheme is summarized in Table 2.2. In general, auditory dyslexics appear to have difficulty in synthesizing sounds into words. The language disorder group (Kinsbourne & Warrington, 1963), the auditory–linguistic group (Pirozzolo, 1979), the linguistic or syntactic–semantic group (Bakker, 1979) and the auditory types (Johnson & Myklebust, 1967) all belong to this category. In contrast, the visual dyslexics (Johnson & Myklebust, 1967; Bakker, 1979; Pirozzolo, 1979) are said to have visual discrimination and related visual perceptual problems.

A second group of researchers (Bannatyne, 1971; Prechtl, 1962; Rabinovitch, 1968; Zangwill, 1962) have based their classification more directly on neurological functions. Zangwill (1962) separated instances of dyslexia that occur in individuals with "normal" cerebral hemispheric specialization (pure dyslexia) from dyslexia associated with incomplete cerebral specialization. From a strictly neurological point of view, Prechtl (1962) divided reading disabilities into two groups: a group with lesions in specific cerebral structures which mediate the function of reading (e.g., lesions in brain areas 17, 18, and 19, which subserve a

Table 2.2
Postulated Dyslexic Classification: Two Subtypes

I. Visual and auditory types	II. Other types
1. Johnson & Myklebust (1967)	1. Zangwill (1962)
a. Visual dyslexia	a. Dyslexia in normal hemispheric
b. Auditory dyslexia	specialization
2. Bakker (1979); Pirozzolo (1979)	b. Dyslexia in incomplete
a. Visual–spatial group	hemispheric specialization
b. Auditory–linguistic group	2. Prechtl (1962)
3. Kinsbourne & Warrington (1963)	a. Specific brain lesions
a. Language retardation group	b. Nonspecific brain lesions
b. Gerstmann's group dyslexia	3. Rabinovitch (1968)
	a. Primary reading retardation
	b. Secondary reading retardation
	4. Bannatyne (1971)
	a. Genetic
	b. Minimal neurological
	dysfunction

visual function, and area 39, which combines both visual and language functions), and a second group with nonspecific lesions in the central nervous system in which impaired reading occurs more or less as a side effect. A classificatory system with a great deal of heuristic value was proposed by Rabinovitch (1968), who classified dyslexia into primary reading retardation, which exists in the absence of brain injury, and secondary reading retardation, which is caused by emotional, motivational, and language disturbances. Bannatyne (1971) classified dyslexia into genetic and minimal neurological dysfunction subtypes. The genetic dyslexics were deficient in verbal skills involving auditory discrimination, auditory closure, and phoneme–grapheme sequencing memory. The minimal neurological dysfunction dyslexics, on the other hand, were deficient in visuospatial and concept formation tasks.

Whereas the investigators mentioned so far have attempted to dichotomize dyslexia, others have proposed that more than two subtypes of dyslexia could exist. Table 2.3 presents studies that suggest the existence of three subtypes of dyslexia. An examination of Table 2.3 reveals that research from several areas could also be marshaled in support of the view that three subtypes of reading disorders may exist. Some of these evidences will be examined in the following paragraphs.

Studies Based on Clinical Approaches

Numerous studies undertaken since the 1960s indicate that there may exist three subtypes of dyslexia. Of course, the three subtypes are

Table 2.3
Postulated Dyslexic Classification: Three Subtypes

I. *Clinical observation and study*
  1. Bateman (1968)
     a. Good visual memory but poor auditory memory
     b. Good auditory memory but poor visual memory
     c. Mixed
  2. Smith (1970)
     a. Deficiency in sequencing ability
     b. Deficiency in simultaneous ability
     c. Mixed
  3. Quadfasel & Goodglass (1968)
     a. Symptomatic reading retardation
     b. Specific reading disability
     c. Secondary reading retardation
  4. Nicholls (1968)
     a. Congenital or developmental dyslexia
     b. Slow reader
     c. Mixed type
  5. Ingram, Mason, & Blackburn (1970)
     a. Audiophonic
     b. Visuospatial
     c. Mixed
  6. deQuiros & Shrager (1978)
     a. Visual–perceptual handicap
     b. Visual–auditory handicap
     c. Vestibular and proprioceptive integration handicap
  7. Birch (1962)
     a. Visual–auditory integration impairment
     b. Visual–kinesthetic integration impairment
     c. Visual–tactual–kinesthetic integration impairment
II. *Neuropsychological profiles*
  1. Mattis, Rapin, & French (1975)
     a. Language disorder
     b. Articulatory–graphomotor disorder
     c. Visual–perceptual disorder
  2. Aaron & Baker (1982)
     a. Posterior dyslexia
     b. Anterior dyslexia
     c. Central dyslexia

III. *Factor-analytic studies*
  1. Doehring & Hoshko (1977); Doehring, Hoshko, & Bryans (1979)
     a. Language deficit
     b. Phonological deficit
     c. Naming deficit
  2. Petrauskas & Rourke (1979)
     a. Auditory-verbal memory deficiency
     b. Sequencing, finger localization deficiency
     c. Psychomotor skills impairment
IV. *Reading and spelling patterns*
  1. Boder (1973); Boder & Jarrico (1982)
     a. Dysphonetic
     b. Dyseidetic
     c. Mixed dysphonetic–dyseidetic
  2. Mann & Suiter (1978); Jordan (1977)
     a. Auditory deficiency
     b. Visual deficiency
     c. Manual deficiency
V. *Computerized brain scan*
  1. Hier, Lemay, Rosenberger, & Perlo (1978)
     a. Left parieto-occipital region wider than right
     b. Right parieto-occipital region wider than left
     c. No difference between the left and the right regions
VI. *Alexia research*
  1. Benson (1977); Albert (1979)
  2. Marshall & Newcombe (1973)
     a. Visual dyslexia
     b. Surface dyslexia
     c. Deep dyslexia
  3. Kremin (this volume)
     a. Pure alexia without agraphia
     b. Literal, deep and/or phonological alexia
     c. Surface dyslexia

described and labeled differently by different authors, and these differences may suggest that all these investigators do not refer to the same three subtypes. According to Quadfasel and Goodglass (1968) the three types are symptomatic reading disability, where reading disability is due to brain deficits; specific reading disability, where reading disability occurs in the absence of brain deficits; and secondary reading retardation, where reading disability is due to external factors such as environment and health. Bateman (1968) and Smith (1970) delineated three types of reading disabilities based on profiles obtained from Illinois Test of Psycholinguistic Abilities (ITPA) and Wechsler Scales of Intelligence, respectively. The three groups, according to Bateman, were dyslexic children with good visual memory but poor auditory memory; good auditory memory but poor visual memory; and both poor visual and auditory memory. The subtypes suggested by Nicholls (1968) were the congenital or developmental dyslexic, the slow reader, and the mixed type. Ingram, Mason, and Blackburn (1970) proposed the following three subgroups of dyslexics: audiophonic dyslexics, who could not successfully discriminate between words such as *bun* and *but*; visuo-spatial dyslexics who encounter difficulty in distinguishing between visual stimuli such as *b*, *p*, and *d*; and the mixed type.

Although these studies all suggest a threefold classification of dyslexia, it has to be pointed out that some investigators have included subjects with brain damage who may not fit exactly the definition of dyslexia. However, a majority of the studies that have selected dyslexic subjects on the basis of criteria suggested by the definition of the World Federation of Neurology also have described three independent dyslexic syndromes.

Studies Based on Neuropsychological Data

As indicated earlier, a majority of the studies were not designed specifically to investigate the heterogeneous nature of dyslexia. A few studies, however, have directly addressed this question. Two such studies will be reviewed here. In the first study, Mattis, Rapin, and French (1975) classified 113 8–18-year-old children into brain-damaged readers, brain-damaged dyslexics, and non-brain-damaged dyslexics. The neuropsychological profile of the dyslexic children revealed three distinct types of dyslexia presenting the following symptoms: visuo-perceptual disorders (14% of the sample); language disorder (28% of the sample); and articulatory and graphomotor dyscoordination syndrome (48% of the sample). An analysis of neuropsychological test performance of 17 college dyslexics by Aaron and Baker (1982) also showed that three distinct profiles exist. On the basis of the similarity of dyslexic symptoms exhibited by the subgroups to those of different alexic groups, Aaron and Baker labeled the subgroups as anterior, central, and posterior dyslexics. Posterior dyslexics had visuoperceptual deficiencies; anterior dyslexics had language defects, particularly of a syntactic nature; and central dyslexics were poor in listening comprehension.

Studies Based on Factor-Analytic Procedures

Several investigators have applied factor-analytic techniques to study the heterogeneity of dyslexia. Doehring and Hoshko (1977) applied the Q-technique factor analysis to data obtained from 31 tests of rapid reading skills administered to 31 children with reading problems. Three factors emerged corresponding to three subtypes; namely, the language deficit group, the phonological deficit group, and the naming deficit group. Jorm (1979b) questioned the validity of this classification because Doehring and Hoshko did not "include the results of a normal control group in the factor analysis [p. 431]." This deficiency was rectified when Doehring, Hoshko, and Bryans subsequently (1979) added 31 normal readers matched for age and sex to the original sample of 31 children with reading problems. In the second factor analysis, the same three subtypes emerged.

Petrauskas and Rourke (1979) randomly divided 133 retarded readers and 27 normal readers into two groups and administered 44 tests. Results of the Q-factor analysis revealed three reliable subtypes of dyslexics marked by deficiencies in verbal fluency and sentence memory, immediate visual–spatial memory, and verbal coding.

Fisk and Rourke (1979) obtained evidence for the existence of three subtypes among 11–14-year-old learning-disabled children by employing multivariate statistical analysis. This study included children who were poor in reading, as well as deficient in spelling and arithmetic.

Other Relevant Studies

Boder (1973; Boder & Jarrico, 1982), on the basis of reading and spelling error patterns, delineated three subtypes of dyslexia which she classified into the following groups: (a) a dysphonetic group which processed written material in a global or simultaneous fashion; (b) a dyseidetic group which used a sequential or analytic strategy; and (c) a mixed dysphonetic–dyseidetic group which had deficiencies in both simultaneous and sequential processing. Boder's classification has received support from Aaron (1978) who found that children in the dysphonetic group remembered and recognized significantly more photographs of faces than those in the dyseidetic group did—that is, their holistic ability was good although their sequential ability was poor—whereas the dyseidetic group recalled more digits in a sequence than the dysphonetic group did—that is, their sequential ability was good but their holistic ability was poor. In this volume, Rosenthal, Boder, and Calloway establish construct validity for Boder's classification.

A threefold classification of dyslexia also derives support from anatomical evidence. For instance, Hier, LeMay, Rosenberger, and Perlo (1978) analyzed computerized brain tomograms in 24 dyslexics whose age ranged from 14 to 47 years. Their analysis showed that in 10 dyslexics the right parieto-occipital region was wider than the left; in 8 dyslexics the left parieto-occipital region was wider than the right; and in 6 dyslexics there was no difference between the left and right regions.

In summary, the results of a large number of studies which used a variety of techniques and assessment procedures support a threefold classification of dyslexia.

A relatively small number of studies has suggested that the number of dyslexia subtypes may be in excess of three. We will briefly review some of them, but it has to be noted that the kind of data gathered in some of these studies are rather unconventional in that they were collected in a clinical setting. Table 2.4 presents studies that have provided evidence for four types of dyslexia.

Table 2.4
Postulated Dyslexic Classification: Four Subtypes

I. Clinical observation
Mattis (1978)
a. Language disorder
b. Articulatory–graphomotor disorder
c. Visual–perceptual disorder
d. Sequencing disorder
II. Genetics study
DeFries & Decker (this volume)
a. Visual–spatial deficiency
b. Short-term memory deficiency
c. Reading disability without the above two deficiencies
d. Mixed
III. EEG study
Hughes (this volume)
a. Positive spikes
b. Excessive slow occipital waves
c. Sharp waves or spike discharges
d. Diffuse or generalized asymmetry

In the first of these, Mattis (1978) has reported evidence for the existence of a fourth subtype of dyslexia in addition to the three sub-types presented earlier (Mattis *et al.*, 1975). Subjects in the fourth group were deficient in sequencing ability and made up about 10% of the total sample. DeFries and Decker (this volume), in an extensive family pedigree study, found evidence suggesting the existence of four sub-types of reading disability. Children placed in Subgroup 1 (23%) were deficient in spatial reasoning; children belonging to Subtype 2 (18%) were deficient in symbol processing. The largest group (subtype 3), accounting for 41% of the subjects, had normal spatial reasoning and symbol-processing abilities but still had reading disability. Subtype 4, representing only 9% of the sample, showed deficiencies in both spatial reasoning and symbol processing. This group can be considered as a mixed type or an unclassified type.

Hughes (this volume), after reviewing the literature on EEG patterns of dyslexics, identified four different types of wave patterns: positive spikes, excessive slow occipital waves, sharp waves and spike dis-charges, and diffuse and generalized asymmetries. To be noted is the fact that whereas the EEG patterns in three of the types were clear, in the fourth type the EEG pattern was not easily discernible.

Cluster analysis of the reading scores of 98 children aged 8–13 years led Naidoo (1972) to conclude that four types of reading disorders were identifiable, although nearly one-third of the subjects could not be placed unambiguously into any of the four groups. The largest of the four groups—31% of the sample—had linguistic difficulties; 6% of the sample had visuospatial problems; and the other two groups were difficult to characterize. Vernon (1977) proposed four types of dyslexia on the basis of deficiency in the following abilities: (*a*) analysis of com-plex, sequential visual and/or auditory linguistic structures; (*b*) linking of visual and auditory linguistic structures; (*c*) establishment of regu-larities in various grapheme–phoneme correspondences; and (*d*) group-ing words into meaningful phrases.

A few investigators have gone one step farther, discussing the pos-sibility of yet another subgroup of dyslexia. Studies that have classified dyslexia into five types are presented in Table 2.5. According to Keeney (1968), the five basic forms of dyslexia are: (*a*) specific developmental dyslexia; (*b*) secondary dyslexia, as a result of organic pathology, slow maturation, uncontrolled seizure states, or environmental disturbances; (*c*) slow readers (bradylexia) as a result of sensory and other handicaps without symbolic confusion; (*d*) acquired dyslexia, as a result of brain lesion; and (*e*) mixed forms. It should be noted that Keeney, in his classification, has included a group of alexic patients whose reading

Table 2.5
Postulated Dyslexic Classification: Five Subtypes

I. Keeney (1968)
  a. Specific developmental dyslexia
  b. Secondary dyslexia
  c. Slow reader or bradylexia
  d. Acquired dyslexia (alexia)
  e. Mixed
II. Denckla (1977)
  a. Global–mixed language disorder
  b. Articulatory–graphomotor disorder
  c. Visual–perceptual disorder
  d. Dysphonemic–sequencing disorder
  e. Verbal learning (memorization) deficiency

disorder originated from brain lesions. If the term dyslexia is restricted to reading disorders which are purely developmental in nature, one may not find more than three subtypes of dyslexia in Keeney's classification.

Denckla (1977), on the basis of her clinical observations, reported the following five types of dyslexic children: (a) visuospatial; (b) articulatory–graphomotor; (c) language disorder; (d) deficient verbal memorization, and (e) right hemisyndrome with mixed language disorder.

Satz and Morris (1981) applied cluster-analytic techniques to data obtained from four neuropsychological tests administered to 89 learning-disabled children. Five subtypes of learning disability emerged from the cluster analysis which accounted for 86 children. Of the five subtypes in this classification, four had impairment in global language, verbal fluency, global language and perception, and visual–perceptual motor tasks. Three of these subgroups also reportedly had soft neurological signs. The fifth subtype showed no impairment as assessed by the neuropsychological tests and was called "unexpected" group. It should be pointed out, however, that, as in the Fisk and Rourke (1979) sample, subjects in the Satz–Morris study included learning-disabled children who, in addition to reading, were also deficient in spelling and arithmetic.

Recently Denckla (1979), in addition to her original classification of five subtypes of dyslexia, proposed a sixth subgroup which was "correlation (sequential–simultaneous?) deficient." However, according to Denckla, children with this disorder are rarely seen in the clinic. These children had superior intelligence and read at grade level but showed imbalances in information-processing strategy. However, surprisingly, their deficiency disappeared at about the time of puberty without any special remedial treatment.

Although the present review of the literature was restricted mainly to developmental dyslexia, there is ample evidence to show that acquired reading disorder (alexia) also could be classified into subtypes. Just as studies of aphasia could contribute to an understanding of normal language functions (Caramazza & Berndt, 1978), so could studies of alexia contribute to the elucidation of the reading process. Benson and Geschwind (1969), Benson (1977), and Albert (1979) present clinical evidence to show that there are at least three subtypes of alexia. From a neurolinguistic perspective, Marshall and Newcombe (1973) classified alexic patients into three categories: visual dyslexics, who predominantly made visual confusion errors (e.g., *bug* for 'rug', *robe* for 'rob'); surface dyslexics, who had problems in grapheme–phoneme conversion (e.g., reading *izland* for 'island', *reply* for 'reapply'); and deep dyslexics, who made semantic substitutions while reading (e.g., *talk* for 'speak', *necklace* for 'diamond'). After reviewing the literature, Kremin (this volume) also classified alexia into three groups: pure alexia without agraphia; literal, deep and/or phonological alexia; and surface dyslexia.

In general, there seems to be greater consensus regarding the number of subcategories of alexia than dyslexia. Most of the investigations indicate that there exist three forms of alexia.

One cannot but be impressed that the number three emerges more often than any other number in studies that deal in some form or other with the typology of dyslexia. Some of the studies that suggest more than three subtypes of dyslexia might have arrived at the number by placing the "unexplainable" cases in a separate category. Regardless of the diversity of opinion regarding the actual number of subtypes, a general finding that emerges with great force is that dyslexia is not a homogeneous deficit. In fact, as far as we know, there exists no study that expressly set out to investigate the homogeneity–heterogeneity problem and came up with evidence supporting the view that dyslexia is a unitary disorder.

RESOLUTION OF CONFLICTS AMONG RESEARCH FINDINGS AND A DEMONSTRATION STUDY

It was noted earlier that investigations that treat all dyslexic subjects as though they represent a single homogeneous group tend to obscure intergroup differences. Such an approach often results in a failure to find significant differences between reading-disabled and normal children. In this section, an experimental study is described which demonstrates the need for treating the subtypes separately. The study involves the relationship between cerebral lateralization and reading disability. This particular problem was chosen for two reasons. First, this has been an active area of research and a number of papers have been published in recent years. Second, at least two major reviews of these studies (Satz, 1976; Naylor, 1980) have appeared and both have concluded that there is no substantive evidence to show that cerebral lateralization is an important factor in reading disability. More importantly, both reviews point to the numerous inconsistencies among the many research studies, inconsistencies that prevent any consensus from emerging.

The aim of the study reported here is to investigate the possibility that the frequently reported failure to find significant difference in lateralization between dyslexic and normal children could be due to the failure of experimental designs to isolate the dyslexic subgroups and study them separately. In order to accomplish this objective, the following procedure was adopted. First, the data relating to dichotic listening scores of all the dyslexic children studied were pooled together and were compared with those of the control subjects. In this respect, the experimental treatment followed the traditional pattern of treating all the dyslexic subjects as though they belong to a single, homogeneous group. Subsequently, the dyslexic subjects were classified into subgroups on the basis of certain criteria and each subgroup was then compared to the control group. If incorporating the "heterogeneity variable" in experimental design is an important factor, then the two approaches should yield different results.

Orton, as early as 1937, postulated that faulty or incomplete cerebral lateralization might be responsible for reading disability. Since 1961, it has become possible to put Orton's hypothesis to rigorous test with the aid of dichotic listening and visual field techniques. A study conducted by Zurif and Carson (1970) found that dyslexics tended to have a left ear advantage for words (not statistically significant) whereas normal readers recalled words that were presented to the right ear. Sparrow and Satz (1970) found that 9–12-year-old dyslexics showed a higher frequency of left ear superiority for dichotic listening tasks. In studies by Leong (1976) and Yeni-Komshian, Isenberg, and Goldberg (1975), significant right-ear advantage was found in normal and disabled readers, although Leong found a greater magnitude of right-ear advantage for normal male readers than for the dyslexics.

Thomson (1976) presented dichotic listening tasks involving digits, three-letter words from the Thorndike–Lorge count, reversible words (*saw/was*), similar-looking words (*big/pig*), and reversible nonsense syllables (*mag/gam*) to 20 dyslexics who ranged in age from 9 to 12 and an equal number of normal readers matched for age, sex, socioeconomic status, and intelligence. Normal readers showed a significant right ear advantage for digits, three-letter words, reversible words, and similar-looking words. There was no significant difference among dyslexics on digits and reversible words. Witelson (1976, 1977) who had separated dyslexic boys from dyslexic girls, found that dyslexic boys had a different form of hemispheric specialization than the boys with normal reading ability.

These studies, in general, lack a consensus as far as the findings are concerned. This view is well expressed by Satz (1976), who after reviewing the relevant literature, concluded that there is still a lack of proper information on the relationship between cerebral dominance and dyslexia. Naylor (1980) also concluded that the cerebral asymmetry hypothesis as an etiological factor in reading disabilities lacks firm basis. In contrast to the conclusions arrived at by these reviews, the few studies that have isolated the dyslexic subtypes and investigated them separately have yielded more consistent results. These studies are, however, too few in number to permit any firm conclusions.

Keefe and Sweeney (1979) administered dichotic listening digits task to 19 dyslexic right-handed boys with an average age of 10 years and to a matched group of 19 normal readers. An interesting finding of this study was that the frequency polygon of normal readers approached normal distribution with a single mode, whereas the frequency polygon of dyslexic readers was bimodal, with two peaks, one on either side of the group mean. Keefe and Sweeney concluded from this study that

> there appears to be at least two categories of dyslexic children with respect to hemispheric specialization of linguistic material. One type demonstrated what might be labelled, at least in comparison to the normal controls, a Left-Hemisphere-Deficit and the other demonstrates, again by comparison, a Right-Hemisphere-Deficit [p. 479].

Fried (1979) compared the auditory event related potential among normal readers, dysphonetic readers, and dyseidetic readers. There were significant wave form differences in the left hemisphere between dyseidetic subjects and dysphonetic subjects but no significant differences between dyseidetic and normal readers.

Pirozzolo (1979) divided dyslexics into auditory–linguistic dyslexics, who may be considered to be similar to Boder's dysphonetic group, and visual–spatial dyslexics, who may be comparable to Boder's dyseidetic group. Auditory–linguistic dyslexics did not show the right visual field superiority for words that is observed in normal readers. Visual–spatial dyslexics, on the other hand, showed a right visual field superiority for words although their performance was poorer than that of normal readers. Even though these three studies are not sufficient to draw any firm conclusions, they point to the need for having more studies that make a priori distinction between dyslexic subtypes.

As mentioned earlier, the present study is an attempt to demonstrate the difference in the outcome of results when subgroups are treated separately. Forty-six dyslexic children from the first and second grades were selected from a population of 256 children attending local elementary schools. These 46 children had normal intelligence (teachers' reports and Peabody Picture Vocabulary Test, Dunn, 1965) and had no known gross neurological problems as determined by the Quick Neurological Screening Test (Mutti, Sterling, & Spalding, 1978). According to screenings conducted by the school, none of the subjects had any visual or auditory problem. Those children who were reading at least one grade level below their expected level on the Gates–MacGinitie test were considered as reading disabled. (As the reading tests were administered at the end of the school year, Level B of the Gates–MacGinitie test was used.)

Of the 46 dyslexic subjects, 35 were males and 11 were females. The retarded readers were further classified as dysphonetic and dyseidetic on the basis of Boder's diagnostic testing (Boder & Jarrico, 1982). Only those subjects who could be clearly classified as dysphonetic or dyseidetic were included in the study. On this basis, 14 dysphonetics and 14 dyseidetics were chosen; they were matched for age, sex, and IQ with a group of normal readers who were reading at or above the grade level according to the Gates–MacGinitie reading test. All were right-handed as determined by the Quick Neurological Screening Test.

The subjects were administered a dichotic listening task individually. The dichotic listening tape contained 30 items, each item consisting of three pairs of digits. The tape was played on a Sony (Model TC-630) stereophonic tape recorder through a pair of audiometric headphones (TDH-39) equipped with MX/41 AR cushions. Sufficient test trials were given to insure that the subjects understood the instructions. The subjects were encouraged to do their best and to guess when necessary.

The scores on the dichotic listening test were scored by using the following formula:

$$\frac{R - L}{R + L} \times 100$$

where R and L are the total number of digits recalled from the right ear and left ear respectively. The means of the IQ scores, reading levels, and dichotic listening scores for all the three groups, as well as the results of analysis of variance, are shown in Table 2.6.

The dichotic listening scores of both subgroups of dyslexic children (dysphonetic and dyseidetic) were first pooled and compared with the scores of normal children by means of a t test. The result showed that there was no significant difference between dyslexic and normal readers, the critical value being 1.62 ($p > .10$). Most of the dichotic listening investigations usually stop here and conclude that there is no difference in cerebral asymmetry between normal and retarded readers. However, with a view to prove the point, we went ahead and compared the scores of the two dyslexic subgroups separately with those of the control group. The outcome of this procedure was entirely different.

The result of one way analysis of variance showed that there was a significant difference among dysphonetic, dyseidetic, and normal readers [$F(2, 39) = 4.38$; $p < .05$]. Further, Tukey's honestly significant difference (HSD) method was applied to find out which groups differed significantly from each other. The critical value for any two groups to be significantly different from one another at .05 significant level was found to be 10.18. Such statistical analysis showed that there is a significant difference between dysphonetic and normal readers. The difference between the means of dichotic scores of dysphonetic and dyseidetic dyslexics was 10.04, which just failed to reach the level of significant critical value of 10.18. However, there was no significant difference between dyseidetic and normal readers on the dichotic listening.

A second analysis of the data was carried out by classifying dyslexic children into three subcategories on the basis of an entirely different criterion. An examination of scores on the Gates–MacGinitie's and Boder's oral reading of the disabled readers revealed that some subjects had obtained an above average score on the Gates–MacGinitie vocabulary test but a below average score on the Gates–MacGinitie comprehension test and vice versa. These groups may, therefore, be considered as "semantic intact" and "semantic deficient" subgroups. Further, some subjects had scored above average on the Gates–MacGinitie vocabulary test, which is read silently, and below average on Boder's word recognition inventory, which is read orally, and vice versa. These groups may, therefore, be considered as "phonetic intact" and "phonetic deficient" subgroups. Similarly, some subjects had above average scores on the Gates–MacGinitie comprehension test but below average scores on Boder's task and vice versa. These groups may be considered as "comprehension intact" and "comprehension deficient" subgroups.

Table 2.6
Mean Dichotic Listening Scores of Dyslexic and Normal Readers and the Results of Analysis of Variance

| | Groups | | | | Group comparisons (Tukey's HSD) | | |
	Normal readers (N = 14)	Dysphonetic readers (N = 14)	Dyseidetic readers (N = 14)	F	1 vs 2	2 vs 3	1 vs 3
Chronological age (in months)	94.68	94.00	92.33				
IQ	102.32	99.84	98.53	1.41			
Reading levels (grade)	3.1	1.3	1.2				
Dichotic listening scores	7.40	-3.92	6.12	4.38*	11.32*	10.04	1.28

* Significant at .05 level.

Table 2.7
Means, Standard Deviations, and the Results of the t *Test of Dyslexic Subgroups on Dichotic Listening Tasks*

	N	Mean	SD	t
1. Good oral reading but poor silent reading (phonetic intact subgroup)	9	9.33	6.53	3.09; $p < .01$
2. Good silent reading but poor oral reading (phonetic deficient subgroup)	11	−2.61	9.97	
3. Good comprehension but poor oral reading (comprehension intact subgroup)	10	4.76	9.88	1.75; $p < .10$
4. Good oral reading but poor comprehension (comprehension deficient subgroup)	9	−5.50	15.60	
5. Good semantics but poor comprehension (semantic intact subgroup)	12	−3.12	13.22	2.31; $p < .05$
6. Good comprehension but poor semantic (semantic deficient subgroup)	9	4.98	11.46	

The details concerning the number of subjects and their mean scores on the dichotic listening digits task are shown in Table 2.7.

In order to find the significant differences between the various subgroups, *t* tests were employed. Significant differences in dichotic listening scores were obtained between phonetic intact and phonetic deficient ($t = 3.09$; $p < .01$); and between semantic intact and semantic deficient subgroups ($t = 2.31$; $p < .05$). The critical *t* value between the comprehension intact and comprehension deficient group was 1.75 ($p < .10$).

The results of the present study lend support to the view that subgroups of dyslexia exist and that these subgroups differ in their hemispheric information-processing strategies from one another as well as from normal readers.

CLINICAL SUBTYPES OF DYSLEXIA AND REMEDIATION

As mentioned earlier, accurate diagnosis of reading problems should lead to improved remediation procedures. There exists a possibility that different subgroups may respond differently to the different methods of treatment. For instance, Wepman (1962) has suggested that "there are notable individual differences in children relative to the modality of learning . . . reading in our schools should not be by a single approach, but rather one directed toward the capacities of the individual child [p. 186]."

Different remedial techniques have been recommended for different dyslexic groups in the literature. For example, Boder (1973) recommended the following remedial techniques for different subgroups of dyslexia: whole-word approach for the dysphonetic group; phonics approach for the dyseidetic group; and tactile-kinesthetic approach for the mixed group. Nonetheless, we could locate only two studies that have tried different methods with different types of learners. Such a paucity of remedial studies is possibly due to the general notion that all dyslexic children are alike.

Pask and Scott (1972) divided 16 18–24-year-old college students into serial learners and holistic learners based on their strengths of learning styles. The performance of both the groups was better when zoology was taught in a serial fashion to serialists and holistically to holistic learners. It should be pointed out, however, that the subjects in this study were not necessarily dyslexics. In another study, Aaron, Grantham, and Campbell (this volume) divided a group of dyslexics into dysphonetics and dyseidetic readers according to Boder's classification. The results showed that after one academic year of training dysphonetic readers made some gains in reading when taught by whole-word method and dyseidetic readers made significant gains when taught by phonetic–sequential method. It is interesting to note that both the studies reported success when teaching method utilized the strengths rather than weaknesses of the subjects. The pathetically small number of studies described here indicate that this is a neglected area of investigation. Clearly more research is needed.

CONCLUSION

The present chapter reviewed the research on reading disability that is relevant to the hypothesis that subtypes of dyslexia exist. A majority of studies support the possibility that dyslexia is a group of disorders composed of three subtypes. A few studies report evidence for the existence of a fourth type which frequently is of an undetermined nature. The "unexpected" group found by Satz and Morris (1981) in their factor-analytic study, the "mixed" group found in the genetic study of DeFries and Decker (this volume), and the group displaying diffuse or generalized wave patterns reported by Hughes (this volume) are examples of the unexpected group. A study that demonstrated the need for separate experimental treatment of dyslexic subgroups was described, as were two studies that showed that remediation techniques were more successful when subgroups were identified and teaching was aimed at the cognitive strengths of the students. In conclusion, resolution of problems regarding dyslexia in all likelihood depends on our identifying specific subgroups of dyslexia and treating them separately rather than continuing to view dyslexia as a unitary syndrome.

REFERENCES

Aaron, P. G. (1978) Dyslexia, an imbalance in cerebral information processing strategies. *Perceptual and Motor Skills, 47,* 699–706.

Aaron, P. G. (1980) Research in reading disability: Riddles and resolutions. *Journal of Reading, 24,* 116–119.

Aaron, P. G., & Baker, C. (1982) The neuropsychology of dyslexia in college students. In R. N. Malatesha & L. C. Hartlage (Eds.), *Neuropsychology and cognition* (Vol. 1). Alphen aan den Rijn, The Netherlands: Sijthoff and Noordhoff.

Albert, M. L. (1979) Alexia. In K. M. Heilman & E. Valenstein (Eds.), *Clinical neuropsychology,* New York: Oxford University Press.

Bakker, D. J. (1979) Hemispheric differences and reading strategies: Two dyslexias? *Bulletin of the Orton Society, 14,* 84–100.

Bannatyne, A. (1971) *Language, reading, and learning disabilities.* Springfield, Ill: Charles C. Thomas.

Bateman, B. C. (1968) *Interpretation of the 1961 Illinois Test of Psycholinguistic Abilities.* Seattle: Special Child Publications.

Bender, L. (1958) Problems in conceptualization and communication in children with developmental alexia. In P. H. Koch & J. Zubin (Eds.), *Psychopathology of communication.* New York: Grune & Stratton.

Benson, D. F. (1977) The third alexia. *Archives of Neurology, 34,* 327–331.

Benson, D. F., & Geschwind, N. (1969) The alexias. In P. J. Vinken & G. W. Bruyn (Eds.), *Handbook of clinical neurology* (Vol. 4). New York: American Elsevier.

Benton, A. L. (1964) Contributions to aphasia before Broca. *Cortex, 1,* 314–327.

Birch, H. G. (1962) Dyslexia and the maturation of visual function. In J. Money (Ed.), *Reading disability: Progress and research needs in dyslexia.* Baltimore: Johns Hopkins University Press.

Boder, E. (1973) Developmental dyslexia: A diagnostic approach based on three atypical reading–spelling patterns. *Developmental Medicine and Child Neurology, 15,* 663–687.

Boder, E., & Jarrico, S. (1982). *Boder Reading and Spelling Pattern Test: A diagnostic screening test for developmental dyslexia.* New York: Grune & Stratton.

Caramazza, A. A., & Berndt, R. S. (1978) Semantic and syntactic processes in aphasia: A review of the literature. *Psychological Bulletin, 85,* 898–918.

Critchley, M. (1970) *The dyslexic child.* Springfield, Ill: Charles C. Thomas.

Cruikshank, W. M. (1968) The problem of delayed recognition and its correction. In A. H. Keeney & V. T. Keeney (Eds.), *Dyslexia: Diagnosis and treatment of reading disorders.* St. Louis: C. V. Mosby.

Delacato, C. H. (1959) *The treatment and prevention of reading problems.* Springfield, Ill.: Charles C Thomas.

Denckla, M. B. (1977) Minimal brain dysfunction and dyslexia: Beyond diagnosis by exclusion. In M. I. Blaw, I. Rapin, & M. Kinsbourne (Eds.), *Topics in child neurology.* New York: Spectrum.

Denckla, M. B. (1979) Childhood learning disabilities. In K. M. Heilman & E. Valenstein (Eds.), *Clinical neuropsychology.* New York: Oxford University Press.

Denhoff, E. (1976) Medical aspects. In W. M. Cruikshank (Ed.), *Cerebral palsy: A developmental disability* (3rd ed.). Syracuse, N.Y.: Syracuse University Press.

deQuiros, J. B., & Shrager, O. L. (1978) *Neuropsychological fundamentals in learning disabilities.* San Rafael, Calif.: Academic Therapy Publications.

Doehring, D. G., & Hoshko, I. M. (1977) Classification of reading problems by the Q-technique of factor analysis. *Cortex, 13,* 281–294.

Doehring, D. G., Hoshko, I. M., & Bryans, B. N. (1979) Statistical classification of children with reading problems. *Journal of Clinical Neuropsychology, 1,* 5–16.

Drew, A. L. (1956) A neurological appraisal of familial congenital word-blindness. *Brain, 79,* 440–460.

Dunn, L. M. (1965) *Peabody Picture Vocabulary Test.* Circle Pines, Minn.: American Guidance Service.

Fisk, J. L., & Rourke, B. P. (1979) Identification of subtypes of learning disabled children at three age levels: A neuropsychological, multivariate approach. *Journal of Clinical Neuropsychology, 1,* 289–310.

Freud, S. (1953) *On aphasia.* New York: International Universities Press.

Fried, I. (1979) Cerebral dominance and subtypes of developmental dyslexia. *Bulletin of the Orton Society, 14,* 101–112.

Frostig, M., & Maslow, P. (1973) *Learning problems in the classroom: Prevention and remediation.* New York: Grune & Stratton.

Gastaut, H. (1970) Clinical and electroencephalographic classification of epileptic seizures. *Epilepsia, 11,* 102–113.

Gates–MacGinitie Reading Tests, Level B. (1978) Boston: Houghton Mifflin.

Hermann, K. (1959) *Reading disability.* Copenhagen: Munksgaard.

Hier, D., LeMay, M., Rosenberger, P., & Perlo, V. P. (1978) Developmental dyslexia. *Archives of Neurology, 35,* 90–92.

Hinshelwood, J. (1917) *Congenital word blindness.* London: Lewis.

Ingram, T. T. S., Mason, A. W., & Blackburn, I. (1970) A retrospective study of 82 children with reading disability. *Developmental Medicine and Child Neurology, 12,* 271–281.

Johnson, D. J., & Myklebust, H. R. (1967) *Learning disabilities.* New York: Grune & Stratton.

Jordan, D. R. (1977) *Dyslexia in the classroom.* Columbus, Ohio: Charles E. Merrill.

Jorm, A. F. (1979a) The cognitive and neurological basis of developmental dyslexia: A theoretical framework and review. *Cognition, 7,* 19–33.

Jorm, A. F. (1979b) The nature of the reading deficit in developmental dyslexia: A reply to Ellis. *Cognition, 7,* 421–433.

Keefe, B., & Sweeney, D. (1979) On the relationship of hemispheric specialization and developmental dyslexia. *Cortex, 15,* 471–481.

Keeney, A. H. (1968) Comprehensive classification of the dyslexias. In A. H. Keeney & V. T. Keeney (Eds.), *Dyslexia: Diagnosis and treatment of reading disorders.* St. Louis: C. V. Mosby.

Kephart, N. (1960) *The slow learner in the classroom.* Columbus, Ohio: Charles E. Merrill.

Kinsbourne, M., & Hiscock, M. (1978) Cerebral lateralization and cognitive development. In J. S. Chall & A. F. Mirsky (Eds.), *Education and the brain.* Chicago: University of Chicago Press.

Kinsbourne, M., & Warrington, E. K. (1963) Developmental factors in reading and writing backwardness. *British Journal of Psychology, 54,* 145–156.

Kline, L., & Lee, N. (1972) A transcultural study of dyslexia. *Journal of Special Education, 6,* 9–26.

Leong, C. K. (1976) Lateralization in severely disabled readers in relation to functional cerebral development and synthesis of information. In R. M. Knights & D. J. Bakker (Eds.), *The neuropsychology of learning disorders.* Baltimore: University Park Press.

Mann, P., & Suiter, P. (1978) *Handbook in diagnostic teaching.* Boston: Allyn & Bacon.

Marshall, J. C., & Newcombe, F. (1973) Patterns of paralexia: A psycholinguistic approach. *Journal of Psycholinguistic Research, 2,* 175–199.

Mattis, S. (1978) Dyslexia syndromes: A working hypothesis that works. In A. L. Benton & D. Pearl (Eds.), *Dyslexia: An appraisal of current knowledge.* New York: Oxford University Press.

Mattis, S., French, J. H., & Rapin, I. (1975) Dyslexia in children and young adults: Three independent neuropsychological syndromes. *Developmental Medicine and Child Neurology, 17,* 150–163.

Morgan, W. P. (1896) A case of congenital word-blindness. *British Medical Journal, 2,* 1378.

Mutti, M., Sterling, H. M., & Spalding, N. V. (1978) *Quick Neurological Screening Test.* San Rafael, Calif.: Academic Therapy Publications.

Naidoo, S. (1972) *Specific dyslexia.* London: Pitman.

Naylor, H. (1980) Reading disability and lateral asymmetry: An information processing analysis. *Psychological Bulletin, 87,* 531–545.

Nicholls, J. V. V. (1968) Responsibilities of the opthalmologist. In A. H. Keeney & V. T. Keeney (Eds.), *Dyslexia: Diagnosis and treatment of reading disorders.* St. Louis: C. V. Mosby.

Orton, S. T. (1937) *Reading, writing, and speech problems in children.* New York: Norton.

Pask, G., & Scott, R. C. E. (1972) Learning strategies and individual competence. *International Journal of Man–Machine Studies, 4,* 217–253.

Petrauskas, R. J., & Rourke, B. P. (1979) Identification of subtypes of retarded readers: A neuropsychological, multivariate approach. *Journal of Clinical Neuropsychology, 1,* 17–37.

Pirozzolo, F. J. (1979) *The neuropsychology of developmental reading disorders.* New York: Praeger.

Prechtl, H. E. R. (1962) Reading difficulties as a neurological problem in childhood. In J. Money (Ed.), *Reading disability: Progress and research needs in dyslexia.* Baltimore: Johns Hopkins University Press.

Quadfasel, F. A., & Goodglass, H. (1968) Specific reading disability and other specific disabilities. *Journal of Learning Disabilities, 1,* 590–600.

Rabinovitch, R. D. (1968) Reading problems in children: Definitions and classification. In A. H. Keeney & V. T. Keeney (Eds.), *Dyslexia: Diagnosis and treatment of reading disorders.* St. Louis: C. V. Mosby.

Satz, P. (1976) Cerebral dominance and reading disability: An old problem revisited. In R. M. Knights & D. J. Bakker (Eds.), *The neuropsychology of learning disorders.* Baltimore: University Park Press.

Satz, P., & Morris, R. (1980) The search for subtype classification in learning disabled children. In R. E. Tarter (Ed.), *The child at risk.* New York: Oxford University Press.

Satz, P., & Morris, R. (1981) Learning disability subtypes: A review. In F. J. Pirozzolo & M. C. Wittrock (Eds.), *Neuropsychological and cognitive processes in reading.* New York: Academic Press.

Smith, D. E. P., & Carrigan, P. M. (1959) *The nature of reading disability.* New York: Harcourt, Brace, and Company.

Smith, M. M. (1970) *Patterns of intellectual abilities in educationally handicapped children.* Unpublished doctoral dissertation, Claremont College.

Sparrow, S., & Satz, P. (1970) Dyslexia, laterality, and neuropsychological development. In D. J. Bakker & P. Satz (Eds.), *Specific reading disability: Advances in theory and method.* Rotterdam, The Netherlands: Rotterdam University Press.

Thomson, M. E. (1976) A comparison of laterality effects in dyslexics and controls using verbal dichotic listening tasks. *Neuropsychologia, 4,* 243–246.

Vellutino, F. R. (1979) *Dyslexia: Theory and research.* Cambridge, Mass.: MIT Press.

Vernon, M. D. (1977) Varieties of deficiency in the reading process. *Harvard Educational Review, 47,* 396–410.

Wepman, J. M. (1962) Dyslexia: Its relationship to language acquisition and concept formation. In J. Money (Ed.), *Reading disability: Progress and research needs in dyslexia.* Baltimore: Johns Hopkins University Press.

Witelson, S. F. (1976) Sex and the single hemisphere: Specialization of the right hemisphere for spatial processing. *Science, 193,* 425–427.

Witelson, S. F. (1977) Developmental dyslexia: Two right hemispheres and none left? *Science, 195,* 309–311.

Yeni-Komshian, G. H., Isenberg, S., & Goldberg, H. (1975) Cerebral dominance and reading disability: Left visual field deficit in poor readers. *Neuropsychologia, 13,* 83–94.

Zangwill, O. L. (1962) Dyslexia in relation to cerebral dominance. In J. Money (Ed.), *Reading disability: Progress and research needs in dyslexia.* Baltimore: Johns Hopkins University Press.

Zurif, E. F., & Carson, G. (1970) Dyslexia in relation to cerebral dominance and temporal analysis. *Neuropsychologia, 8,* 351–361.

Chapter Three

Typology of Developmental Dyslexia: Evidence for Its Construct Validity[1]

JOSEPH H. ROSENTHAL
ELENA BODER
ENOCH CALLAWAY

HISTORICAL PERSPECTIVES AND BACKGROUND

The *learning disabilities* are the clinically noted, functionally expressed problems that professionals in psychology, education, medicine, and other associated disciplines encounter in children and adults who have difficulty with cognition, behavior, or both. The learning disabilities comprise four symptom-complexes, which are not mutually exclusive (Johnson & Myklebust, 1967; Tarnopol, 1971): (*a*) the dyslexia–dysgraphia syndromes; (*b*) the motor–perceptual dysfunction syndromes; (*c*) the language delays; (*d*) the syndromes of distractibility, hyperactivity, and decreased attention span.

[1] This research was supported in part by the Community Service Program of Kaiser Foundation Hospitals; the Ciba Pharmaceutical Company; the Earl C. Anthony Fund, University of California, San Francisco; the Computer Center, University of California, San Francisco; and the Office of Naval Research, Contract No. N00014-75-C-0398.

93

The learning disabilities are usually the expression of those primary neurophysiological and neuropsychological states termed the *minimal cerebral dysfunctions:* deviations of the central nervous system manifested by various combinations of impairments in perception, conceptualization, language, reading, memory, and in control of attention, impulse, or motor function. These minimal cerebral dysfunctions occur in children or adults who (*a*) can see; (*b*) can hear; (*c*) have a general IQ within normal limits (although IQ scores often show wide discrepancy between verbal and performance abilities); (*d*) manifest no obvious neurological damage; (*e*) have no primary emotional disturbance; and (*f*) have been given adequate educational opportunity (Clements, 1966).

The minimal cerebral dysfunctions relate pathophysiologically to some definitive and some as yet unknown genetic problems and to deleterious prenatal, perinatal, and postnatal factors. The effects of the pathophysiological deviations are markedly influenced by the interactions of a child with the environment and by training and education.

The position of the dyslexias within the broad area of *reading incompetence* has only recently begun to assume clear outlines. Rabinovitch (1968) estimated that at least 10% of all children in the United States are handicapped by reading incompetence before they reach the seventh grade. An accepted definition of reading incompetence is a significant discrepancy between actual and expected reading levels for performance mental age; considered significant are 1 year's reading delay in children up to 10 years of age and 2 years' delay in those older than 10 years.

Previously, the diagnosis of the syndromes of the dyslexias involved a process of exclusion of the individual from a universe of children and adults with reading incompetence due to other causes. Saunders (1962) calculated that 20–30% of schoolchildren showed reading incompetence. The estimate referred to children considered normal, specifically excluding those who, in definable categories, were in specific treatment and educational programs, such as the trainable mentally retarded, the physically handicapped, the autistic or primarily emotionally disturbed, and the visually and hearing impaired. Some children with reading incompetence are also found in classes for the educationally or neurologically handicapped or the learning disabled.

In about two-thirds to three-fourths of the children with reading incompetence, this handicap can be traced to a lack either of motivation or of educational opportunity of a sociocultural nature. About one-fourth to one-third have *developmental dyslexia,*[2] hypothesized as a neu-

---

[2] The terms *dyslexia, specific developmental dyslexia,* and *specific reading disability* are used here interchangeably with *developmental dyslexia.* None is used as a broad term encompassing nonspecific reading disorders.

rophysiologically based state. In rare instances in children, dyslexia is attributable to psychopathology or to a definitive acquired cerebral lesion. Blanchard (1946), approaching the learning disabilities from a psychoanalytic point of view, stressed the motivational aspects of learning and the primary neurotic causes of difficulties in these areas, especially those pertaining to reading and writing. Differences of opinion persist between those who propose organic causes for the learning disabilities and those who suggest psychogenic causes. As many clinicians attest, however, *secondary psychopathology* soon assumes great importance in developmental dyslexia because of the pressures to read and the early appearance of social, academic, and practical handicaps experienced by the person who is unable to read without discernible cause (Orton, 1925; Rawson, 1968; Cronin, 1968; Rosenthal, 1973).

Primary reading incompetence has been termed developmental dyslexia (Critchley, 1970b; Eisenberg, 1966; Gofman, 1969; Rabinovitch, 1968; Saunders, 1962). Persons with developmental dyslexia are deficient in the ability to cope with letters and words as symbols and thus to integrate the meaning of written material. Children and adults with this disorder have no visual or hearing difficulties. Their general intellectual functioning is normal or above, although they may show marked divergence in responses to subtests. They have no *obvious* neurological deficit. They have had adequate conventional educational opportunities. They have no *primary* emotional disturbance, were originally well motivated, and came from culturally adequate homes. Yet, they cannot learn to read, spell, and write with normal proficiency. About 5–10% of the general population is said to have developmental dyslexia (Critchley, 1970b).

Although hotly contested, the hypothesis has been proposed that developmental dyslexia reflects a basically disturbed pattern of neurological organization. Most observers have held that the condition is endogenous, biological, and perhaps genetic in etiology (Rosenthal, 1977, 1980).

Developmental dyslexia is still largely diagnosed by exclusion, hampered by the problems inherent in that process. Complicating these problems is the fact that the condition often does not exist alone but may occur together with one or more of the three other major clinical entities within the framework of the learning disabilities: the motor–perceptual dysfunction syndromes; the language delays; and the syndromes of distractibility, hyperactivity, and decreased attention span.

Since developmental dyslexia has been recognized, the burden implied for the affected individual and for society has become increasingly evident. Theoretical and therapeutic interest in this entity has been growing. Three subtypes have been defined (Boder, 1971), and a number of workers have sought to develop type-specific therapeutic approaches to the education of the dyslexic child and adult.

Both diagnosis and therapy, however, demand further refinement. The diagnosis of developmental dyslexia is still made by exclusion of at least six forms of reading incompetence due to other causes. This inefficient and confusing procedure can be significantly reduced if neurophysiological and anatomical bases of dyslexia and its subtypes can be specified. Such delineation can also be expected to have positive implications for improvements in therapy.

Developmental dyslexia is a specific, often genetically determined, difficulty in learning to read and spell. The condition occurs in persons who (*a*) have average or above general intelligence; (*b*) have no obvious brain pathology; (*c*) have no significant hearing impairment; (*d*) have no significant visual impairment; (*e*) have shown no initial resistance to conventional instruction methods; and (*f*) manifest no primary emotional disturbance.

BODER'S CONSTRUCT: READING–SPELLING PATTERN DYSFUNCTION

Boder (1971, 1973) developed, clarified, and established developmental dyslexia as a useful neuropsychological construct of *reading–spelling–writing* dysfunction. Through her empirically evolved diagnostic screening tool for developmental dyslexia she also established the existence of three subtypes: dysphonetic, dyseidetic, and mixed dysphonetic–dyseidetic. Rosenthal (1977) suggested that these subtypes are related to differential neurophysiological dysfunctions (which may have genetic causes).

Stressing that the reading–spelling–writing *patterns* have diagnostic, prognostic, and therapeutic implications, Boder defined three subtypes of dyslexia:

> Group I, *dysphonetic,* by far the largest of the subtypes, manifests deficit in integrating symbols with their sounds, with resulting *disability in developing phonic word-analysis skills* but without gross deficit in visual gestalt function. (The typical misspellings are dysphonetic, or phonetically inaccurate, e.g., "sleber" for "scrambled." The typical misreadings are word substitutions based on minimal clues, e.g., "diesel" for "dress," and gestalt substitutions, e.g., "book" for "block;" the most striking misreadings are semantic substitutions, e.g., "funny" for "laugh" and

"planet" for "moon.") Group II, *dyseidetic*, manifests deficits in visual perception and memory for letters and whole-word configurations, or gestalts, with resulting *disability in developing a sight vocabulary* but without disability in developing phonic skills. (The typical misspellings are phonetically accurate and decodable, e.g., "laf" for "laugh" and "toc" for "talk." The typical misreadings are phonetic renditions of nonphonetic words, e.g., "talc" for "talk"; visuospatial letter and word reversals in reading and writing are also typical, e.g., "bib" for "did," "no" for "on.") Group III, *mixed* dysphonetic–dyseidetic or *alexic*, combines the cognitive deficits of the dysphonetic and dyseidetic subtypes, with resulting *disability in developing both sight vocabulary and phonic skills;* they may be virtually nonreaders and nonspellers. (Typical misspellings are dysphonetic, as in Group I, but usually more bizarre, often only a single wrong initial letter, e.g., "R" for "stop"; letter and word reversals, as in Group II, are also typical.) [Boder & Jarrico, in press].

To raise the level of diagnosis of developmental dyslexia from being one of exclusion to one of discrimination, Boder has developed a direct diagnostic screening test which not only discriminates dyslexics from normal readers and those with nonspecific or secondary reading retardation, but also distinguishes among dysphonetic, dyseidetic, and mixed subtypes of dyslexia by assessing the reader's differential ability to read and then spell "known" and "unknown" words.

CONVERGENT AND SUPPORTIVE DATA

Clinical Data

Convergent and supportive clinical data, suggesting the existence not only of dyslexia but also of these subgroups, are found in other sources.

THE CATEGORIES OF JOHNSON AND MYKLEBUST: VISUAL AND AUDITORY DYSLEXICS

Johnson and Myklebust (1967), using a wide variety of psychoeducational testing procedures, were able to standardize tests for reading readiness and reading diagnosis and to identify subtypes of developmental dyslexia, which they termed *visual dyslexia* and *auditory dyslexia*. The visual dyslexic usually cannot learn the word as a whole; has problems with visual discrimination, memory, analysis, synthesis, and sequencing; and tends to make reversals in reading, writing, and spelling. The auditory dyslexic may be able to associate the word *milk* with the liquid in a carton but cannot relate the visual components of the word to their auditory equivalents. These subjects manifest problems with auditory discrimination, analysis and synthesis, and sequencing.

THE CATEGORIES OF KINSBOURNE AND WARRINGTON:
A LANGUAGE RETARDATION GROUP AND A GERSTMANN GROUP

Kinsbourne and Warrington (1966) studied a group of 13 backward readers and were able to divide them into subgroups on the basis of at least a 20-point disparity between their verbal and performance IQ scores on the Wechsler Intelligence Scale for Children (WISC). In Group I, the *language-retardation group*, were the children with a lower verbal than performance IQ, who showed other language problems such as disorders in verbalization and receptive language difficulties. The children of this group were often male, had a positive family history of learning difficulty, showed few or no soft signs on neurological examination, and were rather slow to acquire language. In Group II, *the Gerstmann group*, with lower performance than verbal IQ, the children showed specific problems on tests of finger differentiation and order, as well as impaired performance on constructional tasks and mechanical arithmetic, but had neither expressive nor receptive speech or language disorders. This group was composed of children, as often female as male, in whom soft signs did appear at neurological examination. Left–right discrimination problems and confusion in letter sequence caused misreading and misspelling and also poor visual memory. These children misread and misspelled by using letters that sounded right, suggesting that they were approaching the word phonetically.

BATEMAN'S CATEGORIES: VISUAL LEARNERS, AUDITORY
LEARNERS, CHILDREN WITH DEFICITS IN BOTH VISUAL
AND AUDITORY SKILLS; THERAPEUTIC IMPLICATIONS

Bateman (1968), on the basis of characteristic profiles on the Illinois Test of Psycholinguistic Abilities (ITPA), identified three subgroups among children with reading disabilities: (*a*) those who have poor auditory memory but good visual memory; (*b*) those with poor visual memory but good auditory memory; and (*c*) those with deficits in both visual and auditory memory, whose reading disability is severe and persistent. Bateman suggested that remedial measures for each group might include a sight-word method of reading instruction in the first group, a phonics approach in the second group, and a tactile–kinesthetic approach in the third group.

SMITH'S CATEGORIES: THREE PATTERNS BASED
ON THE WISC AND THE WAIS TESTS

Smith (1970), using the WISC and the Wechsler Adult Intelligence Scale (WAIS) as diagnostic and research tools, drew conclusions similar to those of Boder. Smith investigated patterns of cognitive–perceptual abilities in 300 educationally handicapped Anglo boys of first through sixth grade age, using a control group of 74 Anglo boys attending regular classes. Three patterns of functioning were delineated in the learning-disabled group; none of these was present in the control group. Pattern I (67.33%) had strength in spatial ability and spatial organization, earned lower scores in symbol manipulation than in spatial organization, and were deficient in sequencing ability. Pattern II (14.66%) had deficits in spatial organization and/or spatial ability and/or perceptual organization, and frequently had deficits in visual–motor coordination. Pattern III (18%) had characteristics of both Patterns I and II.

THE DYSLEXIC CATEGORIES OF MATTIS, FRENCH, AND
RAPIN: A LANGUAGE DISORDER GROUP, AN ARTICULATORY
AND GRAPHOMOTOR DYSCOORDINATION GROUP, AND A
VISUOSPATIAL PERCEPTUAL DISORDER GROUP

In an attempt to delineate causal factors in dyslexia, Mattis, French, and Rapin (1975) assessed 113 children referred for evaluation of learning and behavior disorders. The age range was 8–18 years.

Of the 113 tested, all had verbal or performance IQs greater than 80, had normal visual and auditory acuity, had adequate academic exposure, and showed no evidence of psychosis or thought disorder.

The 113 subjects were divided into three groups: (*a*) those with brain damage who could read ($N = 31$); (*b*) those with brain damage who were dyslexic ($N = 53$); and (*c*) those without brain damage who were dyslexic ($N = 29$).

Brain damage was diagnosed on the basis of a history of an encephalopathic event and subsequent abnormal development; abnormal findings on the clinical neurologic examination; significant abnormalities on the electroencephalogram or skull x-ray films; and abnormality on special neuroradiographic study (pneumoencephalogram or arteriogram).

Dyslexia was operationally defined as reading retardation on the Jastak Wide Range Achievement Test (WRAT) of two or more grades below the level appropriate for age. Eighty-two children were classified as dyslexic. The authors felt that a most significant finding was the *similarity* between the developmental dyslexic and the brain-damaged dyslexic groups. Subsequent neuropsychological examinations often did not indicate reliably whether a given dyslexic child had experienced an early encephalopathic event. Mattis *et al.* felt that, in both developmental dyslexia and in the dyslexia associated with recognizable brain damage, *brain dysfunction can be presumed.*

Interestingly, 23 (79%) of the 29 children in the dyslexic group without brain damage had a family history of reading disability.

On the basis of a battery of subsequent neuropsychological examinations, the dyslexic children—both the developmental dyslexic group and the brain-damaged dyslexic group—were divided according to three syndromes. Although the three syndromes were not evenly distributed between the developmental dyslexics and brain-damaged dyslexics, there were no differences between the two dyslexic groups within the same syndrome.

Syndrome I: Language Disorder (N = 31). The children with this syndrome presented with anomia, disorder of comprehension, disorder of imitative speech, and disorder of speech-sound discrimination. They had intact visual and constructional skills and adequate graphomotor coordination.

Syndrome II: Articulatory and Graphomotor Dyscoordination (N = 30). These children had an assortment of gross or fine motor coordination disorders but especially with buccolingual dyspraxia with resultant poor speech and graphomotor dyscoordination. These children possessed intact visuospatial perception, language, and constructional skills.

Syndrome III: Visuospatial Perceptual Disorder (N = 13). These children possessed a verbal IQ at least 10 points higher than the performance IQ. Their constructional ability was poor, and their visuospatial perception markedly poorer. Storage and retrieval of visual stimuli were very inefficient. These children maintained intact language, graphomotor coordination, and speech-blending skills.

The authors stressed that their results support a model representing dyslexia as caused by multiple independent defects in higher cortical functioning.

Neurological Data

Convergent and supportive neurological data suggesting the existence both of dyslexia and of the subgroups have come from other sources.

CRITCHLEY'S DIVISION OF ALEXIA INTO TWO SUBTYPES:
AGNOSIC (SPATIAL) AND SYMBOLIC (LANGUAGE)

Critchley (1970a), working with adult neurologically impaired patients, defined two types of alexia—the agnosic and the symbolic type. Critchley stated that agnosic alexia represents an underlying disorder of spatioconstructional manipulations, whereby geometric and other figures cannot be either assembled or interpreted as letters. In contrast are the more usual cases, in which what cannot be understood is the symbolic nature of the print or writing—the grapheme–phoneme relationship. Critchley also stated that left parietal dysgraphia can be distinguished from right parietal dysgraphia, the latter being characterized by gross defects in spatial arrangements, often with an inordinately broad left margin.

HECAEN'S DISTINCTION BETWEEN LEFT AND RIGHT
PARIETAL ALEXIAS AND AGRAPHIAS

Subdivisions of the alexias were noted by Hécaen (1967) in his discussion of brain mechanisms. In studies of the parietal lobes, Hécaen noted that the alexias and agraphias of right parietal lesions differ from those caused by left-sided lesions: The latter bear on the comprehension or transcription of the graphic code. The alexias and agraphias due to right parietal lesions are disturbances in writing and reading which come from perceptual difficulties with the spatial arrangement of letters and sentences. Spatial dyslexia is characterized not only by neglect of the left side of the text and sometimes by neglect of one or more words (or, more likely, of a part of a word) but also by difficulty in passing from one line to another. Occipital as well as parietal lesions may be involved. Those features of spatial dysgraphias that separate them from the dysgraphias due to lesions of the left hemisphere include writing on the right side of the page, inability to write in a straight line (diagonal or wavy writing), and alterations involving mainly the vertical strokes (*m, n, i, v*) and, more rarely, letters or words. These alterations usually do not destroy the actual structure of the word, which remains legible, and the grammatic structure of sentences is never altered.

LURIA'S CONTRIBUTION RELATING TO DIFFERENCES
IN SEQUELAE OF LEFT AND RIGHT BRAIN LESIONS

Luria (1973) discussed the differences in pathology between lesions of the left and right hemispheres. Massive lesions of the right parieto-occipital region interfere with processes of spatial gnosis and praxis. A significant feature of spatial gnosis and praxis is unawareness of the left half of the visual field, manifested not only when complex drawings are examined during reading but also in the patient's spontaneous writing and drawing. On the other hand, lesions of the parieto-occipital zones of the left hemisphere at times specifically relate to components of reading from the points of view of higher symbolic processes, complex logical grammatic structures, and phonetic analysis. Disturbances of phonemic hearing arise only in lesions of the left temporal lobe. At times, the principal feature of the clinical picture is that the patient cannot retain even a short series of sounds, syllables, or words in the memory (i.e., auditory sequencing difficulty). The patient either confuses their order or simply states that some of the elements of the sequence have been forgotten.

Scientific Data

Supportive and convergent scientific data from different sources exist that strengthen the concept of differential and specialized cerebral (hemispheric) functioning in adults. In recent years, testing for and information relating to cerebral dominance (differential functioning and lateralized specialization) have come from (a) cortico-anatomical techniques (hemispherectomy, Lenneberg, 1967; cortical mapping, Penfield & Roberts, 1966; split-brain surgery, Sperry & Gazzaniga, 1967); (b) intracarotid sodium amytal techniques (Wada & Rasmussen, 1960); (c) dichotic listening techniques (Bakker, 1969); (d) dichoptic techniques (Kimura, 1969); and (e) regional cerebral blood flow techniques (Ingvar & Schwartz, 1974).

The two hemispheres are probably not functionally equivalent: The left hemisphere can process analytic, language, verbal, and linear reasoning tasks; the right hemisphere can be involved with processing gestalt, holistic, synthetic spatial–geometric–relational information.

Electrophysiological Data

Supportive and convergent electrophysiological data exist that strengthen the concepts of cortical specialization and differential hemispheric utilization in adults. The comprehensive reviews by Callaway (1975) and Donchin, Kutas, and McCarthy (1977) summarize and integrate earlier work. Asymmetry of cortical functioning can be reflected in asymmetric electroencephalograms (EEGs) and averaged evoked cortical potentials, depending upon the evoking stimulus and the type and location of the cognitive process that the stimulus sets into motion. Tasks presumed to utilize the left hemisphere differentially have included composing letters, word-search tasks, mental arithmetic, and "verbal" listening. Right hemisphere tasks have included modified Kohs blocks, seashore tonal memory, drawing tasks, spatial imagery tasks, and music listening tests.

An overview of most of these studies indicates that the *independent variable* is defined in terms of tasks assigned to the subject. The *dependent variable* is some parameter of the scalp-recorded EEG activity. Studies are of two categories, according to the dependent variable utilized (Donchin *et al.*, 1977).

ELECTROENCEPHALOGRAPH FREQUENCY DOMAIN PARAMETERS

Those studies which focus on the ongoing EEG activity measure *frequency domain* parameters.

Until recently, neurophysiological studies attempting to establish correlations between specific reading disabilities and EEG tracings (Klasen, 1972) have not been particularly helpful, even though the incidence of abnormal EEGs is higher in children with minimal brain dysfunction than in normal controls (Hughes, 1971). Critchley (1970b), reviewing EEG studies in dyslexia, noted that mild dysrhythmias suggestive of cortical immaturity are often found, and these are most evident in the parieto-occipital areas bilaterally. Among the problems mentioned by Critchley in the interpretation of EEG data are the co-existing positive "soft" neurological findings, which are more conspicuous in younger dyslexics, and the confused diagnostic standards for dyslexia in older groups, wherein psychiatric overlays are quite prominent.

Recognizing that differences between the EEGs of dyslexics and normals exist, but that refinements of technique were required, Sklar (1971) examined 12 dyslexics (10 boys and 2 girls, aged 9–18 years), in whom all of Boder's three subgroups were represented, although most were of Subgroup I (dysphonetic). The EEGs were evaluated by a computer search for disparities, not by direct visual inspection, following which normal and dyslexic children were classified by computer from spectral analysis of their EEGs. Sklar found that the two groups could be differentiated especially well during the rest, eyes-closed phase. The most prominent spectral differences appeared in the parieto-occipital region; the dyslexic children had, on the average, more energy in the 3–7 Hz and 16–32 Hz bands—the normals, in the 9–14 Hz band (Hz refers to a unit of frequency in the EEG equal to one cycle per second). However, during the actual reading task, the autospectral disparity between the two sample populations was reversed in the 16–32 Hz band, at which normals had greater energy. The mean coherences for all activity within the same hemisphere were higher for dyslexics, whereas the coherences tended to be higher for normals between symmetric regions across the midline. However, if the EEG, or, more specifically, the coherences between hemispheres, is taken as an index of the transfer of information in the central nervous system, the greatest differences between normals and dyslexics might have been expected to occur during the reading task rather than during the state of rest with eyes closed.

Hanley (1975), working with adult dyslexics (diagnosed by Boder, but studied as a group without reference to the Boder subtypes), noted that, in general, the findings with respect to shared activity calculated from the coherence function were similar to those in children in that those without dyslexia showed greater shared activity between symmetric placements across the hemispheres. Hanley took this to be valuable evidence of the robustness of the coherence findings in the face of known maturational processes in the EEG in the progression from childhood to adulthood. In addition, Hanley believed he could *visually* assess the standard EEG to diagnose dyslexia. He believed that dyslexics generate more theta activity (4–7 Hz) from the parieto-occipital areas bilaterally than do nondyslexics, and that the dyslexics show, at the same time, broadband alpha, which is poorly defined and spread out over the 8–14-Hz band.

Callaway and Harris (1974) described a new way to assess how the central nervous system processes data by intrahemispheric measures of coupling between cortical areas. When two areas of the brain are in active functional communication, some relationship should exist between the EEGs from these two areas. The two EEGs can at any instant be classified on the basis of polarity and direction of change of potential (that is, slope), and the results of such a classification can be used to measure coupling. Functional communications between the visual area and each of the left and right hemispheres were manipulated by assigning verbal (left hemisphere) and spatial (right hemisphere) tasks to nine right-handed subjects. Their results indicated that appositional (right hemisphere) processing of visual data (examining a picture) tends to increase coupling between the occiput and the right hemisphere; propositional (read silently—left hemisphere) processing tends to increase coupling to the left. Changes in EEG coupling that accompany changes in cognitive processing support the idea that the EEG is actually related to electrical events involved in information processing of the central nervous system.

Bali, Callaway, and Naghdi (1975) cited the work of Davis and Wada (1974), who measured coherences between averaged evoked potentials recorded from temporal and parietal leads, findings that clicks induced more coherence in the speech-dominant hemisphere than on the other side and that flashes produced more coherence in the other, non-speech-dominant hemisphere. Bali *et al.* (1975) replicated the Davis and Wada data by using the same stimulus paradigm but a method of EEG analysis by cortical coupling. In right-handed subjects, the left–right ratio for clicks was found to be greater than the left–right ratio for flashes for frontoparietal lead pairs. In a preliminary study, Bali *et al.* (1975), working with 11 older dyslexics (not divided into clinical subgroups) found a reversal of the results obtained with normal subjects. Of the 11 dyslexics, 9 showed left–right ratios of coupling higher for flashes than for clicks.

ELECTROENCEPHALOGRAPH TIME DOMAIN STUDIES

Those studies which analyze the EEG in the time domain are concerned with waveforms of event-related potentials (ERPs) taken from the EEG by signal averaging.

Comprehensive reviews exist of the development of measures for averaged evoked cortical potentials (Callaway, 1975; Donchin *et al.*, 1977; Yingling, 1978; Halliday, in preparation; Regan, 1979). The EEG is a continuous record of ongoing variations in electrical potential (voltage) between pairs of electrodes. The correlation between a *particular sensory signal* and the *ensuing electrical response* of the brain was firmly established in the mid and late 1930s but much refined just since the early 1960s. These potential fluctuations may be referred to as ERPs. The ERP technique has greatly assisted the neurophysiologist in tracing sensory impulses along specific afferent systems to their terminals in the cortex. However, because the sensory ERP, recorded from the scalp, is relatively small (4–15 μV) with respect to the background EEG (20–100 μV), the accurate mapping of the minute current fields set up by the deliberate stimulation of a sense organ had to await the development of special-purpose computers (averagers). With these devices, repetitive samples of EEGs are automatically summated. Electrical activity that is unrelated to the onset of a stimulus tends to cancel with successive sweeps, whereas the ERP, initiated by the stimulus, reinforces itself so that it can be quantified. Because the EEG background activity (noise) is not correlated with the stimulus (signal) but varies randomly in relation to it, the summed background noise builds up much less rapidly than the summed evoked potential. Thus the signal-to-noise ratio is enhanced. When an adequate number of individual ERPs (30–100) have been summed and stored, the automatic averaging computer calculates the average amplitude of each point on the trace and displays the average curve.

An EEG–ERP system requires high-quality, high-gain amplifiers (to amplify the signal with a minimum of distortion), an analog-to-digital converter (to digitize the signal), a device to average the digitized signal, a means of storing the data for later analysis, and peripheral equipment to generate signals.

The ERP is a complex sequence of polarity reversals consisting of a series of voltage changes (peaks, amplitudes) that occur at reliable time points following a stimulus. The ERPs may endure for 500 msec or more. Each deflection varies somewhat, depending on the modality stimulated and on the locus from which it was recorded. Although there is some specificity of response following auditory, somatosensory, and visual stimulation, a certain degree of similarity across modalities is also apparent. Several specific measurement techniques are used, designed to reduce the large data volume of ERPs (one ERP may consist of 25,000 data points):

1. Measures of latency and amplitude for each component of the ERP waveform are obtained. Special-purpose computer programs have been developed to sample these measures sequentially.
2. These measurements focus on the broad features of the ERP. Computer programs exist that can measure power amplitude of the entire ERP waveform or any latency band components therein.
3. Multivariate statistical procedures are applied to the ERP waveform.

Specific applications of one or more of these measurement techniques depend on theoretical, technical, and instrumental considerations.

Numerous classification systems have been devised to describe the various undulations of the ERP response. The most universal scheme divides the ERP waveform into early (*exogenous*) and later (*endogenous*) components. The poststimulus exogenous components (up to 60–100 msec) represent stages in the afferent stream, and these deflections can only be recorded in association with some sensory stimulus. Their scalp distribution depends on the modality of the stimulus (e.g., auditory, visual), and their morphology on the physical parameters of the stimulus.

Very early components of the ERP (up to 10 msec) are called the far-field or brainstem response. For example, in response to an auditory stimulus, the far-field response would include the first five waves (components) which are thought to reflect the activity of various relay nuclei in the auditory pathway. Because the brainstem response does not require voluntary cooperation, it can be elicited in newborns and others with limited behavioral repertoires. The exogenous components are sensitive to changes in the intensity of a stimulus but do not reflect higher cognitive activity. By contrast, the later ERP components are affected by psychological factors, are sensitive to task parameters, and are believed to be manifestations of cortical information-processing activities invoked by task demands. A distinct class of pre-event endogenous components relate to preparatory or anticipatory cortical activity and can occur when subjects just expect a stimulus (contingent negative variation or expectancy wave at about 500 msec).

Naming late components is a problem and even a danger if the assignment of a name lulls us into thinking that naming something is the same as knowing what it is (Callaway, 1975). All waves from 30 msec on are not equivalent, regardless of whether components can be named. Positive potentials do not have the same significance as negative potentials. Good arguments exist for using *monopolar recordings* (one active scalp electrode and a relatively inactive reference electrode such as linked ears). Some laboratories favor bipolar recordings, resulting in a mixed contribution from both active electrodes. Modality differences in ERPs occur (e.g., somatosensory, auditory, visual). Still, some general thoughts exist about the endogenous components. Waves from about 100 to 200 msec may reflect simple attention or perhaps early selective attention. Components from about 200 to 400 msec may reflect more complex recognition, discrimination, and perhaps stimulus categorization.

Recent efforts have established the diagnostic utility of the ERP technique, particularly in the assessment of sensory integrity, the tracking of central nervous system maturation, and the anatomical localization of lesions. Cortical auditory, visual, and somatosensory ERPs, respectively, have provided valuable information on hearing loss; visual disorders; and peripheral, spinal cord, and cerebral lesions. Computer-based averaging procedures have been used to study central nervous system development. Changes in amplitude, latency, and waveform of the cortical evoked responses have been shown to correlate highly with cerebral maturation. For example, with increasing age, ERP late components become more stable, and ERP variability and latencies decrease. Attempts to correlate abnormalities in specific brainstem ERP components with localized brainstem lesions have demonstrated the usefulness of this method in determining the site of neurological damage. Starr and Anchor (1975) used the brainstem ERP to distinguish structural from metabolic conditions affecting brainstem pathways. Drug-induced coma did not alter the brainstem response. However, the anatomic localization of brainstem and midbrain tumors was greatly facilitated by brainstem ERP recordings. In a study of over 100 patients, Stockard and Rossiter (1977) correlated parameters of the auditory brainstem ERP with postmortem or radiological identification of brainstem lesions. They found that neurological embarrassment (tumors, vascular lesions, infarcts, hemorrhage) at the level of the pontomedullary junction, caudal pons, rostral pons, midbrain, thalamus, and thalamic radiations coincided with modifications of waves II–VII, respectively.

These studies combined demonstrate the potential diagnostic and prognostic value of the ERP technique. The success thus far achieved with regard to specific neurophysiological and anatomical dysfunction has encouraged the application of ERP technology to the understanding of brain organization in general, especially in more subtle areas of cerebral dysfunctioning and learning disabilities. Particular emphasis has been placed on lateralized specialization of function.

Callaway (1973) has shown positive correlations between ERPs and more conventional measures of intelligence. More important, these positive correlations show that one can obtain a reflection of the relation between ongoing neurophysiological and cognitive states. Callaway found that brighter subjects show shorter latencies, lower ERP variability, and plasticity of the evoked response. The plasticity correlates with intelligence only when intelligent subjects would be expected to be more plastic, that is, they would be expected to show more change than the less bright, from task to task, in their cognitive responses. In broader terms, the issue is not whether ERPs can predict intelligence but whether the ERP measures individual differences in brain function (Halliday, in preparation). The relation between ERPs and intelligence probably reflects the differences in subjects' ongoing cognitive processing rather than hard-wired differences in neurophysiological organization. Therefore, it is probably more appropriate to examine how specific psychologic processes such as attention, memory, and different task requirements affect the ERP.

Beck and associates (Dustman, Schenkenberg, & Beck, 1976) were among the first to examine the hemispheric distribution of evoked cortical activity. They found that responses to simple visual stimuli (flashes) were consistently larger over the right parietal area of children and adults. Left–right amplitude differences were not seen in Down's syndrome or mentally retarded children.

Buchsbaum and Fedio (1970) reported hemispheric differences in ERPs to verbal and nonverbal stimuli presented to the left and right visual fields. Activation of the left hemiretinal hemisphere (dominant) yielded greater differences in ERP waveforms for the two classes of stimuli.

Yet, inconsistencies appear in studies of the laterality of visual ERPs (Donchin *et al.*, 1977). Studies of hemispheric differences in visual ERPs have been particularly hampered by the need to assure that the ERP elicited by stimulation of a retinal half-field is generated entirely within a single hemisphere. Whereas it has been well established that stimulation of different visual half-fields elicits different scalp distributions, the comparison of the hemispheric distributions of visual ERPs is not as straightforward. Several investigators have reported that visual ERPs recorded over homologous regions in normal subjects are symmetrical. Other researchers, however, have maintained that visual ERPs recorded from the right hemisphere are larger than those recorded from the left hemisphere.

Galin and Ellis (1975) suggest that asymmetries in evoked potential amplitude might depend in part on asymmetries in the alpha amplitude of the background EEG, which they consider to be a function of the particular and preferred cognitive mode used by the subject. Galin and Ellis recorded flash-evoked potentials and background EEG in six right-handed adults from left and right temporal and parietal areas—not while the subjects were at rest, but while they performed specific verbal (writing from memory) and spatial (modified Kohs block design) tasks. Previous studies had shown that the alpha ratio (right–left) was lower in spatial tasks (right hemisphere) than in verbal tasks (left hemisphere); the hemisphere engaged by the task develops proportionately less alpha power. In this study, the authors found that the overall power and peak-amplitude characteristics of the evoked potential asymmetry reflected lateralization of cognitive processes but not as consistently as the concomitant asymmetry in EEG alpha power. Such results suggest that baseline asymmetry in ERPs may depend upon variability in ongoing EEG activity, which may, in turn, depend upon subject state variables.

Considerable controversy exists regarding the lateral distribution of the various components of auditory ERPs (Donchin *et al.*, 1977). The maximal contralateral projection to the auditory cortex and the often-observed dominance of one ear over the other in dichotic listening tasks suggest that, at least under certain conditions, different auditory ERPs should be recorded over the two hemispheres. Most investigators concur that right and left ear stimulation generate different scalp distributions, but there is no agreement on the specifics of these distributions. The majority of reports maintain that the contralateral response generally predominates: Some find the difference to be a shorter latency response; others find it to be a larger amplitude response; a few find a difference in both of these measures of the contralateral response.

Some investigators reported a small but consistent tendency for larger responses to appear contralateral to the stimulated ear, but the effect was greater over the left hemisphere in response to right ear stimulation. Other researchers report that the right hemisphere response is consistently larger only for left ear stimulation.

Morrell and Salamy (1971) studied hemispheric response differences to natural speech stimuli (phonemic sounds and nonsense words) compared to pure tones. They were able to show that verbal ERPs were larger on the left side of the head. The greatest asymmetry occurred over the temporoparietal region. This effect reversed when tone stimuli were presented. They also observed a posteroanterior gradient with the size of the ERP becoming progressively smaller as the recording electrode was moved forward. This relationship was most orderly over the left hemisphere in response to speech sounds.

However, different results were found by Davis and Wada (1974), who computed the coherence functions between occipital and temporal scalp regions following simple click and flash stimuli. The ERP to clicks generated greater occipitotemporal coherence on the speech-dominant side, whereas the nondominant side showed a greater degree of similarity (in the 6–15 Hz band) to flashes of light. These results, according to the authors, indicate that hemispheric asymmetries exist for unstructured, nonverbal stimuli, suggesting that coherent processes of the brain, as seen in surface recordings, are related to the perception of visual and auditory forms. ERP asymmetry may not necessarily depend on cognitive-complex stimuli only. Davis and Wada (1974) assumed that high coherence on a side indicates increased data processing on that side. However, Callaway (1975) expressed an alternative view. Perhaps, as Davis and Wada (1974) suggested, clicks are processed on the dominant side more than are flashes—but that does not seem necessarily to follow, as evoked potentials may show more differentiation (with lower coherences) on the side where the principal processing is being carried out. Even if the explanation given by Davis and Wada is not entirely satisfactory, their observation is apparently reliable (Bali *et al.*, 1975).

Callaway (1975) stated that asymmetry of cortical function can be reflected in asymmetric ERPs and EEGs. He hypothesized that the ERP is more differentiated when recorded from the hemisphere presumed to be most involved with cognitive processing of the evoking stimulus. With simpler processes, the ERP over the engaged hemisphere may be larger; with more complex processes, the ERP may be more complex and smaller—perhaps due to a less homogeneous set of ERPs being included in the average.

Experimental data based upon more involved and sophisticated designs relating to ERP asymmetries associated with cognitive functioning and linguistic processing are available. Earlier experiments used tasks and discriminations pertaining to more basic perceptual units—clicks, tones, and flashes. More recent studies of ERPs are designed more to assess higher cognitive processing such as verbal versus nonverbal variables, relevant versus irrelevant stimuli, different language types, and noun–verb differences. Usually, either an auditory or a visual modality is involved; at times, both are included.

Matsumiya, Tagliasco, Lombroso, and Goodglass (1972) compared the auditory ERPs from two bipolar recordings, $W_1–P_3$ and $W_2–P_4$, in four conditions: (a) undiscriminated words; (b) undiscriminated sounds; (c) discriminated sounds (task was to tally the different types of sounds); and (d) meaningful speech.

The conditions were designed to contrast low-significance and high-significance levels of noises—Conditions (b) and (c)—as well as low-significance and high-significance levels of words—Conditions (a) and (d). The wave (W wave) with peak asymmetry occurred 100 msec after stimulus onset. When the subject had to use the meaning of each word maximally—that is, Condition (d)—the asymmetry was largest, seen as increased peak-to-peak amplitude of the W wave in the left hemisphere relative to the right ($p \leq .01$). The same was true, but to a lesser extent, for the sounds—that is, Condition (c) ($p \leq .05$). No group statistical significance was found between words in Condition (a) and sounds in Condition (b). The authors ascribed this hemispheric asymmetry, for both words and sounds, to the *significance* (or meaningfulness) of the auditory stimuli for the subject rather than to the linguistic features of the stimulus (verbal versus nonverbal materials).

Goto, Adachi, Utsunomiya, and Chen (1979) studied ERPs during processing of linguistic information to determine whether ERPs could be useful for testing the recognition of Japanese sentences and words. In the Japanese orthography, two types of symbols, *kana* (phonetic symbols for syllables) and *kanji* (logographic symbols representing lexic morphemes) are used in combination. For sentence recognition, subjects were required to respond by pressing different keys when sequentially presented sentences, visual or aural, were recognized as meaningful or meaningless on the basis of key information in the presentation. In healthy subjects, P300 amplitudes (from C_3 and C_4 referenced to ipsilateral mastoid processes) to the beginning of information and to the key information were larger than those to the other parts of the presented information. A delayed semantic matching paradigm using synonym, antonym, and semantically neutral word pairs was used in the word recognition test; subjects were required to press a different switch according to semantic match or mismatch between either two successive kanji or two successive kana words, presented visually only. In healthy right-handed subjects, P300 and P650 amplitudes (temporal and parietal leads referenced to linked ears) to the second kanji showed a right greater than left asymmetry. The P300 amplitudes to the second kana words showed the same, but P650 amplitudes to the second kana words showed a left greater than right asymmetry.

These findings, according to Goto *et al.* (1979), were compatible with the hypothesis that kana and kanji are processed differentially in the hemispheres.

Research by Brown and Lehmann (1977) focused upon ERPs evoked by noun and verb meanings of homophones (*a pretty rose–the boatman rows*). Comparing the ERP scalp field topographies, the maps were searched for the location of maximal positive values (peaks) and negative values (troughs). They found a general tendency for the peaks of the noun fields to be located to the right of the verb fields and vice versa for the troughs. A second group of three Swiss–Germans who listened to comparable Swiss–German sentences demonstrated similar tendencies but lower reliability. Brown and Lehmann (1977) believe that these results show that neural fields are differentially activated by nouns and verbs, which suggests that topographically different neural populations process nouns and verbs.

Because higher cortical functions are beginning to be studied in normal subjects, recent research has been aimed at disclosing subtle differences in the brain organization of cognitively impaired subjects. These studies employ the cortical ERP as a means of distinguishing normal from learning-disabled children. Emphasis has been directed toward the problem of developmental dyslexia in the experiments of Fenelon (1968, 1978), Conners (1971); Shields (1973); Preston, Guthrie, and Childs (1974); Preston, Guthrie, Kirsch, Gertman, and Childs (1977); Weber and Omenn (1977); Sobotka and May (1977); Lux (1977); Symann-Louett, Gascon, Matsumiya, and Lombroso (1977); Njiokiktjien, Visser, and de Rijke (1977); Shelburne (1978); Musso and Harter (1978); and Fried, Tanguay, Boder, Doubleday, and Greensite (1980).

OVERVIEW OF PREVIOUS ERP–DYSLEXIA STUDIES

Although some ERP asymmetries and differences between the normal and "dyslexic" groups were found in all of the reported studies, either by principal components analyses or some other parameter, significant difficulties arise in the interpretation of the results.

Clinical and Subject Considerations

Consistent definition is lacking, which creates confusion with regard to the makeup of, and qualifications for entry into, the experimental groups. An experimental group composed of subjects with developmental dyslexia—children or adults—should be reading at least 2 years below expected grade level by standardized reading examinations and (*a*) have no significant problems with vision (by standardized examination); (*b*) have no significant problems with hearing (by standardized examination); (*c*) have a general IQ within normal limits; (*d*) manifest no obvious neurological damage; (*e*) manifest no primary emotional disturbance; and (*f*) have had adequate conventional educational opportunity.

In addition, subgroups of dyslexics to be considered as subjects in experimental groups should be selected by standardized assessments that fulfill the psychological requirements of test reliability and validity.

Electrophysiological Considerations

Standardization is lacking in the methodology, experimental design, and measurement of the assessments of neurophysiological functioning in the perceptual–cognitive processes in developmental dyslexia (Evans, 1977). This lack of standardization is seen in the following areas: (*a*) the nature of the stimulus to be presented—tones, flashes, chords, tachistoscopically presented words, patterns, dictated words (e.g., sense modality, intensity, duration, interstimulus interval, number, order of presentations); (*b*) cortical areas and corresponding scalp electrode sites from which ERPs are to be recorded; (*c*) aspects of ERPs to be measured (e.g., overall amplitude, amplitudes at specific times after onset of stimulus, variability of the ERP, latencies to specified points of the ERP); (*d*) EEG frequencies that will be involved in the ERP measure; (*e*) rate of sampling of the EEG by the computer; and (*f*) methods of statistical analyses.

Yet, given the convergent and supportive data enumerated from clinical, neurological, diverse scientific, and electrophysiological sources, we conclude that differential and specialized cerebral (lateralized hemispheric) functions exist. We further conclude that a specific syndrome—*developmental dyslexia*—exists and that *dysphonetic, dyseidetic,* and *mixed subgroups* may be discerned.

Anecdotal evidence from educators has suggested that some children are auditory learners, some are visual learners, and some are both. Is there a preferred cognitive style that is particular to each person? In many ordinary activities, "normal people" simply alternate or integrate between cognitive modes as the need arises—if they are neurophysiologically able to alternate and/or integrate. An "interference hypothesis" might describe a situation in which an inefficient and inappropriate *but required* cognitive style is being used to process a certain task while at the same time preventing the more efficient mode from working (Galin & Ornstein, 1973)—for example, when a teacher specifically requires a phonics approach to the learning of reading–spelling–writing of a student whose preferred cognitive mode is that of visual–spatial–gestalt (sight–say) approach. The implication is that a person's preferred (innate) cognitive style (which may now be assessed by EEG and ERP measures) may facilitate learning of one type of subject matter, such as spatial–relational, while hindering the learning of another type, such as verbal–analytic.

Boder's dysphonetic subgroup may be an extreme version, neurophysiologically (and genetically) based, of those markedly dysfunctional in the auditory (verbal–left hemisphere) cognitive style. Boder's dyseidetic subgroup may be an extreme version, neurophysiologically (and genetically) based, of those markedly dysfunctional in the visual (spatial–right hemisphere) cognitive style. Boder's mixed subgroup may be a combination of both auditory and visual dysfunctioning.

CURRENT ERP–DYSLEXIA STUDY

An experiment was designed to assess possible electrophysiological correlates in developmental dyslexia and its subgroups (Rosenthal, 1980). By using the Camp and Dolcourt modification (1977) of the Boder diagnostic screening test for developmental dyslexia (Boder, 1971), 33 adult subjects with developmental dyslexia were discriminated from a population of adults with reading incompetencies; further subgrouping rendered 12 dysphonetics, 11 dyseidetics, and 10 mixed. Twelve control subjects were used. The dyslexic subjects satisfied criteria relative to vision, hearing, IQ, neurological status, emotional status, and adequacy of a conventional educational opportunity.

Using the montage, P_3–C_z and P_4–C_z, 12 event-related potential (ERP) types were recorded from each subject for each of the combinations of state (visual attending, auditory attending, passive), mode (visual, auditory), and condition (target, standard). The task was to discriminate and silently count targets (30 dim flashes or 30 soft clicks, depending on the attending state, visual or auditory) from the bimodally presented 150 flashes and 150 clicks. There were three runs (visual attending, auditory attending, and passive).

Inspection of the grand-averaged visual and auditory ERPs determined designated latency bands for the dependent variables, which were measures of amplitude power (by computer program) for the total latency band (0–450 msec) and for its component latency bands (50–150, 125–250, and 250–450 msec).

To assess possible ERP correlates in this design of signal recognition between and within modalities, the data were analyzed by a mixed model, five factor, repeated measures analysis of variance (ANOVA). Among the significant interactions (p = .05 level of significance) were Mode × Lead for total power, 50–150 msec power, and 125–250 msec power; Group × Lead for 250–450 msec power; State × Condition × Lead for total power and 250–450 msec power; Mode × Condition × Lead for total power, 50–150 msec power, and 125–250 msec power; Group (dysphonetic versus dyseidetic) × State × Lead for 250–450 msec power; Group (dysphonetic versus dyseidetic) × Mode × Condition for 250–450 msec power; Group (dysphonetic versus dyseidetic) × State × Mode × Condition for 50–150 msec power; Group (dysphonetic versus dyseidetic) × State × Condition × Lead for 250–450 msec power.

The dysphonetics and dyseidetics were compared for P_4 power (visual attending state–visual target) minus P_3 power (auditory attending state–auditory target) in the 250–450-msec latency band.

Low values of P_4 were associated with high values of P_3 in 4 of 11 dyseidetic subjects; low values of P_3 were associated with high values of P_4 in 4 of 12 dysphonetic subjects. Analysis by the χ^2 statistic indicated that the distributions of the dyseidetics and dysphonetics were significantly different, lending support to the construct validity of the Boder typology for subgroups of dyslexia.

COMPARISONS WITH PREVIOUS
ERP–DYSLEXIA STUDIES

A comparison of previous ERP–dyslexia studies is difficult because of the great variations in the experimental designs regarding criteria for group selection, task (independent) variables, the parameters of the EEG used as dependent variables, montage, measurement techniques, and data quantification and analysis. Nonetheless, differences have been elicited which manifest some convergence. Increased ERP latencies have been noted in dyslexics in the studies by Shields (1973), Weber and Omenn (1977), Sobotka and May (1977), Symann-Louett et al. (1977), Njiokiktjien et al. (1977), and Musso and Harter (1978). The explanation has usually pertained to diminished neural capacity resulting in the need for more time to process information. Generally, smaller ERP amplitudes have been found in dyslexics, usually in the left hemisphere in the studies by Fenelon (1978), Conners (1971), Preston et al. (1974), Preston et al. (1977), Symann-Louett et al. (1977); and Shelburne (1978). The explanation has usually pertained to diminished (selective) neural capacity, implying that, in some sense, amplitude *is* related to functional power. Several studies have found increased ERP amplitude in dyslexics (Shields, 1973; Sobotka & May, 1977; Njiokiktjien et al., 1977). The .explanation has usually pertained to diminished (selective) neural capacity resulting in a greater work effort or greater focusing of attention manifested by greater ERP amplitude. Several studies have suggested, either because of contradictory results (Conners, 1971; Symann-Louett et al., 1977) or because of clinically based hypotheses (Weber & Omenn, 1977; Musso & Harter, 1978; Fried et al., 1981), that subgroups of dyslexics with differential dysfunctions might exist.

The present study (Rosenthal, 1980), because of its experimental design, had predetermined latency bands as dependent variables (based on grand averaging).

A reason why most of the ERP studies of dyslexics have shown decreased amplitude at P_3 only may relate to the percentage distribution of subgroups. Boder (1971) and anecdotal evidence from educational sources have indicated that a population of dyslexics typically includes about 60% dysphonetics, 20% dyseidetics, and 20% mixed. Given this percentage distribution and the relatively few subjects in previous experimental groups, we suspect that most of these subjects were dysphonetics with dysfunctions in an area of the left hemisphere, the electrode site for which was usually P_3. In the present study, the four groups were almost equal in numbers of subjects (12 dysphonetics, 11 dyseidetics, 10 mixed, 12 controls).

In the present study (Rosenthal, 1980), differences were significant in the 250–450-msec latency band, which encompasses the P300, wherein categorization and decision-making processes are presumed to occur. Previous studies, except those of Symann-Louett et al. (1977), Njiokiktjien et al. (1977), and Fried et al. (1981), noted ERP amplitude differences, when they occurred, at earlier latencies. A possible reason for this is that, in the present study, three states, two modes, and two conditions were factors, and a task of silent counting was involved, via a bimodal presentation of visual and auditory stimuli. Given the complexities inherent in this design, any differences in group and lead could be expected to occur at or about the P300 since higher order processes beyond just gating and channel selection are probably involved.

SUMMATION

A major purpose of this study was to assess possible ERP-evoked hemispheric asymmetries in a dyslexic population. Cumulative and convergent data from clinical studies (Johnson & Myklebust, 1967; Bateman, 1968; Smith, 1970; Boder, 1971), neurological studies (Hecaen, 1967; Critchley, 1970a; Luria, 1973), diverse scientific studies (Sperry & Gazzaniga, 1967; Bakker, 1969; Ingvar & Schwartz, 1974) and electrophysiological studies supported the concept of at least two subgroups of dyslexia, one based upon language–symbolic dysfunction in the left hemisphere, the other based on spatial–gestalt dysfunction in the right hemisphere. Despite much previous clinical evidence for the existence of subgroups of dyslexics, this was not a testable hypothesis until an instrument to measure dyslexic subgroups was constructed which could satisfy the scientific requirements of reliability, validity, and replicability.

Noting the recent ERP studies in the more subtle aspects of information-processing and related dysfunctions, future research might focus on tachistoscopically presented and auditorily presented known and unknown words to carefully defined subgroups of dyslexics in an attempt to differentially engage the left and right hemispheres. If electrophysiological measures can allow for an early noninvasive and predictive diagnosis of dyslexia and can also infer hemispheric utilization in subgroups of dyslexia, especially in younger children, early detection can establish *early differential remedial education.* Moreover, early detection can establish understanding and diagnosis in a previously amorphous area, thereby aiding in the prevention of the psychopathologies which are frequent sequelae in subjects with developmental dyslexia.

REFERENCES

Bakker, D. (1969) Ear asymmetry with monaural stimulation: Task influences. *Cortex, 5,* 36–42.

Bali, L., Callaway, E., & Naghdi, S. (1975) *Hemispheric asymmetry in cortical coupling for visual and auditory nonverbal stimuli.* Unpublished manuscript. (Available from Enoch Callaway, M.D., Langley Porter Neuropsychiatric Institute, University of California Medical Center, San Francisco, CA 94143.)

Bateman, B. (1968) *Interpretation of the 1961 Illinois Test of Psycholinguistic Abilities.* Seattle: Special Child Publications.

Blanchard, P. (1946) Psychoanalytic contributions to the problems of reading disabilities.

In *The psychoanalytic study of the child* (Vol. 2). New York: International Universities Press.

Boder, E. (1971) Developmental dyslexia—Prevailing diagnostic concepts and a new diagnostic approach through patterns of reading and spelling. In H. Myklebust (Ed.), *Progress in learning disabilities* (Vol. 2). New York: Grune & Stratton.

Boder, E. (1973) Developmental dyslexia: A diagnostic approach based on three atypical reading–spelling patterns. *Developmental Medicine and Child Neurology, 15,* 663–687.

Boder, E., & Jarrico, S. *Boder Reading–Spelling Pattern Test: A diagnostic screening test for developmental dyslexia.* New York: Grune & Stratton, in press.

Brown, W., & Lehmann, D. (1977) Different lateralization for noun and verb evoked EEG scalp potential fields. *Electroencephalography and Clinical Neurophysiology, 43,* 469.

Buchsbaum, M., & Fedio, P. (1970) Hemispheric differences in evoked potentials to verbal and non-verbal stimuli in the left and right visual fields. *Physiological Behaviour, 5,* 207–210.

Callaway, E. (1973) Correlations between averaged evoked potentials and measures of intelligence. *Archives of General Psychiatry, 29,* 553–558.

Callaway, E. (1975) *Brain electrical potentials and individual psychological differences.* New York: Grune & Stratton.

Callaway, E., & Harris, P. (1974) Coupling between cortical potentials from different areas. *Science, 183,* 873–875.

Camp, B., & Dolcourt, J. (1977) Reading and spelling in good and poor readers. *Journal of Learning Disabilities, 10,* 300–307.

Clements, S. (1966) Minimal brain dysfunctions in children. *National Institute of Neurological Diseases and Blindness Monograph No. 3.* Washington, D.C.: U.S. Department of Health, Education, and Welfare; U.S. Government Printing Office.

Conners, C. (1971) Cortical visual evoked response in children with learning disorders. *Psychophysiology, 7,* 418–428.

Critchley, M. (1970a) *Aphasiology.* London: Edward Arnold.

Critchley, M. (1970b) *The dyslexic child.* Springfield, Ill.: Charles C Thomas.

Cronin, Sister E. (1968) *The holistic aspect in the approach to reading problems: Psychological, social and somatic principles as practiced at the Ellen K. Raskob Learning Institute.* Oakland, California: Holy Names College.

Davis, A., & Wada, J. (1974) Hemispheric asymmetry: Frequency analysis of visual and auditory evoked responses to nonverbal stimuli. *Electroencephalography and Clinical Neurophysiology, 37,* 1–9.

Davis, A., & Wada, J. (1977) Hemispheric asymmetries in human infants: Spectral analysis of flash and click evoked potentials. *Brain and Language, 4,* 23–31.

Donchin, E., Kutas, M., & McCarthy, G. (1977) Electrocortical indices of hemispheric utilization. In S. Harnard, R. W. Doty, J. Jaynes, L. Goldstein, and G. Krauthamer (Eds.), *Lateralization in the nervous system.* New York: Academic Press.

Dustman, R., Schenkenberg, T., & Beck, E. (1976) The development of the evoked response as a diagnostic and evaluative procedure. In R. Karrer (Ed.), *Developmental psychophysiology of mental retardation.* Springfield, Ill.: Charles C Thomas.

Eisenberg, L. (1966) Reading retardation: Psychiatric and sociologic aspects. *Pediatrics, 37,* 352–365.

Evans, J. R. (1977) Evoked potentials and learning disabilities. In L. Tarnopol & M. Tarnopol (Eds.), *Brain function and reading disabilities.* Baltimore: University Park Press.

Fenelon, B. (1968) Expectancy waves and other complex cerebral events in dyslexic and normal subjects. *Psychonomic Science, 13,* 253–254.

Fenelon, B. (1978) Hemispheric effects of stimulus sequence and side of stimulation on slow potentials in children with reading problems. In D. Otto (Ed.), *Multidisciplinary perspectives in event-related brain potential research.* Washington, D.C.: U.S. Environmental Protection Agency, Office of Research and Development.

Fried, I., Tanguay, P., Boder, E., Doubleday, C., & Greensite, M. (1981) *Developmental dyslexia: Electrophysiological corroboration of clinical subgroups. Brain and Language, 12,* 14–22.

Galin, D., & Ellis, R. (1975) Asymmetry in evoked potentials as an index of lateralized cognitive processes: Relation to EEG alpha asymmetry. *Psychophysiology, 13,* 45–50.

Galin, D., & Ornstein, R. (1973) Hemispheric specialization and the duality of consciousness. In H. Wildroe (Ed.), *Human behavior and brain function.* Springfield, Ill.: Charles C Thomas.

Gofman, H. (1969) The physician's role in early diagnosis and management of learning disabilities. In L. Tarnopol (Ed.), *Learning disabilities. Introduction to educational and medical management.* Springfield, Ill.: Charles C Thomas.

Goto, H., Adachi, T., Utsunomiya, T., & Chen, I. (1979) Late positive component (LPC) and CNV during processing of linguistic information. In D. Lehmann & E. Callaway (Eds.), *Human evoked potentials. Applications and problems.* New York: Plenum.

Halliday, R. (in preparation) Electrical images of the developing brain.

Hanley, J. (1975) Personal communication.

Hecaen, H. (1967) Brain mechanisms suggested by studies of parietal lobes. In C. Millikan & F. Darley (Eds.), *Brain mechanisms underlying speech and language.* New York: Grune & Stratton.

Hughes, J. (1971) Electroencephalography and learning disabilities. In H. Myklebust (Ed.), *Progress in Learning Disabilities* (Vol. 2). New York: Grune & Stratton.

Ingvar, D., & Schwartz, M. (1974) Blood flow patterns induced in the dominant hemisphere by speech and reading. *Brain, 97,* 273–288.

Johnson, D., & Myklebust, H. (1967) *Learning disabilities: Educational principles and practices.* New York: Grune & Stratton.

Kimura, D. (1969) Spatial localization in left and right visual fields. *Canadian Journal of Psychology, 23,* 445–458.

Klasen, E. (1972) *The syndrome of specific dyslexia.* Baltimore: University Park Press.

Kinsbourne, M., & Warrington, E. (1966) Developmental factors in reading and writing backwardness. In J. Money (Ed.), *The disabled reader: Education of the dyslexic child.* Baltimore: Johns Hopkins University Press.

Lenneberg, E. (1967) *Biological foundations of language.* New York: Wiley.

Luria, A. (1973) *The working brain.* New York: Basic Books.

Lux, J. (1977) Detection of learning disabilities using the visual evoked cortical potential. *Journal of Pediatric Ophthalmology, 14,* 248–253.

Matsumiya, Y., Tagliasco, V., Lombroso, C., & Goodglass, H. (1972) Auditory evoked response: Meaningfulness of stimuli and interhemispheric asymmetry. *Science, 175,* 790–792.

Mattis, S., French, J., & Rapin, I. (1975) Dyslexia in children and young adults: Three independent neuropsychological syndromes. *Developmental Medicine and Child Neurology, 17,* 150–163.

Morrell, L. K., & Salamy, J. G. (1971) Hemispheric asymmetry of electrocortical responses to speech stimuli. *Science, 174,* 164–166.

Musso, M., & Harter, M. (1978) Contingent negative variation, evoked potential, and psychophysical measures of selective attention in children with learning disabilities. In D. Otto (Ed.), *Multidisciplinary perspectives in event-related brain potential research.* Washington, D.C.: U.S. Environmental Protection Agency, Office of Research and Development.

Njiokiktjien, C., Visser, S., & de Rijke, W. (1977) EEG and visual evoked responses in children with learning disorders. *Neuropaediatrie, 8,* 134–147.

Orton, S. Word-blindness in school children. (1925) *Archives of Neurology and Psychiatry, 14,* 581–615.

Penfield, W., & Roberts, L. (1966) *Speech and brain mechanisms.* New York: Atheneum.

Preston, M., Guthrie, J., & Childs, B. (1974) Visual evoked responses (VERS) in normal and disabled readers. *Psychophysiology, 11,* 452–458.

Preston, M., Guthrie, J., Kirsch, I., Gertman, D., & Childs, B. (1977) VERS in normal and disabled readers. *Psychophysiology, 14,* 8–14.

Rabinovitch, R. (1968) Reading problems in children: Definitions and classifications. In A. Keeney & V. Keeney (Eds.), *Dyslexia.* St. Louis: C. V. Mosby.

Rawson, M. (1968) *Developmental language disability.* Baltimore: Johns Hopkins University Press.

Regan, D. (1979) Electrical responses evoked from the human brain. *Scientific American, 241,* 134–146.

Rosenthal, J. (1973) Self-esteem in dyslexic children. *Academic Therapy, 9,* 27–39.

Rosenthal, J. (1977) *The neuropsychopathology of written language.* Chicago: Nelson-Hall.

Rosenthal, J. (1980) *Neuropsychological studies of primary developmental dyslexia.* Unpublished doctoral dissertation, University of California, San Francisco.

Saunders, R. (1962) Dyslexia: Its phenomenology. In J. Money (Ed.), *Reading disability.* Baltimore: Johns Hopkins University Press, 35–44.

Shelburne, S. (1978) Visual evoked potentials to language stimuli in children with reading disabilities. In D. Otto (Ed.) *Multidisciplinary perspectives in event-related brain potential research.* Washington, D.C.: U.S. Environmental Protection Agency, Office of Research and Development.

Shields, D. (1973) Brain responses to stimuli in disorders of information processing. *Journal of Learning Disabilities, 6,* 501–505.

Sklar, B. (1971) *A computer classification of normal and dyslexic children using spectral estimates of their EEGs.* Unpublished doctoral dissertation, University of California, Los Angeles.

Smith, M. (1970) *Patterns of intellectual abilities in educationally handicapped children.* Unpublished doctoral dissertation, Claremont College.

Sobotka, K., & May, J. (1977) Visual evoked potentials and reaction time in normal and dyslexic children. *Psychophysiology, 14,* 18–24.

Sperry, R., & Gazzaniga, M. (1967) Language following surgical disconnection of the hemispheres. In J. Millikan & F. Darley (Eds.), *Brain mechanisms underlying speech and language.* New York: Grune & Stratton.

Starr, A., & Anchor, J. L. (1975) Auditory brainstem response in neurological disease. *Archives of Neurology, 32,* 761–768.

Stockard, J. J., & Rossiter, V. S. (1977) Clinical and pathologic correlates of brainstem auditory response abnormalities. *Neurology, 27,* 316–325.

Symann-Louett, N., Gascon, G., Matsumiya, Y., & Lombroso, C. (1977) Waveform difference in visual evoked responses between normal and reading disabled children. *Neurology, 27,* 156–159.

Tarnopol, L. (1971) Introduction to neurogenic learning disorders. In L. Tarnopol (Ed.), *Learning disorders in children.* Boston: Little, Brown. Pp. 1–22.

Wada, J., & Rasmussen, T. (1960) Intracarotid injections of sodium amytal for the lateralization of cerebral speech dominance. *Journal of Neurosurgery, 17,* 266–283.

Weber, B., & Omenn, G. (1977) Auditory and visual evoked responses in children with familial reading disabilities. *Journal of Learning Disabilities, 10,* 153–158.

Yingling, C. (1978) *Developmental dyslexia: Neurophysiological assessment.* Grant application to U.S. Department of Health, Education, and Welfare.

Chapter Four

Component Processes in Reading Disabilities: Neuropsychological Investigation of Distinct Reading Subskill Deficits

H. GERRY TAYLOR
JACK M. FLETCHER
PAUL SATZ

INTRODUCTION AND RATIONALE

The need to specify characteristics that would allow more homogeneous groupings of children with reading difficulties is well recognized (Benton, 1978). Although the concept of "dyslexia" has not proven helpful in this regard (Taylor, Satz, & Friel, 1979), evidence suggests that poor readers whose problems are not predicted by age and IQ are distinct from those whose problems are more predictable (Rutter & Yule, 1975). Nevertheless, isolation of those with "unexpected" or "specific" reading problems fails to yield a set of common characteristics (Rutter, 1978). The implication is that complex and varying factors contribute to this latter class of reading failure, commonly referred to as "reading disability," and that the isolation of these factors will require careful differentiation among individuals.

Realization that individual differences are relevant to the study of reading disabilities undoubtedly has been behind research on subtyping, critically reviewed by Satz and Morris (1981). These studies generally make use of one of two basic methodologies. The first, exemplified by Boder (1973) and by Sweeney and Rourke (1978), involves formal assessment of the nature of errors made in reading and spelling. The second consists of examining differential patterns of performance

121

on neuropsychological batteries (Mattis, French, & Rapin, 1975; Petrauskas & Rourke, 1979; Satz & Morris, 1981).

Application of these two methods for classifying disabled readers has been successful in several respects. It has permitted subtyping of large numbers of disabled readers, and several subtypes have met the challenge of cross-validation (e.g., Denckla, 1977; Doehring & Hoshko, 1977a; Fisk & Rourke, 1979; Mattis, 1978). Furthermore, there is notable similarity of results across investigations. In view of the different methods used in these studies, the frequent commonalities imply progress in the search for ways to reliably subgroup disabled readers.

Despite its promise, however, appraisal of the subtyping research reveals significant limitations. To begin with, some poor readers have overlapping deficits (Satz & Morris, 1981) and many defy subtyping efforts altogether. Boder (1973), for example, placed 23 of 107 disabled readers into a mixed dysphonetic–dyseidetic group, and she found 7 more who did not seem to fit the pattern of even the mixed group. Denckla (1973), using a classification scheme similar to that of Mattis et al. (1975), observed that about 70% of her disabled readers either had mixed deficits or did not fit into any a priori categories. Rourke and his associates (Petrauskas & Rourke, 1979; Fisk & Rourke, 1979) also report an appreciable number of children who could not be readily subtyped (20–50%). Evidently there are a fair number of children for whom performances on various neuropsychological tasks do not fit any clear pattern. As subtyping research progresses, these results are likely to improve. More recently, Satz and Morris (1981) were able to classify 95% of their learning-disabled children. But the problems of overlapping deficits and of some children not fitting any classification are likely to remain.

A second problem represents what may be the major shortcoming of contemporary subtyping research. Specifically, this research has tended to rely on either examination of reading errors or a battery of cognitive/neuropsychological tests as a basis for their classification schemes. With the exception of Sweeney and Rourke (1978), those studies which have attempted to break down the reading problem have generally failed to integrate these results with neuropsychological evaluation (e.g., Boder, 1973; Doehring & Hoshko, 1977a). And, despite evidence for the relevance of examining the profile of reading, spelling, and math skills in the search for subtypes of neuropsychological dysfunction (Rourke & Finlayson, 1978; Rourke & Strang, 1978), studies of neuropsychological performances have failed to evaluate the reading dysfunction in detail. Typically, only a single measure of reading such as word recognition has been employed for sample identification. Failure to integrate information on the nature of the reading problem with neuropsychological results has limited the effectiveness of the subtyping research in working toward a model of reading failure.

Because of these limitations, the present chapter argues for an additional, idiographic approach to the analysis of individual variations within the general class of reading disabilities. We feel this alternative will complement group-based, or nomothetic, subtyping efforts and in so doing extend the search for component processes underlying reading failure. In brief, we propose that reading subskills be analyzed more comprehensively and that those disabled readers with select problems be studied in depth. Administration of neuropsychological measures would permit exploration of possible cognitive deficits unique to each particular reading problem. This approach will no doubt involve only a small proportion of disabled readers, for experience suggests that most disabled readers have deficits in a number of reading subskills. In essence, this additional approach assumes that most reading problems arise from various cognitive and social–emotional factors which can occur simultaneously and interactively (Applebee, 1971) and that studies of individual cases highly selected according to the nature of their reading deficit may be particularly effective in isolating individual antecedents for reading failure.

Special advantages accruing to an idiographic or case study method are discussed by Shallice (1979). Shallice, using adult neuropsychology as his frame of reference, argues that patterns of association and dissociation among skills in brain-damaged individuals are telling with respect to the "functional organization of cognitive systems." By this he means that only certain cases in which specific lesions have produced select impairments of function may permit us to adduce differential syndromes. These syndromes can then be subjected to more formal study, which might involve attempts to demonstrate the specificity of the processing deficit or to further delineate its nature or clinical utility.[1] He cites a number of examples of the fruitfulness of this strategy from the field of adult neuropsychology. Presuming that constitutional factors are important determinants of learning disorders (Bortner, 1971; Denckla, 1973; Rourke, 1975), there is good reason to believe that this strategy may be equally applicable to the study of childhood reading disorders.

---

[1] The procedure of first adducing different symptom-complexes and then testing these to further clarify their nature or utility needs to be followed regardless of whether one takes the case study or group subtyping approach. The fundamental difference between the two strategies is in the first stage, which specifies how symptom-complexes might be best discovered.

Two considerations provide an empirical groundwork for the viability of this approach. The first is evidence that reading subskills are in fact dissociable at least in some poor readers. Research indicates that the normal process of learning to read consists of acquisition of several distinct subskills, including awareness of sight words, grapheme–phoneme correspondences, orthographic rules, and semantic and syntactic relationships among words (Carroll, 1970; Gibson & Levin, 1975; Guthrie, 1973; Smith, 1971). Although weaknesses in any of these may lead to poor performance on a single measure, a specific weakness may be reflected more prominently on some reading tasks than on others. It is well known that some children fail to comprehend what they read yet show normal ability to recognize and even understand individual words (Cromer, 1970; Isakson & Miller, 1976; Johnson & Myklebust, 1967; Wiener & Cromer, 1967). Others seem to make good use of context in reading passages orally despite limited ability to recognize single words in isolation (Johnson, 1980; Perfetti, 1980). When selecting disabled readers on the basis of a composite reading measure, one also finds considerable variation in phonics skills (Tallal, 1980). This breakdown is surely not complete, and various component functions may contribute to one type of skill. Nonetheless, there is ample evidence that reading is a multiple process ability and that poor readers may be particularly liable to differential patterns of breakdown (Guthrie, 1973; Guthrie & Siefert, 1977; Maliphant, Supramaniam, & Saraga, 1974).

A second consideration in favor of the proposed research strategy is the success that the logically similar approach to aphasic and alexic disorders has enjoyed in adult neuropsychology. Recent research on varieties of alexia exemplifies this approach and is also relevant to the study of reading disability. According to Benson (1976), there are at least three distinct forms of alexia. One of these, referred to as primary alexia, involves a deficit in visual–sensory function wherein the individual has no language deficiencies but cannot interpret sensory information provided via the visual channel. This subtype of alexia is associated with medial occipital damage. A second type, secondary alexia, is associated with language deficits and often with constructional problems. In this type, writing and reading are equally disrupted. In contrast to primary alexia, the patient has difficulty saying words spelled aloud as well as in reading words; and cortical damage is typically in the dominant parietotemporal lobe. A third type, tertiary alexia, involves difficulty in comprehension which extends beyond the difficulty that the patient has in single-word reading. Often accompanying this disorder is visual–motor dysfunction and difficulty on tasks that require temporal sequencing. The third subtype is linked with frontal pathology. Further breakdowns of alexia are detailed in Coltheart, Patterson, and Marshall (1980) and by Derouesne and Beauvois (1979) and Marshall and Newcombe (1973).

The potential productivity of a search for parallel dissociations among reading-disabled populations has been raised by Benton (1978). Damasio (1977) also alludes to this in concluding that "the clinical variation of alexias and the multiplicity of loci of brain dysfunction with which they associate provide a basis for the construction of neuropsychological models of reading . . . [p. 326]." Finally, Denckla (1973), in a discussion of "neurometrics," points out the several advantages of combining the more traditional search for syndromes characteristic of behavioral neurologists with the concern about developmental context emphasized by psychologists. She states that "although localization in the traditional sense is not a reasonable goal, utilization of analogies and critical differences between childhood and adult syndromes sharing similar complaints brings us closer to a clinical classification scheme [p. 449]." Of course, one must be careful in applying models developed for adults with brain damage to developing organisms without established neurological disorder (Fletcher, 1981; Yule, 1978). What recent studies of alexia make clear is that fine-grained analysis of the reading problem itself may be useful in exploring the functional organization of reading-related processes. The next section presents a preliminary attempt to assess the utility of this approach as applied to a learning-disabled population.

PRELIMINARY APPLICATION

Method

INTELLECTUAL AND ACADEMIC SCREENING

As a first step in the application of the proposed approach, a screening procedure was established for children referred to two child neuropsychological services (Marshfield Clinic, Marshfield, Wisconsin; Texas Research Institute of Mental Sciences, Houston, Texas). According to this procedure, a battery of academic tests was administered to children between 8 and 13 years of age who were referred for learning problems and whose prorated verbal, performance, or full-scale IQs on the WISC–R (Wechsler, 1974) fell at 85 or above. Academic tests included the Reading Comprehension, Reading Recognition, and Spelling subtests of the Peabody Individual Achievement Test (PIAT) (Dunn & Markwardt, 1970); the Spelling and Arithmetic subtests of the Wide Range Achievement Test (WRAT) (Jastak & Jastak, 1965); and the Word Attack subtest of the Woodcock Reading Test (Woodcock, 1973). The three reading measures were chosen in order to tap what might be considered major elements of reading acquisition: single-word decoding, presumably dependent to some extent on sight word recognition ability; comprehension of sentences read silently; and phonemic decoding skill. The Gilmore Oral Reading Test (Gilmore & Gilmore, 1968) was also given to a majority of children to obtain an index of the child's ability to orally decode words in context, but this test was not considered a formal part of the academic battery. Academic subskills other than reading were assessed to allow comparison of reading subskills with other academic performances. Raw scores on each of the academic tests were converted to standard scores to permit meaningful comparisons among the various measures of academic skill.[2]

NEUROPSYCHOLOGICAL BATTERY

Children who obtained a standard score of 85 or less on one or more of the academic tests (Gilmore excluded) were then administered a battery of neuropsychological tests assessing linguistic skills, memory and learning, spatial and constructional ability, and fine motor proficiency. The neuropsychological tests were selected to measure a broad range of abilities. In most cases, measures were chosen for which normative standards were available; in a few instances, existing tasks were modified or new ones created to enhance the comprehensiveness of the battery. In the latter instances, age-appropriate norms are not yet available.

The language tasks were chosen to assess skills in naming, comprehension, phonemic analysis, and semantic production. The tests used for this purpose included Rapid "Automatized" Naming (Denckla & Rudel, 1974); the Peabody Picture Vocabulary Test (PPVT) (Dunn, 1965); the Spellacy–Spreen (1969) short form of the Token Test to which a set of more grammatically difficult items given by Whitaker and Noll (1972) was added; the Double-Object Comprehension Test (Fletcher, Satz, & Scholes, 1981); the Phoneme Discrimination Test (Varney & Benton, 1979); the Auditory Analysis Test (Rosner & Simon, 1971); Word Fluency (Gaddes & Crockett, 1975); and the McCarthy Scales' Verbal Fluency Test (McCarthy, 1970).

---

[2] Grade equivalencies, although more typically employed than standard scores, are independent of raw score variance (Durost & Prescott, 1962) and do not measure deviancy relative to that performance regarded as normal for age. Only standard scores permit meaningful comparison of performances across various academic measures.

In the spatial–constructional area, tasks were chosen to assess copying, visual matching, tactile–visual matching, and tactile recognition. Tasks employed were the Beery Developmental Test of Visuo–Motor Integration (VMI) (Beery, 1967); an extended version of Recognition–Discrimination Test (Satz & Friel, 1973); the Stereognosis Test (Spreen & Gaddes, 1969); and our own Finger Localization Test. In the latter test, children were touched on one finger of either one or (simultaneously) both hands and asked to identify the finger(s) touched via a finger movement (i.e., no verbal label was required).

Verbal memory and learning were assessed according to the selective reminding method (Buschke, 1974). The desirable feature of this procedure is that it allows a measure of initial learning as well as retrieval of information previously learned. A visual–spatial learning task was designed to allow parallel assessment, in the nonlanguage area, of the same aspects of memory and learning. This nonverbal memory–learning task was constructed to satisfy the need for a visual memory task that would place minimal demands on verbal or fine motor skills (Denckla, 1973).

Assessment of fine motor skills included tasks of repetitive movement (Finger Tapping) and manipulative dexterity (Grooved Pegboard Test—Knights & Moule, 1968).

SAMPLE

Over approximately a 6-month period, 62 cases (mean age = 129 months) were accumulated who met the criteria detailed earlier. Of these, 36 were 8–10-year-olds and 26 were 11–13-year-olds. The sample was heavily biased toward males (28 of the 36 8–10-year-olds and 21 of the 26 11–13-year-olds). Math and spelling deficits without reading problems were present in 17 of the 62 cases, leaving 45 with reading disabilities. Most of these latter children had math or spelling deficits in addition to reading problems. Among the 45 with reading disorders, most failed to show a selective reading problem. In only 18 cases was the standard score for one reading measure five or more points below those for both of the other measures. In 5 of these cases the low point was in Reading Recognition; in 7 the low point was in Reading Comprehension; and in 6 the low point was in Word Attack.

Results

CHARACTERISTICS OF DISABLED LEARNERS AS A GROUP

Mean verbal, performance, and full-scale IQs for the group of 62 children were 92.4, 98.6, and 94.7, respectively. Mean standard scores on the academic measures were fairly even, all falling at about 85, or one standard deviation below normative expectations.

There was a high degree of correlation among reading subskills, even with IQ and age partialed out (see Table 4.1). Similar findings are reported by others (Doehring & Hoshko, 1977b; Golinkoff, 1975–1976; Guthrie, 1973; Kieffer & Golden, 1978). The present results also document observations that reading relates closely to spelling (Rutter, 1978) but not to written math (Goodstein & Kahn, 1974; Rourke & Strang, 1978). The substantial correlations among reading subskills themselves, of course, do not rule out distinct differences among reading subskills in some poor readers.

Further correlational analyses revealed significant relationships between reading subskills and many of the neuropsychological measures, even with full-scale IQ and age partialed out. Linguistic abilities as a whole showed particularly close association with reading and spelling although not with math. Significant partial correlations with at least one academic test were found for every linguistic measure except the Token Test. Correlations for some linguistic measures were particularly robust. As an example, the Auditory Analysis Test, which involves breaking down aurally presented words into their component sounds, correlated significantly with every reading and spelling subskill. Coefficients ranged from .55 to .75 ($p < .01$). Partial correlations of academic subskills with other neuropsychological measures evidenced weaker associations than those generally found for the language measures— an observation that has also been made by Rutter and Yule (1976). Among the memory and learning measures, only verbal long-term storage related to some reading and spelling subskill performances. In these cases, partial correlation coefficients fell between .23 and .30 ($p < .01$). Spatial–constructional measures of design copying (VMI) and visual matching (Recognition–Discrimination) correlated significantly with written math but not with reading or spelling. Finally, except for nondominant hand performance on the Grooved Pegboard Test, the measures of fine motor skill also failed to show correspondence with reading performances among the total sample of learning-disabled children.

Although any of a broad range of neuropsychological tests may be helpful in deciphering the cognitive correlates of specific cases of reading disability, only a handful of these may be of general usefulness. Still, the major implications of these data stand: Several cognitive–neuropsychological measures do in fact correlate with reading and other academic skills, and these correlations cannot be attributed to age or IQ differences alone. Previous studies have revealed similar relationships between academic abilities and nonacademic cognitive

Table 4.1
Partial Correlations between Academic Subskill Raw Scores, Controlling for Age and Full-Scale IQ

| | Reading | | | | | | | | Spelling | | | | Math | |
| | RR | | RC | | WA | | OR | | WS | | SR | | WM | |
Measure	N	r	N	r	N	r	N	r	N	r	N	r	N	r
RR	62	—	62	.77**	62	.77**	52	.86**	62	.53**	62	.74**	62	.14
RC	62	.77**	62	—	62	.68**	52	.69**	62	.39**	62	.63**	62	.11
WA	62	.77**	62	.68**	62	—	52	.77**	62	.51**	62	.69**	62	.18
OR	52	.86**	52	.69**	52	.77**	52	—	52	.37**	52	.72**	52	.05
WS	62	.53**	62	.39**	62	.51**	52	.37**	62	—	62	.39**	62	.78**
RS	62	.74**	62	.63**	62	.69**	52	.72**	62	.39**	62	—	62	.01
WM	62	.14	62	.11	62	.18	52	.05	62	.78**	62	.01	62	—

* $p < .05$.   RR: Reading Recognition (PIAT)
** $p < .01$.   RC: Reading Comprehension (PIAT)
WA: Word Attack (Woodcock)
OR: Oral Reading (Gilmore)
WS: Written Spelling (WRAT Spelling)
RS: Recognition Spelling (PIAT Spelling)
WM: Written Math (WRAT Arithmetic)

skills (Klinge, Rennick, Lennox, & Hart, 1977; Richardson, DiBenedetto, Christ, & Press, 1980; Rosner & Simon, 1971; Samuels & Anderson, 1973; Taylor et al., 1979). In several of these, academic achievement has been found more closely associated with certain cognitive and neuro-developmental skills than with IQ.

CASE STUDIES

As noted earlier, inspection of the total group of disabled readers revealed a few with relatively specific subskill deficits (defined by a standard score on one of the three main reading tests that was five or more points below scores on the other two tests). Results of intelligence and academic testing for illustrative cases, depicted in Figures 4.1–4.3, are discussed in what follows:

Deficit in Word Recognition. Figure 4.1 presents the standard scores for a 12-year-old boy who had great difficulty in recognizing single words on the PIAT Reading Recognition Test. Word attack skills were well within the broad normal range despite several problems in calling out single words. Spelling and written math were both impaired. Verbal and performance IQs were similar.

Deficit in Reading Comprehension. Figure 4.2 shows the intellectual and academic profile of an 11-year-old boy who had a specific problem in the PIAT Reading Comprehension Test. Relative to comprehension, word attack and oral reading skills were good. In contrast to the previous case, written spelling was within the normal range and verbal IQ was much lower than performance IQ.

Deficit in Word Attack. The performances of an 8-year-old boy with relatively specific deficit on the Woodcock Word Attack Test are presented in Figure 4.3. As opposed to the child with reading comprehension deficit, this child had greater difficulty in written spelling than in spelling recognition. One might speculate that spelling to dictation places heavy demands on the child's ability to associate graphemes with phonemes, an ability that this child apparently lacked. Also of note is the discrepancy between scores on the Woodcock Word Attack and Gilmore Oral Reading tests. Generally one would think that the ability to read a passage aloud would be highly dependent on aptitude in phonics. The lack of close association between these two skills in this case corroborates the dissociations of reading subskills often observed in poor readers (Guthrie, 1973; Guthrie & Seifert, 1978). To

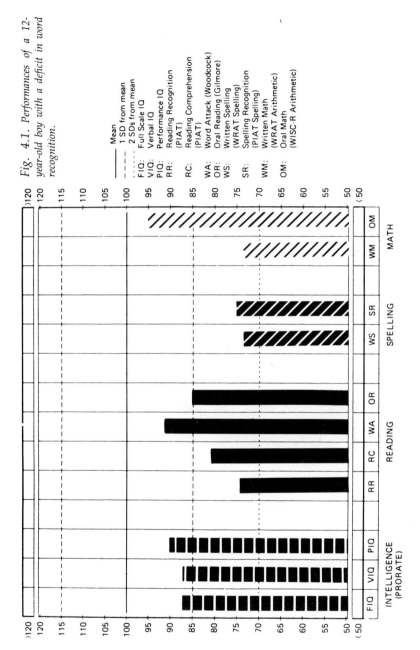

Fig. 4.1. Performances of a 12-year-old boy with a deficit in word recognition.

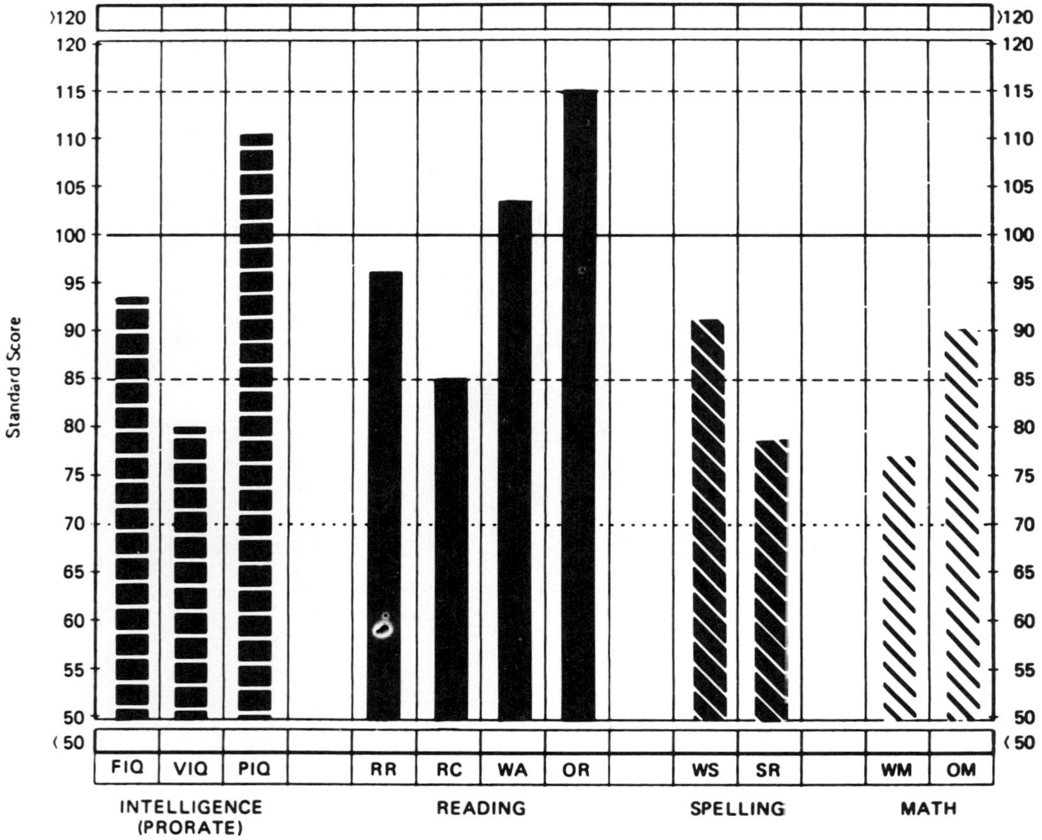

Fig. 4.2. Performances of an 11-year-old boy with a deficit in reading comprehension.

132

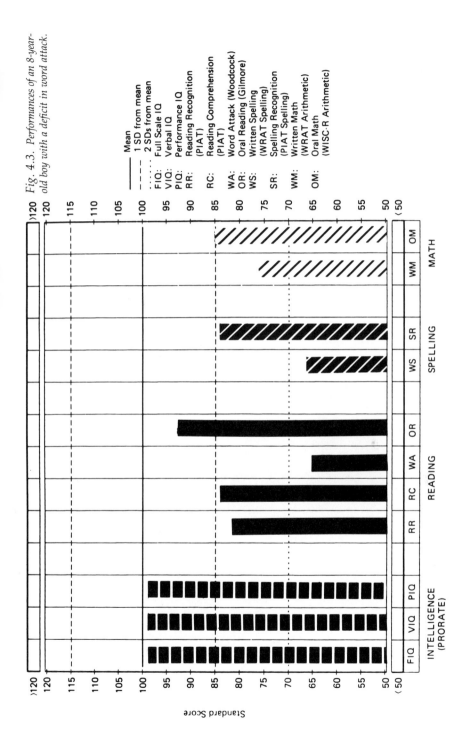

Fig. 4.3. Performances of an 8-year-old boy with a deficit in word attack.

Legend:
—— Mean
– – – 1 SD from mean
· · · · 2 SDs from mean
FIQ: Full Scale IQ
VIQ: Verbal IQ
PIQ: Performance IQ
RR: Reading Recognition (PIAT)
RC: Reading Comprehension (PIAT)
WA: Word Attack (Woodcock)
OR: Oral Reading (Gilmore)
WS: Written Spelling (WRAT Spelling)
SR: Spelling Recognition (PIAT Spelling)
WM: Written Math (WRAT Arithmetic)
OM: Oral Math (WISC-R Arithmetic)

Standard Score

INTELLIGENCE (PRORATE): FIQ, VIQ, PIQ
READING: RR, RC, WA, OR
SPELLING: WS, SR
MATH: WM, OM

133

explain the dissociation, one must conjecture that this boy had a sufficient recognition vocabulary or could make use of linguistic context to the extent of being able to read a passage aloud with remarkable fluency.

DIFFERENTIAL NEUROPSYCHOLOGICAL PROFILES

Deficit in Word Recognition. Although the limited number of cases within each of the relative subskill deficit groups does not permit statistical comparison of their patterns of neuropsychological performance, casual inspection suggests some distinctive features. Table 4.2 shows the pattern of deficits manifested by three children with specific deficit on the PIAT Word Recognition Test. Despite the variability among

Table 4.2
Neuropsychological Deficits for Cases with Relative Subskill Deficit in Word Recognition

			Cases		
Ability area	Neuropsychological skill	Test[a]	W.C. Age 9	J.H. Age 12	L.U. Age 12
Language	Naming	Rapid naming-time	−		
	Comprehension	PPVT			
	Phonemic analysis	Auditory analysis			− −
		Word fluency			
	Learning and memory	Verbal long-term storage			
		Verbal Consistency Retrieval			
Spatial–Constructual	Visual–Visual matching	Recognition-Discrimination	−	− −	− −
	Tactile–Visual Matching	Stereogn.-dominant hand		− −	− −
		Stereogn.-nondominant hand		− −	− −
Fine Motor	Repetitive	Finger Tapping–Dominant hand	−		− −
		Finger Tapping–Nondominant hand	−		
	Manipulative	Grooved Pegboard–Dominant hand	−	− −	
		Grooved Pegboard–Nondominant hand		− −	

− 1 SD below mean for normative group.
− − 2 SDs below mean for normative group.
[a] Only those with age appropriate norms included.

these children in terms of the kinds of deficits exhibited, each was deficient on some visually related task and each showed fairly intact language functions. One child displayed a tendency in oral reading to guess at words based on linguistic context and seemed to ignore visual aspects of words. This child, for example, read the word *girl* as "cat" (the word *cat* having appeared in the previous line). Results of the visual–spatial learning and memory task, along with those of several other tasks, are not presented in Table 4.2 because of unavailability of age-related norms at this time. Relative to the total group of disabled readers, however, children having specific word recognition deficits performed poorly on this visual–spatial task. The aspect of their performance most impaired was that involving consistent retrieval of to-be-remembered target locations from one trial to the next.

Examination of individual cases within the group with a word recognition deficiency raises the possibility of important developmental differences. The youngest of the three children (W.C.), for example, was slow on Rapid "Automatized" Naming, whereas an older child (J.H.) was not. Perhaps even in dysnomic children the naming of familiar objects or pictures becomes more automatic with age. If so, naming deficiencies may be evident on simple naming tasks only at earlier ages. Later on in development, other tasks, perhaps the ones that stress the ability to name relatively unfamiliar stimuli, may be necessary to reveal naming problems.

Deficit in Reading Comprehension. Table 4.3 presents two case illustrations of a pattern of neuropsychological dysfunction seen in children with specific deficit on the PIAT Reading Comprehension Test. In contrast to the group with defective word recognition, there were relatively few striking neuropsychological impairments. The only problem shared by these two poor comprehenders was their inability to consistently retrieve words from a memorized list on the verbal selective reminding procedure. It should be noted that Payne, Davenport, Domangue, and Soroka (1980) also found auditory memory problems common in children deficient in reading comprehension.

Not apparent in Table 4.3 but suggested by examination of the individual cases within this group was an additional tendency toward low verbal IQs. Of the seven children in this subgroup, five had verbal IQs of less than 87 and three had Peabody IQs of less than 87. Despite these deficits, several of the children were relatively free of difficulties in what might be termed "lower order" language skills such as naming and phonetic analysis. Rather than involving the more automatic features of language learning, the impairment appeared to be in the child's

Table 4.3
Neuropsychological Deficits for Cases with Relative Subskill Deficit in Reading Comprehension

Ability area	Neuropsycho- logical skill	Test[a]	Cases C.A. Age 10	M.N. Age 11
Language	Naming	Rapid naming		
	Comprehen- sion	PPVT		
	Phonemic analysis	Auditory analysis word fluency		
	Learning and memory	Verbal long-term storage	−	−
		Verbal consistent retrieval		
Spatial– constructional	Visual–Visual Matching	Recognition–discrimination		−
	Tactile–Visual Matching	Stereognosis—dominant hand		
		Stereognosis—nondominant hand		
Fine motor	Repetitive	Finger tapping—dominant hand		
		Finger tapping nondominant hand		
	Manipulative	Grooved pegboard—dominant hand		
		Grooved pegboard—nondominant hand	−	

− 1 *SD* below mean for normative group.
[a] Only those with age appropriate norms included.

overall ability to accumulate linguistic information and perhaps also to make use of linguistic information in problem solving (as suggested by difficulties in consistent retrieval of verbal information).

In light of the associations that have been observed between reading comprehension and oral comprehension (Berger, 1978), one might have expected members of this group to be defective in the latter area. Casual inspection of the data did not confirm this suspicion. Cases with select reading comprehension problems did not display obvious difficulties on the Token Test. Moreover, despite evidence for a relationship between poor reading comprehension and appreciation of syntax (Isakson & Miller, 1976), the Double-Object Comprehension Test also failed to surface as a useful one in isolating poor comprehenders as a group.

Deficit in Word Attack. Neuropsychological deficiencies associated with three instances in which word attack appeared relatively depressed are presented in Table 4.4. In contrast to the type of language deficits suggested by relatively poor reading comprehension, these cases seem to be characterized by selective difficulty in the lower order features

Table 4.4

Neuropsychological Deficits for Cases with Relative Subskill Deficit in Word Attack

Ability area	Neuropsychological skill	Test[a]	R.P. Age 8	C.B. Age 8	G.L. Age 9
Language	Naming	Rapid naming-time		− −	
	Comprehension	PPVT			
	Phonemic Analysis	Auditory analysis	− −	− −	−
		Word fluency	− −	−	−
	Learning and memory	Verbal long-term storage	−	−	
		Verbal consistent retrieval	− −	−	
Spatial–constructional	Visual–Visual Matching	Recognition–Discrimination	− −		
	Tactile–Visual Matching	Stereognosis–Dominant hand	− −		
		Stereognosis–nondominant hand			
Fine motor	Repetitive	Finger Tapping–Dominant hand	−		− −
		Finger Tapping–Nondominant hand	−		− −
	Manipulative	Grooved Pegboard–Dominant hand			
		Grooved Pegboard–Nondominant hand			

− 1 *SD* below mean for normative group.
− − 2 *SD*s below mean for normative group.
[a] Only those with age appropriate norms included.

of language referred to earlier. Phonemic analysis was affected in each of the cases. The possibility that defective phonics skills may reflect lower order auditory–perceptual dysfunction, in contrast to higher order semantic or syntactic difficulties, is supported by Tallal (1980). She reported a relatively high correlation between word attack skills and the ability to make auditory–temporal judgments. Reading errors committed by one child with a selective word attack deficit fostered the impression of a basic auditory deficit in the context of otherwise normal linguistic functioning. In reading a passage from the Gilmore Oral Reading Test, this child read the word *Mary* as "mother" and the word *gray* as "gold." The WRAT spelling performance of this same child revealed an inability to apply the rules of phonics in attempting to spell words to dictation.

Clinical impression suggests that children with selectively impaired word attack skills tend to be deficient on a variety of neuropsychological tasks (see Table 4.4). Generalization based on such observations is of course premature, but this trend does raise the possibility that the range of developmental problems accompanying reading failure may differ to some extent depending on the specific reading subskill most affected.

The importance of heeding developmental differences was most apparent in this group for individuals who, at least by intermediate elementary school age, seemed to have been able to overcome some of their difficulties. There were several individuals with selective impairment on the Woodcock Word Attack Test who fit the descriptions given here in many ways yet who did not exhibit all primary identifying features. The most obvious example was a child who performed normally on the test measuring phonemic segmentation skills (Auditory Analysis Test). Clinical impressions suggested that this child may have had difficulties with such a test previously, for his history was replete with many years of speech and language therapy. But in this case and others we have observed like it, the child appears to have developed a method for compensating for any residual weaknesses. Frequently, informal observation of oral reading errors and of difficulties in repeating multisyllabic words exposes a pattern reminiscent of children described by Denckla (1977) and Johnson (1980). Denckla has labeled this pattern as a "dysphonemic sequencing" disorder. A residual deficit is obviously present but the child's compensatory abilities apparently render some formal test procedures insensitive to it.

Discussion

COMPARISONS TO CURRENT SUBTYPING RESEARCH

Review of the subtypes proposed by contemporary studies of reading disability and of alexia reveals obvious correspondences with some of the features associated with the specific cases described here. The children in the present sample with specific word recognition deficits, for example, are similar in some ways to the Petrauskas–Rourke (1979) Type 2 subgroup. Both sets of children appear to have deficits in visual–spatial memory. These children are also similar to Boder's (1973) dyseidetic group and the subgroup identified by Mattis et al. (1975) as having visual–perceptual disorders. Moreover, there is some basis for comparison of this group to Benson's (1976) primary acquired alexia, the latter disorder reflective of a specific dysfunction in visual processing.

Those with relatively poor reading comprehension scores are roughly comparable to the subgroup Petrauskas and Rourke (1979) found impaired in verbal coding and concept formation (Type 3). The language disorder groups of Mattis *et al.* (1975) and Kinsbourne and Warrington (1963) also share similar features. Of those subtypes specified by Satz and Morris (1981), Subtype 1 (global language impairment) would seem the most analogous. The alexic disturbance most closely paralleling that seen in the selectively poor comprehender is that which Benson (1976) labels tertiary dyslexia. In these cases, the more mechanical aspects of reading are intact but there is inability to integrate this information in a meaningful way.

The disabled readers with relatively isolated word attack problems are comparable to the dysphonetic readers described by Boder (1973). An analogy may also be drawn between this group and Type 1 of Petrauskas and Rourke (1979)—a group characterized by severely impaired verbal fluency and mildly impaired word blending. A similar subtype emerged in the Fisk and Rourke (1979) study, identified as Subtype B and characterized by deficiencies in phonemic hearing, verbal coding and immediate auditory–verbal memory. The group with especially poor word attack skills is also comparable to Johnson and Myklebust's (1967) auditory dyslexia and to the speech and graphomotor dyscoordination syndrome of Mattis *et al.* (1975). The common occurrence of speech articulation problems and language delays in the histories of children we have observed with relative impairment in phonics lends special support to the latter comparison. With reference to patterns of alexia, this group resembles Benson's (1976) secondary alexia and the "deep" or phonemic alexia mentioned in several studies (Coltheart *et al.*, 1980).

Similarities between the present groups of highly selected children and the more established subgroups of existing studies of acquired and developmental reading disorders are heartening. They suggest that closer examination of children with specific problems may bring the deficits that have emerged from previous subtyping efforts into clearer focus. Moreover, the correspondences lend support to the value of drawing analogies between childhood reading disability and various forms of alexia.

Still, it is important to recognize that, unlike adult alexics, the subjects of study do not have established neurological disease. They are developing organisms in whom the nature of the constitutional anomaly as well as the reading problem may change with age. The developing child's tendency to apply compensatory strategies may be another source of dissimilarity. In contrast to contemporary subtyping approaches to childhood reading disabilities, sample selection depends on how the reading deficit itself is analyzed. With progress in analysis of the reading problem, sample selection will no doubt change, and with these changes, different neuropsychological associates may well emerge. As an example, difficulties in phonics may arise for various reasons. Clinical experience suggests that phonics deficits are in some cases due to difficulties in sequencing phonemes rather than in the mere awareness of single grapheme–phoneme correspondences. Gradual differentiation of reading-related dysfunctions would thus be expected with progress in breaking down the reading deficit. As this occurs, comparisons to nomothetic classification, or group subtyping, studies are likely to become less and less direct, unless of course these latter studies also begin to apply much more refined criteria for sample selection.

LIMITATIONS

In light of the small number of selectively disabled readers emerging from this study and the descriptive nature of comparisons made, no definite conclusions can be drawn. The purpose of examining these few subjects was to illustrate the proposed approach for analyzing component processes in disabled readers. Admittedly, not all children within a given group fit a common description. The children represented in Tables 4.2–4.4 were those who showed more extreme variations among reading subskills and who appeared on inspection to share similar neuropsychological features. Further collection of cases is required to substantiate or reject the present descriptors for each group and to establish other features.

As in any study of clinical samples, referral biases represent a potential problem. Many of the present children were seen in a service to which children are referred for learning problems not easily recognized or treated by school staff. It is possible that a greater proportion of nonreferred learning disabled children might show distinct deficits than was the case in the present sample. Another procedural limitation was that many of the present children exhibited attentional as well as learning problems. Disabled readers free of attentional problems may be difficult to come by in any setting. But again, it might be possible to form purer subskill deficit groups from a nonreferred school sample.

It is also important to note the length of the battery administered. The fatigue resulting from demands of the testing procedure itself (3 hours) may have depressed some test scores. A fair test of the present approach would require more concerted effort to obtain reliable measures.

The choice of the tasks used to breakdown reading deficits may be especially critical. A basic problem with available academic measures is that they do not allow clear differentiation of component reading skills (Maliphant et al., 1974). Word recognition tests, for example, may be as much a measure of phonics as of sight word recognition. Words from the PIAT Reading Recognition Test are in fact biased toward those which can be phonetically analyzed (Dunn & Markwardt, 1970). This of course is at odds with the present purpose of this test (namely, isolation of children having relatively good or poor sight word recognition memory per se). Tests providing clues as to the means by which single words are actually "processed" by the reader would also be of considerable value. Massaro (1975) hypothesizes three processes: direct semantic access, visual features, and phonemic recoding. The construction of tests designed to measure each of these processes, and others that might similarly break down comprehension (Doehring & Hoshko, 1977b; Layton, 1979) and decoding (Marshall & Newcombe, 1973), may well carry this method much farther than would be possible with currently available academic measures. Careful examination of errors in reading may be of additional benefit. Marshall and Newcombe (1973) and several others (see Coltheart *et al.*, 1980) have shown how identification of visual, phonetic, and semantic errors in reading can be used to differentiate varieties of alexia. Bakker (1981), Boder (1973), and Sweeney and Rourke (1978) have already used error analyses effectively in exploring variations among disabled readers.

More careful attention may also have to be paid to the degree of discrepancy between academic subtest scores that would be regarded as significant. In the present study a reading subskill standard score that was five or more points below the other two subskill scores was used to identify the three distinct disability groups. A more rigorous method would have been to use reliabilities and correlation coefficients to statistically determine reliable subskill discrepancies (Payne & Jones, 1957; Shallice, 1979).

Finally, as analyses of reading subskill deficits proceed, there will undoubtedly be impetus to develop new neuropsychological tasks. Such tasks may be aimed at a better understanding of the cognitive bases for isolated reading problems. Critical examination of those skills required for adequate performance on existing neuropsychological tasks may also be necessary. Innovations developed in the study of alexia and of other neuropsychological disorders bear strong consideration as candidates for use with reading-disabled children.

CONCLUSIONS

The approach presented in this chapter assumes that processing deficits responsible for reading failure may be present in isolated form in only a small proportion of reading-disabled children, and that the study of these unique cases may contribute in a vital way to the construction of a multicomponent model of reading failure. The present approach further assumes that such processing deficits may be best explored by breaking down the reading deficit and by searching for relationships between distinctive forms of breakdown and neuropsychological variables.

The theoretical merits of this approach are twofold. One virtue is the implicit emphasis on a detailed description of the target behavioral dysfunction—in this case, the reading problem itself (cf. Yule, 1978; Doehring, 1978). By virtue of this emphasis, the proposed approach acknowledges the diversity and complexity of component reading skills (Maliphant *et al.*, 1974; Rutter, 1978) and the need to consider developmental variations in the manner by which reading takes place (Gibson & Levin, 1975; Guthrie & Seifert, 1977; Fletcher & Satz, 1980). As Benton (1978) aptly stated, "it is within this framework of a more adequate description of the disability itself, both in terms of the characteristics of reading performance and of syndromes defined by correlative cognitive performances, that the question of its genetic, neurological, cognitive, and social determinants can be most fruitfully attacked [p. 476]."

The other theoretical merit is the potential of this strategy to facilitate identification of critical antecedents of reading failure. Disabled readers commonly exhibit not one but a variety of deficits. A major source of frustration in working with these children is the problem of determining how processing deficits themselves might contribute to the learning problem. Without this knowledge, it is difficult to judge the impact of social–emotional or attentional factors on learning, to identify compensatory strategies, or to prescribe the remedial approach most likely to enhance academic achievement. The working assumption of the strategy advocated here is that knowledge of the neuropsychological bases of reading disability will permit separation of factors representing necessary antecedents from factors that may play more interactive roles (e.g., social–emotional). The manner in which this separation is brought about might consist of accumulating cases having similar reading subskill deficits. One could then look for consistent patterns of neuropsychological performance within groups of related cases, compare different groups in search of contrasting features, or even apply existing subtyping approaches (e.g., Q-type or cluster analysis) to explore what distinct patterns of deficit might yield similar academic problems.

The more practical advantages of an approach such as that considered here are given by Torgesen (1979). Through its focus on processing deficiencies underlying reading failure, this approach should foster systematic differentiation between individuals with learning disabilities as opposed to general reading backwardness or underachievement. Knowledge of processing deficits should also have implications for re-mediation. One might work directly with a presumed precursor skill, based on the inferred processing deficit, to determine if improvement enhances learning. And if the precursor skill is not amenable to change, an alternative means of achieving the desired goal might then be formulated.

The primary purposes of this chapter have been (*a*) to show that children with distinct reading problems do in fact exist within the broad category of learning disabilities, and (*b*) to offer tentative support for the possibility that these problems may have differential neuropsy-chological correlates. Results cannot be taken as proof that the proposed approach will be successful but rather as sufficiently promising to justify further applications. The ultimate goal is creation of a functional model of reading failure in which it will be possible to identify component cognitive deficits. Once isolated, these deficits might be studied in interaction with each other and with influences less intimately tied to the basic learning deficiency itself. As the subjects of study are children whose cognitive skills and approach to reading most likely change with age, any functional model of reading disability will of necessity be developmental (Fletcher, 1981). The proposed research strategy, which could be equally well applied to the study of spelling and math, has the potential of leading us to a better understanding of reading failure in the individual child, what to do about it, and what might we expect with development.

In some ways this strategy, essentially idiographic or clinical–in-ferential in nature, is different from the more nomothetic classification methods employed in subtyping research. The idiographic approach consists of neuropsychological assessment of specific cases in which the reading problem is unique. The discovery of factors contributing to more typical cases of reading disability, although a long-term goal, is of little immediate interest. In contrast, the nomothetic approach looks for patterns of neuropsychological deficit in broadly defined groups of disabled readers. Analysis of reading disorders in more typ-ically presenting cases is of greater concern. Seen from a different perspective, however, the idiographic approach advocated in this chap-ter complements the presently more popular nomothetic classification approach. The two approaches merely represent different ways of ex-amining individual variations within the reading-disabled population in order to identify different sources of reading disorder.

ACKNOWLEDGMENTS

Most of the data for this study were collected while the first author was at the Marshfield Clinic in Marshfield, Wisconsin. The authors are indebted to Drs. Philip G. Zerfas and Frederick W. Theye for their cooperation; to psychometrists Jane Anderson, Mary Gropp, Andrea Iwonski, Pat Spencer, and Pona Martin for their assistance in data collection; and to medical stenographer Colleen Whitney for typing the manuscript.

REFERENCES

Applebee, A. N. (1971) Research in reading retardation: Two critical problems. *Journal of Child Psychology and Psychiatry, 12,* 91–113.
Bakker, D. J. (1981) Hemisphere-specific dyslexia models. In R. N. Malatesha & L. C. Hartlage (Eds.), *Neuropsychology and cognition* (Vol. 1). Aalphen aan den Rijh, The Netherlands: Sijthoff and Noordhoff.
Beery, K. E. (1967) *Developmental test of visuo-motor integration: Administration and scoring manual.* Chicago: Follett.
Benson, D. F. (1976) Alexia. In J. T. Guthrie (Ed.), *Aspects of reading acquisition.* Baltimore: Johns Hopkins University Press.
Benton, A. I. (1978) Some conclusions about dyslexia. In A. L. Benton & D. Pearl (Eds.), *Dyslexia: An appraisal of current knowledge.* New York: Oxford University Press.
Berger, N. S. (1978) Why can't John read? Perhaps he's not a good listener. *Journal of Learning Disabilities, 11*(10), 31–36.
Boder, E. (1973) Developmental dyslexia: A diagnostic approach based on three atypical reading patterns. *Developmental Medicine and Child Neurology, 15,* 663–687.
Bortner, M. (1971) Phrenology, localization, and learning disabilities. *Journal of Special Education, 5,* 23–29.
Buschke, H. (1974) Components of verbal learning in children: Analysis by selective reminding. *Journal of Experimental Child Psychology, 18,* 488–496.
Carroll, J. B. (1970) The nature of the reading process. In H. Singer & E. Ruddell (Eds.), *Theoretical models and processes of reading.* Newark, Del.: International Reading Association.
Coltheart, M., Patterson, K. E., & Marshall, J. C. (Eds.) (1980) *Deep dyslexia.* London: Routledge & Kegan Paul.
Cromer, W. (1970) The difference model: A new explanation for some reading difficulties. *Journal of Educational Psychology, 61,* 471–483.
Damasio, A. R. (1977) Varieties and significance of alexia. *Archives of Neurology, 34,* 325–326.
Denckla, M. B. (1973) Research needs in learning disabilities. A neurologist's point of view. *Journal of Learning Disabilities, 6,* 44–50.
Denckla, M. B. (1977) Minimal brain dysfunction and dyslexia: Beyond diagnosis by exclusion. In M. E. Blau, I. Rapin, & M. Kinsbourne (Eds.), *Topics in child neurology.* New York: Spectrum Publications.
Denckla, M. B., & Rudel, R. (1974) Rapid "automatized" naming of pictured objects, colors, letters, and numbers by normal children. *Cortex, 10,* 186–202.
Derouesne, J., & Beauvois, M. F. (1979) Phonological processing in reading. Data from alexia. *Journal of Neurology, Neurosurgery and Psychiatry, 42,* 1125–1132.
Doehring, D. G. (1978) The tangled web of behavioral research on developmental dyslexia. In A. L. Benton & D. Pearl (Eds.), *Dyslexia: An appraisal of current knowledge.* New York: Oxford University Press.

Doehring, D. G., & Hoshko, I. M. (1977a) Classification of reading problems by the Q-technique of factor analysis. *Cortex, 13,* 281–294.

Doehring, D. G., & Hoshko, I. M. (1977b) A developmental study of the speed of comprehension of printed sentences. Bulletin of the Psychonomic Society, 9, 311–313.

Dunn, L. M. (1965) *Expanded manual for the Peabody Picture Vocabulary Test.* Circle Pines, Minn.: American Guidance Service.

Dunn, L. M., & Markwardt, F. C. (1970) *Peabody Individual Achievement Test manual.* Circle Pines, Minn.: American Guidance Service.

Durost, W. N., & Prescott, G. A. (1962) *Essentials of measurement for teachers.* New York: Harcourt, Brace, and World.

Fisk, J. L., & Rourke, B. P. (1979) Identification of subtypes of learning disabled children at three age levels: A neuropsychological, multivariate approach. *Journal of Clinical Neuropsychology, 1,* 289–310.

Fletcher, J. M. (1981) Linguistic factors in reading acquisition: Evidence for developmental change. In F. J. Pirozzolo & M. C. Wittrock (Eds.), *Neuropsychological and cognitive processes in reading.* New York: Academic Press.

Fletcher, J. M., & Satz, P. (1980) Developmental changes in the neuropsychological correlates of reading achievement: A six-year longitudinal followup. *Journal of Clinical Neuropsychology, 2,* 23–37.

Fletcher, J. M., Satz, P., & Scholes, R. (1981) Developmental changes in the linguistic performance correlates of reading achievement. *Brain and Language, 13,* 78–90.

Gaddes, W. H., & Crockett, D. J. (1975) The Spreen–Benton aphasia tests—Normative data as a measure of normal language development. *Brain and Language, 2,* 257–280.

Gibson, E. J., & Levin, H. (1975) *The psychology of reading.* Cambridge, Mass.: MIT Press.

Gilmore, J. V., & Gilmore, E. C. (1968) *Gilmore Oral Reading Test: Manual of directions.* New York: Harcourt Brace Jovanovich.

Golinkoff, R. (1975–1976) A comparison of reading comprehension processes in good and poor comprehenders. *Reading Research Quarterly, 11,* 623–659.

Goodstein, H. A., & Kahn, H. (1974) Pattern of achievement among children with learning difficulties. *Exceptional children 41,* 47–49.

Guthrie, J. T. (1973) Models of reading and reading disability. *Journal of Educational Psychology 65,* 9–18.

Guthrie, J. T., & Seifert, M. (1977) Letter–sound complexity in learning to identify words. *Journal of Educational Psychology, 69,* 686–696.

Guthrie, J. T., & Seifert, M. (1978) Education for children with reading disabilities. In H. Myklebust (Ed.), *Progress in learning disabilities* (Vol. 4). New York: Grune & Stratton.

Isakson, R. L., & Miller, J. W. (1976) Sensitivity to syntactic and semantic cues in good and poor comprehenders. *Journal of Educational Psychology, 68,* 787–792.

Jastak, J. F., & Jastak, S. R. (1965) *The Wide Range Achievement Test: Manual of instructions.* Wilmington, Del.: Guidance Associates.

Johnson, D. J. (1980) Persistent auditory disorders in young dyslexic adults. *Bulletin of the Orton Society, 30,* 268–276.

Johnson, D. J., & Myklebust, H. (1967) *Learning disabilities: Educational principles and practices.* New York: Grune & Stratton.

Kieffer, D. M., & Golden, C. J. (1978) The Peabody Individual Achievement Test with normal and special school populations. *Psychological Reports, 42,* 395–401.

Kinsbourne, M., & Warrington, E. K. (1963) Developmental factors in reading and writing backwardness. *British Journal of Psychology, 54,* 145–156.

Klinge, V., Rennick, P. M., Lennox, K., & Hart, Z. A matched-subject comparison of underachievers with normals on intellectual, behavioral, and emotional variables. *Journal of Abnormal Child Psychology, 5*(1), 61–68.

Knights, R. M., & Moule, A. D. (1968) Normative and reliability data on the motor steadiness battery for children. *Perceptual and Motor Skills, 25,* 717–720.

Layton, J. R. (1979) *The psychology of learning to read.* New York: Academic Press.

Maliphant, R., Supramaniam, S. & Saraga, E. (1974) Acquiring skill in reading: A review of experimental research. *Journal of Child Psychology and Psychiatry, 15,* 175–185.

Marshall, J. C., & Newcombe, F. (1973) Patterns of paralexia: A psycholinguistic approach. *Developmental Medicine and Child Neurology, 2,* 175–199.

Massaro, D. W. (1975) Primary and secondary recognition in reading. In D. W. Massaro (Ed.), *Understanding language.* New York: Academic Press.

Mattis, S. (1978) Dyslexia syndromes: A working hypothesis that works. In A. L. Benton & D. Pearl (Eds.), *Dyslexia: An appraisal of current knowledge.* New York: Oxford University Press, 43–58.

Mattis, S., French, J. H., & Rapin, I. (1975) Dyslexia in children and young adults: Three independent neuropsychological syndromes. *Developmental Medicine and Child Neurology, 17,* 150–163.

McCarthy, D. (1970) *Manual for the McCarthy Scales of Children's Abilities.* New York: Psychological Corporation.

Payne, M. C., Jr., Davenport, R. K., Domangue, J. C., & Soroka, R. D. (1980) Reading comprehension and perception of sequentially organized patterns: Intramodal and cross-modal comparisons. *Journal of Learning Disabilities, 13,*(1), 39–44.

Payne, R. W., & Jones, H. G. (1957) Statistics for the investigation of individual cases. *Journal of Clinical Psychology, 13,* 115–121.

Perfetti, C. A. (1980) Verbal coding efficiency, conceptually guided reading, and reading failure. *Bulletin of the Orton Society, 30,* 197–208.

Petrauskas, R. J., & Rourke, B. P. (1979) Identification of subtypes of retarded readers: A neuropsychological, multivariate approach. *Journal of Clinical Neuropsychology, 1,* 17–37.

Richardson, E., DiBenedetto, B., Christ, A., & Press, M. (1980) Relationship of auditory and visual skills to reading retardation. *Journal of Learning Disabilities, 13*(2), 26–31.

Rosner, J. & Simon, D. P. (1971) The auditory analysis test: An initial report. *Journal of Learning Disabilities, 4*(7), 40–48.

Rourke, B. P. (1975) Brain–behavior relationships in children with learning disabilities: A research program. *American Psychologist, 30,* 911–920.

Rourke, B. P., & Finlayson, M. A. (1978) Neuropsychological significance of variations in patterns of academic performance: Verbal and visual-spatial abilities. *Journal of Abnormal Psychology, 84,* 412–421.

Rourke, B. P., & Strang, J. D. (1978) Neuropsychological significance of variations in patterns of academic performance: Motor, psychomotor, and tactile-perceptual disabilities. *Journal of Pediatric Psychology, 3*(2), 62–66.

Rutter, M. (1978) Prevalence and types of dyslexia. In A. L. Benton & D. Pearl (Eds.), *Dyslexia: An appraisal of current knowledge.* New York: Oxford University Press.

Rutter, M., & Yule, W. (1975) The concept of specific reading retardation. *Journal of Child Psychiatry, 16,* 181–197.

Rutter, M. & Yule, W. (1976) Reading difficulties. In M. Rutter & L. Hersov (Eds.), *Child psychiatry: Modern approaches.* London: Blackwell Scientific.

Samuels, S. J., & Anderson, R. H. (1973) Visual recognition memory, paired-associate learning, and reading achievement. *Journal of Educational Psychology, 65,* 160–167.

Satz, P. & Friel, J. (1973) Some predictive antecedents of specific reading disability: A preliminary one-year follow-up. In P. Satz & J. J. Ross (Eds.), *The Disabled learner: Early detection and intervention*. Rotterdam: University Press, 79–98.

Satz, P. & Morris, R. (1981) Learning disability subtypes: A review. In F. J. Pirozzolo & M. C. Wittrock (Eds.), *Neuropsychological and cognitive processes in reading*. New York: Academic Press, 1981.

Shallice, T. (1979) Case study approach in neuropsychological research. *Journal of Clinical Neuropsychology*, 1, 183–211.

Smith, F. (1971) *Understanding reading: A psycholinguistic analysis of reading and learning to read*. New York: Holt, Rinehart & Winston.

Spellacy, F. J., & Spreen, O. (1969) A short form of the token test. *Cortex*, 5, 390–398.

Spreen, O., & Gaddes, W. H. (1969) Developmental norms for 15 neuropsychological tests, age 6 to 15. *Cortex*, 5, 171–191.

Sweeney, J. E., & Rourke, B. P. (1978) Neuropsychological significance of phonetically accurate and phonetically inaccurate spelling errors in younger and older retarded spellers. *Brain and Language*, 6, 212–225.

Tallal, P. (1980) Auditory temporal perception, phonics, and reading disabilities in children. *Brain and Language*, 9, 182–198.

Taylor, H. G., Satz, P., & Friel, J. (1979) Developmental dyslexia in relation to other childhood reading disorders: Significance and clinical utility. *Reading Research Quarterly*, 15(1), 84–101.

Torgesen, J. K. (1979) What shall we do with psychological processes? *Journal of Learning Disabilities*, 12(8), 16–23.

Varney, N. R., & Benton, A. L. (1979) Phonemic discrimination and aural comprehension among aphasic patients. *Journal of Clinical Neuropsychology*, 1(2), 65–73.

Wechsler, D. (1974) *Manual for the Wechsler Intelligence Scale for Children—Revised*. New York: Psychological Corporation.

Whitaker, H. A., & Noll, J. D. (1972) Some linguistic parameters of the token test. *Neuropsychologia*, 10, 395–404.

Wiener, M., & Cromer, W. (1967) Reading and reading difficulty: A conceptual analysis. *Harvard Educational Review*, 37, 620–643.

Woodcock, R. W. (1973) *Woodcock Reading Mastery Tests manual:* Circle Pines, Minn.: American Guidance Service.

Yule, W. (1978) Diagnosis: Developmental psychological assessment. In A. F. Kalverboer, H. M. vanProag, & J. Mendlewicz (Eds.), *Advances in biological psychiatry* (Vol. 1). Basel: Karger.

Section Two

Cognitive Aspects

Chapter Five

Cognitive Models of Reading: Implications for Assessment and Treatment of Reading Disability[1]

ROBERT CALFEE

INTRODUCTION

Of those students who experience difficulty in learning to read in school today, a substantial number are tagged with one or another of the labels in the category of learning disability: dyslexia, perceptual handicaps, minimal brain dysfunction, developmental aphasia, and hyperactivity, among others.

Benton (1975) comments on the shortcoming of diagnosis that is diffuse and poorly defined:

> Because developmental dyslexia is [at least one form of] reading failure of unknown origin, its defining characteristics are for the most part of a negative nature. Since it is essentially a diagnosis by exclusion, it shares

[1] Research reported in this chapter was funded in part by Grant No. G007903258 from the Department of Education, Office of Special Education.

151

the weaknesses of all diagnoses of this type. As already noted, it is failure to learn to read by a child who is of adequate intelligence, who is endowed with adequate vision and hearing, whose oral language skills are suffi- ciently developed to serve as a basis for learning to read, and who at least at the beginning of schooling had normal motivation to learn to read. That the condition is due to some type of neurological maldevel- opment is a likely presumption—but only a presumption [p. 3].

There is general agreement among all concerned—teacher, psychol- ogist, learning specialist, parent, and even the student—that something is wrong with our current procedures. Global descriptors provide little insight into the diversity of symptomatic behaviors that characterize problem students. Broad labels permit neither precise diagnosis nor focused remediation.

The instruments available for diagnostic assessment are especially problematic. Coles (1978), after reviewing validation studies of the ten most commonly used procedures for assessing students with learning problems, found a troubling disarray:

> Some studies, for example, show inconsistencies among similar learning disabilities tests in their effectiveness in distinguishing learning-disabled students from non-learning-disabled students or good readers from poor ones. Other studies looking at more than one trait found that the pre- dictability of a learning disabilities test fell below statistical significance when intelligence was partialled out. In investigations in which a learning disabilities test could divide students into high- and low-scoring groups, the students could not be separated by commensurate academic achieve- ment scores [p. 327].

Programs for remediation can be sorted into those that are test- dependent and those that are "more of the same with smaller class size." An instance of a test-dependent program occurs when the student who is thought to suffer a "visual perceptual deficit" is trained to perform tasks that help him to do better on the visual perception test— unfortunately, such training has no demonstrated value for improving reading skills (Coles, 1978; Hallahan & Cruickshank, 1973; Hamill, Goodman, & Wiederhold, 1974). Within the more-of-the-same category, smaller classes and individual attention may "feel good" to both student and teacher, but the approach is expensive and relatively ineffectual above student–teacher ratios of 10:1 (Smith & Glass, 1980).

THE NEED FOR A THEORY
OF READING DISABILITY

Why is there so little rationality in the way we handle such a vital problem as reading disability? In my opinion, the confusion can be traced in large measure to the reliance on intuition and empiricism, and the absence of any guiding theoretical framework. Folklore, mysticism, and witchcraft are no substitutes for systematic analysis; factor analysis and discriminant functions are not a great deal more helpful when used in a strictly empirical fashion.

Is it possible to construct a theory of reading and of reading disability? Some experts would argue that it is not. One position—"don't fool with Mother Nature"—holds that the human mind is beyond rational description and simplification. So is a sunset, but physicists can nonetheless provide a systematic analysis of the optics of the setting sun. Their account enhances our understanding without detracting from our appreciation.

Another position takes refuge in idiosyncracy—"every child is a unique individual!" True enough. So is very snowflake, yet we possess a theory of snowflakeness. So is every automobile driver, yet we act as if these individuals behave in regular ways—"you stay in your lane, and I'll stay in mine."

I agree with Suppes's (1974) statement about the potential for theory development in the behavioral and social sciences. We have far richer resources for development and application of theory than we have begun to take advantage of. Present-day cognitive psychology provides a rich array of theoretical concepts that are readily applicable to the diagnosis and treatment of reading disability (Calfee, 1981). In the remainder of this chapter, I will illustrate this point by a concrete example. A theoretical technique known as *independent process analysis* will be applied to normal reading, and then to potential sources of reading disability. I will show how this theoretical approach can serve not only to increase our understanding, but also to provide a framework for assessment and a guide for design of curriculum and instruction programs.

INDEPENDENT PROCESS ANALYSIS

The theoretical approach presented in this section builds on the concept of *process independence*. This concept, proposed originally by Sternberg (1963), assumes that the mental activities underlying performance on a task comprise a relatively small set of separable cognitive processes. In the model of normal reading, for instance, the independent processes include elements to carry out decoding, definition of words, parsing of sentences, and comprehension of both small and large passage structures. The proposal thus stands midway between the notion that intellectual functioning is a single dominant trait, and the postulation that thinking depends on a complex interactive network unique to the individual.

For each of the independent processes in a model, it is assumed that the theorist can identify a set of *factors* that uniquely influence the process, and a set of *measures* that are unique indicators of the process (Calfee & Spector, 1981). An independent process model for a task, therefore, provides a specification of the input–output relations for each process. It is a formally testable model. The researcher states which variables affect each process at the level of the individual student. For the model to be valid for the student, variation in the factors associated with a particular process should influence the measures for that process, but should not affect the measures of other processes.

What are the mental processes that underlie normal reading? Psychologists tend to answer this question with terms from the traditional analysis of general intellectual traits—perception, attention, memory, cognition, motivation, and so on. It is clear that these traits are important resources, along with general language ability, in the development of reading ability and in skilled reading performance.

If I were going to program a computer to read, however, I would probably not begin by constructing "subroutines" to handle perception, attention, and so on. These domains, which are foundations of cognition, are too broad, diffuse, and undefined to work with. I would, instead, find out how the computer already handles certain basic functions—how does it take in data, how does it "compute," is the power on, does the printer work? These resources play the same role as attention, memory, and so on. Then I would prepare programs to carry out the specific functions that are unique to reading—decoding, vocabulary analysis, parsing of the sentences, and comprehension of the text. I am recommending a similar approach to describe the cognitive processes in reading.

Reading Aloud

The young child often begins to acquire literacy by being read to, looking at pictures, "reading" simple stories from memory, and pronouncing familiar and salient words (*STOP, McDonald's,* etc.). The school places more formal demands on the youngster. What independent processes are fundamental to oral reading in a school setting? I assume the stress is on accuracy of pronunciation, that speed is important, and that "comprehension" is not given high priority.

Under these circumstances, three processes can be identified as essential to the reading task. First, the youngster must be able to pronounce each word. *Decoding*, as this process is commonly called, may take place in several ways. Some words, because they occur so frequently, are recognizable on sight. Words like *the, is, says*, and so on, which often serve a syntactic function in early reading, are probably handled by immediate recognition. Other words are decoded by application of the letter–sound correspondences that underlie English writing (Venezky, 1970). Because modern English is an agglomerate language (Pei, 1968), the written language no longer follows the simplest version of the alphabetic principle—one letter standing for one sound. Nonetheless, English is founded on an alphabetic base, and the beginning reader will progress in decoding only as he gains an understanding of this principle.

The decoding process is affected most directly by the complexity of the letter–sound correspondences in a particular word. Increasing the number of letters in a word puts a greater load on the process, because more correspondences have to be handled. The number of syllables also matters—*cable* takes more effort to decode than *stand*, because the reader must first segment the word and then apply the appropriate letter–sound rules. Like most modern languages, English relies heavily on word compounding; thus, many words must first be divided into morphemic elements, and then parsed into syllables and spelling–sound units. Words like *hotdogging* and *international* can be pronounced only with great effort (if at all) if the student tries to decode them as a single unit from left to right. Breaking them into their base morphemes (*hot–dog(g)–ing* and *inter–nation–al*) makes it easier for the reader because the smaller chunks are more readily translated.

The second process in oral reading is *vocabulary*, or word meaning. One might be surprised at the decision to include this process in an admittedly stripped-down model of reading. Most youngsters have a speaking vocabulary far in excess of anything they are likely to read. Moreover, most of us are able to "read" texts (foreign language, or technical material) even when we have little or no knowledge of word meaning. Both of these points are well taken. Nonetheless, I think that the young child does need to work toward the development of a vocabulary process that is appropriate to the reading task, and that growth in this process is essential to skill in reading. A critical change occurs during school in the nature of how the child understands a word. In natural language settings, word meanings are concrete and functional— *A hole is to dig. An apple is red. A penny is for spending.* In formal language settings (like books), words must be understood as part of a highly elaborated network of concepts and abstractions. The youngster begins to grasp formal definitions, and words are employed with increasing precision and sensitivity to nuance. Writing becomes more than "speech on paper" (Calfee & Freedman, 1981).

Skill in understanding meanings is an important part of integrating the information in a word string. Without such integration, the reader's short-term memory capacity is quickly exceeded, and the entire process may come to a halt. Your apparent skill in reading jargon out loud has limits, which you may not appreciate under normal circumstances—try reading the following sentence aloud and "with meaning":

> *In allocameloarithing pundinwroutches, euchormonuatistic psazods can be ortre-manched grophatraepicarly by prancresilioum pharbismentramin.*

Each word can be "decoded," but, because meaning is altogether lacking, the task rapidly becomes intolerable for most readers. We rely on access to lexical meaning far more than we may realize.

The third process in the model is *sentence comprehension*. The major job of this component is to combine the semantic and grammatical information in the string of words. Any given word is subject to various interpretations. By dividing or parsing the sentence into its basic syntactic units, the reader is able to select the proper interpretation for each word, after which he can weave the sentence elements into a comprehensible whole.

As in the case of vocabulary, the typical first-grader has considerable command of the grammar; he has mastered many of the most common sentence patterns of spoken English. Nonetheless, the grammar of written English poses new challenges. For one thing, the child encounters sentence forms that are not commonly found in speech. For instance, in the appositive construction *Tom, the boy in the brown sweater, has a new book, Tom* and *the boy in the brown sweater* are combined with economy of words. Listening to a beginning reader struggle to interpret such a sentence makes one recognize that the written language does place novel demands on the child.

The beginning reader also grows in his awareness of grammatical forms. The child acquires language in a natural manner, and uses it in free form, elliptical fashion. Sentence fragments, an occasional "ya know what I mean," and other irregularities are all acceptable in informal speech. In contrast, textbooks follow conventions, and printed sentences must conform fairly closely to proper grammar. The reader is at an advantage to the extent that he learns the conventions and becomes consciously aware of how sentences are constructed. To be sure, this knowledge often remains in the background, emerging only when needed. Most of us can read aloud fluently and "with meaning," totally unaware that we are dividing sentences into clauses and phrases. We reveal only by the prosodic flow of our intonation pattern that we know a great deal about how to parse even the most complex sentences.

This, then, is the model of a competent oral reader. The model helps in two ways to understand performance on this task. First, it highlights three critical elements, which are functionally distinct, in a way that makes assessment of each element fairly straightforward. Second, it provides guidance for the design and implementation of the instructional program. Teaching a child to read aloud can be a complex and demanding task. The three elements that have been described here can be used as a simple roadmap for instruction—simpler by far than overly detailed scope and sequence charts and teacher's manuals.

Reading for Comprehension

During the middle primary grades, the child is gradually (sometimes subtly) shifted from a reading program that emphasizes fluent oral reading to one in which the emphasis is on comprehension. I say that the shift is subtle because it is seldom clear to either student or teacher when this shift occurs, or what the shift is to. Durkin (1978–1979), after a survey of comprehension instruction in the late elementary grades, reached two disturbing conclusions: First, she found little consensus on what should be meant by comprehension; second, however the concept may be defined, teachers spend scarcely any time in direct instruction on this component. Students may be taught decoding more or less directly, and may be encouraged to read aloud with fluency. When it comes to the mysteries of comprehension, however, they are generally left to their own devices and to the mercies of workbooks and reading labs.

In my opinion, this situation reflects the lack of a clear-cut conception of what is to be taught under the rubric of comprehension. The usual terms—"main idea," "literal detail," "inferential comprehension," and so on—when examined in detail, turn out to be vacuous and self-contradictory. In this section, I will propose a model of reading comprehension that builds on the preceding model of oral reading but incorporates the results of rhetorical analysis and psycholinguistic research.

My proposal is simple enough on the surface—I assume that the "process" of reading comprehension actually consists of two independent processes. One process, *paragraph comprehension*, handles small amounts of prose in a "bottom-up" fashion. A second process, *text comprehension*, handles large amounts of prose in a "top-down" manner.

The notion that paragraphs and texts follow different stylistic conventions is found in many books on composition (e.g., Baker, 1977; Crews, 1977). Psychologists have debated whether reading comprehension is bottom-up (i.e., requiring analysis of individual sentences or propositions, with gradual accretion of the overall structure) or top-down (i.e., with a priori knowledge of text structure providing a basic framework which is elaborated by specific propositions). The most reasonable resolution of the debate seems to be that both levels of analysis are called for (Rumelhart, 1975, 1977).

The paragraph comprehension process operates in the following manner. A well-constructed paragraph consists of a single, well-defined idea, along with a few supporting statements or elaborations. The initial sentence generally introduces the theme of the paragraph, and prepares the reader for what is to follow. Paragraphs vary in length, but 3–10 sentences are typical. Paragraph structures fall into a relatively small number of categories:

1. A general principle is followed by a list of supporting examples.
2. A list of details is presented, ending with a generalization.
3. A series of logical deductions is put forward, leading to a general conclusion.
4. Related events are linked by a more general cause–effect link.
5. A proposition is stated, and clarified by "comparing"/"contrasting" instances that are similar/dissimilar to the proposition.

The reader's task in comprehending a paragraph is to pick out the main idea and figure out the linkage with the supporting details. To untangle the relations in a paragraph, the reader examines each statement, determines how it is related to what has already been said, and, much as in building a tinkertoy, an organization emerges. The optimal framework for a paragraph will depend on the writer's purpose and style, as well as on the topic being discussed.

Now a few words about the text comprehension process. A text is a collection of partial ideas that make a complete thought when taken as a whole. Texts come in several varieties. A story text, for instance, is a series of episodes, generally starting with an introductory setting and ending with some resolution of the problems that confront the various characters along the way. Another variety of text is used to describe the operation of a scientific process. The reader is taken step-by-step through an explanation of how some natural event operates, with the emphasis on underlying mechanisms. Biological descriptions are organized in yet another way. The writer may begin with the taxonomic classification of the animal, followed by an account of the physical appearance of the animal. Next the functional characteristics are noted—eating habits, sex life, and so on. Finally come a few words about unusual features of this particular beast.

It is best to think of a text as an article or book—an extended and complete exposition of a topic. The critical feature of a text, however, is not length, but sufficiency. Sentences and paragraphs are usually not designed to be fully understood in isolation; they cannot stand alone. A text is sufficient unto itself.

During the past 10 years, psychologists and linguists have made considerable progress in understanding the role of text structures on comprehension. For instance, it is now clear that simple narratives have a formal structure, the "story grammar," which underlies most stories found in western culture (Bower, Black, & Turner, 1979; Mandler, 1978; Meyer, 1977; Stein & Glenn, 1979; Thorndyke, 1977). If a particular story does not follow these grammatical rules, it will be more difficult to understand and to be remembered. The grammar is quite pervasive, and is found in the linguistic repertoire of children as young as 4–5 years (Applebee, 1978).

Research is just beginning on the grammars of expository prose (Calfee & Curley, in press). We do know several things. First, most texts in the early primary grades employ narrative passages. The beginning reader is exposed at first to texts that have relatively familiar structures, and so he needs to learn relatively little about comprehension. (To be sure, many primers and pre-primers are an exception to this generalization, in that the passages at this level often have no discernible structure, and are for all intents and purposes incomprehensible.) Second, in the middle of elementary school, the student encounters increasing amounts and new styles of expository writing—in science, in social studies, and in literature. Third, the standard reading curricula provide little in the way of systematic instruction in these new textual forms. Apparently the student is expected to acquire an understanding of expository structures by induction—by self-discovery. Instructional research suggests that only the most able students are likely to grasp such complex concepts on their own (Cronbach & Snow, 1977).

I will have a few more comments about reading comprehension later in the chapter. For now, let me simply note that the two-process model provides an interesting perspective for evaluating current practices in assessment and instruction. The widespread use of group-administered multiple choice tests means that most current information about reading comprehension in this country is restricted to the paragraph level of analysis. Indeed, it is not unusual to test the student's comprehension on a fragment of a paragraph, and to assess only localized knowledge of that fragment. To assess comprehension of larger text structures is not easy. First, it is essential to start with a coherent, well-constructed text. Second, it is necessary to have the student produce that structure in some way—by discussion, by synopsis, by outline, or the like. Present-day assessment systems, by focusing on relatively low level analysis of prose, leave us in the dark about the status of higher level reading comprehension skills. Moreover, the absence of systematic instruction on higher level comprehension skills in reading curricula and the disappearance of text level composition in the language arts curriculum (Applebee, 1980) may mean that our high school graduates comprehend far less than most citizens realize.

SOURCES OF READING DISABILITY

Why might a child read poorly? The independent process model provides a sericeable framework for considering various answers to this question.

First, the student might be lacking in fundamental psychological and linguistic resources. Mental retardation places limits on the ease with which a child learns, the facility with which he or she performs. Inadequate or improper nutrition, insufficient sleep, impoverished experience, instability in the home environment, mistreatment—each of these sources of disadvantage and others that might be mentioned—can affect all cognitive functions, reading included. If you have a headache, if you are sleepy, if you are worried or hungry, you may expect your reading fluency and comprehension to suffer. These problems cannot be ignored by the teacher, nor are they easily remedied by changing the curriculum.

Second, the student may have had so little opportunity to practice reading that he or she cannot perform with speed or accuracy sufficient to meet the demands of the school program. These problems can be traced to one or another of the specific processes in the model, although deficiencies in one process may restrict the student's learning or performance in another process. For instance, it appears that many problem readers have not gained sufficient fluency and skill to insure that decoding is a smooth and automatic operation—for them translation from print to a familiar form of the language is slow, arduous, and attention demanding (Lesgold & Curtis, 1980; Perfetti & Hogaboam, 1975). Not too surprisingly, these students do poorly on all other reading tasks for which decoding is a prerequisite.

For example, let me mention briefly some findings that I will describe in more detail later. In assessing students who are poor readers or who have been identified as learning disabled, we have found that their ability to define words, even when the task is completely oral, remains relatively constant from the second to the sixth grade, a time when their peers are showing considerable growth. From our knowledge of curriculum and instruction in the elementary grades, we conclude that the failure to improve in vocabulary arises not because of the students' inability to learn, but rather as a consequence of the curricular reliance on decoding as the chief vehicle for vocabulary growth. If the student is not a facile decoder, then books are of no help in the attainment of a richer lexicon. The observed correlation between decoding skill and vocabulary level is not a sign of interaction between the decoding and vocabulary processes; rather it is an indication of built-in constraints within the reading curriculum.

In any event, a student may read in the fashion described by the independent process model, but one or more of the processes may operate sluggishly or inefficiently, either because of shortcomings in the training program which the student has undergone, or because of the individual's particular configuration of strengths and weaknesses. In such instances, the teacher and learning specialist can be of most help to the student through a program of assessment and instruction that is sensitive to the individual's profile of skills across the set of process areas. Broad-band assessment and scatter-shot instruction waste time and prove little benefit.

Third, there appear to be certain children who do not read in the manner described by the independent process model (e.g., Juel, 1977). The defining characteristic of these students is that variation in any factor may affect any measure. They seem unable to focus on any specific task, whether it is decoding, vocabulary, or comprehension. For them, reading is truly a "psycholinguistic guessing game" (Goodman, 1967).

I suspect that many individuals can read selected materials reasonably well, even though they lack clearly differentiated resources for the task—the human mind is a remarkably flexible organ. Nonetheless, our data suggest that a distinctive characteristic of many poor readers is the nonindependence of the reading processes. Lesgold and Curtis (1980) have reported similar results in their longitudinal investigation of beginning readers. It may be that poor readers operate according to an alternative model, and that I have simply not been clever enough to discover this alternative. Perhaps so, but I would propose as a working hypothesis that these youngsters read poorly because they have not acquired a clear conception of the components of competent reading. Their "reading mind" is a tangled jumble, which fails them in all but the simplest situations. For these students, major restructuring of the reading process is needed—I doubt that much is gained by remedial "patching up," but more about this matter in the next section.

The fourth reason does not really involve a disability—some students read poorly, not because of a lack of cognitive resources, but because they have not discovered how to make effective use of the cognitive resources at their disposal. Certain of these students might benefit from speed-reading courses. Although it is unlikely that such courses really teach a person to read better (Carver, 1971), it appears that many individuals can learn to apply their skills more effectively to the variety of reading demands that confront them. It is unfortunate that many adults with high school diplomas must spend substantial amounts of money to gain this additional knowledge—a program of reading instruction stretching from kindergarten through high school surely should have room for training strategies for skilled reading and efficient study, and such training would seem a worthwhile investment by the public schools.

The fifth and last category comprises readers who have acquired the rudiments of reading skill, and perform reasonably well on group-administered multiple choice tests, but are nonetheless functionally disabled as readers. They do not like to read, and they find it laborious and not worth the time and trouble. They have little or no understanding of what reading is about, of how they read, or of how to approach different kinds of reading tasks—they handle *Time* magazine and a text on physics in the same way. These students would benefit from additional practice, and from help in becoming consciously aware of how to apply their cognitive skills to different reading stiuations. *Practice* is a hard word, but research on acquisition of perceptual–motor skills points up the importance of achieving mastery. *Consciousness* has reentered the vocabulary of experimental psychology, and is not only respectable, but probably essential (Mandler, 1975). Research on metacognitive awareness has convincingly demonstrated the importance to the individual of an explicit understanding of how he or she comprehends problems and plans a solution strategy. (Flavell coined the term metacognition to designate a person's knowing about what he knows, [Flavell & Wellman, 1977]; Brown [1978] provides a cogent discussion of the importance of this concept in education.)

ASSESSMENT OF READING DISABILITY

How can the teacher or clinician pin down the problems troubling a reader? The key to more precise diagnosis, in my opinion, lies in an assessment system designed to give a "clean" picture of the student's relative strengths and weaknesses in domains of reading performance that can be directly linked to the reading curriculum (Calfee *et al.*, 1972). I think this strategy makes pedagogical sense, and I think it meshes well with the emerging conceptions of the cognitive psychology of the educated person (Calfee, 1981).

Assessment of Decoding Skills

Of the independent processes that have been proposed as essential to reading, let me focus first on the decoding process. What are some ways to discover how well the student can handle this component of the reading task? The independent process method directs attention toward two issues: What factors influence the decoding process, and what are suitable measures of this process? Measurement is fairly straightforward, at least on the surface. The most direct way to assess a student's decoding skills is to have him or her pronounce a list of test words. (Some investigators would recommend that the student be given the test words in the context of meaningful sentences; in my opinion, context-free pronunciation of words in isolation provides a "cleaner" assessment of decoding.) To be sure, the teacher needs to know how to interpret the student's response:

- Is the student responding to the full array of letter–sound correspondences, or only to the general configuration and a few literal elements (the student looks at the first letter and the length, and then guesses)?
- Is the student quick to respond, or is the answer slow and halting?
- Can the student explain how he pronounced the word, or does the answer just "come to mind"?

These performance features cannot be assessed in typical group-administered multiple choice tests. Indeed, the most informative method for assessing decoding skills is to discuss with children the reasons for their responses.

Now to the first-mentioned issue—What factors influence the decoding process? One can easily become overwhelmed by the candidates that come to mind, and the research literature provides only limited guidance. Nonetheless, enough is known to make a beginning. Table 5.1 shows a portion of the design that we have used in our research on reading disability. The importance of familiarity, number of syllables, and word length is obvious from both research and practice. The linguistic origins of a word are also a significant factor, and one that has

Table 5.1
Design of Word List for Assessing Decoding Skills

Word origin, letter–sound correspondence, word length	Frequency of occurrence		
	High	Low	Synthetic
Anglo-Saxon			
Simple			
Short	win	lag	hin
	came	lame	pame
Long	strong	sprint	scrong
	plane	crunch	throve
Complex			
Short	join	whey	sark
	care	tern	knod
Long	ground	strewn	splare
	third	thrall	wrudge
Romance			
Short	famous	subdue	dacture
	object	inject	refarl
Long	direction	restoration	conspartable
	necessary	miscellaneous	affremiation

generally been overlooked (Pei, 1968). The letter–sound correspondences that underlie the Anglo-Saxon words in English are variegated and complex. Those English words with origins in the Romance languages follow a somewhat different set of letter–sound correspondences, a set that is generally consistent. Words from the Romance languages are relatively infrequent and "unfamiliar," but for that very reason they are more informative. Thus, it becomes increasingly important for the student in the later grades to gain the knowledge needed to pronounce words like *international* and *impartiality.*

The student's performance across the factorial variations in Table 5.1 can provide important diagnostic information about the operation of the decoding process. The student who is affected by variation in the familiarity factor (frequency is the prime index of this factor) is operating mentally in a different manner than the student who is primarily influenced by variation in the letter–sound correspondence rules. Students of the first type are operating on the basis of familiarity—if they have previously seen the word in print, they may be able to handle it on the test. Such students lack any principled understanding of the relation between the printed and spoken forms of the language, however, and thus will experience difficulty in extending their knowledge to new words encountered in a text. The diagnosis is different for the student who can handle words from Anglo-Saxon origins, but has trouble with Romance-based words. This student has probably acquired the basic concept of decoding, and can apply this knowledge to those words that are emphasized in most phonics programs. In contrast, the student has not learned the morphological, syllabic, and letter–sound principles for pronouncing words from Romance origins—these principles are not covered in many phonics programs. The first student needs help in acquiring the basic concepts of the alphabetic system; the second student needs training on higher-level correspondences in the English language.

Assessment of Comprehension Skills

My second example comes from passage comprehension. As noted in a previous section, students are likely to be more familiar with narrative prose than with exposition. Multiple choice comprehension questions are not designed to differentiate between these two types of prose structure; the ability to recognize information is not influenced by the individual's deeper understanding of text, but depends only on superficial exposure to the raw facts (Kintsch, 1977). Requiring students to actually recall what they have read, in contrast, is a far more sensitive indicator of the students' structural knowledge. By using a recall task, the diagnostician can determine if the student has a general language deficit, or has yet to learn the structures of expository prose, or simply needs to approach the task of understanding text in a more disciplined and responsible manner.

Suppose that the student is presented with the four kinds of passages shown in Table 5.2. Again, the pattern of relative strengths and weaknesses serves as a clue to the underlying cognitive mechanisms. If the student cannot reproduce a simple narrative passage, this shortcoming indicates a severe language deficit. More typically, a "poor" reader can handle both easy and difficult narratives—details from the difficult passage may be left out, but the main themes will be retold in the correct order. However, this reader will experience considerable trouble in retelling the expository passages. This shortcoming may be more indicative of weaknesses in the curriculum than disability in the student. The lower ability reader is often restricted to a diet of easy vocabulary, high interest narrative passages. Because these readers have little exposure to expository passages, it is not surprising to discover that they have trouble comprehending such texts. They will grow in reading only as they learn to deal with more demanding texts. To "protect" them from reality is a shortsighted instructional strategy, to say the least.

Table 5.2
Design of Texts for Assessing Comprehension Skills

Narrative	Expository
Easy Text	
It is a sunny day. Ann is on her bike. Tom wants to play ball. He asks Ann to play with him. She will not play ball now, she wants to ride.	You should see Ann's dog. He is bigger than Ann. His coat is yellow, but the hair on his head is brown. He has long, thin legs and big fat feet.
Tom is sad. He asks Ann, "Can we take a ride and then play ball?"	Ann thinks he is funny. He can run like a rabbit, but he eats like a pig.
"Yes," says Ann. "That will be fun." So Tom gets his bike and they play.	
Difficult Text	
The moon had risen as Jan looked toward the old deserted house. She was waiting for Ellen. They had planned to find out if the house was haunted.	The seahorse is an odd kind of fish. It is three inches tall and looks like a matchstick frame covered with fine cloth. Its skin is brown, it has a snout like a tube and has long hairs on its head.
When Ellen arrived the two walked nervously up the path. A strange shadow passed across the window next to the porch. Both girls were scared, but pretended not to notice. Ellen held the flashlight, Jan pushed open the door.	When it is time to reproduce, the female lays eggs like all other fish. But it is the male that takes care of them. He babysits the eggs by keeping them in a pouch until they hatch.
Ellen flashed the light. They both realized what was haunting the house. . . . an old cat who had made the house its home.	Thus, although the seahorse is a fish, the way it looks and hatches its eggs makes it a very unusual fish, indeed!

THE INDEPENDENCE OF READING SKILLS: RECENT FINDINGS

To those knowledgeable about research on reading skills, and to those immersed in the pragmatics of reading assessment, it may seem surprising, if not foolhardy, to postulate independence among the various skills that make up reading. Correlations among the subtests of standardized reading achievement tests are uniformly high, and factor analyses of reading tests generally reveal a single dominant factor (Davis, 1972). In my opinion, such findings reflect a lack of systematic design and contamination by uncontrolled factors that in the aggregate cause most tests to converge on an academic "testwiseness" trait. These characteristics of standard tests pose no major problems when measuring a student's overall adjustment to schooling; they are altogether undesirable, however, when test performance is the basis for instructional decisions (Calfee & Drum, 1979). In several recent investigations, I have studied a reading assessment system designed to reveal the independent processes in reading (Calfee & Spector, 1981). Most recently, I have compared the performance of three groups of readers: students identified as learning-disabled; bottom quartile readers who, however, were not identified as disabled; and students who were average readers. I do not have space in this chapter for complete details on this project, but the following discussion of the results gives an idea of the unique profiles for readers from the three categories.

The Sample and the Assessment System

Briefly, we tested students from the second, fourth, and sixth grades who were learning disabled, bottom quartile, and average readers. (A sprinkling of third- and fifth-graders were also tested, and these have been grouped with the second- and fourth-graders, respectively.) An interactive reading assessment system (IRAS; Calfee & Calfee, 1981) provided measures of decoding, vocabulary, sentence-reading skill, and comprehension. The assessment battery was individually administered to each student during a test session of approximately 1 hour.

To assess decoding skills, the student was asked to pronounce words from a list created according to a design like the one in Table 5.1. In addition to the list of real words, the student was asked to read a list of synthetic words constructed to span a broad range of English letter–sound correspondences. A word attack index was calculated from the student's performance on synthetic words. A word recognition index was obtained from performance on real words; this index measured letter–sound knowledge as well as the extent of previous encounters with words in print.

Vocabulary—defined as knowledge of word meaning—was measured by asking the student to define words from a list that was systematically varied in terms of both frequency of occurrence and degree of abstractness of the words. The task was completely oral—the tester pronounced a word, and subsequently asked the student a series of questions designed to probe knowledge of the word.

The student was then asked to read a series of sentences which varied in length, vocabulary difficulty, and syntactic complexity. Here are the easiest and the hardest sentences in the test:

A	*Ann wants Mom to make a cake. Mom cannot do it. She has to go to work.*

F	*Harriet made many heroic attempts to lead other slaves to freedom in the North. Her courage and determination made her an important figure in the nation's history.*

The Findings

The test results are shown in Table 5.3, and are plotted in Figure 5.1. Not surprisingly, students identified as learning disabled (LD) did most poorly, and the average (AV) readers did best. The size of the gap between the bottom quartile (BQ) and LD samples was a surprise to us—there were large variations from school to school in the procedures and criteria for identification of learning disability, and we expected greater overlap between the two low-ability groups. In fact, if you examine the standard deviations in the table, you will notice that variability among students is greatest in the LD sample, followed next by the BQ group, and then the AV group.

Although it is true in general that the LD students did most poorly and the AV students did best, examination of Figure 5.1 reveals distinctive patterns that vary from one index to another. For instance, the LD group shows little growth in decoding through fourth grade, and is still performing poorly in sixth grade (more than one standard deviation below the AV group). The BQ students, in contrast, make steady progress in decoding from second through sixth grade. Nonetheless, it is apparent that both the BQ and LD groups are better at recognizing real words than at decoding synthetic words. These students appear unable to transfer their knowledge of letter–sound correspondences to novel words, in contrast to the pattern of performance in the AV sample.

The pattern of results in the word-meaning panel, which was alluded to earlier in the chapter, is both striking and disturbing. The three groups of students do not differ from one another in second grade, but the AV group pulls steadily ahead of the other two groups and has advanced by a full standard deviation by sixth grade. To be sure, our design is cross-sectional rather than longitudinal, and so we cannot be sure that the populations are fully comparable at all points in time. Nonetheless, the data are consistent with the thesis advanced earlier, to the effect that poor readers of all varieties may experience a relative decline in vocabulary knowledge compared with their classmates who have greater access to the knowledge contained in textbooks.

The sentence-reading results in the next two panels of Figure 5.1 show that the LD students have special problems in oral reading. The shortcomings are substantial at all grades. These students read much more slowly than either AV or BQ students, and, in particular, they do little to adjust their reading rate to the demands of the text. The BQ students, in contrast, show the same pattern of performance and growth as the AV students, except that they begin at a lower starting level in second grade. One interpretation of these data is that the BQ

Table 5.3
Standard Scores for Seven Indices from Interactive Assessment of Independent Reading Skills (Standard Deviation in Parentheses)[a]

	Student classification and grade[b]								
	Average			Bottom quartile			Learning disabled		
Reading measure[c]	2(+3)	4(+5)	6	2(+3)	4(+5)	6	2(+3)	4(+5)	6
Decoding									
Word attack	-21	71	101	-73	-12	59	-84	-87	-20
$m = 42$ $s = 37$	(90)	(72)	(69)	(76)	(77)	(81)	(60)	(42)	(86)
Sight word	07	69	71	-98	40	67	-129	-82	04
$m = 76$ $s = 29$	(52)	(23)	(16)	(93)	(54)	(18)	(108)	(107)	(91)
Word meaning	-73	45	121	-61	-40	18	-91	-34	15
$m = 56$ $s = 17$	(61)	(69)	(68)	(63)	(78)	(93)	(95)	(70)	(97)
Sentence reading									
fluency	-08	53	82	-75	20	45	-111	-65	-03
$m = 69$ $s = 37$	(52)	(36)	(31)	(81)	(41)	(82)	(121)	(139)	(83)
Flexibility	-08	31	48	-47	19	28	-111	-01	-25
$m = 13$ $s = 22$	(52)	(26)	(12)	(125)	(21)	(24)	(219)	(53)	(174)
Comprehension									
Reading	-26	63	98	-98	15	67	-123	-76	10
$m = 66$ $s = 27$	(41)	(48)	(27)	(83)	(68)	(42)	(86)	(91)	(83)
Listening	-45	64	84	-101	13	59	-115	-47	21
$m = 81$ $s = 30$	(57)	(40)	(16)	(105)	(78)	(38)	(95)	(107)	(64)
Number of cases	14	22	34	34	22	31	12	27	21

[a] Two-place decimals omitted for standard scores.
[b] Small number of third- and fifth-grade students are grouped with second- and fourth-graders, respectively.
[c] m and s shown for each index are percentages, except fluency (seconds per word) and flexibility (seconds per word per grade).

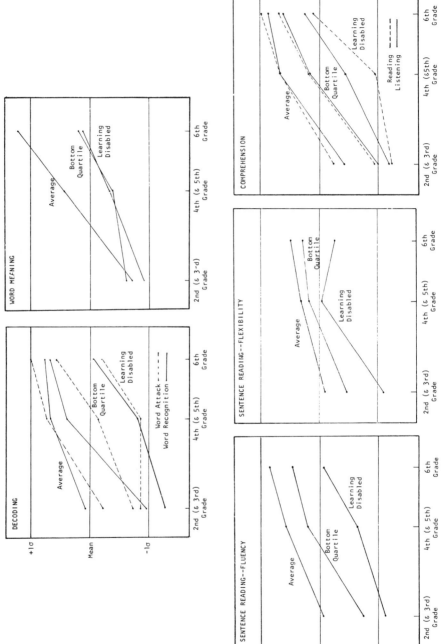

Figure 5.1. Performance patterns as a function of grade and diagnostic category. All scores are standardized to mean of 0 and standard deviation of 1.

group lacks the "head start" of the AV group, whereas the LD students are qualitatively different in their pattern of growth. The motley of "diagnostic" procedures used (or not used) to classify youngsters as LD makes me cautious about this conclusion; but the line of reasoning is worth pursuing with more trustworthy assessment procedures (similar thoughts have been presented by Lesgold & Curtis, 1980).

In the last panel are the results of the comprehension tests. Again, the AV and BQ groups follow similar growth patterns, except that BQ has a lower starting level at second grade. In particular, notice that reading and listening comprehension are fairly well balanced in these two groups; if anything, these students understand what they read slightly better than what they listen to. The LD group performs less well than the other two groups on both comprehension tests, and their reading comprehension is generally inferior to their listening comprehension.

Over the set of seven indices in our assessment, students in different diagnostic categories can be distinguished by unique patterns of performance and growth, despite the rough-and-ready procedures used for classification in this sample. If one simply averages the seven measures to obtain the typical aggregate index, the distinctive patterns disappear, and the picture is the usual one of generalized deficiencies on the part of the LD and BQ students. More carefully planned design and more refined analysis of the data reveal patterns of relative strength and weakness, patterns that can aid the practitioner in making instructional decisions.

Profile Analysis of the Individual Students

The method of profile analysis can be applied to the performance of individual students as well as to group data. In order to locate students with unusual profiles, we computed the total variance among the indices for each student. In Figure 5.2 are two contrastive profiles which were identified in this fashion. Student A, who is in the sixth grade and has been categorized as learning disabled, has a mean standard score over all seven indices of -2.45σ, and a standard deviation about this mean of 2.5σ. Student B, a second-grader in the bottom quartile, has a mean of -1.45σ and a standard deviation of 1.05σ about the mean. Both of these profiles have an unusual amount of between-index variability—the typical student has a standard deviation of less than $.5\sigma$. Variability in the profile indices is in general far greater among the LD students in our sample; more than two-thirds of these students

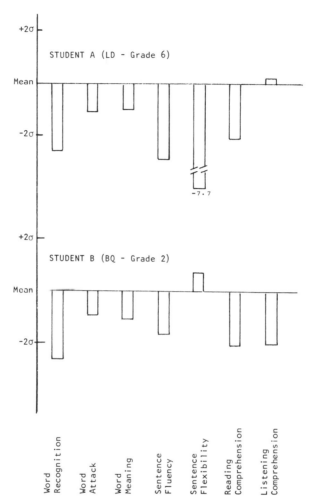

Figure 5.2. Summary profiles for two students with high profile variance.

have a profile standard deviation of .5 or greater, compared with fewer than half of the BQ students and fewer than a third of the AV group.

The profiles in Figure 5.2 highlight the similarities and the differences between the performance patterns of these two students. Both are weak in decoding skills and are low in word meaning and reading comprehension. Student A lacks oral reading fluency, and shows no sign of adjusting his reading rate to the difficulty of the text. His listening comprehension is markedly superior to his reading comprehension. Student B reads somewhat slowly, but is sensitive to the difficulty of the text. His reading and listening comprehension are both low, but are well balanced and are not too far from the expected level for a second-grader.

The two profiles appear on the surface to call for quite different instructional responses. At this point, in the absence of much-needed research on validation of instructional treatments, our advice is based largely on common sense. Student A needs further work on decoding, but more important, he needs help in gaining fluency. He reads with great hesitation, and with little attention to the demands of the text. He is capable of understanding text when it is presented orally, and he could probably extend his facility in comprehension by being encouraged in active participation during class discussions. Student B also needs further work on decoding, but most of all he needs to do a lot of reading, followed by discussion and other activities that foster growth toward the mastery of comprehension.

ASSESSMENT AND INSTRUCTION

The "diagnostic–prescriptive" model is frequently recommended today for students who are experiencing trouble in learning to read. The implication is that some children have an "academic illness" and so require individual help. These diagnoses are seldom confirmed by hard neurological or psychophysiological evidence (however, see the research of Tallal, 1980, and Vellutino, 1979, and the survey by Jorm, 1979).

In line with the medical model, disabled students are often isolated from their peers, and given such aid and comfort as smaller classes and special teachers allow. The instructional treatment is generally "more of the same," but in smaller doses and at a slower pace. With the passage of Public Law 94-142, this approach to problem learners has been disallowed. The mandated remedy is individualized instruction: The classroom teacher, using such resources as may be available, is to prepare an individualized educational plan (IEP) appropriate to the child's needs and satisfactory to the various participants in the process— parents, psychologist, learning specialist, and so on (Wallace & Larsen, 1978).

Ideally, the IEP formalizes those events that occur during the normal course of classroom instruction (Walker, 1979): The teacher assesses the students' strengths and weaknesses, and modifies the normal curriculum to take advantage of the students' strengths and to build up their competence in areas of weakness. Yet, the current state of affairs is clearly far from ideal—IEPs serve mainly to document the mismatch between diagnostic instruments and curriculum programs. The tests seek to measure psychological traits that have little demonstrated relevance to reading performance. The curriculum programs are splintered collections of instructional objectives, and both teacher and student may find it difficult to see clear direction to the programs. Under these circumstances, IEPs are one more distraction, taking up precious educational resources with no clear benefit to the student (Rauth, 1980; Shanker, 1980).

Lest my last remarks seem unduly pessimistic, let me emphasize my belief that psychological analysis of reading (and other educational skills) can serve a useful purpose in solving problems like the one that has been addressed bureaucratically by the IEP. The analysis must be rooted in a careful examination of the subject matter and of the cognitive resources needed to acquire the skill and to perform it in a competent manner. I think that this approach works best when the psychologist seeks the counsel of the classroom teacher, and the program of instruction builds upon the skills and knowledge of the teacher as an active participant in the development and implementation of that program. Efficient assessment systems and effective instructional programs are important ingredients in the teaching of reading, but these ingredients realize their full value only when presented by a teacher whose conception of reading meshes with the rest of the program. The discussion in this chapter suggests one direction for such a conceptualization (see also Calfee & Shefelbine, 1981). My focus has been on assessment; I hope it is clear that this is only the beginning of the process.

REFERENCES

Applebee, A. N. (1978) *The child's concept of story.* Chicago: University of Chicago Press.
Applebee, A. N. (1980) A study of writing in the secondary school. (Final Report NIE-G-79-0174.) Urbana, Ill.: National Council of Teachers of English.
Baker, S. (1976) *The complete stylist and handbook.* New York: Thomas Y. Crowell Company.
Benton, A. L. (1975) Developmental dyslexia: Neurological aspects. In W. J. Friedlander (Ed.), *Advances in neurology* (Vol. 7). New York: Raven Press, 1975.
Bower, G. H., Black, J. B., & Turner, T. J. (1979) Scripts in memory for text. *Cognitive Psychology, 11,* 177–220.
Brown, A. L. (1978) Knowing when, where, and how to remember: A problem of metacognition. In R. Glaser (Ed.), *Advances in instructional psychology* (Vol. 1). Hillsdale, N.J.: Lawrence Erlbaum.
Calfee, R. C. (1981) Cognitive psychology and educational practice. In D. C. Berliner (Ed.), *Review of Research in Education.* Washington, D.C.: American Educational Research Association.

Calfee, R. C., & Calfee, K. H. (1981) *Interactive reading assessment system (IRAS)*. Unpublished manuscript, Stanford University.

Calfee, R. C., Chapman, R., & Venezky, R. L. How a child needs to think to learn to read. In L. W. Gregg (Ed.), *Cognition in learning and memory*. New York: Wiley, 1972.

Calfee, R. C., & Curley, R. G. (in press) Structures of prose in the content area. In J. Flood (Ed.), *Understanding reading comprehension*. Newark, Del: International Reading Association.

Calfee, R. C., & Drum, P. A. (1979) How the researcher can help the reading teacher with classroom assessment. In L. B. Resnick & P. A. Weaver (Eds.), *Theory and practice of early reading* (Vol. 2). Hillsdale, N.J.: Lawrence Erlbaum.

Calfee, R. C., & Freedman, S. (1981) *Understanding and comprehending*. Unpublished manuscript, Stanford University.

Calfee, R. C., & Shefelbine, J. L. (1981) A structural model of teaching. In A. Lewy & D. Nevo (Eds.), *Evaluation roles in education*. New York: Gordon and Breach.

Calfee, R. C., & Spector, J. E. (1981) Separable processes in reading. In F. J. Pirozzolo & M. C. Wittrock (Eds.), *Neuropsychological and cognitive processes in reading*. New York: Academic Press.

Carver, R. P. (1971) *Sense and nonsense in speed reading*. Silver Spring, Md.: Revrac.

Coles, G. S. (1978) The learning-disabilities test battery: Empirical and social issues. *Harvard Educational Review*, *48*, 313–340.

Crews, F. (1977) *The Random House handbook*. New York: Random House.

Cronbach, L. J., & Snow, R. E. (1977) *Aptitudes and instructional methods*. New York: Irvington Publishers.

Davis, F. B. (1972) Psychometric research on comprehension in reading. *Reading Research Quarterly*, *7*, 628–678.

Durkin, D. (1978–1979) What classroom observations reveal about reading comprehension instruction. *Reading Research Quarterly*, *14*, 481–533.

Flavell, J. H., & Wellman, H. M. (1977) Metamemory. In R. V. Kail, Jr., & J. W. Hagen (Eds.), *Perspectives on the development of memory and cognition*. Hillsdale, N.J.: Lawrence Erlbaum.

Goodman, K. S. (1967) Reading: A psycholinguistic guessing game. *Journal of the Reading Specialist*, *6*, 126–135.

Hallahan, D. P., & Cruickshank, W. M. (1973) *Psycho-educational foundations of learning disabilities*. Englewood Cliffs, N.J.: Prentice-Hall.

Hammill, D., Goodman, L., & Wiederhold, J. L. (1974) Visual–motor processes: Can we train them? *The Reading Teacher*, *27*, 469–480.

Jorm, A. F. (1979) The cognitive and neurological bases of developmental dyslexia: A theoretical framework and review. *Cognition*, *7*, 19–33.

Juel, C. L. (1977) *An independent-process model of reading for beginning readers*. Unpublished doctoral dissertation, Stanford University.

Kintsch, W. (1977) On comprehending stories. In M. A. Just & P. Carpenter (Eds.), *Cognitive processes in comprehension*. Hillsdale, N.J.: Lawrence Erlbaum.

Lesgold, A. M., & Curtis, M. E. (1980) Learning to read words efficiently. In A. M. Lesgold & C. A. Perfetti (Eds.), *Interactive processes in reading*. Hillsdale, N.J.: Lawrence Erlbaum.

Mandler, G. (1975) Consciousness: Respectable, useful, and probably necessary. In R. Solso (Ed.), *Information processing and cognition: The Loyola Symposium*. Hillsdale, N.J.: Lawrence Erlbaum.

Mandler, J. M. (1978) A code in the node: The use of a story schema in retrieval. *Discourse Processes*, *1*, 14–35.

Meyer, B. J. F. (1977) The structure of prose: Effects on learning and memory and implications for educational practice. In R. C. Anderson, R. J. Spiro, & W. E. Montague (Eds.), *Schooling and the acquisition of knowledge.* Hillsdale, N.J.: Lawrence Erlbaum.

Pei, M. A. (1968) *What's in a word?* New York: Hawthorn Books.

Perfetti, C. A., & Hogaboam, T. (1975) The relationship between single word decoding and reading comprehension skill. *Journal of Educational Psychology, 67,* 461–469.

Rauth, M. (1980) Testimony to Subcommittee on Selection Education Committee on Education and Labor, U.S. House of Representatives.

Rumelhart, D. E. (1975) Notes on a schema for stories. In D. Bobrow & A. Collins (Eds.), *Representation and understanding: Studies in cognitive science.* New York: Academic Press.

Rumelhart, D. E. (1977) Understanding and summarizing brief stories. In D. LaBerge & J. Samuels (Eds.), *Basic processes in reading: Perception and comprehension.* Hillsdale, N.J.: Lawrence Erlbaum.

Shanker, A. (1980) Testimony presented to the United States Senate Subcommittee on the Handicapped, July 31, 1980.

Smith, M. L., & Glass, G. V. (1980) Meta-analysis of research on class size and its relation to attitudes and instruction. *American Educational Research Journal, 17,* 419–434.

Stein, N. L., & Glenn, C. G. (1979) An analysis of story comprehension in elementary school children. In R. Freedle (Ed.), *New directions in discourse processing.* Norwood, N.J.: Ablex.

Sternberg, S. (1963) *Retrieval from recent memory: Some reaction-time experiments and a search theory.* Paper presented at the meeting of the Psychonomic Society, Niagra Falls, August 1963.

Suppes, P. (1974) The place of theory in educational research. *Educational Research, 3,* 3–10.

Tallal, P. (1980) Auditory temporal perception, phonics and reading disabilities in children. *Brain and Language, 9,* 182–198.

Thorndyke, P. W. (1977) Cognitive structures in comprehension and memory of narrative discourses. *Cognitive Psychology, 9,* 77–110.

Vellutino, F. R. (1979) *Dyslexia: Theory and Research.* Cambridge, Mass.: MIT Press.

Venezky, R. L. (1970) *The structure of English orthography,* The Hague: Mouton.

Walker, H. M. (1979) The Individualized Educational Program (IEP) as a vehicle for delivery of special education and related services to handicapped children. In *Exploring issues in the implementation of P.L. 94-142: IEP—Developing criteria for evaluation of Individualized Education Program provisions.* Philadelphia, Pa.: Research for Better Schools, Inc.

Wallace, G., & Larsen, S. C. (1978) *Educational assessment of learning problems: Testing for teaching.* Boston, Mass.: Allyn & Bacon.

Chapter Six

Reading Disorders as Information-Processing Disorders

J. RISPENS

INTRODUCTION

The Study of Reading Disorders: Some Problems

The study of reading disorders has a rather long history. The first reports of children who failed to learn to read appeared at the end of the nineteenth century (Morgan, 1896). It is surprising to note that most research since then has been dominated by a simple paradigm, and that nearly all researchers today follow a traditional, rather obvious procedure.

In the first place, researchers focus on a small group of children with reading disorders—most research being concerned with so-called specific (or developmental) dyslexia. However, children suffering from this condition are only a small part of the total group of children who have problems learning to read. Moreover, it must be noted that there is still considerable disagreement among researchers as to how "dyslexia"

177

should be defined (Benton, 1975; Rutter, 1978). Some researchers go so far as to deny the very existence of dyslexia (Schlee, 1976) or reject the relevance of the concept. The same situation characterizes attempts to construct subdivisions within the group of dyslexic children.

Second, reading research has a strong child-centered orientation (Torgesen, 1979). By this, I mean that research tries to identify disturbances in psychological and neurological processes that are thought to underlie the reading disorder. A search for the etiology, therefore, remains the main purpose of the research. Most researchers seem to be unaware that such an approach implies a formidable reduction. A reading disorder is traditionally seen as a condition within the child. The basic idea is that there must be a deficit or dysfunction to which the failure can be ascribed. But what about the influence of extraneous factors such as reading instruction? A further reduction has to do with the tendency to adopt a single factor theory (Doehring, 1978; Carr, 1981). As Carr observes, most researchers try to be as parsimonious as possible. This leads to a theory in which a single basic factor underlying the disability is postulated. About the nature of this factor, however, there is no consensus (Vellutino, 1979).

A third characteristic of the conventional research is its naive belief in the applicability of research findings to remediation. Most researchers seem to assume that the concept of dyslexia can be used as a diagnostic label and that based on the notions of etiology, remedial programs can be constructed. However, the assumption that research findings are readily translatable into remedial programs is a questionable one. This is not merely because of the quality of the research conducted—although its internal validity in most cases can seriously be criticized—but also because of the general problem of the use of research results to improve educational programs (Clifford, 1973; Samuels & Pearson, 1980). The notion of ecological validity is very relevant here. One can wonder whether the traditional reading disorder research paradigm, which entails so much reduction, can contribute substantially to the planning and content of educational programs.

It is not our intention to analyze thoroughly the shortcomings of the traditional paradigm. We want, rather, to give a brief presentation of an alternative view of reading disorders. It will be shown that the study of reading from an information-processing point of view is a profitable undertaking.

An Alternative Paradigm

Recent developments in the study of reading disorders are partly inspired by experimental findings in cognitive psychology. Particularly promising is the connection between cognitive psychology—and, more specifically, the information-processing theories—and instructional psychology (Glaser, 1978).

Our view of reading disorders is the following. Reading disorders can be seen as a manifestation of the problem of adaptation of instruction to individual differences. Reading disorders arise in the course of reading instruction when some children do not succeed. That is, children fail to show the expected results, or need much additional time to reach a specified goal. The inclusion of the factor "instructional context" should, of course, not be taken to mean that learning disorders are simply seen as cases of "dyspedagogy" (Cohen, 1971) for which the school can be blamed. What is needed, in fact, is the formulation of a starting point of research in which the limited traditional idea of a child-centered basis of reading disorders is broadened. From our point of view a reading disorder results from an *interaction* between the child and an educational setting which usually aims at an "average" child. As such, this view is neither spectacular nor new. It has, however, important implications for redefining the objectives of research.

First, if the study of reading disorders incorporates more of the instructional context, it becomes possible to avoid the a priori and arbitrary reductions of the traditional paradigm, in which reading failure is seen as having to do only with the learner. In the second place, such an approach brings up the question of whether there is any reason to make a sharp distinction between dyslexia and reading disorders in general. We think there is no need for such a separation. A simple argument can be found in the fact that the distribution of reading scores is not at all bimodal (Doehring, 1978; Carr, 1981). This can lead to the conclusion that there is only one group of children with reading disorders, and not two. This group contains all children with a reading retardation (or disorder) identified by means of their scores on a reading test. Such children can be called "backward readers." We agree with Rutter and Yule (1973) and Rutter (1978) that within the group of children who are backward readers, a division into two groups seems warranted: The validity of the differentiation between specific reading retardation and general reading backwardness is demonstrated by the finding that the two conditions differ with respect to sex distribution, neurological disorder, neurodevelopmental functions, educational attainments, and prognosis (Rutter & Yule, 1973, p. 36). Nevertheless, the question remains of whether from a remedial point of view this subdivision is useful. Although Zigmond (1977) thinks it is, this question is yet to be answered by investigations in which the effects of remedial programs designed for each of the two groups are tested. In this chapter we will not pay further attention to this differentiation.

We will simply speak of reading disorders, referring to both groups.

Finally, when reading disorders are seen as a problem of how instruction has to be adapted to individual differences, the question as to the precise nature of such differences has to be taken into account. We do not have to leave the traditional child-centered orientation; on the contrary, a process orientation remains necessary. However, the search for processes should be preceded by a thorough analysis of the act of reading (or of what is going on during reading instruction). The starting point for such research is a careful analysis of the reading tasks the child is confronted with (Resnick, 1976; Resnick & Beck, 1976).

In our opinion, such task analysis is particularly important in view of the serious shortcomings of correlational approaches, which are so often used in reading disorders research. In the case of young children who fail to learn to read, task analysis could provide information regarding what the child is doing, what the child is really doing wrong, and which strategies the child uses in trying to decipher the riddle of the written word. It may be that this clinical approach can also add something to our insight about the nature of individual differences in general (Pellegrino & Glaser, 1979; Sternberg, 1977).

In the following section, we shall concentrate on the process aspects of reading retardation. The questions we shall ask are: What processes are involved in reading and what leads to the mismatch between child and reading instruction? Why do some children fail, and what does their failure mean? What, in fact, is a reading disorder? What goes wrong when a child does not profit from instructions? One of the sources of information wherein an answer to these questions can be sought is reading theory. Recent developments in reading theory are very promising in this respect, particularly insofar as they take advantage of the progress in cognitive psychology, and especially information-processing theory. In what follows, we will deal with information-processing models and the way in which they are utilized in reading theory.

Reading Theory and the Information-Processing Model

The use of the information-processing metaphor has given a considerable impetus to the study of cognition, as has been demonstrated by recent studies in the field of intelligence. Here, the shift from a traditional psychometric approach to the information-processing-based analysis of intellectual activities and problem solving strategies seems very promising (Carroll, 1979; Sternberg, 1977). Another interesting development in cognitive psychology should be mentioned here: It is our impression that the gap between scientific (laboratory-oriented) psychology (e.g., the psychology of learning) and the practical use of psychology in educational settings is becoming smaller as a result of recent research in cognitive psychology—although there still is a considerable distance between a theory represented in the usual flow chart format and what goes on in a reading class (Glaser, Pellegrino, & Lesgold, 1978).

In the next part of this chapter we shall discuss some general aspects of reading models that fit within the information-processing theory. These models try to describe in some detail the way in which the extraction of information from a text takes place and to identify the processes involved in reading.

The third part of this chapter reports in some detail recent discussions on the decoding aspects of reading and reading disorders. It is common practice to assume that in reading two basic processing stages are involved (Golinkoff & Rosinski, 1976). The first has to do with decoding, the "translation" of the written text into spoken words, the second with apprehending the meaning of the words. The decoding aspect of reading has received a considerable amount of attention in recent research. (From an educational point this much seems rather self-evident: Once a child has mastered the decoding skills, he can read words never seen before.) The question arises as to whether children with reading difficulties can be considered as having decoding difficulties; and, if so, why they manifest such difficulties.

READING MODELS AND INFORMATION-PROCESSING THEORY

The LaBerge–Samuels Model

Reading models are attempts to represent what goes on during the act of reading. Several models have been proposed in recent years (Mackworth, 1972; Gough, 1972; LaBerge & Samuels, 1974; Calfee & Drum, 1978; Rumelhart, 1977; Goodman, 1968). Most models utilize the formalism of information-processing theory and are presented in the well-known flow chart format. As an example, we shall discuss here the LaBerge–Samuels model (LaBerge & Samuels, 1974). Figure 6.1 shows a schematic representation of their model. It omits several relevant aspects of their presentation, such as the role of attention, as well as the episodic memory and response system.

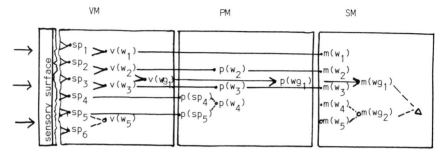

Figure 6.1. Schematic representation of the LaBerge–Samuels model.

The model consists of three memory systems; between these systems there are associative links. The graphemic input (i.e., letters, words) can take different routes thorugh the systems.

1. *Visual memory.* This system contains visual representations. Graphemic information is analyzed by feature detectors (f) and recoded into letter codes (l). They activate spelling pattern codes (sp), which in turn feed into a visual word-group code (vw).

2. *Phonological memory.* This system contains acoustic and articulatory representations. Here the visual codes are recorded into phonological codes. LaBerge and Samuels state that it would be possible to construct separate systems for acoustic and articulatory inputs, respectively, as is in fact done in some other models. They also assume that a visual code may activate a phonological code indirectly, by means of the episodic memory system. This memory system contains codes of temporal and physical events. Together with the visual and phonological codes the episodic memory codes form a superordinate code. This code is supposed to function in the early stages of learning.

3. *Semantic memory.* In this system the visual or phonological codes feed into word meaning or word group meaning codes. Here comprehension takes place.

One of the attractive aspects of the model is that between the graphemic input and the grasping of meaning several process routes are posited. The authors describe five optional routes. For instance, according to Option 1, a graphemic stimulus is directly coded into a visual word code, which automatically activates the meaning code. Alternatively (Option 3) the graphemic stimulus is coded into a visual word-group; this activates the phonological word-group code, feeding directly into the meaning code. In other words, the model can take into account the level of difficulty of the text, or strategy adopted by the reader.

This brief presentation of the LaBerge–Samuels model will serve us as a basis for discussing some questions raised by reading models in general. Although these models represent in a rather straightforward manner the flow of information, several dimensions of the reading process remain obscure. We will discuss here two aspects of a reading model constructed within the information-processing perspective.

The Ecological Validity of a Reading Model

The first question that can be raised about the model has to do with the processing orientation. One can argue that this orientation has a number of limitations that make this approach inappropriate for the representation of complicated cognitive processes (Neisser, 1976; Claxton, 1980). One line of argument runs as follows. Reading is a complex cognitive skill in which several subskills are involved. The model represents this by indicating that various process routes are available. However, the question is which route is chosen at any given time. A possible answer might be that the context in which reading takes place determines which route is utilized. Reading serves many purposes, and depending on the purpose we have in mind, we choose to skim or to scan a passage, or to read it carefully, or even to reread words or sentences. However, even within these different contexts, the decoding techniques could vary. There are a tremendous number of words (or word groups) that we do not spell or sound out. We grasp their meaning at once; but for that, reading would be a very time-consuming affair. The question remains of how a reading model can account for this (i.e., where in the model is there a place for an agent making decisions?). This question takes us from the information-processing approach to a philosophical level. One well-known issue here is whether we perceive the world directly or indirectly. In the latter case, some mediating system would have to be assumed. And what exactly would be the nature of such a system? Attempts to answer this question in terms of information-processing theory lead us to an infinite regression.

For this reason, Shaw and Bransford, in their comparison of the ecological approach with the information-processing orientation, conclude: "We now see that such questions as, Where does the last stage of perceptual processing occur? or Where in the sequence of stages can we fit the knowing agent? are philosophical red herrings which lead our theories astray [Shaw & Bransford, 1977, p. 10]." They argue that in the ecological approach the knowing agent is the process itself; we extract meaning directly from the world surrounding us by means of the perceptual system. No epistemic mediational system (e.g., a memory system) has to be constructed; we know directly. It is not our intention to discuss at length the merits of the ecological approach. Nevertheless, some attention has to be paid to the ecological validity of reading models. Again the question can be asked whether reading models account for the different functions involved in reading. This holds not only for skilled readers, but also for young inexperienced readers. It may be that classroom reading makes specific demands. It may be that for the study of reading disorders this aspect is very important. The function of emotion also must be understood, since it is possible that a sense of failure can influence the cognitive functioning of children. These points—as well as the possible gap between what has to be read and what the child feels is relevant for him—are omitted in reading models. Olson (1977) stresses the role of such factors. He observes that reading books are often not appropriate: "They fail to address the particular child in the personal, direct way that speech does. There is no possibility of the text speaking to the child and the child speaking back. There is no negotiating of meaning, expressions, or ways in which those expressions are used [p. 77]." A reading model describes the reading process without a context, in an abstract sense. It therefore has serious limitations, although we have to admit that the complex reality indicated by the term "reading" could hardly be represented in one model. This does not mean that models are useless. They certainly have a heuristic value in that they generate research questions. And of course, the more they rest upon a real life task analysis, the closer they get at what really happens during reading. However, a model should not have excessive pretentions. The ecological validity of reading models is limited.

Bottom Up or Top Down?

Even if we stay within the framework of information-processing theory, a number of problems remain. First, there is the problem that models use a number of concepts (e.g., memory system, knowledge, perception) which are in themselves liable to discussion and further research. Consider, for example, the changes in theories of the memory system (Craik & Lockhart, 1972; Baddely, 1976; Hitch, 1980)—changes which will be reflected in the reading model. With progress in psychology, any model risks becoming out of date.

Another example of such changes involves the important concept of processing. The LaBerge–Samuels model is an example of a data-driven (or bottom-up) model: Information enters the system via the receptors and is processed by means of various subsystems linked together by different pathways until the flow of information reaches its end and the message is understood. The model reflects this concept, indicating that understanding takes place by the use of information already present in the system. The meaning of a word is understood when the graphemic input is fed into the internal lexicon. (This means that we cannot comprehend what we do not know already in some form.)

Yet this interpretation of the way processing takes place has become subject to serious debate (Rumelhart, 1977; Norman, 1979). The function of the already present knowledge is particularly interesting. In the first place, it is useful to make a distinction between two types of knowledge. A traditional distinction (Broudy, 1977) is between "knowing what" and "knowing how." The latter aspect has been studied recently as an instance of "metacognition" (Brown, 1978). Flavell (1976) describes this metacognition as follows: "Metacognition refers to one's knowledge concerning one's own cognitive processes and products or anything related to them, e.g., the learning-relevant properties of information or data [p. 232]." Metacognition is probably highly relevant for the study of reading disorders, and we shall devote more attention to it later in this chapter.

The "knowing what" aspect also has its influence, especially in those stages in the process of learning to read in which reading comprehension is important (e.g., in tasks like reading a text merely for information). It has to be noted that reading research has paid surprisingly little attention to this comprehension aspect. After Bartlett's (1932) seminal study, there was a long period of relative silence before interest in the topic was eventually renewed (Marshall & Glock, 1978; Juel, 1980). With regard to the study of reading disorders, one additional remark must be made. The limited comprehension capacity of some youngsters diagnosed as suffering from a reading disorder may have to do more with their limited knowledge of the world than with a defect in their reading technique as such. It is a common experience in special education and other kinds of enrichment programs that the teaching of reading, and especially the comprehension aspect, goes hand in hand with (and depends on) an enrichment of the reasoning capacity of these youngsters. A full treatment of this theme is beyond our present scope, as it would require discussion of problems such as the representation of knowledge in memory—for example, in the form of a schema (Rumelhart & Ortony, 1977; Norman, 1979)—and the linguistic aspects of a text. Instead, we confine ourselves here to the processing aspects of the information flow and to the influence of already present knowledge on the recognition of the text.

This influence is demonstrated in a second processing route: the top-down route. There is ample evidence to show that reading involves more than just a flow from lower to higher levels of analysis: Higher level factors also influence lower level ones. This top-down phenomenon inspired Goodman (1968) to develop a reading theory in which he views reading primarily as a problem-solving process analogue: The reader makes guesses about the text and then checks whether these guesses are correct. The existence of the top-down—or conceptually driven—processing route can easily be demonstrated. Rumelhart (1977) describes five domains in which the influence of a higher level of analysis on a lower level is apparent. The idea is that processing is initiated by the context, and that expectations which thus arise then activate the lower levels of analysis. An everyday experience confirms this: We may easily fail to note an incorrectly spelled word in a sentence. Sometimes it takes time to become aware of the fact that something is wrong. The already present knowledge, activated by the context (which in turn is activated by an initial global data driven processing stage) plays an important part. Straightforward models like the La-Berge–Samuels model are incomplete in this regard. However, some attempts have been made to construct models in which both processing ways as well as the interactions between them are accounted for. An example is Rumelhart's (1977) interactive model, shown in Figure 6.2.

Rumelhart comments upon his own model:

> Although the model . . . may, in fact, be an accurate representation of the reading process, it is of very little help as a model of reading. It is one thing to suggest that all of these different information sources interact (as many writers have), but quite another to specify a psychologically plausible hypothesis about how they interact. . . . All that is interesting in the model takes place in the box labeled 'pattern synthesizer'. The flow chart does little more than list the relevant variables. We need a representation for the operations of the pattern synthesizer itself. To represent these we must develop a means of representing the operation of a series of parallel interaction processes [1977, pp. 588–589].

Another attempt to represent the (partially parallel and partially serial) processing dimensions was undertaken by Norman (1979). This schema-driven analysis concept is schematically represented in Figure 6.3. (The model depicts perceptual processing in general, not only reading.)

It can be seen that Norman attaches a lot of weight to the concept "schema." As we have already stressed, this is a very relevant aspect

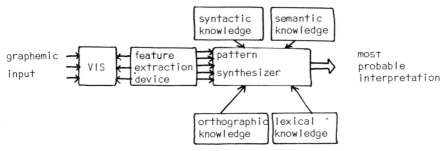

Figure 6.2. Schematic representation of Rumelhart's interactive model of reading.

of reading in the last stage. Norman's model should be very useful for the reading theorist. However, a problem similar to that noticed by Rumelhart arises. The problem inherent to models is that in their presentation of the processes involved they cannot adequately show the complicated parallel interactions between the levels. With the representation of parallel interactions we come to a general problem of information-processing methodology. One solution is the independent stage model—as presented in the domain of reading by Calfee (Calfee, 1977; Calfee & Drum, 1978)—which relies on the componential analysis technique, as proposed by Sternberg (1976). The basic assumption here is that cognitive processes can be decomposed into relatively independent subprocesses. Such an assumption is questionable however in the case of reading; we seriously doubt the psychological reality of dividing the reading process into a number of independent subprocesses. The interplay between top-down and bottom-up processing, in particular, cannot be handled adequately in componential analysis. It must be noted that one difficulty arises as a result of conflating the concepts "processes" and "skills." It may be possible to discover relatively independent skills in reading. However, this is not the same

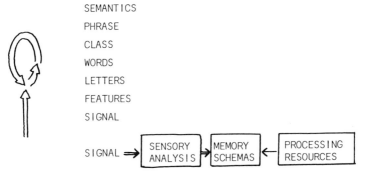

Figure 6.3. Schematic representation of the schema analysis process (Norman, 1979).

as having discovered independent processes. Before ending our brief review of reading models we should introduce another important concept from the processing theory: the concept of strategy.

The model indicates that one can choose between several processing routes; a strategy is chosen that is adequate for the particular level of difficulty of the text, amount of time available, possible uses of the information. This is a general feature of information processing. There is no predetermined route, and the individual must decide what to do (within the limits of the task requirements). Examples of this are the use of context information and the strategy to fragment a text when reading (using the cues in the text). It may be that bad readers have never learned to use such strategies in handling information flow. This concept of strategy is highly relevant for the study of reading disorders. Apart from structural deficiencies (possibly as a result of a neurological disorder) the behavioral disorder might be the result of a lack of the use of adequate strategies.

DECODING PROCESSES AND READING DISORDERS

Introduction

Reading involves an interplay between the decoding, data-driven processes and the conceptually guided top-down process. One can therefore wonder whether reading disorders depend primarily on deficiencies in decoding skills or whether they are due to disabilities of the conceptual domain.

It must be noted that reading disorders manifest themselves when reading instruction begins. The nature of the disorder clearly depends on the stage that the instruction is has reached, although the tendency in much of the research has been to treat reading disorders as a unitary phenomenon. Yet there are a great variety in the ways in which reading failure and mistakes manifest themselves (Vernon, 1977).

The initial stages of reading emphasize the "cracking of the code." Reading (as it is presented in many instructional methods) initially entails the learning of several decoding techniques—the learning of the letter names, the blending of letters, and so on. It is likely, therefore, that young reading-disabled children suffer from decoding disorders. In later stages (the higher grades of the school) the comprehension of the text is emphasized. At these stages, it is possible that reading disorders arise from conceptual deficiencies, as was discussed earlier. It is also possible that deficient or inefficient decoding techniques could continue to exert an influence even in the higher stages of reading. Thus there could be an asymmetry in the relation between the data-driven and the top-down routes (Perfetti, 1980). On the other hand, we do not know to what extent the learning of decoding is influenced by concepts and knowledge already present. It may well be that even in the initial stage of reading, word identification (assuming that this is what children have to perform) depends on the use of context. Paradoxically, the blending of a word based on the constituting letters becomes possible only when the reader knows what the word will be. It is not quite certain, however, that in the teaching of reading this aspect is sufficiently appreciated. We think that children often use strategies invented by themselves, or at least not taught explicitly. In short, we can distinguish between two types of reading disorders— decoding disorders and comprehension problems (Perfetti, 1980; Perfetti & Lesgold, 1980). Before discussing the former, let us briefly consider the latter. In order for the meaning of a sentence to be comprehended, the relevant word meanings have to be present in short-term memory (which we shall here call working memory). Given that the capacity of working memory is limited, an overload of the memory capacity has to be prevented. Comprehension disorders, therefore, can have several causes. As mentioned earlier, decoding ability, as such, can be deficient. As a consequence, decoding can absorb too much attention and cause capacity overload. (This—the role of automatic decoding—was a topic of central importance in the LaBerge–Samuels model.) Another potential factor—namely, the extent of the internal lexicon—has already been discussed. A limited knowledge of the outside world places restrictions on the reading of texts that refer to this knowledge. Third, there is the strategy factor. The use of strategies to structure the text—reading in meaningful units, seeing where a paragraph ends—helps to canalize the information flow. In addition, the proper use of strategies, including metacognition, helps to reduce the overload.

This, in a nutshell, is what research on comprehension disorders tries to discover. We already stressed that there is a real danger in separating processes and dimensions that normally function together in an integrated manner. We want to mention again two problems. The first is that of individual differences. In working with children with reading disorders, it is always striking to observe that they use idiosyncratic strategies. This brings us to the second problem, that of reading instruction which does not explicitly teach children the use of strategies. One of the effects is that children resort to their own strategies—

often not to their benefit. In the next section we will now consider in more detail the decoding aspect of reading and reading disorders.

Decoding Reconsidered

THE UNIT OF READING AND DECODING PROBLEMS

Often a relatively arbitrary unit of reading is chosen as a starting point. Some models (e.g., Gough, 1972) conceive of reading as based on the perception of single—or an assembly of—letters. Proponents of the top-down models, on the other hand, propose more complex units of reading. Such units may be words, but could be sentences, paragraphs, clauses, and so on. Reading, however, does not involve reading of letters, syllables, or words alone. We get an idea of the text based on a sample we scan. Sophisticated reading models appreciate all these aspects, and do not, therefore, propose a single standard unit of reading. We can conclude that both step-by-step and holistic sampling strategies are employed by the normal reader. Sampling of entire words and ignoring phonological information in the word almost never proceed to the extent wherein the reader could readily comprehend a word whose letters are scrambled. Yet readers appear not to be reading letter by letter (Rozin & Gleitman, 1977, p. 73).

We fully agree with Gibson and Levin (1975, p. 286) that neither a stimulus–response paradigm nor a view favoring a relatively simple paired-associate learning model can account fully for the reading process. The process as such can best be described in terms of rule learning in a situation in which the context is very important. In our opinion, the sounding aspect of reading acquisition is also of central importance. Our own research clearly demonstrates that the auditory aspects of reading are relevant, and that a lot of reading problems are due to a failure in this domain. Table 6.1 shows the relation between auditory analysis and auditory blending and reading. These data are from a study in which we compared 50 good readers at the end of the first grade, with 50 poor readers (Rispens, 1974, p. 111). The high correlations obtained in the case of poor readers indicate that these readers are still heavily dependent on the phonetic aspects of the printed material whereas good readers have moved on to a stage wherein they can utilize linguistic and contextual cues in reading. It is our opinion that learning to read goes from the (meaningful) sound via the analysis of the sound stream to the symbol, and then back, from the symbol (conceived as something that represents a part of a meaningful unit) to the spoken word.

Table 6.1

Intercorrelations between Auditory Discrimination, Analysis, and Blending and Performance on Three Different Reading Tests[a]

	Auditory discrimination	Auditory analysis	Auditory blending
Poor readers			
Reading test 1	.12	.59	.70
Reading test 2	.09	.48	.65
Reading test 3	.08	.45	.59
Good readers			
Reading test 1	−.13	.20	−.12
Reading test 2	−.05	.16	.21
Reading test 3	−.07	−.01	.03

[a] Reading test 1 consisted of a number of words; the score is the number of words read within one minute; reading test 2 was a word recognition test; and reading test 3 consisted of a number of sentences.

To summarize: For skilled readers there is not one single unit of reading. What the unit will be depends on the text, reader's intention, the task, expectations, etc. In the process of reading acquisition, however, the unit of reading instruction will center on the letter-sound correspondence. How exactly this correspondence will be presented to children depends on the reading materials used. It is our conviction that the phonetic aspect is of crucial importance.

DECODING, SPEECH, AND READING

We have discussed decoding problems in the initial stage of reading. In this section we want to present an overall description of the decoding process, focusing on the following points:

1. In decoding several pathways from the printed word to the comprehension of the text are involved. These pathways are sometimes used simultaneously.

2. During reading the graphemic input is recoded in some verbal code. This means, that speech plays an important role in the reading process.

3. The level of reading skill is an important factor in the use of the decoding technique.

4. Disorders in decoding can be interpreted as disorders in verbal processing.

Decoding. We consider here especially the reading of a text, and not the lexical decision task. We believe that during reading decoding takes place by means of several pathways. There is evidence that some elements in the text are recognized directly; mere sight gives access to their meaning. The possibility of direct access to the internal lexicon is demonstrated, for example, in word recognition experiments (Levy, 1978). However, there is also ample evidence that lexical access may sometimes involve a phonological recoding and the graphemic input is recoded into a verbal code (Coltheart, Besner, Jonasson, & Davelaar, 1979).

Recoding. Initially recoding was studied in the context of short-term memory research. The basic idea was that storage in short-term memory of visually presented material requires some recoding, because of the very limited storage capacity of short-term memory. Another claim for the recoding hypothesis comes from the limited storage capacity of short-term memory per se. Comprehension of a text consisting of more than a few words, or comprehension of an unexpected or unknown word, possibly involves recoding. The limited memory span makes it necessary to recode stimuli into a verbal code. Recoding is also useful in preventing the overloading of attention. It must be noticed that recoding and comprehension can be conceived of as taking place simultaneously. It is possible that a "multiple pathway" is functioning here. Each processing route plays a role in the system and processes information adequate to the task of this route in the whole system. The often-discussed issue of the relation between speech and reading (Conrad, 1972; Levy, 1978) does not mean converting the written text into spoken language, even though at times the process seems to have features analogous to the simple reading–speech conversion. We have to notice, however, that recoding into speech does not mean speaking aloud. It may well be that this speech recoding uses covert or fragmentary speech (Hochberg, 1976).

Articulatory Recoding. Theories of short-term memory make this process easily conceivable. We refer especially to the theories of Baddeley (1976) and Hitch (1980), and their concept of working memory. One aspect of their theories has special relevance for the decoding aspect of reading. They assume that the articulatory subsystem functions in the working memory and that this articulatory subsystem accounts for internal speech. The importance of this articulatory subsystem for reading is demonstrated by Kleiman (1975). He made clear, using an interference task, that articulatory recoding does take place. The concept of the articulatory loop is important because it enables us to conceive of how we can store in memory the recoded graphemic information. Reading does mean to speak for oneself, even though not necessarily aloud.

Level of Skill. This general picture of decoding which assumes decoding to have several forms needs one further elaboration. The question is, how beginning readers find their way through the decoding pathways? It seems reasonable to assume that the reader frequently uses explicit decoding and especially the articulatory slave system. Direct access will be used less, because of the fact that the beginning reader has yet to learn to use context cues, as well as syntactic and semantic information.

Decoding Disorders. In our view, decoding disorders have to do with the verbal recoding strategies. The perceptual deficit hypothesis appears to neglect the most relevant factors. Of course, visual perception is involved. The first processing stage always uses the graphemic features of the reading material. However, in the processing stages as such, verbal aspects are also of crucial importance. We believe the main factor in reading disorders has to do with the phonemic recoding and the use of articulatory, productive, internal speech.

CONCLUDING REMARKS

In this chapter we discussed some aspects of reading theory from an information-processing point of view. We argued that viewing reading as a form of information pick-up opens the possibility of studying this process from a broad cognitive perspective. It was concluded that the concept of parallel, interactive processing is relevant here and that the simple serial model cannot account for complicated cognitive processes like reading.

Reading implies at least an interaction (or maybe an integration) between a bottom-up, data-driven direction, and a top-down, conceptually guided pathway. The first refers to the fact that in reading a graphemic input is picked up, and an information flow takes place, until the meaning of what is read is grasped. However, this information flow interacts with, and is influenced by, the knowledge we already have.

A source of reading disorders can be located in this bottom-up decoding process. One can, however, seriously doubt the possibility of separating decoding disorders from conceptually based deficits. In this decoding process we stressed the role of phonemic awareness, the ability to handle the flow of sounds. As an extension of this, we think verbal coding is very important for reading. This verbal coding implies the use of phonemic recoding as well as some form of internal speech. The idea is that not only declarative knowledge is relevant here, but also metacognitive aspects of knowledge.

ACKNOWLEDGMENTS

In this chapter we made use of reports produced by members of our research team (the DRaF research project). The work of Bouwe Span was especially important. Dr. Kees van den Bos was of great help in the preparation of the text. Dr. Brian Hopkins assisted with the translation into English. Rietje van der Oort typed the several drafts of the manuscript.

REFERENCES

Baddeley, A. D. (1976) *The psychology of memory.* New York: Harper & Row.

Bartlett, F. C. (1977) *Remembering. A study in experimental and social psychology.* Cambridge: Cambridge University Press. (Originally published, 1932.)

Benton, A. L. (1975) Developmental dyslexia: Neurological aspects. In W. J. Friedlander (Ed.), *Advances in neurology, Vol. 7: Current review of higher nervous system dysfunctions.* New York: Raven Press.

Brewer, F. B. (1972) Is reading a letter-by-letter process? A discussion of Gough's paper. In F. Kavanagh & F. G. Mattingly (Eds.), *Language by ear and by eye.* Cambridge Mass.: MIT Press.

Broudy, H. S. (1977) Types of knowledge and the purpose of education. In R. C. Anderson, R. J. Spiro, & W. E. Montague (Eds.), *Schooling and the acquisition of knowledge.* Hillsdale, N.J.: Lawrence Erlbaum.

Brown, A. L. (1978) Knowing, when, where, and how to remember: A problem of metacognition. In R. Glaser (Ed.), *Advances in instructional psychology* (Vol. 1). Hillsdale, N.J.: Lawrence Erlbaum.

Calfee, R. C. (1977) Assessment of independent reading skills. In A. S. Reber & D. Scarborough (Eds.), *Toward a psychology of reading.* Hillsdale, N.J.: Lawrence Erlbaum.

Calfee, R. C., & Drum, P. A. (1978) Learning to read: Theory, research and practice. *Curriculum Inquiry, 8,* 183–249.

Carr, T. N. (1981) Building theories of reading ability: On the relation between individual differences in cognitive skills and reading comprehension. *Cognition, 9,* 73–114.

Carroll, J. B. (1979) How shall we study individual differences in cognitive abilities? In R. J. Sternberg & D. B. Detterman (Eds.), *Human intelligence: Perspectives on its theory and measurement.* Norwood, N.J.: Ablex.

Claxton, G. (1980) Cognitive psychology: A suitable case for what sort of treatment? In G. Claxton (Ed.), *Cognitive psychology: New directions.* London: Routledge & Kegan Paul.

Clifford, G. J. (1973) A history of the impact of research on teaching. In R. W. Travers (Ed.), *Second handbook of research on teaching.* Chicago: Rand McNally.

Cohen, S. A. (1971) Dyspedagogy as a cause of reading retardation. In B. Bateman (Ed.), *Learning disorders, Vol. 14: Reading.* Seattle: Special Child Publications.

Coltheart, M., Bener, D., Jonasson, J. T., & Davelaar, E. (1979) Phonological encoding in the lexical decision task. *Quarterly Journal of Experimental Psychology, 31,* 489–507.

Conrad, R. (1972) Speech and reading. In F. Kavanagh & I. G. Mattingly (Eds.), *Language by ear and by eye.* Cambridge, Mass.: MIT Press.

Craik, F. I. M., & Lockhart, R. S. (1972) Levels of processing: A framework for memory research. *Journal of Verbal Learning and Verbal Behavior, 11,* 671–684.

Doehring, D. G. (1978) The tangled web of behavioral research on developmental dyslexia. In A. Benton & D. Pearl (Eds.), *Dyslexia: An appraisal of current knowledge.* New York: Oxford University Press.

Flavell, J. H. (1976) Metacognitive aspects of problem solving. In L. Resnick (Ed.), *The nature of intelligence.* Hillsdale, N.J.: Lawrence Erlbaum.

Gibson, E. J., & Levin, H. (1975) *The psychology of reading.* Cambridge Mass.: MIT Press.

Glaser, R. (1978) Introduction: Toward a psychology of instruction. In R. Glaser (Ed.), *Advances in instructional psychology* (Vol. 1). Hillsdale, N.J.: Lawrence Erlbaum.

Glaser, R., Pellegrino, J. W., & Lesgold, A. M. (1978) Some directions for a cognitive psychology of instruction. In A. M. Lesgold, J. W. Pellegrino, S. D. Fokkema, & R. Glaser (Eds.), *Cognitive psychology and instruction.* New York: Plenum Press.

Gleitman, L. R. & Rozin, P. (1977) The structure and acquisition of reading. In A. S. Reber & D. L. Scarborough (Eds.), *Toward a psychology of reading.* Hillsdale, N.J.: Lawrence Erlbaum.

Golinkoff, R. M., & Rosinski, R. R. (1976) Decoding, semantic processing and reading comprehension skill. *Child Development, 47,* 252–258.

Goodman, K. S. (1968) The psycholinguistic nature of the reading process. In K. S. Goodman (Ed.), *The psycholinguistic nature of the reading process.* Detroit: Wayne State University Press.

Goodman, K. S. (1973) Analysis of oral reading miscues: Applied psycholinguistics. In F. Smith (Ed.), *Psycholinguistics and reading.* New York: Holt, Rinehart & Winston.

Gough, P. B. (1972) One second of reading. In J. F. Kavanagh & I. G. Mattingly (Eds.), *Language by ear and by eye.* Cambridge, Mass.: MIT Press.

Hitch, G. J. (1980) Developing the concept of working memory. In G. Claxton (Ed.), *Cognitive psychology: New directions.* London: Routledge & Kegan Paul.

Hochberg, J. (1976) Toward a speech-plan eye-movement model of reading. In R. A. Monty & J. W. Sanders (Eds.), *Eye movements and psychological processes.* Hillsdale, N.J.: Lawrence Erlbaum.

Juel, C. (1980) Comparison of word identification strategies with varying context, word type, and reader skill. *Reading Research Quarterly, 15,* 358–377.

Kleiman, G. (1975) Speech recoding in reading. *Journal of Verbal Learning and Verbal Behavior, 14,* 323–339.

LaBerge, D., & Samuels, S. J. (1974) Toward a theory of automatic information processing in reading. *Cognitive Psychology, 6,* 293–323.

Levy, B. A. (1978) Speech processes during reading. In A. M. Lesgold, J. W. Pellegrino, S. D. Fokkema, & R. Glaser (Eds.), *Cognitive psychology and instruction.* New York: Plenum Press.

Liberman, A. M., Cooper, F. S., Shankweiler, D. P., & Studdert-Kennedy, M. (1967) Perception of the speech code. *Psychological Review, 74,* 431–461.

Liberman, I. Y., Shankweiler, D., Liberman, A. M., Fowler, C. A., & Fischer, F. W.

(1977) Phonetic segmentation and recoding in the beginning reader. In A. S. Reber & D. L. Scarborough (Eds.), *Toward a psychology of reading*. Hillsdale, N.J.: Lawrence Erlbaum.

Mackworth, J. F. (1972) Some models of the reading process: Learners and skilled readers. *Reading Research Quarterly, 7,* 701–733.

Marshall, N., & Glock, M. D. (1978) Comprehension of connected discourse: A study into the relationships between the structure of text and information recalled. *Reading Research Quarterly, 14*(1), 10–57.

Mattingly, I. M. (1972) Reading, the linguistic process, and linguistic awareness. In J. F. Kavanagh & I. M. Mattingly (Eds.), *Language by ear and by eye*. Cambridge, Mass.: MIT Press.

Morgan, W. P. (1896) A case of congenital wordblindness. *The British Medical Journal, 11,* 378.

Neisser, U. (1976) *Cognition and reality*. San Francisco: W. H. Freeman.

Norman, D. A. (1979) Perception, memory, and mental processes. In L. G. Nilsson (Ed.), *Perspectives on memory research*. Hillsdale, N.J.: Lawrence Erlbaum.

Olson, D. R. (1977) The language of instruction: On the literate bias of schooling. In R. C. Anderson, R. J. Spiro, & W. E. Montagnue (Eds.), *Schooling and the acquisition of knowledge*. Hillsdale, N.J.: Lawrence Erlbaum.

Pellegrino, J. W., & Glaser, R. (1979) Cognitive correlates and components in the analysis of individual differences. In R. J. Sternberg & D. K. Detterman (Eds.), *Human intelligence: Perspectives on its theory and measurement*. Norwood, N.J.: Ablex.

Perfetti, C. A. (1980) Verbal coding efficiency, conceptually guided reading and reading failure. *Bulletin of the Orton Society, 30,* 197–226.

Perfetti, C. A., Lesgold, A. M. (1980) Coding and comprehension in skilled reading and implications for reading instruction. In L. B. Resnick (Ed.), *Theory and practice in early reading*. Hillsdale, N.J.: Lawrence Erlbaum.

Resnick, L. B. (1976) Task analysis in instructional design: Some cases from mathematics. In D. Klahr (Ed.), *Cognition and instruction*. Hillsdale, N.J.: Lawrence Erlbaum, 51–80.

Resnick, L. B., & Beck, I. L. (1976) Designing instruction in reading: Interaction of theory and practice. In J. T. Guthrie (Ed.), *Aspects of reading acquisition*. Baltimore: Johns Hopkins University Press.

Rispens, J. (1974) *Auditieve aspekten van leesmoeilijkheden*. Utrecht: Elinkwijk.

Rozin, P., & Gleitman, D. R. (1977) The reading process and the acquisition of the alphabetic principle. In A. S. Reber & D. L. Scarborough (Eds.), *Toward a psychology of reading*. Hillsdale, N.J.: Lawrence Erlbaum.

Rumelhart, D. E. (1977) Toward an interactive mode of reading. In S. Dornic (Ed.), *Attention and performance* (Vol. 6). Hillsdale, N.J.: Lawrence Erlbaum.

Rumelhart, D. E., & Ortony, A. (1977) The representation of knowledge in memory. In R. C. Anderson, R. J. Spiro, & W. E. Montague (Eds.), *Schooling and the acquisition of knowledge*. Hillsdale, N.J.: Lawrence Erlbaum.

Rutter, M. (1978) Prevalence and types of dyslexia. In A. L. Benton & D. Pearl (Eds.), *Dyslexia: An appraisal of current knowledge*. New York: Oxford University Press.

Rutter, M., & Yule, W. (1973) Specific reading retardation. In L. Mann & D. Sabatino (Eds.), *The first review of special education*. Philadelphia: Button Wood F.

Samuels, S. J., & Pearson, P. D. (1980) Using research in applied settings. *Reading Research Quarterly, 15,* 317–323.

Schlee, J. (1976) *Legasthenie forschung am Ende?* Munich: Luchterhand.

Shankweiler, D., & Liberman, I. Y. (1976) Exploring the relationship between reading and speech. In R. M. Knights & D. J. Bakker (Eds.), *The neuropsychology of learning disorders: Theoretical approaches*. Baltimore: University Park Press.

Shaw, R., & Bransford, J. (1977) Introduction: Psychological approaches to the problem of knowledge. In R. Shaw & J. Bransford (Eds.), *Perceiving, acting and knowing: Toward and ecological psychology*. Hillsdale, N.J.: Lawrence Erlbaum.

Sternberg, R. J. (1977) *Intelligence, information processing, and analogical reasoning: The componential analysis of human abilities*. Hillsdale, N.J.: Lawrence Erlbaum.

Sternberg, R. J., & Detterman, D. K. (Eds.) (1979) *Human intelligence: Perspectives on its theory and measurement*. Norwood, N.J.: Ablex.

Torgeson, J. K. (1979) What shall we do with psychological processes? *Journal of Learning Disabilities, 12*(8), 16–23.

Vellutino, F. R. (1979) *Dyslexia: Theory and research*. Cambridge, Mass.: MIT Press.

Vernon, M. D. (1977) Varieties of deficiency in the reading processes. *Harvard Educational Review, 47*, 396–410.

Zigmond, N. (1978) Remediation of dyslexia. In A. Benton & D. Pearl (Eds.), *Dyslexia: An appraisal of current knowledge*. New York: Oxford University Press.

Chapter Seven

The Role of Selective Attention in Reading Disability

MARCEL KINSBOURNE

THE SELECTIVE ASPECTS OF ATTENTION

The term attention means several different things, and can be applied to several distinct mental operations implicated in children's learning. One connotation is attention as concentration: maintaining attention on the same issue over time. Deficient concentration is central to hyperactivity, and is sometimes referred to as the attention deficit disorder (ADD). In this chapter we will, however, focus on attention as selection—the ability to test for and pick out particular objects or attributes from the mass of simultaneously impinging percepts. We will argue, as have others (Gibson, 1969) that it is in the domain of selective attention that the bulk of perceptual development in childhood occurs; and that the impediments to flexible selective attending experienced by young children can usefully be hypothesized to apply also to many older children who are learning disabled—that is, selectively handicapped in their ability to retain information and acquire skills in a particular academic field. The principles that obtain for perceptual development will be found also to apply to the development of language,

199

and to have heuristic value for a better understanding of those subtypes of learning disability that are linguistically rather than perceptually based.

The essence of selective attention is preparation. Whereas the unprepared observer falls automatically under control of the most salient event that happens, the prepared observer can ignore events that, although salient, are outside the class of his interest. He has adopted a categorical mental set. Mental set is based on selective activation of corresponding brain areas. Failure of selective brain activation is a potentially useful construct for inquiry into learning disability.

READING DISABILITY AS
COGNITIVE IMMATURITY

When for constitutional reasons some children find it harder to learn to read than would be expected at their age and in view of their generally normal intelligence, what exactly about learning to read do they find so disproportionately difficult? At the normative achievement level, one can often specify a subject area, or even the subset of operations within an area, that a particular child seems persistently to fail to understand or remember. But this only pushes the question back one step, rather than answering it. What set of mental operations is unavailable to this child, although available to others of that age and general developmental status? The neuropsychologist's answer takes the form of suggesting a selective deficit or syndrome, which compromises the development of certain mental operations, leaving others intact. The educator, thinking in terms of deficient readiness skills, picks out as best he can the ones that are deficient from the total subset. If a child were suffering simultaneously from all the syndromes of development differentiated by the neuropsychologist, or from lack of readiness skills in all areas of learning, then that child would be regarded as mentally retarded. The neuropsychological and educational approaches are different perspectives on the same issue, which is an issue in developmental psychology. Which particular mental operation has failed to mature to the expected extent (and, by its unavailability, impaired the child's ability to benefit from conventional education within the pertinent subjects)? That the core issue is one of cognitive development is easy to see. The neuropsychologist's inferences of deficiencies in particular mental operations are based on scores on a set of tests that purport to tap such operations. Similarly, the educator's estimate of readiness derives from test scores on instruments that purport to measure the efficiency with which those same mental operations can be employed. Yet, in both cases, the choice of test, of items within the test, and of manner of scoring is largely an arbitrary matter legislated by the test designer without validity check. Whereas the test results themselves may be objectively collected, the way the tests are labeled— that is, the mental operations to which they are supposed to refer—is usually arbitrarily determined by the test's inventor. In order to gain validity, such claims should make contact with what is known about how mental skills develop in the normal individual. Presumably any selective deficit that compromises the ability to learn to read for cognitive (rather than emotional) reasons must involve the nonavailability of one or more task-relevant mental operations—in other words, some delay, at least, or, at worst, arrest, of one or more developmental sequences. If educators and neuropsychologists take issue with each other, it is generally that the neuropsychologist, operating from the vantage point of the highly selective acquired deficits in mature individuals, postulates sharply delineated selective deficits. The neuropsychologist's theorizing lends itself to monothetic modeling. The educator, confronted by the continuous variation in children's abilities attributable to genetic diversity and its environmental overlay, inclines to a polythetic viewpoint. In criterion-referenced tests, the educator looks not for sharply selective deficits in particular, but more generally for those factors which most limit the child's progress at any time (keeping in mind that were one such factor corrected, other factors would now limit performance). We need not legislate between these two points of view (and cannot, as the evidence is not at hand). Instead, we will discuss the form that the solution is likely to take ultimately, regardless of whether it fits into a sharply selective or more continuously variable mold.

We arrive at our position by simple logic; there are some things that normal reading calls for that an immature child can do and others that the child cannot do. The child can see clearly. The child's visual acuity is quite equal to the task of discriminating writing and print. Similarly, auditory acuity is sufficiently developed to permit the child to distinguish accurately even the most confusable speech sounds, and well before grade school entry the child can also articulate most of them correctly and distinctively. Many of the ingredients that coordinate into a successful approach to the task of learning to read are available not merely just before the age at which children are conventionally judged ready to learn to read, that is, the age of entering into grade school, but years earlier or even soon after birth. It is reasonable to suppose that deficiency in such skills is less likely to be at the root of most selective reading problems than is deficiency in skills that even in the normal course of events take some years to develop, or are only precariously and intermittently available even to normal children when they first attempt to learn to read. By what further logic can we converge on the general nature of these "at risk" mental operations?

We will first concentrate on those aspects of perceptual development which, given adequate general verbal function, are necessary to facilitate the decoding of the written letter, word, and paragraph. Which particular ones are most taxed depends upon the method of reading instruction. But, clearly, we must include the ability to make certain visual discriminations, remember what has been discriminated, and to make certain auditory discriminations and, again, to remember them. With respect to each modality we will ask ourselves: What is it that develops in normal perceptual development? What is it that the older child can do which the younger child finds difficult and the infant insuperable, within each modality, and with respect to those of its stimulus attributes that are pertinent to one of the forms of reading instruction?

PERCEPTUAL DEVELOPMENT AND LEARNING TO READ

When children approach the age at which reading instruction begins, they are by no means novices at the task of learning. They have learned the essentials of the relevant aspects of the structure of the physical world, and they have also learned the great bulk of at least one arbitrary conventional communication system—their first language. This learning begins in the second year of life at an age well before that at which humans are credited with the ability to concentrate and apply themselves specifically and reliably to a given complex task. Nor does the learning process seem effortful. Rather, children "pick up" language, apparently as they pick up invariances in their physical environment. Yet all it takes is a modality change from audible to visible speech, and a significant, protracted, and often extremely strenuous effort is required to master, in that modality, a language that they already know. To extract information from the written word calls for mental skills that are different and become available later in maturation than the operations that derive meaning from the spoken word. Why this difference?

The written and spoken word differ from each other in many ways, and we will suppose that these differences are necessary (i.e., that our written language approximates the most efficient conceivable way of presenting language visually to a developing child). We will not attempt to redesign writing and print in such a way that it can be learned as "naturally" as is spoken language, because we do not know how to do that. We can, however, point out some mental operations called for by the written language which are less essential to the task of comprehending the spoken word. These are the analytic operations involved in selective attending.

Visual Attention

Soon after birth infants can see detail as well as older children. They can differentiate between colors, and discriminate fine detail and difference in depth and focus to the extent called for by the display. They are in a position to see whatever it is that adults can see. But there is reason to suppose that what they see, is not, in fact, the same because they do not look at things the way that adults do.

Almost all visual environments in the natural world are overwhelmingly populated with detail. Each glance confronts a wealth of information, any element of which could serve as a basis for decision making and the control of behavior. Were all such elements, or many of them, to take control of behavior at the same time, the organism would be neutralized into conflict-ridden immobility. Instead, there is provision for selective attention to specified objects or attributes in the environment and the ability to shift attention from element to element as necessary and at will. When this ability is maximally developed, one can scan a vast field, in perceptual readiness for unexpected events anywhere in it. Or one can focus selectively on minutiae, oblivious of the vast amount of excluded information which impinges on the retina and, though conducted centrally, has no influence on behavior. Gibson (1969) has pointed out that focus on the informative portions of a display is the essence of perceptual learning. "The criterion of perceptual learning is thus an increase in specificity. What is learned can be described as detection of properties, patterns, and distinctive features [p. 77]."

This ability to attend selectively is in the first instance given by the distinction between focal and peripheral attention. Whereas the visual field is wide (210°), that central part of it at which resolving power is greatest, the fovea, subtends only a small angle (2°). Only around the fixation point can people discern significant detail. By shifting fixation they can control the amount and nature of the detail that they discern and to which they attend. However, even within the arena of central or macular vision, one can select to a high degree of exclusiveness. One can prearrange to be alert for some minor detail, a particular configuration or relation between configurations, and permit one's gaze to stray over a wide field undistracted by other detail, remaining open to the envisaged attributes' embodiment, should it appear. This expert selective vision is used to different but great effect by the detective, the inspector of commercial products, the talent scout, and the pathfinder in a wilderness.

This ability to attend selectively is not available to young children. When young children survey a scene they cannot do so in such methodical fashion, and when they search out detail what they notice depends on what is there. Children's "visual search" strategies are ill developed. They search incompletely, redundantly, and unsystematically (Day, 1975). When inspecting a display they often omit to look at parts of it (even though those parts might be important), and, instead, look over and over at what they have already seen although nothing further can be gained by so doing. Also, they may, on successive viewings of the same scene or display, approach it by different patterns of head orientation and gaze (they then notice different things in different order on different occasions and so cannot become progressively familiar with what they are looking at). The best example of this type of difficulty comes from Vurpillot's (1968) study of normal preschool children's ability to judge drawings as same or different. She had children look at sketches of houses and asked them whether the two houses were the same or different. She found many instances of errors in both directions and was able to relate the nature of the error to the pattern of the children's eye movements as they scanned the display (which she had recorded, experimentally). Where children judged two dissimilar houses the "same," they had happened to look at only those parts of the houses which were indeed the same. When children judged two identical houses dissimilar, they had looked at one part of one house and a different part of the other. Note that these are simple pictures. The owner of mature visual attention cannot imagine such irregularities of attention as he looks at them.

If the display at which children look contains stimuli high on the perceptual hierarchy, the children will fail to notice details that they otherwise would be well able to discriminate. Children's ability to detect nonsalient attributes is at the mercy of the other content of the display at which they are looking. It can be enhanced by environmental reorganization, for instance, by the teacher.

This constraint on immature perception explains how some children can fail to notice what is obvious to the instructor. One cannot assume that the child is noticing what one oneself is noticing. Given that one can only tell approximately what a person is looking at (as opposed to what he is touching) it is clear that the teacher will need to verify that the child is attending to the relevant attribute by naming it, pointing to it, or having the child point or even touch it.

The perceptual hierarchy is particularly controlling in the case of reversals. Children labeled dyslexic are customarily supposed to show striking tendencies to reverse mirror image letters, notably those which when reversed assumed new meanings, such as lowercase b and d and p and q, but also any other letter or digit that is not symmetrical around its vertical axis (Orton, 1937). Workers in child development and those who attempt to teach the preschool child to read are equally aware that the reversal tendency is normal in the developing child, and is greater the younger the child (Schonell, 1948). So, in the case of dyslexic reversals, we have not a "disease manifestation" which is diagnostic of this problem, but undue persistence over time of what in a younger child would be completely normal (that is, a soft neuropsychological sign). The reversal tendency is due to the fact that orientation differences of a mirror image kind are relatively low in the perceptual hierarchy. The children will notice a form and whether its alignment is along a vertical or horizontal axis, and yet at times invert and frequently reverse the form. Note, however, that such reversals tend not to be systematic. A child will not at all times write a particular letter backward. Instead, if one takes enough samples, one will find that each graphic symbol that is subject to reversal is reversed about half the time. The mirror image aspect of the letter's or digit's orientation is being left to chance. The child just has not noticed or does not remember which way round it was or should be. Whether the child does pay attention to orientation or not depends on what else he is doing. Liberman, Shankweiler, Orlando, Harris, and Bell (1971) found more reversals for letters embedded in words than letters shown in isolation, and different patterns of reversal depending on whether the words were meaningful or meaningless. Where other matters constrain attention, orientation may remain unattended. But one can show that the child is quite capable of handling orientation by either removing or holding constant those other attributes of the letters which are higher than the mirror image attribute in the perceptual hierarchy. This can be done by zeroing in gradually on the feature under study. First, the child is oriented toward the letter, which is presented in vertical axis. Then the bulge is shown to be at the top or at the bottom of the vertical axis, and only then when the child is well switched into orientation as a relevant dimension is it pointed out that the bulge looks to one side or to the other. Care is taken not to complicate the matter by using letter names or the names of the directions right and left. So by working through an aspect of the shape that ranks higher in the hierarchy than the mirror image distinction—namely, its form and its orientation in lateral and vertical aspects—one enables children to detach their attention from each of these in turn and permit their attention to range down to that lower but necessary rung on the hierarchical ladder. Once attention is restored into the appropriate attribute, the children are found to be fully equipped to perform the discrimination in question. Their previously observed limitation was not absolute, but depended on the context within which they were constrained to perform. As we have seen, a simple manipulation of that context removes the barrier to attention (and therefore to learning).

Auditory Attention

The influx of potentially meaningful auditory information is typically much less voluminous than visual information flow. The important acts of selection occur, not so much between signals, or with respect to different attributes of a given signal, but with respect to the phonetic components of the signal—morphemes, phonemes. Here is a glaring discrepancy between the young child's good ability to discriminate different speech sounds (not only at the level of words, but also down to individual speech sounds), and the child's analytic ability to establish, in recognition and imaginal representation, the sequence of speech sounds into which the word sound may be segmented. This analytic skill is, like analytic skills in general, slow to develop, and becomes spontaneously available at around the sixth or seventh year of life. Yet it is this analytic skill—of attending one at a time to the speech sounds embedded in word sounds—that is called for by word attack by the phonics method. If we need to acquaint a child with phonemic analysis, then a logical approach would parallel the one recommended with respect to vision. Start with easily discriminable speech sounds (differing in several critical features) and segments of two only, and, having focused the child's attention on the mental operation called for, gradually complicate the task to the point necessary for the phonics process. Indeed, this type of teaching might be desirable at whatever age reading is taught. Morais, Cary, Alegria, and Bertelson (in press) have shown that adult illiterates cannot analyze speech sounds. The reading instruction helps realize the potential to do so.

SELECTIVE ATTENTION AT THE
LINGUISTIC LEVEL

When young children attend to sentences, they begin by attending to relatively gross attributes of word order, making such distinctions as noun preceding verb versus noun following verb. Where the meaning of the sentence is ambiguous, the children, if they can, disambiguate it on a perceptual basis. Each noun or verb has a perceptual referent, and the sentence is interpreted in line with the child's experience of how these referents interact. Years have to pass before sentences that violate perceptual expectancies are correctly decoded. It takes substantial mental development for children to be able to use purely linguistic attributes, such as word order, and functors to override the salient percepts evoked by some of the words in isolation (Lempert & Kinsbourne, 1981).

A substantial subset of children with reading disability have difficulty in comprehension even for sentences formed out of words which they demonstrably understand in isolation. At least some of these children find it about as difficult to understand such sentences when they hear them as when they see them in print. It may be that their attention is constrained by salient key words, and they are therefore precluded from using the more subtle grammatical aspects of the sentence as a foundation for understanding.

In the language domain, more than in the perceptual modes, attention as preparation is an issue. Whereas in the natural world appearances are by and large what they appear to be, when signaling systems are involved the signals always convey double messages—about their physical characteristics, and about their referential value. Both with spoken and with written speech, one has to attend selectively to the meaning of the message, rather than to the message as physical pattern. Insofar as the physical characteristics of the message may, particularly for the young child, be salient, an act of selective attention is called for—the adoption of a verbal (semantic) set.

Like any act of selective attention, maintaining a categorical mental set might involve the selective activation of particular brain loci, and the inhibition of potentially competing neural systems. If the mechanism of this selective activation is ill developed, or fluctuatingly effective, then the observer's attention will be constantly or periodically preempted by the surface characteristics of the signal, and meaning is not extracted. This could be the mechanism of the effect noted by Moore, Kagan, Sahl, and Grant (1982). They found among severely dyslexic teenagers, a subgroup of children who showed increased latency in judging spoken sentences "true or false." It was as if, on occasional trials, these children wandered from verbal mental set, and had to retrieve it before they could then correctly respond.

A clinical test that has proven effective in distinguishing dyslexics from others is the rapid automatic naming test (Denckla & Rudel, 1976; Wolf, 1981). Subjects are asked to name items from a familiar set (letters, digits, colors, objects) recurring randomly within an extended series. The dyslexic group shows hesitancy in this naming task (increasing over time) although it knows the names well. This procedure may be sensitive to the variable of maintaining verbal mental set (that is, attending selectively to specific names rather than other qualities of referents).

It is perhaps no accident that naming, which is the first speech skill to develop, is the most pervasively impaired performance after damage anywhere in the language area (or when points in the language areas are stimulated—Ojemann & Whitaker, 1978). The ability to specify precisely, in words, appears to call for a higher level of integrity of the language area than other functions that unroll more automatically (i.e., with little need for inhibiting competing percepts and mental sets).

AT WHAT AGE IS A CHILD READY TO LEARN TO READ?

If a dyslexic schoolchild is, in some aspect of reading readiness, at the level of a prereading preschooler, then we should try to specify at what age normal preschoolers can first be considered ready to learn reading. The simple answer—at school entry—will not do. School entry age varies from 5 to 7 in different countries, without corresponding variation in the mental skills of the children. Further, there is reason to believe that preschoolers could in fact be taught to read. Early reading programs using conventional methods have been shown to be effective at least from age 4 onward.

In a recent sample that Martha Light and I studied an individually administered "language experience" reading program was successful for most of a group of relatively underprivileged 4–5-year-olds though it involved only 20 min per weekday. The children's readiness skills were measured before and after the experience. Not only were the children's readiness scores comparable to that of untaught matched controls before, but they remained so after. So the teaching did not enhance readiness skills. It follows that many normal 4-year-olds are quite ready for reading instruction. Why, then, do even normal 6-year-olds labor at reading, and some fail?

Given that the reading program was of a customary type, the simplest explanation for the success of the preschoolers is that, in fact, 4-year-old readiness is sufficient for the cognitive operations drawn upon by the beginning reading instruction. What was different about the early reading program was the individualization. This released the young children from the need to maintain concentration in a formal group situation, and provided them with an easily accessible adult to "mediate" between their cognitive potential and its realization in performance (Feuerstein, Rand, & Hoffman, 1979). As we have discussed, young children are not so much limited in the discriminations they can make (and remember) as in the range of circumstances under which they can make them spontaneously. This "production deficit" (Flavell, 1977) of normal young children can be overcome by informed rearrangements of the situation by an instructor. We suspect that many children who have fallen behind in grade school reading did so for want of "mediation" early on, and, once having fallen significantly behind, fail to understand what is being taught and consequently suspend any attempt to do so. Some or even many "dyslexias" may be of this kind. And yet it would be futile to attempt to include such cases in a neuropsychological or "unreadiness" classification, as they would not show the corresponding deficits. Rather than undertake wholesale test battery studies of children who fail to reach some criterial level of reading achievement, one should first sort out those who are in fact teachable by conventional methods, *administered individually*. Only those who are not, are candidates for taxonomy and further study.

A dyslexic subtype, whether arrived at by neuropsychological case study, or by some empirical means, does not resolve the question, Why cannot the children learn? It merely circumscribes the area of their difficulty. A learning problem can only be elucidated by studying how the children learn. This has not been done for any subtype.

Regardless of the nature of the syndrome, or area of difficulty, the diagnostic learning testing could take a similar form. This amounts to determining what kind and degree of external support it takes to enable the child to achieve *specificity* within the area of difficulty (be it breaking a word up into constituent speech sounds, or responding differentially to mirror image exemplars). Only when the typology is refined to this degree of detail can it make contact with the practical need for an individualized curriculum. So the developmentally oriented testing amounts to a curriculum in microcosm. Anything short of that restricts the advice given to the teacher after assessment to such broad generalities that insofar as it is accurate it is tritely obvious.

DO DYSLEXICS READ DIFFERENTLY FROM OTHER IMPAIRED READERS?

The diagnosis of dyslexia is made on exclusionary grounds (no mental retardation, no sociocultural deprivation, no thought disorder, no undermotivation in the classroom), and this is correctly regarded as a weakness of the concept (Rutter, 1978; Satz & Morris, 1980). Vigorous attempts have been made to find neurological, prognostic, or behavioral group differences between children whose reading failure meets exclusionary criteria for dyslexia, and equally poor readers whose reading failure is related to one or more of the factors, presence of which invalidates the diagnosis. The best available information is that no such differences could be found (Taylor, Satz, & Friel, 1979). We should reflect, however, that no such differences are necessarily to be expected. Reading failure would result if one or more of the mental operations necessary to the process of learning to read in the classroom fails to be deployed. Failure to deploy a mental operation may occur because that mental operation failed to develop normally although other mental operations did. That would be consistent with the dyslexia concept. Alternatively, it may have failed to develop as a component of a general failure of mental development. Such reading failure would be in a context of mental retardation, but in itself it might be quite similar, in terms of error pattern and other psychoeducational variables, to the reading failure of dyslexics. But even if a child has competence in a mental operation, he might not deploy that competence in performance—because of undermotivation, fear of failure, anxiety, distractability, and so forth. In such cases, the appropriate mental set is not adopted, and therefore the skill remains latent and unused. The performance might be quite similar to that which obtains when deployment is not even a possibility, because the neural substrate for this form of processing has not matured.

This is not to imply that all causes of reading failure would be expected functionally to converge upon the same performance pattern. Several different mental operations must be rate-limiting in learning to read, and the various causes for nondeployment of mental operations could differentially involve one of another. So one would expect there to be subtypes of selective reading failure (dyslexia). One would, however, be quite ready to observe similar subtypes among other reading failure groups, in which the same pattern of cognitive deficit or non-use occurs for other reasons.

TYPOLOGY OF READING DISORDERS

If dyslexia is not a unitary well-defined syndrome, what is it? Two answers are conceivable. One is that it represents the arbitrary dichotomizing of one or more continuous variables. That is, the set of readiness functions that enable beginning reading vary continuously (perhaps on account of genetic diversity). When a given child fails to meet the criteria for one or a combination of such variables, that child encounters difficulty in the regular classroom and, falling behind academically, is identified as dyslexic. Thus, encompassing all these children within normal variation implies that each case is to some extent unique. An alternative view is that subtypes of dyslexia exist; clusters of children who share a cognitive "family resemblance," just as do different patients classified within a particular neuropsychological category. Note that selecting patients as demonstration cases cannot resolve these alternative (continuity versus discontinuity) positions. Kinsbourne and Warrington (1963) first demonstrated two quite distinct subtypes of dyslexia—the "language" and the "sequential" deficit types (see Pirozzolo & Hansch, this volume). They deliberately chose extreme cases of delayed readers to highlight the differences, and thus to provide some guidelines for choosing appropriate behavioral measures for the group of delayed readers as a whole. It was left to further research to determine whether most children can be objectively classified into these two, or some larger set of discrete categories, or whether the sampled cases represent extremes along certain relevant continuously variable behavioral dimensions. To address that issue, multivariate approaches are suitable, with two major provisos: (a) that they use measures that have neuropsychological or developmental psychological validity (i.e., tap known sequences of behavioral development) rather than represent someone's arbitrary choice of procedures that seem to have something to do with the underpinnings of reading; and (b) that the tasks be criterion-referenced. Reading, like any coordinated task, requires a sufficient skill in each of its components. Extreme skill in any one component cannot raise the general reading level. For example, if saccadic eye movements are pathologically slow, the resulting inertia in fixation shift must limit fluency of reading across a page. But beyond a sufficient speed, further increase in saccadic rate would be useless. Now the interpretation of the display viewed at each fixation becomes performance limiting, and the potential for rapid shift to the next locus remains unrealized, and without influence on performance. So an empirical analysis must focus on the weakest (performance-limiting) mental operation. Otherwise, one will find the same cognitive clusters as those which can be isolated among normal and superior readers as well, indicating the meaningless outcome of this form of dyslexia analysis. Existing multivariate approaches fail for reasons stated here; a proper multivariate analysis has not been done, and cannot be, until (*a*) the relevant *development sequences* have been isolated; (*b*) valid measures of the child's status with respect to each have been developed; and (*c*) criteria of performance on each sequence sufficient for each level of reading instruction have been established. Pending such developments, the clinical approach (Kinsbourne & Warrington, 1963; Boder, 1973; Mattis, French, & Rapin, 1975; Pirozzolo, 1978) remains the only useful one, even if it leaves the status of some or many retarded readers uncertain.

The task of developing proper measures is forbidding unless informed by an understanding of mental development. If developmental principles are applied to the neuropsychological leads that we have, the matter might become manageable. For each presumptive subtype, a relevant developmental sequence can be defined, using the principles mentioned earlier. That is, it is necessary to begin with the developmentally simplest case, the most clear-cut distinction in the least distracting context. Then the task is progressively complicated, not by arbitrarily throwing in extraneous variables (e.g., hard-to-comprehend instructions, heavier short-term memory load, and the use of schematic abstractions—cf. Benton, 1959), but by using subtle distinctions embedded in distracting (i.e., perceptually more salient) contexts. For instance, were one to study ability to remember orientation, one would begin with the most clear-cut case—vertical versus horizontal—in the absence of distractors, and end with the most complex case that has ecological validity for reading—the mirror image distinction in the context of a hard-to-read or hard-to-spell word. Further, one would test not merely for success versus failure, but for the presence of automatic fluency in the task, as indexed by minimal decision latency—given that it represents a component process in reading, facility in which is useful only to the extent that it approximates the fluency of an automatized skill.

The alternative approach to subtyping is error analysis, best exemplified by Boder's (1973) useful dichotomy of dysphonetic versus dyseidetic readers. It may well be true that some children are limited by inability to analyze word sounds into speech sounds, and others by inability to retain letter patterns as visual forms. But even patterns have a history. They represent the resultant of the child's initial difficulty and the attempts made to correct it. Take dyseidetic reading as a case in point.

Dyseidetic children read laboriously, as if seeing each word for the first time. They practice word attack to an extreme degree, sound out, often correctly, speech sound by speech sound, but do not transcend this accomplishment by the attainment of any fluency.

The question is what is cause and what is effect. Do these children sound out because they cannot visualize, or can they not visualize because they keep sounding out? One cause of slavish word attack is overinstruction in a phonetic approach to reading, such as Orton–Gillingham. This results in the "phonic cripple" who behaves precisely as if dyseidetic, but does so because of ill-advised instruction, regardless of what the basic defect is.

This instance is instructive with respect to the division of attention. The children selectively attend to the task of phonemic analysis. Insufficient attention is left over for a visual overview of the completed grapheme–phoneme correspondence. Failing that review, each attempt at reading the word is unaided by any recollection of the outcome of the problem-solving activity that went into its deciphering on previous occasions; and nothing is learned.

In concluding overview, issues of attention are *integral* to beginning reading skill—not only attention over time, the concentration that is a precondition to the mastery of any complex skill for which we are not biologically predisposed, but also the selective attention that analyzes stimuli and organizes occupied space. An element of analysis is essential not only to the verbal, but also the visual-spatial aspects of reading and writing, and analysis can only occur if attention selects some attribute to the temporary exclusion of all others while retaining the rest in retrievable form in memory. In this way the specific imaginative alignments can be made to compare and contrast, and thus extract and convey the specifics of the message. As the process is practiced, it becomes fluent, and the component operations occur quickly in coordination and unpunctuated by conscious monitoring. But the precision of their articulation remains a testimonial to the finesse of selective attention that contributed to their working.

REFERENCES

Benton, A. L. (1959) *Right–left discrimination and finger localization.* New York: Harper & Row.

Boder, E. (1973) Developmental dyslexia: A diagnostic approach based on three atypical reading–spelling patterns. *Developmental Medicine of Child Neurology, 15,* 663–687.

Day, M. C. (1975) Developmental trends in visual scanning. *Advances in Child Development and Behavior, 10,* 153–193.

Denckla, M. B., & Rudel, R. (1976) Rapid 'automatized' naming (R.A.N.): Dyslexia differentiated from other learning disabilities. *Neuropsychologia, 14,* 471–479.

Feuerstein, R., Rand, Y., & Hoffman, M. B. (1979) *The dynamic assessment of retarded performers.* Baltimore: University Park Press.

Flavell, J. H. (1977) *Cognitive development.* Englewood Cliffs, N.J.: Prentice-Hall.

Gibson, E. J. (1969) *Principles of perceptual learning and development.* New York: Appleton.

Kinsbourne, M., & Warrington, E. K. (1963) Developmental factors in reading and writing backwardness. *British Journal of Psycholoqy, 54,* 145–156.

Lempert, H., & Kinsbourne, M. (1981) Perceptual constraints on the acquisition and use of language by young children. In K. Nelson (Ed.), *Children's language* (Vol. 3). New York: Gardner Press.

Liberman, I. Y., Shankweiler, D., Orlando, C., Harris, K. S., & Berti, F. B. Letter confusions and reversals of sequence in the beginning reader: Implications for Orton's theory of developmental dyslexia. *Cortex, 7,* 127–142.

Mattis, S., French, J., & Rapin, E. (1975) Dyslexia in children and young adults: Three independent neuropsychological syndromes. *Developmental Medicine of Child Neurology, 17,* 150–163.

Moore, M., Kagan, J., Sahl, M., & Grant, S. (1982) *Retrieval and evaluation in reading disability.* In *Genetic Psychology Monograph.*

Morais, J., Cary L., Alegria, J., & Bertelson, P. (1979) Does awareness of speech as a sequence of phones arise spontaneously? *Cognition. 7,* 323–331.

Ojemann, G. A., & Whitaker, H. A. (1978) Bilingual brain. *Archives of Neurology, 35,* 409–412.

Orton, S. T. (1937) *Reading, writing and speech problems in children.* New York: Norton.

Pirozzolo, F. J. (1978) *The neuropsychology of developmental reading disorders.* New York: Praeger.

Rutter, M. (1978) Prevalence and types of dyslexia. In A. L. Benton & D. Pearl (Eds.), *Dyslexia: An appraisal of current knowledge.* New York: Oxford University Press.

Satz, P., & Morris, R. (1980) Learning disability subtypes: A review. In F. J. Pirozzolo & M. C. Wittrock (Eds.), *Neuropsychological and cognitive processes in reading.* New York: Academic Press.

Schonell, F. J. (1948) *Backwardness in the basic subjects* (4th ed.). Edinburgh: Oliver and Boyd.

Taylor, H. G., Satz, P., & Friel, J. (1979) Developmental dyslexia in relation to other childhood reading disorders: Significance and ability. *Reading Research Quarterly, 15(1),* 84–101.

Vurpillot, E. (1968) The development of scanning strategies and their relation to visual differentiation. *Journal of Experimental Child Psychology, 6,* 632–650.

Wolf, M. (1981) The word-retrieval process and reading in children and aphasics. In K. Nelson (Ed.), *Children's language* (Vol. 3). New York: Gardner Press.

Section Three

Biological Aspects

Chapter Eight

The Neurobiology of Developmental Reading Disorders

FRANCIS J. PIROZZOLO
EDWARD C. HANSCH

INTRODUCTION

Children who experience unexpected reading failure have been the subject of intense scientific investigation for almost a century. In the field of neuropsychology, there is probably no topic that draws greater attention than developmental reading disability. Despite this phenomenal interest the most tenable hypothesis for the pathophysiology of reading disability is one that was given by the very first researcher to recognize the disorder. After reading the contemporary theories of the causation of acquired reading disability given by James Hinshelwood (1895), W. Pringle Morgan (1896) recognized that an otherwise normal, healthy schoolboy under his care had reading deficits similar to those seen in Hinshelwood's brain-damaged patients. Morgan speculated that the area of cerebral cortex that was then recognized as the "center of written word images" was probably underdeveloped in the child with this unusual cognitive disability. Although neurobiological and neuropsychological scientific methods have improved greatly since the late

215

nineteenth century, Morgan's suggestion remains a reasonable theory as to why normal children fail to learn to read on a level expected of them.

In this chapter we will review the recent attempts to understand the neurobiological underpinnings of developmental reading disability. Although studies of the cognitive deficits of disabled readers have contributed a great deal to a descriptive understanding of dyslexia, they have not aided considerably in the investigation of the causal mechanisms of the disorder. Studies that have directly mapped the electrical activity of the dyslexic's brain, that have evaluated the dyslexic's neurophysiological function, or that have examined a dyslexic's brain at autopsy are the subject matter of this chapter. If a better understanding of the cause of developmental reading disability is to be achieved, then it will undoubtedly come from a thorough investigation of the dyslexic's neurobiological, neurophysiological, and neuroelectric function.

THE ANATOMY OF DEVELOPMENTAL DYSLEXIA

Cytoarchitectonic Studies of
Developmental Reading Disability

Most neurological disorders have life-threatening consequences. In contrast, although dyslexic children face a wide range of unfortunate dilemmas, such as potential academic and social failure, their disorder is not one that demands immediate medical attention. Because dyslexia is not associated with progressive brain disease, or even verifiable brain damage, systematic autopsies have not been carried out. However, two anatomical studies of the brains of boys with developmental reading disability have been done and have led to some understanding of the pathophysiology of this disorder.

The first such study was performed by Drake (1968). The patient was a 12-year-old boy who died from a cerebellar hemorrhage. Significant medical background included a history of enuresis, asthma, hyperactivity, dizzy spells and "blackouts," moderately severe emotional disturbance, and recurrent left frontal headaches. During infancy the boy had achieved most age-appropriate developmental milestones. His school progress was delayed by reading, writing, and calculation difficulties. Neurological evaluation was unremarkable, except for the aforementioned deficits in reading, writing, and calculation. Tests for cerebellar, motor, and sensory functions were all normal. Psychological evaluation revealed that the boy had a verbal IQ of 99, a performance IQ of 105, and a full-scale IQ of 103.

The child's death was caused by a massive hemorrhage involving the inferior vermis of the cerebellum extending into the subarachnoid and ventricular spaces. Gross examination of the cerebral hemispheres revealed an atypical gyral pattern in both parietal lobes. Gyri were unusually wide and the corpus callosum was equivalently atrophied. Microscopic examination showed that the cerebellar hemorrhage was caused by an angioma (capillary telangiectases). The cerebral cortex was thicker than normal and its lamination was columnar. There were many ectopic neurons lying deep in the white matter.

On the basis of this autopsy, Drake argued that the headaches experienced by this patient were related to the vascular malformation, and that this condition was either an atypical migraine or a minor seizure disorder. He was reluctant to speculate that the parietal anomalies were responsible for the child's reading disability. The cerebellar, white matter, and corpus callosal abnormalities were also not discussed.

The second cytoarchitectonic study was carried out by Galaburda and Kemper (1979). The patient was a left-handed 20-year-old man who died as a result of a construction accident. There was a family history of left-handedness and reading disability. The patient's medical history showed evidence of late onset of speech (age 3), reading and writing difficulties, seizure disorder (controlled by phenytoin), and evidence of EEG abnormality (a single sleep study revealing borderline slowing over the right hemisphere). Gross neuropathological examination of this young man's brain found that it was of normal size (1,576 gm after formalin fixation) and appearance. There was no suggestion of abnormality on visual inspection of the white matter or subcortical structures. The corpus callosum and ventricular system were intact. The left cerebral hemisphere was wider than the right, but the left planum temporale (the region roughly corresponding to Wernicke's area) was equivalent in length to the right planum temporale.

In normal brains, microscopic analysis reveals qualitatively different areas of the cortical surface, as well as a 6-layered organization of cells running from the cortical surface to the white matter. Although the cytoarchitectonic structure of different areas varies from one brain to another, the basic characteristics have been well described (Lorenté de Nó, 1949) and the individual regions studied carefully (e.g., Galaburda & Sanides, 1977). On microscopic examination of this dyslexic's brain several abnormalities were discovered, all of which were confined to the left hemisphere. Polymicrogyria was observed in the posterior parts of Heschl's gyrus and the planum temporale. The molecular layers in this region were fused and were not well differentiated. In addition, areas of mild cortical dysplasia were found in the auditory association cortex. Abnormally large neurons were found, not only in all lamination layers of cortex, but also in the white matter. Dysplasia was also seen in the cingulate and anterior insular areas. The right hemisphere was without abnormality, both in gross appearance and on microscopic examination.

As in the Drake case, a clinicopathological correlation was difficult to draw. In addition to the usual idiographic problems of ascribing the reading disability to the neuropathological findings, this dyslexic case is further complicated by the fact that the subject also suffered from a seizure disorder. However, this excellent study has provided an important beginning for future attempts to determine the anatomy of developmental dyslexia.

Structural Cerebral Asymmetries in
Developmental Reading Disability

Studies of normals have shown that cerebral asymmetries exist in the areas presumed to be specialized for language functions (Geschwind & Levitsky, 1968; Wada, Clarke, & Hamm, 1975; Witelson & Pallie, 1973; Galaburda, LeMay, Kemper, & Geschwind, 1978. Geschwind and Levitsky were the first to demonstrate that a region involved in speech comprehension (the left planum temporale) is larger than the corresponding region of the right hemisphere. Subsequently, studies using carotid arteriography and computerized tomography (LeMay, 1976, 1977) have shown that morphological differences exist. These structural asymmetries are believed to provide a favorable anatomical substrate for language development.

Hier, LeMay, Rosenberger, and Perlo (1978) have examined computerized tomograms (CTs) of the brains of 24 developmental dyslexics in an attempt to find evidence of structural anomalies that may be responsible for the clinical syndrome of dyslexia. Of the 24 dyslexic subjects studied, 10 patients showed a reversal of this cerebral asymmetry (right larger than left). None of the CTs revealed evidence of brain damage. These data are in support of the "reversed cerebral dominance" hypothesis of developmental reading disability. Interestingly, Rosenberger and Hier (1980) have found that children with verbal learning deficits frequently have this so-called reversal of cerebral dominance. In a study of 53 children with academic difficulties, these investigators found that a high percentage (42%) showed a wider right than left parieto-occipital region on CT scan. Furthermore, depressed verbal IQ performance was highly correlated with increased size of the right parieto-occipital region.

EVIDENCE INFERRING ANOMALOUS
CEREBRAL ORGANIZATION

Indirect evidence of anomalous cerebral organization in cases of dyslexia has come from studies of perceptual and perceptual-motor asymmetries which are reviewed elsewhere in this volume. These studies have employed techniques that have been used to show that, in normal right-handed subjects, the left hemisphere is specialized for language functions and that the right hemisphere is specialized for certain visual-spatial functions. Studies of the visual half-field effect (Pirozzolo, 1977a) have frequently found that children with reading disorders do not show the usual right visual field–left hemisphere advantage (e.g., Marcel, Katz, & Smith, 1974; Pirozzolo & Rayner, 1979; Pirozzolo, 1979; Pirozzolo, Rayner, Hansch, & Hynd, 1981). The nature of this variance (cf. Yeni-Komshian, Isenberg, & Goldberg, 1975) and the implications for reading disability are, however, still not well understood at this time. Similarly, studies employing the dichotic listening technique (Kimura, 1961) have shown that children with reading disability do not show the normal right ear–left hemisphere effect (e.g., Obrzut, 1979; Bakker, 1980). Once again, however, a wide variety of findings are reported in these studies and, thus, a clear picture of the neuropsychological deficit has not been generated (Pirozzolo *et al.*, 1981). Finally, there have been a small number of studies of the dichaptic shape effect (e.g., Witelson, 1977) showing differences between normals and dyslexics and suggesting the role of cerebral hemispheric specialization.

BIOCHEMICAL ABNORMALITIES
IN LEARNING DISORDERS

It has been argued that learning disabilities are caused by biochemical imbalances in the brain (e.g., Wender, 1971). There are numerous clinical observations that would lead to such a conclusion, and most evidence seems to point to a monoaminergic deficiency. Children with the so-called minimal brain dysfunction (MBD) symptom complex (attentional deficits, hyperactivity, and learning disorders) often respond favorably to substances such as methylphenidate, dextroamphetamine, and caffeine, which are thought to act directly upon the bioamines, dopamine, serotonin, and norepinephrine. The "paradoxical effect," that of improvement of attentional and learning capacity and a decrease in purposeless hyperactivity, after the use of these agents suggests that deficiencies in one or more of the monoamines may be causally linked to this notorious symptom complex. More recent evidence indicates, however, that this drug effect may not be as specific as it has been held to be (Rapoport, Buchsbaum, Zahn, Weingartner, Ludlow, & Mikkelson, 1978).

Other evidence from a variety of sources also seems to suggest a biochemical abnormality. Blood serotonin levels are known to be characteristically lower in MBD children and have been shown to increase as a function of improvement in clinical symptomatology (Brase & Loh, 1978). Children who were infected in the Von Economo encephalitis pandemic early in this century did not get the Parkinsonian symptoms that were observed in adult encephalitis victims, but instead revealed the MBD symptom complex. It is widely accepted now that Parkinsonian symptoms (bradykinesia, tremor, and rigidity) are associated with an imbalance in monoaminergic–cholinergic neurotransmitter systems. With respect to specific developmental reading disorders, investigators have administered a gamma aminobutyric acidlike substance, Piracetam, and have achieved improved reading skills in dyslexic children (Wilshire, Atkins, & Smith, 1979; Pirozzolo & Maletta, 1981). Further research is clearly needed to determine what the specific causes of developmental reading disorders are before a clear interpretation can be given for the favorable results of the administration of the drugs discussed here.

THE ROLE OF EYE MOVEMENTS IN THE NEUROPHYSIOLOGY OF DEVELOPMENTAL READING DISABILITY

Fluent reading depends upon the rapid processing of visual symbols and the transformation of this visual information into meaning (see reviews by Rayner, 1978a; 1981). Eye movements play a key role in the comprehension of text. Reading can be disrupted by a variety of lesions in the central nervous system that interfere with the normal performance of the oculomotor mechanism, even when all cognitive functions remain intact (Pirozzolo & Rayner, 1978b). Early studies of reading disability that tested the notion that abnormal eye movements caused dyslexia were unable to show a relationship between defective eye movements and dyslexia. When text difficulty is carefully controlled, most studies have found no differences in the reading eye movements of dyslexics and normals (Pirozzolo, 1979). Thus, a higher level neurolinguistic problem can be assumed to be the underlying factor in most instances of abnormal reading eye movements.

Recently, however, several studies have shown more basic oculomotor deficiencies in some groups of disabled readers. These studies have employed nonreading tasks in order to eliminate the possible confounds, such as the higher level neurolinguistic problem mentioned here, of previous studies. Studies of saccadic eye movement reaction time have produced particularly interesting results in this respect (Lesevre, 1968; Pirozzolo, 1979; Pirozzolo, 1981). Normal right-handed adults (Rayner, 1978b; Pirozzolo & Rayner, 1980) and children (Pirozzolo, 1979) show shorter saccadic latencies when stimuli are presented in the right parafoveal and near peripheral vision. Pirozzolo and Rayner (1980) have shown this effect to be related to hemispheric specialization, as left-handers as a group do not demonstrate this asymmetry. Some right-handed dyslexics, as might be expected, have shorter reaction time for eye movements made to the left than to the right, suggesting reversed "cerebral dominance" for this physiological function. Some dyslexic readers have great difficulty with return sweeps (Pirozzolo, 1979; Pirozzolo & Rayner, 1978a; Zangwill & Blakemore, 1972), an ability considered to be independent of the neurolinguistic disturbances responsible for most cases of reading disability. Pavlidis (1981) has found that dyslexics are poorer than normal readers in making saccades to horizontally moving light emitting diodes. Taken together, these studies suggest that some dyslexics do have deficits in basic spatial-oculomotor function. Most evidence suggests that these deficits are not the cause of reading disability, but rather are the effects of the underlying pathophysiology that causes dyslexia.

NEUROELECTRIC CORRELATES OF BRAIN DYSFUNCTION IN READING DISORDERS

A number of studies investigating the electroencephalogram (EEG) in learning-disabled children have pointed to an increased presence of electrophysiological deficits in this group. Early studies reported incidence of EEG abnormalities ranging from 36 to 75% in reading-disabled children (Hughes, Leander, & Ketchum, 1949; Webb & Lawson, 1956; Kennard, Rabinovitch, & Wexler, 1952; Muehl, Knott, & Benton, 1965;

Ayers & Torres, 1967; Hughes & Park, 1968; Hughes, 1971). However, several reports of relatively high percentages of EEG abnormalities in normal control or "conduct problem" children without specific reading disability (Kennard *et al.*, 1952; Cohn, 1961; Bryant & Friedlander, 1965) suggested that the observed EEG aberrations were not necessarily pathognomic in nature. Typical EEG abnormalities found in developmental reading disorders have included slowing at posterior (especially occipital) leads, focal sharp waves, and 14 and 6 per second positive spike patterns during sleep; with the latter abnormality being reported most consistently across investigations. Somewhat disappointingly, a lack of positive correlation between degree of reading retardation and the extent of EEG abnormalities has been the rule, as shown by studies such as Muehl *et al.*, 1965 and Hughes, 1971, the latter of which actually describes a paradoxical higher frequency of abnormalities in a borderline as opposed to a more severely learning-disabled group.

More recent studies of quantitative EEG employing power spectrum analyses of electrical activity in various frequency domains have offered compelling evidence for neurophysiological dysfunction in children with reading disorders. Ahn, Prichep, John, Baird, Trepetin, and Kaye (1980) utilized the neurometric approach to examine a set of 32 developmental equations based on topographical location and frequency band computed for 60 sec of EEG. Children with either a specific or more generalized learning disability showed increased percentages of significant deviation on many of the EEG parameters compared to normal controls. Most common were increases in power in the theta–delta range, particularly at parieto-occipital and temporal derivations. Significantly diminished alpha power at these sites was considered as a by-product of this increased slow activity. The brain electrical activity mapping (BEAM) technique of Duffy, Denckla, Bartels, and Sandini (1980), employing topographical images of EEG activity in the theta and alpha spectral range, has proved to be promising in elucidating the regional dynamics of electrical activity at rest and during mental processing tasks in dyslexia. Group differences were characterized by increase in mean alpha and to a lesser extent, theta, activity, with power differences observed bilaterally over medial frontal regions as well as the expected left temporal and occipital regions. Although the recording of EEG during "active" tasks engaged time points resulted in greater group differences, significant regional increases in mean alpha and theta activity occurred during rest as well. A clinical classification schema derived from the BEAM technique correctly classified 90% of normal and dyslexic children (Duffy, Denckla, Bartels, Sandini, & Kiessling, 1980). In the only study examining the EEG during reading in dyslexics, Sklar, Hanley, and Simmons (1973) found decreased beta range (16–32 Hz) activity compared to normal age-matched counterparts. However, the reverse relationship was observed in resting EEG, with increased beta as well as more prominent 3–7 Hz theta activity in the dyslexics as compared to normals; this resting measure actually better differentiated the groups. Finally, Fuller (1977) has described decreased alpha attenuation over the left hemisphere in learning-disabled boys compared to normal boys during initial instruction, immediate recall, and arithmetic computation tasks. This relative increase in alpha activity during mental processing in learning-disabled children over normals is in agreement with the Duffy, Denckla, Bartels, & Sandini (1980) findings, and gains neurophysiological significance from the notion that greater alpha activity "iclling" represents underactivation of underlying cortical structures (Gevins, Zeitlin, Doyle, Yingling, Schaffer, Callaway, & Yeager, 1979) and conversely alpha attention or "blocking" signifies cortical arousal (Glass, 1959; Glass, 1964). The finding in the Ahn *et al.* (1980) study of decreased power in the 7.5–12.5 Hz alpha range for learning-disabled groups during resting EEG would not be discordant with this interpretation.

These investigations examining EEG under conditions of complex task involvement, particularly those tasks involving various aspects of reading and other linguistic processes, represent a step forward in the assessment of neuroelectric correlates of brain dysfunction in children with reading disorders. Chief among the EEG's advantages as an electrophysiological technique is its adaptability to recording under conditions of ongoing mental processing, which permits a more flexible and complex array of experimental cognitive tasks to be examined in reading-disabled children for electrocortical manifestations. As topographical distribution and quantitative analysis techniques become more sophisticated, clinical diagnostic utility can be expected to improve.

Event-related potentials (ERP) have been investigated more recently as an electrophysiological index of neurological function with reading disorders. Consisting of discrete epics of brain electrical activity following specifiable sensory, motor, or internal processing events, ERPs have been obtained across stimulus modalities and may exhibit latency, amplitude, and/or topographical distribution shifts according to experimental condition. A useful dichotomy in considering the ERP has been the categorization of "exogenous" and "endogenous" components (Sutton, Bararen, Zubin, & John, 1965). Stimulus-evoked, or "exogenous," components usually occur under 200 msec in latency, range in topographical location according to stimulus modality, and vary directly as a function of the physical characteristics of the eliciting stimulus.

These components are thought to reflect the physiological integrity of the afferent neural network. In contrast, the "endogenous" components occur at much longer latencies. They are less related to physical parameters of the stimulus, and, instead, are believed to reflect information-processing-related activities in humans and to represent relatively diverse psychological constructs. Studies of ERPs in children with developmental reading disorders have focused primarily on the stimulus-evoked or "exogenous" components. Several papers (Goodin, Squires, & Starr, 1978; Syndulko, Hansch, Cohen, Pearce, Montan, Goldberg, Tourtellotte, & Potvin, 1980; Hansch, Syndulko, Cohen, Tourtellotte, Potvin, & Goldberg, 1981) have reported increased differentiation of clinical neurological groups with associated cognitive symptomatology with the endogenous component P300 of ERPs as opposed to earlier sensory related components. The review of ERP studies of dyslexic and other learning disabled groups to follow will refer to this distinction of primarily sensory versus more cognitively based components, and proceed to suggest the need to further study the "endogenous" components in gaining insight into the electrophysiological significance of the primary reading and cognitive disturbance in this population.

The studies of Connors (1971) that examined the flash-evoked response in a family of severely retarded readers and in several groups of children with learning disabilities gave considerable impetus to subsequent ERP studies concerned with the electrophysiology of dyslexia. Bipolar EEG from O_1, O_2, P_3, and P_4 referred to the vertex was averaged with amplitude and latency of Waves V and VI, positive and negative with latencies of approximately 140 and 200 msec, respectively, serving as the criterion measures. Attenuation of amplitude at the left parietal P_3 electrode for Waves V and VI compared to the other sides was observed in family members with reading problems but not in the normal reading mother. In a study of 27 children with reading difficulties, scores on the spelling and reading substests of the Wide Range Achievement Test (WRAT) correlated significantly only with Wave VI amplitude at the P_3 electrode. A further study of "good" and "poor" readers within a learning-disabled group revealed that significant amplitude differences existed only at the P_3 electrode for the N200 Wave VI, with more negativity reported for the better readers. Unfortunately, Connors did not study normal controls on the flash-evoked response measure, rendering the left parietal sites amplitude effects difficult to interpret. Although Connors discusses the attenuated amplitude af P_3 in terms of a selective effect on a "late" component possibly related to "*attentiveness*," the task demands as well as the latency suggest that this component primarily reflects sensory-related "exogenous" neuroelectric activity.

Binocular color flash ERPs were studied in children with various kinds of reading disability by Ross, Childers, and Perry (1973). Electrode placement was accomplished by denoting a scalp site 5 cm anterior to the inion and then placing four electrodes in a "cross" 5 cm away. Bipolar recordings from the left and right occipital regions and anterior and posterior midline were obtained. The most prominent feature of the results was a phase reversal of the right occipital electrode with respect to the posterior midline site in 20 of 30 children. Speculations that there was an "inversion of polarity between the hemispheres" or that "the hemispheres could be working asynchronously" were raised by the authors. Again, failure to include an appropriate control group and, more seriously, to specify the time parameters or component latencies effectively limit the conclusions that can be drawn.

Preston and colleagues (Preston, Guthrie, & Childs, 1974; Preston, Guthrie, Kursch, Gertman, & Childs, 1977) have considerably improved on these earlier studies by including normal controls as well as referencing to an "inactive" site, easing the interpretation of regional cortical distribution differences. In their first study, reading-disabled children were found to display significantly decreased amplitude in a negative component occurring at about 180 msec at the P_3 electrode to both flashes of light and the word *cat*. Essential agreement was postulated by the authors to the decreased amplitude to the N200 component in poor readers in the Connors study. Of critical importance to an interpretation for a neuroanatomical origin for the ERP differences between normals and reading-disabled children was the lack of ERP differences between two groups of normal children, one matched for chronological age and the other for reading level age. Adult normal and disabled readers were examined in a separate study on a simple light flash ERP paradigm and a word flash condition in which subjects silently counted the occurrence of a target word. Disabled readers showed a significantly larger amplitude differential of word condition compared to flash condition for both a P200 and late positive component (LPC) at the P_3 electrode only. Earlier latency components did not show this group–condition–electrode site interaction, leading the authors to suggest the possibility of an electrophysiological access of differences in the processing of written materials between normal and reading-disabled adults. While Preston's group had offered compelling evidence for ERP differentiation of these groups at the electrode nearest to the left parietal (angular gyrus) cortical region, selective access of "endogenous" or cognitive related neural activity remains open to question.

In their counting paradigm, target and nontarget stimuli were averaged together, effectively dampening an endogenous P300 component to targets which occurs in this "oddball stimulus" paradigm (see Donchin, Ritter, & McCallum, 1978 for review). Separate averages of task-relevant and nontarget stimuli would seem to be essential in assessing the observed component's relationship to attentional and/or language-related information-processing activity.

Increased peak to peak amplitude for P_1-N_1 at parietal sites and a similar effect for N_1-P_2 amplitude over the occipital region for dyslexic children in a visual flash ERP procedure has been reported by Sobotka and May (1977). In contrast to earlier reports, no differential hemispheric effects were observed. Symann-Louett, Gascon, Matsumiya, and Lombroso (1977) have recorded visual ERPs to flashed word stimuli under conditions where normal and reading-disabled children were expecting a subsequent recall test. Dyslexic children displayed significantly fewer waves (defined as amplitude deflections of at least 2.5 μV above the previous peak) in the first 200 msec at the P_3 electrode and at a site over Wernicke's area compared to normals. A nonsignificant trend toward increased waves of latencies exceeding 200 msec in dyslexics opens the possibility that a latency increase for the same components, pushing a component past 200 msec, could account for the data as well as an interpretation centered on the absence of early components. Hemispheric asymmetries in visual and auditory ERP records were also noted in the BEAM technique of Duffy, Denckla, Bartels, and Sandini (1980). Enhanced detection of significant amplitude differences between dyslexics and normal children occurred at electrode sites over the left posterior temperoparietal region.

Although only two groups have studied the endogenous P300 and contingent negative variation (CNV) wave forms in dyslexia, their initial application comprised the earliest published electrophysiological investigation of reading disorders. Fenelon, in 1968, failed to observe the CNV or positive component to an imperative trigram stimulus, while the record of an 8-year-old dyslexic was comparable to that of a 6-year-old normal reading child. Fenelon argued that age must be taken into account when evaluating the cortical electrophysiological response in dyslexia. In a small group of problem readers, Fenelon (1978) described significantly decreased CNV amplitude compared to normal readers during bimodal (visual–auditory) pairings of warning and imperative stimuli. Mean amplitude of the CNV was decreased in the reading-disabled group most clearly over the left parietal region, although this effect did not reach statistical significance. Musso and Harter (1978) used visual P300 tasks to study two groups of reading-disabled children with disorders classified as stemming from visual or auditory perceptive problems. Latencies for the P300 component at both the vertex and O_2 were delayed for the visual problem as compared to the auditory problem dyslexic group, which in turn displayed significantly increased latencies over a normal reading control group. Increased amplitude differentiation at O_2 when the stimulus was task relevant as opposed to irrelevant for the visual problem dyslexics when compared to the normal readers was interpreted to reflect enhanced attention in compensating for slowing in sensory–neural information processing in the visual dyslexic group. Despite restriction of recording sites to the midline and failure to report P300 latency for visual flash and linguistic stimuli separately, the study of Musso and Harter stands as strong evidence for neurophysiological correlates of abnormal cognitive information processing in dyslexia.

In summary, ERP studies of reading disorders have supported the notion of associated primary sensory related and cognitive electrophysiological deficits. Many studies have supported increased localized waveform aberrations, mainly amplitude decrements, on topographical sites overlying the angular gyrus and left parietal cortex, consistent with other neuroanatomical evidence for involvement of this region in dyslexia (Galaburda & Kemper, 1979). Discrepancies in ERP findings between studies can probably be accounted for in part by variant age ranges of the groups studied, inclusion criterion for learning-disabled groups, and nonstandard employment of reference electrodes. Only a few studies have investigated the longer latency endogenous components of ERPs in dyslexia, a disorder marked by specifiable cognitive deficits, despite the intrinsic relationship of these components to neurocognitive events involved in information processing. Investigations of endogenous components of ERPs in normals during engagement in more complex tasks involving word or sentence processing (Kutas & Hillyard, 1980; Neville, 1980; Chapman, McCrary, Chapman, & Martin, 1980) when applied to the reading-disabled child may contribute considerably to our knowledge of the neurophysiology of dyslexia.

SUMMARY

Although a considerable amount of knowledge about developmental reading disability has accumulated during the past decade, our understanding of the causes of these disorders is still relatively primitive.

One of the basic problems is that we are far from having a true understanding of the reading process. Reading is not a single stage psychological process; it depends upon brain mechanisms that govern such functions as visual perception, memory, and sequencing; auditory perception, memory, and sequencing; and language abilities such as lexical analysis and syntactic comprehension. Furthermore, brain functions for such disparate skills as oculomotor control and abstract thinking must also be intact for fluent reading to take place. Although neuropsychological and cognitive studies of reading have greatly increased in number during the last two decades, due in part to the rejection of behaviorist doctrine, our understanding of the component processes in reading is still far from complete (Pirozzolo & Wittrock, 1981).

Studies have shown that developmental dyslexia is not a single homogeneous clinical entity (Mattis, French, & Rapin, 1975; Pirozzolo, 1977b). It now appears that a single cause does not underlie all cases of developmental reading disability. Moreover, clinical data clearly show that the potential etiologies for the related disorder known as minimal brain dysfunction are so diverse that it is extremely unlikely that impairment of, for example, a single biochemical process will explain the various clinical manifestations of MBD.

Recent data indicate that dietary factors play an important role in learning disorders. Careful consideration must be given to a wide variety of other brain biochemical factors that could impair normal mental function. Studies of inborn enzymatic defects are slowly beginning to specify the biochemical balances that are essential for normal intellectual development, but further research is needed before any firm conclusions can be drawn about the biochemistry of learning.

In this chapter we have reviewed evidence that developmental reading disorders are associated with neurobiological, neurophysiological, and neuroelectric abnormalities. Neuropathological studies have shown that dyslexic children do not have brain damage, but have a number of neuronal abnormalities. By inference, neurophysiological studies suggest a compromise in neuronal or glial function. Still other studies employing electrophysiological techniques, pharmacological treatment, and dietary regulation suggest that an alteration in synaptic function may be a key to the learning problems of these children. If an alteration in intercellular communication is a contributing factor, then the complexity of synaptic function will further delay our understanding of the pathogenesis of learning disorders. If a biochemical impairment in synaptic function is demonstrated, it remains to be seen whether the localization of the problem is at the level of the presynaptic or postsynaptic cell membrane, neurotransmitter metabolism, axoplasmic flow, ion conductance in the soma or axon hillock, or neurotransmitter release, uptake, and so on. Although some important insights into the clinical symptomatology and causal factors of reading disorders have been gained in recent years, further research efforts should be aimed at a better description of normal brain–behavior relationships, which will undoubtedly provide clues to the pathogenesis of developmental reading disability.

REFERENCES

Ahn, H., Prichep, L., John, E. R., Baird, H., Trepetin, M., & Kaye, H. (1980) Developmental equations reflect brain dysfunction. *Science, 210,* 1259–1262.

Ayers, F. W., & Torres, F. (1967) The incidence of EEG abnormalities in a dyslexic and a control group. *Journal of Clinical Psychology, 23,* 334–336.

Bakker, D. J. (1980) Cerebral lateralization and reading proficiency. In Y. Lebrun & O. Zangwill (Eds.), *Lateralization of language in the child.* Lisse: Swets & Zeitlinger.

Brase, D. A., & Loh, H. H. (1978) Possible role of 5-hydroxytryptamine in minimal brain dysfunction. *Life Sciences, 16,* 1005–1016.

Bryant, N. D., & Friedlander, W. J. (1965) "14" and "6" in boys with specific reading disability. *Electroencephalography and Clinical Neurophysiology, 19,* 318–322.

Chapman, R. M., McCrary, J. W., Chapman, J. A., & Martin, J. K. (1980) Behavioral and neural analyses of connotative meaning: Word classes and rating scales. *Brain and Language, 11,* 319–339.

Cohn, R. (1961) Delayed acquisition of reading and writing abilities in children. *Archives of Neurology, 4,* 153–164.

Connors, C. K. (1971) Cortical visual evoked response in children with learning disorders. *Psychophysiology, 7,* 418–428.

Donchin, E., Ritter, W., & McCallum, W. C. (1978) Cognitive psychophysiology: The endogenous components of the ERP. In E. Callaway, P. Teuting, & S. H. Koslow, *Event related potentials in man.* New York: Academic Press.

Drake, W. (1968) Clinical and pathological findings in a child with a developmental learning disability. *Journal of Learning Disabilities, 1,* 468–475.

Duffy, F. H., Denckla, M. B., Bartels, P. H., & Sandini, G. (1980) Dyslexia: Regional differences in brain electrical activity by topographic mapping. *Annals of Neurology, 7,* 412–420.

Duffy, F. H., Denckla, M. B., Bartels, P. H., Sandini, G., & Kiessling, L. S. (1980) Dyslexia: Automated diagnosis of computerized classification of brain electrical activity. *Annals of Neurology, 7,* 421–428.

Fenelon, B. (1968) Expectancy waves and other complex cerebral events in dyslexic and normal subjects. *Psychonomic Science, 13,* 253–254.

Fenelon, B. (1978) Hemispheric effects of stimulus sequence and side of stimulation on slow potentials in children with reading problems. In D. A. Otto (Ed.), *Multidisciplinary perspectives in event-related brain potential research.* Washington, D.C.: Government Printing Office.

Fuller, P. W. (1977) Computer estimated alpha attenuation during problem solving in children with learning disabilities. *Electroencephalography and Clinical Neurophysiology, 42,* 149–156.

Galaburda, A. M., & Kemper, T. (1979) Cytoarchitectonic abnormalities in developmental dyslexia: A case study. _Annals of Neurology, 6_, 94–100.

Galaburda, A. M., LeMay, M., Kemper, T. L., & Geschwind, N. (1978) Right–left asymmetries in the brain. _Science, 199_, 852–856.

Galaburda, A. M., & Sanides, F. (1977) The human auditory cortex: A new cytoarchitectonic map. _Neuroscience Abstracts, 3_, 67.

Geschwind, N., & Levitsky, W. (1968) Human brain: Left–right asymmetries in temporal speech region. _Science, 161_, 186–188.

Gevins, A. S., Zeitlin, G. M., Doyle, J. C., Yingling, C. D., Schaffer, R. E., Callaway, E., & Yeager, C. L. (1979) Electroencephalogram correlates of higher cortical functions. _Science, 203_, 665–668.

Glass, A. (1959) Blocking of the occipital alpha rhythm and problem-solving efficiency. _Electroencephalography and Clinical Neurophysiology, 11_, 605.

Glass, A. (1964) Mental arithmetic and blocking of the alpha rhythm. _Electroencephalography and Clinical Neurophysiology, 16_, 595–603.

Goodin, D. S., Squires, D. C., & Starr, A. (1968) Long latency components of the auditory evoked potential in dementia. _Brain, 101_, 635–648.

Hansch, E. C., Syndulko, D., Cohen, S. N., Tourtellotte, W. W., Potvin, A. R., & Goldberg, Z. (1981) Delays in an event related potential waveform associated with cognitive function in Parkinson's disease. _INS Bulletin_, November.

Hier, D. B., LeMay, M., Rosenberger, P., & Perlo, V. P. (1978) Developmental dyslexia. _Archives of Neurology, 35_, 90–92.

Hinshelwood, J. (1895) Wordblindness and visual memory. _Lancet, 2_, 1564–1570.

Hughes, J. R. (1971) Electroenchaphalography and learning disabilities. In H. R. Myklebust (Ed.), _Progress in learning disabilities_. New York: Grune & Stratton.

Hughes, J. R., Leander, R., & Ketchum , G. (1949) Electroencephalographic study of specific reading disabilities. _Electroencephalography and Clinical Neurophysiology, 1_, 377–378.

Hughes, J. R., & Park, G. E. (1968) The EEG in dyslexia. In P. Kellaway & I. Petersen (Eds.), _Clinical electroencephalography of children_. Stockholm: Almquist and Wiksell.

Kennard, M. A., Rabinovitch, R., & Wexler, D. (1952) The abnormal electroencephalogram as related to reading disability in children with disorders of behavior. _Canadian Medical Association Journal, 67_, 330–333.

Kimura, D. (1961) Cerebral dominance and the perception of verbal stimuli. _Canadian Journal of Psychology, 15_, 166–171.

Kutas, M., & Hillyard, S. A. (1980) Reading between the lines: Event related brain potentials during natural sentence processing. _Brain and Language, 11_, 354–373.

LeMay, M. (1976) Morphological cerebral asymmetries of modern man, fossil man, and non-human primate. _Annals of the New York Academy of Sciences, 280_, 349–366.

LeMay, M. (1977) Asymmetries of the skull and handedness. _Journal of Neurological Sciences, 32_, 243–253.

Lesevre, N. (1968) L'organisation du regard chez infants d'age scolaire, lecteurs, normaux et dyslexiques. _Revue de Neuropsychiatrie Infantile, 16_, 323–349.

Lorenté de Nó, R. (1949) Cerebral cortex: architecture. In J. F. Fulton (Ed.), _Physiology of the nervous system_ (3rd ed.). New York: Oxford University Press.

Marcel, T., Katz, L., & Smith, M. (1974) Laterality and reading proficiency. _Neuropsychologia, 12_, 121–139.

Mattis, S., French, J., & Rapin, E. (1975) Dyslexia in children and young adults: Three independent neuropsychological syndromes. _Developmental Medicine and Child Neurology, 17_, 150–163.

Morgan, W. P. (1896) A case of congenital word blindness. *British Medical Journal, 2*, 1378.

Muehl, S., Knott, J. R., & Benton, A. L. (1965) EEG abnormality and psychological test performance in reading disability. *Cortex, 1*, 434–440.

Musso, M. R., & Harter M. R. (1978) Contingent negative variation, evoked potential, and psychophysical measures of selective attention in children with learning disabilities. In D. A. Otto (Ed.), *Multidisciplinary perspectives in event-related brain potential research*. Washington, D.C.: Government Printing Office.

Neville, H. J. (1980) Event-related potentials in neuropsychological studies of language. *Brain and Language, 11*, 300–318.

Obrzut, J. E. (1979) Dichotic listening and bisensory memory skills in qualitatively diverse dyslexic readers. *Journal of Learning Disabilities, 12*, 304–314.

Pavlidis, G. (1981) Do eye movements hold the key to dyslexia? *Neuropsychologia, 19*, 57–64.

Pirozzolo, F. J. (1977a) Lateral asymmetries in visual perception: A review of tachistoscopic visual half-field studies. *Perceptual and Motor Skills, 45*, 695–701.

Pirozzolo, F. J. (1977b) *Visual-spatial and oculomotor deficits in developmental dyslexia: Evidence for two neurobehavioral syndromes of reading disability*. Unpublished doctoral dissertation, University of Rochester.

Pirozzolo, F. J. (1979) *The neuropsychology of developmental reading disorders*. New York: Praeger.

Pirozzolo, F. J. (1981) Eye movements and visual information processing in developmental reading disability. In R. N. Malatesha & L. C. Hartlage (Eds.), *Neuropsychology and cognition*. Aalphen aan den Rijn: Sijthoff & Noordhoff.

Pirozzolo, F. J., & Maletta, G. J. (1981) *The efficacy of Piracetam in children with specific written language disturbances*. FDA IND #18267.

Pirozzolo, F. J., & Rayner, K. (1978a) Disorders of oculomotor scanning and graphic orientation in developmental Gerstmann syndrome. *Brain and Language, 5*, 119–126.

Pirozzolo, F. J., & Rayner, K. (1978b) The neural control of eye movements in acquired and developmental reading disorders. In H. Whitaker & H. A. Whitaker (Eds.), *Studies in neurolinguistics* (Vol. 4). New York: Academic Press.

Pirozzolo, F. J., & Rayner, K. (1979) Cerebral organization and reading disability. *Neuropsychologia, 17*, 485–489.

Pirozzolo, F. J., & Rayner, K. (1980) Handedness, hemispheric specialization, and saccadic eye movement latencies. *Neuropsychologia, 18*, 225–229.

Pirozzolo, F. J., Rayner, K., Hansch, E., & Hynd, G. (1981) The measurement of cerebral hemispheric asymmetries in children with developmental reading disability. In J. Hellige (Ed.), *Cerebral hemisphere asymmetry: Theory, method, and application*. New York: Praeger.

Pirozzolo, F. J., & Wittrock, M. C. (Eds.) (1981) *Neuropsychological and cognitive processes in reading*. New York: Academic Press.

Preston, M. S., Guthrie, J. T., & Childs, B. (1974) Visual evoked responses (VERs) in normal and disabled readers. *Psychophysiology, 11*, 452–457.

Preston, M. S., Guthrie, J. T., Kirsch, J. T., Gertman, D., & Childs, B. (1977) VERS in normal and disabled adult readers. *Psychophysiology, 14*, 8–14.

Rapoport, J. L., Buchsbaum, M. S., Zahn, J. P., Weingartner, H., Ludlow, C., & Mikkelson, E. J. (1978) Dextroamphetamine: Cognitive and behavioral effects in normal prepubertal boys. *Science, 199*, 560–563.

Rayner, K. (1978a) Eye movements in reading and information processing. *Psychological Bulletin, 85*, 618–660.

Rayner, K. (1978b) Saccadic latencies for parafoveally presented words. *Bulletin of the Psychonomic Society, 11,* 13–16.

Rayner, K. (1981) Eye movements and the perceptual span in reading. In F. J. Pirozzolo & M. C. Wittrock (Eds.), *Neuropsychological and cognitive processes in reading.* New York: Academic Press.

Rosenberger, P., & Hier, D. (1980) Cerebral asymmetry and verbal intellectual deficits. *Annals of Neurology, 8,* 300–304.

Ross, J. J., Childers, D. G., & Perry, N. W. (1973) The natural history and electrophysiological characteristics of familial language dysfunction. In P. Satz & J. J. Ross (Eds.), *The disabled learner: Early intervention and treatment.* Rotterdam: University of Rotterdam Press.

Sklar, B., Hanley, J., & Simmons, W. W. (1973) A computer analysis of EEG spectral signatures from normal and dyslexic children. *IEEE Transactions on Biomedical Engineering, 20,* 20–26.

Sobotka, K. R., & May, J. G. (1977) Visual evoked potentials and reaction time in normal and dyslexic children. *Psychophysiology, 14,* 18–24.

Sutton, S., Bararen, M., Zubin, J., & John, E. R. (1965) Evoked potential correlates of stimulus uncertainty. *Science, 150,* 1187–1188.

Symann-Louett, N., Gascon, G. G., Matsumiya, Y., & Lombroso, C. T. (1977) Waveform differences in visual evoked responses between normal and reading disabled children. *Neurology, 27,* 156–159.

Syndulko, K., Hansch, E. C., Cohen, S. N., Pearce, J. W., Montan, B. I., Goldberg, Z., Tourtellotte, W. W., & Potvin, A. R. (1980) Long latency event related potentials in normal aging and dementia. *Transactions of the American Neurological Association, 105.*

Wada, J. A., Clarke, R., & Hamm, A. (1975) Cerebral hemispheric asymmetry in humans: Cortical speech zones in 100 adult and 100 infant brains. *Archives of Neurology, 32,* 239–246.

Webb, E. M., & Lawson, L. (1956) The EEG in severe speech and reading disabilities of childhood. *Electroencephalography and Clinical Neurophysiology, 8,* 168.

Wender, P. H. (1971) *Minimal brain dysfunction in children.* New York: Wiley.

Wilshire, C., Atkins, G., & Manfield, P. (1979) Piracetam as an aid to learning in dyslexia. *Psychopharmacology, 65,* 107–109.

Witelson, S. F. (1977) Neural and cognitive correlates of developmental dyslexia: Age and sex differences. In C. Shagass, S. Gershon, & A. J. Friedhoff (Eds.), *Psychopathology and brain dysfunction.* New York: Raven Press.

Witelson, S. F., & Pallie, W. (1973) Left hemisphere specialization for language in the newborn: Neuroanatomical evidence of asymmetry. *Brain, 96,* 641–646.

Yeni-Komshain, G., Isenberg, D., & Goldberg, H. (1975) Cerebral dominance and reading disability: Left visual field deficit in poor readers. *Neuropsychologia, 13,* 83–94.

Zangwill, O., & Blakemore, C. (1972) Dyslexia: Reversal of eye movements during reading. *Neuropsychologia, 10,* 371–373.

Chapter Nine

The Electroencephalogram and Reading Disorders

JOHN R. HUGHES

In 1978 I published a review of the electroencephalogram (EEG) in dyslexia, based mainly on studies in which EEGs were systematically done on a large number of children with reading disorders. In the following years other types of studies were published that illustrate the usefulness of the electroencephalogram to further our understanding of dyslexia in children. The same problems that made this type of study difficult in the past have continued to the present time, namely, the imprecise definition of the groups under study, the reporting of questionable EEG abnormalities, and the relatively high incidence of positive EEG findings in control groups. However, statistically significant differences between dyslexic and control groups continue to appear, as

do significant correlations between EEG and clinical findings. The new-
est EEG studies add evidence to the understanding of dyslexia, especially to an appreciation of the complexity of this disorder. Scientific
truth regarding any human phenomenon seems to develop out of early
studies that present simple concepts which then become necessarily
more complex as further data accumulate. This type of development
is readily apparent in the neurological and neurophysiological literature
on reading disorders.

INCIDENCE OF ABNORMAL EEG IN DYSLEXIA

Because much of the relevant data are dealt with in the already-
mentioned review on the EEG in dyslexia (Hughes, 1978), these data
will only be briefly discussed here. Table 9.1 lists the authors who have

Table 9.1
Incidence of EEG Abnormality in Dyslexics

Patients N	Percentage Abnormal	Percentage controls	Comment	Investigators
33	27	0	Mainly delta waves and focal	Fenelon *et al.*, 1972
62	34		More abnormality (84%) in general "learning disability"	Ingram *et al.*, 1970
60	35	7	Abnormality (50%) if inadequate visual perception	Black, 1972
157	36		Positive spikes (21%), occipital slowing (10%)	Hughes & Park, 1968
58	45		Mild (37%) and borderline (8%)	Njiokiktjien *et al.*, 1977
46	50	10	Slowing, especially occipital, and generalized paroxysms	Cohn, 1961
31	55	29	Most common abnormality was temporal spike	Torres & Ayres, 1968
76	57		Nonspecific (39%) and positive spikes (18%)	Kenny *et al.*, 1972
41	59		Also with speech retardation, 27% focal abnormality	Webb & Lawson, 1956
50	62		Positive spike (41%), occipital slowing (50%)	Knott *et al.*, 1965
34	71		All with behavior disorders as well	Kennard *et al.*, 1952
16	88		Slow alpha and pathological features	Roudinesco *et al.*, 1950
664	47			

systematically studied dyslexia in children and also correlated the EEG findings with clinical features in these same patients. From a total of 664 individuals the table shows a grand mean of 47%, representing the EEG abnormality in dyslexia. The cursory review of the column labeled "comments" indicates that four different kinds of positive EEG findings are often found in patients with dyslexia. These patterns are (a) positive spikes, (b) excessive occipital slow waves, (c) temporal lobe sharp waves or spikes, and also (d) generalized or diffuse EEG findings. In the studies that included control groups significant differences were found between those groups and the dyslexic patients. In the studies that did not incorporate such controls other questions were asked of the data, especially with the aim of uncovering electroclinical correlations. The 47% incidence in Table 9.1 is relatively high under any circumstances and would likely be significantly different from any kind of control group. It is similar to the 41% incidence of positive EEG findings found in a double blind study on underachievers (Hughes, 1971). Although the latter group included subjects with any form of learning disability, many of them had a specific dyslexia. The incidence of positive EEG findings in this underachiever group was very significantly different ($p = .007$) from a carefully controlled group of normally achieving children who were of the same age, the same sex, and from the same classroom.

ELECTROCLINICAL CORRELATIONS

Abnormal EEG

An abnormal EEG in dyslexia has been correlated with both positive neurological findings and a positive birth history (Ingram, Mason, & Blackburn, 1970; Gerson, Barnes, Mannino, Fanning, & Burns, 1972), in addition to inadequate visual perception (Black, 1972). Also, positive EEG findings have been correlated with a better clinical response to various kinds of medication, especially methylphenidate or nitrazepam (Satterfield, Lesser, Saul, & Cantwell, 1973; Fenelon, Holland, & Johnson, 1972). On the other hand, in the study by Muehl, Knott, and Benton (1965) no relationship could be found between the degree of severity of the dyslexia and the degree of EEG abnormality.

Positive Spikes

Positive spikes at 6–7 and 14 per second continue to be a controversial finding in electroencephalography, although at present a majority would likely report them as a normal variant. On the other hand, 40 new papers, appearing in the literature in the past 10 years, continue to argue for the clinical significance of this controversial EEG finding. The incidence of positive spikes in dyslexics has shown great variability, and these values range from 21% (Hughes & Park, 1968) to 30–35% (Knott, Muehl, & Benton, 1965; Bryant & Friedlander, 1965), to the relatively high value of 55% (Muehl *et al.*, 1965). No significant differences were found between the incidence of positive spikes in the dyslexic groups and their controls in the studies of Bryant and Friedlander (1965) and of Torres and Ayers (1968). A trend, but without statistical significance ($p = .09$), was found by Hughes (1971) in the 20% incidence of positive spikes in 214 underachievers, compared to the 15% incidence of the control group.

A few studies have reported correlations with clinical findings in dyslexics who have positive spikes. For example, Smith, Philippus, and Guard (1968) found that the patients with positive spikes showed significant improvement in both verbal and full-scale IQ when placed on the medication ethosuximide. Hughes and Park (1968) found that the dyslexics with this waveform were the brightest children among four different EEG groups, but also showed the greatest difference between their potential and their actual achievement in reading. These same patients scored high on different tests measuring tension and anxiety, in addition to metabolic rate. On the other hand, Muehl *et al.* (1965) reported that positive spikes did not correlate with any psychological test score.

Excessive Occipital Slow Waves

Excessive occipital slow waves are usually defined as bursts of organized, rhythmical delta patterns (under 4 per second) found on the posterior regions, rather than the common slow transient, representing only a piece of a slow wave, that usually appears in all normal children. In the study by Hughes (1971) of underachievers with some form of learning disability, a significantly increased incidence of slow waves was seen in this group compared to normal controls. Although occipital slow waves were seen more often than slowing from other areas, it was not the occipital, but rather the temporal, slow waves that proved to be significantly different from the controls. The 10% incidence of occipital slow waves in this study was exactly the same incidence that Hughes and Park (1968) reported in their dyslexic patients. This incidence contrasts with the 50–54% incidence reported by Knott *et al.* (1965) and by Murdoch (1974).

The clinical correlations that have been reported with excessive occipital slow waves are not numerous, but I found (Hughes, 1971) a relationship between these slow waves and a disturbance within the visual system in the form of a decreased photic driving response in deaf children. Pavy and Metcalf (1965) have shown more specifically the relationship between excessive occipital slow waves and abnormal visuomotor performance. In a study of dyslexics (Hughes & Park, 1968), it was reported that occipital slow waves tend to be found in the poorest of readers, also with poor potential, and with a decreased visual responsivity in the form of a deficient visual duction. On the other hand, another study (Chiofalo, Bravo, Perez, & Villavicencio, 1971) found that patients with excessive occipital slowing tended to have a less impaired learning disability than the other children included in the study and also usually had normal IQs. Although some studies have shown a correlation between abnormal visuomotor performance and excessive occipital slow waves, these same slow waves are often considered non-specific in that they have also been correlated with other kinds of deficits, especially behavior disorders (Cohn & Nardini, 1958).

Diffuse or Generalized Abnormality

Only a few studies have reported on diffuse findings and these studies show a variation with regard to the incidence of such a finding in dyslexics. In a group with minimal brain dysfunction or learning disability, Capute, Niedermeyer, and Richardson (1968) reported that one-half of these subjects had abnormal slowing that was nonfocal or diffuse. On the other hand, Hughes and Park (1968) found only 3 of 157 dyslexics with diffuse slow waves. Also, Roudinesco, Trelat, and Trelat (1950) reported that slowed alpha frequencies sometimes are found in patients with dyslexia and this particular finding could be considered a diffuse or generalized disorder.

The clinical correlations found with diffuse or generalized EEG findings include the findings on learning disorders by Chiofalo *et al.* (1971) who reported that these diffuse patterns were noted in patients with a low IQ and also visuomotor deficiencies. In dyslexics, in particular, Roudinesco *et al.* (1950) reported that these EEG findings were noted especially in patients with retarded speech and motor development.

Epileptiform Activity

Epileptiform activity includes the EEG terms of spikes, spike and wave complexes, and sharp waves, and is the type of EEG event seen in patients with a seizure disorder. However, these same patterns, although indicating the presence of a focus, can be found in patients without any kind of episodic symptoms that would qualify as a seizure. As with other EEG patterns, the literature seems to show considerable variability in the incidence of such patterns in dyslexics. On the one hand, relatively few of these EEG events were found in the study by Hughes (1971) on underachievers (6%) or in the study of Hughes and Park (1968) on dyslexics (4%). Consistent with these findings is the study by Ingram *et al.* (1970) who reported only at 7% incidence in dyslexics. On the other hand, Torres and Ayers (1968) reported that the most common EEG abnormality found in patients with dyslexia was a sharp wave discharge recorded from the temporal areas. Also, Murdoch (1974) reported that there was more of this type of activity in their patients with minimal cerebral dysfunction than in their control group. Fenelon *et al.* (1972) claimed that eight of the nine patients with dyslexia and an abnormal EEG had some type of discharge in the form of spike or sharp wave. In a study of patients with occiptial sharp waves or spikes, Volterra and Giordani (1966) reported that some of these patients were dyslexics. Finally, Lairy and Harrison (1968) have shown that patients with occipital spike foci frequently demonstrate visual or oculomotor disorders.

The electroclinical correlations in dyslexic or learning-disabled patients with sharp waves or spikes have emphasized that these patients tend to have short attention span or impaired attention. Evidence on this point comes from the studies of Green (1961) and Stores (1973). There is also evidence (Hughes & Park, 1968) that dyslexics with epileptiform activity tended to have relatively high thyroid levels in the blood, but also visual deficiencies in the form of abnormal duction and stereopsis. Also, Corcelle, Rozier, Dedieu, Vincent, and Faure (1968) reported that dyslexics with epileptiform activity showed a relatively high incidence of verbal and spatial disorders. A very specific pattern, called the bilaterally synchronous and symmetrical 3 per second spike and wave complex, is found in patients with absence (petit mal) seizures and specifically is associated with the impaired retrieval of information rather than impaired storage. The impairment lasts for the duration of these complexes and even when the presentation of the stimulus is 2–4 sec before the complexes (Hutt, Lee, & Ounsted, 1963; Geller & Geller, 1970; Woodruff, 1974). Chiofalo *et al.* (1971) reported that occipital discharges tend to be associated with a relatively normal IQ, but with visuomotor defects, although minor in most instances. Finally, Lairy and Netchine (1963) found that partially sighted patients tended to have a relatively high (25%) incidence of occipital and temporal discharges, especially on the left occipital area. This latter study places further emphasis on the fact that occipital discharges at times may correlate with some type of visual disorder.

CONCLUSIONS FROM AN EARLY REVIEW OF THE LITERATURE

Benton and Bird (1963) have acknowledged that an increased incidence of abnormal EEGs is found in patients with dyslexia, but conclude that "a specific association between EEG and reading disability has not been unequivocally demonstrated [p. 531]." The statement is justified, especially with use of the terms "specific" and "unequivocally." However, the statement also does point out both that dyslexics show a higher incidence of positive EEG findings than control groups and that the kind of EEG patterns that are found in individuals with reading disabilities are not of one variety, but of different types (see also Benton, 1975). The previous discussion has shown that four kinds of EEG findings are usually reported, namely, positive spikes, excessive occipital slow waves, epileptiform discharges, and generalized, diffuse abnormalities. The demonstration that there are different kinds of EEG findings in dyslexia may lead to the conclusion that these electrographic patterns are of no clear significance and can lead to no further understanding of the problem of dyslexia. On the other hand, such a demonstration of varied findings may lead to the appropriate conclusion that dyslexia is the final common, clinical pathway for a disorder which may arise from different etiologies, involving various areas of the brain and associated with a number of related deficits. Thus, the different kinds of EEG findings in patients with dyslexia may essentially reflect the multifaceted aspects of a reading disability. For example, dyslexics with positive spikes may have as a common problem relatively high levels of tension and anxiety, in addition to high thyroxine levels leading to hyperactivity and behavior disorders, but appearing in the classroom first as a reading disability. Patients with excessive occipital slow waves may have as their special problem a deficit in visuomotor performance that also manifests itself as a dyslexia. Those with different kinds of epileptiform activity may specifically have a disorder of attention that may also appear first in a scholastic setting as a dyslexia. Finally, patients with generalized, diffuse findings may have protean clinical deficits, including retarded speech and motor development, but the first major problem encountered in the classroon may be a dyslexia. In short, individuals with a reading problem may, in fact, have specific disorders that are not clearly recognized and are labeled in the classroom as a dyslexia, because the first major, scholastic difficulty encountered in the classroom is reading retardation. Attempts have been made by various investigators to control for related disorders and to study only dyslexia, but dyslexia in its pure form may be nonexistent. Therefore, it is possible that most studies on dyslexia will necessarily include patients with various related disorders, even though the definition of the dyslexia can be as specific or operational as possible. The usefulness of the EEG may be to underscore the particular part of the brain involved, pointing to a special class of EEG findings and possibly leading to other studies that will specifically determine the precise nature of the major underlying deficit in any given child. In the remaining portion of this review the same theme will appear—namely, that the difficulty or inability to read can arise from many different causes, involving different areas of the brain.

ALPHA ASYMMETRY

Some of the newer EEG studies have demonstrated the usefulness of the EEG in determining the dominant hemisphere, in order to investigate the relationship of hemispheral dominance to dyslexia. The studies are predicated on a reasonable assumption that the greater desynchronization or lower amplitude of alpha is found over the dominant hemisphere. One such study is by Galin and Ellis (1975) who reported on an asymmetry of alpha power (more consistent than differences in the visual evoked potential) which changed according to whether the subjects were involved in verbal or spatial tasks. The highest correlation between the alpha asymmetry and the different cognitive processes was found on the temporal areas. In addition, the changes in the asymmetry of the evoked potential amplitude paralleled the task dependent asymmetry of the alpha. In another similar study, Dumas and Morgan (1975) attempted to determine whether alpha asymmetry was a function of occupation and for this purpose investigated the alpha of artists and engineers, performing linguistic and spatial tasks. They found no differences according to occupation of the subjects or the degree of difficulty of task, but they reported a significant relationship for the type of task performed. Evidence of left-sided dominance in the form of greater desynchronization was found during linguistic or mathematic endeavors, and right-sided laterality was noted for spatial tests. In a further investigation on the same kind of problem, Hirshkowitz, Earle, and Paley (1978) reported on EEG alpha asymmetry in musicians and nonmusicians. Their conclusion was that the alpha asymmetry of the nonmusicians and musicians was different only during musical stimulation, with right hemisphere activation accompanying musical stimuli only among the nonmusicians. These data seemed to indicate that hemispheric specialization was related to perceptual processing and past experience, and not merely to the acoustical properties of the stimulus. In a very similar study, Willis, Wheatley, and Mitchell (1979) reported on alpha power as related to a task varying along a spatial analytic continua. The data supported the hypothesis that hemispheric processing was a function of task processing demands, not just perceptual requirements.

EEG IN SELECTIVE CASES

We will now deal with the EEG in certain selective cases, mainly patients with alexia without agraphia. This disorder is relevant to the subject of dyslexia since reading difficulty can be viewed as a continuum from a developmental dyslexia, gradually appearing in the young child, to an alexia, precipitously appearing from a given brain lesion usually in older patients. Although the term alexia implies the complete *inability* to read, in most instances patients with this disorder share with the dyslexic child the *difficulty* in reading, without a specific disorder of writing (agraphia). Therefore, alexia without agraphia refers to the same kind of clinical disorder as is seen in developmental dyslexia; the determination of the locus of the lesions in alexia should provide evidence of the brain areas involved in dyslexia. The emphasis in this section will be on demonstrating the various kinds of EEG abnormality that can be found in patients with alexia without agraphia.

In some instances the EEG is *normal* and fails to show any clear abnormal pattern. In one interesting patient presented by Streifler and Hofman (1976) a slight concussion resulted in mirror writing and a difficulty in the patient's sinistral writing and reading, but left the dextral system unimpaired. The EEG was normal in this patient. In view of the other types of impairment in this patient the authors suggested that there was pathology within both parietal–occipital areas. In another patient described by Orgogozo, Pere, and Strube (1979), the EEG was again normal, but the neurological examination revealed a mild quadrantopsia in the upper visual field. Finally, Assal and Hadj-Djilani (1976) discussed a patient with a normal EEG with alexia but without hemianopsia.

A slow wave abnormality has appeared on the left temporal area in some other patients with alexia. For example, Holtzman, Rudel, and Goldensohn (1978) described a patient who at first had a normal EEG, but later developed a left temporal slow wave focus with a paroxysmal alexia progressing to a persistent alexia without agraphia. The authors considered this paroxysmal disorder to be a partial seizure, reflecting a disturbance of the dominant hemisphere involving the outflow from the occipital fissure to the angular gyrus, although the slow wave abnormality was noted on the left temporal area. In another patient (Greenblatt, 1973), the EEG showed a delta slow wave focus (under 4 per second) on the left temporal area, in addition to a diffuse slowing, and later the patient was shown to have a left occipital glioma. The patient had an alexia without agraphia and hemianopsia. Finally, one other patient described by Debray-Ritzen, Hirsch, Pierre-Kahn, Bursztejn, and Labbe (1977) showed a great amount of delta slow waves on the left temporal area, also involving the left frontal area. This patient was an adolescent who developed a reading disorder on the basis of a hematoma that was limited to the medial part of the second left temporal convolution. The evacuation of the hematoma resulted in the disappearance of the reading disorder. In this patient concordance occurred in that the slow waves appeared maximal on the left temporal area and the pathology was also located within that same region. However, it is well known that slow waves may appear maximal on the temporal areas in patients whose major pathology may be located not within the temporal area but rather in neighboring regions.

Other patients with alexia without agraphia have presented with slow wave abnormalities from the *left occipital* area. In the second patient of Orgogozo *et al.* (1979), the EEG showed delta slow waves and also low amplitude background activity from the left occipital area. This alexic patient also had a severe lower quadrantopsia. The computerized tomography (CT) scan showed a necrosis of the internal part of the left occipital lobe, but also showed some atrophy especially within the left temporal area. In another patient described by Levitt, Gastinger, McClintic, and Lin (1978), the EEG showed slow waves on the left posterior region and a brain scan showed an increased uptake within the same area. A hematoma located in the left occipital area from an aneurysm was the likely cause of this alexia without agraphia.

The *right occipital* area may also be the localization of abnormal slow waves in alexia, as demonstrated by a patient of Aptman, Levin, and Senelick (1977). In this patient the brain scan confirmed a right occipital lobe lesion as did the CT scan with postinfusion studies demonstrating an enhancement of the lesion in that region.

Finally, *both the temporal and occipital* areas may demonstrate slow wave abnormalities. For example, Levine and Calvanio (1978) reported on three patients with verbal alexia-simultanagnosia. The EEG in one of these patients showed slow wave abnormalities on both posterior temporal areas. However, the CT scan suggested that only the left occipital-temporal area was involved with structural pathology. In another patient, reported on by Lühdorf and Paulson (1977), the EEG showed theta rhythms and sharp waves on both temporal and occipital areas, more on the left side. In this patient with alexia without agraphia the brain scan was normal, as was the angiogram, but the authors concluded that a left occipital lobe infarction had occurred. Finally, Heilman, Rothi, Campanella, and Wolfson (1979) described three patients with aphasia, one of whom developed an alexia when a right hemispheral lesion was added to a left-sided lesion. The EEG in this patient showed bilateral slow waves greater over the right side, the hemisphere with the more recent lesion.

In this section the EEG findings have been described as either normal, left temporal in location, left occipital or right occipital, or, finally, as involving both temporal and occipital areas. Patients with normal EEGs but with some type of neurological deficit represent no theoretical problem in view of the fact that some lesions may be so deep with reference to the surface EEG electrodes that the EEG may not "see" an abnormality. Also, if the rate of destruction of neurons is very slow, no clear slow wave abnormality may be recorded. The variations in the EEG findings of the other patients demonstrate the general point made in this section of the review, namely, that lesions of different parts of the brain may result in the same clinical picture of alexia (or dyslexia).

DEMONSTRATED PATHOLOGY IN PATIENTS WITH ALEXIA WITHOUT AGRAPHIA

This section will emphasize the location of the demonstrated pathology in patients with alexia without agraphia who may or may not have had an EEG. These data will provide further evidence for the neurophysiological basis of reading disabilities by showing that lesions found in various locations can result in alexia.

In some alexic patients a *left occipital* lesion may be found, as exemplified by one patient of Dejerine, described by Geschwind (1965). This patient also had a lesion of splenium of the corpus callosum. In four patients of Johansson and Fahlgren (1979), lateral or medial infarction was demonstrated of the left occipital lobe. Michel, Schott, Boucher, and Kopp (1979) summarized the world literature on alexia without agraphia and concluded that in the majority of instances this disorder is related to an infarction from a disorder of the left posterior cerebral artery, involving mainly the left occipital lobe, but in some cases also extending into other (subcortical) areas. In a summary of the reading and writing disorders by Heilman (1975), alexia without agraphia was considered to represent a lesion within the left occipital (visual) cortex.

In other instances authors have specified both the left parietal and left occipital area as the important region to explain this condition. In Geschwind's (1965) discussion of Dejerine's two patients of 1891 and 1892 one of them had a lesion in the left angular gyrus, in addition to the left occipital area. In the patient of Assal and Hadj-Djilani (1976), an angiogram showed a vascular lesion involvinq both the left parietal and occipital areas.

In still other instances the combination of *left temporal and occipital* areas seems to form the basis of the pathology to explain alexia without agraphia. An example is the one patient of Orgogozo *et al.* (1979) who showed atrophy especially in the left temporal area and also necrosis of the left occipital lobe.

The right parietal or occipital area is implicated in still other patients with alexia without agraphia. Patients described by Kinsbourne and Warrington (1962) showed evidence of a neglect of left-sided space, resulting in the conclusion by the authors that a right parietal lesion was indicated. These patients were right-handed. In one non-right-handed patient with alexia described by Erkulvrawatr (1978), a right occipital lobe infarction was demonstrated, especially by a CT scan and a brain scan. In a patient presented by Hirose (1978), a CT scan revealed a lesion within the right occipital area consistent with an infarction from a disorder of the right posterior cerebral artery. Finally, in the patient described by Fincham, Nibbelink, and Aschenbrener (1975), an alexia was found in a patient with a right parietal–occipital lesion, as demonstrated by the brain scan also showing a lesion in the left posterior parietal area. The author concluded that none of the demonstrated lesions seemed to involve the left occipital area or the pathways connecting this region to the left angular gyrus.

Finally, some evidence exists that *both parietal–occipital* areas may be involved in some patients with alexia without agraphia. For example, in the case of the patient of Streifler and Hofman (1976) who had a slight concussion leading to both mirror writing and a dyslexia, there was evidence that both parietal–occipital areas were involved. However, there was no clear demonstration of bilateral lesions. One interesting patient described by Skoglund (1979) with mitochondrial myopathy and lactic acidemia also had an alexia without agraphia. The CT scan demonstrated lesions within both parietal–occipital areas.

In summary, of the patients with alexia but without agraphia described in this section, some have demonstrated a lesion in the left occipital area, others in left parietal and occipital regions or left temporal and occipital areas, still others in the right parietal–occipital area, and finally in some other instances bilateral parietal–occipital lesions are indicated. These patients thus add further evidence to the general point that a multiplicity of lesions can show up with the same general clinical manifestation of an alexia or dyslexia.

NEUROPHYSIOLOGICAL THEORIES
OF DYSLEXIA

The patients that have been described in the previous sections have led to various neurophysiological theories to explain dyslexia or alexia. One theory, popularized by Geschwind (1965), is the *disconnection theory*, which proposes that a functional or structural separation of cortical regions from their white matter connections or from their association areas may explain this type of deficit. In the two cases described by Dejerine and subsequently discussed by Geschwind, the lesions were found in the left angular gyrus and left occipital area in one instance and in the left occipital lobe and splenium of the corpus callosum in the other. Geschwind has suggested that the lesion within the splenium of the corpus callosum is important to disconnect the right visual cortex region from the angular gyrus of the left side. Evidence in favor of the importance of the callosal lesion comes from the work of Badian and Wolff (1977) who demonstrated that young males with dyslexia demonstrate normal tapping ability when one hand is used alone but not when alternating the two hands. These authors present these data as evidence in favor of a disturbance of the interhemispheric cooperation required for normal reading and as pointing to some disturbance within the corpus callosum. Further evidence for this position comes from the work of Kreuter, Kinsbourne, and Trevarthen (1972), who showed that patients with hemispheric deconnection could not alternate their finger tapping in a normal manner. Other theories, not necessarily mutually exclusive with the disconnection syndrome, also come from Geschwind (1965), who suggested that dyslexia involves the *delayed development* of the angular gyrus, probably with a bilateral involvement. The *parietal* lobe has been the center of attention in other studies on developmental dyslexia, as exemplified by the work of Jorm (1977) who presented to dyslexic children five tests that were considered sensitive to parietal lobe function. The dyslexic subjects performed poorly in two of these five tests. A factor analysis led the author to conclude that two separate functional systems involving the parietal lobe are needed to explain developmental dyslexia. Evidence for a parietal involvement also comes from visual evoked potentials, as exemplified by the studies of Symann-Louett, Gascon, Matsumiya, and Lombroso (1977). These authors showed that the visual evoked potentials of dyslexics were deficient in early components by virtue of the fewer waves, especially on the left parietal area. Some of these patients did have bilateral parietal abnormalities, but it was the left parietal area that was especially distinctive. Preston, Guthrie, Kirsch, Gertman, and Childs (1977) have provided further evidence by showing that disabled adult readers demonstrate differences from normals on the left parietal area, especially for the two waveforms called P200 (positivity at 200 msec) and also LPC (late positive component).

Further emphasis on a left-sided disorder to explain dyslexia comes from various theories that suggest that these patients are using the *right hemisphere,* rather than the left, for a function for which the left is better suited. For example, Kershner (1977) showed that dyslexic patients demonstrated an inferior performance when visual stimuli were presented to the right visual field, but scored high with left field stimuli. These data suggested to the author that dyslexia may be related to hemispheral differences in processing reading material and that these patients were utilizing the right hemisphere for localized coding strategy for reading. Such a strategy may be inefficient and inappropriate, considering the important demands of also comprehending the text. Further evidence on this point comes from McKeever and Van Deventer (1975) who reported that right-handed dyslexics have normal interhemispheric processing delays for single letter stimuli, but impaired efficiency of visual and auditory processing of simple language stimuli. Their conclusion was that dyslexics may have a deficit in the function of the left hemisphere visual association area. Consistent with this conclusion is the finding by Hier, LeMay, Rosenberger, and Verlo (1978) that the CT scan tends to show a wider right parietal–occipital area in dyslexics, as opposed to normals who show a reversed asymmetry. Witelson (1977) has suggested a similar left hemispheral deficiency in these patients with developmental dyslexia in whom there may be "two right hemispheres and none left." This author speculates that a bilateral involvement in spatial processing may interfere with left hemispheric processing, and the result could therefore be a deficient linguistic sequencing for cognitive processing and the overuse of spatial cognitive modes. Thus, the dyslexic child may be attempting to read predominantly with a spatial, holistic cognitive strategy, neglecting the phonetic sequencing strategy, and such an approach in learning to read phonetically coded language may be inefficient.

Further complication to the understanding of the neurophysiological basis of reading difficulties comes from evidence presented by Pöppel and Shattuck (1974). These authors discussed 22 patients with a penetrating head injury, 12 of whom had lesions within the central visual pathways leading to visual field defects. These latter patients were not aware of any reading difficulty, but their reading time for given material was twice that of control patients. One interesting finding was that the visual field defects per se did not seem to affect the results of these tests. The authors concluded that the lesions in the central visual pathways, clinically manifesting themselves as a reading difficulty, resulted in simply a *slowing down* of the analysis of visual information.

In the search for a specific defect in dyslexia some evidence on this question may be found in the studies of Yeni-Komshian, Isenberg, and Goldberg (1975). In contradistinction to the findings of Kershner (1977), these investigators showed that the deficit in poor readers was most evident when digits were presented in the left visual half field. These data suggested to these authors that poor readers may suffer from some form of *degraded processing within the right hemisphere* or possibly a problem involving transmission from the right to the left hemisphere.

Finally, one other theory in dyslexia relates to the question of an uncertain establishment of *cerebral dominance,* suggested by Orton in 1937. Evidence for this hypothesis came later from Klasen (1968), who reported that 44% of dyslexics showed crossed laterality or lack of correspondence of hand, eye, and foot dominance. Also, Thomson (1976) found that controls showed right ear superiority for auditory stimuli, but dyslexics demonstrated either no difference or varied superiority according to the type of stimulus presented. He concluded that these data indicate a less well-established hemispheral dominance in dyslexics than normals as the underlying difficulty in processing visual information. Further investigation into the question of cerebral dominance in dyslexics has taken the form of the incidence of left-handedness in this disorder. The results vary from the 15% of Kagen (1943) (4% in controls), to the 27% of Naidoo (1972) (9% in controls), to the 75% of Roudinesco (see Matejcek, 1968).

On the other hand, evidence can be found that conflicts with the concept of poorly established hemispheral dominance in dyslexics. For example, Abigail and Johnson (1976) found in dichotic listening experiments that right-handed dyslexics did *not* differ from normal readers with regard to ear dominance. Kershner's (1978) data go yet one step further from the concept of a poorly established dominance by showing

that dyslexic children have a *strong* degree of early lateralized concordance for hand, eye, ear, and foot preference. These data contradict
the idea that a delay in early lateralization may underlie a subsequent
reading impairment. Kershner suggests that normal maturation involves the development of bisymmetry and a slowly maturing child,
at risk for dyslexia, is one with a delay in developing bisymmetrical
functions by demonstrating persistent lateralization for hand, eye, ear,
and foot usage. This suggestion is consistent with the data of Gesell
and Ames (1974) who maintained that newborns show a propensity
of right-sided tonic neck reflexes, related to a later hand preference.
The suggestion is also consistent with the conclusion of Kinsbourne
(1974), who claimed that sensory–motor lateralization is present from
birth. Thus, some data argue that dyslexics have a developmental immaturity in the form of strongly lateralized functions with inadequate
symmetry whereas other data suggest that the immaturity is in the
form of a poorly established hemispheral dominance.

    The major theme of this review is well summarized by Mattis, French,
and Rapin (1975) who argue for multiple, independent defects in higher
cortical function, as opposed to any theory of a single causal defect,
to explain a reading disability. The theories presented in this section,
the demonstrated lesions in the individual patients with alexia without
agraphia, in addition to the EEGs of those patients and the EEG findings
in large groups of dyslexic children, all argue strongly for a multiplicity
of defects or lesions to explain reading disabilities.

SUMMARY OF THE USEFULNESS OF THE EEG IN
THE STUDY OF DYSLEXIA

    The first section of this chapter summarized the studies that dem-
onstrate an increased incidence of positive EEG findings in patients
with developmental dyslexia. Four types of EEG patterns have been
described in these patients: (*a*) positive spikes—a controversial phenomenon, (*b*) excessive occipital slow waves, (*c*) epileptiform sharp
waves or spike discharges, and (*d*) diffuse or generalized abnormalities.
If the evidence in patients with dyslexia or alexia were to point toward
a single cause or lesion to account for this type of deficit, these varied
EEG findings could be considered insignificant, as their variability
would not be consistent with such a monocausal defect. However, this
review has shown that the evidence argues for a multiplicity of causes
and of locations of lesions to explain a reading difficulty, and, therefore,
a multiplicity of positive EEG findings may be considered consistent

with these data. Also, John (1977) found in 50 learning-disabled children that "no single pattern emerged" and that many different kinds of abnormality appeared—from excessive occipital slow waves, through abnormal polarity coincidence correlations, to abnormal signal ratios.

Children labeled dyslexic do not automatically have the same kind of basic underlying problem. The actual disorder in these patients may be single or multiple and may only *indirectly* relate to a problem in acquiring visual information, but the first clinical presentation in a scholastic setting may be a difficulty in reading. Thus, the presence of positive spikes (although very controversial) could argue for a (diencephalic) hyperactivity, leading to a behavioral disorder, but showing as a dyslexia in school. The parietal–occipital slow wave abnormality might prove to be a more specific finding related to deficiencies in visuomotor performance. The presence of epileptiform activity has often been associated with defects of attention, and diffuse EEG abnormalities have correlated with multiple defects, in addition to a reading disorder, but either type of EEG finding, if clinically manifested, may show up first as a dyslexia in the classroom. Thus, the EEG may point to some specific problem related to a dyslexia, and the electrographic results may lead to undercovering some of the many factors that are involved in a child learning to read. Further research is required in order to determine whether specific EEG patterns relate to specific disorders that can appear as a dyslexia.

In the search to incorporate the concept of hemispheral dominance into theories to explain developmental dyslexia, the EEG has been valuable as a noninvasive test to provide evidence. The EEG has also been very useful in studying patients with alexia without agraphia, confirming that the lesions may either be within the right parietal and/ or occipital area or on the left parietal and/or occipital region or on both sides. All of the data on patients with alexia without agraphia, the EEGs in these patients, and the results of systematic studies of the EEG in developmental dyslexia point toward a multiplicity of lesions that can clinically manifest themselves as a reading disorder or dyslexia. As suggested in the introduction, simplistic theories always seem to give way to more complicated ones when more data appear. The act of reading and the acquisition of visual information are obviously very complicated tasks involving complex systems within the brain, including oculomotor, sensory afferent and efferent, perceptual and association systems, incorporating the classic visual afferent system, subcortical oculomotor pathways, both parietal and occipital (possibly temporal) areas, and their interconnections within and between hemispheres, all under the influence of the reticular activating system. If any part of these complex pathways is involved either with a discrete lesion or as a developmental delay, a reading difficulty or dyslexia may result. The electroencephalogram has contributed to the body of knowledge on dyslexia by providing further evidence for a multiplicity of causes, neurophysiological disturbances, or lesions in this disorder.

REFERENCES

Abigail, E. R., & Johnson, E. G. (1976) Ear and hand dominance and their relationship with reading retardation. *Perceptual and Motor Skills, 43,* 1031–1036.

Aptman, M., Levin, H., & Senelick, R. C. (1977) Alexia without agraphia in a left-handed patient with prosopagnosia. *Neurology* (Minneapolis) *27,* 533–536.

Assal, G., & Hadj-Djilani, M. (1976) Une nouvelle observation d'alexia pure sans hémianopsie. *Cortex, 12,* 169–174.

Ayers, F. W., & Torres, F. (1967) The incidence of EEG abnormalities in a dyslexic and a control group. *Journal of Clinical Psychology, 23,* 334–336.

Badian, N. A., & Wolff, P. H. (1977) Manual asymmetries of motor sequencing in boys with reading disability. *Cortex, 13,* 343–349.

Benton, A. L. (1975) Developmental dyslexia. Neurological aspects. In W. J. Friedlander (Ed.), *Advances in neurology* (Vol. 7). New York: Raven.

Benton, A. L., & Bird, J. W. (1963) The EEG and reading disability. *American Journal of Orthopsychiatry, 33,* 529–531.

Black, F. W. (1972) EEG and birth abnormalities in high- and low-perceiving reading retarded children. *Journal of Genetic Psychology, 121,* 327–328.

Bryant, N., & Friedlander, W. J. (1965) "14" and "6" in boys with specific reading disability. *Electroencephalography and Clinical Neurophysiology, 19,* 318–322.

Capute, A. J., Niedermeyer, E. F. L., & Richardson, F. (1968) The electroencephalogram in children with minimal cerebral dysfunction. *Pediatrics, 41,* 1104–1114.

Chiofalo, N., Bravo, L., Perez, M., & Villavicencio, C. (1971) The electroencephalogram in children with learning disorders. *Acta Neurologia Latino-Americana, 17,* 164–171.

Cohn, R., & Nardini, J. (1958) The correlation of bilateral occipital slow activity in the human EEG with certain disorders of behavior. *American Journal of Psychiatry, 155,* 44–54.

Cohn, R. (1961) Delayed acquisition of reading and writing abilities in children. *Archives of Neurology, 4,* 153–164.

Corcelle, L., Rozier, J., Dedieu, E., Vincent, J. D., & Faure, L. (1968) Variations of cortical evoked potentials according to the modality of sensory stimulation in dyslexic children. *Revue de Laryngologie, Otologie, Rhinologie, 89,* 458–468.

Debray-Ritzen, P., Hirsch, J.-F., Pierre-Kahn, A., Bursztejn, C., & Labbe, J.-P. (1977) Atteinte transitoire du langage écrit en rapport avec un hématome du lobe temporal gauche chez une adolescente de quatorze ans. *Revue Neurologique, 133,* 207–210.

Dumas, R., & Morgan, A. (1975) EEG asymmetry as a function of occupation, task and task difficulty. *Neuropsychologia, 13,* 219–228.

Erkulvrawatr, S. (1978) Alexia and left homonymous hemianopia in a non-right-handers. *Annals of Neurology, 3,* 549–552.

Fenelon, B., Holland, J. T., & Johnson, O. (1972) Spatial organization of the EEG in children with reading disabilities—A study using nitrazepam. *Cortex, 8,* 444–464.

9. The Electroencephalogram and Reading Disorders

Fincham, R. W., Nibbelink, D. W., & Aschenbrener, C. A. (1975) Alexia with left homonymous hemianopia without agraphia. *Neurology, 25,* 1164–1168.

Galin, D., & Ellis, R. R. (1975) Asymmetry in evoked potentials as an index of lateralized cognitive processes in relation to EEG alpha asymmetry. *Neuropsychologia, 13,* 45–50.

Geller, M., & Geller, A. (1970) Brief amnestic effects of spike-wave discharges. *Neurology, 20,* 1089–1095.

Gerson, I. M., Barnes, T. C., Mannino, A., Fanning, J. M., & Burns, J. J. (1972) EEG of children with various learning problems, I: Outpatient study. *Diseases of the Nervous System, 33,* 170–177.

Geschwind, N. (1965) Disconnection syndromes in animals and man. Part I. *Brain, 88,* 237–294.

Gesell, A., & Ames, L. (1974) The development of handedness. *Journal of Genetic Psychology, 70,* 155–175.

Green, J. B. (1961) Association of behavior disorder with an EEG focus in children without seizures. *Neurology, 11,* 337–344.

Greenblatt, S. H. (1973) Alexia without agraphia or hemianopsia. *Brain, 96,* 307–316.

Heilman, K. M. (1975) Reading and writing disorders caused by central nervous system defects. *Geriatrics, 30,* 115–118.

Heilman, K. M., Rothi, L., Campanella, D., & Wolfson, S. (1979) Wernicke's and global aphasia without alexia. *Archives of Neurology, 36,* 129–133.

Hier, D. B., LeMay, M., Rosenberger, P. B., & Verlo, V. P. (1978) Developmental dyslexia. *Archives of Neurology, 35,* 90–92.

Hirose, G. (1978) Alexia without agraphia with right occipital lesion. *Journal of Neurology, Neurosurgery and Psychiatry, 41,* 1152.

Hirshkowitz, M., Earle, J., & Paley, B. (1978) EEG alpha asymmetry in musicians and non-musicians: A study of hemispheric specialization. *Neuropsychologia, 16,* 125–128.

Holtzman, R. N. N., Rudel, R. G., & Goldensohn, E. S. (1978) Paroxysmal alexia. *Cortex, 14,* 592–603.

Hughes, J. R. (1971) Electroencephalography and learning disabilities. In H. R. Myklebust (Ed.), *Progress in learning disabilities* (Vol. 2). New York: Grune & Stratton.

Hughes, J. R. (1978) Electroencephalographic and neurophysiological studies in dyslexia. In A. L. Benton & D. Pearl (Eds.), *Dyslexia: An appraisal of current knowledge.* New York: Oxford University Press.

Hughes, J. R., & Park, G. E. (1968) The EEG in dyslexia. In P. Kellaway & I. Petersén (Eds.), *Clinical electroencephalography of children.* Stockholm: Almqvist and Wiksell.

Hutt, S. J., Lee, D., & Ounsted, D. (1963) Digit memory and evoked discharges in four light-sensitive epileptic children. *Developmental Medicine and Child Neurology, 5,* 559–577.

Ingram, T. T. S., Mason, A. W., & Blackburn, I. (1970) A retrospective study of 82 children with reading disability. *Developmental Medicine and Child Neurology, 12,* 271–281.

Johansson, T., & Fahlgren, H. (1979) Alexia without agraphia: Lateral and medial infarction of left occipital lobe. *Neurology, 29,* 390–393.

John, E. R. (1977) *Neurometrics: Clinical applications of quantitative electrophysiology.* New York: Wiley.

Jorm, A. F. (1977) Parietal lobe function in developmental dyslexia. *Neuropsychologia, 15,* 841–844.

Kagen, B. (1943) On word blindness. *Pedagogeska Shriften, 60,* 179–180.

Kennard, M. A., Rabinovitch, R., & Wexler, D. (1952) The abnormal electroencephalogram as related to reading disability in children with disorders of behavior. *Canadian Medical Association Journal, 67,* 330–333.

Kenny, T. J., Clemmens, R. L., Cicci, R., Lentz, G. A., Jr., Nair, P., & Hudson, B. W. (1972) The medical evaluation of children with reading problems (dyslexia). _Pediatrics, 49_, 438–442.

Kershner, J. R. (1977) Cerebral dominance in disabled readers, good readers and gifted children: Search for valid model. _Child Development, 48_, 61–67.

Kershner, J. R. (1978) Lateralization in normal 6 year olds as related to later reading disability. _Developmental Psychobiology, 11_, 309–319.

Kinsbourne, M. (1974) The mechanism of hemispheric interaction in man. In M. Kinsbourne & L. Smith (Eds.), _The disconnected cerebral hemisphere._ Springfield, Ill.: Charles C Thomas.

Kinsbourne, M., & Warrington, E. K. (1962) A variety of reading disability associated with right hemispheral lesions. _Journal of Neurology, Neurosurgery and Psychiatry, 25_, 339–344.

Klasen, E. (1968) _Legasthenie._ Bern: Huber.

Knott, J. R., Muehl, S., & Benton, A. L. (1965) Electroencephalograms in children with reading disabilities. _Electroencephalography and Clinical Neurophysiology, 18_, 513.

Kreuter, C., Kinsbourne, M., & Trevarthen, C. (1972) Are deconnected cerebral hemispheres independent channels? A preliminary study of the effect of unilateral loading on bilateral finger tapping. _Neuropsychologia, 10_, 453–461.

Lairy, G. C., & Harrison, A. (1968) Functional aspects of EEG foci in children: Clinical data and longitudinal studies. In P. Kellaway & I. Petersén (Eds.), _Clinical EEG of children._ Stockholm: Almqvist and Wiksell.

Lairy, G., & Netchine, S. (1960) Signification psychologique et clinique de l'organization spatiale de l'EEG chez l'enfant. _Revue Neurologique, 102_, 380–388.

Lairy, G., & Netchine, S. (1963) The electroencephalogram in partially sighted children related to clinical and psychological data. _Proceedings, First International Meeting on Technology and Blindness, 2_, 267–284.

Levine, D. N., & Calvanio, R. (1978) A study of the visual defect in verbal alexia-simultanagnosia. _Brain, 101_, 65–81.

Levitt, L. P., Gastinger, J., McClintic, W., & Lin, F. (1978) Alexia without agraphia due to aneurysm. _Pennsylvania Medicine, 81_, 86–87.

Lühdorf, K., & Paulson, O. B. (1977) Does alexia without agraphia always include hemianopsia? _Acta Neurologica Scandinavia, 55_, 323–329.

Matejcek, Z. (1968) Dyslexia, an international problem—A report from Czechoslovakia. _Bulletin of the Orton Society, 18,_

Mattis, S., French, J. H., & Rapin, I. (1975) Dyslexia in children and young adults: Three independent neuropsychological syndromes. _Developmental Medicine and Child Neurology, 17_, 150–163.

McKeever, W. F., & Van Deventer, A. D. (1975) Dyslexia adolescents: Evidence of impaired visual and auditory language processing associated with normal lateralization and visual responsivity. _Cortex, 11_, 361–378.

Michel, F., Schott, B., Boucher, M., & Kopp, N. (1979) Alexie sans agraphie chez un malade ayant un hémisphère gauche de afferente (hémianopsie, hémianesthésie, hémianacousie). _Rev. Neurol., 15_, 347–364.

Muehl, S., Knott, J. R., & Benton, A. L. (1965) EEG abnormality and psychological test performance in reading disability. _Cortex, 1_, 434–440.

Murdoch, B. D. (1974) Changes in the electroencephalogram in minimal cerebral dysfunction. Controlled study over 8 months. _South African Medical Journal, 48_, 606–610.

Naidoo, S. (1972) _Specific dyslexia._ London: Pitman.

Njiokiktjien, C. J., Visser, S. L., & de Rijke, W. (1977) EEG and visual evoked responses in children with learning disorders. *Neuropaediatrie, 8,* 134–147.

Orgogozo, J. M., Pere, J. J., & Strube, E. (1979) Alexie sans agraphie, "agnosie", des couleurs et atteinte de l'hémichamp visuel droit: Un syndrome de l'artère cérébrale postérieure. *Semaine des Hopitaux de Paris, 55,* 1389–1394.

Orton, S. T. (1937) *Reading, writing and speech problems in children.* New York: Norton.

Pavy, R., & Metcalfe, J. (1965) The abnormal EEG in childhood communication and behavior abnormalities. *Electroencephalography and Clinical Neurophysiology, 19,* 414.

Pöppel, E., & Shattuck, S. R. (1974) Reading in patients with brain wounds involving the central visual pathways. *Cortex, 10,* 84–88.

Preston, N. S., Guthrie, J. T., Kirsch, I., Gertman, D., & Childs, B. VERs in normal and disabled adult readers. *Psychophysiology, 14,* 8–14.

Roudinesco, J., Trélat, J., & Trélat, M. (1950) Étude de quarante cas de dyslexic d' evolution. *Enfance, 3,* 1–32.

Satterfield, J. H., Lesser, L. I., Saul, R. E., & Cantwell, D. P. (1973) EEG aspects in the diagnosis and treatment of minimal brain dysfunction. *Annals of the New York Academy of Science, 205,* 274–281.

Skoglund, R. R. (1979) Reversible alexia, mitochondrial myopathy and lactic acidemia. *Neurology, 29,* 717–720.

Smith, W. L., Philippus, M. J., & Guard, H. L. (1968) Psychometric study of children with learning problems and 14–6 positive spike EEG patterns, treated with ethosuximide (Zarontin) and placebo. *Archives of Diseases of Children, 43,* 616–619.

Stores, G. (1973) Studies of attention and seizure disorders. *Developmental Medicine and Child Neurology, 15,* 376–382.

Streifler, M., & Hofman, S. (1976) Sinistrad mirror writing and reading after brain concussion in a bi-systemic (oriento-occidental) polyglot. *Cortex, 12,* 356–364.

Symann-Louett, N., Gascon, G. G., Matsumiya, Y., & Lombroso, C. T. (1977) Wave form difference in visual evoked responses between normal and reading disabled children. *Neurology, 27,* 156–159.

Thomson, M. E. (1976) A comparison of laterality effects in dyslexics and controls using verbal dichotic listening tasks. *Neuropsychologia, 14,* 243–246.

Torres, F., & Ayers, F. W. (1968) Evaluation of the electroencephalogram of dyslexic children. *Electroencephalography and Clinical Neurophysiology, 24,* 287.

Volterra, V., & Giordani, L. (1966) Considerazioni electrocliniche su 193 soggetti con EEG caratterizzato da punte e punte-onda in regione occipitale *Giornale di Psichiatria e di Neuropatologia, 94,* 337–373.

Webb, E. M., & Lawson, L. (1956) The EEG in severe speech and reading disabilities of childhood. *Electroencephalography and Clinical Neurophysiology, 8,* 168.

Willis, S. G., Wheatley, G. H., & Mitchell, O. R. (1979) Cerebral processing of spatial and verbal–analytic tasks: An EEG study. *Neuropsychologia, 17,* 473–484.

Witelson, S. F. (1977) Developmental dyslexia: Two right hemispheres and none left. *Science, 195,* 309–311.

Woodruff, M. L. (1974) Subconvulsive epileptiform discharge and behavior impairment. *Behavioral Biology, 11,* 431–458.

Yeni-Komshian, G. H., Isenberg, D., & Goldberg, H. (1975) Cerebral dominance and reading disability: Left visual field deficit in poor readers. *Neuropsychologia, 13,* 83–94.

Chapter Ten

Genetic Aspects of Reading Disability: A Family Study

J. C. DeFRIES
SADIE N. DECKER

INTRODUCTION

That reading disability tends to be familial has been known for many years. For example, in 1905, Thomas described the familial nature of "congenital word-blindness" as follows: "In this connection it is to be noted that it frequently assumes a family type; there are a number of instances of more than one member of the family being affected, and the mother often volunteers the statement that she herself was unable to learn to read, although she had every opportunity [p. 381]."

One of the cases described by Thomas (1905) in that report was especially noteworthy:

> J. H., aged 14, has been five years in a Special School. In March, 1901, it was noted: "Improving in everything but reading; cannot interpret any word."
> In November, 1904, no progress has been made in reading, although his attainments in other respects were normal. He did difficult problems in mental arithmetic with ease; drawing is good; and manual subjects excellent.

255

READING DISORDERS

He cannot read the word "cat," although when spelt aloud, he recognised it at once.

A sister, S. H., passed through this school, and her final note states that she could do everything but read on leaving.

The mother states that she herself could never learn to read, although she had every opportunity. Five other children in the same family have been unable to learn to read [italics in original, pp. 383–384].

A more recent example of the familial transmission of reading disability is depicted in Figure 10.1. Upon learning that we were conducting a family study of reading disability, a former colleague provided us with this pedigree of his own family. As he realized, the pedigree is unusual because it is cross-cultural. Two brothers, both of whom were born and educated in the USSR, experienced serious difficulties learning to read despite normal or above average intelligence. After World War II, the brothers became separated. One remained in Russia, where he later married and had three daughters. Like her father, one daughter is reading disabled. The other brother emigrated to the United

CROSS-CULTURAL PEDIGREE OF READING DISABILITY (RD)

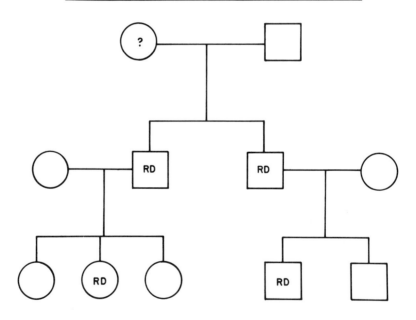

BORN AND RAISED IN U.S.S.R.   BORN AND RAISED IN U.S.A.

Figure 10.1. Familial transmission of reading disability in both the USSR and the United States.

States, where he married and had two sons. One of the sons is also reading disabled. The native languages of the two affected cousins are considerably different (Russian is a phonetically regular language, whereas English is not), and the educational systems of the United States and the Soviet Union are highly dissimilar. Nevertheless, familial transmission occurred in both cultural settings.

Although individual cases of familial transmission are of intrinsic interest, systematic family studies and twin studies are far more informative. Earlier twin and family studies of reading disability have been reviewed in detail by Finucci (1978), Herschel (1978), and Owen (1978), and will not be described here. However, the most extensive family study of reading disability, the Colorado Family Reading Study (FRS), has just recently been completed and only a few brief published accounts are currently available. The study is unique in that extensive psychometric data were collected on relatives of both reading-disabled children and their matched controls. Thus, the primary objective of the present chapter is to provide an overview of the Family Reading Study, including summaries of previously published and unpublished results.

COLORADO FAMILY READING STUDY

The primary objectives of the FRS, a 3-year project funded by the Spencer Foundation, were (a) to construct a battery of tests that differentiates children with diagnosed reading problems from controls; (b) to assess for possible cognitive and reading deficits in parents and siblings of children with reading problems; and (c) if such deficits were found, to study their transmission in families, that is, to conduct genetic analyses.

Subjects were ascertained by referral from personnel of the Boulder. Valley and St. Vrain Valley School districts in Colorado. The criteria employed for selection of the reading-disabled children (probands) were as follows: an IQ score of 90 or above as measured by a standardized intelligence test; a reading achievement level of one-half of grade level expectancy or lower as measured by a standardized reading test (e.g., a child in the fourth grade who is reading at or below second-grade level); chronological age between 7.5 and 12 years; residence with both biological parents; no known emotional or neurological impairment; and no uncorrected visual or auditory acuity deficits.

Control children were matched to reading-disabled children on the basis of age (within 6 months), sex, qrade, school, and home neighborhood. Each control child met all the criteria for probands, except that their reading level was equal to or greater than their current grade placement. In addition to the probands and matched controls, parents and siblings (7.5–18 years of age) were also tested. Typically, families were middle-class Caucasians, and the primary language spoken in the home was always English.

The design of the FRS, illustrated in Figure 10.2, provides for several informative comparisons. In addition to the obvious comparison of probands versus their matched controls, we can also compare siblings of probands versus siblings of controls, fathers of probands versus fathers of controls, and mothers of probands versus mothers of controls. If reading disability is to any degree heritable, then relatives of probands should manifest some deficits on our reading measures.

A 3-hour battery of psychometric tests was individually administered by trained examiners to members of 58 matched pairs of families during the first phase of the study. The most discriminating and reliable tests were then retained for a 2-hour battery which was employed during the remainder of the study. As may be seen in Table 10.1, two versions of the reduced battery were used: one for children under 10 years of age, the other for subjects 10 years of age or older. However, 10 tests were given to all subjects irrespective of age. Tests in the reduced battery were individually administered in two 1-hour blocks, separated by a 15-min break for rest and refreshment.

PROBAND FAMILY   **CONTROL FAMILY**

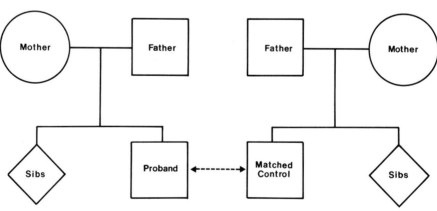

Figure 10.2. Design of the Colorado Family Reading Study.

Table 10.1
Family Reading Study Tests: Reduced Battery

Tests Administered to All Subjects
Peabody Individual Achievement Tests
  Mathematics (MATH)
  Reading recognition (REC)
  Reading comprehension (COMP)
  Spelling (SPELL)
Nonverbal Culture Fair Intelligence Test (IPAT "g")
Primary Mental Abilities Test
  Spatial relations (PMASR)
Colorado Perceptual Speed Test: Rotatable letters and numbers (CPS)
Wechsler Intelligence Scale for Children
  Coding B (CODE)
Illinois Test of Psycholinguistic Abilities
  Auditory closure
Benton Right–Left Discrimination Test

Tests for Subjects Under 10 Years of Age
Educational Testing Service
  Hidden patterns
Illinois Test of Psycholinguistic Abilities
  Grammatic closure
  Visual closure
  Auditory reception
  Visual reception
  Auditory association
  Auditory sequential memory

Tests for Subjects 10 Years of Age or Older
Educational Testing Service
  Concealed words
  Gestalt completion
American Council on Education
  Verbal analogies
Wechsler Intelligence Scale for Children or Adult Scale
  Digit span

During the 3-year project, 125 probands, their parents and siblings, and members of 125 control families were tested. The total number of subjects tested in these 250 families was 1044. Test descriptions and mean individual test scores for the various groups were previously reported by Foch, DeFries, McClearn, and Singer (1977) and DeFries, Singer, Foch, and Lewitter (1978). In this chapter, only results based upon composite measures will be summarized.

Individual test scores were age adjusted to facilitate comparisons among subjects of different ages. The sample was divided into three age groups (children under 10 years of age, children 10 and older, and parents), and each subject's score was expressed as a deviation from expectation based upon the linear and quadratic effects of age in the corresponding control sample. Resulting age-adjusted scores for all subjects on eight tests that had been administered to everyone (MATH, REC, COMP, SPELL, IPAT "g," PMASR, CODE, and CPS) were intercorrelated and then subjected to principal component analysis with Varimax rotation (Nie, Hull, Jenkins, Steinbrenner, & Bent, 1975).

Principal component analysis is basically a data reduction procedure. When a battery of cognitive tests is administered to a group of subjects, the tests are always found to be correlated. However, some tests are more highly correlated than others. With principal component analysis, one can determine if the observed pattern of correlations is due to one or more underlying abilities.

As shown in Table 10.2, three readily interpretable ability dimensions were found to account for the pattern of correlations among the eight FRS tests that were administered to all subjects. The reported "loadings" are equivalent to correlations between the test scores and the underlying abilities. The first principal component has highest loadings on REC, COMP, and SPELL; thus, it is a measure of single word decoding and sentence comprehension, or more simply, of general reading ability. The second component, which correlates most with IPAT "g," PMASR, and MATH, is identified as a general spatial/reasoning measure. The spatial tests are thought to measure spatial visualization and, to some extent, spatial/reasoning and nonverbal IQ. The third component

Table 10.2
Varimax Rotated Principal Component Loadings

Test	Reading	Spatial/reasoning	Symbol processing speed
MATH	.57	.58	.08
REC	.87	.16	.22
COMP	.82	.30	.13
SPELL	.83	.02	.34
IPAT "g"	.37	.76	.14
PMASR	−.01	.85	.22
CODE	.13	.20	.87
CPS	.36	.16	.80
Eigenvalues[a]	4.11	1.09	.98
Common variance (%)[b]	44	29	27

Note. From "Cognitive Abilities in Families of Reading-Disabled Children" by S. N. Decker and J. C. DeFries, *Journal of Learning Disabilities*, 1980, 13, p. 519. Copyright 1980 by The Professional Press, Inc. Reprinted by permission.
[a] Unrotated.
[b] Rotated.

has highest loadings on CODE and CPS, two measures of the ability to process and code symbols rapidly, hence the name "symbol processing speed."

From these principal component loadings and the correlations among the tests, we can compute "factor score coefficients" (really just beta weights) to predict component scores from observed test scores. Three composite scores were thus computed for each subject, one representing each of the three underlying abilities.

Group Means

Average principal component scores of probands and controls are presented in Table 10.3. As the composite scores for the complete data set (probands, controls, and their siblings and parents) have been standardized to have a grand mean of zero and a standard deviation of one, negative entries in Table 10.3 indicate average performance below the mean. An unweighted means analysis of variance with unequal subclass numbers yielded the F-values for family type (probands versus controls), sex, and their interaction.

With regard to each of the three composite measures, the difference between probands and controls is significant. However, the difference for the reading measure is considerably larger than that for the other two measures. This is not very surprising, given the fact that the probands were referred to us because of their reading problems. If we were unable to find a significant difference between probands and controls on our reading measure, we would have a serious problem ourselves. However, as may be seen in Table 10.3, the difference between probands and controls for the reading measure is substantial. If the measure was transformed to a scale with a standard deviation of 15 (comparable to an IQ scale), the difference between probands and controls would exceed 25 points. However, it is interesting to note that significant differences between probands and controls were also found for spatial/reasoning and symbol processing speed. Although these differences are considerably smaller than that for reading, this result indicates that at least some reading-disabled subjects are also deficient in other "independent" cognitive domains. This issue will be discussed in greater detail in a later section.

Significant sex differences for spatial/reasoning and symbol processing speed are also indicated in Table 10.3. The differences are in the expected directions, with boys obtaining higher spatial/reasoning scores than girls, and vice versa for symbol processing speed.

Table 10.3
Mean Principal Component Scores: Reading-Disabled Probands versus Matched Controls

	Mean scores				F-values		
	Males		Females				
Composite	Proband	Control	Proband	Control	Family type	Sex	Family type × Sex
Reading	-1.21	.43	-1.39	.55	336.21*	.07	1.91
Spatial/reasoning	-.14	.41	-.50	-.39	14.40*	17.11*	2.49
Symbol processing speed	-.25	-.04	.32	.66	5.29*	25.99*	.26
N	96	96	29	29			

Note. From "Cognitive Abilities in Families of Reading-Disabled Children" by S. N. Decker and J. C. DeFries, *Journal of Learning Disabilities*, 1980, *13*, p. 520. Copyright 1980 by The Professional Press, Inc. Reprinted by permission.
* $p \leq .05$.

It is of some interest to note that there is no significant interaction between sex and family type for any of the composites. This lack of an interaction suggests that reading-disabled girls, taken as a group, are no more or less impaired than reading-disabled boys. Thus, there apparently was little or no bias in diagnosis as a function of sex in the FRS sample, despite the considerable difference in prevalence rate. As indicated in Table 10.3, there were 96 male probands and only 29 female probands in the FRS sample, a sex ratio (3.3 : 1) that is highly consistent with previous studies.

Corresponding data for siblings of probands and siblings of controls are summarized in Table 10.4. As for the probands, a highly significant family type difference is indicated for the reading measure. However, there is also a significant interaction between family type and sex. This interaction is due to the fact that brothers of probands are more impaired than sisters of probands. As shown in Table 10.4, brothers of probands score almost .8 standard deviations below brothers of controls. Again, if this were converted to an IQ scale with a standard deviation of 15, this difference is equivalent to 12 points. In contrast, sisters of reading-disabled children differ from those of controls by only about .2 standard deviations, equivalent to a difference of only about 3 points. This finding suggests that both a child's sex and family history should be considered in risk assessment for reading disability. Brothers of reading-disabled children are clearly at higher risk for reading problems than are sisters.

It may be seen in Table 10.4 that siblings of reading-disabled children are also significantly impaired with regard to symbol processing speed, but not for spatial/reasoning. As was the case for the probands and controls, significant sex differences are present for both spatial/reasoning and symbol processing speed and they are in the expected directions.

The pattern of significant main effects for the FRS parents, shown in Table 10.5, exactly parallels that for siblings. Again, the largest difference between parents of probands and those of controls is for the reading measure. Although the interaction between family type and sex is not significant, fathers of probands tend to be somewhat more affected than mothers. Employing a transformed scale with a standard deviation of 15, the difference between fathers of probands and fathers of controls is equivalent to about 10 points, whereas that between mothers of probands and mothers of controls is about 6 points. As is the case for siblings, there is a significant difference between parents of probands and parents of controls for symbol processing speed (but not spatial/reasoning) and the two significant sex differences are again in the expected directions. It is noteworthy that neither the siblings nor

Table 10.4
Mean Principal Component Scores: Siblings of Reading-Disabled Probands versus Siblings of Controls

| | Mean scores of siblings | | | | F-values | | |
| | Brothers | | Sisters | | | | |
Composite	Proband	Control	Proband	Control	Family type	Sex	Family type × Sex
Reading	-.35	.44	.03	.24	28.69*	1.34	8.77*
Spatial/reasoning	-.02	.14	-.26	-.23	.76	7.00*	.37
Symbol processing speed	-.41	-.25	.37	.78	6.34*	66.14*	1.27
N	81	76	77	60			

Note. From "Cognitive Abilities in Families of Reading-Disabled Children" by S. N. Decker and J. C. DeFries, *Journal of Learning Disabilities*, 1980, 13, p. 520. Copyright 1980 by The Professional Press, Inc. Reprinted by permission.
* $p \leq .05$.

Table 10.5
Mean Principal Component Scores: Parents of Reading-Disabled Probands versus Parents of Controls

| | Mean scores of parents | | | | F-values | | |
| | Fathers | | Mothers | | | | |
Composite	Proband	Control	Proband	Control	Family type	Sex	Family type × Sex
Reading	-.24	.40	.02	.43	41.85*	3.29	2.00
Spatial/reasoning	.33	.55	-.32	-.36	1.19	88.06*	2.37
Symbol processing speed	-.53	-.17	.07	.43	17.16*	46.44*	0.00
N	125	125	125	125			

Note. From "Cognitive Abilities in Families of Reading-Disabled Children" by S. N. Decker and J. C. DeFries, *Journal of Learning Disabilities*, 1980, 13, p. 520. Copyright 1980 by The Professional Press, Inc. Reprinted by permission.
* $p \leq .05$.

the parents of probands demonstrated any deficits on the spatial/reasoning measure. Thus, any tendency toward pervasive cognitive deficits in families of probands may be ruled out.

The FRS parental data not only substantiate findings from the sibling data, they also demonstrate that the reading impairment persists to some extent in adulthood. The problem of adult reading disability, discussed elsewhere in this volume, is obviously of considerable social and economic significance. Because almost all previous reading disability research has focused upon problems of children, it would appear that adult reading disability is a neglected area that merits additional research.

The FRS sibling and parental data conclusively demonstrate the familial nature of the difference *between* probands and controls. But what about individual differences *within* the proband and control groups? Are they also familial? To answer this question, correlation and regression methods, rather than mean comparisons, are required.

Within-Group Familial Resemblance

Parent–offspring and sibling correlations are both mathematical functions of the spouse correlation. Therefore, before presenting evidence for parent–child and sibling resemblance, we shall first consider husband–wife similarity.

Spouse correlations for the three composite measures are presented in Table 10.6. It may be seen that there is a striking similarity in spouse resemblances within the two parental groups. For both parents of probands and those of controls, spouse correlations are relatively large for the reading measure, intermediate for symbol processing speed, and near zero for spatial/reasoning. As reported elsewhere, spouse correlations for verbal tests tend to be greater than those for nonverbal measures (see DeFries, Johnson, Kuse, McClearn, Polovina, Vandenberg, & Wilson, 1979).

Table 10.6
Spouse Correlations for Composite Measures[a]

Principal component	Parents of probands	Parents of controls
Reading	.27	.31
Spatial/reasoning	.01	− .04
Symbol processing speed	.18	.11
N (pairs)	125	125

[a] Correlations of .18 or larger are significant ($p \leq .05$).

Table 10.7
Regression of Offspring on Mid-Parent for Composite Measures[a]

Principal component	Families of probands	Families of controls
Reading	.30	.18
Spatial/reasoning	.56	.38
Symbol processing speed	.21	.20
N (families)	125	125

[a] All coefficients are significant ($p \leq .05$).

Although parent–offspring resemblance is usually assessed by correlations in family studies, regression coefficients are preferable. One important advantage of the regression of mid-child on mid-parent value as an index of parent–child resemblance is that it is not a mathematical function of the spouse correlation (DeFries et al., 1979). As spouse correlations for the reading measure are significant, the regression of offspring on mid parent was used as our measure of parent–child resemblance. Regressions of offspring on mid-parent value for the three composite measures are presented in Table 10.7. All of the coefficients are significantly different from zero, but none of the differences between the regressions estimated from the two groups (families of probands versus families of controls) is significant. For both groups, the regressions are largest for the spatial/reasoning measure and somewhat lower for reading and symbol processing speed.

In the absence of common-family environmental influences, the regression of offspring on mid-parent value estimated from a random sample of families provides a direct estimate of heritability in its narrow sense (see DeFries et al., 1979). However, because at least some family environmental influence seems likely for mental abilities, the coefficients reported in Table 10.7 should not be regarded as estimates of heritability. In fact, because of the manner in which the FRS families were ascertained, these coefficients do not even provide unbiased estimates of "familiality," that is, familial resemblance due to genetic factors, environmental factors, or both (DeFries et al., 1979).

The same problem pertains to the sibling correlations presented in Table 10.8. As is the case for the parent–child regressions, the sibling correlations are largest for spatial/reasoning and somewhat lower for reading and symbol processing speed in both groups. In the absence of common-family environmental influences, the sibling correlation estimated from a random sample provides an estimate of one-half of

Table 10.8
Sibling Intraclass Correlations for Composite Measures[a]

Principal component	Siblings and probands	Siblings and controls
Reading	.05	.10
Spatial/reasoning	.26	.27
Symbol processing speed	.20	.11
N (offspring)	255	223
N (families)	97	87

[a] Correlations of .20 or larger are significant ($p \leq .05$).

heritability. In fact, when the values in Table 10.8 are doubled, they roughly approximate the parent–offspring regressions in Table 10.7. However, because of the likelihood of environmental influences being shared by siblings, and because of the nature of the sample, the sibling correlations in Table 10.8 should not be regarded as simple functions of either population heritability or familiality.

The large and significant differences between the mean reading scores of relatives of probands versus those of controls, in addition to the within-group parent–offspring and sibling resemblance, conclusively demonstrate the familial nature of reading disability. Such familial resemblance is necessary, but not sufficient, evidence for genetic influence. In the following sections, we shall utilize the FRS data to test the adequacy of various genetic models to account for the familial transmission of reading disability.

Polygenic Threshold Model

The polygenic threshold model (Carter, 1969, 1973) assumes an underlying liability or predisposition toward a condition that is a function of both genetic and environmental influences (see Figure 10.3). Individuals beyond the "risk threshold" manifest the condition. To the extent that the condition is heritable, relatives of affected individuals will have a higher average liability and thus will be at greater risk for the condition than members of the general population. For conditions in which there is a different prevalence rate in the two sexes, it is assumed that there are different thresholds for males and females. When the prevalence rate is higher in males (as it is in the case of reading disability), then females must have the higher threshold. Consequently, in order for females to be affected they must have a greater

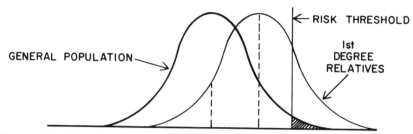

Figure 10.3. The polygenic threshold model (after "Multifactorial Genetic Disease" by C. O. Carter, in V. A. McKusick and R. Clairborne (Eds.), Medical Genetics, 1973, New York, HP Publishing Company).

genetic loading (i.e., more "risk" genes) than affected males. Thus, the polygenic threshold model predicts that a greater proportion of the relatives (brothers, sisters, fathers, and mothers) of reading-disabled girls should be affected than those of affected boys; that is, relatives of female probands are at higher risk for reading disability than relatives of male probands.

In order to test the polygenic threshold model, scores for the reading measure were dichotomized. A comparison of the reading composite scores of probands and their matched controls revealed a break between their distributions at approximately $-.50$ standard deviations. Therefore, scores equal to or below this point were interpreted as indicating a disability, whereas higher scores were considered to be within the normal range. This dichotomous classification system was also applied to the parent and sibling data.

The proportions of "affected" relatives of male probands versus female probands are shown in Table 10.9. For each relationship (father, mother, brother, and sister), relatives of female probands are at greater risk for reading problems; the differences are highly significant for fathers, mothers, and the overall comparison between relatives of male and female probands. Thus, these results are consistent with the polygenic threshold model.

Unfortunately, the polygenic threshold model is rather complex, assuming both multiple genetic and environmental factors. Moreover, other threshold models (single-locus or environmental) could account for the observed pattern of results. In contrast, classical single-gene models are more parsimonious and are more likely to suggest modes of amelioration (e.g., phenylketonuria). In the following sections, we shall test for possible major-gene influence.

Table 10.9
Proportion of Affected Relatives by Sex of the Proband[a]

	Reading disabled (RD) male probands		Reading disabled (RD) female probands		
	Percentage RD	Total N	Percentage RD	Total N	χ^2
Fathers	36.5	96	75.8	29	12.40*
Mothers	29.2	96	58.6	29	7.17*
Brothers	48.2	56	64.0	25	1.15
Sisters	32.7	61	37.5	16	.00
Overall	35.5	309	61.6	99	20.72*

* $p < .01$.
[a] χ^2 with Yates correction based on frequencies of affected versus not affected; $df = 1$ for each individual comparison and 4 for overall.

Variance Ratios

One prima facie test for major gene influence is to compare the variances obtained by relatives of affected individuals to those of controls. Genetic variance in a population is a function of gene frequency; thus, a rare major gene will contribute relatively little to the population variance. However, because relatives of affected individuals will have the gene in higher frequency, they should manifest greater genetic variance.

Variances for the reading measure in probands, controls, and their siblings and parents are presented in Table 10.10. It may be seen that the variances for the probands and controls are homogeneous. However, siblings and parents of probands have larger variances than those

Table 10.10
Reading Score Variances[a]

Group	Males		Females		Variance ratios (Proband/Control)	
	Proband	Control	Proband	Control	Males	Females
Children	.50 (96)	.67 (96)	.36 (29)	.41 (29)	.75	.88
Siblings	.93 (81)	.51 (76)	.71 (77)	.59 (60)	1.82*	1.20
Parents	1.23 (125)	.73 (125)	.86 (125)	.47 (125)	1.69*	1.83*

* $p \leq .05$.
[a] Sample size is shown in parentheses.

of controls, and three of the four variance ratios are significant. Thus, results of the variance comparison test are consistent with the hypothesis of major-gene influence. We shall next test the adequacy of several specific single-gene models, beginning with sex-linked, major-gene influence.

Sex Linkage

One of the most consistent findings in the reading disability literature is the higher prevalence rate in boys than in girls. It has been suggested that this difference could be accounted for by sex-linked, recessive inheritance (Symmes & Rapoport, 1972). It is well known that males are at higher risk for sex-linked, recessive conditions such as color blindness. Females have two X chromosomes (in addition to the 22 pairs of autosomes), whereas males have one X and one Y chromosome. Thus, for a female to express a sex-linked, recessive disorder, she must carry the recessive allele on both sex chromosomes. In contrast, the presence of a sex-linked, recessive gene on the one X chromosome in males is sufficient to cause the condition to be expressed. If the frequency of a sex-linked, recessive gene in a population is q, then q of the males will manifest the condition, but only q^2 of the females. For example, if q is .1, then 10% of the males will be affected, but only 1% of the females.

In the case of reading disability, it is generally found that the sex ratio is between three or four males to each affected female. We shall assume a value of 3.5 : 1. From this information we can predict the frequency of the hypothesized sex-linked, recessive gene: $q^2/q = 1/3.5 = .29 = q$. But 29% of the boys and 8% of the girls are not reading disabled. Thus, the sex-linked, recessive gene hypothesis does not adequately account for the different prevalence rates of reading disability in boys and girls.

Additional tests also provide little or no evidence that reading disability is caused by a sex-linked, major gene. Fathers transmit their only X chromosome to their daughters and sons receive their only X chromosome from their mothers. Thus, father–daughter resemblance should approximately equal mother–son resemblance, both of which should exceed mother–daughter resemblance (mothers and daughters each have two X chromosomes, but share only one). Since fathers transmit their Y chromosome (not their X chromosome) to their sons, father–son resemblance should be near zero for sex-linked, recessive conditions. Because parent–child resemblance for sex-linked characters is a function of the sex of the family members, one may examine the pattern of single-parent–single-child correlations for evidence of sex linkage. However, as discussed by DeFries, Vandenberg, and McClearn (1976), the pattern of familial correlations, by itself, does not yield a rigorous test of the sex-linkage hypothesis. With small samples, the correlations may be in the expected order, but differences among them may not be significant. On the other hand, because of the problem of sampling variation, the expected pattern may sometimes not occur even for characters that are sex linked.

A more rigorous test of the sex-linkage hypothesis that utilizes a hierarchical multiple regression analysis (Cohen & Cohen, 1975) has been proposed (see DeFries *et al.*, 1979). As shown in Table 10.11, a child's score is expressed as a function of the child's sex (coded 1 or 2), mother's score, father's score, and their interactions. The interactions are represented by products of variables from which the main effects and lower-order interactions have been partialed. The significance of the main effects, the two-way interactions, and the three-way interaction are tested sequentially. A significant two-way interaction indicates a conditional relationship between the child's score and the two variables. For example, a significant interaction between mother's score and child's sex would indicate that mother–child resemblance differs as a function of the child's sex. This, of course, is exactly what is expected for a sex-linked character. For such characters, the two-way interaction between father's score and child's sex and the three-way interaction should also be significant.

Table 10.11
Hierarchical Regression Model

$$\hat{C} = \underbrace{B_1S + B_2M + B_3F}_{} + \underbrace{B_4SM + B_5SF + B_6MF}_{} + \underbrace{B_7SMF}_{} + A$$

| (Step 1) | (Step 2) | (Step 3) |

$\hat{C}$ = child's expected score
S = child's sex (coded 1 or 2)
M = mother's score
F = father's score
B_1 = partial regression of C on S (a measure of the importance of sex on child's score)
B_2 = partial regression of C on M (a measure of mother–child resemblance)
.
.
.
A = regression constant

Note. From "Mental Abilities: A Family Study" by J. C. DeFries, *Current Developments in Anthropological Genetics*, Vol. 1, 1980, New York, Plenum, p. 413.

Table 10.12
Single-Parent–Single-Child Correlations for Reading Measure

	Father–son		Mother–daughter		Mother–Son		Father–Daughter
Expected order for a sex-linked character	r_{FS}	<	r_{MD}	<	r_{MS}	=	r_{FD}
Observed correlations:[a]							
Families of probands	.06 (177)		.35 (106)		.19 (177)		.34 (106)
Families of controls	.14 (172)		.24 (89)		.10 (172)		.04 (89)

[a] Number of paired comparisons in parentheses.

When the reading scores of proband and control families were subjected to hierarchical multiple regression analysis, only one of the six interactions that are informative with regard to sex linkage was found to be significant (B_5, $p = .04$, families of probands). When one or more of these interactions is significant, it is imperative to examine the order of the parent child correlations, as they may arise in several different ways (see DeFries, 1980). The single-parent–single-child correlations for the proband and control families are presented in Table 10.12. It may be seen from this table that father–child resemblance in the proband families does indeed differ as a function of child's sex. However, the father–daughter correlation is actually somewhat smaller than the mother–daughter correlation. Among control families, the father–daughter correlation is even lower than the father–son correlation. Thus, these results provide little or no evidence for the hypothesis that reading disability is due to a sex-linked, recessive gene.

Segregation Analysis

The FRS data were subjected to segregation analysis to test for possible autosomal (not sex-linked), major-gene influence (Lewitter, DeFries, & Elston, 1980). Tests for major-gene influence on animal behavioral characters are relatively direct, usually involving controlled crosses (see Plomin, DeFries, & McClearn, 1980). In contrast, in the case of human behavioral characters, genetic hypotheses can be tested only indirectly. Segregation analysis involves the fitting of probability models to family data, based upon the principles of population genetics and statistics (for an elementary exposition, see Cavalli-Sforza & Bodmer, 1971).

Classical segregation analysis is concerned with the transmission of qualitative (all-or-none) characters. However, continuously distributed characters may also be influenced by major genes. A more general method of segregation analysis that detects the influence of a single gene on the distribution of a quantitative character was developed by Elston and Stewart (1971). This theory was utilized by Elston and Yelverton (1975) in their computer program GENSEG, which provides maximum-likelihood estimates of genetic parameters and tests of goodness of fit of various genetic models.

Lewitter *et al.* (1980) subjected the FRS data to segregation analysis using the GENSEG program. A continuous composite score was derived for each subject, based upon a two-group discriminant function analysis of probands versus controls. The resulting measure is highly similar to the reading composite measure previously discussed, the coefficient of congruence (Rummell, 1970) between the factor loadings and discriminant weights being .82.

Preliminary analyses indicated that a mixture of two normal distributions fit the composite data significantly better than a single normal distribution; thus, segregation analysis was deemed appropriate and the five hypotheses listed in Table 10.13 were tested. When data from the families of all probands were analyzed, chi-square tests of goodness of fit indicated that each of the five hypotheses must be rejected. Thus, neither the single-locus models nor the within-family environmental model adequately accounts for the transmission of reading disability in the families of probands. When similar analyses were applied to families of male probands only, similar results were obtained. However, when data from families of female probands only were analyzed (31 families; 135 individuals), the hypothesis of recessive inheritance (Hypothesis 2) could not be rejected. Lewitter *et al.* (1980) argued that the lack of significance for the recessive-gene hypothesis was not due to the smaller number of subjects, because the reduction in chi-square was greater than could be accounted for on the basis of sample size alone. Although by no means definitive, this evidence for autosomal; recessive inheritance in females is consistent with the finding, discussed

Table 10.13
Hypotheses Tested by Segregation Analysis

1. Mendelian segregation at a single autosomal dominant locus with two alleles.
2. Mendelian segregation at a single autosomal recessive locus with two alleles.
3. It is sufficient to postulate two rather than three phenotypic distributions.
4. Mendelian segregation at a single autosomal locus with two alleles.
5. Within-family environmental influence only, that is, there is no familial transmission involved.

Note. From "Genetic Models of Reading Disability" by F. I. Lewitter, J. C. DeFries, and R. C. Elston, *Behavior Genetics*, 1980, *10*, 9–30. Copyright 1980 by Plenum Publishing Corporation. Reprinted by permission.

earlier, that families of female probands are more affected than those of male probands.

Heterogeneity of Reading Disability

One possible explanation for the lack of adequate fit of any of the various single-gene models to the *total FRS data set* may be that reading disability is a heterogeneous disorder. There may be several etiologically distinct forms of reading disability, some of which may be heritable and others not. Of the heritable forms, one might be polygenic; another sex linked; another due to autosomal, recessive inheritance; etc. If this were the case, it would not be surprising to find that no single genetic model accounts for the transmission of all forms of reading disability.

In an initial attempt to assess heterogeneity using the three principal component scores (Decker & DeFries, 1981), a profile was plotted for each proband and then classified as to subtype. The same dichotomous classification system was used for each measure as described previously in the test of the polygenic threshold model. That is, subjects who obtained scores of −.50 or lower for an ability dimension were considered disabled, whereas those with higher scores were considered to be within the normal range. Using this procedure, four subtypes that contained a minimum of eight probands were identified. Average composite scores for probands within each subtype and for their matched controls are plotted in Figure 10.4.

From Figure 10.4 it may be seen that Subtype 1 is characterized by reading and spatial/reasoning scores in the disabled range, but symbol processing speed (or coding speed, symbolized here as C/S) within the normal range. This subtype, which represented 23% of the proband sample, bears some similarity to the deficient visuospatial group of Mattis, French, and Rapin (1975). However, the spatial/reasoning deficit found in Subtype 1 should not be interpreted as a simple visual–perceptual impairment. Instead, it may be due to a combination of difficulties in visualization, spatial representation, and/or reasoning ability.

Subtype 2 subjects (18% of the proband sample) obtained scores within the disabled range for reading and symbol processing speed, but are within the normal range for spatial/reasoning. The poor performance of these subjects on symbol processing speed may be due to deficits in automatic encoding or short-term memory (Morrison, Giordani, & Nagy, 1977). A sex ratio of 10 : 1 (i.e., 10 affected males to each affected female) in Subtype 2 was the highest of any subtype, presumably due to its more typical male pattern of lower symbol processing speed and higher spatial ability.

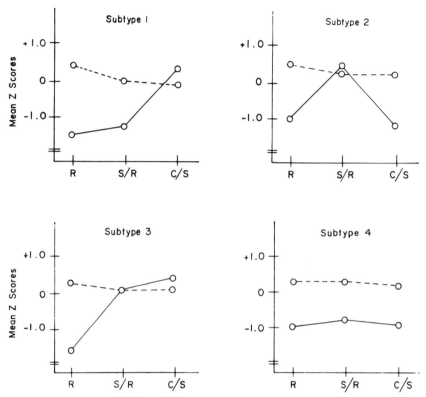

Figure 10.4. Subtypes of reading disability. Ability profiles are based on reading (R), spatial reasoning (S/R), and coding or symbol processing speed (C/S) composite scores. Solid lines and dashed lines represent average z scores of probands and their matched controls, respectively. (From "Cognitive Ability Profiles in Families of Reading-Disabled Children" by S. N. Decker and J. C. DeFries, Developmental Medicine and Child Neurology, *1981, 23, p. 223.*

Subjects in Subtype 3 appear to be more specifically reading disabled; that is, they have reading scores within the disabled range, but they are within the normal range for spatial/reasoning and symbol processing speed. This is the largest subtype, accounting for 41% of the proband sample.

Subjects of Subtype 4, the smallest subtype (only 9% of the probands), are within the disabled range for all three measures. The flat profile of subjects in this subtype suggests that they are more pervasively impaired than those of the other subtypes, and the diagnosis of a more specific type of reading disability in their case is questionable.

Although all four subtypes are deficient in reading, an analysis of variance indicated that differences among the subtypes for the reading measure were significant. Post hoc comparisons revealed that Subtypes 1 and 3 are significantly lower on the reading measure than Subtypes 2 and 4. In contrast, there are no significant differences among subtypes with regard to the age of the probands.

Is such a typology really meaningful? It is our conviction that a family study can provide a strong test of the biological validity of a typology in exactly the same manner that family studies have been used to test for heterogeneity of the psychoses (for a review, see DeFries & Plomin, 1978). If a given subtype has any biological reality, then relatives of reading-disabled subjects of a particular subtype should be more likely to be of the same subtype than expected on the basis of chance alone.

In order to subject our typology to this validity test, reading-disabled siblings and parents were categorized using the same classification system as that employed for probands and then cross-tabulated as a function of proband's subtype. Familial resemblance for subtype would be indicated by an excess number of relatives on the main diagonal of the cross-classification table. From Table 10.14 it may be seen that there is at least some suggestive evidence for sibling subtype resemblance. For example, almost half (13/27) of the siblings of probands of Subtype 3 are also of Subtype 3. As shown in Table 10.15, however, this familial resemblance for subtype does not generalize to the parental data. Needless to say, it would be interesting to see how other typologies would fare when put to the same validity test.

CONCLUDING REMARKS

The FRS data conclusively demonstrate the familial nature of reading disability, both from a comparison of the mean scores of relatives of

Table 10.14
Cross-Classification of RD Siblings as a Function of Proband Subtype

RD proband subtypes	RD sibling subtypes			
	1	2	3	4
1	7	3	8	4
2	2	1	2	4
3	5	7	13	2
4	1	4	0	1

Note. From "Cognitive Ability Profiles in Families of Reading-Disabled Children" by S. N. Decker and J. C. DeFries, *Developmental Medicine and Child Neurology,* 1981, *23,* p. 224. Copyright 1981 by Spastics International Medical Publications. Reprinted by permission.

Table 10.15
Cross-Classification of RD Parents as a Function of Proband Subtype

RD proband subtypes	RD parent subtypes			
	1	2	3	4
1	6	9	10	11
2	0	4	2	6
3	9	13	11	7
4	2	2	2	2

Note. From "Cognitive Ability Profiles in Families of Reading-Disabled Children" by S. N. Decker and J. C. DeFries, *Developmental Medicine and Child Neurology*, 1981, *23*, p. 224. Copyright 1981 by Spastics International Medical Publications. Reprinted by permission.

probands versus those of controls and from within-group familial resemblance (parent–offspring regressions and sibling correlations). Such evidence is necessary, but not sufficient, for demonstrating genetic influence.

When several different genetic models were tested using the FRS data, some positive evidence was obtained for the polygenic threshold model and for autosomal, recessive inheritance in females. However, no single-gene model was found to account adequately for the transmission of reading disability in all of the proband families.

The lack of strong evidence for any particular genetic model may be due to inherent limitations in the design of the FRS. Segregation analysis and linkage analysis are more likely to yield positive evidence when applied to a few large families rather than many small families. In fact, the most definitive evidence for major-gene influence may come from linkage studies, where an association between a chromosome marker and reading disability is observed to occur over several generations. Tentative evidence for such a relationship between a marker on chromosome 15 and a dominantly inherited form of reading disability has been found (Smith, 1978), and confirmatory evidence is currently being sought (Kimberling, personal communication).

The lack of adequate fit of any single-gene model to the entire FRS data set may also be due to the fact that reading disability is a heterogeneous disorder. In order to explore this possibility, a classification system was devised that employed principal component score profiles. The validity of this typology was then assessed by classifying siblings and parents and cross-tabulating them as a function of proband's subtype. It was predicted that relatives of reading-disabled subjects of a given subtype should be more likely to be of the same subtype than expected on the basis of chance if the subtype has biological reality and psychological reliability. Although some suggestive evidence for profile similarity between probands and their affected siblings was found, this evidence for subtype similarity did not generalize to the parental data. It is conceivable, of course, that subtypes of children are not isomorphic with parental subtypes. Nevertheless, since no evidence for profile similarity between probands and parents was found, it must be concluded that this particular typology has not met our validity criterion.

The results summarized in this chapter demonstrate that family studies provide tests of various genetic models as well as a unique opportunity to assess the validity of alternative typologies. We strongly urge that other typologies of reading disability be put to similar validity tests.

ACKNOWLEDGMENTS

This work was supported in part by grants from the Spencer Foundation and NICHD (HD-11681) to J. C. DeFries. We wish to acknowledge the invaluable contributions of staff members of the Boulder Valley and St. Vrain Valley school districts and of the families who participated in the study. We also thank Samuel A. Kirk, Winifred D. Kirk, and William Meredith for their help in planning the study and Rebecca G. Miles for expert editorial assistance.

REFERENCES

Carter, C. O. (1969) Genetics of common disorders. *British Medical Bulletin, 25,* 52–57.

Carter, C. O. (1973) Multifactorial genetic disease. In V. A. McKusick & R. Clairborne (Eds.), *Medical genetics.* New York: HP Publishing Company.

Cavalli-Sforza, L. L., & Bodmer, W. F. (1971) *The genetics of human populations.* San Francisco: Freeman.

Cohen, J., & Cohen, P. (1975) *Applied multiple regression/correlation analysis for the behavioral sciences.* Hillsdale, N.J.: Lawrence Erlbaum.

Decker, S. N., & DeFries, J. C. (1980) Cognitive abilities in families of reading-disabled children. *Journal of Learning Disabilities, 13,* 517–522.

Decker, S. N., & DeFries, J. C. (1981) Cognitive ability profiles in families of reading-disabled children. *Developmental Medicine and Child Neurology, 23,* 217–227.

DeFries, J. C. (1980) Mental abilities: A family study. In J. H. Mielke & M. H. Crawford (Eds.), *Current developments in anthropological genetics* (Vol. 1). New York: Plenum.

DeFries, J. C., Johnson, R. C., Kuse, A. R., McClearn, G. E., Polovina, J., Vandenberg, S. G., & Wilson, J. R. (1979) Familial resemblance for specific cognitive abilities. *Behavior Genetics, 9,* 23–43.

DeFries, J. C., & Plomin, R. (1978) Behavioral genetics. *Annual Review of Psychology, 29,* 473–515.

DeFries, J. C., Singer, S. M., Foch, T. T., & Lewitter, F. I. (1978) Familial nature of reading disability. *British Journal of Psychiatry, 132,* 361–367.

DeFries, J. C., Vandenberg, S. G., & McClearn, G. E. (1976) Genetics of specific cognitive abilities. *Annual Review of Genetics, 10,* 179–207.

Elston, R. C., & Stewart, J. (1971) A general model for the genetic analysis of pedigree data. *Human Heredity, 21,* 523–542.

Elston, R. C., & Yelverton, K. C. (1975) General models for segregation analysis. *American Journal of Human Genetics, 27,* 31–45.

Finucci, J. M. (1978) Genetic considerations in dyslexia. In H. R. Myklebust (Ed.), *Progress in learning disabilities* (Vol. 4). New York: Grune & Stratton.

Foch, T. T., DeFries, J. C., McClearn, G. E., & Singer, S. M. (1977) Familial patterns of impairment in reading disability. *Journal of Educational Psychology, 69,* 316–329.

Herschel, M. (1978). Dyslexia revisited: A review. *Human Genetics, 40,* 115–134.

Lewitter, F. I., DeFries, J. C., & Elston, R. C. (1980) Genetic models of reading disability. *Behavior Genetics, 10,* 9–30.

Mattis, S., French, J. H., & Rapin, I. (1975) Dyslexia in children and young adults: Three independent neuropsychological syndromes. *Developmental Medicine and Child Neurology, 17,* 150–163.

Morrison, F. J., Giordani, B., & Nagy, J. (1977) Reading disability: An information processing analysis. *Science, 196,* 77–79.

Nie, N. H., Hull, C. H., Jenkins, J. G., Steinbrenner, K., & Bent, D. H. (1975) *Statistical package for the social sciences* (2nd ed.). New York: McGraw-Hill.

Owen, F. W. (1978) Dyslexia—Genetic aspects. In A. L. Benton & D. Pearl (Eds.), *Dyslexia: An appraisal of current knowledge.* New York: Oxford University Press.

Plomin, R., DeFries, J. C., & McClearn, G. E. (1980) *Behavioral genetics: A primer.* San Francisco: Freeman.

Rummel, R. J. (1970) *Applied factor analysis.* Evanston, Ill.: Northwestern University Press.

Smith, Shelley D. (1978) *Genetic studies and linkage analysis of specific dyslexia: Evaluation of inheritance in kindreds selected for the parent autosomal dominant transmission.* Unpublished doctoral dissertation, Indiana University.

Symmes, J. S., & Rapoport, J. L. (1972) Unexpected reading failure. *American Journal of Orthopsychiatry, 42,* 380–385.

Thomas, C. J. (1905) Congenital "word-blindness" and its treatment. *Ophthalmoscope, 3,* 380–385.

Chapter Eleven

An Approach to the Combined Study of Acquired and Developmental Reading Disorders[1]

MARYANNE WOLF

INTRODUCTION

In this chapter, research from the cognitive and neurosciences is used to examine two traditionally separate areas of concern: the developmental dyslexias and acquired (adult) reading disorders. The working assumption throughout this chapter is that both acquired and developmental dyslexias include a continuum of reading disorders; childhood disorders will be defined by a reading performance more than 1.5 years below grade level without evidence of social–environmental, emotional, intellectual, or gross neurological handicaps. Although there exists a long, well-founded tradition eschewing comparisons between developmental and acquired disorders, an underlying purpose of this chapter will be to suggest that an approach to reading disorders that integrates knowledge from both developmental and neurological dysfunction perspectives will increase our theoretical understanding of the reading process across time and has the potential to give new direction to remediation efforts. In addition, such a framework has implications for differentiating aspects of the controversy surrounding maturational lag and neurological deficit as explanations for the dyslexias in children.

[1] This and the following chapter by Epstein emerged as the result of a year-long series of discussions between the two authors. Although each author is responsible for the respective content, both chapters have been shaped by this exchange.

Because of the preliminary nature of these efforts, several points of caution are necessary. First, there will be no attempt to summarize research in the various fields; rather, several issues have been selected to demarcate where future research efforts should be directed. Second, cross-disciplinary comparisons, not unlike correlations, raise the sticky problem of confusing contiguity with causality; this chapter is not about conclusions but about an approach.

I will begin with impaired reading development in the child. Our chief sources of information are varied and somewhat unconnected: (a) theoretical and clinical constructs about acquired and developmental dyslexia from a variety of disciplines (Benton & Pearl, 1978; Chall, 1979; Coltheart, Patterson, & Marshall, 1980; Denckla, 1978; Mattis, French, & Rapin, 1975; Rudel, 1980; Vellutino, 1979; Vernon, 1977); (b) parallels with alexia or the adult acquired disorders of reading (Aaron, Baxter, & Lucenti, 1980; Albert & Geschwind, 1980; Ellis, 1979; Holmes, 1978; Jorm, 1979; Marcel, 1980); (c) case studies of dyslexic children who have come to autopsy, two of which exist to date (Drake, 1968; Galaburda & Kemper, 1979); (d) literature about normal child development during the reading acquisition years, especially the neurophysiological under-pinnings of language development; and (e) cognitive and psycholin-guistic theory about the development of the reading process. Described amply in other parts of this volume, contributions from each of these five areas will be used to construct a developmental (i.e., across time) framework for reading disruption.

A traditional method of investigating normal processes is to study aberrant or dysfunctional processes. The assumption is that if one can identify the specific subprocesses or factors that cause the dysfunction, one can infer that such subprocesses and variables are necessary for the intact process to operate (Wolf, 1981). In this way, the study of adult acquired reading disorders has been one means through which to understand what occurs in *fluent* reading; the developmental ana-logue of such an approach is an implicit concern in this chapter.

Of the major models of adult reading breakdown, two are of par-ticular interest: (a) the neuroanatomically based model of alexia with and without agraphia, first proposed by Dejerine in 1892 and described extensively by Geschwind (1962), Benson and Geschwind (1974), and Albert and Geschwind (1980); and (b) the psycholinguistic, information-processing model of acquired dyslexia, introduced by Marshall and Newcombe (1966, 1973, 1980) and elaborated by a group of cognitive psychologists and neuropsychologists (see Coltheart *et al.*, 1980). Al-though both models deal with neuroanatomical and behavioral features of the disorders, their emphases are quite different. In the Dejerine model, a patient could be designated as belonging to a particular form of alexia on the basis of the location of the lesions. In contrast, in the psycholinguistic model, the disorder is characterized as *deep, surface,* or *visual* dyslexia according to the neurolinguistically defined symptom complex (Marshall & Newcombe, 1980). Morton and Patterson (1980) indicate the difference in emphasis between the cognitive and anatomically based models: "In principle, we agree with Oatley's recent assessment of lesion studies: we look to such studies for identifying components of behavior rather than localizing them [p. 96]."

The complementarity of the two models has been discussed by Geschwind (1980) and Newcombe (1980). It is a major premise in this chapter that a theoretical integration of the two models will be of particular import to the study of both acquired *and* developmental disorders of reading by providing a foundation for understanding what must occur in the normal reading process over development.

PARALLELS BETWEEN ACQUIRED AND DEVELOPMENTAL DISORDERS OF READING

Many investigators have correctly pointed out the dangers inherent in any strict one-to-one correspondences between acquired reading disorders in the brain-damaged adult and developmental disorders in the child. It may be equally injudicious to ignore what can be learned from the literature on adult disorders. For example, the literature on acquired disorders has begun to contribute substantively to our theories of fluent reading; it may also contribute to refining our notions of the differences and similarities between the developing and adult systems. Within the psycholinguistic paradigm, Marcel (1980) illustrates an important aspect of this approach by comparing beginning reading prerequisites and particular patterns of breakdown in one form of acquired dyslexia called *surface dyslexia* (Marshall & Newcombe, 1973) in which grapheme–phoneme errors predominate. Other literature on adult dyslexia also suggests how the symptom complexes of particular acquired syndromes may correspond to specific subsyndromes of developmental dyslexia (see Aaron *et al.*, 1980; Ellis, 1979; Holmes, 1978; Jorm, 1979; Wolf, 1979).

It is my position that the information-processing paradigm offers a useful framework not only for analyzing areas of breakdown in acquired disorders but also for developing stages of reading acquisition that apply to childhood reading disorders (see Chall, 1979, for one account of developmental stages in reading). An information-processing framework will, however, be most useful in defining childhood disorders of reading when conceptually linked to both a construct of cognitive-based *stages* of reading development and the cluster (or subsyndrome) approach to developmental dyslexias (Denckla, 1978; Kinsbourne & Warrington, 1962; Mattis *et al.*, 1975). Table 11.1 presents the results of an attempt to integrate these approaches.

Although the evolving state of our knowledge about the reading process and its disorders makes Table 11.1 very tentative, the major purpose of the table is heuristic. Within it, reading is conceptualized as a continuum of cognitive and linguistic subprocesses that follow a developmental sequence in reading acquisition and which must function automatically in adult fluent reading. Developmental disorders can be grouped according to where their breakdown occurs in the stages of cognitive requirements. These groups would then be compared to acquired cases with similar patterns of reading breakdown. Our ability to give more specific information about intact and dysfunctioning processes in acquired cases may, in turn, inform our notions of compensation strategies for children's remediation.

More immediate implications emerging from information in the table concern issues within the developmental-delay–neurological-deficit controversy in the developmental dyslexias. Whatever process disrupts reading ability in the adult brain might also be implicated in the child's brain. It could be either a neuroanatomical lesion or neurobiologically based failure to develop, or both. A developmental failure in any stage of processing (indicated by the information-processing models) or a lesion in any anatomical area that mediates reading (as indicated by the neuroanatomical data) might result in a child's inability to learn to read efficiently. Thus, some children's reading disorders may best be described in terms of neurodevelopmental factors whereas others may correspond to syndromes similar to those found in lesion-caused disorders in adults.

Such a notion combines two popular views of the etiology of children's reading disorders: the delay hypothesis and the neurological deficit hypothesis. (Proponents of the delay or lag hypothesis emphasize that hard-core developmental reading disorders are usually caused by a failure to develop on schedule; the functions or subprocesses are not aberrant, but delayed. Proponents of the neurological deficit model suggest that reading disorders are caused by a specific deficit or breakdown of eventually localizable subprocesses due to various neurological factors.) I propose here a continuum of reading disorders based on the integrity and interaction of specifiable perceptual, cognitive, and linguistic subprocesses. The cluster or syndrome approach (e.g., Denckla, 1978; Mattis *et al.*, 1975, 1980; Rourke, 1980) is consistent with such a continuum depiction, but we still must tease apart—for every stage of processing—dysfunction from development immaturity. The severe methodological problems encountered by the cluster approach (Doehring, 1980) may well be the result of attempting to classify children without reference to an underlying model of reading development. I suggest here a *developmental* classification based on a model of cognitive stages of reading (described at a most general level by Table 11.1).

In the developmental classification, groups will first be characterized by stage of breakdown and then grouped, whenever possible, by discrete neurological dysfunction of a particular subprocess, developmental delay, or unidentified etiological factors. The obvious methodological issues involved in isolating such developmental–dysfunctional indices are formidable and may prove ultimately unnecessary. Holding the latter consideration in suspension, however, there are several potential means of isolating these indices opened by the approach outlined in Table 11.1. First, it is possible that a detailed comparison between patterns of errors in children and adults—on tests designed to measure systematically levels (or stages) of expertise in model-specified components of reading—will shed light on what is general immaturity or discrete damage in the child. Second, without reference to adults, there is some evidence (Wolf, 1981) that these two dimensions may be distinguishable when probed by measures designed to examine the integrity of subprocesses in the underlying linguistic system. Similar to the methodological principles suggested in Table 11.1, a sequence was first outlined of the general stages of naming or word-retrieval—a process that incorporates an extensive range of linguistic subprocesses and that is frequently indicated in dyslexic children. Next, a refined model of word-retrieval and reading was constructed and tasks were selected to tap each of the specified components. Last, the battery of naming and reading tests was administered to average and poor readers from 6 to 11 years of age. Certain measures, like a confrontation naming test with refined error analyses and varying word-frequency conditions indicated a normal developmental curve in average readers and a very different curve in poor readers. Furthermore, some poor readers were simply developmentally delayed (as shown, for example, by a lowered score with a clean breakoff point in responses as word frequency drops), whereas others were distinctly different (lowered score with no clear word-frequency effect). In addition, children in the latter group often made highly idiosyncratic naming errors (e.g., *hippochondriac* for *rhin-*

Table 11.1
Stages of Information Processing and Disorders of Reading

Information-processing stages in reading development	Developmental reading disorders		Acquired reading disorders
	Mattis, French, and Rapin (1975) subsyndromes and description	Denckla (1978) subsyndromes[a]	
1. Input functions Perception Perceptual integration	1. Visuospatial perceptual disorder High verbal score Low Raven's Colored Progressive Matrices Low Benton Test of Visual Retention	1. Visuospatial (defined as in Mattis *et al.* but found to be also *anomic*)	1. Visual dyslexia: predominance of visual confusions (Marshall & Newcombe, 1973, 1977)
2. Central processing Perceptual–conceptual integration Semantic–phonological information integration Lexical access and retrieval Comprehension	2. Language disorders Anomic Imitative speech Speech-sound discrimination Comprehension	2a. Language disorders Mixed (i.e., poor naming, comprehension, repetition, and phonemic memory sequencing Anomic and repetition poor (poor on Oldfield–Wingfield, RAN, and repetition tests; normal on comprehension) Anomic pure (as above but normal on repetition) Dysphonic sequencing (poor repetition and phonemic substitutions and missequencing; comprehension and naming normal)	2a. Surface dyslexia Breakdown of phonological rules for grapheme–phoneme correspondence (Holmes, 1978; Marcel, 1980)

3. Translation to output Integration of phonological and articulatory information Motoric aspects	3. Articulatory and graphomotor dyscoordination: Poor sound blending Low graphomotor skills Normal acoustosensory and receptive language	3. Articulatory–graphomotor (similarly defined in Mattis et al., 1975)
		2b. Verbal memorization disorder (poor sentence repetition and paired associate learning)

2b. Deep dyslexia:
  Semantic errors predominate
  Derivational errors present
  Some visual errors
  Poor with functor words
  Some problems with nonsense syllables (see case studies in Coltheart et al., 1980)

2c. Most cases of alexia with agraphia fall here (see Geschwind, 1973)

2d. Some cases of alexia without agraphia (see Greenblatt, 1976)

2e. Wernicke's aphasic cases with accompanying reading loss

3. Some forms of phonological or surface dyslexia closer to output stage; many Broca's aphasics with accompanying reading disorders here

---

[a] Denckla also includes a right hemisphere syndrome and most recently, an account of an attentional syndrome.

ocerus); together, these effects point to a very different system of lexical processing in this group. Finally, the detailed analyses of errors (perceptual, phonological, semantic, perseverative, etc.) on the confrontation task, the Boston Naming Test (Goodglass, Kaplan, & Weintraub, 1976), in combination with response patterns from other naming measures in the battery, provided profiles capable of still further differentiation into several dyslexia subgroups (e.g., one subgroup, similar to the visual groups of Mattis *et al.* and Denckla, was found to have a high percentage of visually based confrontation errors and a low score on a visually reduced naming measure—see Wolf, 1981, and longitudinal work by Wolf & Bally, 1981).

SUMMARY

Within this entire approach, the need for developing constructs of the reading process that better integrate neuroanatomical data cannot be overemphasized. Little substantive work has been directed to abstracting reading process requirements from process breakdown in existing case reports of alexia with and without agraphia (see, however, Geschwind's modified version of the reading process in Manter & Gatz, 1975). A model of reading that could accommodate the existent and future data bases of both information-processing and neuroanatomical models would provide a powerful tool for examining the components and stages in reading acquisition and breakdown.

Another reason for work toward such a model is the rapid expansion of neuroanatomical information and the increased sophistication of methodologies now available. For example, Galaburda and Kemper (1979) have made a substantial contribution toward developing a neuroanatomical basis for some developmental disorders. In their cytoarchitectonic examination of the brain of a dyslexic young man killed in an accident, they found abnormal cellular architecture in the posterior portion of the planum temporale and part of Wernicke's area, regions typically implicated in the acquired alexias. Other sources of neuroanatomical data about reading disorders include CAT scan studies (Hier, LeMay, Rosenberger, & Perlo, 1978) and brain electrical activity mapping research (Duffy, 1979). Few applications of these methodologies are, however, based on theoretical constructs of the reading process. It is critically important that hypotheses and methodologies from the neurosciences be informed by evolving, experimentally based models of reading.

In summary, this chapter has presented a bifurcated argument for (*a*) the combined study of developmental and acquired reading disorders through (*b*) an integration of the cognitive sciences paradigm with methodologies and data bases from the neurosciences. It is my belief that such an approach will yield more refined models of the reading process across human development. These theoretical models will provide the basis for systematic, comprehensive testing of the cognitive and linguistic subprocesses underlying reading. Such measures will increase our capacity to draw comparisons between developmental and acquired disorders of reading, which will, in turn, give added insight into what compensating strategies are being used when (in development), and by whom. Such comparisons may also illumine both the composition of some developmental subgroups and also shed fresh light on the neurological deficit versus lag issues. Finally, the steady growth of knowledge about reading disruption, the various forms of compensation available, and the nature of reading disorder subgroups may give new direction to our ongoing attempts to remedy loss.

REFERENCES

Aaron, P. G., Baxter, C., & Lucenti, J. (1980) Developmental dyslexia and acquired alexia: Two sides of the same coin? *Brain and Language, 11*, 1–11.

Albert, M., & Geschwind, N. (1980) Acquired disorders of reading. In M. Wolf, M. McQuillan, & E. Radwin (Eds.), *Thought and language/Language and reading.* Cambridge, Mass.: Harvard Educational Review.

Benson, F., & Geschwind, N. (1974) The alexias. In N. Geschwind, *Selected papers on language and the brain.* Boston, Mass.: Reidel.

Benton, A., & Pearl, D. (1978) *Dyslexia: An appraisal of current knowledge.* New York: Oxford University Press.

Chall, J. (1979) The great debate: Ten years later, with a modest proposal for reading stages. In L. Resnick & P. Weaver (Eds.), *Theory and practice in early reading* (Vol. 1). Hillsdale, N.J.: Laurence Erlbaum.

Coltheart, M., Patterson, K., & Marshall, J. (Eds.). (1980) *Deep dyslexia.* London: Routledge & Kegan Paul.

Denckla, M. (1978) Minimal brain dysfunction. In J. Chall & A. Mirsky (Eds.), *Education and brain.* Chicago: National Society for Study of Education.

Doehring, D. (1980) *Classification of children with reading problems by cluster analysis.* Paper presented at International Neuropsychological Society, San Francisco, January 1980.

Drake, W. E. (1968) Clinical and pathological findings in a child with a developmental learning disability. *Journal of Learning Disabilities, 1,* 486–502.

Duffy, F. (1979) *Brain electrical activity mapping (BEAM).* Psychiatry colloquium, The Children's Hospital Medical Center, Boston, March 1979.

Ellis, A. (1979) Developmental and acquired dyslexia: Some observations on Jorm. *Cognition, 7,* 413–420.

Galaburda, A., & Kemper, T. (1979) Auditory cytoarchitectonic abnormalities in developmental dyslexia. *Annals of Neurology, 6,* 94–100.

Geschwind, N. (1962) The anatomy of acquired disorders of reading. In John Money (Ed.), *Reading disabilities: Progress and research needs in dyslexia*. Baltimore: Johns Hopkins University Press.

Geschwind, N. (1974) *Selected papers on language and the brain*. Boston: Reidel.

Geschwind, N. (1980) Discussion remarks. World Conference of Neurology, Boston, October 3, 1980.

Goodglass, H., Kaplan, E., & Weintraub, S. (1976) *Boston Naming Test*. (Experimental edition).

Greenblatt, S. (1976) Subangular alexia without agraphia or hemianopsia. *Brain and Language, 3*, 229–245.

Hier, D., LeMay, M., Rosenberger, P., & Perlo, V. (1978) Developmental dyslexia: Evidence for a subgroup with a reversal of cerebral asymmetry. *Archives of Neurology, 35*, 90–92.

Holmes, J. (1978) "Regression" and reading breakdown. In A. Caramazza & E. Zurif (Eds.), *Language acquisition and language breakdown*. Baltimore: Johns Hopkins University Press.

Jorm, A. (1979) The cognitive and neurological basis of developmental dyslexia: A theoretical framework and review. *Cognition, 7*, 19–33.

Kinsbourne, M., & Warrington, E. (1962) A variety of reading disability associated with right hemisphere lesions. *Journal of Neurology, Neurosurgery and Psychiatry, 25*, 339–344.

Kinsbourne, M., & Warrington, E. (1963) Developmental factors in reading and writing backwardness. *British Journal of Psychology, 54*, 145–156.

Manter & Gatz (1975) *Essentials of clinical neuroanatomy and neurophysiology* (5th edition by R. Clark). Philadelphia: Davis.

Marcel, T. (1980) Surface dyslexia and beginning reading: A revised hypothesis of the pronunciation of print and its impairments. In M. Coltheart, K. Patterson, & J. Marshall (Eds.), *Deep dyslexia*. London: Routledge & Kegan Paul.

Marshall, J., & Newcombe, F. (1966) Syntactic and semantic errors in paralexia. *Neuropsychologia, 4*, 169–176.

Marshall, J., & Newcombe, F. (1973) Patterns of paralexia: A psycholinguistic approach. *Journal of Psycholinguistic Research, 2*, 175–199.

Marshall, J., & Newcombe, F. (1977) Variability and constraint in acquired dyslexia. In H. Whitaker & H. A. Whitaker (Eds.), *Studies in neurolinguistics* (Vol. 3). New York: Academic.

Marshall, J., & Newcombe, F. (1980) The conceptual status of deep dyslexia: An historical perspective. In M. Coltheart, K. Patterson, & J. Marshall (Eds.), *Deep dyslexia*. London: Routledge & Kegan Paul.

Mattis, S., French, J., & Rapin, I. Dyslexia in children and young adults: Three independent neurological syndromes. *Developmental Medicine and Child Neurology, 17*, 150–163.

Morton, J., & Patterson, K. (1980) A new attempt at an interpretation, or an attempt at a new interpretation. In M. Coltheart, K. Patterson, & J. Marshall (Eds.), *Deep dyslexia*. London: Routledge & Kegan Paul.

Newcombe, F. *Reading without phonology—An update*. Paper presented at World Conference of Neurology, Boston, October 2, 1980.

Rourke, B. P. (1980) *Reading and spelling problems: A neuropsychological approach*. Paper presented at European International Neuropsychological Society, Chianciano-Terme, Italy, June 2, 1980.

Rudel, R. (1978) Neuroplasticity: Implications for development and education. In J. Chall & A. Mirsky (Eds.), *Education and the brain*. Chicago: National Society for Study of Education.

Vellutino, F. (1979) *Dyslexia: Theory and research.* Cambridge, Mass.: MIT Press.

Vernon, M. D. (1977) Varieties of deficiencies in the reading process. In E. Radwin & M. Wolf (Eds.), *Reading, language and learning.* Cambridge, Mass.: Harvard Educational Review.

Wolf, M. (1979) *The relationship of word-finding and reading disorders in children and aphasics.* Unpublished doctoral dissertation, Harvard University.

Wolf, M. (1981) The word-retrieval process and reading in children and aphasics. In K. Nelson (Ed.), *Children's language* (Vol. 3). New York: Gardner.

Wolf, M., & Bally, H. (1981) *From "Unicorns" to "Screwhorses": A longitudinal investigation of Kindergarten naming and First-Grade reading.* Paper presented at Boston University Language Conference, Boston, October 10, 1981.

Wolf, M., & Bally, H. (In preparation) *A longitudinal study of dysnomia in children with reading disorders.*

Chapter Twelve

Developmental Biology and Disorders of Reading

HERMAN T. EPSTEIN

NEUROBIOLOGICAL DEVELOPMENTAL FEATURES

Although brain function is clearly dependent on brain structure, we are only beginning to understand the specifics of that relationship. In this chapter we will explore just one of its aspects: the connection between the *development* of function and the *development* of structure at various ages. That is, changes in one should be correlated with changes in the other. We are not likely to transcend correlations because the brain–mind problem is really one of manifestations and observations on two different levels: biology and psychology.

Such correlations serve, however, to generate working hypotheses about the development of functions, in that they provide us with constraints on functions arising from the natures of the developing biological structures. In this section, we present facts about brain growth that will lead to inferences and hypotheses about functions, particularly language and reading.

Brain Growth Data

Autopsy data on brain weight at various ages is rather limited, so inferences about patterns of growth require utilization of other data.

293

Copyright © 1982 by Academic Press, Inc.
All rights of reproduction in any form reserved.
ISBN 0-12-466320-6

This can be done by exploiting the quantitative connection between brain weight and head circumference which has been shown (Epstein & Epstein, 1978; Epstein, 1979) to be constant from brain weights of about 15–2000 gm, the brain weight being proportional to the cube of the head circumference. Longitudinal data from the Berkeley Growth Study and cross-sectional data from the standardization information for pediatricians both give growth stage age spans similar to those from the brain weight data: 3–10 months, 2–4, 6–8, 10–12+, and 14–16+ years (Epstein, 1979). The possibility that the changes could, at least in part, be manifestations of changes in skull bone thickness was ruled out by ascertaining that those changes are small compared with the overall head circumference increments. The single study (Vignaud, 1966) of human cranial capacity shows volume changes precisely parallel the inferred brain/head growth stages up through age 10 years (at which the data stop).

Thus, the brain growth stages apply to about 85% of children, with girls on the early side of the age spans and boys on the later side. The reasons why some 15% of children do not follow this paradigm are not known to us.

The studies of Dobbing and Sands (1973) provide the additional information needed: They found a virtual cessation of net DNA increases after 18–24 months, so the later growth of the brain amounts to about 30% in weight without much increase in the total number of brain cells. As most of the brain weight is in neurons (Kuffler & Nichols, 1976) most of the weight increase must reflect the elongation and branching of axons and dendrites.

Such neuronal changes must be presumed to signal the creation of new connections among neurons, for the elongation and branching would not otherwise occur. Four studies bear on this point. The indirect but more general evidence comes from developmental studies of cortical thickness and from electroencephalographic (EEG) studies in humans. Data on cortical thickness are not abundant, but Rabinowicz (1979) gave a compilation of his own data and those of Conel from birth through age 10 years. Summed over all regions of the brain, these data show increases in cortical thickness during the first year of life and at ages 2–4 and 6–8 years, with much less or no overall increase during the age spans 1–2, 4–6, and 8–10 years. This finding is in excellent accord with the brain weight growth data. Interestingly, only in the inferior parietal lobule is the overall picture precisely paralleled; the sampling was actually done somewhat away from the angular gyrus end of the lobule, but there is no reason to suppose that a difference would be found in the area of the angular gyrus.

Although the specific interpretation of EEG data remains a matter of controversy, the use of the data for information about gross changes over time is not affected by such questions. Electrical currents in the cortex may be expected to change appreciably if the networks themselves are changing. Accordingly, we have looked at the developmental aspects of the EEG and found a parameter of importance: the percentage of total EEG energy to be found in the alpha frequencies of 8–13 Hz. This percentage rises from zero at birth to about 70% in adults, and the rise is in stages occurring quite precisely at the ages of the brain growth stages (Epstein, 1979, 1980a). Here again, the regional concordance is precise in the junction of the parietal, occipital, and temporal lobes, or the angular gyrus region. It is also worth noting that the one study (Henry, 1944) giving data separately for males and females exhibits the same sexual dimorphism as is found in the brain weight data.

The direct evidence about changes in elongation and branching of axons and dendrites is less general because the two studies focused on single regions of the brain. For some time it has been believed that creation of novel synapses meant a net creation of new synapses, although recent studies of neuronal cell death during development strengthened the likelihood that shifting of synapses might be a causal factor. Huttenlocher (1979) measured synapse density in one of the human frontal gyri and found that, after a substantial (about tenfold) increase during the first year of life, there is no appreciable change in synapse density at least to age 7, followed by a twofold decrease by the next measuring age of 16 years. Thus, if changes in synapses are to occur mainly as a result of the large increase in axonal and dendritic sprouting or arborization, they reflect mainly the shifting of synapses, presumably associated with the maturation of some synapses which, in turn, would free other synapses to move their locations, thereby altering the neural networks in substantial ways. Of course, the absence of net increases in synapse density may reflect only what is happening in the particular part of the frontal lobe, and other parts of the cortex could still manifest substantial net increases in density as well as some shifting of synapses.

The occipital cortex was studied by LeVay and Stryker (1979) in their investigation of the development of ocular dominance columns in the cat. They pointed out that

The changing autoradiographic picture seen in layer IV between 2 weeks and maturity seems likely to result from roughly synchronous changes in the arborization of thousands of overlapping geniculo-cortical axons. . . . It could be seen that synapses were formed with neighboring dendritic elements along the course of the axon. These synapses were, for the most part, quite elementary in construction. . . . The glial wrapping, which is prominent in the adult synapse, was either absent or poorly developed. . . . [The] adult arborizations differ from those seen in young kittens in being myelinated. . . . The boutons on the mature arborizations are very distinct bulbous structures . . . packed with synaptic vesicles. . . . The rearrangement of axonal arbors in normal development envisioned here takes place during a "critical period" [pp. 87, 90, 91, 95].

The studies just discussed all give substantial support to the picture of changes in neural network arborization inferred from brain weight and brain DNA data.

It is also of significance that stages of EEG changes were described and emphasized by Pampiglione (1971, 1977a, 1977b) in his studies of EEG development in dogs, lambs, pigs, and humans. We have located similar evidence for cats and monkeys (Epstein, 1979) showing a parallel between EEG changes and the putative brain growth stages in two species.

This concludes the sketch of those facts about human brain growth essential to our discussion of neurological bases of language and reading. Before turning to that discussion, it is interesting to note briefly how stages in brain growth may be used to draw certain inferences about learning in general.

We do not know what happens in the brain during the slow growth periods, but it is plausible that such periods might be manifested in a slow mental growth. This hypothesis has received some support from data concerning the parameter of mental age (Epstein, 1978, 1979, 1980b). What is less clear at present is the proposition that *learning capacity* itself may be lower during such periods. The few developmental studies purporting to measure something related to inherent learning capacity yield supportive data (Rosenthal & Jacobson, 1968; Cattell, 1971). And I have pointed out a suggestive parallel between slow brain growth periods and the schooling problems encountered by children in Head Start programs (4–6 years) and in junior high school (12–14 years, Epstein, 1978).

Blood Flow Measurements

Blood flow measurements in the brain may be obtained by a variety of techniques. The measurements discussed here were made by injecting radioactive substances into the artery leading to the brain and studying the subsequent location of those substances while the individual was carrying on a variety of activities.

The Swedish group led by Ingvar, Lassen, and their associates (Ingvar, 1976) measured blood flow with the aid of radiation detectors placed at different points on the head. They first checked to see if activation of various systems (e.g., motor, sensory) caused an increased blood flow in the brain region where such activity is generally known to be mediated. Having confirmed their expectations, they then asked individuals to do things such as speaking, reading, taking an IQ test.

Their study showed that, while the subject tried to "reason," the increase in blood flow in the back part of the brain was confined to the angular gyrus region. While the subject was involved in reading, there was, as expected, increased blood flow in the visual cortex and Wernicke's and Broca's areas. Totally unexpected was the observation that the blood flow in the angular gyrus region not only did not increase during reading, but actually decreased substantially. Even if the individual were merely reading mechanically, which requires little beyond automatic decoding, the least that would be expected is that the blood flow in the angular gyrus would remain unaffected. The finding of a large, significant decrease in blood flow probably means that blood that would have flowed through that region was being actively diverted to some other region.

It appears that, as reading abilities develop, the transfer of energy from vision to comprehension bypasses regions that in the beginning reader, are actively involved. Perhaps some groups of children who have difficulty reading are not able to make this direct transfer to comprehension but continue to require the extra step of transfer to hearing, which slows up the whole process and thus makes reading much less efficient.

EVOLUTIONARY ASPECTS OF BRAIN GROWTH

We know that the brain has undergone evolution, for *Homo sapiens* have about three times as much brain as some of their earliest forerunners. Even our earliest ancestors presumably grew in developmental stages which corresponded to childhood, adolescence, and a mature period. What can we say about the ways in which additional brain growth may have occurred? A brain mutation, if it occurred within the period from conception to maturation, would have disrupted the set of connected processes that permit growth to maturity. Therefore, such a mutation would probably be deleterious, if not lethal. This is a very general insight of geneticists about all mutations, but it would hold especially for mutations affecting the control system—the brain. Accordingly, the only mutations that might not upset the normal developmental sequence are those that occur at the end of the normal maturation period of the brain. That is, possibly nonlethal mutations are those that affect the postmaturity period of brain development.

Evidence has already been cited showing that in humans net cell formation ceases very early in brain development, so mutation after maturation almost certainly must effect changes in the connections among existing neurons. If these changes do not happen to affect seriously the existing functions of the brain, then the new networks can survive.

What kinds of new networks can we expect to survive? Because they are new, they can have no predefined function. So, their use will depend on their being adaptable to new functions which are learned, presumably by trial and error. Once someone has discovered functions that could be performed by these new networks, these functions could be taught to others. Therefore, the functioning of the new networks is clearly learning dependent; it must be taught to others, especially to succeeding generations.

Can there be further evolution of these networks so as to preprogram some of the changes of connections that are brought about by learning? There is no way to make such an estimate, but we *can* say that unless they perform the new functions sufficiently better to make a difference in survival through selection, the usual selection pressures will not operate. Such kinds of preprogramming are believed to be unlikely. Therefore, it is probable that these additional brain growth stages remain learning dependent. In the case of humans, as will be shown later, the last three brain growth stages take place after the known programmed functions are already in place. Therefore, we believe that the utilization of the last three human brain growth stages should depend on adequate and timely instruction. This means that from age 4, the essentially human functions should depend on effective interaction between organism and environment. From this point of view, all of our learning depends on adequate instructional input.

THE ORIGINS OF LANGUAGE AND READING

Brain growth stages permit us to make cross-species comparisons by pointing out similarities among the main events in brain growth stages in various species. Consider, for example, brain growth stages in two species, mice and men. For reasons presented in the preceding study of evolutionary aspects of brain growth, mutations affecting brain growth preceding maturity are not likely to have been conserved. Thus, the brain growth stages should remain pretty much as they were in the common vertebrate ancestor. That is, we expect the *main events*— anatomical, biochemical, and physiological—to remain pretty much unaltered. Therefore, we look at brain growth stages in the two species and examine the main events. During the second postnatal brain growth stage of rodents (8–12 days) myelination has just started; there is a very substantial growth of the cerebellum; sensory functioning is rudimentary; and there is substantial DNA net synthesis in all parts of the brain, especially the cerebellum. If we consider the first postnatal brain growth stage of humans (3–10 months) we find the same main events in addition to some other changes that are not relevant to this discussion. Thus, we can make a preliminary identification of those stages as originating in a common vertebrate ancestor. Next, between 17 and 23 days, the rodents have just finished their main net DNA synthesis. Sensory functioning of all senses is initiated, and myelination of those sensory tracts is extensive. During the next brain growth stage of humans, between 2 and 4 years, the same main events take place. Thus, we make a second set of identifications presumably due to their having been originated in the common vertebrate ancestor.

Now, the rodent has no more brain growth stages, so the later stages in humans are associated entirely with the postdivergence of the evolutionary history of the lines leading to *Homo sapiens*. Whatever functions are subserved by the networks developed through age 23 days in rodents and 4 years in humans are presumed to be still subserved as remnants of their common ancestry. It is obvious that all those networks had functions, for "nature" should not be expected to create networks for some future use. Thus, it is believed that we share functions with the rodents in the early stages of development.

Rodents do not speak. Humans, however, begin to speak by the end of the first year and certainly make enormous progress in speech by the end of the fourth year. Thus, we may suppose that the networks being used for language are ones that existed in our common ancestor and were being used for other purposes. It might even be possible to study those uses in rodents of preweaning age and humans before age 1. It is quite possible that, when language begins to appear, it must use existing neuronal networks developed and evolved for entirely different purposes. The only way this can happen without serious deleterious effects is for language to use networks that are redundant. Thus, language could have been inserted into just one side of the human brain, leaving the networks on the other side to take care of the functions that were previously subserved by both sides. Accordingly, both language and the old functions are now at risk, each being singly represented.

The important aspect of this hypothetical analysis is that it indicates that language may have been grafted on to networks already serving other functions. Indeed, by studying other activities that occur during speech (hand waving, facial movements, etc.), we may gain an idea of what the networks once did.

It then follows that, since many children can learn to read by the end of their fourth–sixth year of life, reading, too, may utilize networks that evolved for other purposes and thus also be grafted onto human functioning by placing previous functions at risk because of lack of redundancy.

CONCLUSION

The investigation of any human function requires examination of extant models within a context of trying to unify the observations. An additional problem lies in the tendency of investigators of human behavior to work at studies aimed at defining the validity of their individual models at the expense of looking at the larger picture showing how each model explains a subset of the observations. What we have attempted to do in this chapter is to present a kind of ecumenical approach to the origins of reading disorders. We hope we have shown the feasibility of such an approach, as well as why we believe the study of reading processes demands such a multidimensional view.

REFERENCES

Cattell, R. B. (1971) The structure of intelligence in relation to the nature–nurture controversy. In R. Cancro (Ed.), *Intelligence*. New York: Grune & Stratton.

Dobbing, J., & Sands, J. (1973) Quantitative growth and development of human brain. *Archives of Diseases in Childhood, 48,* 757–767.

Epstein, H. (1978) Growth spurts during brain development: Implications for educational policy and practice. In J. S. Chall & A. Mirsky (Eds.), *NSSE Yearbook: Education and the Brain.* Chicago: University of Chicago Press.

Epstein, H. (1979) Correlated brain and intelligence development in humans. In M. Hahn, C. Jensen, & B. Dudek (Eds.), *Development and evolution.* New York: Academic Press.

Epstein, H. (1980a) EEG developmental stages. *Developmental Psychobiology, 13,* 629–631.

Epstein, H. (1980b) Some biological bases of cognitive development. *Bulletin of Orton Society, 30,* 157–177.

Epstein, H. T., & Epstein, E. B. (1978) The relationship between brain weight and head circumference from birth to age 18 years. *American Journal of Physical Anthropology, 48,* 471–474.

Henry, C. E. (1944) Electroencephalograms of normal children. *Monographs of Society for Research in Child Development, 9,* 1–71.

Hubel, D., Wiesel, T. S., & LeVay, S. (1977) Plasticity of ocular dominance columns in monkey striate cortex. *Philosophical Transactions, Royal Society of London,* Part B, *278,* 377–409.

Huttenlocher, P. R. (1979) Synaptic density in human frontal cortex—Developmental changes and effects of aging. *Brain Research, 163,* 195–205.

Ingvar, D. H. (1976) Functional landscapes of the dominant hemisphere. *Brain Research, 107,* 181–197.

Kuffler, J., & Nichols, H. (1976) *From neuron to brain.* Sunderland, Mass.: Sinauer Associates.

LeVay, S., & Stryker, M. P. (1979) The development of ocular dominance columns in the cat. In J. A. Ferrendelli (Ed.), *Aspects of developmental neurobiology.* Bethesda, Md.: Society for Neuroscience.

Pampiglione, G. (1971) Some aspects of the development of cerebral function in mammals. *Proceedings of the Royal Society of Medicine, 64,* 429–435.

Pampiglione, G. (1977a) Development of rhythmic E.E.G. activities in infancy (waking state). *Reviews of E.E.G. and Neurophysiology, 7,* 327–334.

Pampiglione, G. (1977b) Development of some rhythmic activity in the E.E.G. of young pigs, lambs, and puppies. *Reviews of E.E.G. and Neurophysiology, 7,* 255–262.

Rabinowicz, T. (1979) The differentiate maturation of the human cerebral cortex. In F. Falkner & J. M. Tanner (Eds.), *Human growth: 3, Neurobiology and Nutrition.* New York: Plenum Press.

Rosenthal, R., & Jacobson, L. (1968) *Pygmalion in the classroom: Teacher expectation and pupils' intellectual development.* New York: Holt, Rinehart and Winston.

Vignaud, J. (1966) Radiological study of the normal skull in premature and newborn infants. In F. Falkner (Ed.), *Human development.* Philadelphia. W. B. Saunders.

Part Two

Acquired Alexia

Chapter Thirteen

Acquired Alexia

NILS R. VARNEY
ANTONIO R. DAMASIO

INTRODUCTION

The term "alexia" refers to those disturbances of reading in which previously literate individuals lose their ability to comprehend written language as the result of acquired disease of the central nervous system (CNS). The term does not refer to those impairments (congenital or acquired early in life) which prevent the normal acquisition of reading skills (generally referred to as "developmental dyslexia" or merely "dyslexia"). There is, however, an exception to this usage: The reader will find the terms alexia and dyslexia used almost interchangeably in the British literature.

Alexia may be descriptively divided into two major subtypes: verbal alexia and literal alexia. In verbal alexia, understanding of the written word is impaired whereas letter "recognition reading" is intact: There is "word blindness" without "letter blindness." In literal alexia, both letter reading and word reading are defective: There is both letter blindness and word blindness. Some authors have applied the term literal alexia to a disturbance of letter naming (literal anomia) which can occur in the context of relatively normal oral word reading (Benson, 1977;

305

READING DISORDERS

Hécaen & Kremin, 1977). However, the validity of what Hinshelwood (1900) called "letter blindness without word blindness"—that is, disturbed letter recognition in the context of normal reading comprehension—is questionable. Occasionally patients with "literal alexia" can read a few overlearned words (e.g., *stop, love*), but this possibly reflects iconographic recognition rather than actual reading comprehension.

Alexia can reflect a variety of neuropathological and neurolinguistic disorders. The defect figures prominently in classic aphasia nosology. Impaired reading comprehension is a diagnostic criterion for the following different syndromes: (*a*) "pure" alexia (alexia without agraphia), (*b*) alexia with agraphia, (*c*) transcortical sensory aphasia, (*d*) Wernicke's aphasia, and (*e*) global aphasia. Alexia can appear in other disturbances, such as Broca's aphasia, although less prominently.

The diagnosis of alexia may not be immediately apparent. For instance, patients may read aloud correctly without comprehending any of the words they read. Visuomotor (oral) "transcoding" remains intact despite impaired reading for meaning. But the opposite can occur, too. It is quite common to find nonfluent aphasics with articulatory problems whose oral reading aloud is moderately or even grossly defective but who nevertheless retain normal or near normal reading for meaning. Thus, regardless of the status of oral reading, it is essential that reading comprehension be assessed formally.

Assessment of letter "reading" can pose additional problems. The examiner can usually assume that patients able to name individual letters correctly or point to them when named by the examiner have intact letter recognition. On the other hand, failure on such tasks can result from defects other than disturbed letter recognition (e.g., anomia, impaired aural comprehension). To guarantee the presence of letter recognition impairment patients should be requested to match upper- and lowercase letters. In the general aphasic population, disturbances in letter matching are less than half as common as defects in letter name recognition (Faglioni, Scotti, & Spinnler, 1969; Marshall, Kushner, & Philips, 1978).

As a general rule, the evaluation of alexic patients should include the following: (*a*) assessment of spontaneous writing, writing from copy, writing from dictation, written spelling, and oral spelling; (*b*) assessment of aural comprehension in relation to reading comprehension; (*c*) assessment of visual naming in relation to auditory and tactile naming; (*d*) assessment of numeral reading and arithmetic ability; and (*e*) assessment of tactile and auditory recognition of words spelled letter by letter.

PURE ALEXIA (ALEXIA WITHOUT AGRAPHIA)

This syndrome is characterized by a major impairment of reading comprehension with an equally striking preservation of writing.

The impairment in "visual" reading comprehension is not paralleled in "tactile" or "auditory" reading. Most patients with pure alexia are able to read words "written" letter by letter on the palm of their hand, and can read by touch letters and words printed in relief. Similarly, they can recognize words that are spelled aloud.

Writing to dictation or spontaneously is linguistically correct, but the spatial arrangement of the written production as well as the design of letters itself may be slightly disturbed. A similar problem besets writing from copy, which can become a complex or even impossible task for pure alexics. Aural comprehension, naming of three-dimensional objects, and repetition are intact.

There was at one time considerable disagreement as to the relationship between letter recognition and reading comprehension in "pure" alexia. Some authors argued that disturbance in letter recognition was indicative of severity of alexia whereas others suggested that letter recognition could be affected independently of word reading. Studies by Hécaen (Hécaen, 1967; Hécaen & Kremin, 1977) have helped resolve this issue. It appears there may be three subtypes of "pure" alexia. In one, termed "verbal alexia," reading of words is severely impaired while recognition and oral reading of letters is intact. In another, "global alexia," letter recognition and word reading are both severely impaired. In the third variety, termed "literal alexia," the patients are unable to name letters but occasionally are able to read single words. At the same time, reading comprehension is severely impaired but letter recognition is well preserved.

Most patients with "pure" alexia retain numeral reading (Alajouanine, Lhermitte, & DeRibaucort-Ducarne, 1960). Although reading of numbers and recognition of names of numbers are usually less than optimal, the level of impairment tends to be moderate, and arithmetic competence may be preserved. In this regard, it may be noted that normal subjects usually show better recognition of tachistoscopically presented numerals in the left hemifield (when numerals are compared to words—White, 1969), suggesting that the frequent intactness of number reading in pure alexia may reflect normal right hemisphere mediation of recognition of numerals.

There are few studies of music reading in "pure" alexia, but it appears that virtually all patients who were musically literate premorbidly are as impaired in music reading as in word reading (De Ajuriaguerra & Hecaen, 1949). Interestingly, all retain their ability to "comprehend" music, enjoy it, learn new musical pieces by ear, and perform both old and newly learned material. That is, the motor and auditory aspects of musical processing are as intact as the motor and auditory aspects of language.

One of the interesting signs accompanying "pure" alexia is color anomia. Many such patients lose their ability to name colors or to point to colors given their names. However, they are not achromatopsic. Most patients with color anomia retain color imagery, remember the color names typical of certain objects (e.g., yellow for banana, red for blood), and can even associate abstract, "affective" concepts with colors that could appropriately symbolize them (e.g., sadness with blue) (Damasio, McKee, & Damasio, 1979).

The most frequent sign accompanying pure alexia is a right homonymous hemianopia. Often that is the chief complaint and the cause for seeking medical attention. A considerable number of patients with pure alexia are first seen by ophthalmologists; some are even referred to psychologists, as suspected conversion hysterics. But hemianopia is not indispensable, and pure alexia may present without a field defect altogether or with hemiachromatopsia. Cerebral vascular accidents are responsible for the majority of cases with pure alexia although glial tumors can produce the syndrome.

In addition to the disturbances that have been outlined, the following may be moderately abnormal in patients with pure alexia: (a) visual naming of line drawings, particularly in cases with color anomia; (b) the digit symbol subtest of the WAIS, which will be particularly difficult for patients with disturbed letter recognition; and (c) the paired associate learning subtest of the Wechsler Memory Scale.

The pathological changes associated with pure alexia can be found, almost invariably, in the dominant occipital lobe. More often than not the lesion is caused by infarction in the territory of the left posterior cerebral artery, but neoplasms—generally gliomas—are frequently responsible for the syndrome. Whatever the cause, the lesion effectively disconnects visual information (arriving in both the right and left visual cortices) from the language cortices located in the temporoparietal cortices of the left hemisphere. Different loci of damage can produce that effect. For instance, the lesion may involve the mesial visual cortex of the left hemisphere and compromise the white matter of the forceps major, a structure that continues the splenium of the corpus callosum within the substance of the occipital lobe. Both visual information corresponding to the right visual field (which enters the cerebral cortex in the left visual region) and information corresponding to the left visual field (which arrives in the left hemisphere mainly via the forceps major) will be prevented from reaching the dominant language cortex. Recent evidence from studies using CT scan (A. Damasio & H. Damasio, to be published) show that two separate lesions can produce this same effect, the first located, for instance, in the mesial visual cortex of the left hemisphere or in the left lateral geniculate body, and the second located in the splenium of the corpus callosum itself. Finally, a single lesion, involving neither visual cortex nor corpus callosum, but strategically located at a point in which pathways from either structure converge to reach the left lateral language cortices, can be associated with pure alexia. This lesion is seen in cases of so-called subangular alexia.

Whether the corpus callosum itself is damaged or not, the anatomical mechanism responsible for the disorder is that of disconnection. This was hinted at by Dejerine in his original description of 1892, and extensively elaborated on by Geschwind (1965). In addition to the case of Dejerine, the standard anatomical description of the syndrome can be found in Geschwind and Fusillo (1966). For details on the correlates of subangular alexia the reader is referred to Greenblatt (1976). For a discussion on the role of the splenium in the appearance of alexia see Damasio (1980; 1982).

ALEXIA WITH AGRAPHIA

In alexia with agraphia, reading and written language are impaired to a comparable extent. However, this disorder is more than the sum of "pure" alexia and disturbed writing. Most cases have word finding difficulties and paraphasic speech. The distinction between the syndrome of alexia with agraphia and those of the posterior fluent aphasias (Wernicke's, transcortical sensory) rests on the magnitude of the reading and writing defects in comparison with the impairments of speech, naming, and aural comprehension.

Some authors have referred to alexia with agraphia as a state of "acquired illiteracy." Insofar as reading and writing are concerned, that is correct. The disturbance in reading comprehension is not limited to "visual" reading, as in "pure" alexia, and it affects word recognition in a tactile mode or by means of oral spelling. In additon, disturbances in letter and number reading are frequent, though not necessary, and most cases show partial or complete acalculia, both in oral and written forms.

Writing spontaneously and to dictation is severely disturbed, with abnormal spelling (oral spelling is equally disturbed). There may be paraphasias of the global type, or, more commonly, neologisms, as a result of poor spelling, but writing is often complicated by graphomotor apraxia, and can be entirely illegible. The ability to write from copy is variable, this being the only aspect of written expression that can be partially preserved.

Other than aphasia, the most common accompanying signs of alexia and agraphia are right hemisensory dysfunction and visual field defects. The latter are less common than in pure alexia. Components of the Gerstmann syndrome can be observed. Because alexia with agraphia can result from either vascular or neoplastic lesions, onset can be acute or gradual, and the disturbances in reading and writing can be variable in severity.

As a result of the associated aphasia and acalculia, Verbal IQ and verbal memory are generally below expected premorbid levels. In addition, many affected patients will show both graphomotor and constructional apraxia, with the result that the WAIS Performance IQ will also appear defective (i.e., Block Design, Object Assembly, and Digit Symbol subtests of the WAIS are all compromised by apraxia).

Alexia with agraphia is generally associated with vascular or neoplastic lesions that involve the inferior parietal or posterolateral temporal regions of the dominant hemisphere. Damage to both cortex and white matter have been noted to produce the syndrome. Lesions located superiorly to the angular gyrus often fail to produce alexia or agraphia, and lesions located caudally to the parieto-temporal junction may be associated with alexia but not agraphia.

THE THIRD ALEXIA

The designation "third alexia" or "frontal alexia" applies to disturbances of reading comprehension associated with Broca's aphasia. Observations of Broca's aphasics with disturbed reading date back to the nineteenth century (Lichtheim, 1885), but the disorder has been recognized only recently as a distinct variety of alexia. This is the result of Benson's (1977) finding that a majority (57%) of Broca's aphasics have severely disturbed reading comprehension, and that only a small minority (16%) show normal reading. Benson argued against the long-standing view that postrolandic lesions were essential for the development of alexia, and his "third alexia" has, consequently, important implications for the understanding of both impaired and normal reading comprehension.

Virtually all patients with the third alexia have Broca's aphasia, and so their speech is nonfluent and telegrammatic. Spontaneous writing is similarly nonfluent, with frequent blocking and grossly abnormal spelling. Oral spelling and recognition of orally and tactually spelled words are also impaired. Writing from dictation and from copy is as disturbed as spontaneous writing. As with all other perisylvian aphasias, repetition is impaired.

Patients with the third alexia show a far greater disturbance in reading sentences for meaning than in reading single words, and are more likely to understand substantive words than relational words. For example, a patient with the third alexia may be able to understand the written words *boy, running,* and *house,* but fail in reading *The boy is running away from the house.*

A further distinguishing feature of the third alexia is "literal anomia," which is sometimes mistaken for literal alexia (Benson, Brown, & Tomlinson, 1971). This means that oral reading (naming) of individual *letters* of the alphabet may be appreciably poorer than oral *word* reading, with the occasional result that a patient can read a word aloud correctly, but cannot name the component letters. Nevertheless, these same patients typically show well-preserved aural comprehension of letter names and presumably have no problems with letter recognition.

Benson (1977, 1979) has proposed that the reading impairments characteristic of the third alexia result from deterioration of one or more of the following functions essential for normal reading: (*a*) left-to-right visual scanning; (*b*) sequential logic and memory; and (*c*) appreciation of syntactic/grammatic aspects of written language. The literal anomia shown by these aphasics has been somewhat more difficult to interpret, particularly as these patients usually show normal letter recognition.

The behavioral and anatomical descriptions available with regard to the third alexia are by no means complete. Reading defects have been classified as severe or mild, neuroanatomical features have been inferred from neurological and neuropsychological data, and little is known about the status of aural comprehension. The latter is of particular import because the characteristic reading disturbances of the third alexia may also be present in aural comprehension. It has been repeatedly observed that Broca's aphasics usually show good aural word recognition but perform poorly on tasks that contain many relational words or sentence length material (e.g., the token test) (Poeck, Kerschensteiner, & Hartje, 1972). Should the aural comprehension and reading comprehension defects of third alexia prove comparable, the status of this disorder as a true alexia would be open to question.

DEEP DYSLEXIA

The term "deep dyslexia" was introduced by Marshall and New-combe (1973) to label those rare cases of reading disorder that contained abundant semantic paraphasic errors. Patients with deep dyslexia will, for instance, read *cow* as "milk," *dad* as "father," *gnome* as "pixie," or *liberty* as "freedom." This type of error is not present in spontaneous speech, visual naming, or repetition. Thus, the frequent semantic par-alexias appear to reflect a specific disturbance of the reading process.

The paralexic responses which hallmark deep dyslexia have been found to occur more frequently with picturable, concrete words than with nonpicturable, abstract words. Nouns are more likely to elicit semantic paralexias than adjectives, and adjectives are more likely to do so than verbs. Contextual clues usually facilitate oral reading per-formance for both correct and paraphasic responses. For example, pa-tients may be unable to read a word like *zebra* unless told that the word is an animal name, in which case they may say "zebra" or "giraffe."

The argument that deep dyslexia is a syndrome is based on the fact that patients with semantic paralexias typically make four other types of error in oral reading. The first of these is designated "visual error"— the misreading of a word by substituting one that has similar appear-ance in print (e.g., *shock* → "stock," *flow* → "flower"). This type of error does not include substitution of phonologically similar word with different "visual form" (e.g., *phrase* → "freeze"). The second type of error is called "derivational." In this instance, words are misread as a different part of speech; for example, *birth* is read as "born," *wise* as "wisdom." A third type of error involves the substitution of function, producing any oral reading response to function words. The usual reply is "don't know." However, if an error is made, it typically involves substitution of another function word (e.g., *our* → "by," *she* → "he"). The fourth type of error involves the inability to read pronounceable nonsense words such as *tud* or *nol* (cf. Marshall & Newcombe, 1980).

Coltheart (1980) has reviewed 21 cases of deep dyslexia, and found that all showed those errors in oral reading. In addition, all of these patients showed defects in spontaneous writing, writing from dictation, and aural–verbal short-term memory. However, all patients were aphasic, and so these symptoms, all common in aphasia, can hardly be considered specific to deep dyslexia. Speech was reported to be of both fluent and nonfluent types, variably paraphasic, and with variable weakness of word finding. Occasionally speech was well preserved in comparison to oral reading. Motor, sensory, and visual field findings were just as variable. Unquestionably, deep dyslexics show a charac-teristic constellation of oral reading defects, but it is fair to say that they form a linguistically and neurologically heterogeneous group. The pathological correlates of those defects are difficult to predict and the anatomical information gleaned from CT scans thus far is clearly insufficient.

APHASIC ALEXIA

Some mention should be made of "aphasic alexia," an acquired reading defect occurring in the context of a receptive aphasia. Whereas most research and theoretical discussion concerning the alexias has been concentrated on its purer varieties, the great majority of patients who develop alexia have Wernicke's, global, or transcortical sensory aphasias. Because such patients present multiple incapacitating linguistic defects, their reading disorder has not captured much attention.

There are two fairly standard views of aphasic alexia. The first is that impaired reading is a secondary sign, the primary defect being in aural comprehension, and the responsible lesion being in the posterior left temporal lobe (De Massary, 1932; Hécaen & Kremin, 1977). The second view is that aphasic alexia is a syndrome of alexia with agraphia complicated by linguistic defects, and that it reflects a parietal lesion (Albert, 1979; Benson, 1979). These views are not mutually exclusive and may well apply, in combination, to most cases of aphasic alexia.

There is an increasing body of data to suggest that reading defects occurring within the context of Wernicke's or global aphasias can be classified into descriptive and diagnostic and subtypes. For example, our own material suggests that aphasic alexia can be differentiated into verbal and literal alexic subtypes (Varney, 1981), and Kertesz (1979) has shown that there is great linguistic variability in the reading performances of patients with receptive aphasic syndromes. The nature, number, and anatomical significance of these distinctions have yet to be established. Nevertheless, there are sufficient data to indicate that aphasic alexia is not a unitary entity, even within established aphasia diagnostic groups.

REFERENCES

Alajouanine, T., Lhermitte, F., & De Ribaucort-Ducarne, B. (1960) Les alexies agnosiques et aphasiques. In T. Alajouanine (Ed.), *Les grandes activités du lobe occipital.* Paris: Masson.

Albert, M. (1979) Alexia. In K. Heilman & E. Valenstein (Eds.), *Clinical neuropsychology.* New York: Oxford University Press.

Benson, F. (1977) The third alexia. *Archives of Neurology, 34,* 327–331.

Benson, F. (1979) *Aphasia, alexia, and agraphia.* New York: Churchill Livingstone.

Benson, F., Brown, J., & Tomlinson, E. (1971) Varieties of alexia: Word and letter blindness. *Neurology, 21,* 951–957.

Coltheart, M. (1980) Deep dyslexia: A review of the syndrome. In M. Coltheart, K. Patterson, & J. Marshall (Eds.), *Deep dyslexia.* London: Routledge and Kegan Paul.

Damasio, A. (1980) Notes on the anatomical basis of pure alexia and of color anomia. In Martha Taylor Sarno & Olle Hook (Eds.), *Aphasia.* New York: Masson .

Damasio, A. (1982) Pure Alexia. *Trends in the Neurosciences,* in press.

Damasio, A., McKee, J., & Damasio, H. (1979) Determinants of performance in color anomia. *Brain and Language, 7,* 74–85.

Dejerine, J. (1892). Contribution a l' étude anatomo-pathologique et clinique des differentes varietés de cécité verbale. *Memories Societé Biologique, 4,* 61–90.

De Ajuriaguerra, J., & Hécaen, H. (1949) *Le cortex cerebral.* Paris: Masson & Cie.

De Massary, J. (1932) L'alexie. *Encèphale, 27,* 134–164.

Faglioni, P., Scotti, G., & Spinnler, H. (1969) Impaired recognition of written letters following unilateral hemispheric damage. *Cortex, 5,* 120–133.

Geschwind, N. (1965) Disconnexion syndromes in animals and man. *Brain, 88,* 237–294, 585–644.

Geschwind, N., & Fusillo, M. (1966) Color-naming defects in association with alexia. *Archives of Neurology, 15,* 137–146.

Greenblatt, S. H. (1976) Subangular alexia without agraphia or hemianopsia. *Brain Language, 2,* 229.

Hécaen, H. (1967) Aspects des troubles de la lecture (alexie) au cours des lésions cérébrales en foyer. *Word, 23,* 265–287.

Hécaen, H., & Kremin, H. (1977) Neurolinguistic research on reading disorders resulting from left hemisphere lesions. In H. Whitaker & H. A. Whitaker (Eds.), *Studies in neurolinguistics* (Vol. 2). New York: Academic Press.

Hinselwood, J. (1900) *Letter, word and mind blindness.* London: H. K. Lewis.

Kertesz, A. (1979) *Aphsia and associated disorders.* New York: Grune & Stratton.

Lichtheim, L. (1885). On aphasia. *Brain, 7,* 434–484.

Marshall, J., & Newcombe, F. (1973) Patterns of paralexia. *Journal of Psycholinguistic Research, 2,* 175–199.

Marshall, J., & Newcombe, F. (1980) The conceptual status of deep dyslexia: A historical perspective. In M. Coltheart, K. Patterson, & J. Marshall (Eds.), *Deep dyslexia.* London: Routledge and Kegan Paul.

Marshall, R., Kushner, K., & Philips, D. (1978) Letter recognition ability of aphasic subjects. *Perceptual and Motor Skills, 47,* 1231–1238.

Poeck, K., Kerschensteiner, M., & Hartje, W. (1972) A quantitative study on language understanding in fluent and non-fluent aphasia. *Cortex, 8,* 299–304.

Varney, N. R. (1981) Letter recognition and visual form discrimination in aphasic alexia. *Neuropsychologia, 19,* 795–800.

White, M. J. (1969) Lateral differences in perception: A review. *Psychology Bulletin, 72,* 387–405.

Chapter Fourteen

Acquired Reading Disorders: A Diagrammatic Model

KENNETH M. HEILMAN
LESLIE J. ROTHI

THE ACQUIRED ALEXIAS

Definition

Alexia is a term used to denote a loss of the ability to comprehend written language (Benson & Geschwind, 1969), but, as is true with naming many other clinical syndromes, this definition is further refined by a process of exclusion. Alexia is not the isolated inability to read aloud nor is it induced by a primary sensory (visual) disturbance. Although these and other problems can be associated, the crucial symptom of alexia is a compromise of reading comprehension.

315

Occasionally the terms *dyslexia* and *alexia* are used synonymously, or dyslexia is used to indicate mild impairments, and alexia to indicate a severe disorder of reading comprehension. More commonly, dyslexia is used in reference to disorders of reading acquisition, whereas alexia refers to loss of previously acquired reading skills. We shall respect these latter definitions, and this chapter will deal specifically with the problem of alexia—loss of reading comprehension.

Various brain lesions can induce attentional disorders. Although these attentional disorders may induce a defect in reading comprehension (e.g., the unilateral paralexia associated with neglect or simultanagnosia), we shall not discuss the attentionally induced reading disorders in this chapter.

Methods of Studying Acquired Reading Disorders

As discussed by Hughlings Jackson (see Taylor, 1932), the abnormal behavior noted after brain ablation is induced not only by a loss of the function processed by the affected area but also by how the remainder of the brain responds to that loss. Ablation of active brain alters other functional areas that were previously inhibited or facilitated by the ablated area. In addition, other nonablated areas may possibly substitute functionally for the damaged areas. These ablation-induced alterations of the nondamaged tissue make it difficult to deduce normal processing mechanisms from the behavioral effects of brain lesions.

Ideally, one would like to know how the normal brain processes written language because with this knowledge plus the knowledge of potential abilities of other brain areas to substitute, one could predict the type of dysfunction resulting from a given lesion. This would result in a predictive as well as generative diagnostic system; not only would known syndromes be better understood, but new syndromes and symptomatology could be predicted. In addition, localization of a lesion from behavioral symptoms would be better refined.

Unfortunately, most of what we now know about the brain processes underlying normal and disordered reading comes from studies of brain lesions. However, a technological revolution is under way that will dramatically influence neuropsychology. In the immediate future, techniques using radioisotopes (positron emission tomography scans, xenon blood flow), electrophysiological studies (evoked potentials, power spectra analysis), and electromagnetic studies may provide researchers with investigative techniques that do not have the shortcomings of the present ablative paradigm.

In this chapter, however, we shall use the ablative paradigm in an attempt to build a model of how the brain normally processes written language. Because our main objective is to build a model, we do not intend this chapter to be an exhaustive review, and we refer the reader interested in more detail to the excellent chapters written about alexia by Benson and Geschwind (1969), Hécaen and Kremin (1976), Albert (1979), and Kremin (this volume). Like many models of brain processing, ours should not be accepted as an accurate depiction of brain processing but rather as a metaphor which we hope will have heuristic value.

THE APHASIAS

Disorders of written language (alexia plus agraphia) often coexist with disorders of spoken language (aphasia). Because written language and spoken language often require the same or similar brain processes and because the processes underlying verbal/language processing form the framework of our reading model, we will first dicuss the disorders of spoken language—the aphasias. A detailed review of the aphasias would be beyond the scope of this chapter, but we shall give a brief review to aid in developing our model of language processing.

The Perisylvian Aphasias

Broca's aphasics produce nonfluent agrammatic speech comprising mainly major lexical items such as nouns and verbs. Repetition and naming are also impaired. In contrast, comprehension of spoken language would appear relatively spared, except that these patients have difficulty comprehending sentences when the meaning depends on syntactic relationships (e.g., word order, inflection) (Heilman & Scholes, 1976). Although there has been some controversy as to precisely the locus of the lesion that induces Broca's aphasia (Mohr, 1978), most investigators would agree that left anterior suprasylvian lesions are associated with this disorder (Figure 14.1).

Unlike Broca's aphasics, *Wernicke's aphasics* are fluent and have difficulty comprehending major lexical items. They often speak in jargon, and their spontaneous speech contains not only neologisms (nonsense words) but also semantic and phonemic paraphasias (incorrect words or words with the incorrect phonemes). Like Broca's aphasics, Wernicke's aphasics also have difficulty repeating and naming.

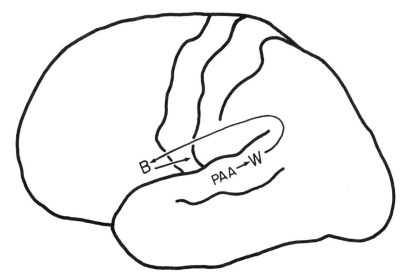

Figure 14.1. *Wernicke's reflex arc. PAA, primary auditory area; W, Wernicke's area; B, Broca's area.*

The lesion that induces Wernicke's aphasia is in the posterior portion of the superior temporal gyrus (Figure 14.1). Wernicke (1874) thought that this anatomic area, which is adjacent to the auditory area, contained memories or engrams of sound and word images. Destruction of this area, which hereafter shall be referred to as Wernicke's area or the area of auditory word images, would induce defects of comprehension and repetition because without these engrams the patient could not analyze the incoming auditory message. In addition, Wernicke proposed a hierarchical model of language processing. He thought that Broca's area may contain the engrams required to program the muscle sequences used to produce phonemes (speech sounds). To encode language correctly, Broca's area needs to be directed by Wernicke's area of auditory word images. Without this direction, the intact Broca's area may encode the wrong phonemes or phonemic sequences (e.g., phonemic paraphasia).

With this model of hierarchical processing as a basis, Wernicke (1874) also suggested that a lesion that spared but disconnected this posterior portion of the superior temporal gyrus (Wernicke's area of auditory word images) from Broca's area could induce an aphasia in which a patient would comprehend language (because the area of auditory images would be intact) but, because of the disconnection of this area from Broca's area, would make paraphasic errors. Most strikingly, the patient would have great difficulty with repetition. This constellation of symptoms has been termed *conduction aphasia*, which may be induced by insular lesions and anterior inferior parietal lesions that destroy the supramarginal gyrus and arcuate fasciculus (Damasio & Damasio, 1980). The site of this lesion is well suited to disconnect Wernicke's and Broca's areas (Figure 14.1). Conduction aphasics also have difficulty understanding sentences whose meaning depends on syntax (Heilman & Scholes, 1976).

A lesion in the temporal lobe anterior to Wernicke's area may destroy the primary auditory area on the left (Heschl's gyrus) and the projections that reach the left temporal lobe from the primary auditory area on the right. This lesion would spare Wernicke's area but would prevent any auditory stimuli from being processed by Wernicke's area. Patients with such a lesion therefore cannot comprehend spoken language but can understand written language. They cannot repeat but have normal spontaneous speech and naming. This disorder has been termed *pure word deafness*. These patients are often able to comprehend environmental sounds and the emotional tones of voice. This probably occurs because the right primary auditory area and its connections to the right hemisphere are intact and are able to process this information. Although pure word deafness is not an aphasia, the importance of Heschl's gyrus to language processing models requires that this disorder be included in any discussion of aphasic syndromes.

Thus far we have described four regions in which lesions may induce a language processing disorder: Broca's area (inferior frontal lobe), Wernicke's area (posterior portion of the superior temporal gyrus), the insula–supramarginal gyrus–arcuate fasciculus region, and the primary auditory areas with their projections to Wernicke's area. These critical areas and their connections form an arc (termed *Wernicke's reflex arc*) around the sylvian fissure (Figure 14.1). As discussed, lesions in various portions of this arc induce different symptoms; however, a defect in repetition is the one symptom common to lesions in any part of the arc.

Aphasias Induced by Lesions outside the Perisylvian Area

Lichtheim (1885) described a patient who, like a Wernicke's aphasic, could not comprehend speech, was fluent, made paraphasic errors, and had difficulty with naming. However, unlike a Wernicke's aphasic, this patient was able to repeat. This type of aphasia has been termed *transcortical sensory aphasia* (Goldstein, 1948) and is usually caused by lesions in the parietal lobe. Because patients with transcortical sensory aphasia are unable to comprehend major lexical items, it is difficult to test their ability to comprehend spoken sentences in which the meaning depends on syntactic relationships. If, however, these patients are asked to repeat a spoken agrammatic sentence, they will often spontaneously correct it. For example, when asked to repeat *The boy fell down a flight of **stair,*** they will correct it to *The boy fell down a flight of* ***stairs.***

Lichtheim recognized that the schema proposed by Wernicke did not fully explain how one developed transcortical sensory aphasia nor did it account for how speech is volitionally initiated. To account for transcortical sensory aphasia, he elaborated on Wernicke's schema by adding an area of concepts (semantic field), as shown in Figure 14.2. Lichtheim suggested that transcortical sensory aphasia was induced by a disconnection of Wernicke's area from the semantic field. According to Lichtheim's schema, although patients with transcortical aphasia may be capable of performing an auditory analysis at the primary auditory area and a phonemic analysis in Wernicke's area, they are incapable of performing semantic analysis. Because their Wernicke's reflex arc is

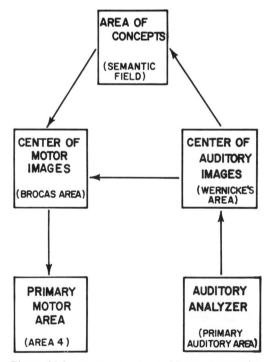

Figure 14.2. Lichtheim's schema of language processing.

intact, patients with transcortical sensory aphasia can perform an auditory and phonemic analysis. They also can perform phonetic encoding and are thus able to repeat and echo.

The anatomic localization of the semantic field, if it can be localized, is not known. Luria (1966) believed the semantic field was in the parietal lobes, but it is not clear whether a parietal lesion induces transcortical sensory aphasia because it destroys the area of concepts or whether it disconnects the area of concepts from the perisylvian speech regions.

Although Lichtheim's schema can explain the mechanism underlying transcortical sensory aphasia, as well as the perisylvian aphasias, his schema cannot explain several other known phenomena. For example, there are patients who have difficulty naming objects in any modality (e.g., visual or somatesthetic) but can tell what they are used for or can show how they are used. When they speak spontaneously these patients may also have word-finding difficulty and circumlocute. They can comprehend spoken language, are fluent, and can repeat well. This condition has been termed *anomic aphasia* (the terms *amnestic aphasia* and *nominal aphasia* are also used). Lichtheim's schema cannot explain this aphasic disturbance. In addition, according to Lichtheim's schema, spontaneous speech is initiated in the area of concepts which projects directly to Broca's area. Since spontaneous speech bypasses Wernicke's area in Lichtheim's schema, lesions of Wernicke's area should not induce abnormalities of spontaneous speech. As mentioned previously, however, Wernicke's aphasia is associated with abnormal spontaneous speech.

Kussmaul (1877) proposed a schema (Figure 14.3) that also incorporated Broca's and Wernicke's work and was similar to that of Lichtheim, except for an important difference. There is no direct projection from the area of concepts (semantic area, ideational center) to the motor centers to coordinate sound movements into spoken words (Broca's area). Rather the area of concepts first projects back to the area of auditory word images (Wernicke's area). According to Kussmaul's schema, a disconnection between the area of concepts and the area of auditory word images (Wernicke's area) would induce an anomia, and since Wernicke's area is not bypassed in spontaneous speech, lesions of this area could induce abnormal spontaneous speech.

Also according to Kussmaul's schema (Figure 14.3) and our modification of it (Figure 14.4), a lesion can interrupt information processed by the area of auditory word images from gaining access to the area of concepts but allow information processed by the semantic area to gain access back to the area of auditory word images. This would induce a syndrome in which the patient would comprehend poorly but be able

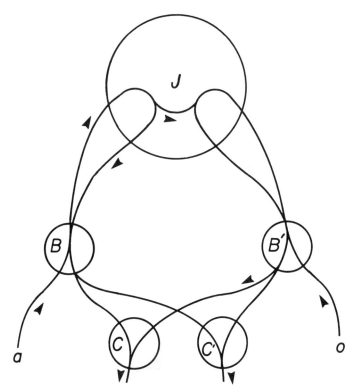

Figure 14.3. Kussmaul's schema of language processing. J, ideogenic center; B, acusticosensory center; B', opticosensory center; C, spoken word coordination center; C', written word coordination center; o, optic nerve; a, acoustic nerve.

to repeat, name, and speak spontaneously. We have examined a patient with this disorder and have termed it *transcortical aphasia with intact spontaneous speech and naming* (Heilman, Rothi, McFarling, & Rottman, 1981).

Transcortical motor aphasia is a disorder in which speech is nonfluent and language comprehension is spared. Unlike Broca's aphasics, these patients are not agrammatic and their repetition is good. This deficit is thought by some to reflect a cortical activation or intentional disorder rather than a true language disorder and is not accounted for in our language model. This syndrome is produced by lesions of the left dorsolateral frontal lobe, superior to Broca's area, left medial frontal lobe (cingulate gyrus and supplementary motor areas), or left thalamus.

Transcortical motor and transcortical sensory aphasia may sometimes coexist. This syndrome has been termed *mixed transcortical aphasia* (isolated speech area) because the lesion that induces it does not damage

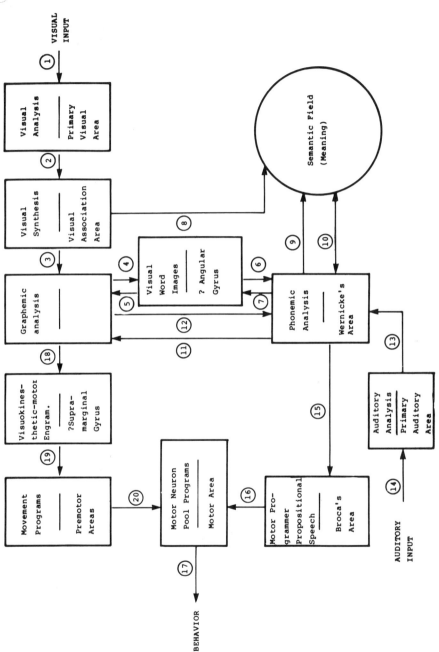

Figure 14.4. Heilman and Rothi's schema of the processing of written and spoken language.

the perisylvian arc but disconnects it both anteriorly and posteriorly from the remainder of the cortex. Left thalamic lesions may also induce this syndrome.

Reading disorders may coexist with disorders of spoken language or may occur independently (aphasic alexia versus nonaphasic alexia). Reading disorders not associated with spoken language disorders may or may not be associated with writing disorders (alexia with agraphia versus alexia without agraphia). The language model developed thus far provides a framework upon which we can build a model of reading. We shall first discuss the significance of the presence or absence of writing disorders in conjunction with alexia, and then review the reading disturbances associated with various forms of aphasia.

NONAPHASIC ALEXIAS

Alexia without Agraphia (Pure Alexia, Agnosic Alexia,
Subcortical Alexia, Pure Word Blindness, Primary Alexia)

In 1872, Broadbent described an intelligent and energetic man who after suffering from cerebral symptoms lost entirely the power to read printing and writing. The patient saw the text but did not understand it, although he could still write easily and correctly both from dictation and spontaneously. His conversation was good and his vocabulary large. Kussmaul (1887) described another patient with alexia without agraphia, who was noted to be hemianopic. Subsequently Dejerine (1892) and many others have described cases of alexia without agraphia.

Patients with alexia without agraphia are usually able to comprehend spelled words and can spell them aloud. With the use of anagram tiles or graphesthesia, these patients can recognize letters and single words. Although they can write spontaneously and to dictation, they often have difficulty when asked to transcode a message from print to script and vice versa. When they are not required to transcode, they copy well. If distracted, they make errors because they cannot identify "where they were." They poorly orient their writing on the paper and write as if they were blind. That they can copy, however, shows that they do not have a severe perceptual disorder that would induce the alexia.

Some patients with alexia without agraphia, though they are not anomic, may be unable to name colors. In contrast, they may be able to match colors and respond appropriately to questions about colors (e.g., *What color is the sky?*) (Geschwind & Fusillo, 1966). Agnosia for objects and amnesia are also occasionally reported.

Dejerine's (1892) famous patient had a second cerebral infarction after which he died. On postmortem examination, the brain showed two infarctions. The older one, which presumably accounted for the alexia without agraphia, affected the medial and inferior aspects of the left occipital lobe and the splenium of the corpus callosum. Subsequently many authors have confirmed that lesions of left fusiform and lingual gyri together with lesions of the splenium of the corpus callosum are usually associated with this syndrome (Geschwind & Fusillo, 1966; Cumming, 1970). However, Greenblatt (1976) has demonstrated that alexia without either agraphia or hemianopia may be induced by a lesion undercutting the angular gyrus. This lesion presumably isolates the angular gyrus from input from the visual analyzers.

Kussmaul (1877) postulated that there was an area of optical text images similar to Wernicke's area of auditory word images. He thought that lesions that induced "text blindness" with a retention of the ability to write spontaneously and from dictation involved a destruction of the tract between the area of optical text images and the area of concepts (Figure 14.4). Kussmaul's (1877) schema preceded Dejerine's (1892) observations and failed to explain several phenomena. For example, according to Kussmaul's schema the area of optical text images was intact in alexia without agraphia and was connected both to optical input and to the area of speech output. If this were true, these patients should not have been able to comprehend written material read silently but should have been able to read aloud and comprehend what they read aloud. Unfortunately, patients with alexia without agraphia are unable to read aloud.

Redlich (1895) and Brissaud (1900) proposed that in these patients the left hemisphere infarction that induced hemianopsia also prevented graphic stimuli from reaching the left hemisphere language areas. The lesion described by Dejerine and subsequent authors (e.g., Greenblatt, 1973), would be well suited to disconnect the language area from visual input. That is, a lesion in Pathway 3 in our revision of Kussmaul's schema (Figure 14.4) would disconnect visual information not only from the area of optical text images but also from the remainder of the language areas. Patients with a lesion in this area would be incapable of reading either silently or aloud. However, because the area of concepts has normal connections to those areas important for writing, these patients should be able to write spontaneously.

Patients with alexia without agraphia are not only able to write spontaneously and to dictation but also can spell and comprehend spelled words (Albert, 1979). Although Kussmaul thought that the transcoding of sound images into text images occurred in the area of concepts, normal subjects can transcode phonemes to graphemes and vice versa without accessing meaning. Therefore, in our modification of Kussmaul's model, phonemic–graphemic transcoding does not require prior semantic analysis (see Figure 14.4, Pathways 11 and 12).

Alexia with Agraphia

In 1891 Dejerine described a patient who was suddenly unable to read or write. The patient also had some mild speech disturbances which eventually cleared. The severe alexia with agraphia persisted. On postmortem examination, the lesion was noted to be in the left angular gyrus and extended into the subcortical white matter down to the occipital horn of the lateral ventricle.

Subsequent to Dejerine's description of alexia with agraphia, the syndrome has been described by many authors. The patients may be unable to read sentences and words written in print or script. In addition, unlike patients with alexia without agraphia, these patients cannot spell words aloud, cannot comprehend words spelled to them, and cannot comprehend words written on their hands (somesthetic reading). In regard to the writing disturbance, although these patients are often able to write letters legibly, they may select incorrect letters (paragraphia). Similarly they have difficulty with writing to dictation whether it be sentences, words, or even letters. Alexia with agraphia is often associated with other signs of dominant cortical hemisphere dysfunction, including anomia, right–left confusion, finger agnosia (Benton, 1979), acalculia (Levin, 1979), and constructional apraxia (Benton, 1979).

Because lesions of the dominant angular gyrus are associated with alexia and agraphia as well as an inability to spell aloud or recognize spelled words, it would appear that this area conforms to what Kussmaul termed the area of optical text images. Dejerine (1891) also thought that the syndrome of alexia with agraphia resulted from a lesion of the center for written words (visual word images).

Alexia and Agraphia with the Spared Ability to Spell Aloud and Recognize Spelled Words

Although most patients with alexia and agraphia are incapable of spelling out loud or comprehending spelled words, Dejerine and André-

Thomas (1904) described a patient with alexia and agraphia who could spell out loud and comprehend orally spelled words. The patient also appeared to have had two insults separated by 2 years. Dejerine and André-Thomas argued that the area of visual word images had been spared but isolated from both visual input and graphic output. They suggested that the patient had originally had an infarction that resulted in alexia without agraphia, and that 2 years later a second infarction caused a dysfunction of the motoric execution of written language. That is, the patient had had a right hemiplegia and had to use his left hand to write. The authors thought that the second lesion disconnected the left hand from the left (language dominant) hemisphere. Their analysis was, in part, borne out by autopsy, which showed sparing of the left angular gyrus and an old lesion of the left occipital lobe and projection fibers to the angular gyrus. The newer, second lesion, hypothesized to be in the right hemisphere and disrupting the path of fibers connecting the left angular gyrus to the right motor areas, was not confirmed because the patient had died of a massive hemorrhage of the right hemisphere.

More recently, several cases of alexia and agraphia with spared oral spelling ability have been reported (Albert, Yamadori, Gardner, & Howes, 1973; Mohr, 1976). Kinsbourne and Rosenfield (1974), for example, described a patient with left posterior parietotemporal ischemia resulting in mild aphasia and symptoms associated with the Gerstmann syndrome. This patient also displayed reading and writing difficulties in conjunction with relatively preserved oral spelling. Because writing was impaired when the patient used his right hand, Kinsbourne and Rosenfield postulated that the defect proposed by Dejerine and André-Thomas, instead of being interhemispheric, could be intrahemispheric. Kinsbourne and Rosenfield suggested that there is a "supraordinate letter selection system," which for purposes of oral spelling can send appropriate motor programs to the area responsible for programming speech musculature, and that in their patient the process was intact. In contrast, they proposed that for writing, information leaving this supraordinate letter selection system must first undergo transformation from letter sounds or names into a visual representation and it was this mechanism that was impaired.

We (Rothi & Heilman, 1981) have also described a patient who had alexia with agraphia but with intact spelling and comprehension of spelled words. Although normal subjects can transcode between the verbal–phonemic and orthographic codes, these codes are independent and in English are not directly related (Gibson & Levin, 1975, pp. 178–180). If our patient had been spelling aloud because he was directly transforming letter sounds to letter names (Figure 14.4, Pathway 11), he should not have been able to spell irregular words that do not have a direct phoneme-to-grapheme representation but require special conversion rules (e.g., *knife*). Our patient could comprehend and correctly spell such words aloud, which suggests that his orthographic code (visual word images) was intact and that the verbal code had access to and from the orthographic code (Figure 14.4, Pathways 6 and 7).

To explain alexia with agraphia with intact oral spelling ability and ability to comprehend spelled words, we proposed that in addition to the area of visual word images, which contains the orthographic code, there is a graphemic area. Unlike the area of word images, which contains engrams of letter clusters or words, the graphemic area is responsible both for distinguishing the individual features of a grapheme and for grapheme production. This area, however, does not contain the visual kinesthetic motor engrams that program how the hand is going to be moved in space. A destruction or a disconnection of the graphemic area from the area of visual word images may be responsible for this form of alexia with agraphia in which spelling and comprehension of spelled words are intact (Figure 14.4, Pathways 4 and 5).

There is an alternative mechanism that could explain how one lesion induced alexia and agraphia in our patient. Greenblatt's (1973) patient with pure alexia had a subcortical lesion that disconnected visual input. In our patient the lesion may have been either larger or more anterior than the one in Greenblatt's patient and could have interrupted not only visual input to the language areas but also output from language areas that are important in programming the movement used in writing letters.

APHASIC ALEXIAS

Although a mild anomic aphasia can be associated with the syndrome of alexia with agraphia, the speech disturbance is mild and qualitatively different from the reading disturbance. In contrast, in aphasic alexia the reading disorder usually mirrors the speech disorder. In this section we shall describe the reading disorders sometimes associated with language disorders and discuss their underlying mechanisms.

Wernicke's and Global Aphasia

Wernicke suggested that the acquisition of visual language is by reference to the initial auditory acquisition. Although Lichtheim elab-

orated on Wernicke's schema (see Figure 14.2), he, too, proposed that
written language had to be analyzed by the area of auditory word
images (Wernicke's area) before it could undergo semantic analysis.
Unfortunately, neither of these authors postulated the level at which
this visual-to-auditory transcoding took place. That is, was there a
grapheme-to-phoneme (Figure 14.4, Pathway 12) transcoding, or were
visual *word* images transcoded into auditory *word* engrams (Figure 14.4,
Pathway 6)? Luria (1966) proposed that reading starts with visual perception and analysis of a grapheme and that these graphemes are
recoded into the corresponding phonemic structure. In contrast with
Wernicke, Lichtheim, and Luria, Kussmaul believed that after visual
input is processed by the area of visual word images, it directly (without
transcoding) enters the semantic field (see Figure 14.3).

The observation that most patients with Wernicke's aphasia are also
alexic provides support for the schemas of Wernicke, Lichtheim, and
Luria. A lesion, however, that destroys Wernicke's area (posterior portion of the superior temporal gyrus) may also destroy the area of visual
word images or damage the semantic field. Hier and Mohr (1977) described a patient with Wernicke's aphasia whose reading comprehension was modestly superior to auditory comprehension. They postulated a reading mechanism similar to that proposed by Kussmaul and
suggested that most Wernicke's aphasics cannot read because the lesion
inducing Wernicke's aphasia routinely extends outside the superior
temporal plane. Nielson (1939), however, described 16 patients who
showed left temporal lobe lesions that did not involve the angular gyrus
(area of visual word images). All these patients were not only aphasic
but also alexic. Nielson's observations would appear to refute Kussmaul's notion that the area of visual word images has direct access to
the semantic field.

Transcoding may take place at both levels—grapheme to phoneme
and visual *word* images to auditory *word* engrams (see Figure 14.4).
Therefore, a temporal lobe lesion might tend to impair the former type
of transcoding, whereas parietal lobe lesions would tend to impair the
latter. Hécaen and Albert (1978) described two types of Wernicke's
aphasia: In one, reading ability was worse than the ability to comprehend spoken language; in the other, the opposite was the case. When
word deafness overshadows reading disturbance, there is greater abnormality in the first temporal gyrus, involving fibers approaching the
primary auditory cortex; when word blindness is greater, the abnormality is probably more posterior and involves the junction of the
angular gyrus and the dominant temporal lobe (Hécaen & Albert, 1978).
These observations would tend to support a dual transcoding process.

Although it remains possible that there are Wernicke's aphasics who cannot comprehend speech because they cannot perform a phonemic analysis but can read because they can perform transcoding of visual word images to auditory word engrams, we described two aphasics who could read better than they could comprehend speech and had lesions that destroyed not only Wernicke's area but also the angular gyrus (Heilman, Rothi, Campanella, & Wolfson, 1979). Therefore, although the aforementioned mechanisms may explain the cases reported by Hier and Mohr (1977) and by Hécaen and Albert (1978), these mechanisms cannot explain the disorder in our two patients, whose lesions were outside the temporal lobe and appeared to involve the inferior parietal lobule, including the angular gyrus.

One patient from our study, in spite of having a severe global aphasia from a large perisylvian lesion was able not only to read but also to learn to communicate using Amerind. (Amerind is a pantomime-based system of gestural communication, in which hand posture and motions represent iconic images of major lexical items [ideograms]; for example, the gesture for "spouse" is to point to the ring finger on the left hand [see Skelly, Schinsky, Donaldson, & Smith, 1972].) Subsequently this patient had a right temporoparietal infarction and lost his ability to read and to use Amerind. We postulated that although this patient's left hemisphere lesion may have impaired his ability to perform phonemic decoding (which induced his speech comprehension disturbance), he could read because he was not relying on a visual–verbal (grapheme to phoneme or visual word image to auditory word image) transcoding process to gain access to the semantic field. Instead, he was using an ideographic strategy to gain direct access to the semantic field (Figure 14.4, Pathway 8). We subsequently examined a patient with Wernicke's aphasia who, like our first patient, was unable to comprehend spoken language but was able to read. To learn whether this patient was using an ideographic strategy to gain access to the semantic field, we performed a printed rhyming test. We found that if words looked similar, the patient thought that they rhymed regardless of whether they actually did rhyme (e.g., *beard–heard*). He also had difficulty in perceiving that visually dissimilar words rhymed (e.g., *hate–eight*). These results suggest that he was using an ideographic strategy because he could read words but could not transcode them into the phonemic–verbal mode.

Because left hemisphere lesions appear to impair the visual–verbal transcoding strategy and permit continued use of the ideographic strategy, the right hemisphere, which has been shown to be an efficient visuospatial and gestalt processor, may be mediating this behavior.

Several observations support this postulate: One is that our first patient subsequently had a right temporoparietal lesion and lost the ability both to read and to use Amerind. The second source of support comes from the Japanese literature. Japanese orthography contains two types of nonalphabetic symbols: Kana are phonetic–syllabic symbols, and kanji are nonphonetic logographic symbols representing lexical morphemes. Because of a possible parallel to the distinction in reading English between the visual–verbal transcoding and the ideographic system, the 1977 report by Sasanuma, Itoh, Mori, and Kobayashi is of interest. They presented kana and kanji words tachistoscopically to the left or right visual fields of normal right-handed subjects and found a right field superiority for kana words and a trend for left field superiority for kanji words. Another study in Japan (Sugishita, Iwata, Toyokura, Yoshioka, & Yamada, 1978) revealed that in patients who had undergone section of the splenium, a 2-year retest using tachistoscopic methods showed selective impairment of kana in the left visual half field. This suggested that the right hemisphere was necessary to support that function. Other studies have shown that lesions resulting in aphasia (Sasanuma, 1975), especially nonfluent aphasias (Sasanuma & Fujimura, 1971), can also result in a reading impairment that more selectively involves kana processing than kanji. A similar dissociation has been noted in a patient with alexia with agraphia (Yamadori, 1975).

Finally, in manual communications for the deaf, American Sign Language (ASL) could be considered ideographic. McKeever, Joemann, Florian, and VanDeventer (1976) presented ASL tachistoscopically to subjects with normal hearing who were familiar with the system. These investigators found a left visual field, right hemisphere superiority for processing this information. In summary, the information about the lesions in our patient, the Japanese literature, and the study on ASL all support the hypothesis that the processing of visually received ideograms can be mediated by the right hemisphere.

It therefore appears that perhaps both the hypothesis that visual images are transcoded to auditory–phonemic images before being comprehended and the hypothesis that visual word images can be comprehended without auditory–phonemic transcoding may be correct but for different hemispheres. The left hemisphere relies on a system of grapheme (visual images) to phoneme (auditory images) transcoding, whereas the right hemisphere processes visual word images without phonemic transcoding. We do not know whether the left hemisphere is also capable of ideographic processing, and we also do not know what effects training and individual variations may have on these abilities.

Syntactic Alexia and Broca's Aphasia ("The Third Alexia")

As previously discussed, Broca's aphasia induced by anterior left hemisphere perisylvian lesions is usually associated not only with agrammatic speech but also with a disorder of syntactic comprehension. Benson (1977) and Samuels and Benson (1979) demonstrated that these patients also have a reading disorder in which major lexical items (content words) are comprehended better than relational words. That is, the reading disorder of these patients was similar to their disorder of speech expression and comprehension. Benson termed this the "third alexia" to contrast it with the other two major forms (alexia with agraphia induced by posterior perisylvian lesions and alexia without agraphia induced by occipital and splenium lesions).

Conduction Aphasia

Patients with conduction aphasia may have lesions in the inferior parietal lobe, and often the angular gyrus is destroyed. It is therefore not surprising that many of these patients have a severe alexia. In the clinic, however, one occasionally sees conduction aphasics who are able to read. We recently tested the ability of two patients with conduction aphasia to comprehend graphically presented sentences when the meaning depended on syntax. Although both patients were able to comprehend the major lexical items, they were unable to comprehend sentences when the meaning depended on syntax.

We term this form of alexia, which occurs in patients with Broca's and conduction aphasia, *syntactic alexia*. We are uncertain why the lesions that induce Broca's or conduction aphasia also induce syntactic alexia. Possibly the posterior conduction aphasia that is associated with destruction of the angular gyrus, like that in Wernicke's and global aphasia, cannot transcode from the visual–grapheme code to the phonemic–verbal code and therefore must rely on the right hemisphere ideographic system, which is asyntactic.

We are also not certain why the right hemisphere is asyntactic, but syntax does provide the relational significance between major lexical items. The right hemisphere has been described as a gestalt processor (Levy-Agresti & Sperry, 1968), yet given that the syntactic component of language provides relational significance, the right hemisphere would seem to be poorly suited for this type of function. In Broca's aphasia and in some cases of anterior conduction aphasia, the area important for transcoding should be intact. Therefore, these patients would not need to depend solely on the right hemisphere asyntactic ideographic system. The manner in which the brain mediates syntax remains to be elucidated.

Transcortical Aphasias—Reading Aloud without Comprehension

It has been noted that patients with a mixed or sensory transcortical aphasia (Heilman, Tucker, & Valenstein, 1976; Heilman *et al.*, 1981) can read aloud (including irregular words such as *comb*) almost flawlessly but are unable to comprehend what they have read. These patients are able to read nonsense words and words that are misspelled but phonetically correct. It would appear that these patients are capable both of performing grapheme-to-phoneme transcoding and of gaining access to the left hemisphere perisylvian region (see Figure 14.4), important in allowing them to verbalize the written message. These patients, however, cannot gain access to the semantic field.

As previously discussed, patients with either anterior (i.e., Broca's aphasia) or posterior (i.e., conduction aphasia) perisylvian lesions appear to have syntactic incompetence (e.g., cannot comprehend spoken and written sentences when the meaning depends on syntactic relationships). It has been noted that patients with mixed and sensory transcortical aphasia, in spite of poor comprehension, appear to have syntactic competence as measured by a task of spoken repetition. We presented asyntactic written sentences (e.g., *The boy are going*) to a patient with a form of transcortical sensory aphasia, and he was usually able to recognize or correct the error (Heilman *et al.*, 1981). In contrast, he had difficulty recognizing or correcting semantic errors (e.g., *The airplane swam to Bermuda*). Based on these and other observations discussed in the section on aphasia, it would appear that there is a dichotomy between perisylvian- and nonperisylvian-induced language disorders. Whereas perisylvian-induced language disorders (i.e., Broca's, conduction, and Wernicke's aphasia) are associated with phonemic–phonetic and syntactic disorders, nonperisylvian-induced language disorders (i.e., transcortical sensory, transcortical motor, and mixed transcortical aphasias) are not associated with phonemic–phonetic or syntactic disorders. Instead, they are associated with activational–intentional disorders (e.g., akinesia of speech) and semantic disorders.

To summarize this section on the alexias, we have proposed a model of reading based on the clinical syndromes. There appear to be two processes for attaching meaning to graphically presented material. The first process depends upon left hemisphere language processes that transform the visual information into phonemic information before accessing meaning. In the second process, meaning is directly applied to the visual analysis. The two processes are apparently supported by different cerebral mechanisms.

ALTERNATIVE STRATEGIES

Authors such as Marshall and Newcombe (1973) view the reading of alexic patients as output of the defective processing system. We have already discussed the idea that multiple strategies are available to the skilled reader. We believe that the errors of the alexic patient may also in fact reflect the compensatory strategies they have available to them to overcome their deficits. The effectiveness of these strategies is certainly lesion dependent, but the choice of strategies may depend on premorbid factors. Therefore, different error types may occur in patients with similar lesions and similar error types may occur in patients with different lesions. It is thus important for clinical and research purposes to analyze the types of errors made by the patient so that we may establish the integrity of alternative or compensatory strategies accounting for residual reading skills.

In discussions of alexia, whether with or without agraphia or aphasia, most authors seem to agree on three common types of reading errors. *Semantic errors* involve the production of words within the same semantic category as the target word. These can include responses that are overly general ("vehicle"–*truck;* "fruit"–*oranges;* "furniture"–*chair*), or responses that are constituents of a category in common with the target word ("car"–*truck;* "apple"–*orange;* "table"–*chair*).

Phonemic errors are responses that sound like the target word. These errors take two forms: errors in grapheme-to-phoneme conversion or errors in application of the rules of English orthography. The patient who has difficulty with grapheme-to-phoneme conversion will be unable to "sound out" words and will often simply refuse to attempt to read the word. Such a patient will also be unable to identify graphemes when the corresponding phonemes are spoken by the examiner or will be unable to produce the phonemes represented by particular graphemes. If the difficulty is with the rule system, the patient will be able to sound out completely predictable words (e.g., *bat, top, hand*) but not words that require application of the rules of English orthography. For example, *bait* might be read as "bat," *tape* as "tap," or the stress on *begin* might be shifted from the second to the first syllable (Marshall & Newcombe, 1973).

Haselrud and Clark (1957) have shown that normal rapid reading involves the analysis of the first and last graphemes of a word. As the length of the word approaches the span of apprehension, the last letter is less often analyzed with more medial graphemes being noted. In some patients we see errors that might be interpreted as resulting from deficits of such a visual analysis (e.g., "telephone" for *television*, "chain" for *chair*). *Visual errors*, however, do not necessarily involve only the last elements of the target word. There may be difficulties with earlier portions of the word as well (e.g., "shirt" for *skirt*, "book" for *hook*, "age" for *cage*).

These three types of errors can each be found to some degree in each alexic patient, but some forms predominate more than others in the various classifications. For example, there are patients who can recognize familiar (high frequency) words whether they are phonologically predictable, require conversion rules, or are irregular. They often make visual as well as semantic errors in word reading. Few, if any, phonemic errors of any type are noted. These patients cannot read nonsense words or function words like prepositions and articles. They have less difficulty reading concrete words or words in context than reading abstract words or words in isolation. They cannot name letters but can tell if letters are consonants or vowels. This has been termed *deep dyslexia* (Marshall & Newcombe, 1973), *phonemic dyslexia* (Shallice & Warrington, 1975), or *literal alexia* (Hécaen & Kremin, 1976).

As mentioned early in this chapter, Hughlings Jackson proposed that the behavior that occurs after brain ablation is caused not only by the loss of function induced by the lesion but also by how other portions of the brain respond to this loss. We have already discussed the idea that multiple strategies are available to the reader and that some aphasics with global or Wernicke's aphasia can have direct access to the semantic field. Also possible is that nonaphasic alexic patients who have the aforementioned syndrome of literal alexia have direct access to the semantic field (Figure 14.4, Pathway 8). These literal alexics, when asked to read aloud, can pronounce the word only after its meaning is understood (Saffran, Schwartz, & Marin, 1979). That is, according to our schema, when these patients read aloud, they go from the visual association area to the semantic field and then to Wernicke's area. It is therefore not surprising that, like Wernicke's and global aphasics, the literal alexics when reading aloud often confuse semantically similar but phonologically different words. They rely solely on visual analysis before semantic access, allowing for an increasing incidence of visual error relating to decreased visual skills (e.g., span of apprehension) and poor visual analyses (e.g., the ability to detect the difference between *p* and *d*). Caplan and Hedley-Whyte (1974) and Albert, Yamadori, Gardner, and Howes (1973) have confirmed in these patients a surprising integrity of semantic analysis of words they claim they cannot read. Because, as we proposed earlier, these patients are using their right hemisphere, which is asyntactic, it is not surprising that they have difficulty reading function words. Again, our emphasis here is that the compensatory mechanism of right hemisphere processing results, in part, in the reading errors.

In *verbal alexia* (Hécaen & Kremin, 1976) or *spelling dyslexia* (Warrington & Shallice, 1980) the patient is able to read words by naming the letters aloud. We believe this can also be accounted for by the use of compensatory strategies. Although some patients may be able to treat individual letters as ideograms, premorbid factors may limit them from reading entire words as ideograms. When such patients have alexia without agraphia, which spares Wernicke's area (the area of auditory word engrams) and the angular gyrus (the area of visual word engrams), they may be able to gain access to these areas by treating single letters as ideograms and spelling words aloud or to themselves. By a transcoding process that converts visual to verbal stimuli, they thereby gain access to both the phonological processors and the semantic field. This strategy is only successful when reading single words or short phrases, presumably because of the memory load required for this type of processing.

Some alexic patients appear to read words aloud incorrectly; however, unlike those with deep dyslexia, these patients make paralexical errors that may not be in the same semantic field as the target word but may be phonologically similar to the target word. Typically, the most difficult words for these patients to read are the irregular words for which there is no direct grapheme-to-phoneme correspondence. Marshall and Newcombe (1973) termed these patients *surface dyslexics* (as opposed to deep dyslexics). We suspect that these patients have alexia with agraphia, with destruction of the area that in our model is termed the *area of visual word images.* They therefore have lost the rules of English orthography. They are performing a direct letter-by-letter grapheme-to-phoneme transcoding, in order to read aloud and to gain access via the phonemic area to the semantic field (Figure 14.4, Pathway 12).

In summary, patients may use a direct visual-to-semantic (ideographic) strategy if the following areas of our model have been destroyed: the phonemic area (area of auditory word engrams, Wernicke's area), the graphemic area, or the area of visual word images. Patients with destruction of the area of visual word images may use direct grapheme-to-phoneme transcoding. Patients with destruction of the graphemic area or those who have a disconnection between the graphemic and visual areas may use a direct access route or may spell words aloud.

REFERENCES

Albert, M. L. (1979) Alexia. In Heilman, K. M., & Valenstein, E. *Clinical neuropsychology.* New York: Oxford University Press.

Albert, M. L., Yamadori, A., Gardner, H., & Howes, D. (1973) Comprehension in alexia. *Brain, 96,* 317–328.

Benson, D. F. (1977) The third alexia. *Archives of Neurology, 34,* 327–331.

Benson, D. F., & Geschwind, N. (1969). The alexias. In P. J. Vinken & G. W. Bruyn (Eds.), *Handbook of clinical neurology* (Vol. 4). New York: American Elsevier.

Benton, A. (1979) Body schema disturbances: Finger agnosia and right–left disorientation. In K. M. Heilman & E. Valenstein (Eds.), *Clinical neuropsychology.* New York: Oxford University Press.

Brissaud, E. (1900) Cécité verbale sans aphasie ni agraphie. *Revue Neurologique, 8,* 757.

Broadbent, W. (1872) Cerebral mechanisms of speech and thought. *Medical and Chirurgical Transactions (London), 55,* 148–194.

Broca, P. P. (1861) Remarques sur le siège de la faculté du langage articulé suivies d'une observation d'aphémie. *Bulletins de la Société Anatomique de Paris, 36,* 330–357.

Caplan, L. R., & Hedley-Whyte, T. (1974) Cuing and memory disturbance in alexia without agraphia. *Brain, 97,* 251–262.

Cumming, W. J. (1970) Anatomical findings in a case of alexia without agraphia. *Journal of Anatomy, 106,* 170.

Damasio, H., & Damasio, A. R. (1980) The anatomical basis of conduction aphasia. *Brain, 103,* 337–250.

Dejerine, J. (1891) Sur un cas de cécité verbale avec agraphie, suivi d'autopsie. *Comptes Rendus Hebdomadaires des Seances et Memoires de la Société de Biologie, 3,* 197–201.

Dejerine, J. (1892) Contribution à l'étude anatomo-pathologique et clinique des différentes variétés de cécité verbale. *Comptes Rendus Hebdomadaires des Seances at Memoires de la Société de Biologie, 4,* 61–90.

Dejerine, J., & André-Thomas, J. (1904) Un cas de cécité verbale avec agraphie suivi d'autopsie. *Revue Neurologique, 12,* 655–664.

Geschwind, N., & Fusillo, M. (1966) Color-naming defects in association with alexia. *Archives of Neurology, 15,* 137–146.

Gibson, E. J., & Levin, H. (Eds.) (1975) *The psychology of reading.* Cambridge, Mass.: MIT Press.

Goldstein, K. (1948) *Language and language disturbances.* New York: Grune & Stratton.

Greenblatt, S. H. (1973) Alexia without agraphia or hemianopsia. *Brain, 96,* 307–316.

Greenblatt, S. H. (1976) Subangular alexia without agraphia or hemianopsia. *Brain and Language, 3,* 229–245.

Haselrud, G. M., & Clark, R. E. (1957) On the redintegrative perception of words. *American Journal of Psychology, 70,* 97–101.

Hécaen, H., & Albert, M. (1978) *Human neuropsychology.* New York: Wiley.

Hécaen, H., & Kremin H. (1976) Neurolinguistic research on reading disorders. In H. Whitaker & H. A. Whitaker (Eds.), *Studies in neurolinguistics* (Vol. 2). New York: Academic Press.

Heilman, K. M., Rothi, L., Campanella, D., & Wolfson, S. (1979) Wernicke's and global aphasia without alexia. *Archives of Neurology, 36,* 129–133.

Heilman, K. M., Rothi, L., McFarling, D., & Rottman, A. (1981) Transcortical sensory aphasia with relatively spared spontaneous speech and naming. *Archives of Neurology, 38,* 236–239.

Heilman, K. M., & Scholes, R. J. (1976) The nature of comprehension errors in Broca's, conduction, and Wernicke's aphasics. *Cortex, 12,* 258–265.

Heilman, K. M., Tucker, D. M., & Valenstein, E. (1976) A case of mixed transcortical aphasia with intact naming. *Brain, 99,* 415–426.

Hier, D. B., & Mohr, J. P. (1977) Incongruous oral and written naming: Evidence for a subdivision of the syndrome of Wernicke's aphasia. *Brain and Language, 4,* 115–126.

Kinsbourne, M., & Rosenfield, D. B. (1974) Agraphia selective for written spelling. *Brain and Language, 1,* 215–255.

Kussmaul, A. (1877) *Die Störungen der Sprache.* Leipzig: Vogel-Verlag.

Levin, H. S. (1979) The acalculias. In K. M. Heilman & E. Valenstein (Eds.), *Clinical neuropsychology.* New York: Oxford University Press.

Levy-Agresti, J., & Sperry, R. W. (1968) Differential perceptual capacities in major and minor hemispheres. *Proceedings of the National Academy of Sciences, 61,* 1151.

Lichtheim, L. (1885) On aphasia. *Brain, 7,* 433–484.

Luria, A. R. (1966) *Higher cortical functions in man.* New York: Basic Books.

Marshall, J. C., & Newcombe, F. (1973) Patterns of paralexia: A psycholinguistic approach. *Journal of Psycholinguistic Research, 2,* 175–199.

Marshall, J. C., & Newcombe, F. (1977) Variability and constraint in acquired dyslexia (Spelling dyslexia). In H. Whitaker & H. A. Whitaker (Eds.), *Studies in neurolinguistics* (Vol. 3). New York: Academic Press.

McKeever, W. F., Joemann, H. W., Florian, V. A., & VanDeventer, A. D. (1976) Evidence of minimal cerebral assymetries for the processing of English words and American sign language in the congenitally deaf. *Neuropsychologia, 14,* 413–423.

Mohr, J. P. (1976) An unusual case of dyslexia with dysgraphia. *Brain and Language, 3,* 324–334.

Mohr, J. P. (1978) Broca's aphasia: Pathologic and clinical. *Neurology, 28,* 311–324.

Nielson, J. M. (1939) The unsolved problems in aphasia, II: Alexia resulting from a temporal lesion. *Bulletin of the Los Angeles Neurological Society, 4,* 168–183.

Redlich, E. (1895) Ueber die sogenannte subcorticale Alexie. *Jahrbuecher fuer Psychiatrie und Neurologie, 13,* 1–60.

Rothi, L. J., & Heilman, K. M. (1981) Alexia and agraphia with spared spelling and letter recognition abilities. *Brain and Language, 12,* 1–13.

Saffran, E. M., Schwartz, M. F., & Marin, O. S. M. (1979) *Neuropsychological evidence for mechanisms of reading, I: Deep dyslexia.* Paper presented at the annual meeting of the International Neuropsychology Society, New York City, 1979.

Samuels, J. A., & Benson, D. F. (1979) Some aspects of language comprehension in anterior aphasia. *Brain and Language, 8,* 275–286.

Sasanuma, S. (1975) Kana and Kanji processing in Japanese aphasics. *Brain and Language, 2,* 369–383.

Sasanuma, S., & Fujimura, O. (1971) Selective impairment of phonetic and non-phonetic transcription of words in Japanese aphasic patients: Kana vs Kanji in visual recognition and writing. *Cortex, 7,* 1–18.

Sasanuma, S., Itoh, M., Mori, K., & Kobayashi, Y. (1977) Tachistoscopic recognition of Kana and Kanji Words. *Neuropsychologia, 15,* 547–553.

Shallice, T., & Warrington, E. K. (1975) Word recognition in a phonemic dyslexic patient. *Quarterly Journal of Experimental Psychology, 27,* 187–199.

Skelly, M., Schinsky, L., Donaldson, R., & Smith, R. W. (1972) *Amerind sign: Gestural communication for the speechless.* Paper presented at the Annual Meeting of the American Speech and Hearing Association, San Francisco, 1972.

Sugishita, M., Iwata, M., Toyokura, Y., Yoshioka, M., & Yamada, R. (1978) Reading of idiograms and phonograms in Japanese patients after partial commissurotomy. *Neuropsychologia, 16,* 417–426.

Taylor, Y. (Ed.) (1932) *Selected writings of John Hughlings Jackson.* London: Hodder and Stoughton.

Warrington, E., & Shallice, T. (1980) Word form dyslexia. *Brain, 103,* 99–112.

Wernicke, E. (1874) *Der aphasiche Symptomencomplex.* Breslau: Cohn and Weigart.

Yamadori, A. (1975) Ideogram reading in alexia. *Brain, 98,* 231–238.

Chapter Fifteen

Alexia: Theory and Research

HELGARD KREMIN

INTRODUCTION

The suggestion that acquired reading disorders are associated with disorders of spoken language is an old one (see Benton & Joynt, 1960, for review). Early authors also claimed that difficulties of reading could occur independently of disorders of oral expression and even independently of disorders of writing. As the literature devoted to the topic of alexia is very extensive, this review can only be concerned with some main approaches of research and theory. Acquired reading disorders have been described as clinical syndromes with reference to cerebral localization; they have been assessed by linguistically oriented approaches focusing on reading behavior in terms of error analysis; and, finally, they have been studied in the framework of information-processing models.

Early authors also recognized the existence of developmental dyslexia (Hinshelwood, 1895, 1900). Ever since developmental reading disorders

341

have been considered in neurological terms (Critchley, 1970; see also Jorm, 1979a, for a review). Although it is dangerous to identify a developing system with a system disturbed by pathology, the analysis and comparison of these two distinct entities should help us to acquire knowledge about the functional components and mechanisms involved in the processing of written material. Both acquired and developmental reading disorders represent good candidates for furnishing data for theoretical approaches to reading as well as testing the psychological reality of the proposed models.

This article deals only with acquired reading disturbances due to brain damage, reviewing the literature with reference to the three approaches of research and theory mentioned earlier. Two varieties of reading impairment, so-called deep dyslexia and surface dyslexia, will also be reviewed rather extensively, as they sometimes are considered to represent features that can also be found in developmental dyslexia (see Holmes, 1973, 1978; Jorm, 1979a, 1979b; Marcel, 1980).

SYNDROMIC AND ANATOMOCLINICAL APPROACH

Alexia with and without Agraphia

Following the publication of Kussmaul's (1884) book, alexia, under the name of *word blindness*, took on a special status. However, it was Dejerine (1891, 1892) who provided the impetus for further study of the syndrome by two case reports which included post mortem findings. Dejerine argued for the clinical reality of two different reading disorders: word blindness with agraphia, produced by a lesion in the center of visual verbal images (the left angular gyrus), and pure word blindness, with both spontaneous writing and writing to dictation intact, produced by a subcortical lesion (white matter of the lingual gyrus) that interrupted the connections between the angular gyrus and the visual cortex.

For Dejerine, alexia in its pure form was a specialized variety of aphasia. Dejerine did not separate alexia with agraphia from Wernicke's aphasia. Marie (1906), however, argued that pure alexia fits best within the general framework of the visual agnosias. His interpretation of pure alexia as a particular subgroup of the agnosias became more generally accepted as new cases were presented. Thus, although most authors agreed with Dejerine's conjectures concerning localization, pure alexia came to be known as agnosic alexia, and alexia with agraphia as aphasic (or "parietal") alexia. Alajouanine, Lhermitte, and Ribaucourt-Ducarne (1960) studied a series of patients in whom reading impairment was the predominant feature. The study established that the two types of alexia may be distinguished on the basis of location of the lesion as well as on the basis of different reading behavior. In *agnosic alexia* (with writing intact) the reading of words and sentences is dramatically impaired but the reading of isolated letters only slightly affected. Words are "deciphered" with great difficulty, letter by letter and syllable by syllable. Alajouanine *et al.* (1960) state that "this dissociation between the overall reading loss and the relative intactness of analytical reading is a characteristic element of agnosic alexia [p. 239]." The anatomically verified cases show an occipital lesion (lingual and fusiform gyri and the splenium of the corpus callosum). In *aphasic alexia* (with agraphia) there is always, at least in the initial stages, an impairment in oral language. The most characteristic feature, however, is that the reading of letters is often more affected than the reading of words. The reading behavior is "global"—patients do not resort to a literal analysis of words. The authors also observed a frequent dissociation between reading aloud and comprehension of the stimulus (this dissociation never being found in agnosic alexia). Aphasic alexia occurred with lesions of the parietotemporal region (territory of the sylvian artery). Alajouanine *et al.* formally distinguish between these two types of alexia, but they explictly maintain the specificity of agnosic alexia among the agnosias and, with certain reservations, the specificity of alexia with agraphia among the aphasias.

Like many other authors, Hécaen (1967) subdivides the alexias on an anatomoclinical basis into three major groups: (*a*) alexia without agraphia (or "pure" or agnosic alexia), (*b*) alexia with agraphia (or parietal alexia), and (*c*) alexia associated with sensory aphasia. In the third group the reading disturbance is part of an aphasic syndrome arising from lesions of the dominant posterior temporal lobe.

Benson, Brown, and Tomlinson (1971) and Benson (1977) distinguish yet another type of reading impairment. This impairment is seen in patients with Broca's aphasia and frontal lobe pathology: They comprehend content words better than syntactic relations and appeared more letter than word blind. In this respect studies by Marin, Saffran, and Schwartz (1976) and Friederici and Schoenle (1980) are worth mentioning. These authors clearly established the parallelism of reading performance and aphasia type: For agrammatic and fluent aphasics they found a double dissociation of content words versus function words in reading aloud. The same dissociation has been found for the comprehension of written material (von Stockert, 1972; von Stockert & Bader, 1976; Kremin & Goldblum, 1975). Thus studies focusing on aphasic reading performances do not seem to provide any special insight into the primary process of reading, but rather accumulate evidence that the (central) lexicon may be divided into two distinct vocabularies according to the grammatical nature of the stimulus.

Characteristics of Alexia without Agraphia

Reading disturbances may either be global in nature, relating to both letters and words, or they may affect them more or less selectively. Since Dejerine, the distinction between literal and verbal alexia has been standard, although usually interpreted only as different degrees of the reading impairment. Péré (1978), reviewing 100 cases in the literature, pointed out that there exists virtually no observation of alexia without agraphia where literal alexia is predominant over verbal alexia. Most frequently verbal alexia is predominant over literal alexia, but 19 out of the 100 cases show a pure verbal alexia. Verbal alexia thus represents the most characteristic symptom of pure alexia without agraphia. Indeed, in Dubois-Charlier's (1970) groups of "literal" alexics, writing was more or less affected in all its different aspects, and in Hécaen and Kremin's (1976) study only the group of patients with "verbal" alexia was unimpaired in spontaneous writing and dictation.

The reading behavior of patients with verbal alexia without agraphia is rather stereotypic. Patients are described as reading by an analytical deciphering strategy, reading letter by letter or syllable by syllable. With longer words this reading by spelling aloud often fails: the reconstruction of the whole word seems to be hindered by an impairment in identifying (naming) the isolated letters and/or by "forgetting" the letters already read. Sometimes this "spelling dyslexia" has been integrated into the more general impairment of simultanagnosia (Kinsbourne & Warrington, 1962) with perceptual analysis being impaired (Levine & Calvanio, 1978). (See also Shallice and Warrington, 1977, who described two patients with a different type of "literal" alexia: They could read isolated letters and words, but naming the constituent letters of the word just read was impaired. This type of dyslexia was due to an "attentional" impairment not specific to letters: Visual presentation of more than one stimulus belonging to the same category "overloaded" the system and impaired performance.)

For some patients the reading difficulty may indeed be correlated with a perceptual problem (see Hécaen & Kremin, 1976, for a review). However such problems do not always occur in verbal alexia. One of Pötzl's patients read all letters without being able to read the word, and all patients with verbal alexia reported by Hécaen and Kremin (1976) were able to match nonsense syllables up to eight letters in a multiple choice paradigm. Warrington and Shallice (1980) demonstrated experimentally that the letter-by-letter reading of their patients could not be attributed to visual or perceptual deficits.

Reading performance of patients with (verbal) alexia without agraphia is characterized by the parallelism between reading aloud and comprehension: What is not read is not understood. (Only two exceptions to this general pattern have been reported: Caplan & Hedley-White, 1974; Stachowiak & Poeck, 1976.) Kremin (1981) furnished normative data for a patient with verbal alexia without agraphia. Patient A could match graphic stimuli perfectly, but reading and comprehension of isolated words were equally impaired in all tasks: reading of words, 50%; reading of nonsense syllables, 48%; lexical decisions, 50%; comprehension of words with a multiple choice of words, 50%; and comprehension of words with a multiple choice of pictures, 50%. Overall performances improved only 8% when the patient was told the category of the stimuli.

Patients with alexia without agraphia are reported to read shorter words more rapidly (Gardner & Zurif, 1975; Warrington & Shallice, 1980) and more accurately (Hécaen, 1967). There is no effect of part of speech (Dubois-Charlier, 1970) on reading, but function words may be better read because they are short (Gardner & Zurif, 1975; Hécaen & Kremin, 1976). There is no influence of the abstract–concrete dimension (Warrington & Shallice, 1980). Reading errors are visually similar to the stimulus (Poppelreuter, 1917; Marshall & Newcombe, 1973; Hécaen & Kremin, 1976; Levine & Calvanio, 1978). The meaningfulness of the stimulus exhibits no crucial influence on the reading performance (Hécaen, 1967; Assal & Hahj-Djilani, 1976; Hécaen & Kremin, 1976; Warrington & Shallice, 1980; Kremin, 1981).

When the patient is bilingual, reading may be impaired in both languages. Sroka, Solsi, and Bornstein (1973) presented a Hebrew patient who was impaired in both script from right to left and script from left to right. And in Japanese patients suffering from alexia without agraphia, reading of kana and kanji script is equally disturbed (Hirose, Kin, & Murakami, 1977). This parallelism is in sharp contrast with the dissociations found when reading impairment is associated with aphasic and/or writing disturbances.

LINGUISTICALLY ORIENTED APPROACHES

Classification of Reading Disturbances according to the
Linguistic Level of the Deficit

As has been mentioned, the distinction between literal and verbal alexia, although standard since Déjérine, was usually seen only as one of degree, resulting from differences in the severity of the lesions or from differences in educational level of the patients. Hinshelwood (1900) was one of the rare authors who considered the different types of alexias as distinct forms, which should be observable in pure states. Alajouanine *et al.* (1960) distinguished them within the framework of agnosic versus aphasic alexia. Hécaen (1967) finally claimed that they cannot be considered to be just variations in intensity of a basic disorder: The nature of errors and the types of paralexic responses suggested that these different types of reading impairments could be interpreted as structurally different forms. Dubois-Charlier (1970, 1971) confirmed the structural independence of literal and verbal alexias and furthermore suggested the presence of an additional type of reading disturbance, that of sentence alexia. These different forms were each represented by one patient without any language impairment. The other patients, in whom oral language disorders were encountered, could be classified into one of the three types. Hécaen and Kremin (1976) analyzed new cases of severely alexic patients without disorders of oral language and compared them with patients suffering from left hemispheric lesions and associated syndromes. The neurolinguistic study established that there was not only a quantitative difference between pure alexia and the other reading impairments, but also a qualitative difference. Moreover, the authors confirmed that within the category of "pure" alexia, the clinically different aspects corresponded to different structural forms. Their analyses took into account three contrasts that stem from the implicated cognitive processes or from the linguistic character of the material presented: recognition versus reading aloud, meaningfulness versus nonmeaningfulness, and combination versus global apprehension. Hécaen and Kremin (1976) maintained the classification of the alexias according to the different linguistic levels (letters, words, sentences) at which the disturbance was predominantly found, but they specified for each the similarities and differences with regard to the three contrasts described.

1. *Verbal alexia:* "At the level of graphemes, this type of alexia is characterized by a good ability to read and good recognition of individual letters. There appears, however, to be a deficit in categorization which manifests itself when the patient has to recognize the same letter

in different graphic shapes. At the level of words, reading difficulties caused by combination difficulties are observed. These are more or less independent of the factor of "meaningfulness." The recognition of words seems to depend on the nature of the task. Presentation of pictures in a multiple choice task and presentation of words in a foreign language facilitate the recognition, whereas presentation of part of the letters which make up a word in the form of mutilated words does not. The strategy of reading used is deciphering by successive spelling. An overall (global) understanding of a word is totally impossible [p. 318]."

2. *Literal alexia:* "Individual letters may be recognized but not read. There is no deficit in categorization. Words (even mutilated words) and nonsense syllables are easily recognized. The ability to read is, however, impaired. Nonsense syllables cannot be read at all, and the responses have no resemblance to the stimulus. The reading strategy is 'global, ' which produces visual and semantic paralexias [p. 319]."

3. *Sentence alexia:* "Individual letters are well read, but a deficit in categorization is also found in this form. Recognition of nonsense syllables and words is good. Words may be relatively well read, but nonsense syllables create serious problems. The major impairment is found at the level of written text and sentences, for which both reading and recognition are very deficient. Reading is accomplished on the basis of an overall comprehension of the word. Combination difficulties are found, but at a higher level. They appear to be characterized by the loss of principles of sequence, choice, or coordination of the morphemic items of a sentence or text. Sentence alexia is thus characterized by the same deficit in categorization as verbal alexia. Combination difficulties also seem to be a common feature of these two types of alexia, but are found at different linguistic levels. At the same time, sentence alexia also has features in common with literal alexia, for example, the use of a global comprehension strategy for reading words and the influence of the factor of meaningfulness on the reading performance [p. 319]."

Despite all the reservations that can and should be made with regard to this classification, the fact remains that it corresponds to a certain clinical reality which appears to be confirmed both by the literature (see Péré, 1978, for a review) and by systematic anatomoclinical correlations (Hécaen, 1975).

Classification of Reading Behavior in Terms of Error Analysis

Holding that the structural nature of reading errors places one of the most important constraints upon theories of reading, Marshall and

Newcombe (1973) carried out a taxonomic analysis of reading errors made by subjects in whom the dyslexic component was predominant. They distinguished three types of acquired dyslexia in terms of performances in reading isolated words: (*a*) visual dyslexia, in which the paralexias consist of confusions of visually similar letters and words; (*b*) deep dyslexia, due to an impairment of grapheme-to-phoneme reading, in which direct access to meaning is preserved; and (*c*) surface dyslexia, in which the paralexias result from a partial failure of grapheme–phoneme correspondence rules, and in which a large number of neologisms are produced.

The authors propose a theoretical model which postulates that deep dyslexia cannot occur unless other aphasic features are present. By the same token, their model allows for the possibility of "pure" visual dyslexia without other aphasic involvement. Although Marshall and Newcombe insisted that "dyslexic impairment must be related to other aspects of aphasic performance [p. 195]," subsequent studies in this field established deep—or "phonemic" (Shallice & Warrington, 1975)— dyslexia as a clinical entity by means of a list of reading performances, and the possible effects of the disturbance upon linguistic tasks other than reading have not yet been studied systematically. Nevertheless, the case descriptions—most of them focusing on deep dyslexia, some of them on surface dyslexia—cast some light on the mechanisms implicated in the reading of written words. Let us first briefly describe the two syndromes, deep and surface dyslexia, which turned out to be an important matter of theoretical concern.

DEEP DYSLEXIA

Although some authors have listed 20 characteristics of the syndrome (Coltheart, 1977), most authors distinguish four main features: (*a*) production of semantic and derivational paralexias, and, in addition, the occurrence of visual errors and omissions; (*b*) severe if not total impairment of the grapheme-to-phoneme conversion strategy as shown by poor reading of nonsense syllables; (*c*) influence of part of speech— nouns are read best, function words worst; and (*d*) influence of the concreteness/imageability dimension on word-reading performance (Richardson, 1975).

Semantic paralexias being the crucial characteristic of the syndrome (Marshall & Newcombe, 1973; Schwartz *et al.*, 1977), we reviewed the literature in order to check other possible characteristics of the reading performance, the type of verbal impairment, site of lesion, and associated syndromes (when the information was available). The results of this review are given in Table 15.1. We extended our list to some other cases where semantic paralexias were reported in order to have a broader basis for comparison. Indeed, almost all deep dyslexic patients described in the literature were agrammatic aphasics—the patients K.F. (Shallice & Warrington, 1975), A.R. (Warrington & Shallice, 1980), and LEC. (Kremin, 1980b) being the major exceptions.

For some patients, at least, semantic errors have been observed in tasks other than reading. Marshall and Newcombe (1977) explicitly mention that the presence of "semantic errors or circumlocutions is consistent with the type of word-finding difficulties that are apparent in B.R.'s spontaneous speech [p. 273]." For K.U., too, there was evidence of word-finding difficulties in spontaneous speech. Marshall, Newcombe, and Marshall (1970) mention the parallelism between G.R.'s performances in reading and naming. Saffran *et al.* (1976) point out that their patients V. and H. "made similar semantic substitutions in naming and writing to dictation [p. 257]." The patients D.E. and P.W. (cited by Morton & Patterson, 1980) produced errors and circumlocutions on picture and object naming. Patient LEC. (Kremin, 1980b), with normal spontaneous speech and object naming, produced many semantic substitutions in word repetition (see Goldblum, 1979).

Of course, these details are only hints suggesting that semantic errors might not be limited to a specific modality but might be due to a more "central" disturbance. (We will return to this later.) Note that the obvious disproportion of semantic errors in reading versus spontaneous speech and naming might be an artifact of testing; spontaneous speech is "spontaneous" (and not a re-production task), and naming can be tested only for picturable objects and lacks the dimension of abstractness. There is theoretical (Morton & Patterson, 1980) and experimental evidence (Goldblum, 1979; Kremin, 1980b—Case FRA.) that performance in reading and in repetition need not be parallel because of the independence of grapheme-to-phoneme and acoustic–phonological routes. The same is true for writing (see Beauvois & Dérousné, 1979, 1981).

Returning to Table 15.1, it is clear that the differences in the individual reading performances range from an isolated semantic error (BLA.) to a maximum of 69% of total errors (G.R.). One is tempted, indeed, to distinguish a "low production group" not exceeding, let us say, 10% of semantic paralexias and a "high production group." The "low production group" thus stays within the range of semantic errors produced by normal subjects under conditions of visual masking (Allport, 1977); it is possible that such a rate may have been achieved by guessing (Williams & Parkin, 1980). But, as Williams and Parkin point

Table 15.1
Summary of Neuropsychological Characteristics of Patients Showing Deep Dyslexia Symptoms

Patients[a]	Variables of reading							Neuropsychological variables											Examples of semantic paralexias
	Production of semantic paralexias	Influence of part of speech (N, V; Adj.)	Agrammatism (functors worse than lexemes)	Influence of concrete-abstract dimension	Nonsense syllables disturbed	Isolated letters disturbed	Comprehension of words and/or lexical decisions disturbed	Presence and type of aphasia	Problems of the semantic type	Agrammatism in spontaneous speech	Agraphia	Spelling deficit	Motor problems	Visual field defect	Oral comprehension deficit	Localization of the lesion	Time from accident to testing	Occurrence of semantic paralexias (%)	
1 G.R.	+	+	+	+	+	+		+ gl.A.	+ nam.	+	+	+	+	+	+	T.P.	30 years	69	storm → "thunder"
2 K.U.	+	+	+	+			±	+	nam.	±	+	+	+	+	±	P.O.	26 years	2	diamond → "necklace"
3 B.R.	+			+				+ exp.A.	(+)	±			+	+	±	M.C.A.	1 year		parent → "oh, my father and mother"
4 D.E.	+	+	+	+	+		±	+ Broca	+ nam.	+			+	0	±	F.T. Int.C.	5 years	23	
5 P.W.	+	+	+	+	+		0	+ Broca	+	+			+	0	±	F.T.P.O.	10 years	54	edition → "journal"
6 K.F.	+	+	+	+	+		(±)	+	nam.	0		+	±	0	+	P. (T.O.)	13 years	4	air → "fly"
7 V.S.	+	+	+	+			0	+ Broca	+ writ.	+	+?		0	0	+	T. post. + O.	3 years	19	shoulder → "arm"
8 H.	+	+	+				0	+ Broca	+ writ.	+			0	0	+	(vasc.)	4 years	20	olive → "black"

350

Case										Aphasia	nam./rep.					Loc.	Duration	n	Example
9 H.D.	+	+	+	+	+			+		Broca	±	nam.	+		0?	P.T.R.	10 years	5	est → "nord"
10 A.R.	+	0	0	±	+			0	±		±		0	+	+	P.	5 years	10	month → "week"
11 LEC.	+	+	±	+	0			+	+	opt.A.	nam.	+	0	0	±	P.T.O.	5 years		faïence → "porcelaine"
12 BLA.	+	0	0	+	±			+	+	Con.A.	rep.	+	0	0	0	P.O.	20 months	1	dimanche → "c'est un jour de la semaine"
13 L.	+			+		0		0		0	+		0	0					Italie → "république"
14 G.	+			+		0		0		0	+	nam.	0	0					hôpital → "c'est les docteurs"
15 1 case	+	+		+	0	+		+	0	0	+		0	+				(rare)	child → "girl"
16 1 case	+	+	Kanji better than kana					±	0	0	+	nam.	+	+			4 weeks		cold → "winter"
17 1 case	+	Kanji better than kana						0		0	+	nam.	0	0	0	int.C.			hospital → "doctor"
18 Case 23	+	+		0	±			+	±	Sens.A.	+		+	+	+				oven → "hot"
19 LEJ.	+	0	0	0			0	0	+	+	+		±	+	+	P.post.	3 weeks	2**	girafe → "cette grosse bête"
20 DES.	+	0	0	+	0			+	Sens.A.	+	nam.	0	±	+	P.T.O.	2 months	2	sentimentalité → "l'amour est basé la dessus"

0: absence of variable
+: presence of variable
T.: temporal
P.: parietal
O.: occipital
F.: frontal
R.: rolandic
post.: posterior
vasc.: vascular
M.C.A.: middle cerebral artery
Int. C.: internal carotid artery

gl.A.: global aphasia
exp.A.: expressive aphasia
Broca: Broca's aphasia
opt.A.: optic aphasia
cont. A.: conduction aphasia
Sens. A.: sensory aphasia
nam.: naming
writ.: writing
rep.: repetition
**: only in reading sentences

[a] Data are drawn from

1: Marshall & Newcombe, 1966
2: Marshall & Newcombe, 1973
3: Marshall & Newcombe, 1977
4,5: Patterson & Marcel, 1977
6: Shallice & Warrington, 1975
7: Saffran & Marin, 1977
8: Saffran, Schwartz, & Marin, 1976
9: Andreewsky & Seron, 1975

10: Warrington & Shallice, 1979
11: Kremin, 1980b
12: Dubois-Charlier, 1970, 1971
13,14: Hécaen, 1967
15: Low, 1931
16: Sasanuma, 1974
17: Yamadori, 1975
18: Goldstein, 1948
19,20: unpublished personal data

Some of the data are chosen from secondary sources.

out, it might be "unwise to make direct arithmetical comparisons of error rates which may arise in entirely different ways [p. 106]."

Besides the quantitative differences in the production of semantic paralexias, further attention should be drawn to the qualitative difference in the responses: Most of them are in the same field (e.g., *storm* → "thunder"); others are descriptions of the stimulus (e.g., *sentimentalité* → "l'amour est basé la-dessus"); yet others, in contrast, show a rather loose relationship with the stimulus; and, finally, though an omission is produced, some of the patients show that they correctly understood the stimulus, and one patient (A.R.) showed the spared capacity to categorize words he failed to read (forenames versus surnames, etc.).

Table 15.1 also shows that there is no privileged relation between occurrence of semantic paralexias and type of aphasia. Moreover, semantic paralexias are even produced, though to a lesser extent, by patients with normal spontaneous speech although, as we have discussed, there are methodological difficulties in directly comparing spontaneous speech with other production tasks.

Consider now how the patients in Table 15.1 deal with the reading of function words, another constituent variable for deep dyslexia. Actually, most of them have difficulties with functors—but these patients also have telegrammatic speech or, if not, other agrammatic symptoms (as do LEC. and Low's case). Table 15.1 shows that for some of the patients (BLA., LEJ., DES., and A.R.) reading of function words constitutes no major difficulty. It is interesting that one patient had "pure" literal alexia (BLA.), two subjects had sensory aphasia (DES., LEJ.), and one patient (A.R.) had optic aphasia. So it seems that the type of aphasia plays some role in the nature of reading performance. And this is independent of any articulatory problem.

Our list shows that other variables usually associated with deep dyslexia (the concrete versus abstract dimension; nouns versus other lexemes) are not crucial for all patients who produce semantic paralexias even though reading of isolated letters seems in some cases to be. Indeed, the only variables constantly associated with the occurrence of semantic paralexias and/or deep dyslexia are the inability to read nonsense syllables and the presence of writing disturbances. Our review therefore suggests that the loss of the grapheme–phoneme route is the only independent variable among those used to describe the clinical entity of deep dyslexia. The cases reported to date do not represent a homogeneous syndrome; "deep dyslexia" rather seems to be due to the association of several components as reflected in reading of isolated words. Shallice and Warrington (1980) take a position close to this.

Arguments for such a view also come from a case study done by Beauvois and Dérouesné (1979). They described the reading performance of a patient suffering from a parietal lesion, who had normal spontaneous speech, repetition, and naming and good oral comprehension. Oral spelling was intact, but writing was (specifically) disturbed (Beauvois & Dérouesné, 1981). The patient was incapable of reading (long) nonsense syllables. Reading of words was about 80% correct, but frequency, concreteness, and length of words had no main effect. Part of speech did have some effect (nouns were 94% correct, grammatical words 69%, and verb forms 57%). The authors point out that the meaningfulness of the items (whole words and/or root morphemes) is a crucial variable in accounting for their results. The patient produced no semantic error at all, but showed signs of visual and derivational misreadings. The aim of Beauvois and Dérouesné was to show the functional independence of the two reading processes (i.e., R.G. suffered from a disturbance of the phonological reading route without an impairment of the lexical reading route). The impairment in R.G. was located at the phonological processing stage within the grapheme–phoneme translations. This "phonological alexia" thus demonstrates that even a gross impairment of the phonological route is not by itself sufficient to produce the syndromes observed in deep dyslexic patients such as G.R., P.W., and D.E.

SURFACE DYSLEXIA

Marshall (1976) defined four features of surface dyslexia: (*a*) "can read (some nonsense syllables)"; (*b*) "errors are typically phonologically similar to the stimulus"; (*c*) "errors are very frequently phonologically possible but non-existent lexical forms"; and (*d*) "semantic reading of the visual stimulus is determined by the (frequently erroneous) phonology of the response [p. 114]."

Studies dealing with surface dyslexia (Marshall & Newcombe, 1973; Holmes, 1973, 1978; Marcel, 1980) have mostly been based on the reading performances of J.C. and S.T., the two original patients of Marshall and Newcombe (1973), although three more cases have also been published (Deloche, Andreewsky, & Desi, 1980; Kremin, 1980b; Shallice & Warrington, 1980). In the early descriptions of surface dyslexia (Marshall & Newcombe, 1973; Holmes, 1973, 1978) reading of isolated words and assigning meaning to them is supposed to be solely mediated by grapheme-to-phoneme conversion strategies, the direct visual semantic pathway being impaired. (Surface dyslexia thus represents the reverse dissociation to that of deep dyslexia.) If an internal semantic representation is not available one would indeed expect the production of a great number of neologisms. This is indeed true for all cited cases. Marshall and Newcombe (1973) claim that in surface dyslexia the reading errors are due to "partial failure of the grapheme-to-phoneme correspondence rules [p. 179]." It is noteworthy, though, that in some cases the vast majority (Deloche *et al.*, 1980; Kremin, 1980b) if not virtually all (Shallice & Warrington, 1980) reading errors involved the misapplication of a generally valid—but for the particular item inappropriate—grapheme–phoneme conversion rule. This suggests that surface dyslexia might occur as a "purer" syndrome than that of J.C. and S.T.

On the basis of the literature to date, other characteristics of surface dyslexia may be described as follows:

1. No semantic errors are produced.
2. There is a "part of speech" effect (Marshall & Newcombe, 1973; Deloche *et al.*, 1980; Kremin, 1980b). Two patients (Deloche *et al.*, 1980; Kremin, 1980b) had greater difficulties with words than with nonsense syllables, and with content words than with function words. The highest error rate was observed for nouns. For patient A.D. (Deloche *et al.*, 1980) these performance differences were statistically significant.
3. Graphic complexity of the stimulus played a variable role, with length of the letter string influencing the performances of S.T. (Marshall & Newcombe, 1973), FRA. (Kremin, 1980b), and A.D. (Deloche *et al.*, 1980), but not the performances of J.C. (Marshall & Newcombe, 1973) and HAM. (personal data).
4. The complexity of the verbal output did not interact with the reading performance of A.D., in terms of constituent phonemes (Deloche *et al.*, 1980). But, it affected the number of syllables read correctly by FRA. (Kremin, 1980b), as well as the reading time of ROG. (Shallice & Warrington, 1980).
5. Word frequency effect is mentioned for J.C. and S.T. (Marshall & Newcombe, 1973) but not for FRA. (Kremin, 1980b) and HAM. (personal data).
6. Orthography, in terms of regular versus irregular word spellings influenced the reading performance of ROG. and E.M. (Shallice & Warrington, 1980) and of HAM. (personal data). Orthography/ phonology, in terms of words versus homophonic nonwords, induced a high false recognition score in lexical decision tasks for FRA., HAM., and A.D. (though for the latter only in a pattern masking condition, Deloche *et al.*, 1980). Orthography was a crucial variable in writing, too.

7. All patients are reported to have had difficulties in writing and spelling. Deloche *et al.* (1980) and Kremin (1980b) studied the writing performances of their patients most carefully. They stated that in most cases the errors did not affect the phonological form of the word but, rather exclusively, their conventional orthography.
8. In lexical decision tasks, only a few errors are made; function words are better recognized than content words (Deloche *et al.*, 1980; Kremin, 1980b). However, when orthographic and/or phonological variables are introduced into the experimental paradigm, false recognitions occur on words and homophonic nonwords, the good recognition of nonsense syllables being spared (Kremin, 1980b).
9. Comprehension of the written words also seems to be a multi-component variable. When assessed nonverbally in a multiple choice paradigm where written words were to be processed on semantic grounds exclusively, comprehension was almost perfect in A.D. and FRA. (Deloche *et al.*, 1980; Kremin, 1980b). However when a phonological trap was introduced, A.D. derived lexical meaning from the target erroneously by phonology—"It thus appears that the surface dyslexic patient was using either one or both semantic and phonological routes in trying to understand written words [Deloche *et al.*, 1980, p. 19]."

Comprehension while reading aloud shows a somewhat complex picture, too. Usually, words that are correctly read are understood. Items on which a reading error is produced reveal two different reading behaviors. For instance FRA. and A.D. succeeded in self-correcting the vast majority of their initial reading errors, whereas J.C. and S.T. did not (see Holmes, 1973). Usually it is argued that the (former) patients "can help themselves by providing information that can be processed in the intact auditory channel [Holmes, 1973, p. 78]." Although this is probably true in some instances, comprehension by auditory feedback cannot account for the performances of all surface dyslexics. Patient FRA., for example, suffered from an impairment in the processing of auditory linguistic stimuli (see Goldblum, 1979), and it is difficult to conceive that the patient's numerous self-corrections in reading words (and nonsense syllables) could depend on the auditory channel without reflecting its specific impairment ("auditory analogue of deep dyslexia"). There is another intriguing fact that is difficult to account for by auditory feedback. Patients such as FRA. and HAM. (the latter with normal speech and repetition, *do* comprehend words they do not pronounce correctly [*toast* (tost) → /toas/ /twal/ (what does it mean?) on le mange (= one eats it) . . un /tost/ . . . /to-ast/; *fuel* (fjul) → /fyel/ (what does it mean?) chauffer du /fyl/ . . . /fwal/? . . .]

In the light of the details that have accumulated concerning the performances of patients with so-called surface dyslexia, it seems difficult to account for this reading impairment solely within the framework of Marshall's (1976) definition.

THE INFORMATION-PROCESSING APPROACH

Theoretical Models for Reading

The investigations of acquired reading disturbances turned out to be a matter of theoretical concern. Experimental research, having established that some patients suffer from an impairment of analytical and/or phonological reading (as shown by their inability to read nonsense syllables), made it possible to postulate the existence of a nonphonological route from print to meaning.

On the basis of their analysis of reading errors, Marshall and Newcombe proposed a theoretical model for reading in their 1973 paper. Their model postulates that, after registration of the graphic stimulus in a primary visual register, both phonological and semantic characteristics must be assigned to the stimulus. If, as a consequence of brain damage, the semantic pathway is unavailable, the subject has no other option than reading via grapheme–phoneme correspondence rules. It is consistent with the model that, when a false response is produced by grapheme-to-phoneme conversion, semantic interpretation will correspond with the reading error.

Morton, too, tried to integrate data from pathology into his logogen model (1979). This model of isolated word recognition is based on the assumption that the input is modality specific. It thus separates visual and auditory input and, in its current version (Morton & Patterson, 1980), it separates visual graphemic input from pictorial stimuli, etc. This latter version of the logogen model is based on the assumption that there are three routes by which a phonological output can be obtained given a graphic visual input:

1. "After categorization of the stimulus in the visual input logogen system, information is sent directly to the output system where the appropriate phonological code is produced."
2. "The word is categorized in the visual input logogen system and information is sent to the cognitive system. Here the appropriate

semantics can be found and sent to the output logogen system where the appropriate phonological code could be obtained."

3. "The stimulus is treated as a sequence of graphemes and converted by rule into a phonological code [p. 94]."

It should be noted that only (1) is, in principle, error free; that the logogen system itself contains no semantic information, and that the grapheme–phoneme system has no concept of "word," words and nonwords being treated alike.

Shallice and Warrington (1980) have a somewhat different approach. In their view, there are two main reading routes: (*a*) "the direct (or 'visual') route from the visual word-form system to the semantic system"; and (*b*) "the phonological route from the visual word-form system to phonological processing systems." In this view, phonological recoding "does not just operate on graphemes . . . but also on larger visual units including syllables and words." The actual pronunciation of any letter combination does not depend on rules but on the "frequency with which alternative pronunciations of the letter string occur," the phonological system "accepting the most word-like as valid." As Marcel (1980) pointed out, Shallice and Warrington's formulation of the grapheme–phoneme translation process is not independent of descriptions that yield lexical access.

Marcel's (1980) view bears strong similarities to Shallice and Warrington's proposal. For Marcel the basic process involved in pronouncing is alike for both words and nonwords. (We skip the details of his view as to how parsing and segmentation of the visual input occurs.) The main point of Marcel's approach is that orthographic lexical knowledge intervenes in the segmentation of *any* letter string: When orthographic lexical knowledge is met, the left-to-right segmentation of each letter in the string is "overridden." However, when no lexical knowledge is forthcoming (in the case of nonsense syllables, "there are no segments that can be dealt with other than individual letters. . . . While at first sight this may look like grapheme-to-phoneme conversion its operation is by recourse to lexical knowledge [p. 247]."

In this respect one should not ignore information available on reading disorders in special writing systems, as compared to standard alphabetical systems written from left to right. The study of Japanese cases of alexia is of particular interest, given that Japanese uses more than one writing system, the two main systems being kanji (an ideographic script for lexical items derived from Chinese) and kana (a syllabic writing system used for grammatical elements). Dissociation of the problems experienced in these two writing systems has been confirmed by Japanese authors for both the writing and reading of aphasics (Imura,

Nogami, & Asakawa, 1971; Sasanuma & Fujimura, 1970, 1972). Patients have been observed for whom words written in kana caused more reading problems than words written in kanji (Kotani, 1935; Sasanuma, 1973, 1974; Yamadori, 1975). But the reverse pattern, with reading impairment greater for kanji than for kana, can also be seen (Imura, 1943; Sasanuma & Monoi, 1975; Yamadori & Ikumura, 1975). Both Sasanuma (1973) and Yamadori (1975) interpreted these results to mean that the two scripts are treated differently: Reading words in kanji involves a direct graphic strategy (with a direct access to the semantic representation of items), whereas reading words in kana involves an indirect phonetic strategy, as it requires an intermediary phonological process in order to arrive at the meaning.

Data from Pathology

THE VISUAL WORD-FORM SYSTEM

In alexia without agraphia the semantic processing system seems to be intact: Words that are read correctly are understood. The deficit cannot be accounted for at the level of oral response either, as there is no dissociation between reading aloud and comprehension of the stimuli. Moreover, phonological processing is also intact, as shown by patients' ability to read nonsense syllables (almost) as efficiently as words. It therefore seems necessary to "locate" the deficit at a stage in the reading process that is prior to semantic and/or phonological analysis: Alexia without agraphia is a deficit in attaining the visual word-form or equivalent (Warrington & Shallice, 1980). As mentioned earlier, the deficit cannot necessarily be accounted for by postulating a perceptual deficit. The possible role of selective attention studied by Shallice and Warrington (1977) should be further explored in this type of reading impairment, as the disturbance underlying the letter-by-letter reading strategy remains unclear to date. There is some evidence, though, that "categorization" and/or association of visual stimuli is selectively impaired in posterior lesions of the left hemisphere (De Renzi, Scotti, & Spinnler, 1969), especially in the syndrome of associative visual agnosia (Hécaen, Goldblum, Masure, & Ramier, 1974). Faglioni, Scotti, and Spinnler (1969) confirmed this with reference to the categorization of graphic material (matching of same letters which were visually dissimilar). Difficulties in categorizing letters (e.g., printed capitals versus cursive script) have indeed been reported in cases of verbal alexia without agraphia, and not in cases of "literal" alexia (Hécaen & Kremin, 1976; Kremin, 1976) or "phonological" alexia (Beauvois &

Dérouesné, 1979). Hécaen and Kremin (1976) thus propose that verbal alexia without agraphia may be considered as representing aspects of visual agnosia—this relationship demonstrating either the proximity of the underlying lesions or an impairment, specific to the visual modality, of association and/or categorization involving different types of materials (colors, objects, words): "Verbal alexia appears therefore to be a difficulty in the construction of meaningful units (words) on the basis of elements with known forms [Hécaen & Kremin, 1976, p. 320]."

DIRECT SEMANTIC ACCESS FROM PRINT TO MEANING

The reading performance of patients with impairment of the phonological route should reflect the "nature" of the direct route, that is, "locate" the different components and stages of this reading system. It is clear that, even in patients with deep dyslexia, the visual input system is operating normally. Direct evidence comes from lexical decision tasks (Patterson, 1979; Kremin, 1980b); indirect evidence comes from the production of semantic paralexias. (It is evident that errors related only in meaning to the stimulus item could not arise unless semantic associates had been activated during the reading process.)

But in the comprehension of written words the patients showed inconsistent performances. On the one hand, LEC. (Kremin, 1980b) performed almost perfectly, and P.W., D.E. (Patterson, 1979), and V.S. (Saffran et al., 1977) performed fairly well. But P.D. (Kapur & Perl, 1978) was at chance level in an auditory recognition reading test (where he had to choose between the paralexic response he had made and the correct response). Similarly, P.W. and D.E. were far from perfect in a forced choice recognition test (Patterson, 1978). Moreover, D.E. (Patterson, 1979), K.F., and P.S. (Shallice & Warrington, 1980) failed to comprehend abstract words. These findings suggest that, at least in some deep dyslexic patients, the reading error cannot simply be accounted for by a failure at the level of the correct output. In fact, the comparison of performances in the "naming" (oral response) and in the comprehension of the stimulus should enable us to "locate" the underlying deficit either as a "naming" disturbance or as a more central disturbance in the semantic system (see Shallice & Warrington, 1980). In this respect it is noteworthy that even the deficit in reading function words might be due, at least in some patients, to a "naming" deficit. For instance, G.R. (Marshall & Newcombe, 1966) could not read prepositions aloud, but he had no difficulty in correctly selecting pictures on the basis of descriptions containing prepositions; and one of our patients read personal pronouns "semantically" (e.g., *celles* → "femme . . . pluriel.")

Patterson (1978) established the reality of a functional relation—independent of quantitative performance differences—between error type and recognition and/or confidence ratings of the subjects. The experimental data indicate that semantic paralexias are more frequently recognized as reading errors than are derivational and visual errors. Moreover, it was noted that words yielding visual paralexias are relatively abstract (Patterson, 1980; Shallice & Warrington, 1980; Kremin, 1980b). (Compare Patterson, 1978, and Shallice & Warrington, 1980, for differences in the interpretation of this phenomenon.) It should further be noted that reading for confidence ratings seem to depend on the "nature" of the verbal response and that oral production might interfere with comprehension. For instance, LEC. (Kremin, 1980b) correctly understood the words *univers* and *ténèbres* in a nonverbal written comprehension test, yet in reading aloud he produced *univers* as "un hiver . . . en hiver" and *ténèbres* as /pénèbre/ or /pénègre/. In the first case, where a real word was produced, comprehension paralleled the erroneous response; in the second case, where a neologism was produced, comprehension paralleled the target. The latter suggests that a "naming" error (at the level of verbal output) can occur even when the reading error seems visual in nature.

Semantic errors are less often accepted as correct responses than are visual errors (Patterson, 1979). We have already mentioned the quantitative and qualitative differences in semantic reading errors. The overall pattern of occurrence of semantic errors seems to be adequately described by (*a*) a close synonymous relationship between target and response, and (*b*) the abstractness of the concepts (Shallice & Warrington, 1975; Patterson, 1979). In accordance with the data referring to semantic paralexias, different "loci" of the underlying disturbance may be considered: (*a*) a "naming" problem at the level of the oral output, and (*b*) a weakness within the semantic organization itself. Shallice and Warrington (1980) also discuss the possibility that some semantic errors may occur from difficulties in the access to semantic specifications (as in the patients A.R. and K.F.). Finally, semantic errors may be absent in (nonaphasic) patients although they make use only of the direct reading route (Beauvois & Dérouesné, 1979).

In Japanese patients, semantic paralexias occur exclusively with kanji words (Sasanuma, 1974). By analogy, "global" or direct reading in alphabetical languages has often been, implicitly or explicitly, conceived of as "holistic" or "ideographic" in nature. Saffran and Marin (1977) and Saffran (1980) studied this question more closely in four patients with deep dyslexia. It was found that these patients were not reading "ideographically"; reading performance was not disrupted by distorted printed form and/or the removal of configurational cues. Saffran (1980) thus supposes that "these patients are relying on an orthographic reading mechanism in which letter strings, encoded in some abstract form, are matched to stored orthographic representations [p. 222]" and postulates an orthographic reading system to be operating in deep dyslexia, that is, when reading by the nonphonological route.

READING BY GRAPHEME-TO-PHONEME TRANSLATION

The syndrome of surface dyslexia is characterized by the preservation of grapheme-to-phoneme translation; such patients can read nonsense syllables (Deloche *et al.*, 1980; Kremin, 1980b). Their reading contains a large number of phonological errors due to a misapplication or overgeneralization of existent correspondence rules and, in some cases, to a partial failure in the application of these correspondence rules. Sometimes their reading deficit is limited to irregularly spelled words (Shallice & Warrington, 1980). Their discrimination of words from nonwords and their comprehension of words are preserved when tested solely on semantic grounds (Deloche *et al.*, 1980; Kremin, 1980b). But, with orthographic and/or phonological "traps," the comprehension of words was disrupted for lexical decisions (Kremin, 1980b), as well as for semantic comprehension (Deloche *et al.*, 1980). Orthography thus turned out to be a crucial variable not only in reading aloud, but also in the comprehension of written material and in writing. Indeed, it has been argued that orthography, that is, a disturbance of orthographic specifications in the lexicon, is the main or sole feature of surface dyslexia (Marcel, 1980).

Finally, the question is raised how (or when) the information available from grapheme-to-phoneme translation enters the cognitive system. Most authors of psycholinguistic information-processing models define the phonological route as alexical (Marshall & Newcombe, 1973; Beauvois & Dérouesné, 1979; Morton & Patterson, 1980). In this view access to the cognitive system should take place *after* grapheme-to-phoneme translation, usually by auditory checking procedures. But recent studies on surface dyslexia have tended to accumulate data against such a view. The reading performance of surface dyslexias shows an influence of part of speech, and erroneous responses were often self-corrected, even when the auditory channel was impaired. Moreover, patients understood target items they could not read aloud. In the one patient in whom these variables were studied, the error patterns for words and nonsense syllables were not the same: There were only 10% visual errors for words as opposed to 39% visual errors for nonsense syllables (Kremin, 1980b). This patient also showed an effect of length of the stimuli on the production of words but not nonwords.

These data strongly suggest that reading by grapheme-to-phoneme translation involves—in many if not all surface dyslexics—a lexical dimension. Kremin (1980a) interpreted FRA.'s reading performances within the framework of the logogen model: When "recognition" fails, the patient adopts a sounding out strategy (therefore some words are not understood, even when they are correctly read); when only the output logogen fails, the patient again adopts a sounding out strategy instead of producing an omission (in this case the target is understood). Kremin also advanced an alternative interpretation of the patient's reading behavior, suggesting that, being aware of general output problems, the patient may have freely chosen, for ease of production, the one-to-one mapping for reading aloud in order to overcome the (aphasic) deficit of phonemic combination. (The phonological route had been available even in the acute aphasic state, as had been comprehension of written material.) This interpretation can and should, of course, be rediscussed in the light of the information approaches proposed by Marcel (1980) and Shallice and Warrington (1980). The data on surface dyslexia, nevertheless, seem to indicate that grapheme-to-phoneme reading does not result from a single component syndrome of reading disturbance. They rather suggest that, because of the lexical dimensions, other (aphasic) language disturbances are often associated.

CONCLUSION

The review of acquired reading disturbances shows evidence of a set of reading defects which are remarkably dissociated. Different approaches of research and theory (whether clinically oriented, based on analyses of reading errors, or influenced by information-processing models) confirm the distinction, standard since Déjérine, between pure alexia without agraphia and alexia accompanied by writing disturbances. It has been furthermore suggested that patients with "pure" (or agnosic) alexia tend to be better at letter naming than word reading, whereas the opposite pattern is associated with (aphasic) alexia with agraphia (Alajouanine *et al.*, 1960). These forms of "literal" and "verbal" alexia (Hinshelwood, 1900) were, as an approximation, described according to the linguistic level (letters, words) on which the disturbance was predominantly found (Hécaen, 1967). This approach suggested another variety of reading impairment, that of sentence alexia (Dubois-Charlier, 1971). It was concluded that literal and verbal alexia reflect the selective disturbance of different processes involved in reading. Similarly, different strategies for reading words were demonstrated by the patients: A spelling strategy in (verbal) alexia without agraphia contrasts with a global reading strategy in (literal) alexia with agraphia. Recent research, moreover, established that patients with literal and/or deep dyslexia suffer from an impairment of analytical reading by grapheme-to-phoneme translation, the direct semantic access from print to meaning being spared. In terms of information-processing approaches it can thus be argued that alexia without agraphia reflects a deficit in attaining the visual word-form system (Warrington & Shallice, 1980), whereas in patients using a global reading strategy the visual input system is operating normally.

Besides the global reading strategy common to both literal and deep dyslexia, a certain resemblance between these two types of reading disturbance is revealed by the occurrence (though at different degrees) of semantic paralexias. This has been pointed out by the authors themselves (Hécaen, 1967; Hécaen & Kremin, 1976; Marshall & Newcombe, 1977). It thus can be questioned whether semantic paralexias necessarily occur through inability to use the grapheme to phoneme translation. A study by Beauvois and Dérouesné (1979) suggests, rather, that the production, even of rare semantic paralexias, might be due to (slight) aphasic involvement.

Research has furthermore led to the distinction of another type of reading impairment, so-called surface dyslexia (Marshall & Newcombe, 1973). This type is mainly characterized by the occurrence of phonological reading errors and the spared ability to read by grapheme-to-phoneme conversion. Although the underlying deficit(s) of this reading impairment remain open to further discussion, there is nevertheless evidence that in this type of dyslexia lexical dimensions are involved, just as they are in literal and deep dyslexia. It thus seems that the visual word-form must also be attained prior to phonological analysis as well as to semantic analysis (Warrington & Shallice, 1980).

The data we reviewed from pathology favor possible selective disturbances of each of the components involved in the reading process: the visual word-form system, and the semantic and phonological processing systems.

REFERENCES

Alajouanine, T., Lhermitte, F., & Ribaucourt-Ducarne, B. De. (1960) Les alexies agnosiques et aphasiques. In T. Alajouanine (Ed.), *Les grandes activités du lobe occipital.* Paris: Masson.

Allport, D. A. (1977) On knowing the meaning of words we are unable to report: The effects of visual masking. In S. Dornic (Ed.), *Attention and performance* (Vol. 6). Hillsdale, N.J.: Lawrence Erlbaum.

Andreewsky, E., & Seron, X. (1975) Implicit processing of grammatical rules in a case of agrammatism. *Cortex, 11*, 379–390.

Assal, G., & Hadj-Djilani, M. (1976) Une nouvelle observation d'alexie pure sans hémianopsie. *Cortex, 12*, 169–174.

Beauvois, M. F., & Dérouesné, J. (1979) Phonological alexia—Three dissociations. *Journal of Neurology, Neurosurgery and Psychiatry, 42*, 1115–1124.

Beauvois, M. F., & Dérouesné, J. (1981) Lexical or orthographic agraphia. *Brain, 104*, 21–49.

Benson, D. F. (1977) The third alexia. *Archives of Neurology, 34*, 327–331.

Benson, D. F., Brown, J., & Tomlinson, E. B. (1971) Varieties of alexia: Word and letter blindness. *Neurology, 21*, 951–957.

Benson, D. F., & Geschwind, N. (1969) The alexias. In P. J. Vinken & G. W. Bruyn (Eds.), *Handbook of clinical neurology* (Vol. 4). Amsterdam: North-Holland.

Benton, A., & Joynt, R. J. (1960) Early descriptions of aphasia. *Archives of Neurology, 3*, 205–222.

Caplan, L. R., & Hedley-White, T. (1974) Cueing and memory dysfunction in alexia without agraphia: A case report *Brain, 97*, 251–262.

Coltheart, M. (1977) *Phonemic dyslexia: Some comments on its interpretation and its implication for the study of normal reading.* Paper presented at the International Neuropsychological Society, Oxford, August 1977.

Critchley, M. (1970) *The dyslexic child.* London: Heinemann.

Dejerine, J. (1891) Sur un cas de cécité verbal suivi d'autopsie. *Mémoires de la Société de Biologie*, 197–201.

Dejerine, J. (1892) Contribution à l'étude anatomo-pathologique et clinique des différentes variétés de cécité verbale. *Mémoires de la Société de Biologie, 4*, 61–90.

Deloche, G., Andreewsky, E., & Desi, M. (1980) *Surface dyslexia: A route towards understanding reading?* Paper presented at the International Neuropsychological Society, Chianciano-Terme, Italy, June 1980.

De Renzi, E., Scotti, G., & Spinnler, H. (1969) Perceptual and associative disorders of visual recognition. Relationship to site of lesion. *Neurology, 19*, 634–642.

Dubois-Charlier, F. (1970) *Etude neurolinguistique du problème de l'alexie pure.* Unpublished doctoral dissertation. Facultés des Lettres et Sciences Humaines, Paris X.

Dubois-Charlier, F. (1971) Approche neurolinguistique du problème de l'alexie pure. *Journal de Psychologie Normale et Pathologique, 1*, 39–68.

Ellis, A. W. (1979) Developmental and acquired dyslexia: Some observations on Jorm. *Cognition, 7*, 413–420.

Faglioni, P., Scotti, G., & Spinnler, H. (1969) Impaired recognition of written letters following unilateral hemispheric damage. *Cortex*, 120–133.

Friederici, A. D., & Schoenle, P. W. (1980) Computational dissociation of two vocabulary types: Evidence from aphasia. *Neuropsychologia, 18*, 11–20.

Gardner, H., & Zurif, E. (1975) Bee but not be: Oral reading of simple word in aphasia and alexia. *Neuropsychologia, 13*, 181–190.

Goldblum, M. C. (1979) Auditory analogue of deep dyslexia. In O. Creutzfeld, H. Scheich, & C. Schreiner (Eds.), *Experimental brain research, Supplementum II: Hearing mechanisms and speech.* Berlin: Springer-Verlag.

Goldstein, K. (1948) *Language and language disturbances.* New York: Grune & Stratton.

Hécaen, H. (1967) Aspects des troubles de la lecture (alexies) au cours des lésions cérébrales en foyer. *Word, 23*, 265–287.

Hécaen, H. (1976) Les problèmes des localisations lésionnelles des alexies. *Langages, 44,* 111–117.

Hécaen, H., Goldblum, M. C., Masure, M. C., & Ramier, A. M. (1974). Une nouvelle observation d'agnosie d'objet. Déficit de l'association ou de la catégorisation spécifique de la modalité visuelle. *Neuropsychologia, 12,* 447–464.

Hécaen, H., & Kremin, H. (1976) Neurolinguistic research on reading disorders resulting from left hemisphere lesions. Aphasic and "pure" alexias. In H. Whitaker & H. A. Whitaker (Eds.), *Studies in neurolinguistics* (Vol. 2). New York: Academic Press.

Hinshelwood, J. (1895) Word-blindness and visual memory. *Lancet, 2,* 1564–1570.

Hinshelwood, J. (1900) *Letter-, word- and mind-blindness.* London: H. K. Lewis.

Hirose, G., Kin, T., & Murakami, E. (1977) Alexia without agraphia associated with right occipital lesion. *Journal of Neurology, Neurosurgery and Psychiatry, 40,* 225–227.

Holmes, J. M. (1973) *Dyslexia: A neurolinguistic study of traumatic and developmental disorders of reading.* Unpublished doctoral dissertation, University of Edinburgh.

Holmes, J. M. (1978) Regression and reading breakdown. In A. Caramazza & E. Zurif (Eds.), *The acquisition and breakdown of language: Parallels and divergencies.* Baltimore: John Hopkins University Press.

Imura, R. (1943) Aphasia: Characteristic symptoms in Japanese. *Psychiatrica et Neurologia Japanica, 47,* 196–218.

Imura, T., Nogami, Y., & Asakawa, K. (1971) Aphasia in the Japanese language. *Nippon University Journal of Medicine, 13,* 69–90.

Jorm, A. F. (1979a) The cognitive and neurological basis of developmental dyslexia: A theoretical framework and review. *Cognition, 7,* 19–33.

Jorm, A. F. (1979b) The nature of the reading deficit in developmental dyslexia: A reply to Ellis. *Cognition, 7,* 421–433.

Kapur, N., & Perl, N. T. (1978) Recognition reading in paralexia. *Cortex, 14,* 439–443.

Kinsbourne, M., & Warrington, E. (1962) A disorder of simultaneous form perception. *Brain, 85,* 461–486.

Kotani, S. (1935) A case of alexia with agraphia. *Japanese Journal of Experimental Psychology, 2,* 333–348.

Kremin, H. (1976) Les problèmes de l'alexie pure. *Langages, 44,* 82–110.

Kremin, H. (1980a) *Case study of a patient with surface dyslexia.* Paper presented at the Meeting of the International Neuropsychological Society, Chianciano-Terme, Italy, June 1980.

Kremin, H. (1980b) Deux stratégies de lecture dissociables par la pathologie: Description d'un cas de dyslexie profonde et d'un cas de dyslexie de surface. In *Etudes Neuro-linguistiques* (special issue of *Grammatica*), Université de Toulouse-Le Mirail.

Kremin, H. (1981) Problèmes d'accès lexical et stratégies de lecture. In Processus fon-damentaux en oeuvre dans la lecture et la comprehension du langage écrit, special issue of *Psychologie Française.*

Kremin, H., & Dubois-Charlier, F. (1976) Les troubles de la lecture: L'alexie. *Langages, 44,*

Kremin, H., & Goldblum, M. C. (1975) Etude de la compréhension syntaxique chez les aphasiques. *Linguistics, 154–155,* 31–46.

Kussmaul, A. (1884) *Les troubles de la parole.* (French translation by A. Rueff.) Paris: Baillière.

Levine, D. N., & Calvanio, R. (1978) A study of the visual defect in verbal alexia-simultan agnosia. *Brain, 101,* 65–81.

Low, A. A. (1931) A case of agrammatism in the English language. *Archives of Neurology and Psychiatry, 25,* 556–597.

Marcel, T. (1980) Surface dyslexia and beginning reading—A revised hypothesis of the pronunciation of print and its impairments. In M. Coltheart, K. E. Patterson, & J. C. Marshall (Eds.), *Deep dyslexia*. London: Routledge and Kegan Paul.

Marie, P. (1906) Révision de la question de l'aphasie. In *Travaux et mémoire* (Vol. 1). Paris: Masson et Cie.

Marin, O. S. M., Saffran, E. M., & Schwartz, M. F. (1976) Dissociations of language in aphasia: Implications for normal function. *Annals of the New York Academy of Sciences, 280*, 868–884.

Marshall, J. C. (1976) Neuropsychological aspects of orthographic representation. In R. J. Wales & E. Walker (Eds.), *New approaches to language mechanisms*. Amsterdam: North-Holland.

Marshall, J. C., & Newcombe, F. (1966) Syntactic and semantic errors in paralexia. *Neuropsychologia, 4*, 169–174.

Marshall, J. C., & Newcombe, F. (1973) Patterns of paralexia: A psycholinguistic approach. *Journal of Psycholinguistic Research, 2*, 175–199.

Marshall, J. C., & Newcombe, F. (1977). Variability and constraint in acquired alexia. In H. Whitaker & H. A. Whitaker (Eds.), *Studies in neurolinguistics* (Vol. 3). New York: Academic Press.

Marshall, M., Newcombe, F., & Marshall, J. C. (1970) The microstructure of wordfinding difficulties in a dysphasic subject. In G. B. Flores d'Arcais & M. J. M. Levelt (Eds.), *Advances in psycholinguistics*. Amsterdam: North-Holland.

Morton, J. (1979) Word recognition. In J. Morton & J. C. Marshall (Eds.), *Psycholinguistic series II*. London: Elek Scientific Books.

Morton, J., & Patterson, K. E. (1980) A new attempt at an interpretation or an attempt at a new interpretation. In M. Coltheart, K. E. Patterson, & J. C. Marshall (Eds.), *Deep dyslexia*. London: Routledge and Kegan Paul.

Patterson, K. E. (1978) Phonemic dyslexia: Errors of meaning and the meaning of errors. *Quarterly Journal of Experimental Psychology, 30*, 587–601.

Patterson, K. E. (1979) What is right with "deep" dyslexic patients? *Brain and Language, 8*, 111–129.

Patterson, K. E., & Marcel, T. (1977) Aphasia, dyslexia and the phonological coding of written words. *Quarterly Journal of Experimental Psychology, 29*, 307–318.

Péré, J. J. (1978) *L'alexie sans agraphie*. Unpublished doctoral dissertation, Université de Bordeaux II.

Poppelreuter, W. (1917) *Die psychischen Schädigungen durch Kopfschuss im Kriege, 1914–1916*. Leipzig: Voss.

Pötzl, O. (1928) Die optisch-agnostischen Störungen. Vienna: F. Deuticke.

Richardson, J. T. E. (1975) The effect of word imageability in acquired dyslexia. *Neuropsychologia, 13*, 281–288.

Saffran, E. M. (1980) Reading in deep dyslexia is not ideographic. *Neuropsychologia, 18*, 219–224.

Saffran, E. M., & Marin, O. S. M. (1977) Reading without phonology: Evidence from aphasia. *Quarterly Journal of Experimental Psychology, 29*, 515–525.

Saffran, E. M., Schwartz, M. F., & Marin, O. S. M. (1976) Semantic mechanisms in paralexia. *Brain and Language, 3*, 255–265.

Sasanuma, S. (1973) Kanji and kana processing in alexia without agraphia. *Logopedics–Phoniatrics Annual Bulletin*, University of Tokyo, *7*, 77–92.

Sasanuma, S. (1974) Kanji versus kana processing in alexia with transient agraphia a case report. *Cortex, 10*, 89–97.

Sasanuma, S., & Fujimura, O. (1970). Selective impairment of phonetic and non-phonetic transcription of words in Japanese aphasic patients: Kana vs kanji in visual recognition and writing. *Cortex, 7*, 1–18.

Sasanuma, S., & Fujimura, O. (1972) An analysis of writing errors in Japanese aphasic patients: Kanji versus kana words. *Cortex, 8,* 265–282.

Sasanuma, S., & Monoi, H. (1975) The syndrome of Gogi (word-meaning) aphasia: Selective impairment of kanji processing. *Neurology, 25,* 627–632.

Schwartz, M. F., Saffran, E. A., & Marin, O. S. M. (1977) *An analysis of agrammatic reading in aphasia.* Paper presented at the International Neuropsychological Society, Santa Fe, February 1977.

Shallice, T., & Warrington, E. K. (1975) Word recognition in a phonemic dyslexic patient. *Quarterly Journal of Experimental Psychology, 27,* 187–199.

Shallice, T., & Warrington, E. (1977) The possible role of selective attention in acquired dyslexia. *Neuropsychologia, 15,* 31–41.

Shallice, T., & Warrington, E. (1980) Single and multiple component central dyslexic syndromes. In M. Coltheart, K. E. Patterson, & J. C. Marshall (Eds.), *Deep dyslexia.* London: Routledge and Kegan Paul.

Sroka, H., Solsi, P., & Bornstein, B. (1975) Alexia without agraphia with complete recovery. *Confinia Neurologica, 35,* 167–176.

Stachowiak, F. J., & Poeck, K. (1976) Functional dysconnection in pure alexia and color naming deficit demonstrated by facilitation methods. *Brain and Language, 3,* 135–143.

Stockert, Th. von (1972) Recognition of syntactic structure in aphasia. *Cortex, 8,* 323–334.

Stockert, Th. von, & Bader, L. (1976) Some relations of grammar and lexicon in aphasia. *Cortex, 12,* 49–60.

Warrington, E., & Shallice, T. (1979) Semantic access dyslexia. *Brain, 102,* 43–63.

Warrington, E., & Shallice, T. (1980). Word form dyslexia. *Brain, 103,* 99–112.

Williams, P. C., & Parkin, A. J. (1980) On knowing the meaning of words we are unable to report—Confirmation of a guessing explanation. *Quarterly Journal of Experimental Psychology, 32,* 101–107.

Yamadori, A. (1975) Ideogram reading in alexia. *Brain, 98,* 231–238.

Yamadori, A., & Ikumura, G. (1975) Central (or conduction) aphasia in a Japanese patient. *Cortex, 11,* 73–82.

Part Three

Treatment

Chapter Sixteen

Neuropsychologically Based Remedial Reading Procedures: Some Possibilities

JAMES R. EVANS

INTRODUCTION

The rapidly increasing interest in brain–behavior relationships shown by professionals from many disciplines is reflected clearly in the proliferation of research and writing on the topic. The major emphasis, however, has been on demonstrating the nature of the relationships and methods of evaluating them rather than on the remediation of their abnormalities. This is to be expected considering the relatively short history of fields such as neuropsychology and the recency of many research findings with potential for therapeutic application. Thus, it

371

also is not surprising that in the more specific area of reading disability one finds much more literature dealing with theories and tests of neurological dysfunction and their relationship to reading than with related remedial treatment methods. In fact, many consider that the latter would be premature, that much greater explication of the nature of neuropsychologically based reading disorders necessarily must precede development of remediation strategies. However, I would argue that there are many remedial implications of neuropsychological research findings which, if carefully developed and applied with conservative expectations, might be of great value to many of the present generation of poor readers. Furthermore, the successes and failures of such techniques should facilitate generation of new theories and refinement of present theories of brain–reading-behavior relationships, resulting in greater precision in future remedial procedures.

There already have been some applications of neuropsychological knowledge and theory to remediation of learning disorders, including reading. The main purposes of this chapter are to provide an overview of some such techniques presently in use, and to propose others which have potential application. Although the emphasis will be on techniques that are being used or could be used with reading-disabled children, in most cases the techniques and suggestions could relate as well to adults with reading disorders. Although the techniques discussed might benefit any poor reader, it is likely that they would be most appropriate for persons with severe reading disorders, especially those commonly referred to by terms such as "dyslexia" and "specific reading disability." Persons with a general mental retardation are unlikely to learn to read with comprehension through these methods. And those with reading retardation associated primarily with lack of past educational opportunity should respond to more conventional teaching approaches. This chapter will consider only procedures that could be applied by nonmedically trained persons, such as teachers, psychologists, and physical and occupational therapists. Thus, for example, there will be no coverage of methods involving medications or diet, even though these may be neuropsychological in nature and effective in some cases of reading disorder.

HISTORICAL BACKGROUND

Multisensory Approaches

The first attempts of any significant magnitude to apply knowledge and theory of brain–behavior relationships to reading problems and other specific learning disabilities appear to have been those related to the work of Samuel Orton and of Alfred Strauss and Heinz Werner. Several of Orton's associates (e.g., Beth Stillman, Anna Gillingham, Marion Monroe, and Grace Fernald) devised remedial programs partially based upon his theory of mixed or confused hemispheric dominance as a cause of many cases of severe reading disability. These programs incorporated multisensory approaches, in which visual, auditory, kinesthetic, and/or tactile representations of letters and words were taught. These so-called VAKT techniques are believed by some (e.g., Gillingham & Stillman, 1936) to develop stronger intersensory language-pattern associations in the dominant hemisphere, thus alleviating or eliminating mixed dominance. Such techniques have proven effective in many cases. They remain popular among reading remediation specialists, despite some warnings (e.g., Johnson & Myklebust, 1967) that they may "overload" the nervous systems of some persons and thus actually lower learning efficiency. It is a rather common practice today to "experiment" with the VAKT approach in individual cases by varying systematically the senses simultaneously stimulated (or blocked)—for example, V–A with no K–T, V–K–T with A ignored (or partially or completely blocked, as with ear plugs).

Perceptual–Motor Training

The work of Strauss and Werner with brain-injured mentally retarded children in the 1930s and 1940s stimulated the development of many teaching procedures which were believed to help compensate for some behavioral effects of brain damage. These researchers noted among these children a high incidence of perseveration, need for orderliness, extreme emotional reactivity to some normally innocuous situations, perceptual handicaps, and perceptual–motor problems. Laura Lehtinen, an educator and a colleague of Strauss, coauthored with him a text in which some specific remedial suggestions were made. In this text, *Psychopathology and Education of the Brain Injured Child*, Volume I (Strauss & Lehtinen, 1947) it was recommended, for example, that daily routines be established, that small group instruction be used, and that perceptual processing be facilitated by enhancing the "figure" (stimuli to be attended to) while reducing "background" distractions. The latter was to be accomplished by procedures such as requiring teachers to wear plain clothing, covering windows, permitting the child to face the wall while working, and eliminating decorations from classrooms. Although subsequent research has not strongly supported these environmental manipulation techniques as *generally* applicable to nonretarded children diagnosed as brain injured or learning disabled, there are many individual cases of their successful use reported by clinicians and teachers, including reading teachers.

It seems foolish to ignore these approaches when working with adults with reading disorders. Some may show more efficient learning when remedial procedures are routinized and/or when perceptual problems partially are compensated for by minimizing background distractions. Quiet areas for the remedial sessions, use of wider spacing between words and lines of print, and permitting the use of a finger, a cover sheet, or a paper with a "window" cut out of it to maintain one's place during reading are specific examples of ways to minimize visual perceptual difficulties of the "figure–background differentiation" type.

MOVEMENT THERAPIES

Theoretical Foundations

Several others who worked with Strauss and Werner adapted many of their ideas to remedial work with children of average or higher general intelligence who showed learning and/or behavioral disorders with or without specific evidence of brain injury. Newell Kephart and William Cruickshank have been among the most influential of these. Many specific remedial suggestions can be found in their texts (e.g., Strauss & Kephart, 1955; Kephart, 1971; Cruickshank, 1967). These writers focused on visual perceptual and perceptual-motor aspects of learning disabilities and were responsible in large part for the popularity of "perceptual-motor" approaches to remediation of reading and other learning disorders in the 1950s and 1960s. Although such approaches are less popular today, there are remedial specialists who continue to stress "motor approaches," "movement education," or "somatic education." These tend most often to be specialists in adaptive physical education, occupational therapy, or physical therapy. Most share the beliefs that efficient motor learning is a prerequisite for subsequent normal development of perceptual and cognitive skills. For example, de Quiros and Schrager (1979) hold that "knowledge starts through intentional coordinated motor activities [p. 49]," and Hanna (1980) states that thinking is a motor act and mental abilities are motor abilities. Evidence (de Quiros & Schrager, 1979) that nerve fibers intimately related to movement (e.g., vestibular and cerebellar tracts) are among the first to myelinate is said to give credence to the basic position of the motor system in learning. Furthermore, there are reports that disproportionately large numbers of children with reading and other learning disabilities show indications of vestibular and cerebellar dysfunctions (Frank & Levinson, 1973), have failed to have integrated vestibular impulses adequately with proprioceptive, tactile, and other sensory input, and/or have failed to have outgrown completely various "progravity" reflexes such as the tonic neck reflex (Ayres, 1972). Such neurological abnormalities are said to result in difficulty in organizing, integrating, and timing movements, thus causing some degree of clumsiness and dysrhythmia of movement. Especially relevant to language would be the resultant difficulties with eye movements and the sequential movements required for speech and for handwriting. A related notion is that only when movements are correctly integrated and timed and performed "automatically" (without conscious effort) can higher brain centers be "freed" to permit efficiency in cognitive learning.

Treatment Strategies

Movement therapists use a variety of remedial activities, such as having children engage in specific swinging, spinning, rolling, and balancing activities designed to "trigger" antigravity responses in order to facilitate integration of vestibular–cerebellar impulses with each other and with other senses, and to enable normal or more nearly normal movement patterns in general.

Although most movement therapists work only with children, perhaps some adults with learning problems could profit from attention to motor patterns. Some specialists in neurodevelopmental treatment (NDT), that is, the Bobath (1971) method of working with cerebral palsied persons, have considered the application of movement education to children and adults with reading disabilities. In this approach, emphasis is placed upon both inhibition of abnormal reflexes and other movement and facilitation of normal movement patterns. The Feldenkrais (1972) "functional integration" technique, which stresses a necessary link between thinking and moving, also is being applied with persons of all ages. The Feldenkrais methods are designed to help a person gain conscious awareness and control of movement patterns which formerly were unconscious and maladaptive. Such movement abnormalities supposedly can arise from neurological damage or can be learned responses to frustration, anger, and other negative emotions. Investigation of efficacy of Feldenkrais and NDT methods with certain reading-disabled adults seems warranted, especially where abnormal movement patterns exist and appear to interfere significantly with reading behavior.

HEMISPHERIC SPECIALIZATION OF FUNCTION

As noted earlier, abnormal interaction between the right and left cerebral hemispheres has been implicated for some time as a basic cause of many reading disabilities. Although the notions of Orton regarding lack of hemispheric dominance have been seriously questioned, brain research during the past decade has resulted in revived interest in hemispheric function. It has been demonstrated many times that the left hemisphere in the majority of persons is the more efficient for processing of most aspects of language whereas the right generally is more efficient for holistic functions such as are intimately involved in processing of many visuospatial, musical, and perhaps emotion-arousing stimuli. Evidence for a high incidence of abnormal hemispheric function and/or structure in persons with reading disability has been found, ranging from the often conflicting findings of dichotic listening, visual half field, and dichoptic stimulus presentation research (e.g., Kimura, 1967; Witelson, 1977) to some CAT scan and autopsy evidence which seems indisputable (Hier, LeMay, Rosenberger, & Perlo, 1978; Galaburda & Kemper, 1979).

Theoretical Foundations

In addition to Orton's idea of lack of "dominance" of one hemisphere over the other, there have been other hypotheses regarding hemispheric abnormality. These include (a) left hemisphere dysfunction or weakness; (b) excessive dominance and/or interference by the right hemisphere (possibly, but not necessarily, due to left hemisphere dysfunction); (c) inadequate interhemispheric integration (sometimes discussed as poor spatial–verbal integration); and (d) right hemisphere dysfunction or weakness. Although this last is rarely mentioned as a basic cause of reading disability, it has been seen as a possible factor in cases where visual perceptual problems are the major symptoms. Each of these possibilities seems plausible, and each suggests the basis for a different subtype of reading disability with specific neuropsychologically based remedial procedures. A major problem, of course, involves making accurate diagnoses of the nature of hemispheric dysfunction. Presently available educational and neuropsychological tests permit only indirect inferences concerning brain function. However, such tests are being refined, and, along with somewhat more direct measures such as the "neurometric" computerized EEG measurement approach of E. Roy John (1977), they should make it possible to obtain increasingly accurate information on nature of hemispheric function abnormalities.

Treatment Strategies

There have been some reports of remedial procedures based on theories of hemispheric function. Delacato (1966), somewhat like Orton before him, advocated development of lateral dominance in treatment of reading disorders. In this case lateral dominance apparently was equated with unilateral usage of eye, ear, hand, and foot, and was to be facilitated by patching the eye, blocking the ear, and/or placing the arm in a sling on the side that was to become nondominant. In addition, the reading-disabled person was to refrain from listening to music as this might excessively stimulate the nondominant hemisphere. This approach has been severely criticized as overly rigid, not supported by well-controlled research, and based on scientifically unsound reasoning. For example, patching an eye should not facilitate hemispheric dominance as visual input from each eye now is known to be projected to both hemispheres. It seems probable, however, that there were some successes with use of these procedures; and perhaps these were particularly with persons whose reading problems were based on hemispheric conflict, that is, failure of one hemisphere (presumably the left in the vast majority of cases) to become dominant during most language-processing activities.

More recent research on hemispheric function has led to some creative approaches to remediation. Van de Honert (1977) used a stereo tape recorder and headphones and had learning-disabled children listen to music in the left ear and words from a spelling list in the right. Because left-ear input is known to be projected initially primarily to the right hemisphere, it was felt that the music might engage that hemisphere in a type of processing for which it commonly is specialized, thus freeing the left side from right side interference and enabling it more efficiently to process verbal materials (spelling words in this case). Van den Honert reported major gains in language function, including reading, among two groups of children. Bakker (1981) used very similar techniques in an experimental study of reading remediation techniques in the Netherlands. In addition to the selective ear presentation of musical and verbal stimuli, he selectively presented visual verbal stimuli to be learned (e.g., words) to visual hemifields. Decisions concerning which stimuli were to be presented initially to which hemisphere were based in part on results of dichotic listening tests. Bakker reported encouraging results.

The Van den Honert and Bakker techniques may be most appropriate for those cases of reading disability in which there is interference in language processing (presumably left hemisphere) by strategies less efficient for the analytic, sequential nature of language. Such interference may be in the form of bias toward use of holistic or simultaneous processing strategies (presumably most often functions of the right hemisphere) which, in turn, may be the result of overdevelopment of the right hemisphere, weakness of the left, abnormally great holistic processing-type representation in the left, or some combination of these factors.

There have been other approaches to language skills development using somewhat similar principles. The "suggestology" method developed by Lozanov (1978) purports to teach foreign languages very rapidly by techniques that include listening to classical music simultaneously with hearing the words to be learned. Other features of the approach include exercises in mental imagery and "mental relaxation," as well as the provision of positive suggestions. There have been reports of successful uses of suggestology with children who learn normally, but apparently it has not yet been applied in remedial settings.

Language therapists working with aphasic persons have been able to facilitate rehabilitation of language skills by use of "melodic intonation therapy" (Sparks, Helm, & Martin, 1974; Berlin, 1976). This therapy involves embedding short phrases or sentences to be learned into simple melody patterns. The fact that some aphasic patients with damage to language centers of their left hemispheres can sing the phrases or sentences (and often later speak them and regain much language usage) suggests that music may stimulate and increase the role of the right hemisphere in language. If so, an extension of therapy of this general type to cases of reading disability may be warranted. Persons whose reading disabilities are due to a damaged, dysfunctioning, or otherwise weak language (usually left) hemisphere but who have an intact nonlanguage hemisphere may profit from the presentation in a musical context of words to be learned. Bottari (1980) attempted something similar in a study comparing the memory skills for verbal material of 9–11-year-old learning-disabled children with high visuospatial and low verbal skills (presumably right hemisphere biased) to those of children with the opposite skills pattern (presumably left hemisphere biased). Stories were presented as songs or simply read to the subjects. The method of presentation did not differentially affect retention scores of the high verbal children, but, as predicted, the group with high visuospatial and low verbal skills had significantly better retention scores for verbal material presented via singing.

Growing numbers of educators are showing interest in topics such as the "education of both halves of the brain." Many such educators express the belief that American schools have too long neglected education of presumably "right hemisphere" skills such as music, art, drawing, metaphorical reasoning, visualizing, dream interpretation, body movement (as in dance), and certain forms of creativity. Some have developed specific techniques for teaching development of such skills in the regular classroom. For example, Edwards (1979) discusses methods of drawing designed to "confuse or override" the dominant left hemisphere, such as drawing upside down and drawing just edges and contours which cannot be labeled verbally. There seem to be some implications here for remediation of certain types of reading disability. Perhaps creative uses of art and visualization as a vehicle for learning verbal materials can be developed in a manner similar to that employed by Bottari with music. As Gazzaniga (1974) notes, a cognitive system (imagery, in this case) working in parallel with the language system might come to one's aid following left brain damage. He and others have found major improvement in verbal memory following imagery training. Finally, in those relatively infrequent cases where a reading disability seems due primarily to a right hemisphere weakness (isolated visual perceptual problems), techniques such as those of Edwards may be of rather direct benefit.

Although, as is usually the case, most of the activities discussed have been used primarily with children, there is the strong possibility that they also could be effective with certain adults. In fact, I have known remedial reading specialists who have successfully used with adults techniques that easily can be perceived as "teaching through the right hemisphere" or teaching verbal material via holistic strategies. For example, a severely reading-disabled middle-aged man made his greatest progress when the "experience story" approach was combined with observation of pictures he took of his experiences, and when emphasis was placed on learning to read words with easily visualizable referents and/or with high emotional value.

Disorders of Interhemispheric Integration

Another type of hypothesized hemispheric abnormality in some cases of reading disability is lack of adequate interhemispheric integration. Because of the temporal (sequential over time) nature of much of (auditory) language, and the spatial nature of much visual processing, this topic often is seen as relating to time–space and/or auditory–visual integration. These functions often have been reported as impaired in reading-disabled persons (e.g., Birch & Belmont, 1964; Hatchette, 1979). Occasionally there is reference to possible corpus callosum malfunction in these cases of apparent interhemispheric transfer difficulties.

Galin (1974) has speculated that disruption of hemispheric integration may be learned in some cases. For example, a child who is presented conflicting messages from a parent such as "I love you" stated verbally (left hemisphere), and, "I resent you" communicated nonverbally through gestures (right hemisphere) may avoid this conflict and related anxiety by learning to inhibit corpus callosum activity. If so, this might result not only in lack of ability to verbalize experiences of certain emotions, but also in difficulty in learning to read. The latter would be expected as reading involves both perceiving visual forms (i.e., of letters and words) (right hemisphere) and assigning verbal meaning to them (left hemisphere).

In such cases of learned hemispheric disconnection, psychotherapy may be the most appropriate remedial strategy, and might center around helping the client become able to verbalize emotional experiences. Education-based remedial approaches to facilitate interhemispheric integration could take many forms ranging from movement training using various balancing activities requiring continuous interweaving of right and left body side activities, to practice in activities requiring visual spatial–auditory sequential integration. Other approaches could use tachistoscopic, dichotic, and/or dichaptic procedures to present part of a stimulus to one hemisphere and a second part to the other and then require recognition of the whole.

RHYTHMIC ASPECTS OF LANGUAGE

Theoretical Foundations

Reading involves the sequential processing of words within paragraphs, sentences, or phrases in order to perceive and express correct syntax and meaning, as well as the sequential processing of the order of syllables and letters within words in order to recognize and "call" them. In fact, at even more basic levels it may involve appreciation of correct ordering of aspects of sound within phonemes. Normal oral reading also entails appreciation of accent patterns, that is, the sequential recurrence of strong and weak elements at the word and phrase levels of language. Efficient eye movements during reading also involve a coordinated sequencing of oculomotor muscle activity. Thus, the act of reading appears to necessitate a simultaneous processing or "orchestration" of several different sequences. Each of these sequences is constrained to some degree by the structure of the language; that is, they do not vary randomly. The totality of these sequences, or rhythms, may form a hierarchical pattern unique to reading and, if so, any defect in rhythm appreciation should cause some degree of reading disability.

The movement therapists have, as mentioned earlier, stressed the commonly observed lack of proper timing (rhythmicity) of movements in children with specific learning disabilities. The term "dyssynchronous child" is one of the many terms that have been used synonymously with the currently more popular "learning-disabled child." Perception of synchrony, the simultaneous occurrence in time of two or more events, is probably necessary not only for smooth movement patterns, but also for appreciation of any hierarchically arranged pattern of rhythms (i.e., rhythms embedded within rhythms), as are believed to be involved in reading.

Research Findings

Empirical evidence for the presence of dysrhythmia and dyssynchrony in some reading-disabled children comes from the research of Condon (1975). Using techniques of "linguistic–kinestic" sound–film analysis he observed a "self-synchrony" involving the simultaneous occurrence of organized units (patterns) of a normally functioning person's movement with specific aspects of his or her speech (syllables, words). Furthermore, he found that listeners very often moved in precise shared synchrony with the speaker's speech, as if entrainment were occurring and the two were engaged in a type of dance. This, however, did not occur for a group of 17 autistic children and a group of 8 children with reading problems. These children appeared to respond to sound more than once, when it actually occurred and up to a full second later, thus losing both the self-synchrony and speaker–listener synchrony. Condon suggested that there is "some degree of neurological involvement" in this dyssynchrony, and that such children might benefit by being shielded from excessive noise and spoken to quietly and in short sequences in order to help avoid sound overlap.

Martin (1972) also investigated rhythmic aspects of language, and he found them to be important for aspects of learning to read. Using computer auditing of sound sequences, he disrupted rhythm by deleting bits of sound from spoken passages and measured listener comprehension before and after such deletion. Comprehension scores were lower with the disruption, even though listeners said they were unaware of any sound omissions in the message. Martin, Meltzer, and Mills (1978) have applied findings on the importance of rhythm in language to improvement of reading skills. In this research they used a computer program to present words on a television screen at the same rhythm as a speaker's speech. Oral reading fluency after training with sentences presented in this manner was greater than when reading material was presented in the usual fashion. This, of course, suggests some possible new remedial reading approaches. It also may relate to the "neurological impress" remedial approach (Heckelman, 1969) in which a teacher reads orally at a normal pace, with the reading-disabled student attempting to read the same passage simultaneously. When reading improvement is shown with this technique, it may be because the language dysrhythmia of the pupil has been decreased through a form of entrainment from continuing close exposure to the normal language rhythm of the teacher.

The notion of rhythm hierarchies as basic to language seems consonant with the writings of Pribram (e.g., Pribram & Goleman, 1979), who considers the brain to function as an analyzer of spatial and temporal frequencies. Auditory, visual, and somatosensory perception as well as memory are said to be based largely on the brain's capacity to, in effect, perform a Fourier analysis of a complex stimulus pattern (i.e., a wave form pattern), breaking it down into its component frequencies. Pribram cites research by Bernstein (1967) in which movies were taken, against a black background, of persons dressed in black leotards with white dots painted on their elbows and other joints. Movies of these people in action showed only white dots moving up and down along the film, creating wave forms. Fourier analysis of the wave forms at a point in the sequence enabled accurate prediction of location of subsequent steps in the sequence. Perhaps similar processes are active in normal reading, with the brain constantly performing Fourier analyses of the rhythmic structure of the language. At least for oral reading, it is likely that this would make reading more efficient because sound and movement (speech articulator) patterns at any given point in time would predict subsequent sound and movement patterns. Any deficiency in the brain's frequency analysis capabilities might result in fluency impairments. And, if the latter is impaired it seems likely that comprehension also would suffer.

Possible Treatment Strategies

If dysrhythmia and dyssynchrony are in fact basic to many reading problems, there is a need for remedial procedures that relate directly to these underlying problems. Rhythm training is, of course, an inherent aspect of many of the movement therapies; and, as mentioned earlier, both Condon's suggestions and the neurological impress method may be applicable. Perhaps if there is a characteristic rhythmic structure to the English language, this could be described mathematically and incorporated into the structure of sentences and paragraphs in remedial reading texts, as well as into movement therapies, including dance therapies. I have used a similar notion (Evans, 1972) in an approach labeled "multiple simultaneous sensory stimulation." On the assumption that dysrhythmic brain activity might become more organized by the person's being subjected to organized and correlated multisensory input, severely retarded subjects were exposed to children's songs accompanied by lights which changed in intensity and color in synchrony with amplitude and frequency characteristics of the music. Limited gains in movement and language functions were shown by some subjects. Variations of this procedure might prove useful for both child and adult poor readers who show evidence of dysrhythmia. Modern technology should permit a precise relating of many aspects of rhythmic sound patterns to aspects of visual stimuli; and it may be possible to synchronize these with intentional movements in order, perhaps through a form of entrainment, to develop an inherent and durable rhythmicity within the individual. Improved intersensory integration could be an incidental by-product of such procedures.

BIOFEEDBACK

Research Findings

Several researchers have applied biofeedback procedures to treatment of learning disabilities. The term "biofeedback" refers here to procedures in which an external sensor is used to provide a person with information about the state of some bodily process of which he or she would otherwise not be clearly aware, usually in order to help that person change the process being measured. For a review of the literature on such applications with children see Cobb and Evans (1981). Electromyographic (EMG) and electroencephalographic (EEG) biofeedback procedures most often have been used. Children generally have been able to learn both muscle tension and EEG control, but concomitant improvement in academic skills was infrequent. And those studies in which improvement was found usually were those which were less well designed.

Because anxiety is believed often to accompany and disrupt reading attempts by persons with reading disorders, it seems plausible that exercises in deep relaxation, whether using meditation, hypnosis, biofeedback, or other procedures, could prove useful. The relaxation might transfer to specific life situations, including reading. This may well be true in individual cases, but research to date has not indicated it to be a usual result of biofeedback.

Possible Treatment Strategies

The vast majority of biofeedback research has been done within the last 8 years. Perhaps its earlier promise as a treatment for learning problems will be realized when better controlled studies are completed, providing feedback relating to more complex patterns of internal bodily function. For example, EEG biofeedback might be used to help a reading-disabled person learn to "activate" selectively one cerebral hemisphere while simultaneously "deactivating" the other, for example, to develop a predominance of higher (beta) frequency activity in one hemisphere and a predominance of lower (alpha) frequency activity in the other. Another possibility would be to use feedback to train coupling or coherence of EEG activity among brain sites within and/or between hemispheres. Specific patterns of activation–deactivation or of coherence found to characterize good readers might be developed in poor readers through biofeedback. My finding (Evans, 1977) of a specific pattern of cortical coupling in the left angular gyrus area of the brain in good readers and that of Leisman (1981) regarding a unique coherence pattern among good readers might be used as guides in this regard.

Perhaps, given that reading appears normally to be an act involving simultaneous (or near simultaneous) visuospatial and linguistic processing, it may be that it requires a flexible, reciprocal interweaving or "orchestration" of dominance of right and left hemisphere activity. As is well-known, women and girls have a much lower incidence of specific reading disability. Goleman (1978) cites research indicating that women's cerebral hemispheres not only seem less specialized along verbal–spatial lines, but also show more selective, task-appropriate activation–deactivation patterns. Electroencephalographic biofeedback training of the pattern type described earlier might be conceptualized as training in flexibility of brain electrical activity—and the possibility exists that flexibility in this activity may facilitate flexibility in the perceptual and cognitive processes underlying reading.

SUMMARY AND CONCLUSIONS

This chapter has presented an overview of actual and potential remedial reading procedures based on neuropsychological research.

During the early and mid 1900s observations of the unique learning problems of persons with known brain damage stimulated development of specific activities designed to help remediate reading and other learning disabilities. Most of these activities were based on the belief that perceptual and/or motor disorders are present in children with specific learning problems whether or not there is independent evidence of actual brain damage or dysfunction. Members of several professions involved with reading-disabled populations continue to use some of these activities. This is especially true of those who use multisensory (VAKT) techniques, and of the "movement educators" who believe in the necessity of coordinated movement patterns for efficient learning. Some recent research on behavioral results of dysfunctions of neural structures involving the cerebellum and vestibular apparatus supports these beliefs. The continuing use of perceptual–motor-related treatments suggests their effectiveness with at least some types of reading-disabled children. Their use with certain adults also may be warranted.

Recent research on hemispheric specialization of function has also been applied in innovative ways to remedial activities. In most cases these activities involve either "engaging" the right hemisphere in some activity (e.g., music) during language lessons in an effort to reduce its hypothesized inappropriate interference, or teaching language skills in "right hemisphere" ways, for example, through imagery and music. There remains much opportunity for devising innovative remedial techniques in this area, including some designed to facilitate efficiency of interhemispheric communication.

Speculation on the nervous system's frequency analysis function in perception and memory provides support for the basic role dysrhythmia and dyssynchrony could play in reading disorders. The rhythmic nature of language along with recent research indicating a high incidence of various dysrhythmias among reading-disabled children suggests new directions for remedial approaches. Perhaps rhythmic movement activities coordinated with visual and auditory patterns would decrease reading-related dysrhythmia.

Attempts to use EMG and EEG biofeedback procedures with children evidencing various types of learning problems have not provided strong support for its efficacy. However, investigation of new approaches providing feedback of more complex patterns of body function (e.g., flexibility of hemispheric EEG activation–deactivation patterns) is believed to be warranted.

There was no attempt here to consider all possible applications of neuropsychological research to reading problems. For example, there was no mention of treatment of memory or attentional disorders underlying reading disability; and treatment procedures requiring medical supervision were omitted.

Although all approaches discussed could apply to adults, most have been used primarily with children. The reading problems of adults surely differ considerably from those of children. Adults have had a longer history of reading failure and might be expected to be less optimistic about their chances to improve. The commonly held view that brain plasticity is much less in adults also would be expected to bias remedial teachers toward pessimistic views of chances of remedial success. Furthermore, by adulthood most poor readers have learned to compensate to some degree for basic deficiencies in reading aptitude, and such compensation may have involved development of perceptual and cognitive strategies incompatible with development of efficient reading skills.

Because of these factors, remedial procedures used with adults may be effective only when accompanied by counseling concerning nature of the reading disorder, by the development of positive, yet realistic, expectations of success in both teacher and student, the lowering of reading failure-related anxiety, and by an effort to dismantle existing inefficient reading strategies. And, of course, with reading-disabled persons of all ages, it is important that the techniques used relate to the presumed basic cause of the individual's disability.

Although I would view many of the remedial approaches described in this chapter to be creative, if speculative, they may well be viewed in a less desirable light—for example as "fanciful"—by more conservative researchers and teachers. Educators frequently ignore or even actively oppose neuropsychologically based diagnostic and remedial procedures. This probably results from some combination of lack of training and/or interest in brain–behavior relationships, past failures of "promising" physiologically based techniques, and fear of diminution of the teacher's role in remediation. Fortunately, however, it appears that this situation is changing rapidly. At least one major university is about to begin an educational neurosciences program, seminars on "educating both halves of the brain" are well attended by educators in many parts of the country, and recent brain–behavior research increasingly is demonstrating definite relevance to educational practice. It should be noted that most of the procedures speculated upon in this chapter, if effective, would serve only to develop a state of reading "readiness" in students; more traditional reading instruction would continue to be needed. Yet if ideas such as those presented in this chapter stimulate further basic and applied research and cooperation among neuroscientists and educators, and eventually influence remedial reading activities, there is no doubt that both students and teachers will benefit.

REFERENCES

Ayres, A. (1972) *Sensory integration and learning disorders.* Los Angeles: Western Psychological Services.
Bakker, D. (1981) Hemispheric specific dyslexia models. In R. N. Malatesha & L. C. Harthage (Eds.), *Neuropsychology and cognition* (Vol. 1). Aalphen aan den Rijn, The Netherlands: Sijthoff and Noordhoff.
Berlin, C. (1976) On "Melodic intonation therapy for aphasia" by R. W. Sparks and A. L. Holland. *Journal of Speech and Hearing Disorders, 41,* 287–297.
Bernstein, N. (1967) *The coordination and regulation of movements.* Elmsford, N.Y.: Pergamon.
Birch, H., & Belmont, L. (1964) Auditory–visual integration in normal and retarded readers. *American Journal of Orthopsychiatry, 34,* 852–861.
Bobath, B. (1971) *Abnormal postural reflex activity caused by brain lesions.* London: Heinemann.
Bottari, S. (1980) *Effects of musical context, type of vocal presentation and time on the verbal retention abilities of visual-spatially oriented and verbally oriented learning disabled children.* Unpublished doctoral dissertation, University of South Carolina.
Cobb, D., & Evans, J. (1981) The use of biofeedback techniques with school aged children exhibiting behavioral and/or learning problems. *Journal of Abnormal Child Psychology, 9,* 251–281.
Condon, W. (1975) Multiple response to sound in dysfunctional children. *Journal of Autism and Childhood Schizophrenia, 5,* 37–56.
Cruickshank, W. (1967) *The brain injured child in home, school and community.* Syracuse, N.Y.: Syracuse University Press.
Delacato, C. (1966) *Neurological organization and reading.* Springfield, Ill.: Charles C Thomas.
de Quiros, J., & Schrager, O. (1979) *Neuropsychological fundamentals in learning disabilities.* Novato, Calif.: Academic Therapy Publications.
Edwards, B. (1979) *Drawing on the right side of the brain.* New York: St. Martin's Press.
Evans, J. (1972) *Multiple simultaneous sensory stimulation with severely retarded children.* Paper presented at the meeting of the Southeastern Psychological Association, Atlanta, 1972.
Evans, J. (1977) A cortical coupling pattern differentiating good from poor readers. *International Journal of Neuroscience, 7,* 211–216.
Feldenkrais, M. (1972) *Awareness through movement.* New York: Harper & Row.
Frank, J., & Levinson, H. (1973) Dysmetric dyslexia and dyspraxia. *Journal of the American Academy of Child Psychiatry, 12,* 690–701.
Galaburda, A., & Kemper, T. (1979) Cytoarchitectonic abnormalities in developmental dyslexia: A case study. *Annals of Neurology, 6,* 94–100.
Galin, D. (1974) Implications for psychiatry of left and right cerebral specialization. *Archives of General Psychiatry, 31,* 572–583.

388 *James R. Evans*

Gazzaniga, M. (1974) Determinants of cerebral recovery. In D. Stein, J. Rosen, & N. Butters (Eds.), *Plasticity and recovery of function in the central nervous system*. New York: Academic Press.

Gillingham, A., & Stillman, B. (1936) *Remedial work for reading, spelling and penmanship*. New York: Hackett & Wilhelms.

Goleman, D. (1978) Special abilities of the sexes: Do they begin in the brain? *Psychology Today*, November 1978, pp. 48–59; 120.

Hanna, T. (1980) *The body of life*. New York: Knopf.

Hatchette, R. (1979) *Auditory–visual and temporal–spatial pattern matching performance of two types of learning disabled children*. Unpublished doctoral dissertation, University of South Carolina.

Heckelman, R. G. (1969) A neurological impress method of remedial reading. *Academic Therapy, 4*, 277–282.

Hier, D., LeMay, M., Bosenberger, P., & Perlo, V. (1978) Developmental dyslexia: Evidence for a subgroup with a reversal of cerebral asymmetry. *Archives of Neurology, 35*, 90–92.

John, E. R. (1977) *Functional neuroscience* (Vol. 2). Hillsdale, N.J.: Lawrence Erlbaum.

Johnson, D., & Myklebust, H. (1967) *Learning disabilities: Educational principles and practices*. New York: Grune & Stratton.

Kephart, N. (1971) *The slow learner in the classroom*, (2nd ed.). Columbus, Ohio: Charles E. Merrill.

Kimura, D. (1967) Functional asymmetry of the brain in dichotic listening. *Cortex, 3*, 163–178.

Leisman, G. (1981) Cerebral hemispheres and dyslexia. In R. N. Malstesha & L. C. Harthage (Eds.), *Neuropsychology and cognition* (Vol. 2). Aalphen aan den Rijn, the Netherlands: Sijthoff and Noordhoff.

Lozanov, G. (1978) *Suggestology and outlines of suggestopedy*. New York: Gordon and Breach.

Martin, J. (1972) Rhythmic (hierarchical) versus serial structure in speech and other behavior. *Psychological Review, 79*, 487–509.

Martin, J., Meltzer, R., & Mills, L. (1978) Visual rhythms: Dynamic text display for learning to read a second language. *Visible Language, 12*, 71–80.

Pribram, K., & Goleman, D., (1979) Holographic memory. *Psychology Today*, February 1979, pp. 70–84.

Sparks, R., Helm, M., & Martin, A. (1974) Aphasia rehabilitation resulting from melodic intonation therapy. *Cortex, 10*, 303–316.

Strauss, A., & Kephart, N. (1955) *Psychophathology and education of the brain-injured child: Progress in theory and clinic* (Vol. 2). New York: Grune & Stratton.

Strauss, A., & Lehtinen, L. (1947) *Psychopathology and education of the brain injured child*. Vol. 1: *Fundamentals and treatment*. New York: Grune & Stratton.

Van den Honert, D. (1977) A neuropsychological technique for training dyslexics. *Journal of Learning Disabilities, 10*, 21–27.

Witelson, S. (1977) Developmental dyslexia: Two right hemispheres and none left. *Science, 195*, 309–311.

Chapter Seventeen

Dyslexia in Adolescents

CARL L. KLINE

INTRODUCTION

In 1846 Horace Mann made a prophetic statement:

They, then, who knowingly withhold sustenance from a newborn child, and he dies, are guilty of infanticide. And, by the same reasoning, they who refuse to enlighten the intellect of a rising generation are guilty of degrading the human race! They who refuse to train up children in the way they should go are training up incendiaries and madmen to destroy property and life, and to invade and pollute the sanctuaries of society [Silberman, 1970, p. 53].

The wisdom of Horace Mann's prophecy has been confirmed repeatedly. One example among many is the 1969 report by the Department of Health, Education and Welfare's National Advisory Committee on Dyslexia and Related Reading Disorders. This committee of 100 authorities concluded that the nation's effort to teach reading is mostly an ill-defined, directionless, and uncoordinated "patch work

389

Copyright © 1982 by Academic Press, Inc.
All rights of reproduction in any form reserved.
ISBN 0-12-466320-6

affair." Moreover, their report, "Reading Disorders in the United States," contained some rather startling revelations.

1. Of the children in the United States schools, 15% had severe reading disabilities.

2. The enrollment in the primary and secondary grades of the public schools was 51.5 million. The average annual cost per child was $696. If 1 child in 20 (5%) was not promoted, the national loss expressed in economic terms alone would be $1.7 billion.

3. Children who were of adequate intelligence but retarded in reading often performed adequately in nonreading schoolwork during the early grades. However, as the years of reading failure built up feelings of inadequacy and dissatisfaction with school, their overall academic work was severely affected.

4. A follow-up study showed that sixth grade underachievers continued to be underachievers in the ninth grade, with the resulting tendency to drop out.

5. The American Association of Junior Colleges estimated that from one-third to one-half of new students had significant reading problems and that 20% of the new students in the most disadvantaged areas were unable to profit from their present remedial programs, so severe was their handicap.

6. Every year some 700,000 children dropped out of public school.

7. In Job Core Urban Centers, 60% of enrollees had less than sixth-grade reading ability and about 20% of enrollees read below the third-grade level.

8. Among juvenile delinquents, there was a 75% rate of significant reading retardation. The 1968 cost for detention of juvenile delinquents in federal institutions was $6935 per person.

9. The retention of reading underachievers cost the nation's public education system in excess of $1 billion every year.

10. The state of affairs was such that there could be no assurance that a diagnostic study would be accurate or that related remedial instruction would be sufficient to meet a child's needs—a situation conducive to exploitation and to well-meaning but ineffective effort.

SOME IMPLICATIONS OF THE PROBLEM

For several decades now it has been recognized that the incidence of emotional problems in learning-disabled children is extremely high. Eisenberg (1975) and others have pointed to inadequately treated reading disability as the number one cause of emotional problems in children in North America today. Based upon my 30 years of practice in child and adolescent psychiatry, with a special interest in learning-disabled children, I am convinced that this is indeed the case.

Bender (1975) presented a fascinating and sobering study of 5000 boys who had been admitted to the in-patient psychiatric service at Bellevue Hospital over a period of years. In analyzing these cases, she found that of the boys aged 6–12, 50% had severe reading disabilities, and of those aged 12–17, 75% had severe reading disabilities. Although this study does not prove that these children's emotional problems were due to reading disabilities, this kind of association has to be significant from whatever viewpoint one chooses to regard it. In the face of such facts, it is indeed bewildering that constructive solutions have not been found.

In what follows, I shall present three cases in order to underscore the gravity of the problem, illustrate the association found by Bender, and make some general points about treatment. A 13-year-old boy was seen for evaluation because of marked academic problems and severe behavioral problems. A handsome, husky, angry boy, he had been in special classes since first grade. He faced charges in juvenile court for auto theft and for breaking and entering. He had refused to attend school for several months and spent his time working on an old automobile engine in his back yard.

The drawing in Figure 17.1 reflects his poor self-image, feelings of insecurity, and emotional emptiness. Figure 17.2 indicates the boy's attempt to spell the words dictated to him (i.e., the typed words). He was unable to read a preprimer, and all reading tests reflected his functional illiteracy. He was at a fourth-grade level in math. He had received no remedial help and was designated as a behavioral problem. On the WISC-R his performance IQ was in the bright normal range, but his verbal IQ was below average. He had no knowledge of phonics.

Long letters were written to social agencies indicating the urgent need for specialized intensive remedial help for his severe developmental language problem. It was stated that unless he received help he would most likely end up in jail or in a mental institution. Detailed recommendations were made for an effective program for him. These letters were ignored. Two years later, he was facing six charges of car theft and twelve of breaking and entering, and he had become extremely angry and defiant. He felt I was the only adult who understood him, and he expressed willingness to involve himself in any program that I designed. On testing, he was at the same low achievement levels as 2 years before. Again I wrote desperately urgent letters to the authorities

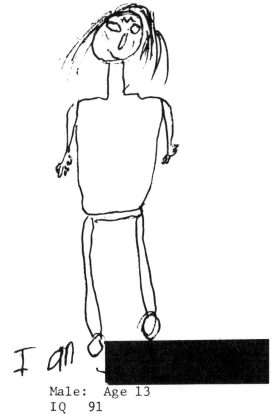

Male: Age 13
IQ   91

Figure 17.1

involved at all levels. The next I heard was that he had been placed in a prison for adult men and was found hanging by the neck from a bedsheet. Although he was revived physically, his basic problems continued to go ignored.

One of the tragic problems with teenagers with serious developmental language problems is that they have often been mistreated and misplaced. Either they have not been diagnosed at all or they have been misdiagnosed. Consequently, if help has been offered at all, it is often inappropriate to the youngster's needs. The result is reinforcement of feelings of negativism and stupidity. Rage builds up inside, and acting out problems become common.

The second case I will present here is that of a 17-year-old eleventh-grade female student with a long history of conflict with the schools.

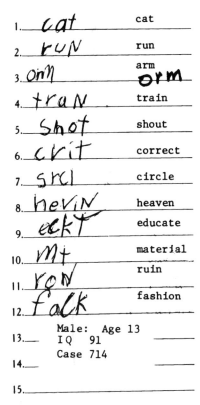

1. *cat*   cat
2. *run*   run
3. *onm*   arm   **orm**
4. *tran*   train
5. *shot*   shout
6. *crit*   correct
7. *srcl*   circle
8. *hevin*   heaven
9. *eckt*   educate
10. *mt*   material
11. *ron*   ruin
12. *falk*   fashion
13. ___   Male: Age 13   IQ 91   Case 714   ___
14. ___
15. _____

Figure 17.2

She was distressed by her inability to cope with schoolwork and by the absence of help or understanding. She had average intelligence and had for several summers held a responsible job as a lifeguard at a community swimming pool.

Figures 17.3 and 17.4 illustrate one of the more dramatic sequencing problems I have seen. Note in Figure 17.4 that even in copying from the chalkboard she made many sequencing errors. Her Draw-a-Person (Figure 17.3) is immature and reflects her negative self-image, her difficulty in ascertaining her own identity, and the feelings of emptiness and isolation she felt.

Because she had rebelled in junior high school and had been expelled from school on several occasions, she was stereotyped as a "troublemaker." She read and spelled only at a fifth-grade level and had only the most rudimentary knowledge of phonics. The school refused to

I dnot luk ot chwa ✱

"I DON'T LIKE TO DRAW".
Patient: Female, C.A.: 17.1
WAIS: V., 103; P. 89, F.S., 97.

Figure 17.3

COPIED: (FROM THE CHALKBOARD): HE SAW NO GIRL ON TOP OF THE BIG OVERWHELMING
MOUNTAIN SEEN FROM BELOW THE RIVER.
Patient: Female; C.A.: 17.1
WAIS: V., 103; P. 89; F.S., 97
Case: C-77

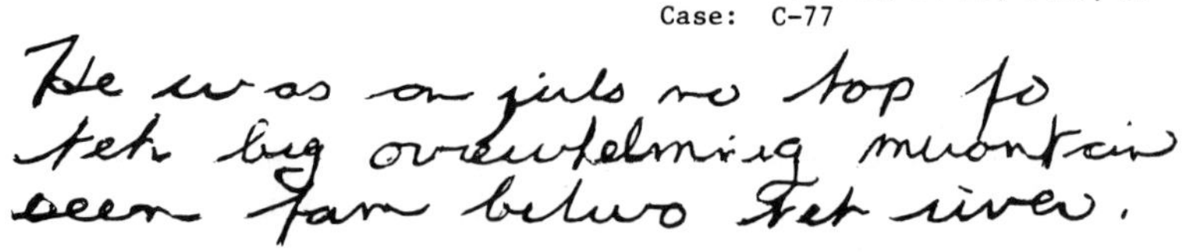

He was on jirls no top to teh big overwhelming muontain seen fam beluo Tet river.

Figure 17.4

recognize the problem, and she initiated her admission to a special school in another district. There she is accepted, supported, and receiving help. She is working hard and making good grades.

My third case is that of a 17-year-old boy with marked emotional difficulties which affect his academic adjustment. His Draw-a-Person (Figure 17.5) dramatically emphasizes his serious plight. The rigidity, facelessness, loneliness, isolation, and sense of being lost "with a long way to go" are all accurate representations of his disturbed emotional

Figure 17.5

state. Even the shadow probably represents his feeling of being split off from himself.

These patients dramatically illustrate the following:

1. There is an urgent need for early diagnosis and early intervention.
2. It is crucially important to relate to a language disability the emotional factors which are secondary to the language disability. It must be recognized that after so many years of emotional battering, psychotherapy must often be given as well as appropriate remedial therapy.
3. Emotional factors are often primary (e.g., Case 3). In such cases the treatment should be intensive psychoanalytically oriented psychotherapy.
4. Making a diagnosis is not enough. The evaluator has a responsibility to formulate a realistic treatment program and to help the patient to become involved in treatment.

THE ROLE OF THE EDUCATIONAL SYSTEM

In the 1970 report of the Joint Commission on Mental Health of Children in the United States, *Crisis in Child Mental Health: Challenge for the 1970's,* a good deal was said about problems in the educational system. Several thoughtful and relevant recommendations deserve special emphasis here:

1. The goals for education should be focused on developmental processes in childhood; sensitivity to the world around; cognitive power and intellectual mastering of the symbolic systems; synthesis of cognitive and affective experiences; differentiated reaction to people; and adaptation to requirements of social situations, self-understanding, and moral judgment. *Achievement criteria are partial, inadequate measures of development.*

2. Instructional methods and technology should be evaluated before adoption by two criteria: (*a*) productivity in advancing intellectual power, and (*b*) positive value for associated emotional factors related to personality.

3. Learning activities should be designed for independent pursuit by an actively involved child; should afford various possibilities to observe, discover, invent, and choose; and should avoid complete dependence on verbal, vicarious transmission of information.

4. Learning activities should encompass and integrate thinking and feeling experiences; children should have opportunities to express feel-

ings directly in relation to people in school, and for indirect reexpression in symbolic form, through creative activities.

5. The organization of learning tasks should make maximum use of the peer group process—for evolving codes of special interaction, for working through interpersonal reactions, and for experience in being part of a forum for the discussion of ideas.

6. The authority structure should be flexible and rational, not arbitrary, not invested in status and position; it should exclude threat, humiliation, or retaliatory punishment; children should participate in formulating regulations; methods of control should be corrective, relevant, and nonpunitive. (It is my experience that recommendations listed here are far from being met in the public school system and that an extensive overhaul of the system is needed in this respect.)

7. Genuine work experiences serving the school and the community should be included as an integral part of the curriculum; the work should be perceived by the children as realistically essential and as a sign of their acceptance into the world of adult concerns. Projects of cross-age teaching are an example of intraschool work activities that have had positive results.

8. The moral climate of the school should be built around attitudes of mutual trust, respect, and "fair-play" as the basis for judgment and behavior; children should be exposed to a diversity of points of view and helped to build up moral principles for judging and guiding behavior; values openly advocated by schools must not be violated covertly.

Bronfenbrenner (1970) has emphasized some of the same ideas. He writes as follows: "It is not primarily the needs of problem children or the disadvantaged that call for change in American schools. If the radical innovations that are required are not introduced it will be all the children who will be culturally deprived—not of cognitive stimulation but of their humanity [p. 158]."

TYPES OF ACADEMIC PROBLEMS SEEN IN ADOLESCENTS

All levels of growth and development—physical, intellectual, and emotional—should be seen in historical perspective. Any given problem should be perceived in terms of the gestalt rather than as an isolated symptom. On the basis of my extensive experience and study of academic problems in adolescents I believe that the types of problems encountered can be divided as follows:

1. *Developmental language disabilities* (Developmental Dyslexia). This category is made up of those young people who have genetically determined functional neurological language disabilities in varying degrees of severity. According to various authorities, this group probably constitutes somewhere around 10% of the population if the milder cases are included. The very severe forms of this problem probably make up about 2% of the population.

Although many definitions have been offered for dyslexia the most incisive is perhaps that of Critchley and Critchley (1978), who define it as:

> a learning disability which initially shows itself by difficulty in learning to read, and later by lack of facility in manipulating written as opposed to spoken words. The condition is cognitive in essence, and usually genetically determined. It is not due to intellectual inadequacy or to lack of socio-cultural opportunity, or to faults in the techniques of teaching, or to emotional factors, or to any known structural brain defects. It probably represents a specific maturational defect which tends to lessen as the child grows older, and is capable of considerable improvement, especially when appropriate remedial help is afforded at the earliest opportunity [p. 149].

This group also includes the less common types of functional neurological disabilities such as dyscalculia and dysgraphia.

2. *Emotional problems.* It is well established that emotional problems are rarely the cause of basic reading disabilities. However, as children grow older the cumulative effect of family problems catalyze emotional problems which may interfere with academic functioning. Even though the youngster is an adequate reader and speller, serious academic problems may appear due to a variety of psychiatric difficulties. Although the majority of these problems are rooted in family psychopathology, many result primarily from unfortunate school experiences due to inappropriate behavior on the part of school personnel, creating problems with which the child or adolescent cannot cope.

3. *Intellectual handicaps.* Some youngsters drift through years of schooling without recognition and acknowledgment on the part of authorities that the youngster is intellectually handicapped and thus unable successfully to cope with academic courses. Here I refer not to overtly retarded children but rather to those with low average, dull-normal, or borderline intellectual functioning. School personnel are often reluctant to level with parents about such problems. This procrastination confronts the child with the frustration of making futile attempts to handle academic work that is beyond his or her grasp.

Sometimes the school system simply has no viable alternatives to offer. Certainly there is a gross lack of facilities for vocational planning and vocational training in the school systems despite the large number of youngsters needing such programs.

A somewhat more complex but, in some ways, more satisfactory classification of the kinds of problems seen in adolescents is adopted from Lorand's chapter "Therapy of Learning Problems" (Lorand, 1961; Kline, 1972).

1. *Chronic dyslexics.* Most adolescent reading problems are the result of long-standing difficulties which have always slowed the child's progress to varying degrees. In some of the mild cases the problem may not become apparent until the upper grades where so much of the work depends on reading and writing proficiency and where there is added time pressure. A youth who requires triple the amount of time to complete the reading assignment or who may know all the answers on a test but has written out only half of them when the time is up is obviously greatly handicapped. (See Critchley, 1970.)

2. *The mini-effort group.* There are many bright children who have managed quite well in the primary grades where minimal effect produced adequate or even above average grades, but who find in junior high or high school that they are unable to produce the sustained effort necessary to succeed. Some are narcissistic youngsters who have difficulty with object relations and expect to be nurtured without having to give of themselves. Brody and Axelrad (1978) have demonstrated convincingly that children whose pattern of object relations in the first year is poor, deficient, or imbalanced will, in their seventh year, show poorer object relations in general and poorer capacity for abstract thinking.

3. *The overindulged.* Some bright children, brought up in an over-permissive environment, never have had to postpone gratification. They are unable to cope with the tension associated with working toward mastering knowledge. Often they focus their attention on activities providing immediate gratification.

4. *The afraid-to-be-curious.* Adolescents whose childhood curiosity was regressed may develop learning difficulties in certain subjects. For example, biology and science threaten the young person who fears the emergence of repressed childhood curiosity about sex.

5. *The emotionally traumatized.* The student previously doing well in school whose performance abruptly drops may be caught up in an acute emotional crisis, often home centered. Teenage romances and the

associated crises may cause temporary disturbances in academic performance.

6. *The afraid-to-know.* The need to avoid knowledge is a primary difficulty in some children with learning problems. The child attempts to avoid pain by avoiding facing certain realities.

7. *The love-to-be-loved group.* Some emotionally starved children suddenly find themselves attractive in adolescence. They derive so much gratification from dates, admiration, and physical contact, from feeling attractive and lovable for the first time in their lives, that they become distracted from the less gratifying academic requirements.

8. *The psychiatrically ill.* Children with severe, specific emotional illness or personality disturbances may suffer secondary language problems and other learning problems. Difficulty in handling aggression associated with excessive guilt and anxiety often coupled with hostile, or sadistic impulses and fantasies may precede difficulties in learning. Although only about 2% of reading-disabled children are in this category, it is important to identify them.

A common prototype of reading disabilities seen in adolescents is the rather bright high school student who reads at or near grade level, but who has a spelling problem, is a slow reader, misreads some words, omits words, substitutes words, and occasionally reverses letters or words. Often these youngsters are unidentified dyslexics or dyslexics with residual problems.

DIAGNOSTIC EVALUATION

History

As previously indicated, the longitudinal history is of basic importance in the diagnostic process. Developmentally, it is essential to know what happened throughout the mother's pregnancy, during delivery, and following birth. Because of the relevance of genetic factors related to specific language disabilities, the family history is important. Knowledge of the developmental time sequences may reveal maturational lags in such important areas as speech. A history of severe febrile illness or of certain other serious physical illnesses could indicate possible brain damage. The developmental emotional history is important in terms of parental relationships, including the absence of one or both parents for extended periods during the early years. Separation, divorce, or death in the family are highly visible problems. But the less obvious, often repressed experiences can cause also long-term emotional problems interfering with learning (e.g., the profound effect upon a child of having a sadistic baby-sitter or of having been seduced by an adult).

Examination of the Patient

The evaluation process should include physical, psychoeducational examination, and psychiatric evaluation. Every adolescent being evaluated should have the benefit of a thorough physical examination including a neurological examination when indicated. If the physical and neurological examinations suggest the possibility of neurological disorders this should be pursued with whatever laboratory tests, including X rays and EEGs, are necessary.

The psychoeducational examination is probably one of the least well-defined and most controversial areas of the entire evaluation. A multitude of tests have been devised, written about, and used by various clinics. Certain tests which were temporarily popular have been discarded following ample research (e.g., the Frostig test). The Illinois Test of Psycholinguistic Abilities (ITPA) is in general disfavor now because the length of time required to administer and score it is not justified by the relevance of the information obtained.

The test battery should include the WISC-R, the Bender Gestalt Test, the Draw-a-Person test (Goodenough, 1926, and also Brody & Axelrad, 1978, pp. 254–298). There is an especially large group of achievement tests to choose from, and the examiner should settle on one balanced battery of tests that suits his or her particular training and needs and stick to it, while continuing to search for more effective evaluation procedures.

Psychological or psychoeducational testing should only be done by qualified examiners. Some of these tests are very complex, requiring considerable training and experience before reliable information can be obtained. To illustrate the importance of this principle, I want to present a fourth case (Figure 17.6). The patient was a 12.5-year-old female who had entered puberty. She presented the typical clinical syndrome of developmental dyslexia. However, on the Bender Gestalt she superimposed all the figures, something I had not seen done in 30 years of observing Benders. When I sent a copy of the test to Doctor Lauretta Bender, she responded that she had seen this in a few instances with schizophrenic patients, but never in dyslexia. However, this patient was distinctly not schizophrenic and was clearly dyslexic, and Bender stated that "it is not inconceivable that a dyslexic could produce such

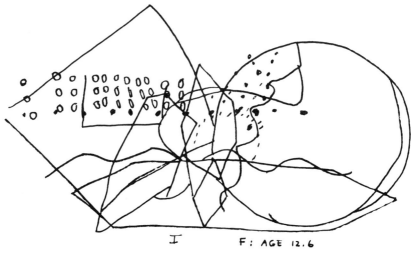

Figure 17.6

a test pattern." Since this time De Hirsch and Jansky (1980) have called attention to the fact that some children with learning disabilities have ambiguous laterality problems, reflecting a lack of differentiation due to a diffuse internal organization: "Some children in the group fail to respond to and reproduce the essential of the Gestalten [Bender Gestalt Test], violating the integrity of the individual figure by cheerfully superimposing one design upon another [p. 230]." In any event, my point is that if the originator of a test which has stood the test of time and which has been written about extensively has never seen a particular production of the test in dyslexia, the need for caution in interpreting any psychological or achievement test is clear.

The psychoeducational evaluation should always include a description of the youngster and of the youngster's behavior and comments during the evaluation procedure. If the test battery given requires more than 3 hours, two sessions should be scheduled. After the test battery has been carefully scored and analyzed, a detailed formal report of the observations should be prepared in time for study prior to the psychiatric evaluation.

The psychiatric evaluation should include interviews with both parents and with the child, together with observation of the youngster— what type of observation depends on the child's age. (With adolescents I usually start by seeing the teenager and parents together and then see each separately.)

After these studies have been completed, the psychiatrist should formulate the diagnosis on the basis of the complete findings. In every instance, the patient and the parents should have the findings explained to them as realistically and honestly as possible. An appropriate treatment plan should be presented with specific recommendations.

Just making a diagnosis and referring the parents back to the school is distinctly unsatisfactory. School personnel often are unable to understand the diagnostic formulation and do not have the background to understand the test results. At times, school personnel are indifferent or openly hostile toward "outside" help and may refuse to cooperate. The parents then have to seek help outside the school and need guidance and support.

It is unwise for the examiner to have any contact with the school without the express request or permission of the child's parents. In the case of an adolescent, his or her permission should be obtained as well. Respect for the confidentiality of the consultation is of the utmost importance. School personnel may sometimes become incensed because a doctor refuses to share information with them without consultation or permission from the parent or patient. It should be explained to them why this cannot be done: Many parents will make a special point of insisting that they do not want information imparted to the school under any circumstance, often because they have had several years of frustrating and unrewarding experiences in trying to communicate with teachers and principals.

Children and adolescents should not be tested over and over again. This tends to reinforce in their minds the all-too-prevalent idea that they must indeed be dumb because of having so many tests. Retesting is unnecessary except in some very severe cases in which progress needs to be closely monitored.

TREATMENT RECOMMENDATIONS

Formulation of the case, based upon the diagnostic findings, should determine the recommended treatment plan. Because of the greater complexity of the learning problems and associated difficulties in adolescents, special care should be exercised in providing a well-balanced treatment program.

After years of frustration, humiliation, and misunderstanding, many young people have resigned themselves to their fate and present an attitude of apathetic indifference. Others are full of anger and involved in major patterns of rebellious acting-out. Then there are those with greater ego strength who, although discouraged, are still trying valiantly to find answers to their perplexing problems (Kline, 1978).

Remedial therapists who work with adolescents should have good basic training in appropriate methodology. They should also be psychologically mature and possess a good self-image, firmness, flexibility, imagination, and a sense of humor. The therapist should have enough knowledge of developmental dynamics to be able to recognize and work with the major defensive maneuvers commonly used by these young people. Transference phenomena are apt to play an important role in many cases, and the therapist should be able to recognize these situations and avoid entanglements.

The methodology used for language remediation in adolescents varies in many respects from that used with younger children, although the principles are the same.

Most patients with primary developmental language disabilities respond best to a modified Gillingham approach (Gillingham & Stillman, 1956; also see Deverell, 1974).

Psychotherapy is indicated for those with specific neurotic illness and for those with developmental personality problems. Psychoanalytically oriented psychotherapy is the method of choice in most instances. The role of medication is extremely limited. Ritalin and the amphetamines should be avoided in adolescents. Operant conditioning has no meaningful role to play in the treatment of these patients.

Patients who have emotional problems secondary to their basic language disability may require psychotherapy along with their remedial program. Others may stabilize emotionally when improvement occurs in their language problem.

Because of the long duration of the problem in adolescents and because of the age–grade factor, it is urgently recommended that treatment be intensive. Remedial sessions should be on a one-to-one basis, 1 hour in length, and 5 days a week. It is preferable to have these sessions during school hours because of the fact that most patients are emotionally drained by the end of a long day in school.

TREATMENT RESULTS AND PREVENTION

Although prevention is always the best treatment, effective treatment techniques are available for helping dyslexic adolescents to achieve maximum language function. Contrary to the poor prognosis articulated by some prophets of gloom, research studies indicate a good outlook (e.g., Kline & Kline, 1975; Rawson, 1968; Monroe, 1932). These studies indicate that, given appropriate methodology and a well-trained therapist, 96% of dyslexic children will make significant progress. Figure 17.7 indicates results by age group in 92 patients who were thoroughly evaluated before and after treatment (Kline & Kline, 1975).

The outlook for prevention is also good. Sufficient evidence, based upon solid research, exists to enable us to test children at kindergarten level and predict with a high degree of accuracy which ones are likely to have a language problem in the first grade. Jansky and de Hirsch (1972) present their extensive research into methods for prediction. Slingerland (1969) has also made significant contributions to this important problem. Moreover, both the de Hirsch and the Slingerland programs are easy to administer and to interpret. The de Hirsch battery has the advantage of better standardization and provides a scale-score with established norms.

Prevention must also be viewed from a transcultural perspective, as there is much of value to be learned from such an approach (Kline,

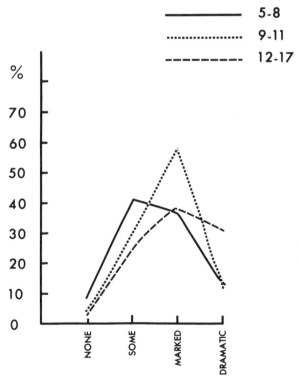

Figure 17.7. *Orton-Gillingham tutored children: Results by age groups* (N = 92).

1977). The evidence is convincing that Japanese children do not have dyslexia. Duke (1977) indicates—on the basis of over a decade of experience in studying and observing Japanese language classes—that the Japanese school program represents one of the most successful mass literacy programs in the world. He states categorically that "learning to read and write in Japanese elementary schools is not a problem for children [p. 230]." He feels that important factors are the totally phonetic nature of the kana script and the effective teaching methods. Another important treatise in transcultural factors has been edited by the Tarnopols (Tarnopol & Tarnopol, 1976), and clearly this is an important area for future research.

SUMMARY AND CONCLUSIONS

Figure 17.8 summarizes this chapter better than words. This boy was 9 when he drew the picture in a fit of rage because his mother did not allow him to continue eating after dinner. He is now 16 and has had 4 years of superior remedial therapy together with periods of psychotherapy. He is self-confident—sometimes too self-assertive—and is functioning well academically in secondary school. Serious trouble and a life of certain frustration and unhappiness have been aborted by a

Figure 17.8

combination of supportive parents, early diagnosis, highly professional intervention, and reasonably good school cooperation. It should be possible for nearly all youngsters with learning problems to have a reasonably happy outcome!

Because of their complex developmental histories, the tensions inherent in the normal adolescent identity struggle, and the cumulative effects of their language disabilities, adolescents with academic difficulties present a very special challenge. In this chapter an approach to the problem has been presented which is holistic and which often enables the patient to succeed in overcoming a serious and crippling problem. Clearly, the complexities of the problem made it impossible to discuss here in a comprehensive way all of the academic difficulties encountered by these adolescents. Perhaps what has been said will enable those who are interested further to pursue the fascinating trails that must be traversed en route to offering meaningful help to these endangered young people.

REFERENCES

Bender, L. (1975) A career of clinical research in child psychiatry. In E. J. Anthony (Ed.), *Explorations in child psychiatry*. New York: Plenum Press.

Brody, S., & Axelrad, S. (1978) *Mothers, fathers and children: Explorations in the formation of character in the first seven years*. New York: International Universities Press.

Bronfenbrenner, U. (1970) Two worlds of childhood: U.S. and U.S.S.R. New York: Russell Sage Foundation.

Crisis in Child Mental Health: Challenge for the 1970's. (Report of the Joint Commission for Mental Health of Children in the U.S.) New York: Harper & Row. 1970.

Critchley, M. (1970) *The dyslexic child*. London: Heinemann.

Critchley, M., & Critchley, A. (1978) *Dyslexia defined*. London: Heinemann.

de Hirsch, K., & Jansky, J. (1980) Patterning and organizational deficits in children with language and learning disabilities. *Bulletin of the Orton Society, 30*, 227–239.

Deverell, A. (1974) *Teaching children to read and write*. Toronto: Holt, Rinehart & Winston of Canada Ltd.

Duke, B. (1977) Why Noriko can read: Some hints for Johnny. *The Educational Forum.*

Eisenberg, L. (1975) Psychiatric aspects of language disability. In D. Duane & M. Rawson (Eds.), *Reading, perception and language*. Baltimore: York Press.

Gillingham, A., & Stillman, B. (1956) *Remedial training for children with specific disability in reading, spelling and penmanship* (5th ed.). New York: Sackett and Wilhelms.

Goodenough, F. L. (1926) *Measurement of intelligence by drawings*. New York: World Book.

Jansky, J., & de Hirsch, K. (1972) *Preventing reading failure: Prediction, diagnosis and intervention*. New York: Harper & Row.

Kline, Carl L. (1972) The adolescents with learning problems: How long must they wait? *Journal of Learning Disabilities, 5*(5), 262–271.

Kline, Carl L. (1977) *Developmental dyslexia: An overview of transcultural factors*. Paper presented to the World Congress on Mental Health of the World Federation of Mental Health, Vancouver, Canada, 1977.

Kline, Carl L. (1978) Developmental dyslexia in adolescents: The emotional carnage. *Bulletin of the Orton Society, 28,* 160–174.

Kline, Carl L., & Kline, Carolyn L. (1975) Follow-up study of 216 dyslexic children. *Bulletin of the Orton Society, 25,* 127–144.

Lorand, R. (1961) Therapy of learning problems. In S. Lorand & H. Schneer, (Eds.), *Adolescents.* New York: Harper-Hoeber.

Monroe, M. (1932) *Children who cannot read.* Chicago: University of Chicago Press.

Rawson, M. (1968) *Developmental language disability: Adult accomplishments of dyslexic boys.* Baltimore: John Hopkins University Press.

Reading disorders in the United States. Report of the Secretary's (HEW) National Advisory Committee on Dyslexia and Related Reading Disorders. August 1969.

Silberman, C. (1970) *Crisis in the classroom.* New York: Random House.

Slingerland, B. (1969) *Pre-Reading screening procedure.* Cambridge, Mass.: Educators Publishing Service.

Tarnapol, L., & Tarnapol, M. (1976) Reading disabilities: An international perspective. Baltimore: University Park Press.

Chapter Eighteen

The Orton–Gillingham Approach to Remediation in Developmental Dyslexia

ALICE ANSARA[1]

The approach to remediation in cases of developmental dyslexia and related language disabilities that is now commonly referred to as the "Orton–Gillingham Approach" was an outcome of intensive research conducted by Samuel Torrey Orton, a neurologist and psychiatrist, and his associates in an interdisciplinary effort. As no description or explanation of the approach can be fully understood without an awareness of Orton's theoretical basis, I will briefly sketch the pertinent history of his work and summarize the hypotheses he developed about language defects and delays. Following this, I will outline his approach to diagnosis and the remedial strategies he developed with the aid of his research associates, most notably with Anna Gillingham.

[1] Alice Ansara passed away on 27 June 1981, shortly after she had completed the writing of this chapter.

409

ORTON'S RESEARCH IN SPECIFIC
LANGUAGE DISABILITIES

Orton's research in specific language disabilities, including developmental dyslexia, had its beginning in the early 1920s at the State University of Iowa where he was professor of psychiatry and neuropathology and the first director of the Iowa State Psychopathic Hospital (Stewart, 1980). During this time, the first published reports on his investigations into specific language disabilities and his hypotheses about their underlying basis began to appear (Orton, 1925, 1928b, 1928c, 1929a, 1929b; Monroe, 1928). Upon his removal to New York, the work was continued there and maintained until his retirement in 1948 (and subsequent death shortly thereafter). In New York, Orton had appointments as professor of neurology and neuropathology in the College of Physicians and Surgeons of Columbia University and as neuropathologist at the New York Neurological Institute. The continued research and his thinking during this period are reflected in published papers (Orton, 1930, 1931, 1932, 1943b; Orton & Gillingham, 1933) and in a book (Orton, 1937).

Early research associates in Iowa included, among others, Lauretta Bender, Marion Monroe, June Lyday Orton, and Lee Edward Travis—all drawn from different disciplines so that the research encompassed a wide range, from the physiology of the brain to language and behavior. The Language Research Project at the New York Neurological Institute also assembled an interdisciplinary group which included, for example, the neurologists Earl Chesher and Edwin M. Cole, the psychiatrists Paul Dozier and David G. Wright, speech pathologist Katrina de Hirsch, and psychologist and educator Anna Gillingham. June Lyday Orton, a psychiatric social worker, served as coordinator of the project and as clinical assistant to Dr. Orton.

The impetus for research specifically in developmental dyslexia and related language disabilities came from the experience with the hundreds of children referred to the Mobile Mental Hygiene Clinic which Dr. Orton organized and sent out into the rural areas of Iowa. Among the children and adolescents referred for behavioral and emotional problems, Orton had found a surprising number who, for reasons not readily discernible, had failed to learn to read or were reading with extreme difficulty and inaccuracy relative to their grade level. He also noted associated problems of a severe nature in their writing. Whether the children were writing spontaneously, copying, or writing from dictation, their spelling errors were often bizarre and unlike the common misspellings of children at their age and grade levels. The intelligence levels of these children and adolescents, however, were well within the normal range, and their educational retardation seemed to be specifically in the language areas. These findings caused Orton to focus on their language problems.

The first group studied included 142 pupils from the county grade and high schools. From this group, 15 children in grades 1–9 were selected for deeper diagnostic study. One of them, an intelligent boy of 16 who could barely read first-grade material, was the subject of Orton's first intensive study of an individual with developmental dyslexia (Orton, 1925). The results of this study convinced Orton that there was a neurological explanation for the disability and that it warranted further research.

With funding from the Rockefeller Foundation in 1926, Orton was then able to organize a full-scale research program which included, in addition to experimental work in basic cerebral anatomy and physiology and the expansion of the Mobile Mental Hygiene Clinic, diagnostic and remedial work with the children with reading and other language disabilities and thus further investigation of developmental dyslexia. Drawing from over 1000 children and adolescents referred to the Mobile Mental Hygiene Clinic, 175 retarded readers were studied and compared with 120 normal readers (Monroe, 1928). Two additional grants from the Rockefeller Foundation enabled continuation of research in New York as well as in Connecticut and Pennsylvania where Orton directed research projects.

The net result of Orton's quarter of a century of research in specific language disabilities was (*a*) a neurological explanation for the disabilities that rejected the earlier views that they were caused by an obscure brain defect or brain damage; (*b*) a view of specific reading disability as a maturational deviation in language development; (*c*) the identification of developmental reading disability (dyslexia) as differentiated from a reading disability caused by mental deficiency, brain damage, or primary emotional disturbance; (*d*) the identification of distinct syndromes in specific language disabilities; and (*e*) principles of diagnosis and remediation for the disabilities.

ORTON'S CONCEPTUAL FRAMEWORK

Although Orton was the first to formulate his particular hypothesis for a neurological basis for dyslexia other than that of brain defect or damage, he was by no means the first to recognize or describe the condition. Referred to mainly as "word-blindness" or "congenital alexia," cases had been reported in a number of papers published from

1896 (Morgan, 1896) through the first two decades of the twentieth century. In addition, although Orton was the first to offer his hypothesis about the neurological basis for a genetic link in developmental dyslexia (Orton, 1930), earlier literature had reported evidence of a family tendency to the condition (Fisher, 1905; Hinshelwood, 1909; Stephenson, 1907; Thomas, 1905). Despite the growing number of investigations into severe reading disability, published reports did not yet reflect a consensus as to causation.. According to Benton (1980), however, two schools of thought had emerged by the 1920s. One attributed the failure in learning to read to perceptual and cognitive disabilities; the other attributed the failure to environmental and characterological variables (cf. Bronner, 1917; Gates, 1922). Orton discarded both of these views of the etiology of specific reading disability.

Prior to his investigations into the cause of reading failure, Orton had already begun his studies of brain functions associated with specific areas, and his interest in language disabilities had been stimulated by his work with stutterers (Orton, 1928b; Orton & Travis, 1929). Moreover, he held a strong belief in the importance of the study of brain structure for both neurology and psychiatry. That belief is best exemplified in the following statement:

> The enormous organ which evolution has developed in man's head has a much wider part to play in his behavior than that of a generator of emotions. . . . *A thorough knowledge of the functions represented in each of the various large areas which show a markedly different histologic structure is of enormous value in the study of many clinical syndromes* [Orton, 1943a, p. 13; italics added].

His observations of the emotional and social problems of stutterers led Orton to the further belief that emotional variations might also be linked to brain structure and functions, and he stated this unequivocally.

> Moreover, I believe not only that emotional variations may modify the efficiency of the various brain functions, but also that differences in physiological activity of specific areas may generate emotional deviations as well, and that *thus observed concurrent emotional disturbances may often be an effect rather than a cause of disordered functions* [Orton, 1943a, p. 13; italics added].

Neurological Concepts

What were the premises on which Orton based his neurological concepts about developmental dyslexia that led to the diagnostic and educational practices that are incorporated within the Orton–Gillingham

Approach? First and foremost, he viewed language as an evolutionary function of the human brain (Orton, 1937, pp. 15–17). Second, as already stated, he believed that brain functions were related to brain structures. Third, he attributed great significance to the fact that one cerebral hemisphere becomes the dominant one for language functions (Orton, 1937, pp. 27–35). Fourth, he attributed an equally great significance to the finding that although the two hemispheres of the brain operate together at the first and second levels of cortical elaboration, at the third or associative level there are important differences between them (Orton, 1928c). Fifth, he believed that the knowledge gained from cases of acquired alexia gave evidence that visual and auditory association at the third cortical level is essential for reading (Orton, 1937, Chapter 1). And, sixth, Orton's study of cases of speech and language disabilities in which there was evidence of a genetic link led him to conclude that there is a neurological basis for the variations in the natural process of growth and development that manifest themselves in reading disorders and other language disabilities (Orton, 1930, 1937).

Orton also had noted that children with severe impairment in reading, spelling, and writing showed great instability, in both the recognition and recall of the spatial orientation and sequencing of letters, syllables, and words,[2] and he attributed this to an innate problem in the associative process (Orton, 1928b, 1928c). In addition, many of these children and adolescents with reversal and sequential problems showed mixed right and left laterality in their motor behaviors. These observations, together with the basic premises that have already been mentioned, led Orton to form his first hypothesis as to the cause of developmental dyslexia.

Cerebral Dominance and Reading Disability

Central to this hypothesis was the concept of cerebral dominance. This concept was based on clinical studies that had shown that impairment of visual associative function, and alexia (loss of the ability to read printed or written words, though the ability to see and read individual letters is retained, occurred when the destroyed area was in the dominant hemisphere but not when it was in the nondominant hemisphere.

---

[2] Persistence (beyond the age at which such tendencies are uncommon) of reversals of letters and words (e.g., *b–d, p–q, big–dig,* and *was–saw*) and the "twisting" of a pair of letters within a word (e.g., *from–form*) in both reading and writing led Orton to coin the term *strephosymbolia,* meaning "twisted symbols." At the time he did so, he felt that the cases he was describing showed a typical symptomatology for which the term then in use, "congenital word blindness," was misleading (Orton, 1928c).

Because the visual spheres of the brain are antitropic, that is, right and left, Orton believed that visual "engrams" register as antitropic pairs and "that either [member of the pair] is competent to become the guide for motor responses." He believed, moreover, that the physiological habits involved in such intricate motor responses as speech and writing, dependent upon the association area of one hemisphere only, developed in early childhood, though at varying ages, with outward expression in the preference for handedness, either left or right. In Orton's view, the establishment of unilateral dominance (as demonstrated in handedness) presupposed the elision of the engrams in the nondominant hemisphere so that they no longer served the motor responses of speech and writing. He applied these concepts to reading:

> It seems probable that only one of these antitropic engrams serves as the basis for associative linkage between the visual sphere and the concept, and that if a clear cut unilateral dominance be not established by the elision of one of them, confusion might readily arise which would prevent that immediately successive linkage between the sensory stimulus (printed word) and its meaning (concept) which constitutes reading [Orton, 1928a, pp. 55–56].

Orton developed his theory about the crucial role of cerebral dominance in relation to developmental dyslexia before the technological developments that have made possible the recent advances in the neurosciences. Yet, as Masland (1975) has pointed out, newly acquired data serve as reaffirmation of Orton's thesis. As an example of such reaffirmation, he cites Gazzaniga (1973) as follows:

> A far more basic and important feature of cerebral dominance seems to be the function of the dominant hemisphere as the central processing site of the brain. According to this concept, if dominance is not clearly established, there is no central point through which various cognitive acts are channeled—where their relative importance is ranked and proper commands for motor responses are programmed. In other words, this theory states that there must be a final cognitive path. One can easily imagine that the lack of a central processing and control system—especially for the subtle and fragile processes of language learning and reading—would lead to great confusion.
>
> The problem of cerebral dominance is real and crucial. It now appears that the dominant hemisphere gathers information from all over the brain for analysis of linguistic information.
>
> The data suggest that in language-related behaviors—in particular, reading—there may be a direct and immediate need for the transfer of information between the cerebral hemispheres. One can begin to see that if this system is not operating normally, obvious deficits would result in both acquiring and utilizing reading skills [cited in Masland, 1975, p. 175].

Genetic Considerations

In the data he assembled from his studies of families of children with reading and other language disabilities, Orton found additional support for his hypothesis about "conflict" between the two hemispheres and the crucial role of cerebral dominance in language learning. In addition to a greater than expected incidence of speech defects and reading disability over two or more generations (including cousins), these studies also revealed a greater than expected incidence of left-handedness and ambidexterity (Orton, 1930, 1943b). In his citation of a number of scientific investigations into the genetics of language and its disorders which show a familial occurrence of a variety of language disabilities and reading difficulties along with poorly established hand preference or frank leftism, Lenneberg (1967, pp. 249–252) provides additional evidence.

The family studies led Orton to postulate a probable genetic basis for opposing right and left tendencies that interfered with the development of language functions, a development dependent upon "mastery" by one cerebral hemisphere. These studies and his studies of patients also led him to conclude that language disorders, including reading disability, are considerably more frequent in males than in females. In the study of patients, for example, he found that out of one sample of 102 subjects with reading disabilities and other language disorders, 84 were boys and 18 were girls (Orton, 1943b). Orton attributed the preponderance of males over females to a probable genetically linked neurological variation.

More recent investigations indicate that there are indeed sex differences in hemispheric specialization and these differences may account for the higher incidence of males over females with developmental dyslexia (Hier, 1979). Furthermore, there now appears to be adequate evidence that neurological variations do exist; the literature contains numerous references not only to hemispheric specialization but also to hemispheric asymmetries (e.g., Bakker, 1979; Geschwind, 1979; Hier, 1979; Hier, Le May, Rosenberger, & Perlo, 1978; Lake & Bryden, 1976; Witelson & Pallie, 1973). Currently, there is strong interest in the question of the precise relationship between innate hemispheric differences and developmental dyslexia, as well as in the question of sex differences (Ansara, Albert, & Galaburda, 1981).

DIAGNOSIS AND REMEDIATION

The Orton–Gillingham Approach to remediation of specific disabilities in reading, spelling, and writing begins with careful evaluation, first to determine the existence and nature of the disability and then to determine the degree of its severity. It was Orton's view that as the disability was a developmental one, the evaluation must take into consideration a number of factors. As a neurologist, therefore, he looked for manifestations of neurological and developmental variations; as a psychiatrist, he evaluated the environmental forces that might have affected the educational development of the child or adolescent. Although he took into account the inherent and hereditary factors that might underlie the disability so that it might be regarded as a congenital one, other aspects could not be ignored, and he discarded the term "congenital alexia" as not appropriate to a total evaluation of the problem. This position, clearly stated, provided the basis for the diagnostic procedures.

> While the importance of heredity is clearly recognized and accepted here, nevertheless we feel that the use of the term congenital tends to overstress the inherent difficulty and to underemphasize the many environmental factors, both specific—such as methods of teaching—and more general— such as emotional and social forces—and we therefore prefer to use the term developmental to congenital since it may be said to include both the hereditary and environmental forces which are brought to play on the individual [Orton, 1937, p. 69].

Thus, by almost half a century, Orton anticipated current practice in the identification of a learning disability as now mandated by the 1975 Act of Congress, Public Law 94-142. This practice is an integral part of the Orton–Gillingham Approach.

Diagnostic Procedures

The first steps in the diagnostic procedures include evaluation of visual and hearing acuity and the level of intelligence; determination of the presence or absence of primary emotional disturbance; a review of the child's educational opportunity; and a family history. When intellectual, emotional, environmental, and peripheral physical factors are ruled out as the cause of the educational retardation, other diagnostic measures are undertaken. The total testing and evaluation, therefore, include both intrinsic and extrinsic factors: analysis of spoken language; assessment of written language; oral and silent reading; motor skills; physical status; social, economic, and educational status; family history; and school reports. Both standardized and informal tests are used, and from the results an educational profile is developed.

Differential Diagnosis

The diagnostic procedures used by Orton in the course of examining hundreds of children, adolescents, and young adults, combined with his neurological concepts, led to his identification of distinct syndromes of language disorders which he labeled as follows: *developmental alexia* (reading disability); *developmental agraphia* (special writing disability); *developmental word deafness* (auditory discrimination disability); *developmental motor aphasia* (motor speech delay); *developmental apraxia* (abnormal clumsiness); *childhood stuttering;* and *combined or mixed syndromes* (Orton, 1937, Chapter 2). In children with developmental apraxia, he found abnormal clumsiness not only in such acts as dressing, the handling of utensils, and childhood games, but also in the motor patterns of speech and writing; and in cases of stuttering, he found an associated difficulty often with writing. In the other syndromes, he found associated difficulties with reading, spellinq, and writing. Because of these associations, special tests were devised (e.g., the *Iota* tests with Marion Monroe, and writing tests) to evaluate the behavioral manifestations of the difficulty in each area of written language and to make the differential diagnoses of the specific language disabilities. In turn, the differential diagnoses served as the foundation for the remedial teaching procedures. These procedures, first developed during the research in Iowa and later in New York, Connecticut, and Philadelphia during both research and clinical practice, are now described in the teaching manual prepared by Anna Gillingham with the assistance of Bessie Stillman (Gillingham & Stillman, 1965).

Remedial Procedures and Sequences

The Orton–Gillingham Approach is often mistakenly referred to as a "method," which implies a rigidity that is the antithesis of its intent and its conceptual framework. Orton was careful to caution against a general formula to be applied to all cases.

Each case of developmental delay forms an individual problem in which factors derived from the neurological status, the emotional reactions, the educational needs and the facilities for carrying on retraining must be evaluated and a program devised to conform to all of these. This point can scarcely be emphasized enough since we are all prone to search for a simplified and universally applicable formula, but no such general "method" can be defined for any of these syndromes and any attempt to apply such a blanket prescription without thorough diagnosis of the individual case would assuredly lead to error and misguided effort [Orton, 1937, pp. 143–144].

The characterization of the Orton–Gillingham Approach as a method rather than an approach to be used judiciously overlooks its basic premises. We cannot overstress this point; indeed, Orton stressed it repeatedly.

For example, after a study of almost 1000 cases—from preschool to college age and from public, private, and parochial schools—Orton concluded that

> *each child presents an individual problem,* not only because of the diverse influence of a considerable number of environmental conditions, but also because *the relative part played by each of the three major functions entering into the language faculty—vision, audition, and kinaesthesis—varies markedly in different children as does the child's emotional reaction to his difficulty* [Orton, 1937, p. 157; italics added].

In his discussion of establishing the phonetic basis for reading, Orton once again made clear the need to avoid a rigid methodology:

> We have tried to avoid overstandardization lest the procedure become too inflexible and be looked upon as a routine method applicable to all cases of non-readers, which would be clearly unwise in view of the wide variation in symptomatology and hence in training needs which these children exhibit [Orton, 1937, pp. 160–161].

The study of large numbers of children, however, also convinced Orton that dyslexic children, *as a group,* exhibited certain "symptoms" related to his neurological concepts. This led him to advocacy of principles of educational remediation along with specific procedures to be applied as each case required for either training or retraining in reading, writing, and spelling. Most notably, he found that as a group, dyslexic children suffered from problems with spatial orientation in both reading and writing, instability of memory for symbols, difficulties with sound–symbol association, and problems of sequencing. Some children were severely handicapped and total nonreaders; others were moderately handicapped but reading below grade level with confusion and inefficiency. Spelling and writing were markedly deficient. The procedures, therefore, were designed to address the various problems that would inevitably be encountered in large measure.

The procedures in the Orton–Gillingham Approach are principally designed to: (*a*) overcome the tendency to reverse symbols and to transpose letters within syllables and words; (*b*) strengthen and ensure visual–auditory association for alphabetic symbols through a kinesthetic linkage; (c) establish the necessary left-to-right sequential process for reading, spelling, and writing; (d) strengthen mnemonic processes; and (e) provide a phonetic and syllabic basis for the building of an accurate and sufficiently extensive reading vocabulary.

The first four aims are based on Orton's theories of cerebral dominance and the establishment of association at the third level of cortical elaboration with "free interplay of visual and auditory implantations in control of both speech and writing [Orton, 1929b, p. 642]." Theoretically, Orton considered the kinesthetic element particularly important for overcoming the tendency to spatial, directional, and sequential confusions; the visual–auditory association reinforced motorically by speech and movement would be strengthened and result in the "elision of the confusing engrams [Orton, 1928a]."

The fifth procedure, the provision of a phonetic–syllabic basis for the building of an accurate reading vocabulary, is related to the other four in that it builds from the smaller units that can be utilized to the larger ones.

> [The] experiences in teaching reading to those children who have suffered from a delay or defect in learning this subject have pointed to the importance of sequence building in such cases and in our experiments in the other syndromes this has led us to look for such units as the child can use without difficulty in the field of his particular disability and to direct our training toward developing the process of fusing these smaller, available units into larger and more complex wholes [Orton, 1937, p. 158].

The necessity for this procedure was strengthened in Orton's view by some of the data that emerged in the 1926–1927 field study carried out in Iowa under the grant from the Rockefeller Foundation. In accumulating the data on reading retardation in a number of communities, the research group found that differences in the percentage of cases of reading disability in comparable schools correlated with differences in teaching methodology. For example, in a community with a relatively low percentage of cases of reading retardation with symptomatic evidence of specific disability, "sight reading methods were employed but when children did not progress by this method they were given help by the phonetic method. In the town with the larger number [of similar cases] no child was given any other type of reading training until he or she had learned ninety words by sight [Orton, 1929c, p. 140]." Orton concluded that although "sight reading" might result in greater progress as measured by a group average, it was clearly an obstacle for some children and that the number of such children, though relatively small, was nevertheless of numerical importance in terms of those severely affected. For others with a less severe disability who eventually did learn to read without special training, there was reason to believe that their achievement would not be commensurate with their ability and their achievement in other areas. Consequently, establishing the link between written or printed language and the phonetic elements it represents is an integral part and purpose of the Orton–Gillingham Approach.

Sound–Symbol Association and Reading Comprehension

The emphasis on sound–symbol association is also based upon the assumption that coding with accuracy and facility is essential for comprehension in reading. This is a view that has found increasing support in more recent times (e.g., Chall, 1967; Perfetti & Hogaboam, 1975) and is summed up somewhat succinctly by Gough and Hillinger (1980):

> Our view of reading, that it consists of decoding plus linguistic comprehension, may be too simple. If so, it should be easy to refute, for it holds that any child with normal comprehension who learns to decode with facility will know how to read, and if any child with normal comprehension fails to read, it is because he has not learned to decode with facility [p. 194].

Thus the initial goal of the Orton–Gillingham Approach is to insure the acquisition of accurate and facile decoding, as the final goal—understanding the concepts within the reading material—is dependent upon this basic skill. But there is a second assumption inherent in the approach toward that final goal, that is, that reading comprehension is also dependent upon vocabulary knowledge, the growth of which is linked to efficient decoding and storage in memory. Perfetti and Lesgold (1979) also relate these two, decoding and word meaning, to preventing "cognitive load" when the reader must extract meaning from the context:

> Knowing the exact meaning of a word . . . makes comprehension more a recognition task and less a problem solving task. . . . When print maps automatically to phonologically referenced words, the decoding requires no monitoring and hence, does not waste limited memory. This is a good example of two conceptually independent components that are functionally intertwined. Because decoding leads to meaning, affecting the efficiency of print decoding affects the efficiency of meaning access [p. 59].

Although the first emphasis in the Orton–Gillingham Approach is to insure decoding with visual accuracy, correct phonological association, and facile performance, decoding is only the foundation in reading. The teaching of decoding encompasses a progression from graphemes to syllables to multisyllabic words with roots and affixes, along with their meanings, so that the structure of the English language is made explicit. Sufficient practice in both reading and writing is provided so that one reinforces the other while moving toward the goal of automatic decoding. Throughout this process, there is the additional emphasis on vocabulary expansion and a steadily growing use of decoding in sentences and paragraphs in both oral and silent reading. Mastery tests are incorporated into the teaching process as a means of insuring that no weak "links" remain to impede the progress of the student.

Distinctive Features of the Approach

The teaching of decoding in the Orton–Gillingham Approach differs from other "phonics" programs in that the sequence, structure, and pedagogical procedures are specifically designed to circumvent the learning problems so often associated with developmental dyslexia. It avoids the workbook approach that is usually an important component of published phonics programs and often requires the child to work silently in the matching of letters and pictures or circling letters for the beginning sound of pictured objects. In the Orton–Gillingham Approach, the building of the visual–auditory (grapheme–phoneme) associations and fixing them firmly in memory is constantly reinforced kinesthetically in the initial learning stage through speech and movement (tracing and/or writing). The pupil sees, hears, says, traces, and writes. He produces the sound for the letter he sees or the letter for the sound he hears. He reads, he spells, he writes.

An important aspect of the approach is that it is synthetic, rather than analytic, in the teaching of the components necessary for decoding. The process begins with the phoneme and grapheme provided to the pupil; it does not require the selection by the pupil on the basis of his analysis of what is similar or different within a group of phonograms or words. Furthermore, it does not require phonemic segmentation from the pupil as a starting point but leads him to the awareness of such segments and how they are blended into larger units of syllables and words. For dyslexic children not aware of, or able on their own to reflect upon, the distinctive features of written language—such as the single grapheme to represent a phonemic segment within a word or, in some cases, the phonemic segments in oral language—this approach brings them to the level of conscious awareness that will enable them to develop their ability for the feature detection essential to accurate and facile decoding.

Early blending is an important aspect of the approach. With a minimum of graphemes learned, a few consonants and a vowel or two, syllables and short words are formed to be read, spelled, and written. As additional consonants and vowels are learned, the pupil reads, spells, and writes detached syllables and pseudowords as well as real words. Not only does this insure that there is a firm grasp of the sound–symbol correspondences but it demonstrates the syllabic nature of the language. Moreover, it is at this point that the foundation is laid for the structural analysis that will be needed for more advanced reading later on. Another important outcome is that by working first with the most predictable elements of the language—one-to-one correspondences of phonemes and graphemes and "regular" syllables—and thus generating rules that they can rely upon, the pupils gain in two ways. First, they develop a self-confidence that serves them well while they are gradually prepared to deal with less predictable components of the written language. Second, and perhaps equally important, they learn that there are rules that govern language.

Still another feature of the approach is the order in which the language components are introduced. For example, the phonograms are ordered, as they are presented, in a sequence that will circumvent visual and auditory confusions and, simultaneously, lead to a secure knowledge of syllable structure. The "short" rather than "long" vowels are introduced first along with selected consonants. Thus the basis is established for learning the most "regular" syllable in English, the "closed" syllable, and for the pupil to begin to grasp the rules that govern English syllable structure. But the *order* in which the vowels are introduced is important to overcoming the vowel confusions so often exhibited by dyslexic children and adolescents.

Using the principle of maximum contrast to avoid or correct visual, auditory, or speech production confusions and writing errors—and also to avoid proximity of shape, sound, and movement in writing—a front, *low* vowel (*a*, /æ/) is taught first and then followed with a front *high* vowel (*i*, /ɪ/). This provides more than contrast in speech alone; it provides also the most distinct contrast that can be obtained between two of the five vowels (*a, e, i, o, u*) for visual and auditory discrimination and the sequence of movement required for writing.

Similarly, using only those that are unequivocal, there is a planned order in the introduction of consonants. For example, voiced and unvoiced pairs (e.g., /b/ and /p/; /v/ and /f/) are spaced apart in the teaching sequence as are "mirror" pairs (e.g., *b* and *d*) or others that are frequently confused (e.g., *sh* and *ch*).

It is important to an understanding of the Orton–Gillingham Approach not to allow emphasis on its initial goal—the secure grasp and firm retention of phoneme–grapheme relationships either for reading acquisition or retraining in reading—to obscure its other equally important aspects. Early in his research to develop remedial procedures for developmental dyslexia, Orton found that merely teaching phonics was "hopelessly inadequate" without synthesis of phonetic elements into meaningful units, and he stated this view forcefully:

> We have repeatedly seen children referred to us as reading disability cases with the statement that the phonetic method had been tried but failed. In these cases examination has revealed the fact that while the teaching of the phonetic equivalents may have been fairly complete, the next and most cardinal step, that of teaching the blending of letter sounds in the exact sequence in which they occur in the word, had not been attempted or had been poorly carried out. It is this process of synthesizing the word as a spoken unit from its component sounds that often makes much more difficulty for the strephosymbolic [dyslexic] child than do the static reversals and letter confusions [Orton, 1937, p. 162].

Space does not allow the discussion of many other features of the Orton–Gillingham Approach that distinguish it from other remedial programs. I will, however, give a brief description of Gillingham's contribution to its development and the teaching manual she prepared with the assistance of her collaborator, Bessie Stillman.

GILLINGHAM'S CONTRIBUTION AND THE TEACHING MANUAL

Anna Gillingham, the school psychologist at one of the divisions of the Ethical Culture School with which she had been associated for many years and where she had developed a remedial department, began her case consultations with Dr. Orton soon after his arrival in New York in 1928. Taking leave from her school post in 1932, Gillingham accepted an appointment to work with Orton as a research associate at the Neurological Institute. Her assignment was "to organize remedial techniques in reading and spelling in conformity with Dr. Orton's neurological explanation [Childs, 1968, p. 8]." By 1933, she had completed this task and had compiled a "Detailed Description of Remedial Work for Reading, Spelling and Penmanship" (Childs, 1968, pp. 111–130).

In addition to quotations from Orton's writings to provide the theoretical framework, the compilation included outlines of procedures (e.g., the steps to ensure visual–auditory–kinesthetic "linkage") and specific details of the sequences to be followed in introducing letters and continuing on into reading, spelling, and writing.

With Bessie Stillman as collaborator, Gillingham expanded this original work and, as it became more widely known and in use in schools and remedial centers, successive editions were published and distributed by the authors. Eventually, the manual was taken over by a publishing house, and the seventh edition (Gillingham & Stillman, 1965) has by now gone through 14 printings with a wide distribution.

The manual is extensive in its detail of each topic, the sequence of topics, and teaching procedures, whether for reading or spelling or penmanship. It is heavily illustrated with examples and word lists for the orthographic representation of each English phoneme and syllable structure, affixes, and spelling rules and generalizations with their occasional "exceptions." The manual makes a distinction, however, between the application of the approach to the younger child and those who are in the upper elementary grades or high school. Although the same principles apply to both age groups—and indeed the older ones may need to cover the same ground as the younger ones—remedial training for upper grade pupils is covered in separate chapters.

Unless the older students are total nonreaders and in need of learning to decode at a rudimentary level, their presenting problems are likely to be slow reading with poor comprehension; almost certainly poor and sometimes bizarre spelling; great difficulty with expressive writing; frequently poor handwriting; and few or no study skills. Although the older student may need to acquire the same basic knowledge and skills as the younger child—as when the root of the problem with reading comprehension is either an inadequate grasp of decoding or inaccuracy and a lack of facility with it—the manual gives recognition to the fact that the work cannot be conducted in precisely the same manner as with the younger child. Discussion of the older students and the approach to be taken with them includes the observation that "their greater maturity and the realization of what they are facing make it possible to proceed more rapidly and with more comprehensive organization [Gillingham & Stillman, 1960, p. 118]."

Even while reviewing and "drilling" at a basic level to insure automatic decoding, less time is spent on this with the older students during the remedial period, and work at several other levels is carried on simultaneously. For example, vocabulary study can begin almost at once; pronunciation symbols and dictionary usage can be introduced;

spelling rules and generalizations can be taught; and notebooks can be organized. Thus, the work with the older student is simultaneously broader than with the younger one and ranges further through the course of remediation. The goal, however, is the same—automatic, facile decoding with reading comprehension at an appropriate level, expressive writing freed from the inhibition of spelling and handwriting problems, and good study skills.

Like the younger child, the older student makes use of the kinesthetic modality to strengthen visual–auditory associations, but it is more apt to be with writing than tracing, and the student also maintains notebooks for rules, vocabulary, word form alterations related to parts of speech, and spelling.

The sequence of topics is carefully structured, as they were for the younger children, so that the older students progress from the smaller units of the language that they already possess or acquire, and which they can utilize, to the larger ones. The work is comprehensive, ranging from insuring accuracy and fluency for decoding to the writing of a precis, and encompasses learning English vocabulary derived from Latin and Greek, learning to recognize grammatical constructions, learning to interpret the meaning in sentences and paragraphs of various constructions, and propositional writing.

Especially with older dyslexic students, the amount of work in any given area will differ from pupil to pupil; it will be determined by the differential diagnosis, stressed in the Orton–Gillingham Approach, and the uniqueness of the set of problems each child or adolescent brings to the remediation setting. The end goals remain the same for all, however—essential word attack skills, vocabulary knowledge, the thinking skills necessary for fluent reading with comprehension, and the ability to deal with spelling to the degree that allows uninhibited expression in writing. Both Orton and Gillingham held the firm conviction that these goals could be accomplished despite the difficulties and seeming obstacles of developmental dyslexia. Nowhere does Orton make this more explicit than in the conclusion to his book, *Reading, Writing, and Speech Problems in Children.*

The view here presented that many of the delays and defects in development of the language function may arise from a deviance in the process of establishing unilateral brain superiority in individual areas, while taking account of the hereditary facts, brings with it the conviction that such disorders should respond to specific training if we become sufficiently keen in our diagnosis and if we prove ourselves clever enough to devise the proper training methods to meet the needs of each particular case [Orton, 1937, p. 200].

That Orton attempted to meet his own challenge is eminently clear, and the "Orton–Gillingham Approach" is the result.

RESEARCH FINDINGS

After half a century of practice in clinics and schools where, according to numerous accounts, tutors and teachers have successfully used the Orton–Gillingham Approach, we should expect to be able to cite studies comparing it with other approaches. This is not the case, however, although there are many anecdotal descriptions of clinic and school programs, as there are case reports, demonstrating the effectiveness of this approach to selected populations of dyslexic children, adolescents, and adults. Yet good research reports remain few, for the Orton–Gillingham Approach as well as for others equally or even better known.

It is highly regrettable that educational research has not yet furnished the necessary, definitive, empirical data that would establish unequivocally the most efficacious remedial approach to dyslexia in general or to subtypes of dyslexia. The paucity of well-designed and properly controlled studies, however, merely reflects the poor caliber of educational research in general—an ongoing problem in education which shows little promise for resolution in the immediate future. For example, in 1967 a committee of the American Educational Research Association conducted a comprehensive study of the quality of educational research reported in articles published in both educational and noneducational journals during 1962. The committee concluded that the majority of the articles contained serious flaws. Furthermore, it considered less than 7% of the research articles published in educational journals as worthy of publication. Replicating this study, Ward, Hall, and Schramm (1975) conducted an evaluation of the educational research studies published during 1971. Agreeing with the conclusions of the earlier study, these authors found most educational research to be "mediocre" in quality. The most frequently cited shortcomings of the research articles were in procedures, data analysis, summaries, and conclusions. Poor design remains a persistent obstacle to obtaining reliable data.

The problem of research for remedial outcomes in dyslexia is especially compounded by the looseness of the terminology surrounding lags in reading and other school achievement and thus the selection and labeling of experimental groups. A "reading-disabled" group or "learning-disabled" group may or may not contain dyslexic children. Criteria for selection differ from study to study and, in many reports, are not even given. In addition, a group labeled "dyslexic" may contain children who are not achieving for one or more of a number of reasons.

As Torgesen and Dice (1980) point out, published reports of research continue to show these serious problems in the selection of reading-disabled and learning-disabled children for study. Torgesen and Dice surveyed eight major journals published during the last 3 years in order to examine the characteristics of recent research on learning disabilities. Excluding studies that focused primarily on "hyperactive" children and studies that were primarily designed to validate an instrument or test the relationship between two instruments, they selected articles that primarily focused on learning- or reading-disabled children, reported empirical data, examined the effectiveness of nonmedical treatment, or provided information about the psychological characteristics of the subjects.

According to Torgesen and Dice, their examination of the selected articles revealed serious problems in the manner of selecting the subjects, in description of the samples, in general methodology, and in the failure of a high proportion of the studies to employ true experimental designs.

Thus, despite the increased sophistication of statistical analysis, which is now aided by computer technology, we are left with little reliable empirical data derived from scientifically based studies that can demonstrate conclusively that one remedial approach or another is the more promising one in a given situation.

My own search for such data on the Orton–Gillingham Approach has turned up a large number of reports that demonstrate impressive results based upon evaluation with pre- and post-treatment testing, although they do not involve comparison with other specific modes of treatment. A significant number of schools also report successful intervention with a modification of this approach in classroom use for children identified through screening as at "high risk" in learning to read or as having specific language-learning disability.[3] Given this evidence in the face of the general deplorable condition of educational

---

[3] One example is the Slingerland program of intervention which is growing in popularity in school systems across the country. Large group screening tests and teaching procedures were adapted from the Orton–Gillingham Approach by Beth Slingerland, an educator who had studied with Anna Gillingham. Children are taught by regular grade school classroom teachers who have received training from Slingerland specialists.

Another example of an adaptation to classroom use is PROJECT READ, developed in Bloomington, Minnesota, by Mary Lee Enfield, Coordinator of Special Learning and Behavior Problems Program in Bloomington's school system. Now adopted by other school systems as well, PROJECT READ provides intensive training to all classroom teachers in the school system through the sixth grade so that they can use with selected groups of children the teaching program based upon the sequences and procedures of the Orton–Gillingham Approach.

research—including research in the area of our particular concern—and further drawing upon the disciplines of neurology, psychology, and psycholinguistics, our conclusion is that the Orton–Gillingham Approach has proven itself as a viable approach to the remediation of developmental dyslexia. In what follows, two studies, of different designs but each involving a careful selection of the population, are presented. The first illustrates the successful application of Orton's theories; the second demonstrates the success of Orton–Gillingham Approach.

Monroe's Study of 235 Children

Monroe's study, as she pointed out in her preface to the monograph *Children Who Cannot Read* (1932) in which she published the results, was an outgrowth of her previous study, undertaken under Dr. Orton in Iowa and reported in *Genetic Psychology Monographs* (Monroe, 1928). Using the diagnostic and teaching procedures developed during the Iowa research, she measured the results of remedial reading instruction given in varying amounts and under varying conditions to 235 children and adolescents drawn from schools in the Chicago area. Treatment was also varied according to the subtype identified during evaluation (i.e., visual, auditory, or motor). Final results were obtained on 189 children from three groups taught under different conditions—two experimental groups and one control group.

One group of 89 subjects received individual instruction at the Institute for Juvenile Research from tutors who used the special teaching procedures under supervision. A second group of 50 received instruction at their schools from their teachers. These teachers had also received training in the use of the special procedures and they came to the Institute for conferences. The work with this second group, however, was neither as intensive nor as controlled as the work with the group taught at the Institute. A third group of 50 children served as the control group and received the instruction that was ordinary for their schools.

The children in all three groups were subject to the same diagnostic procedures, criteria for inclusion in the study, and pre- and posttesting. Moreover, the three groups of children were very similar in their initial reading indices before the remedial instruction. As was to be expected, the intensive instruction group, treated at the Institute, made the greatest progress. The average gain for this group (based on the mean of four reading tests) was 1.39 years in the interval of 6.8 months between pre- and posttesting.

Of special interest, however, is the comparison between the two groups of 50 children taught in their own schools. The experimental group made a gain of .79 year in a 7-month period compared to .14 year by the control group in an 8-month period.

Following Orton's work in Iowa, Monroe's study was an early demonstration that his theories of instruction could be applied effectively within the schools as well as the clinic. The special teaching procedures were demonstrated as more effective than other procedures then in use by teachers within the classroom. Unfortunately, Monroe gives no information about the nature of the reading instruction given to the control group and we know from this study only that "ordinary" methods failed to produce the desired results.

A Follow-up Study of 216 Dyslexic Children

Another interesting report is the follow-up study of 216 dyslexic children by Kline and Kline (1975). The particular value of this study derives from several of its aspects. First, the 216 children were drawn from 750 referred over a 4-year period by family doctors because of suspected severe learning disabilities. Second, all referred children were subjected to the same extensive psychoeducational test battery and to psychiatric evaluation. Third, diagnosis of developmental dyslexia was based upon the 1968 definition by the World Federation of Neurology (Critchley, 1970). And, fourth, Orton–Gillingham therapy by specially trained tutors was advised for the patients diagnosed as having developmental dyslexia.

In the follow-up study, 92 patients who had received the recommended Orton–Gillingham therapy during the 4-year period of referrals (the clinic group) and 29 patients who had not followed the recommendation for similar treatment (the school group) were reevaluated. In place of the recommended treatment, the school group received either one or more of a variety of other treatments (language experience, whole-word reading approach, "Kephart" training, etc.) or, in a few cases, no treatment.

Independent research teams determined the results based on post-treatment evaluation without knowing which patients had or had not received the recommended therapy. Characterizing improvement as "some, marked, or dramatic," they found overall improvement to be 95.7% in the clinic group compared to 44.8% in the school group. "Marked" improvement, that is, reading up to grade level, was shown in the clinic group by 46.7% compared to 13.8% in the school group; "dramatic" improvement, that is, above grade level within a short period of time, was shown by 17.5% of the clinic group compared to 3.4% of the school group.

In addition to these 121 patients in the clinic and school groups who were reevaluated, another 95 patients were followed up through parental interviews by the independent research teams. Analysis of parental responses showed that 95.3% of the Orton–Gillingham treatment group (48 cases) had improved in comparison with 54.8% of the school treatment group (47 cases). Analysis combining the two kinds of follow-up (i.e., reevaluation of patients and parental responses) showed that only 4.3% of the 140 patients in the clinic group failed to improve versus 49% of the 76 patients in the school group.

The Need for Comparative Studies

Unlike many practices that prevail in the schools, the Orton–Gillingham Approach stems from serious scientific inquiry and careful research in its development. It seems ironic, therefore, that so many decades have elapsed with so little continuing scientific scrutiny applied to it. In this respect, unfortunately, it has experienced the same neglect that attends so many other educational innovations. Nevertheless, like all other theoretical constructs, its best use can come only after scientifically designed validation studies are carried out.

The problem of developmental dyslexia is real, and its consequences are severe for millions of children and adults—indeed, for the whole of society. Therefore, even while other disciplines search for the definitive answer to the enigma of developmental dyslexia—for example, in brain structure and its relationship to linguistic development—education must take on the task of finding the most effective ways to circumvent its consequences. To do this, it will have to undertake comparative studies of intervention approaches. These should include good experimental design, adequate control of variables, proper methodology, and appropriate statistical analysis. Equally important, reports of these studies should include the criteria used for the selection of subjects and controls along with full description of the intervention approaches under study.

Every remedial approach to children, including the one discussed in this chapter, should be subject to validation studies. This is no easy task for the busy school administrator, who may lack the training and/or the time for designing and supervising a research project. Collaboration with a nearby university may provide guidance and assistance not only in designing and executing a research project but also in searching for funds to carry out the project. Too often, it is the university that seeks out the school for carrying out a research project of its own design and for its own purpose. Perhaps it is time for the schools to reverse this process and to try to engage the support of the universities directly in the educational practices that are of immediate concern to the schools and the children they are meant to serve.

REFERENCES

American Educational Research Association, Committee on Evaluation of Research. (1967) An evaluation of educational research published in journals. Unpublished report. (Cited in A. W. Ward, B. W. Hall, & C. F. Schramm, Evaluation of published educational research: A national survey. *American Educational Research Journal, 1975, 12,* 109–128.)

Ansara, A., Albert, M., & Galaburda, A. (Eds.) *The significance of sex differences in dyslexia.* Towson, Md.: The Orton Society. 1981.

Bakker, D. J. (1979) Hemispheric differences and reading strategies: Two dyslexias? *Bulletin of the Orton Society, 29,* 84–100.

Benton, A. L. (1980) Dyslexia: Evolution of a concept. *Bulletin of the Orton Society, 30,* 10–26.

Bronner, A. F. (1917) *The psychology of special abilities and disabilities.* Boston: Little, Brown.

Chall, J. S. (1967) *Learning to read: The great debate.* New York: McGraw-Hill.

Childs, S. B. (Ed.) (1968) *Education and specific language disability: The papers of Anna Gillingham, M.A.* Towson, Md.: The Orton Society.

Critchley, M. (1970) *The dyslexic child.* Springfield, Ill.: Charles C Thomas.

Fisher, J. H. (1905) Case of congenital word-blindness. *Ophthalmic Review, 24,* 315–318.

Gates, A. I. (1922) *The psychology of reading and spelling with special reference to disability. Teachers College Contributions to Education, 129.*

Gazzaniga, M. S. (1973) Brain theory and minimal brain dysfunction. *Annals of New York Academy of Medicine, 205,* 89–92.

Geschwind, N. (1979) Asymmetries of the brain—New developments. *Bulletin of the Orton Society, 29,* 67–73.

Gillingham, A., & Stillman, B. W. (1960) *Remedial training for children with specific disability in reading, spelling, and penmanship* (7th ed.). Cambridge, Mass.: Educators Publishing Service.

Gough, P. B., & Hillinger, M. L. (1980) Learning to read: An unnatural act. *Bulletin of the Orton Society, 30,* 179–196.

Hier, D. B. (1979) Sex differences in hemispheric specialization: Hypothesis for the excess of dyslexia in boys. *Bulletin of the Orton Society, 29,* 74–83.

Hier, D. B., LeMay, M., Rosenberger, P. B., & Perlo, V. P. (1978) Developmental dyslexia: Evidence for a sub-group with a reversal of cerebral asymmetry. *Archives of Neurology, 35,* 90–92.

Hinshelwood, J. (1909) Four cases of congenital word-blindness occurring in the same family. *British Medical Journal, 2,* 1229–1232.

Kline, C. L., & Kline, C. L. (1975) Follow-up study of 216 dyslexic children. *Bulletin of the Orton Society, 25,* 127–144.

Lake, D. A., & Bryden, M. D. (1976) Handedness and sex differences in hemispheric asymmetry. *Brain and Language, 3,* 266–282.

Lenneberg, E. H. (1967) *Biological foundations of language.* New York: Wiley.

Masland, R. L. (1975) Samuel T. Orton—Yesterday and today in neurology. *Bulletin of the Orton Society, 25,* 156–159.

Monroe, M. (1928) Methods for diagnosis and treatment of cases of reading disability. *Genetic Psychology Monographs, 4,* Nos. 4 & 5.

Monroe, M. (1932) *Children who cannot read.* Chicago: University of Chicago Press.

Morgan, W. P. (1896) A case of congenital word-blindness. *British Medical Journal, 2,* 1378.

Orton, S. T. (1925) "Word-blindness" in school children. *Archives of Neurology and Psychiatry, 14,* 581–615.

Orton, S. T. (1928a) Foreword. In M. Monroe, Methods for diagnosis and treatment of cases of reading disability. *Genetic Psychology Monographs, 4,* Nos. 4 & 5.

Orton, S. T. (1928b) A physiological theory of reading disability and stuttering in children. *New England Journal of Medicine, 199,* 1046–1052.

Orton, S. T. (1928c) Specific reading disability—Strephosymbolia. *Journal of American Medical Association, 90,* 1095–1099.

Orton, S. T. (1929a) Neurological studies of some educational deviates from Iowa schools. *Journal of Iowa State Medical Society,* April 1929. (Reprinted in J. L. Orton, Ed., *"Word-blindness" in school children and other papers on strephosymbolia by Samuel Torrey Orton.* Towson, Md.: The Orton Society, 1966.)

Orton, S. T. (1929b) The neurologic basis of elementary education. *Archives of Neurology and Psychiatry, 21,* 641–646.

Orton, S. T. (1929c) The "sight reading" method of teaching reading, as a source of reading disability. *Journal of Educational Psychology, 20,* 135–142.

Orton, S. T. (1930) Familial occurrence of disorders in acquisition of language. *Eugenics, 3*(4).

Orton, S. T. (1931) Special disability in spelling. *Bulletin of the Neurological Institute of New York, 1*(2). (Reprinted in J. L. Orton, Ed., *"Word-blindness" in school children and other papers on strephosymbolia by Samuel Torrey Orton.* Towson, Md.: The Orton Society, 1966. Pp. 167–200.)

Orton, S. T. (1932) Some studies in the language function. (Presidential Address) *Proceedings of the Association for Research in Nervous and Mental Disease, 13.* (Reprinted in J. L. Orton, Ed., *"Word-blindness" in school children and other papers on strephosymbolia by Samuel Torrey Orton.* Towson, Md.: The Orton Society, 1966. Pp. 147–166.)

Orton, S. T. (1937) *Reading, writing, and speech problems in children.* New York: Norton.

Orton, S. T. (1943a) The philosophy of psychiatry: Remarks. In F. J. Sladen (Ed.), *Psychiatry and the war.* Springfield, Ill.: Charles C Thomas. (Reprinted in J. L. Orton, Ed., *"Word-blindness" in school children and other papers on strephosymbolia by Samuel Torrey Orton.* Towson, Md.: The Orton Society, 1966. Pp. 10–14.)

Orton, S. T. (1943b) Visual functions in strephosymbolia. *Archives of Ophthalmology, 30,* 707–713.

Orton, S. T., & Gillingham, A. (1933) Special disability in writing. *Bulletin of the Neurological Institute of New York, 3*(1 & 2). (Reprinted in J. L. Orton (Ed.), *"Word-blindness" in school children and other papers on strephosymbolia by Samuel Torrey Orton.* Towson, Md.: The Orton Society, 1966. Pp. 201–232.)

Orton, S. T., & Travis, L. E. (1929) Studies of action currents in stutterers. *Archives of Neurology and Psychiatry, 21,* 61–68.

Perfetti, C. A., & Hogaboam, T. W. (1975) The relationship between single word decoding and reading comprehension skill. *Journal of Educational Psychology, 67,* 461–469.

Perfetti, C. A., & Lesgold, A. M. (1979) Coding and comprehension in skilled reading and implications for reading instruction. In L. B. Resnick & P. A. Weaver (Eds.), *Theory and practice of early reading* (Vol. 1). Hillsdale, N.J.: Lawrence Erlbaum.

Stephenson, S. (1907) Six cases of congenital word-blindness affecting three generations of one family. *Ophthalmoscope, 5,* 482–484.

Stewart, M. A. (1980) Honoring the memory of Dr. Orton at the University of Iowa. *Bulletin of the Orton Society, 30,* 7–9.

Thomas, C. J. (1905) Congenital "word-blindness" and its treatment. *Ophthalmoscope, 3,* 380–385.

Torgesen, J. K., & Dice, C. (1980) Characteristics of research on learning disabilities. *Journal of Learning Disabilities, 13,* 531–535.

Ward, A. W., Hall, B. W., & Schramm, C. F. (1975) Evaluation of published educational research: A national survey. *American Educational Research Journal, 12,* 109–128.

Witelson, S., & Pallie, W. (1973) Left hemisphere specialization for language in the newborn: Neuroanatomical evidence of asymmetry. *Brain, 96,* 641–646.

Chapter Nineteen

Services for College Dyslexics

BARBARA K. CORDONI

INTRODUCTION

In the 1960s, when educators began a concerted effort to address the needs of the learning disabled, this effort coalesced around two factors: remedial programming, and early intervention/identification. Most believed, based on data available at the time, that given appropriate programming at early ages, children could be released from the effects of their disabilities by late adolescence. Relatively little thought was given to secondary and postsecondary training, because it was believed that such training would rarely be needed.

Yet when the children of the 1960s grew up, they all too often were still disabled. Researchers began to look further, and discovered to their sadness that learning disabilities did not disappear so magically, even though teachers were caring and often had discovered the disabilities in children when they were still young. The disabilities remained, having changed form, or, perhaps, having become less obvious, but still restricting the life goals of the individual.

Junior high school programs were developed and, finally, high school programs. Still, such programs were few and limited because of lack of knowledge and materials. Few teachers had then been trained in methods of working with secondary and postsecondary learning-disabled students. Materials which had been developed as remedial tools

435

READING DISORDERS

were oriented toward the elementary-aged student, and as such, were inappropriate for the older student.

Little research had been conducted on the older student, so there was no data base to help determine the effectiveness of various programs, techniques, or intervention systems as they were developed. Many students were dropping out of high school because of the lack of, or at least the inappropriateness of, programs in the high school. Many of these drop-outs became juvenile delinquents. Those who somehow managed to complete high school were not much better off. Ill-prepared for the working world, they found themselves in job situations that offered little opportunity for advancement. Many could not hold a job at all. Vocational education texts were usually written at reading levels above those of the dyslexic student, so even this area was closed to them. Clearly, it was time to act, and new laws provided the power with which to foment change.

There were many difficulties to be overcome. Few tests were available to assess the older student; moreover, as has been mentioned, a data base, from which such tests should emerge, was itself nonexistent. Researchers and educators could only guess as to which techniques, programs, or materials might benefit the student.

Teachers in high schools were sent to training workshops, or went back to college. Gradually, programs at the high school level began serving more needs, but for the student who wanted to continue, who had a special goal in life which required a higher degree, there were few options.

Although more and more educators struggled to meet the needs of this previously unserved population, legislation became the vehicle by which a nationwide effort began. The passage of P.L.94-142, Education of All Handicapped Act, stated that over a period of a few years, all handicapped individuals between the ages of 3 and 21 years must be served. Section 504 of the Rehabilitation Act further stated that no individual could be denied access into educational programs solely on the basis of a handicap. Yet college programs were few.

SPECIAL PROGRAMS FOR THE LEARNING
DISABLED AT THE COLLEGE LEVEL

A few small schools had attempted to develop special programs at the college level. Their programs differed widely with one exception—they were all expensive (the current range is $3000–10,000 per year).

This is not surprising in that any program that attempts to meet special needs is inevitably more expensive, both to begin and to maintain, than is a regular curriculum model. However, the effect was to limit programs to the wealthy or to the occasional scholarship student.

Often, the programs lasted only a short time. Few faculty were trained to work with this population; many did not want to. Administrators did not want to "lower their acceptance standards," fearful of the impact such a move would have on enrollment figures. Many would have liked to help but had no way to begin. As a result, when Gollay and Bennett's *A College Guide for Students with Disabilities: A Detailed Directory of Higher Education Services Programs and Facilities Accessible to Handicapped Students in the United States* was published in 1976, learning disabilities or dyslexia were not mentioned. The situation seems even more deplorable when it is noted that the book was developed under the auspices of the Bureau of Education for the Handicapped. In November 1978, a bulletin of *Education of the Handicapped* identified six colleges and universities that admitted learning-disabled students.

How does one enroll in an institution of higher learning? Generally, a transcript of high school grades, class standing, and one of the college entrance exams are the criteria on the basis of which an applicant is accepted or rejected. Yet, even though learning-disabled students have always been notoriously poor test takers, especially on timed tests, it is only recently that they have been allowed to take untimed college boards.[1] Our research has shown the limitations of this change: Only 1 high school counselor in 20 even knows that such testing is available, the testing must cost no more than a regular test administration, and the test results may not be judged differently from those administered to other students. As far as high school transcripts are concerned, these generally reveal the serious problems these students have in specific academic areas, problems resulting in low class rank and grade point average. Therefore, no matter what the law states, these students were—and still are—denied access because of their handicap.

Unknown to most is the fact that virtually all community colleges, colleges, and universities already have programs and services that would meet the needs of the learning-disabled student, with only minimal modifications, if the student were admitted. With a doctor's signature, dyslexics are eligible to have their textbooks taped, as are blind

---

[1] The ACT Assessment: Special Testing Guide; ACT Test Administration; P. O. Box 168; Iowa City, IA 52243.

students.[2] Students with receptive language problems are eligible to have a note-taker in class, as are the hearing-impaired. Any student is allowed to take tests orally; this, of course, includes students with dysgraphia.

Remedial or support services also exist in different forms at most institutions. Reading Centers, or Basic Skills Laboratories, are usually available, as are counseling centers. Because of the Section 504 regulations, there is usually a staff member on campus responsible for ordering books on tape, acquiring note-takers, or test proctors. Once an institution decides to make a commitment to serve the learning disabled, it is remarkable how few changes need to be made.

Probably the most critical modifications are in the areas of training the faculty and hiring a learning disability specialist. It is not generally a lack of concern that causes a faculty member to reject the learning-disabled student; it is a lack of understanding of his needs. Faculty must be helped to understand that a student who may be articulate in class cannot necessarily read a textbook or write the answer to an essay question. Faculty must learn that atrocious spelling may have nothing to do with intelligence or interest. There are many ways of acquainting the faculty with these facts. Slide/tape productions are available for rent. Professors from institutions that have viable programs often conduct workshops. National conventions have recently presented several sessions aimed at educating educators. Whichever method is chosen, it is critical that this be done.

The type of institution, be it a university or a community college, seems to matter little. What does matter is the presence of a professional who is excited about such a program and dedicated to making it work. The role of the professional must encompass the areas of diagnosis, training of staff, and programming for the students. This professional can be the primary resource for what can best be termed faculty consciousness raising sessions. In the vast majority of cases, with understanding comes acceptance.

Once the student has been accepted into the university or college, the next step is the administration of a diagnostic battery. Previously identified learning-disabled students have usually been tested repeatedly; they are not eager to repeat the process. Sometimes, previously collected diagnostic data can be used. Even data from elementary and secondary school records can be helpful, for it can provide information about a student's previous progress for comparison purposes.

[2] Recordings for the Blind, Inc., 215 East 58th Street, New York, NY 10022; Library Services for the Blind and Physically Handicapped; 1291 Taylor Street, N.W., Washington, D.C. 20542.

The rationale for collecting new diagnostic data is the need for intelligent programming for the student. The beginnings of any well-designed individual educational program must be developed from a thorough understanding of the student's strengths and weaknesses. Only when teachers really understand the modality preferences of a student can they be of any real service.

There are those who, despite the lack of appropriate testing instruments, of a data base, and of trained personnel, nonetheless have attempted to work effectively with the college-aged learning-disabled student, for the simple reason that these students cannot afford to wait.

As has been mentioned, the first colleges to address the issue were small private schools. In the 1970s, several colleges opened their doors and attempted to deal with the needs of a small number of learning-disabled students. Basically, the programs were tutorial in nature; students did not necessarily take part in the regular college curricula, going instead to specifically designed basic skills classes. Some enrolled in a regular class or two in addition to these skills classes, and institutions differed as to whether course credit was given for the skills classes.

Isolated community colleges in various parts of the country also attempted limited programs in the early 1970s, but they were few. In many ways, it was appropriate for the effort to begin in the community colleges: Many community colleges must accept all applicants, and, consequently, the learning disabled often enrolled in community colleges when they could not hope to matriculate elsewhere. The results were varied. Those schools that had a learning disability specialist often were able to help the handicapped student, but the lack of funding and the lack of support services sometimes hampered their efforts. Later in the decade, as more programs were developed, the success rate grew.

Virtually no state institution had any program until the late 1970s. There were many reasons for this. Entrance requirements were often higher, and the very size of the university frightened many students away from applying. Here, as in the other types of institutions, faculty were not exceptionally responsive. Yet a program in a large university has certain advantages over a program in a smaller institution, the proximity of support services being the major one. Because of the existence of these services, what a school must do to provide for students is less a matter of development than simply of organization. It is not necessary to pay development costs or find funds for additional personnel. This fact alone makes administrators more responsive to beginning programs. In addition, when a student comes in contact with a nonsupportive professor, there are others who teach the same course, and there are more students available to work as tutors. Moreover, the effort in the state university systems that have developed programs has been to keep costs as low as possible or to charge no additional fees.

In summary, there are advantages to each type of institution. In smaller schools the teacher–student ratio is often an added blessing, whereas in larger schools more support services are available. Throughout the country, community, private, and public colleges and universities are recognizing a need and attempting to address it. If faculty and administrative support is present, a learning disability specialist can make a significant impact.

So little has been researched about the late adolescent–young adult population that data are scarce and far from complete. Still, there are intriguing hints as to the nature of the disabilities that are prevalent in the student who has graduated from high school and attempted to go to college. Because Project Achieve, at Southern Illinois University–Carbondale, has the most complete data of any institution, much of the reported results must come from that research.

PROJECT ACHIEVE

Project Achieve completed its third year of programming in 1981. Based in a large state university in the Midwest, its foci were the collection of a valid data base for the college-aged, learning-disabled student, and the development of a support system to enable qualified students to overcome their learning disabilities to the extent of acquiring a college degree in their own areas of interest. Federal funding began in 1980, after 2 years of the pilot program.

In 1981, 46 students were members of Project Achieve. Their ages ranged from 17 to 23, and all but 7 were male. Their choices of academic majors utilized the breadth and scope of a major university, as students were enrolled in anthropology, administration of justice, aviation, education, engineering, special education, design, premedicine, chemistry, music, child and family services, and social work.

As the project was in its third year, posttest data were not yet available. However, it was found that the first year is the most difficult for the students, as it is for most college students. If the students are going to get into academic trouble, it is most likely to occur during the second semester of the freshman year. Interestingly, if we can get them through that period, they are generally able to complete a degree program. We have found that the longer they are with us, the less they need us. Although prognosis obviously differs with the severity of the disability, it seems that only a few students need much support help after 2 years. Indeed, most maintain a B average in their chosen field. Four are on the Dean's List, four have already graduated, and only three have dropped out of the university. Of those three, two did not really want to be in college, but had come because of parental expectations. The third had severe disabilities and experienced too much failure in his chosen field. However, his parents report that he now reads newspapers and magazines, something he had not been able to do before.

Virtually all of the students exhibit dyslexia to some degree, although the range of reading scores is enormous. If one simply looks at grade equivalent scores, the range in 70 students tested thus far at Southern Illinois University–Carbondale is 3.9–12.9. Results from other studies are similar. However, it should be noted that even in the students with reading grade scores at the college level, there is a serious problem with comprehension. Often those who attack words less well actually score higher on comprehension than their peers with seemingly better reading skills.

As posttest data were not available, it obviously is not yet possible to give quantitative data as to final reading posttest scores. However, the fact that more than 50% of the students no longer need their books on tape leads one to surmise that reading scores have increased significantly. About 40% of the students are taught using a phonics approach to reading. For the other 60% of the reading disabled, a multisensory approach (such as the Fernald Technique) is used, generally taught by syllables.

Language disabilities are common. Some students speak little and there is a paucity of vocabulary. Research data indicate approximately one-half of the students to be inarticulate. The other half are articulate, but the presence of this ability does not entail written fluency. Only rarely does a student have written language skills. Even those who are articulate are very poor in transferring verbal fluency to written work. All have spelling problems.

The spelling problems become apparent, of course, in all written work, not only in that the students spell poorly, but also in that they tend to choose smaller words, which they think they might be able to spell. Therefore, their written work suffers from both the quality of their spelling and the choices of their vocabulary. Students' writing also suffers from the spelling problem because, being uncertain whether to choose an *i* or an *e* or an *a* in spelling a word, they tend to write sloppily, freely admitting that they hope the teacher will give them the benefit of the doubt. A few spell bizarrely, but the pattern of about 80% of the students shows a phonetic attempt at spelling. For those students, the use of a book such as *The Perfect Speller* (Wittels & Greisman, 1978) supplies a critical need.

An interesting fact noted in a number of the students is that after practice they are able to write/spell the first four or five letters of a word, but this ability then deteriorates and the last few letters of the word are spelled incorrectly. Teaching the students to spell by syllables often ameliorates this problem, as the problem seems to be related to memory span rather than spelling per se.

Visual processing disorders are also common. Some of the students complain of "floating letters," others are still experiencing visual sequencing difficulties with letters and numerals. Reversals of telephone numbers and street addresses still occur. As all of the students receive eye examinations, we know these difficulties are not due to problems of visual acuity. Other visual processing disorders parallel those found in younger students: spacing, forming a gestalt, discrimination, and position in space.

It is interesting that motoric difficulties are still apparent at this age. Sports activities are invariably individual ones, never team sports, and most of the students do not participate in any sport. By far the most popular sport is swimming, with scuba diving a close second. Students report a "freedom" in water which they do not find elsewhere, leading one to question if a vestibular effect is occurring.

Fine muscle coordination is generally poor. All the students have either flunked or received no higher than a D in high school typing courses, a combined visual–motor task. Writing remains awkward; there is a strong tendency to print. Hobbies, when there is one, tend to involve larger muscles. Most students do not have hobbies. A few students want to be engineers, and they seem able to develop the skills necessary for drafting. Others are accomplished artists, but still have writing problems, leading one to suspect that writing a symbol system is more the problem than is fine motor coordination.

Even less has been written about social problems than about the other deficiencies, yet it has been repeatedly noted that what facilitates upward job mobility—indeed, what enables one to get a job in the first place—is how one presents oneself. The socially inept are at risk in all aspects of life, from peer relationships to employability. Consider for a moment how people respond to an inappropriate statement. Generally, in adults, there is little or no feedback, the listener merely turns away. Because learning-disabled students are notoriously weak in "reading" body language, gesture, or facial expression, their methods of assessing response are limited. If they have difficulty with the prosodic elements of speech as well, they are indeed aliens in the social world.

Research results offer intriguing hints as to the nature of the student who is able to complete high school and who will accept the continued trauma of higher education. Basically, Project Achieve data indicate that the degree of reading impairment per se is not as critical as is the student's motivation to go to school. Those who are ambivalent, who are going to school because of parental expectation, do not seem to have the degree of dedication necessary to earn a college diploma and sustain the remedial effort as well.

It is apparent that many students are dependent individuals who seek another's opinion before taking any action. The need to seek direction even when perfectly capable of proceeding on one's own results in students who are less well equipped for adulthood. Such students often tend to feel as though their lives are directed by others, and, consequently, show less ability to accept responsibility for their own mistakes.

In contrast are the students who are capable of self-direction. Generally more mature and less likely to blame others, their success rate is likely to be higher than that of their more dependent peers. However, it should be noted that dependency can be overcome by a general weaning process, which is slow at first—for dependency often stems from fear—but ultimately successful. This weaning process is accomplished by providing all the support asked for until students feel comfortable in their new environment, then gradually requiring that they do more and more for themselves.

For many years, the literature has alluded to depressed IQ scores in the learning-disabled population due to the effects of their handicap, so the possibility of depressed scores must always be considered in programming. There is also the probability that data collected on existing college populations are skewed: It is logical to assume that those who have made it this far are likely to be highly motivated individuals with better than average IQs. However, when one looks at the data, one finds a wide range of IQ levels; Project Achieve data show a range of 98 to 143 with a mean IQ score of 110.3. Differences of as much as 41 points between verbal and performance IQ scores are noted, although this is unusual. Of far more importance is the pattern of disabilities noted.

Efforts to assess children through the use of subtest "patterns" on Wechsler scales have continued for many years. It is therefore interesting to determine if patterns identified in the young learning-disabled child are similar to those found in the young adult. There appear to be important differences. Vance, Wallbrown, and Blaha (1978) identified two groupings of subtest scores which they named "distractibility" and "language-disability pervasive" in their subjects. These patterns are noted in the Project Achieve population as well. Keogh, Witter, McGinty, and Donlon (1973) noted high scores in what they termed "intellectual ability" and low scores in "attention–concentration." Both studies are replicated in our data. Obviously, those students with lowest scores in the language disability pervasive category are the most handicapped in receptive–expressive language, whereas those with low scores in distractibility and attention–concentration experience problems in attending to tasks and sustaining an effort. Neither of these conditions is conducive to rapid learning. These kinds of data serve to alert project staff to programming needs. For instance, the client with a short attention span will be tutored in short time segments rather than in 2–3 hour blocks. The language disability cases will require many techniques and materials, which include tape recorders, language experience activities, and note-taking skills.

Self-concept scores as identified by the Tennessee Self-Concept Scale (Fitts, 1972) reveal deviant scores in feelings of self-worth. Posttesting data indicate, however, that within 3 months of college enrollment, scores are in the normal range for most students. Academic scores change much more slowly. The ranges of academic scores are great. The range of reading scores, as was noted previously, shows a 9-year difference in high and low scores, the range of math scores a 10-year difference. Spelling scores are low for all students, the average being at about the fourth grade level.

Information derived from the Halstead–Reitan neuropsychological battery reveals that only the "learning over time" subtest differentiates between the experimental and control students. Investigators never know whether a learning-disabled student or a control student is being tested, but when that subtest is reached, it becomes obvious to them.

In contrast, the test of dichotic listening and the test of compressed speech differentiated not at all between subjects. Although many studies indicate deviant performance in dichotic listening skills in the learning-disabled child, that appears not to be a problem for the college-aged learning disabled. It is interesting to hypothesize about this: Is this a condition that is simply outgrown, or do people who have abnormal laterality never get this far educationally?

Academically, writing remains the most serious disability. Spelling, organizational, and syntactical difficulties all contribute to this problem. Motorically, the students tend to write slowly, but it is very difficult to determine what revisualization and other problems contribute to this phenomenon. Creativity, on the other hand, tends to be high.

As has been previously stated, remedial programming should always come from a thorough diagnostic base. For that reason, all students in Project Achieve are tested in a variety of ways in the same skill area. Math skills are tested visually through the use of the Peabody Individual Achievement Test (Dunn & Markwardt, 1970), motorically and visually by the Wide Range Achievement Test (Jastak & Jastak, 1965), and orally by the Wechsler Adult Intelligence Scale. Disparities among achievement levels are assessed, for it is often the modality used to question the student rather than the skill itself that causes the attainment of a measured skill level. It has been found, for instance, that in a test of comprehension administered randomly in oral and written form, the students are often able to answer only one or two comprehension questions in writing, but eight or nine orally. When learning styles and preferences are better understood, the time necessary for intelligent programming is lessened and accuracy of programming is enhanced. Therefore, each skill area is assessed in several ways.

Once levels have been determined, programming begins. Virtually all college programs function in this manner, although the quantity and quality of diagnostic workups vary widely. Generally, a student is required to work on several areas of weakness, particularly those which will most limit him academically. Often, of course, the weakest area is reading. Reading programs are chosen on the basis of a student's learning strength. For example, students who are strong auditorily would be programmed into a phonics program such as Gillingham and Stillman's (1960) remedial training program, whereas students who need a multisensory program might work according to Fernald's visual, auditory, kinesthetic, and tactile (VAKT) approach. While this skill was being developed, all books would be taped so that the student would not miss content. The student would be encouraged to listen to the tapes while reading along, for this technique has been shown to increase comprehension. As books are taped free of charge by the Library of Congress, and are also available from Recordings for the Blind, there is no financial burden involved. A program called Scoring High in Survival Reading (Kravitz & Dramer, 1977) is taught to most students, as it teaches such skills as reading a map or a classified advertisement, an income tax form, or a job application.

Organizational skills are taught in a variety of ways. If a student has a term paper to write, he or she would be shown how to look up the topic in the library. Each salient point would be written on a separate card. After the topic is thoroughly researched, the cards would be divided into three piles, one for the introduction, one for the body of the paper, and the last for the summary. The student then begins the writing task, and with the help of a tutor, if necessary, inserts any "carry" sentences which are needed. Finally, the draft copy is looked at for spelling errors. Using *The Perfect Speller* (Wittels & Greisman, 1978), which shows all of the ways a word *might* be spelled in red, and the correct spelling in black, the student corrects the paper, and only then types it. As a part of this whole process, the student is taught through *The Thirty Lessons in Outlining* (Ross & Culliton, 1971) program.

Typing is a skill taught as quickly as possible after enrollment, for students are less likely to reverse on a typewriter and, interestingly, make fewer spelling errors. A fine program which limits stimuli is the *Typing Keys for the Remediation of Reading and Spelling Difficulties* (Davis, 1971). Because of the way it is designed, learning-disabled students have little difficulty learning to type, although they may have been unable to do so before.

Many students have trouble in writing down notes in lecture classes, or in choosing *what* to write down. Students first learn to take a tape recorder to class and to take as many notes as they can. Then the tape is brought into the learning lab and played sentence by sentence. Each sentence is assessed to determine if it contains information that is important and should be remembered, which would then be added to the notes. This process continues throughout the taped lecture. Although this is a lengthy process, it teaches a necessary skill. All of the students also complete the *Thirty Lessons in Notetaking* (Ross & Culliton, 1971) program. Soon they are able to handle this area on their own, although they may still prefer to use the tape recorder for reinforcement.

Social skills training is not so concrete, but is important nonetheless. Students have problems making friends, knowing how to talk to professors, and learning what things not to say. They are often ill at ease in groups. A peer advocate may be assigned to go with the student to a club activity, to acquaint him with the town, or simply to be a good listener. Tutors and advocates are trained to respond to inappropriate comments, instead of not reacting verbally. They may say, "What you just said hurts my feelings. What you could have said was. . . ." Verbal interplay has been called the social sense and must be an important part of a student's training. Because the student has never played a significant role in the social world, a repertoire of behavior must be instilled.

Language disabilities appear in many forms. Receptive abilities are the most severe, in that one must receive before one can express. Often students do not understand assignments or important points because of receptive problems. They will look quizzically at a speaker and often "fill in the blanks" with what they thought was said. This can lead to some serious problems. Our students are taught to repeat the assignment they thought they heard to check for accuracy, and to use a tape recorder until this skill is enhanced.

Expressive difficulties limit one's ability to communicate ideas, thoughts, and feelings. Again, social interaction is affected. Word retrieval difficulties may exist. As most of our students are tested orally because of the writing and spelling problems, expressive difficulties may limit the ability of students to demonstrate what they know. When expressive difficulties also affect writing, students are left with a double handicap. It seems, however, that the student who is not orally fluent can often write things down. When a word will not come, we often say, "Let your hand do it." In this way, fluency increases over time.

Basically, the learning-disabled young adult is afflicted with the same disabilities as are younger children, and six major areas of concern must be addressed in the educational–social climate:

> Social problems
> Dependency
> Lack of organizational skills
> Writing and spelling difficulties
> Academic deficits
> Language problems

In a simple reading of this list, it will be obvious to the most casual reader that the problems listed cross areas usually served by at least three disciplines. Although the need for interdisciplinary research and remediation has been cited for years, little actual work on a long-term basis has been accomplished. It behooves us all to consider the possible contributions of other disciplines and to find methods of integrating them for the benefit of all our students.

REFERENCES

Davis, M. (1971) *Typing keys for remediation of reading and spelling.* San Rafael, Calif.: Academic Therapy Publications.

Dunn, L., & Markwardt, F. (1970) *Peabody Individual Achievement Test.* Circle Pines, Minn.: American Guidance Service.

Fernald, G. (1943) *Remedial techniques in basic school subjects.* New York: McGraw-Hill.

Fitts, W. (1972) *Tennessee Self-Concept Scale.* Nashville, Tenn.: Oede Wallace Center.

Gillingham, A., & Stillman, B. (1960) *Remedial training for children with specific disability in reading, spelling and penmanship.* Cambridge, Mass.: Educators Publishing Service.

Gollay, E., & Bennett, A. (1976) *A college guide for students with disabilities*. Cambridge, Mass.: Abt Associates.

Jastak, J., & Jastak, S. (1965) *The Wide Range Achievement Test (Rev. ed.)*. Wilmington: Guidance Associates.

Kasinin, L., & Hanfmann, E. (1938) An experimental study of concept formation in schizophrenia. *American Journal of Psychiatry, 95*, 35–48.

Keogh, B., Witter, J., McGinty, A., & Donlon, C. (1973) Functional analysis of WISC performance of learning disordered hyperactive and mentally retarded boys. *Psychology in the Schools, 10*, 26–31.

Kravitz, A., & Dramer, D. (1977) *Scoring high in survival reading*. New York: Random House, *10*, 178–181.

Reitan, R., & Davison, L. (1974) *Clinical neuropsychology: Current status and applications*. Washington, D.C.: V. H. Winston.

Ross, E., & Culliton, T. (1971) *Thirty lessons in outlining*. North Billerica, Mass.: Curriculum Associates.

Vance, H., Wallbrown, F., & Blaha, J. (1978) Determining WISC-R profiles for reading disabled children. *Journal of Learning Disabilities, 11*, 657–660.

Wechsler, D. (1955) *Wechsler Adult Intelligence Scale*. New York: The Psychological Corporation.

Wittels, H., & Greisman, J. (1968) *The perfect speller*. New York: Grosset & Dunlap.

Chapter Twenty

Differential Treatment of Reading Disability of Diverse Etiologies[1]

P. G. AARON
SONDRA L. GRANTHAM
NANCY CAMPBELL

INTRODUCTION

There exists a clear possibility that children with specific reading disability constitute a heterogenous group. Boder (1971, 1973) has proposed that there are three subgroups of reading-disabled children: (*a*) the dysphonetics, who have difficulty in symbol–sound association and word analysis, (*b*) the dyseidetics, who are deficient in the perception of whole words, and (*c*) a mixed group. Further, she has shown that writing to dictation provides a convenient means of identifying these three groups. For instance, the dysphonetic child who has phonetic analysis difficulties commits spelling mistakes of a bizarre nature. When asked to write 'stop' he may write *sotp* or *spto,* and for 'mother' he may write *mom.* On the other hand, the dyseidetic child whose visual memory for words is poor tends to spell literally as the word sounds. This results in writing *blu* for 'blue' or *gal* for girl. Boder's dysphonetic and dyseidetic groups signify analytic–sequential and gestalt–spatial difficulties, respectively. Interestingly, the two basic methods of teaching reading are phonics and look–say, the former based on the analytic–sequential and the latter on the gestalt–holistic processes.

[1] The research program was supported by a grant from the Research Committee, Indiana State University. The authors wish to thank Jo Ann Evans for her assistance during the tutorial sessions.

449

It was therefore hypothesized that successful remediation of reading disability should be aimed at overcoming the deficits of children by training the dysphonetic child through the analytic–phonetic method and the dyseidetic child through the whole-word–gestalt method. The results of experimental attempts to test the validity of this hypothesis are reported here.

EXPERIMENT 1

Subjects. From among reading-disabled children attending a special remedial program, seven boys and one girl who could be unambiguously classified as dysphonetic or dyseidetic were selected. All the students had completed the second grade and were of at least average intelligence. Their mean age was 7.9 years and, as determined by the Gates–MacGinitie Reading Test, they were reading at more than one grade level below expectation.

Procedure. Subjects were classified as dysphonetic or dyseidetic on the basis of the errors they made in the writing to dictation task. Following Boder's procedure, four children whose written spelling revealed predominantly sequential errors were placed in the dysphonetic group and four children who tended to spell strictly the way the words sound were placed in the dyseidetic group. Of the four subjects in each group, two were trained through the phonetic–sequential method and two were trained through the gestalt–whole-word method.

Videotapes representing two different instructional modes—phonetic sequential and gestalt–whole-word were prepared. In the phonetic–sequential method, each word in a sentence was broken down into its letter components and each letter of the word, along with its sound, was displayed in the videomonitor. After all the letters of the word had been presented sequentially one at a time, the entire word appeared on the screen along with its sound. After three such repeated presentations, the same sequence was repeated twice without the corresponding sound. During those silent presentations, the tutor urged the subjects, one at a time, to sound the word out. Each word in the sentence was presented in this manner, and finally, the entire sentence appeared on the screen, first with and later without sound. Again, the tutor instructed each subject to read the sentence aloud. In the gestalt–whole-word method, each word in the sentence was presented as a unit, five times with and twice without sound. After each word in the sentence was presented in this manner, the entire sentence appeared on the screen first with and later without sound. Twenty sentences were taught at the rate of one per day for a period of 4 weeks. The children were instructed in groups of four with a tutor present during the entire session which lasted about 25 min. No other reading instruction was provided to these children during the treatment period. Two forms of the Gates–MacGinitie Reading Test were administered as pre- and posttests.

EXPERIMENT 2

Method. The second experiment was initiated in October and lasted the entire academic year. The diagnostic and treatment methods were identical to those of Experiment 1 with the following exceptions: A control group matched for age, sex, and reading achievement score was selected. Children in the control group attended the conventional remedial reading classes for 45 min, 3 days a week. Subjects in the experimental groups maintained a workbook in which they were required to write from memory the sentence they had learned during the treatment session. The total number of sentences taught to the experimental group was 40. Children in the experimental groups received treatment for 30 min per day, 3 days a week.

Subjects. There were six boys and three girls in this treatment group. The control and experimental groups had mean reading grade equivalent scores of 1.29 and 1.24 respectively; their mean ages were 8.4 and 8.3 years; and all were attending the third grade.

Procedure. Of the nine subjects, four were dyseidetic; three of these children were placed in the phonetic training group; the remaining subject received whole-word training. Out of the remaining five dysphonetic subjects, three received training through the phonetic method and two in the whole-word method.

RESULTS

Both experiments yielded essentially the same results. As the small number of subjects does not permit valid statistical analysis, the data from both experiments are combined and the mean scores are shown in Table 20.1. On the Gates–MacGinitie test, greatest gains in terms

Table 20.1

Performance of Subjects Belonging to the Different Diagnostic and Treatment Groups[a]

	Holistic–gestalt deficient subjects		Sequential–phonetic deficient subjects		
	Trained by phonetic method (N = 5)	Trained by whole-word method (N = 3)	Trained by phonetic method (N = 5)	Trained by whole-word method (N = 4)	Control (N = 9)
Gain in vocabulary	.85	.50	.45	.55	.50
Gain in comprehension	.49	.10	.15	.20	.15

[a] Gains are for the Gates–MacGinitie Reading Test, and given in terms of grade equivalents.

of vocabulary and comprehension were shown by the dyseidetic subjects who were trained by the phonetic–sequential method. Among the dysphonetic children, those who were trained in the whole-word method showed greater gains than those trained in the phonetic–sequential method.

DISCUSSION

The observation that the dyseidetics did better under the phonetic–sequential method and the dysphonetics under the whole-word method suggests that reading-disabled children are likely to improve when taught by methods that utilize their strengths rather by those that attempt to strengthen their weaker processes. The hypothesis proposed earlier was, therefore, rejected.

The small number of children involved as well as the lack of statistical analysis of the data are clear limitations of the study. It is reported here simply to stress the need for taking into account the heterogenic nature of reading disability while formulating treatment plans.

REFERENCES

Boder, E. (1971) Developmental dyslexia: Prevailing diagnostic concepts and a new diagnostic approach. In H. R. Myklebust (Ed.), Progress in earning disabilities (Vol. 2). New York: Grune & Stratton.

Boder, E. (1973) Developmental dyslexia: A diagnostic approach based on three atypical reading–spelling patterns. Developmental Medicine and Child Neurology, 15, 663–687.

Chapter Twenty-One

Psychotropic Drugs in the Treatment of Reading Disorders

MICHAEL G. AMAN

INTRODUCTION

Psychotropic or behavior-modifying drugs were first extensively used in children variously described as hyperactive, hyperkinetic, or minimally brain damaged (Conners & Werry, 1979; Werry, 1976; Cantwell & Carlson, 1978). In particular, the stimulant drugs such as the amphetamines and methylphenidate (Ritalin) have proven effective in dampening excessive motor activity, reducing aggressiveness, and improving attention span in grossly hyperactive children. However, there

[1] Preparation of this chapter was supported by a grant from the Medical Research Council of New Zealand to Professor J. S. Werry.

453

has also been a recent trend to employ psychotropic medication in children with specific learning problems, including reading disorders.

It is worth noting at the outset that the state of diagnostic classification in this area has been one of disarray. For this reason, I will use general terms such as "learning problems," further unspecified, when the original usage was unclear or when information was lacking regarding the narrower area of specific reading disorders.

This chapter looks at a variety of issues in relation to the pharmacotherapy of reading disorders. First, an attempt is made to examine the incidence of drug treatment in learning problems. Second, the emergence of the stimulants as a therapy for childhood behavior problems, their subsequent application in treating learning problems, and the research pertaining to effects on reading itself are discussed. Next, the role of antianxiety drugs is presented along with relevant research. Finally, suggestions for future research and overall conclusions are set forth.

DRUG PREVALENCE IN CHILDREN WITH LEARNING PROBLEMS

Gadow (1975, 1976, 1979) surveyed a large group of children in special education programs in Illinois and found that between 12 and 14% of the children in these programs received at least one type of psychotropic or anticonvulsant drug. Anticonvulsants were the most common drugs, followed by stimulants, anxiolytics, then antipsychotic drugs. Gadow relied upon the reports of teachers who were not necessarily informed about all medications received by their pupils, so it is possible that these figures underestimate real levels of drug prescription. Hansen and Keogh (1971) examined the incidence of medication in 239 educationally handicapped pupils in California. They found that 31% of these children were receiving drugs. Sedatives and tranquilizing medication were most frequently prescribed, followed by stimulants. Neither of these surveys focused exclusively on children with specific reading disorders (i.e., children grossly retarded in reading relative to overall intellectual ability) although the populations studied clearly would have included some such children.

The lines of diagnostic demarcation in this area are ill defined and amorphous, with children frequently presenting symptoms of hyperactivity in addition to specific learning disorders. One study of children selected for learning disorders revealed that almost one-half of the children presented hyperactive behavior as the *principal* problem (Schain, 1972). A large majority of children who are diagnosed as hyperactive by their doctors subsequently receive psychotropic medications, particularly the stimulants, for improvement of social behavior and reduction of excessive activity (Gadow, 1981). This suggests that a significant proportion of children with learning disorders may receive psychotropic drugs because of coexisting hyperactivity.

If we take these estimates of drug prevalence in special education classes together with the association between hyperactivity and reading disorders, it appears that psychotropic drugs have become a common form of treatment in this area. With this in mind, it would be instructive to look briefly at the history of stimulant drug therapy in hyperactivity because of its relevance both to the medical treatment of reading disorders and to the greater area of pediatric psychopharmacology.

A BRIEF HISTORY OF STIMULANT TREATMENT

Behavior Disorders

The first major impetus toward pharmacological treatment of behavior problems in children resulted from a widely cited study by Bradley (1937), in which amphetamine (Benzedrine) was administered to 30 children. These children ranged in age from 5 to 14 years, were of normal intelligence, and presented with a wide variety of behavior disorders including specific educational disabilities, anxiety disorders, and aggressive behavior. Bradley's drug trial was poorly controlled by today's standards, but his conclusions were important because they served to encourage both research and treatment of children with stimulants. With regard to school performance, he stated:

> Fourteen children responded in a spectacular fashion. Different teachers, reporting on these patients . . . agreed that a great increase of interest in school material was noted immediately. There appeared to be a definite "drive" to accomplish as much as possible during the school period, and often to spend extra time completing additional work. Speed of comprehension and accuracy of performance were increased in most cases [p. 578].

The children were also described as more "subdued" emotionally; mood swings and noisy, aggressive, and domineering behavior were greatly diminished. Furthermore, excessive motor activity often appeared to be reduced. Thus, Bradley concluded that the stimulant caused improvement in learning and behavior, and reduced excessive motor activity, although he did not present numerical data to support these impressions.

This and other reports by Bradley ultimately led to the extensive use of stimulants and other drugs to treat hyperactivity,[2] a condition characterized by inattention, excessive motor activity, impulsivity, and aggressiveness, and frequently accompanied by learning problems (Conners & Werry, 1979; Gittelman-Klein, Spitzer, & Cantwell, 1978; Werry, 1976). Subsequent research on drug treatment in these children has gradually undergone large improvements in methodology, but most of Bradley's conclusions regarding the effects of stimulants on *social* behavior have been upheld, namely that inappropriate and excessive activity are reduced and behavioral adjustment improved by such treatment (Conners & Werry, 1979).

There has also been substantial work which has looked at the effects of drugs on the learning of hyperactive children. These studies can be characterized as either *laboratory investigations*, which have looked at basic cognitive function in the short term, or *long term follow-up studies*, which have attempted to measure the long range effects of medication in various spheres including academic achievement (see Aman, 1980).

In the laboratory situation, the stimulants tend to improve attention span, verbal memory, short-term memory, and occasionally cognitive style in hyperactive children. Additionally, performance is often found to be enhanced on clinical tests of perception and on tests of planning capacity, such as the Porteus Mazes (Aman, 1978, 1980; Freeman, 1966; Sprague & Werry, 1971; Sroufe, 1975). All of these laboratory findings understandably led to an enthusiastic reception of the stimulants, both by the professions and by the public.

Follow-up educational studies of hyperactive children necessarily lagged behind the more immediate laboratory assessments. Unfortunately, this group of studies has been unable to document lasting educational gains as a result of any of the medications (stimulants, antidepressants, or antipsychotics) used in treating hyperactive children (Aman, 1978, 1980; Barkley & Cunningham, 1978; Hechtman, Weiss, Finkelstein, Werner, & Benn, 1976; Mendelson, Johnson, & Stewart, 1971; Minde, Weiss, & Mendelson, 1972; Quinn & Rapoport, 1975; Riddle & Rapoport, 1976; Weiss, Kruger, Danielson, & Elman, 1975; Weiss, Minde, Werry, Douglas, & Nemeth, 1971).

---

[2] Officially designated as Attention Deficit Disorder with Hyperactivity in the new American Psychiatric Association diagnostic system (DSM III).

The discrepancy between the immediate cognitive assessments and educational follow-up may be explained by the rather specific action of the most common pediatric drugs (particularly the stimulants and antidepressants) in improving the attention span of these children (Barkley & Cunningham, 1978; Douglas, 1974). Most of the laboratory tests that have been cited here place considerable reliance upon uninterrupted attention span. However, it cannot be assumed that heightened scholastic ability would necessarily follow from enhanced attention span.

As the cardinal features of hyperactivity are motor overflow, impulsivity, and excessively short attention span, the failure to document *educational* gains has not been seen as crucial to the legitimacy of pharmacotherapy in this disorder. Nevertheless, the lack of clear-cut educational improvement in the long term has tempered some of the enthusiasm for pharmacotherapy even in hyperactivity.

Children with Learning Disorders

In developments that were later than but parallel to those outlined for hyperactivity, many clinicians began to treat children having specific learning difficulties with stimulant medication. Emphasis has been placed by some authors (e.g., Anderson, Halcomb, & Doyle, 1973; Harris, 1976; Routh, 1979) on research showing attentional deficits in children selected for specific learning problems (see also Kinsbourne, this volume). Because this finding has been so common, poor attention span and excessive distractibility have often been considered as major causes of reading and other learning disorders (e.g., Harris, 1976). This understandably led to the usage of stimulants in children with learning problems because of the reputation of these drugs for improving attention in other groups of children (Aman, 1978; Sroufe, 1975) as well as in adults (Weiss & Laties, 1962). Furthermore, their administration seemed justified by the enthusiastic claims of the earliest uncontrolled trials in children with behavior problems and because of the *impression* of general cognitive facilitation which emerged from laboratory studies.

The failure of follow-up studies to show educational gains in hyperactive children naturally raised the issue of whether the stimulants were being too enthusiastically administered to children with learning problems (e.g., Adelman & Campos, 1977; Rie, Rie, Stewart, & Ambuel, 1976a, 1976b). Research relating directly to the efficacy of the stimulants in severe reading disorders will be presented later.

SOME CONSIDERATIONS OF IMPORT
TO DRUG RESEARCH

Classification

The state of classification and diagnosis in pediatric psychopharmacology has often been one of disarray. No single diagnostic system
has been used to determine selection practices or to render more or
less standardized groupings of subjects. Furthermore, various labels
such as hyperactivity, minimal brain dysfunction, and even learning
disability have at times been applied indiscriminately and often without
objective criteria, sometimes creating the impression that they are in-
terchangeable terms. Such haphazard usage of diagnostic terms has
caused a great deal of confusion and has probably encouraged the use
of pharmacotherapy in learning-disordered children despite lack of
documentation indicating beneficial effects.

An important related issue concerns the measurement and classification of reading disorders in children participating in drug investigations. Rutter and Yule (1973, 1975) have presented a strong case for
the scientific value of defining reading problems in terms of reading
backwardness or alternatively reading retardation. Reading backwardness traditionally refers to a discrepancy between reading age and *chronological age* whereas reading retardation denotes a discrepancy between
reading age and *mental age*. Some studies (see Rutter & Yule, 1973;
Yule, 1973) have shown that academic and social outcome are quite
different for these two groups. Also, reading retardation, which conforms to many people's concept of "specific reading disability," is theoretically interesting due to the unexplained discrepancy between demonstrated intellectual ability and achievement. Finally, these terms are
essentially operational definitions for the disorders in question, making
it possible to compare groups across studies. Unfortunately, as will be
shown later, these relatively objective terms have been used infrequently in drug research relating to reading disorders.

Independence of Behavioral and Cognitive Drug Effects

One issue which has received little attention in the past is the degree
to which behavioral changes concur with cognitive changes. Most children who receive psychotropic medication do so for behavioral control,
whether it be for hyperactivity, extreme aggressiveness, or emotional
problems. Many workers, myself included, have assumed that a fa-

vorable behavioral response would naturally be associated with positive cognitive changes, or at least was unlikely to be associated with adverse cognitive changes. However, findings that have emerged in the research (Gittelman-Klein & Klein, 1975; Lerer, Lerer, & Artner, 1977; Yepes, Balka, Winsberg, & Bialer, 1977) suggest that behavioral change is often quite independent of other changes in the cognitive and scholastic sphere. For example, Gittelman-Klein and Klein (1975) examined a wide variety of psychometric learning measures and compared these to parent, teacher, psychiatrist, and psychologist behavior ratings of children treated with methylphenidate. The results were startling because the number of significant correlations between learning and behavioral measures did not exceed chance levels!

This raises the interesting issue of what dimensions should take priority in children with learning disorders who also happen to be hyperactive or who have other behavioral difficulties. It also suggests that regardless of the *reason* for placing a child on medication, there should be provision for both cognitive and behavioral assessment. Adequate medical supervision of the future may well demand just such a comprehensive evaluation.

STIMULANT DRUG RESEARCH IN CHILDREN WITH READING DISORDERS

I was able to locate eight studies that have evaluated the role of stimulants in children selected for the presence of learning problems. Two additional studies which emphasized drug effects on achievement were also included. The studies are presented in order of publication in Table 21.1.

Methodology

All studies adequately applied the usual methodological controls including the use of placebos, and only one (Conners, Rothschild, Eisenberg, Schwartz, & Robinson, 1969) failed to report a double blind procedure to minimize bias. The only apparent methodological flaw of consequence occurred in the study by Page, Janicki, Bernstein, Curran, and Michelli (1974), in which initial group differences on the achievement measures may have made interpretation of differences at outcome of the trial impossible.

Table 21.1
Studies of Achievement Using Stimulant Drugs

Authors	Subjects	Drugs, group size	Duration	Perceptual–cognitive measures[a]	Achievement measures[b]	
Huddleston, Staiger, Frye, Musgrave, & Stritch (1961)	"Retarded readers" of normal IQ. Primary, secondary, & tertiary level students. Degree of retardation unspecified.	Deanol, 75 mg, twice daily (N = 60); placebo (N = 60).	8 weeks	Differential Aptitude Test a) Clerical speed b) Clerical accuracy (2/2)	Gates Survey Reading Test	(=) N.S.
Conners, Rothschild, Eisenberg, Schwartz, & Robinson (1969)	Children with learning or behavior problems. Extent of learning problem unspecified.	Dextroamphetamine (approx. 25mg/day) (N = 22); placebo (N = 21).	4 weeks	Porteus Mazes Frostig Test of Perception (2) Auditory perception Paired associate learning (4/18)	WRAT a) Reading b) Spelling c) Arithmetic Gray Oral Reading	(↑) N.S. (=) N.S. (↑) * (=) N.S.
Conrad, Dworkin, Shai, & Tobiessen (1971)	Children screened for hyperactivity. Extent of learning problem unspecified.	Dextroamphetamine (10–20mg/day) (N = 33); placebo (N = 35).	4–6 months	Frostig Test of Perception (3) (3/10)	WRAT a) Reading b) Arithmetic	(↓) N.S. (↑) N.S.
Conners, Taylor, Meo, Kurtz, & Fournier (1972)	Children referred for learning or behavior problem. Extent of learning problem unspecified.	Dextroamphetamine (20mg/day) (N = 21); magnesium pemoline (82mg/day) (N = 21); placebo (N = 21).	8 weeks	Porteus Mazes Frostig Test of Perception (3) (4/14)	WRAT a) Reading b) Spelling c) Arithmetic Gray Oral Reading Gates Diagnostic Reading a) Comprehension b) Speed c) Accuracy	(↑) N.S. (↑) * (↑) N.S. (↑) * (↑) N.S. (↓) N.S. (↑) N.S.
Conners (1972)[c]	Children referred for academic problems. Extent of learning problem unspecified.	Methylphenidate (Dose ?) (N = 29); dextroamphetamine (Dose ?) (N = 24); placebo (N = 22).	8 weeks	Frostig Test of Perception (4) Bender Gestalt Draw-a-man test Porteus Mazes Speech discrimination (3) Vigilance (2) (12/18)	WRAT a) Reading b) Spelling c) Arithmetic	(↑) N.S. (=) N.S. (=) N.S.

Study	Subjects	Drug and dosage	Duration	Other measures	Achievement measures	Result
Page, Janicki, Bernstein, Curran, & Michelli (1974)	Children selected for hyperkinesis due to MBD. Extent and nature of learning problem unspecified.	Magnesium Pemoline 2.69mg/kg/day; placebo (total N = 238)	9 weeks	Lincoln Oseretsky (1/7)	WRAT a) Reading b) Spelling c) Arithmetic	(↑) * (↑) N.S. (↑) *

Gittelman-Klein & Klein, 1976	Children backward in reading by at least 2 years, free of cross-situational hyperactivity.	Methylphenidate (52mg/day) (N = 29); placebo (N = 32)	4 & 12 weeks	Porteus Mazes (3)
				Visual motor integration (2)
				Visual sequential memory (2)
				Paired associate learning
				Vigilance task (9/16)
					WRAT
					a) Reading 4 weeks
					  12 weeks
					b) Arithmetic 4 weeks
					  12 weeks
					c) Spelling 4 weeks
					  12 weeks
					Gray Oral Reading
					  4 weeks
					  12 weeks
						(↑) N.S.
						(↑) N.S.
						(↑) *
						(↑) **
						(↑) N.S.
						(↑) N.S.
						
						(↑) N.S.
						(↑) N.S.

Rie, Rie, Stewart, & Ambuel, 1976a	Children backward in reading by at least 6 months.	Methylphenidate (21.1mg/day) (N = 28); placebo (N = 28)	12 weeks	Iowa Test of Basic Skills (word analysis) ITPA (auditory associations) (2/7)	Iowa Test of Basic Skills a) Reading b) Spelling c) Math 1 d) Math 2	(↑) N.S. (=) N.S. (=) N.S. (↑) N.S.
Rie, Rie, Stewart, & Ambuel, 1976b	Children backward in reading by at least 6 months.	Methylphenidate (23.1mg/day) (N = 18); placebo (N = 18)	15 weeks	Iowa Test of Basic Skills (vocabulary) ITPA (auditory closure) (2/7)	Iowa Test of Basic Skills a) Reading b) Spelling c) Math 1 d) Math 2	(↑) N.S. (=) N.S. (=) N.S. (↑) N.S.
Aman & Werry, 1982	Children retarded in reading by at least 2 years.	Methylphenidate (.35mg/kg) (N = 15); Diazepam .1mg/kg (N = 15); placebo (N = 15)	6 days	Vigilance (1/7)	Neale Analysis of Reading a) Accuracy b) Comprehension Psycholinguistic analysis a) Self-correction b) Syntax c) Error rate d) Repetition rate e) Prompt rate Letter recognition Common words	(↑) N.S. (=) N.S. (↑) N.S. (=) N.S. (↑) N.S. (↑) N.S. (↑) N.S. (=) N.S. (=) N.S.

[a] Excluding WISC. Fractions in parentheses (e.g., 2/4) indicate the proportion of dependent measures showing significant change.

[b] Arrows indicate the direction of change in achievement measures—↑ indicates drug-related improvement, ↓ indicates worsening on medication—and the equals sign (=) indicates little or no apparent change. WRAT stands for Wide Range Achievement Test.

[c] The secondary study appearing in this publication (Conners, Rothschild, Eisenberg, Schwartz, & Robinson, 1969) is reported elsewhere in the table.

461

Classification of Reading Problems

In terms of the criteria of reading backwardness and retardation, there was remarkable laxness in screening subjects for magnitude and nature of learning problem (see Column 2 of Table 21.1). Only four of the studies (Aman & Werry, 1980; Gittelman-Klein & Klein, 1976; Rie *et al.*, 1976a, 1976b) confined their samples to children with reading problems and used objective criteria for their selection. In two instances only (Aman & Werry, 1980; Gittelman-Klein & Klein, 1976) were the criteria rigorous enough to result in samples with serious and specific reading disorders.

Dosage Levels

Sprague and Sleator (1973, 1975, 1977) have cogently argued that the optimal dose for learning differs from that required for maximum behavioral improvement. Studies of short-term memory with methylphenidate (Ritalin) suggest that learning performance peaks at relatively *low doses* (0.3 mg/kg) and declines thereafter, whereas improvement in social conduct tends to be greatest at substantially *higher* doses (1.0 mg/kg and higher).

This is an important issue as it is possible that many of the studies of stimulants have exceeded the optimal dose range that might be expected to enhance learning function. In fact, with the exception of the Aman and Werry (1982) study, trials of methylphenidate and dextroamphetamine (Dexedrine) had doses ranging roughly from .84 to 1.62 mg/kg when converted to methylphenidate's equivalent potency. This is far higher than the optimal dose (0.3 mg/kg) recommended by Sprague and Sleator, and it suggests that dosage was being titrated against the most accessible indicator—social behavior.

Critique and Summary of Results

Although the essentials of methodological control have been correctly applied, there has been a regrettable neglect of objective screening procedures in most of these investigations. The result has been a hodge-podge collection of groups, the compositions of which are often unclear and which are impossible to compare across studies. Additionally there has been a disregard for the important dimension of dosage which usually has been titrated against the criterion of social conduct. Finally, there has been too little attention directed to the appropriate measurement of changes in reading itself, a topic that will be addressed later.

Nevertheless, because of the uniformity and sheer weight of their numbers, the results of these studies must be taken seriously. The results are presented under two major headings, perceptual–cognitive measures and achievement measures (Columns 5 and 6, Table 21.1). The perceptual–cognitive measures, which include all forms of learning-related indices except formal IQ tests, indicate an overall level of significant improvement on 40 of the 106 measures. On the other hand, *only 2 of the 26 reading measures* (and only 6 of all 45 achievement measures) were significantly improved as a consequence of stimulant medication.

Thus, the results were almost uniform in indicating a failure of the stimulants to improve reading performance. However, there is an apparent nonspecific enhancement of reading performance due to the drugs since 18 of the 25 comparisons showed (nonsignificant) drug-related gains. These slight gains probably reflect a modest drug effect on motivation or attention span, but they certainly do not justify the use of stimulants for "treating" reading disorders.

ANTIANXIETY DRUGS IN SPECIFIC READING DISORDERS

Rationale for Anxiolytics

Specific reading disorders are frequently accompanied by high anxiety levels which are presumably occasioned by persistent failure (Merritt, 1972). This has led a number of authors (Freed, Abrams, & Peifer, 1959; Millichap, 1968; Westman, Arthur, & Scheidler, 1965) to recommend the use of benzodiazepines and other anxiolytics with these children. The benzodiazepines are popular antianxiety and hypnotic agents which, despite their chemical distinctiveness, are basically similar in clinical action to other sedatives such as barbiturates. However, in usual clinical dosage they are less liable to produce frank sedation because of a much lower dose response gradient (Greenblatt & Shader, 1974).

The effects of antianxiety drugs on cognitive performance in adults have been reviewed by McNair (1973). In general, performance has been shown to deteriorate under these drugs, but there is an apparent relationship between outcome and degree of stress. Thus when anxiety-inducing factors have been introduced experimentally, learning has sometimes been enhanced as a function of the anxiolytics. McNair concluded his summary by noting that there was little sound information about the cognitive effects of these drugs, even in adults.

The benzodiazepines and other anxiolytics have received little study in children and their effects on learning performance have almost been ignored altogether (Rapoport, Mikkelson, & Werry, 1978). Furthermore, despite their occasional usage for treating anxiety disorders in children, their clinical effectiveness has *not* been empirically established (Gittel-man-Klein, 1978; Werry & Aman, 1980). Consequently, there is little objective information available about the general cognitive and anxiolytic effects of these drugs, let alone their effects in specific reading disorders.

Studies in Specific Reading Disorders

I was able to locate only four investigations even remotely related to this area.

Fenelon, Holland, and Johnson (1972) evaluated the effects of nitrazepam (Mogadon) in 33 children with reading backwardness. The children received both drug and placebo in a crossover-type design. Results showed that the spatial index of the EEG increased under the drug. The authors regarded this as signifying a more normal level of cerebral activity and also as suggesting improved attention span. It is a remarkable and unfortunate fact that these investigators reported no attempt to measure the drug's effect on reading performance itself.

In another study, Fenelon and Wortley (1973) assessed the effects of nitrazepam in children who were backward in reading by an average of 24 months. The study was intended to evaluate the drug's effect on two-flash fusion thresholds (TFT), which are inversely related to attention span and arousal level. Three groups were formed: normal readers who received placebo, backward readers who received placebo, and backward readers who received nitrazepam. Unfortunately no pre-medication measures were obtained so that it was impossible to assess whether there were initial group differences, a situation not improved by the fact that there were only eight subjects per group. Results showed the normal readers to have the lowest thresholds but levels for the drug-treated children approximated those of the normal readers, appearing to confirm the authors' hypothesis that nitrazepam would decrease thresholds. However, in the absence of predrug measures, these findings are impossible to evaluate. As in the previous study, no attempt to measure reading itself was reported.

Freed, Abrams, and Peifer (1959) studied the effects of prochlorperazine (Compazine, Stemetil), chlorpromazine (Largactil, Thorazine), and placebo in children with severe reading backwardness. These drugs are pharmacologically quite different from the benzodiazepines and probably act via different neural mechanisms, but they are included because they (particularly prochlorperazine) are considered to have mild anxiolytic actions (Rapoport *et al.*, 1978). Five groups of children were formed yielding the following treatment combinations: (*a*) placebo, (*b*) placebo + tutoring, (*c*) prochlorperazine + tutoring, (*d*) chlorpromazine, and (*e*) chlorpromazine + tutoring. Assessment for reading gains followed a 10-week period of treatment. The results indicated that the drugs in combination with reading instruction—(*c*) and (*e*)—were significantly superior to placebo alone—(*a*)—and also resulted in the greatest *absolute* gains in reading. However, there were no significant differences between the *drugs in combination with instruction* and *placebo with instruction*, although the authors did not discuss this rather crucial point. Unfortunately all analyses were conducted in terms of multiple *t* tests, inappropriate in this case since numerous reapplications of the test inflates the number of "significant" findings. There were additional methodological problems: The study was apparently non-blind and the attrition rate reached the rather serious level of 39%.

Finally, Aman and Werry (1982) evaluated diazepam (Valium) against methylphenidate and placebo in severely reading-retarded children (see Aman & Werry, 1982, Table 1). The design was of the crossover type in which each child eventually received all drug conditions. Medications were given in random order for 6 days each. The measures included cognitive tests on which retarded readers had previously been shown to be deficient (Aman, 1979) and a detailed psycholinguistic analysis of reading. The results indicated that diazepam caused improvement on a vigilance-type task (consistent with decreased TFT thresholds [Fenelon & Wortley, 1973]), but there were no effects of diazepam on several other cognitive tasks, on self-ratings of anxiety level, or on measures of reading.

This survey fails to suggest any role for anxiolytic drugs in specific reading disorders. Although these four studies left much to be desired in terms of design, duration of drug periods, numbers of participants, and so forth, there was no indication that these drugs truly enhanced reading performance in reading-disordered children. Despite the lack of research on the topic, routine usage of anxiolytics (or *any* drug) must surely hinge upon the prior existence of sound evidence attesting to their benefit. So far there is no such evidence.

DIRECTIONS FOR FUTURE DRUG RESEARCH

It is clear that more refined approaches to research are needed in the field of drugs and reading disorders. The need for adopting a more objective way of selecting children has already been addressed. From the foregoing surveys it is also clear that not all or even most children with reading disorders respond positively to medication. In the absence of further refinement, drug treatment simply is not a viable approach for treating learning disorders that are uncomplicated by other difficulties such as behavior problems.

First, this suggests that future research in the area must make a major commitment to identify predictors of outcome. The larger field of specific reading disorders is rich in theories relating to etiological factors (Aman & Singh, in press). However researchers in the drug field have been slow to appreciate the potential significance of these factors in predicting drug response. Subtypes of reading disorders should be examined for their possible value in determining who will benefit from medication, thereby providing an empirical framework for the use of drugs if such therapy is going to be employed at all.

Second, remarkably little attention has been directed to the most suitable ways of assessing reading performance. The dilemma is that these children are assessed in areas where they are most singularly incapable. This causes enormous problems of measurement, as such children seldom perform beyond the lowest levels on most achievement tests, often resulting in a very rough estimate of achievement. Consequently, many achievement tests appear to be insensitive to subtle but potentially important changes in performance, at least in these extreme children. As one solution to the problem, I have employed a psycholinguistic approach which provides qualitative as well as quantitative information about reading performance (see Aman & Werry, 1982; Clay, 1975; Pikulski, 1974). This approach emphasizes the nature of errors made rather than stressing a simple error count which eventuates from many achievement tests. Another resolution to this problem may involve the use of diagnostic reading tests, as these stress relative areas of strength rather than overall levels of performance.

Third, there is no compelling evidence to date that drugs *in isolation* result in improved reading performance. It is probably naive and unreasonable to expect gains from medication used without some mechanism for change. Only two of the studies reported here (Conrad, Dworkin, Shai, & Tobiessen, 1971; Freed *et al.*, 1959) provided for simultaneous remedial teaching. Werry (1968) has suggested that drugs may fulfil a catalytic role accelerating the rate of other treatments such as behavior modification or special education. If this is the case, the most meaningful way to evaluate drug treatment of learning disorders is to assess it *in combination* with acceptable forms of special education.[3]

---

[3] Gittelman and her associates (personal communication, 1979) conducted an investigation that addressed this issue. Children with pronounced reading backwardness were

CONCLUSIONS

No direct figures are available on the incidence of drug treatment in children with reading disorders. Drug prevalence can be expected to vary greatly, depending in part upon severity of the learning problem, presence of behavior problems, philosophy of therapists and parents, and even geographic region. However, based on studies of exceptional children together with the well-known association between learning disorders and hyperactivity, there is good reason to believe that psychotropic drugs are used in a sizeable proportion of these children.

Short-term studies of the stimulants with hyperactive children indicated that these drugs have beneficial effects on learning-related skills, particularly when attention span played a role in such tests. However, long-term follow-up studies which emerged later were unable to document lasting drug-related gains in the scholastic–achievement sphere.

Stimulant drugs gained entry into the learning disability field because of the putative preeminence of attentional deficits in children with learning problems. Also the lax usage of diagnostic terminology may have encouraged the administration of stimulants in specific reading disorders. Most of the research assessing stimulant drugs in children with learning disorders has only appeared recently. These studies have been almost unanimous in failing to demonstrate drug effects either on reading or in other scholastic areas.

Anxiolytic drugs have occasionally been recommended because many children with reading disorders appear also to suffer levels of anxiety which are believed to interfere with the learning process. However, the scattered research in this area fails to support any role for the antianxiety drugs in treating reading disorders.

The consistent failure of past studies to show drug-related changes in reading performance indicates the need for new strategies in future research. Diagnostic factors which may characterize children likely to benefit from treatment must be emphasized. More attention must be directed to appropriate and sensitive ways of measuring reading itself. Dosage should be adjusted against cognitive rather than behavioral criteria. Finally, there should be some provision for remedial teaching in conjunction with medication as it is unlikely that learning will occur without the provision of adequate opportunity.

treated with a combination of remedial teaching plus methylphenidate or remedial teaching plus placebo. Preliminary results suggested some differences between these two groups, but in general the drug did not significantly alter outcome on tests of achievement. Both groups generally did better than another (control) group which received placebo plus attention (i.e., contact with an adult tutor doing tasks other than reading).

It is an unfortunate fact that treatment often tends to go beyond its proven indications. There are many staunch advocates for the adjunctive use of drugs, particularly the stimulants, for treating children rather vaguely referred to as learning disabled. However, there is little evidence to date that drugs produce academic benefit in learning disorders unaccompanied by behavior problems. Psychotropic drugs may improve academic attainment in cases where behavioral deviancy interferes with cognitive development, but even this needs to be demonstrated. When medication is given for a problem that is primarily behavioral, it appears to be important that gains in social adjustment do not come at the expense of cognitive functioning. Further, it is essential that, when medication is given in connection with a learning problem, an acceptable form of educational therapy be provided as well.

Finally, it is worth reflecting momentarily on why Bradley believed that learning itself was improved in stimulant-treated children. Bradley and his staff clearly misinterpreted greater application to schoolwork and improved social demeanor as indicative of improved learning. It is hoped that clinicians and researchers today will be sophisticated enough and well enough informed not to confuse the two domains, social conduct and learning.

REFERENCES

Adelman, H. S., & Compas, B. E. (1977) Stimulant drugs and learning problems. *The Journal of Special Education, 11,* 377–416.

Aman, M. G. (1978) Drugs, learning, and the psychotherapies. In J. S. Werry (Ed.), *Pediatric psychopharmacology: The use of behavior modifying drugs in children.* New York: Brunner/Mazel.

Aman, M. G. (1979) Cognitive, social, and other correlates of specific reading retardation. *Journal of Abnormal Child Psychology, 7,* 153–168.

Aman, M. G. (1980) Psychotropic drugs and learning problems—A selective review. *Journal of Learning Disabilities, 13,* 87–96.

Aman, M. G., & Singh, N. N. (In press) Specific reading disorders: Traditional concepts of etiology. In K. D. Gadow and I. Bialer (Eds.), *Advances in learning and behavioral disabilities.* (Vol. 2), Greenwich, Conn.: JAI Press.

Aman, M. G., & Werry, J. S. (1982) Methylphenidate and diazepam in severe reading retardation. *Journal of the American Academy of Child Psychiatry, 21.*

Anderson, R. P., Halcomb, C. G., & Doyle, R. B. (1973) The measurement of attentional deficits. *Exceptional Children, 39,* 534–540.

Barkley, R. A., & Cunningham, C. E. (1978) Do stimulant drugs improve the academic performance of hyperkinetic children? A review of outcome research. *Clinical Pediatrics, 17,* 85–92.

Bradley, C. (1937) The behavior of children receiving benzedrine. *American Journal of Psychiatry, 94,* 577–585.

Cantwell, D. P., & Carlson, G. A. (1978) Stimulants. In J. S. Werry (Ed.), *Pediatric psychopharmacology: The use of behavior modifying drugs in children.* New York: Brunner/Mazel.

Clay, M. M. (1975) *The early detection of reading difficulties: A diagnostic survey.* Auckland: Heinemann Educational Books.

Conners, C. K. (1972) Symposium: Behavior modification by drugs, II. Psychological effects of stimulant drugs in children with minimal brain dysfunction. *Pediatrics, 49,* 702–708.

Conners, C. K., Rothschild, G., Eisenberg, L., Schwartz, L. S., & Robinson, E. (1969) Dextroamphetamine sulfate in children with learning disorders. *Archives of General Psychiatry, 21,* 182–190.

Conners, C. K., Taylor, E., Meo, G., Kurtz, M. A., & Fournier, M. (1972) Magnesium pemoline and dextroamphetamine: A controlled study in children with minimal brain dysfunction. *Psychopharmacologia, 26,* 321–336.

Conners, C. K., & Werry, J. S. (1979) Pharmacotherapy of psychopathology in children. In H. C. Quay & J. S. Werry (Eds.), *Psychopathological disorders of childhood.* New York: Wiley.

Conrad, W., Dworkin, E. S., Shai, A., & Tobiessen, J. E. (1971) Effects of amphetamine therapy and prescriptive tutoring on the behavior and achievement of lower class hyperactive children. *Journal of Learning Disabilities, 4,* 45–53.

Douglas, V. I. (1974) Differences between normal and hyperkinetic children. In C. K. Conners (Ed.), *Clinical use of stimulant drugs in children.* Amsterdam: American Elsevier.

Fenelon, B., Holland, J. T., & Johnson, C. (1972) Spatial organization of the EEG in children with reading disabilities: A study using nitrazepam. *Cortex, 36,* 444–464.

Fenelon, B., & Wortley, S. (1973) Effect of auxiliary acoustic stimulation on two-flash fusion thresholds of reading disabled children: A study using nitrazepam. *Perceptual and Motor Skills, 36,* 443–450.

Freed, M., Abrams, J., & Peifer, C. (1959) Reading disability: A new therapeutic approach and its implications. *Journal of Clinical and Experimental Psychopathology and Quarterly Review of Psychiatry and Neurology, 20,* 251–259.

Freeman, R. D. (1966) Drug effects on learning in children. A selective review of the past thirty years. *Journal of Special Education, 1,* 17–45.

Gadow, K. D. (1975) *Pills and preschool: Medication usage with young children in special education.* Paper presented at the Illinois Council for Exceptional Children, Chicago, October 1975.

Gadow, K. D. (1976) *Psychotropic and anticonvulsant drug usage in early special education programs, I. A preliminary report: Prevalence, attitude, and training.* Paper presented at the annual meeting of the Council for Exceptional Children, Chicago, 1976. (ERIC Document Reproduction Service No. ED125 198).

Gadow, K. D. (1979) *Children on medication: A primer for school personnel.* Reston, Va.: The Council for Exceptional Children.

Gadow, K. D. (1981) Prevalence of drug treatment for hyperactivity and other childhood behavior disorders. In K. D. Gadow & J. Loney (Eds.), *Psychosocial aspects of drug treatment for hyperactivity.* Boulder, Co: Westview Press.

Gittelman-Klein, R. (1978) Psychopharmacological treatment of anxiety disorders, mood disorders, and Tourette's disorder in children. In M. A. Lipton, A. DiMascio, & K. F. Killam (Eds.), *Psychopharmacology: A generation of progress.* New York: Raven Press.

Gittelman-Klein, R., & Klein, D. F. (1975) Are behavioral and psychometric changes related in methylphenidate-treated, hyperactive children? *International Journal of Mental Health, 4,* 182–198.

Gittelman-Klein, R., & Klein, D. F. (1976) Methylphenidate effects in learning disabilities. *Archives of General Psychiatry, 33,* 655–664.

Gittelman-Klein, R., Spitzer, R. L., & Cantwell, D. P. (1978) Diagnostic classification and psychopharmacological indications. In J. S. Werry (Ed.), *Pediatric psychopharmacology: The use of behavior modifying drugs in children.* New York: Brunner/Mazel.

Greenblatt, D. J., & Shader, R. I. (1974) *Benzodiazepines in clinical practice.* New York: Raven Press.

Hansen, P., & Keogh, B. K. (1971) Medical characteristics of children with educational handicaps. Implications for the pediatrician. *Clinical Pediatrics, 10,* 726–730.

Harris, L. P. (1976) Attention and learning disordered children: A review of theory and remediation. *Journal of Learning Disabilities, 9,* 47–57.

Hechtman, L., Weiss, G., Finklestein, J., Werner, A., & Benn, R. (1976) Hyperactives as young adults: Preliminary report. *Canadian Medical Association Journal, 115,* 625–630.

Huddleston, W., Staiger, R. C., Frye, R., Musgrave, R. S., & Stritch, T. (1961) Deanol as aid in overcoming reading retardation. *Clinical Medicine, 68,* 1340–1342.

Lerer, R. J., Lerer, M. P., & Artner, J. (1977) The effects of methylphenidate on the handwriting of children with minimal brain dysfunction. *Journal of Pediatrics, 91,* 127–132.

McNair, D. M. (1973) Antianxiety drugs and human performance. *Archives of General Psychiatry, 29,* 611–617.

Mendelson, W., Johnson, N., & Stewart, M. (1971) Hyperactive children as teenagers: A follow-up study. *Journal of Nervous and Mental Disease, 123,* 477–479.

Merritt, J. S. (1972) Reading failure: A re-examination. In J. F. Reid (Ed.), *Reading: Problems and practices.* London: Ward Lock Educational.

Millichap, G. J. (1968) Drugs in management of hyperkinetic and perceptually handicapped children. *American Medical Association Journal, 206,* 1527–1530.

Minde, K., Weiss, G., & Mendelson, N. (1972) A 5-year follow-up study of 91 hyperactive school children. *Journal of the American Academy of Child Psychiatry, 11,* 595–610.

Page, J. G., Janicki, R. S., Bernstein, M. S., Curran, C. F., & Michelli, F. A. (1974) Pemoline (Cylert) in the treatment of childhood hyperkinesis. *Journal of Learning Disabilities, 7,* 498–503.

Pikulski, J. (1974) A critical review: Informal reading inventories. *The Reading Teacher, 28,* 141–151.

Quinn, P. O., & Rapoport, J. L. (1975) One-year follow-up of hyperactive boys treated with imipramine or methylphenidate. *American Journal of Psychiatry, 132,* 241–245.

Rapoport, J. L., Mikkelson, E. J., & Werry, J. S. (1978) Antidepressants. In J. S. Werry (Ed.), *Pediatric psychopharmacology: The use of behavior modifying drugs in children.* New York: Brunner/Mazel.

Riddle, K. D., & Rapoport, J. L. (1976) A 2-year follow-up of 72 hyperactive boys. *Journal of Nervous and Mental Disease, 162,* 126–134.

Rie, H. E., Rie, E. D., Stewart, S., & Ambuel, J. P. (1976a) Effects of methylphenidate on underachieving children. *Journal of Consulting and Clinical Psychology, 44,* 250–260.

Rie, H. E., Rie, E. D., Stewart, S., & Ambuel, J. P. (1976b) Effects of Ritalin on underachieving children: A replication. *American Journal of Orthopsychiatry, 46,* 313–322.

Routh, D. K. (1979) Activity, attention, and aggression in learning disabled children. *Journal of Clinical Child Psychology, 8,* 183–187.

Rutter, M., & Yule, W. (1973) Specific reading retardation. In L. Mann & D. A. Sabatino (Eds.), *The first review of special education.* Philadelphia, Penn.: JSE Press.

Rutter, M., & Yule, W. (1975) The concept of specific reading retardation. *Journal of Child Psychology and Psychiatry, 16,* 181–197.

Schain, R. J. (1972) *Neurology of childhood learning disorders.* Baltimore: Williams & Wilkins.

Sprague, R. L., & Sleator, E. K. (1973) Effects of psychopharmacologic agents on learning disorders. *Pediatric Clinics of North America, 20,* 719–735.

Sprague, R. L., & Sleator, E. K. (1975) What is the proper dose of stimulant drugs in children? *International Journal of Mental Health, 4,* 75–118.

Sprague, R. L., & Sleator, E. K. (1977) Methylphenidate in hyperkinetic children: Differences in dose effects on learning and social behavior. *Science, 198,* 1274–1276.

Sprague, R. L., & Werry, J. S. (1971) Methodology of psychopharmacological studies with the retarded. In N. R. Ellis (Ed.), *International review of research in mental retardation* (Vol. 5). New York: Academic Press.

Sroufe, L. (1975) Drug treatment of children with behavior problems. In F. Horowitz (Ed.), *Review of child development research* (Vol. 4). Chicago: University of Chicago Press.

Weiss, G., Kruger, E., Danielson, U., & Elman, M. (1975) Effect of long-term treatment of hyperactive children with methylphenidate. *Canadian Medical Association Journal, 112,* 159–165.

Weiss, B., & Laties, V. G. (1962) Enhancement of human performance by caffeine and the amphetamines. *Psychological Review, 14,* 1–36.

Weiss, G., Minde, K., Werry, J. S., Douglas, V., & Nemeth, E. (1971) Studies on the hyperactive child, VIII: Five-year follow-up. *Archives of General Psychiatry, 24,* 409–414.

Werry, J. S. (1968) The diagnosis, etiology, and treatment of hyperactivity in children. In J. Hellmuth (Ed.), *Learning disorders* (Vol. 3). Seattle: Special Child Publications.

Werry, J. S. (1976) Medication for hyperkinetic children. *Drugs, 11,* 81–89.

Werry, J. S., & Aman, M. G. (1980) Anxiety in children. In G. D. Burrows & B. M. Davies (Eds.), *Handbook of studies on anxiety.* Amsterdam: ASP Biological and Medical Press.

Westman, J., Arthur, B., & Scheidler, E. (1965) Reading retardation: An overview. *American Journal of Diseases of Children, 109,* 359–369.

Yepes, L., Balka, E., Winsberg, B., & Bialer, I. (1977) Amitriptyline and methylphenidate treatment of behaviorally disordered children. *Journal of Child Psychology and Psychiatry, 18,* 39–52.

Yule, W. (1973) Differential prognosis of reading backwardness and specific reading retardation. *British Journal of Educational Psychology, 43,* 244–248.

Chapter Twenty-Two

Adult Outcome of Reading Disorders[1]

OTFRIED SPREEN

INTRODUCTION

The past 25 years have produced a large volume of studies about reading disorders, including numerous projects that deal with epidemiological issues, debates of definitions, early prediction, subtypes, behavioral and biological correlates, treatment and training, and changes during the school years (Benton & Pearl, 1977). These studies reflect a growing concern, an increased understanding, and an interest in helping those children who for one reason or another cannot keep up with the present educational system. Relatively little is known, however, about the long-term effects and the adult outcome of reading disabilities after school-leaving age (Levinson, 1980). The present chapter is an attempt to review and evaluate the information available on this topic. Results of a new study are also included.

One reason for the paucity of major studies on adult outcome lies in the difficulty of conducting long-term follow-up studies, particularly when the studies involve a young, highly mobile population. Although

[1] The work reported in this chapter was supported by grants from the Medical Research Council of Canada and from Health and Welfare, Canada.

473

short-term follow-up research investigating the course of reading disorders with or without specific treatment regimes is relatively easy to conduct with captive school populations, studies beyond school-leaving age tend to be fraught with problems of tracing, early school drop out, unexplained attrition, and refusal to cooperate—all of which make generalizations from existing studies somewhat tenuous. Some optimistic reports suggest that children overcome reading problems in their later school and early adult years, or at least that such problems have no lasting effect on adult adjustment after the subjects leave school. Other studies take a more pessimistic view, suggesting that learning disabilities generally are the forerunners of social and emotional maladjustment related to serious deviancy, delinquency, and social and occupational failure.

Another problem that needs to be stated at the outset of this review is that of definition (Gaddes, 1976). The terms used for the target population in follow-up studies range from "dyslexia" and "reading disorder" to "general learning disabilities." Such differences in terms do not necessarily signify actual differences in the target populations. Although frequently a study is focused on reading failure only, a glance at other school achievement data (if they are provided) suggests that in most cases the disorder is much broader than specific reading disability. There are two possible reasons for this:

1. The reading disorder has interfered with achievement in most other school subjects, resulting in a more general learning disability; this is understandable given that instruction in most school subjects tends to rely heavily on written material after the fourth grade. Moreover, reading failure may very well set a negative attitude toward learning in general so that the problem generalizes to other subjects.

2. The other possible explanation is that "pure" forms of reading disorder are indeed rare and in most cases accompanied by either general "backwardness" in learning ability or at least by a broader deficit in language development which, in turn, generalizes to other academic school subjects (although not necessarily to nonacademic areas), at least to the more "verbally oriented" subject areas, such as English and social studies.

Whatever the reason, adult outcome studies are typically not limited to the outcome of reading disorder, but to a broader range of learning disabilities in the absence of a major general intellectual impairment.

One specific aspect of interest in several studies has been the presence or absence of demonstrated or suspected minimal or definite brain dysfunction. We will deal with this topic briefly in the early part of this chapter. In relation to a long-term follow up, several questions of interest arise—such as the question of whether such "minimal brain dysfunction" persists into adulthood; whether the dysfunction is merely a maturational delay and the growing adult "matures" out of it; and whether the presence of neurological impairment creates specific problems for the health of the person or specific limitations in occupational training and adjustment, in social adjustment, etc.

Adult outcome cannot be narrowly defined in terms of school or even reading achievement. Adult adjustment must take into account the many variables relating to personal and interpersonal satisfaction as well as occupational success and financial and personal independence. Although it remains of interest what reading achievement the disabled reader will eventually achieve, a host of other variables of interest also contribute to the complexity of any follow-up study into adulthood and probably account for some of the heterogeneity of findings.

THE ROLE OF BRAIN DAMAGE IN READING AND LEARNING DISORDERS

One study of the role of "minimal brain-damage" in learning problems (Myklebust, Boshes, Olson, & Cole, 1969) found that among the 15% "underachievers" in a population of 3000 fourth-graders, approximately half (7.5% of the total population) showed indication of brain damage of varying degrees. This agrees with the estimate of 8% of the total population made by other investigators although widely varying estimates have also been reported (Minskoff, 1973; Rubin & Balow, 1971; Silverman & Metz, 1973). The notion of a "continuum of reproductive casualty" at the perinatal stage (Pasamanick & Knobloch, 1960) suggests also that brain abnormalities of varying degrees are involved in the development of many individuals and may be responsible not only for gross mental deficiency but for other developmental problems, even if the defect can no longer be neurologically demonstrated. Authors like Birch (1964), Cruickshank (1966, 1967, 1971), Denckla (1977), Deutsch and Schumer (1970), Hallahan and Cruickshank (1973), Johnson and Mykleburst (1967), Kaspar, Millichap, Backus, Child, and Schulman (1971), Levine, Brooks, and Shonkoff (1980), Mykleburst *et al.* (1969), Rutter, Graham, and Yule (1970), Schain (1972), Wender (1973), and others have described the effects of brain damage on the development of the child from various points of orientation. Two books (Chall & Mirsky, 1978; Rie & Rie, 1980) review some of the progress

made in this area. Reading and language problems have been particularly singled out as being related to problems of cerebral maturation
or brain damage (Bakker & Satz, 1970; Bakker & DeWit, 1977; Critchley,
1966, 1970; Doehring, 1968; Klasen, 1972; Lenneberg, 1967; Muehl,
Knott, & Benton, 1965; Pirozzolo, 1979; Rourke, 1977, 1978; Tarnopol
& Tarnopol, 1977; Wikler, Dixon, & Parker, 1970). Some authors maintain that manifest brain damage can be found, although more frequently
in children with general learning problems, only rarely in the child
with specific reading disabilities. A survey of the concept, epidemiology, and developmental and treatment factors of minimal brain damage
is provided by de la Cruz, Fox, and Roberts (1973). Kinsbourne (1973)
and others view minimal brain damage as a "neurodevelopmental lag."
This notion is somewhat different from, though not incompatible with,
the traditional view of minimal brain damage. Kinsbourne sees such
a "neurodevelopmental" lag to be clearly related to reading retardation,
and he raises the question of how long this lag persists. He calls for
longitudinal studies to clarify the issue.

Given the nature of educational, psychological, and medical counseling, diagnostic inferences of brain damage as a major cause of learning disability are usually made on the basis of relatively short observation and examination periods. Detailed educational and other treatment
prescriptions are frequently given (Gaddes, 1968, 1980; Segal, 1968),
but the results of such treatments are known to the counseling agency
only if the child returns for further assistance. Similarly, although the
validity of some of the indicators of brain damage may be checked by
correlational validation procedures, the persistence of these indicators
during the further development of the child remains unknown. Case
reports may indicate progressing seriousness of the handicap or a complete "remission" of symptoms. Studies following newborns with indications of brain damage at birth (e.g., Apgar & James, 1962; Broman,
Nichols, & Kennedy, 1975; Corah, Anthony, Painter, Stern, & Thurston,
1965; Graham, Ernhart, Craft, & Berman, 1963; Graham, Ernhart, Thurston, & Craft, 1962; Solomons, Holden, & Denhoff, 1963; Kalverboer,
Touwen, & Prechtl, 1973; Pasamanick & Knobloch, 1960) indicate that
a large proportion of "at risk" babies are completely normal and free
of symptoms at age 3 or 7. This outcome cannot necessarily be expected
for children diagnosed as "brain damaged" at a later age. Children
diagnosed as brain damaged between the ages of 2 and 7 showed more
diversification after 4 years with some 25% retaining the same level of
intellectual functioning, 30% showing improvement, and almost 50%
showing further decrease (Roesler, 1971). Roesler and Kurth (1975) also

found a decrease in IQ between the ages of 8 and 11 for children with "slight encephalopathy" as compared to a control group.

One reason for the confusing, often contradictory opinions about the effect of brain damage may be the use of "soft" neurological signs and the concept of "minimal brain dysfunction (MBD). Soft signs include difficulties in rapid alternating movements, skipping, nose touching with eyes closed, graphaesthesia, run–skip–stop, finger tremor, right–left orientation, finger touching, touching tip of nose, standing on one foot, hopping down a line, walking in circles, face and hand sensation, and often include reported hyperactive behavior. Some authors (e.g., Pirozzolo, 1979) rely on only a few, primarily behavioral, "signs" of "minimal brain damage," for example, short attention span, distractibility, impulsivity, poor motor integration, and hyperkinesis. However, Schmitt (1975), among others, has challenged the concept of brain damage based on such signs, maintaining that they "represent transient phenomena and disappear with age [p. 1314]." Adams, Kocsis, and Estes (1974) found that learning-disabled children could not be reliably distinguished from normal children on the basis of such signs; and Stine, Saratsiotis, and Mosser (1975) found in a sample of 575 children that neurological signs were not predictive of a particular form of behavior. Barlow (1974) accepts that some relationship between neurological signs and learning problems may exist, but questions whether such signs are sufficient to predict individual performance ("guilt by statistical association," p. 606). Clements and Peters (1963) concluded that no single sign is pathognomic, but that the total number of signs may be indicative of an MBD diagnosis. This position is also taken by Hertzig, Bortner, and Birch (1969) and Hertzig and Birch (1968). Lucas, Rodin, and Simon (1965) argued that neurological findings are not related to emotional immaturity, withdrawal, and antisocial behavior; Helper (1980) concludes that "risk of psychopathy, lowered SES, antisocial behaviors and psychiatric contact are elevated, but total social and vocational incapacitation are evidently not the rule [p. 110]."

On the other hand, Page-El and Grossman (1973) describe neurological involvement as a common factor underlying learning disabilities. Wolff and Hurwitz (1973) also argue for the importance of neurological signs in the clinical diagnosis of learning disabilities. Werry, Minde, Guzman, Weiss, Dogan, and Hoy (1972) found neurological abnormalities also in a group of 20 hyperactive, emotionally disturbed children and viewed hyperactivity as one specific syndrome.

The search for syndromatic groups was continued by Peters, Romine, and Dykman (1975) and Rie, Rie, Stewart, and Rettemnier (1978). Rie *et al.* accepted Birch's (1964) premise that disturbed behavior is the developmental product of multiple factors. In 80 children with learning problems they found six factors, including factors for verbal–motor functioning, visual–cognitive integration, general ability, age, sex, and hyperactivity, and suggested that these "multiple conditions" are interacting and that "multiple effects of diverse conditions" may have to be considered (p. 45).

Considering the importance of this ongoing debate about the role of brain dysfunction in reading and learning disorders, the results of follow-up studies which include groups of brain-dysfunctioned children should be of special interest.

A SUMMARY OF OLDER FOLLOW-UP RESEARCH

Several older studies have attempted a long-term follow-up of children with learning problems. Many of these studies are concerned with special groups (e.g., hyperkinetic children, autistic children), with specific effects of treatment (e.g., Friedmann, Dale, & Wagner, 1973; Silver & Hagin, 1963, 1964), or with behavioral adjustment problems (e.g., a 30-year follow-up by Kagan & Moss, 1962). Vacc (1972) described the sociometric changes of emotionally disturbed children after 8 months and after 5.5 years. Other long-term studies include a 4-year follow-up of "vulnerable" adolescents by Jones (1973); a 5–6 year follow-up of hyperactive Montreal elementary school children (Minde, Lewin, Weiss, Lavigueur, Douglas, & Sykes, 1971; Minde, Weiss, & Mendelson, 1972; Weiss, Minde, Werry, Douglas, & Nemeth, 1971); a 2–5 year follow-up of hyperactive teenagers by Mendelson, Johnson, and Stewart (1971), a 5-year follow-up of hyperactive subjects (Hechtman, Weiss, Finklestein, Werner, & Benn, 1976); a follow-up of subjects with behavioral disorders with ages ranging from 9 to 24 years (Huessy, Metoyer, & Townsend, 1973, 1974); a 20-year follow-up of similar groups by Menkes, Rowe, and Menkes (1967); a 6-year follow-up of children with speech and perceptual handicaps by Wepman and Morency (1971); and a study of children with learning problems by Hinton and Knights (1971).

Of the more specific long-term follow-up studies of reading-disabled children, the oldest report was published by Hermann (1959) who reviewed the achievement of 72 Danish backward readers at a follow-up age of 23–24 years. He found that on an average their reading ability was approximately at the sixth-grade level, and that 10 could read "very well," 20 were very slow, and 3 were very poor in reading. Their occupational adjustment was fair, and 50% of the sample held skilled jobs. In addition, Hermann reviewed the adjustment of 541 "word-blind" adults and found a remarkable cohort effect, that is, the younger members of his sample had received considerably more special education, although, in general, the number of unskilled or domestic workers and errand boys in the group was disproportionately high. Balow and Blomquist (1965) found that all the 32 children with severe reading disability they had studied had achieved a tenth-grade reading level in a 10–15-year follow-up. Nonetheless, a variety of problems were still evident in this group, and a "negative and defeatist attitude about life in general" was prevalent. Of the subjects, 27 had completed high school and 23 had obtained some continuing education, 10 were still in college or undergoing training, 12 were holding managerial or skilled jobs, and 10 were doing unskilled work. Robinson and Smith (1962) conducted a 10-year follow-up study of 44 former clients of a reading clinic. At an average age of 24, these subjects achieved a median IQ of 120. All except 3 had completed high school, 11 were still in college, and 1 had completed medical school. In general, the occupational adjustment of this group was quite good, and the authors felt that intervention at the reading clinic had in fact cleared up the reading disability in many of their subjects. Silver and Hagin (1964) were the first authors to use a control group and to conduct extensive retesting in a 10–12 year follow-up of 24 former clients of a reading clinic. Although 15 of the disabled readers were judged to have become adequate readers, these subjects belonged to a less impaired group at the time of their first referral.

A dissertation research by Carter (1964) is reported by Herjanic and Penick (1972) in a review of several earlier studies. Carter's study followed 35 former clients of a reading clinic at a mean age of 21 and compared them to control subjects who were normal readers during school. The study found that the reading problem group tended to be self-supporting whereas many of the controls were still continuing their education; that control subjects who were employed earned slightly more than the former reading clinic clients; but that there was no difference on self-reported restrictions on job choice, vocational adjustment rating, and on dependence on financial assistance. Among males, social adjustment was better for the control subjects than for the former clinic clients. Howden (1967) extended the follow-up period into the late twenties for former students with high ($N = 9$), average ($N = 22$) and poor ($N = 22$) reading achievement. The poor reader group was still poor on the Gates reading survey, showed lower socioeconomic status, and had less formal education than average or good readers, but showed equal social participation. Unfortunately, socio-economic status and school-age IQ were uncontrolled and could have acted as confounding variables.

A study by Preston and Yarington (1967) described the results of a follow-up study of 50 former clients of a reading clinic between the ages of 14 and 23. It was found that retarded readers tended to take longer to complete their education, but that their occupational adjustment was not different from the national average. Hardy (1968) followed up, after 7 years, 35 boys originally referred to a reading clinic at age 11. In this study, reading performance was found to be significantly improved, although 60% of the sample was still retarded in reading. Twenty subjects who were still attending school were judged to perform at a satisfactory level although 14 had been in special classes at some time. For those subjects who had completed school, educational achievement was poor. Although only 2 subjects were still unemployed, 55% were employed in semiskilled or unskilled jobs. Yet 65% reported to be satisfied with their jobs and to have felt that they had made a satisfactory vocational adjustment. Regarding other aspects studied, 95% of the subjects reported good relationships with fellow employees, 70% appeared to be reasonably self-confident, and 78% reported satisfactory social adjustment.

Rawson (1968) reported what Herjanic and Penick (1972) described as "the most optimistic follow-up report." Fifty-six former male students of a private school were traced after 23 years (follow-up age between 26 and 40 years). Of this group, 20 were judged to be moderately or severely dyslexic, and 16 as mildly dyslexic. In terms of socioeconomic class, 46 were reported to function in the upper two classes, 7 in Class III, 1 in Class IV and 2 in the lowest class. These subjects did not differ significantly in educational level from their fathers or from boys classified as having had only a mild or no reading problem. All members of the follow-up group had continued schooling after high school, and 48 of the 56 earned college degrees, although former students with low language facility continued to have some problems in spelling and reading. The exceptionally good outcome reported in this study may very well be related to the highly selective sample of children of upper class parents attending private school with special facilities for "specific language disability" during the 1935–1947 period. An additional selection factor that was responsible for such a favorable outcome probably was the relatively high general intelligence of the probands (the mean IQ was 131; only one subject had an IQ between 90 and 100). Similarly, Buerger (1968), in a 5-year follow-up, found strikingly good academic achievement in a follow-up of learning-disabled children from families of high socioeconomic status, but reported little effect of special instruction in comparison with an untreated control group. The reading clinic group did, however, report fewer adjustment problems.

MORE RECENT STUDIES OF OUTCOME DURING SCHOOL AGE AND ADULTHOOD

More recently, some studies that are more comprehensive and better controlled than the earlier follow-up studies have been presented. Ackerman, Dykman, and Peters (1977b) followed up, at 14 years of age, children who had been referred to a clinic at ages 8–11 because of learning problems. Only children with performance or verbal IQs of at least 90 and without obvious emotional or psychiatric illness, cultural disadvantage, or uncorrected visual or auditory defects were retained in the sample. The following results were obtained:

1. Fifteen percent of the learning disabled overcame their deficits.
2. Intervention and special instruction did not seem to help the children to catch up.
3. There were few specific disabilities at follow-up. Language difficulty was usually accompanied by arithmetic difficulty, and the learning disabled were impaired relative to controls in mathematics, English, science, and social sciences.
4. The best predictors of follow-up status were degree of reading impairment and discriminant function weights based on the information, similarities, arithmetic, digit span, and coding subtests of the WISC.

A second report by these authors (Ackerman, Dykman, & Peters, 1977a) stressed that all but the more severely disabled group had continued to progress academically and that they were close in performance to the "below average control" group.

Gottesman, Belmont, and Kaminer (1975) followed up 58 retarded readers 5 years after referral to a clinic. Age range was 7–15 at referral and 10–18 at follow-up. Only children with a full-scale IQ of at least 70 were retained in the study (mean IQ = 88). The results were as follows:

1. The children were, with few exceptions, more reading retarded at follow-up than at referral.

2. There was no difference between a group that received remedial instruction at the clinic and a group that received no remedial instruction (selection criteria for remediation was based on access to the clinic).
3. There was no relationship between reading gain and IQ.
4. The younger group (7–10 years) was less impaired initially (relative to chronological age), but more impaired at follow-up than the older group (11–13 years old).

In a later report, Gottesman (1979) stressed again that academic deficits in learning-disabled children tend to persist over a 5–7 year interval.

Koppitz (1971) followed up over a 5-year period children referred to special classes for the educationally handicapped. They were 6–12 years at the time of referral with an IQ range of more than 79 to less than 120 (mean = 92). The following results were obtained:

1. Seventeen percent were able to return fairly successfully to regular classes.
2. Most progress was made by children with an IQ of at least 85 who were no more than 2 years reading retarded, and who had parents who were interested, cooperative, and supportive.
3. At referral girls were usually more impaired than boys and the younger children were more impaired than the older children. Proportionately fewer girls and fewer of the younger children were able to return to regular class.

Trites and Fiedorowicz (1976) retested three groups of reading-disabled children an average of 2.6 years after initial assessment at a neuropsychology laboratory. The three groups were (*a*) 27 boys with a diagnosis of specific reading disability, (*b*) 10 girls with the same diagnosis, and (*c*) 10 boys with reading disability secondary to neurological disease. The criteria for diagnosis of specific reading disability included average or above average IQ, and no evidence of gross or focal brain damage or severe emotional disturbances. At the time of referral the girls were significantly younger (mean age = 8.9) than the boys (mean age = 11.6). The result for all three groups was an increased discrepancy at follow-up between grade placement and level of achievement in all academic skills measured despite the fact that most children had received remedial help.

Yule (1973) retested two groups of reading-disabled children after 4–5 years. The "backward" readers were those who had accuracy or comprehension scores (on the Neale Analysis of Reading Ability) 2 years and 4 months or more below the level predicted by their chronological age. The "retarded" readers were those who scored 2 years and 6 months or more below the level predicted by their mental age and IQ. Most of the "retarded" readers were also included in the "backward" group. Despite a higher mean IQ (98), the "retarded" readers had significantly lower reading and spelling scores at follow-up than the "backward" readers (mean IQ = 86). The "backward" readers were also poor in arithmetic at follow-up, and both groups continued to be reading disabled. The discrepancy between chronological age and reading age at follow-up was an average of 5.5 years for all the subjects.

Rourke (1975) retested normal and retarded readers after 4 years. He found that most of the normal readers had made more than 4 years' progress during that period. In contrast, most of the retarded readers had made less than two years' progress.

Muehl and Forell (1973–1974) administered the reading subtest of the Iowa Test of Basic Skills (ITBS) to 43 high school students who had been referred 4 years earlier to a remedial reading clinic. The children were an average of 3 years reading retarded at the time of referral. The mean age was 11.6 and the mean IQ was 101.5. At follow-up, only 4% of the sample attained an average or better reading grade on the ITBS. A multiple regression analysis tested the relationship between the ITBS reading grade and six predictor variables: chronological age, grade placement, reading grade, verbal IQ, performance IQ (all at the time of referral), and the number of semesters of remedial instruction. Chronological age and verbal IQ were significantly and independently related to the ITBS reading grade. The authors found less impairment at follow-up among the children referred at an earlier age. This finding is at variance with some of the studies cited earlier, which found younger children to be more impaired than older children at follow-up.

A general conclusion that could be drawn from the studies reviewed in this and the previous section seems to be that most children who are referred to a clinic for a learning or reading disability do not catch up. In fact, their disability is likely to become worse with time. In addition, remedial instruction has in general not been shown to improve the prognosis for these children. Factors that seem important are chronological age at referral (Gottesman, Belmont, & Kaminer, 1975; Koppitz, 1971; Muehl & Forell, 1973–1974); IQ (Koppitz, 1971; Hinton & Knights, 1971; Hardy, 1968); verbal IQ (Muehl & Forell, 1973–1974); language skill test results (Hinton & Knights, 1971); and sex (Koppitz, 1971).

There is also some indication that children with a severe reading disability fare worse in all academic areas than other learning-disabled children (Ackerman *et al.*, 1977a; Koppitz, 1971).

It should be noted, however, that the conclusions reached in these studies by no means represent a general consensus. In fact, contradictory results are often obtained, and some studies present a highly optimistic picture in contrast to the conclusions reached by many other studies. Such optimistic conclusions are usually expressed more for the occupational and social adjustment than for reading achievement, and apply especially to subjects who came from higher socioeconomic status families and received special attention in private schools. Other reasons for contradictory findings are to be found mostly in methodological differences and methodological faults inherent in many studies: Many follow-up projects use small atypical samples, fail to include appropriate control groups, and use inadequate indices of adult achievement; they frequently fail to distinguish between mild and severe disabilities; and they pay little or no attention to intervening variables such as remediation, maturation, and sociocultural factors.

FOLLOW-UP OF LEARNING-DISABLED CHILDREN WITH BRAIN DAMAGE

Whereas the studies reviewed so far present valuable information regarding learning disabilities in general and reading disability in particular, a growing body of information is available on the effect of brain damage on later adjustment. In a review dealing with this topic, Helper (1980) acknowledges that many of the papers are fraught with methodological problems, but concludes that these children "will have a high risk of some lasting deficit of functioning," especially of repeating grades in school, and, if the child is also hyperactive, "an elevated risk of antisocial behavior." Beyond these very broad conclusions, Helper states that "outcomes depend on the nature and extent of the cognitive and behavioral manifestations of minimal brain damage, the child's general intelligence level, and perhaps on the socio-economic status of his family [p. 110]."

Silver and Hagin (1963) already noted that dyslexic children with "organic signs" showed less improvement in reading than children with reading problems but without such signs. A study by Denhoff (1973) that dealt primarily with the infant to preschool age found, over a 10-year span, a changing clinical picture "with diminishing signs of neurological dysfunction and evidence of increasing IQ scores [Denhoff,

Sigueland, Komich, & Hainsworth, 1968, p. 204]." Dykman, Peters, and Ackerman (1973) studied 53 14-year-old returnees, originally tested and reported to have had minimal brain dysfunction, and compared them with 22 controls. They found, not surprisingly, that low IQ scores were predictors of a poor academic career and that many of their subjects suffered from poor self-image and had a dislike for school. The authors speculate that "the younger cases [8–9 years old at the time of the first study] will show greater improvement than . . . the child who is diagnosed MBD at age 10–12 who is more apt to carry the scar at age 14 [p. 107]." Koppitz (1971) reports that 45% of her learning-disabled samples were diagnosed by a neurologist or psychiatrist as having some kind of brain dysfunction. There was no significant relationship between neurological impairment and follow-up achievement. Koppitz did not formally test the difference between children who showed neurological signs and those who did not, but simply states that there was no significant relationship between any one medical or developmental factor and achievement during the follow-up. Not all of her sample had a neurological examination. Johnson and Neumann (1975), in a follow-up of 32 out of 40 clinic cases who ranged in age from 7 to 18 and who had originally been seen 1–7 years earlier, found that "a combination of below-normal IQ and abnormal EEG or serious untreated psychiatric problems [p. 174]" characterized children who did not improve. The study relied on parent reports only and stressed the need for better aftercare.

Borland and Heckman (1976) followed up 20 hyperactive boys after an average of 23 years at the age of 30 and compared them to their brothers. With this rather unique control group, the authors found a residual of at least three indicators of hyperactivity still persisting in 10 of the subjects whereas only one of the brothers in the control group showed this many symptoms. Nevertheless, the adult outcome was reported to be fairly favorable: Although the subjects reported only slightly more lower level jobs and more work hours than were reported by their brothers, they reported considerably more feelings of job dissatisfaction. Although 4 of the 20 were described as "psychopathic," none was imprisoned or institutionalized.

Laufer (1971) reported a follow-up at a mean age of 20 years for 66 former reading-disabled and hyperactive clients. The average follow-up period was 12 years. Of the 37 subjects 19 years or older, 14 were attending college or university, 18 were employed, and only 5 were unemployed. The technique of returned questionnaires employed by the study probably contributed to the highly favorable picture presented. Nevertheless, 20 of the total of 55 respondents admitted that they had needed psychiatric help, though only 3 had been admitted to a hospital for psychiatric treatment. Sixteen reported that they had been in "some kind of trouble with police," but none was in jail.

Kleinpeter and Goellnitz (1976) followed 171 out of 196 more seriously brain-damaged children from age 8–10 to school-leaving age. They found that 42 of their subjects finished school with education provided for the retarded, 27 received special school education, and 15 "got through six or fewer grades of regular school [p. 33]." Only 44% of the children were in the grade corresponding to their age. They also reported that brain-damaged children "tend more frequently to develop neurotic reactions than normal children do [p. 33]." Gottesman, Belmont, and Kaminer (1975) reported that 12% of their reading-disabled children showed neurological "hard" signs and 19% showed "soft" signs on admission to an outpatient clinic. There was no relationship between neurological signs and reading ability either on admission or at follow-up. Only 11 of the 58 children followed up showed "soft" signs. The sample was very heterogeneous with regard to age, IQ, and reading level. A subsequent report on the same group of learning-disabled children (Gottesman, 1979) indicated that reading achievement after 5–7 years remained a persistent deficit. Ackerman *et al.* (1977a) also report there was no difference in achievement (measured by the WRAT) at follow-up among learning-disabled boys classified at referral as having positive, equivocal, or negative neurological signs. The total follow-up sample of 60 learning-disabled boys was divided into nine subgroups (three levels of neurological functioning and three activity levels). These negative findings may not be surprising if the size of these subgroups is taken into account. A 10-year follow-up by Kaste (1972) remains one of the most comprehensive studies to date. She examined 116 children of a target group of 148 (including 15 with established brain dysfunction, 39 mildly brain damaged, and 53 with minimal brain damage, as well as 41 normal controls) originally seen at age 8–12, after a 10-year period, and found that 85% of the cerebral dysfunction group "showed to an even more pronounced degree patterns which previously have been associated with cerebral dysfunction," and that they "did not simply 'grow out of' problems or become more similar to other former child guidance patients with the passage of time [p. 1797]." Flach and Malmros (1972) followed 148 children with severe head injury after an 8–10 year period and found persisting mental disturbances in 46% and social maladjustment in 27% of these patients. One of the most detailed studies, the Isle of Wight study of 5–14-year-old children, was not longitudinal in nature, but some of its retrospective aspects throw some light on educational and intellectual retardation in relation to brain damage (Rutter, Tizard, & Whitmore, 1970).

It appears that, in general, these widely varying and sometimes contradictory findings are based on very small samples from highly selected populations. It seems probable that there is a greater incidence of neurological "soft" signs in a learning-disabled population. However, the demonstration of this phenomenon does not elucidate the implications of a diagnosis of neurological dysfunction for treatment or prognosis. The few studies that compared presence or absence of neurological signs with achievement within a learning-disabled sample found no firm relationship either at referral or at follow-up. However, in all of these studies the neurological factor was a side issue and the methodology was not designed to give a powerful test of its implications.

A NEW LONG-TERM FOLLOW-UP STUDY ON LEARNING-DISABLED CHILDREN

In an attempt to answer some of the many questions regarding the outcome of learning handicap in children, I conducted a study of 203 children and their parents. Both groups were interviewed separately an average of 10 years after the children's initial assessment for learning disabilities at the University of Victoria neuropsychology clinic. The sample was broken down into three groups according to the degree of neurological impairment (definite impairment, suggested impairment, learning problem without neurological impairment). A control group of 52 matched for age, sex, and socioeconomic status, and selected from local secondary school records, was also interviewed. The average age in all groups was 19 years. The interview covered a wide range of issues: school experiences and attitudes (success/failure, special instruction, awards, particular competencies or problems, etc.), employment history, health variables (general health, seizures, accidents; prescription and street drugs), family characteristics and relationships, other personal relationships (dating/marriage, friends, classmates), behavioral problems, involvements with the police, offenses and penalties resulting. In addition, school records as well as behavior ratings by parents, and a personality questionnaire completed by the former students were used.

The results of this follow-up project have been reported in a number of papers (Denbigh, 1979; Hern, 1979; Hern & Spreen, 1982; Peter &

Spreen, 1979; Spreen, 1978, 1981; Spreen & Lawriw, 1980). A number of areas are still under investigation. With respect to academic achievement, it was found that all three learning-handicapped groups were inferior to the control group in all areas of study, including art and industrial education. They also had a poor attitude toward school. There were no differences between the groups in attainment in physical education or in reported involvement in extracurricular activities. Few reliable differences in academic achievement were found between groups with definite, suggested, or no evidence of cerebral dysfunction. Where differences were found, they typically favored the learning disability group without neurological handicap. Analysis of the behavior rating scale and the personality questionnaire (Bell, 1962) revealed consistent and significant relationships between an earlier diagnosis of neurological impairment and behavioral deviance at the time of the follow-up, even when other confounding variables such as age, sex, and intelligence were taken into account (Peter & Spreen, 1979). All learning-handicapped groups reported a greater number of signs of personal maladjustment and more antisocial behavior than the control group. Surprisingly, females were described as having more social and personality problems than males, but males tended to show more "acting-out" or antisocial behavior. In considering health adjustments, females were shown to be more severely impaired than males; this may be related to the more severe social difficulties. In addition, central nervous system illnesses, seizures, birth and pregnancy problems, and behavioral difficulties decreased as the level of neurological impairment decreased (Hern & Spreen, 1982). General health and the number of accidents sustained were not significantly affected by the presence of learning disorder or neurological dysfunction. The latter finding is somewhat contradictory to that of previous researchers (Wender, 1973; Kinsbourne, 1973) who claim that these children are "accident prone." In considering the relationship between delinquency and learning disorders, Spreen (1981) found no increase in the number of encounters with the police or the number of offenses committed by learning-handicapped versus control subjects (although clients with learning disability without neurological impairment tended to receive slightly more and somewhat more severe penalties). This is in contradiction to the reports of some authors (Berman, 1978; Poremba, 1975), who, on the basis of retrospective studies, claim an association between learning disability and delinquency. Children in the control group attended school longer, had slightly higher salaries, and were less likely to have received psychological or psychiatric counseling than learning-handicapped children.

At this point several major findings and conclusions can be outlined as a summary of this study:

1. Perhaps the most important finding is that, on a majority of outcome variables, a definite and significant difference was found between the four groups. Typically this difference was present in a linear fashion—that is, the learning-disabled children without neurological findings fared worse than the controls, the children with evidence of "minimal brain damage" showed poorer outcome than those without neurological impairment, and the definitely brain-damaged group showed the poorest outcome of all four groups. In all areas of long-term adjustment and outcome (social, personal, occupational), the presence of neurological handicap was related to poorer achievement and adjustment, even though the groups did not differ significantly on general intelligence at the time of the original referral nearly 9 years earlier.

This finding may not surprise a neurologist, but is of considerable importance to the educator, counselor, and psychologist, who often consider the presence or absence of neurological impairment an irrelevant or useless piece of information. This study attempts a new approach in that for the first time all three groups (definite neurological impairment, minimal brain damage, no neurological impairment) were compared in the same study and under the same conditions. Previous research has usually been limited to the study of outcome for only one of these groups (or to comparison with a control group without learning disability) and hence remained inconclusive with regard to the relative importance of neurological impairment. The present study fills this gap of information and clearly demonstrated the importance of the dimension of neurological impairment.

2. As described in the review of the literature, much controversy has surrounded the concept of "minimal brain dysfunction." The concept is a weak one in that it often refers to the mere inference of brain damage from behavioral or observational data including hyperkinesis or from "soft signs" which may be merely transient and maturational. This study used the concept in clearly defined operational terms based on neurological examination, not on inferences from other sources. Thus, children falling into this category could be contrasted with those with "hard" evidence of neurological impairment and those without neurological impairment. The results clearly indicate that children with "minimal brain damage" show poorer outcome as compared to those without any evidence of brain damage, but show better outcome in

many respects than the group with definite neurological impairment. The results were not anticipated when the study was designed, but seem to confirm the view that minimal brain damage (defined in operational terms) has a significant impact on the future development of children. One restriction should be stated here: Minimal brain-damage was diagnosed by a neurological examination only in children between the ages of 8 and 12. Our results cannot be generalized to children in whom such evidence was found at an earlier age or at birth. We also do not know at this time whether the neurological evidence itself persisted in these children as they grew into young adults or whether these neurological "soft signs" were outgrown (This question will be addressed in the ongoing Phase II of this study.)

3. The social and economic importance of these findings should be stressed: Not only do these youngsters suffer through a miserable and usually foreshortened school career and live a discouraging social life full of disappointments and failures; they also have a relatively poor chance for advanced training and skilled employment. The need for early educational intervention and appropriate job counseling and training is obvious.

4. Two separate interviews (with clients and with their parents) indicated that parents are well aware of the difficulties encountered by our clients. On questions concerning factual information, the two interviews agreed quite well. Exceptions to this were the areas of delinquency (encounters with the police) and alcohol and drug use, with parents usually reporting less instances than the clients themselves, probably because they were not aware of the full extent of such behavior. On the other hand, parents tended to report much more serious effects on the personal well-being, happiness, and social interaction of their children; that is, they gave a more pessimistic picture than did the clients. This may reflect an overprotective attitude on the part of the parents, as the normal control group did not show this discrepancy between parents' and students' responses. It was also quite apparent that learning-disabled children remembered health-related and behavior problems before the age of 8–12 less well than their parents and less well than the control subjects did; it would appear that their childhood memories were not as clear as those of other children.

5. Our former clients ranged in age from 13 to 25. As their age increased, all of our subjects tended to have firmer plans for the future and better occupational adjustment. However, with increasing degree of neurological impairment, our subjects had more difficulty in finding a permanent job; they also had less earnings. With increasing age, our

clients also gave an increasingly poorer impression of their school experiences.

6. The personal adjustment inventory filled in by the former clients and a behavior ratings scale filled in by their parents explored further personal and emotional adjustment. Here again, we found a consistent and significant relationship between degree of neurological impairment and behavioral deviance and emotional maladjustment. As expected, deviance and maladjustment were also related to intelligence at the time of the original referral. However, the striking difference between males and females showed poorer emotional and social adjustment in females than males.

7. Although our results indicate, in statistical terms, the dissatisfaction with life, the feelings of being "different" and viewed as "different" by others, it should be remembered that these were statistical averages which do not clearly express the range of variability or the personal involvement and suffering that some of our clients experienced. We found a few of our clients in prison and in mental hospitals, others in comfortable homes of their own and in apparent harmony with their community. During the interview, however, many of our former clients "relived" the years since their first referral to our laboratory and often expressed their frustration and anger as well as their depression in forms that cannot be documented on a questionnaire or submitted to statistical analysis.

SUMMARY

This review of our knowledge to date suggests that children who have difficulty acquiring reading skills and children with broader learning handicap for a variety of reasons may be of great concern to society in their adult life. Although little information is available on outcome in later life, studies following such children into their twenties suggest the picture of a group of individuals who, even though initially presented with a specific reading problem, tend to have problems in many school subject areas, and who in growing up encounter problems in many areas and at many age levels, although the type of problems may change as their life progresses.

Adult adjustment problems can be occupational as well as social and personal, and they are strongly influenced by socioeconomic background. In addition, some studies including the study I recently completed, have emphasized the effect of neurological impairment during childhood: The outcome tends to be negatively influenced even by the presence of "minimal" neurological impairment suggested by soft signs. The relationship between delinquency and learning disability has probably been overstated in the past, as prospective studies find only a minor increase or no increase of delinquency in learning-disabled groups nor can the effect of neurological impairment on this relationship be confirmed.

Although many studies report continued progress in reading and other academic subjects for the reading-disabled individuals up into the adult years, personal dissatisfaction and dislike for school remain, and school careers are frequently foreshortened with early entry into low status and low paying jobs. Most reports indicate that former learning-disabled children manage to find employment in spite of some difficulty and to lead independent lives; psychiatric disorders are found very infrequently. The review of outcome studies over the past 25 years tends to show only minimal or no effect of increasing attempts at intervention, except for students with high intelligence attending private schools. Discrepancies between the findings of some of the studies are probably due in part to differences in the IQ range sampled; studies that include low IQ subjects (80 and below) tend to report poor outcomes whereas studies that exclude subjects with an IQ below 90 tend to produce the most optimistic findings. This "IQ effect" does not, however, apply to the actual accomplishment in reading as adults; in fact, several studies stress that they found no relationship between adult reading achievement and IQ of former subjects with reading disability.

REFERENCES

Ackerman, P. T., Dykman, R. A., & Peters, J. E. (1977a) Learning-disabled boys as adolescents: Cognitive factors and achievement. *Journal of the American Academy of Child Psychiatry, 16,* 296–313.
Ackerman, P. T., Dykman, R. A., & Peters, J. E. (1977b) Teenage status of hyperactive and nonhyperactive learning disabled boys. *American Journal of Orthopsychiatry, 47,* 577–596.
Adamas, R., Kocsis, J., & Estes, R. E. (1974) Soft neurological signs in learning disabled children and controls. *American Journal of Diseases of Children, 128,* 614–618.
Apgar, V., & James, L. S. (1962) Further observations on the newborn scoring system. *American Journal of Diseases of Children, 104,* 419–428.
Bakker, D. J., & De Wit, J. (1977) Perceptual and cortical immaturity in developmental dyslexia. In L. Tarnopol & M. Tarnopol (Eds.), *Brain function and reading disabilities.* Baltimore: University Park Press.

Bakker, D. J., & Satz, P. (Eds.) (1970) *Specific reading disability: Advances in theory and method.* Rotterdam: Rotterdam University Press.

Balow, B., & Blomquist, M. (1965) Young adults ten to fifteen years after severe reading disability. *Elementary School Journal, 66,* 44–48.

Barlow, C. F. (1974) Soft signs in children with learning disorders. *American Journal of Diseases of Children, 128,* 605–606.

Bell, H. M. (1962) *The adjustment inventory: Student form.* Palo Alto: Consulting Psychologists Press.

Benton, A. L., & Pearl, D. (Eds.) (1977) *Dyslexia: An appraisal of current knowledge.* New York: Oxford University Press.

Berman, A. (1978) Neuropsychological aspects of adolescent violence. In: Ramos, N. P. (Ed.). *Delinquent Youth and Learning Disabilities.* San Rafael, Calif.: Academic Therapy.

Birch, H. G. (Ed.) (1964) *Brain damage in children: The biological and social aspects.* Baltimore: Williams and Wilkins.

Borland, B. L., & Heckman, H. K. (1976) Hyperactive boys and their brothers. *Archives of General Psychiatry, 33,* 669–675.

Broman, S. H., Nichols, P. L., & Kennedy, W. (1975) *Pre-school IQ: Prenatal and early developmental correlates.* New York: Wiley.

Buerger, T. A. (1968) A follow-up of remedial reading instruction. *The Reading Teacher, 21,* 329–334.

Carter, R. P. (1964) *A descriptive analysis of the adult adjustment of persons once identified as disabled readers.* Unpublished doctoral dissertation, Indiana University.

Chall, J. S., & Mirsky, A. F. (Eds.) (1978) *Education and the brain. The 77th yearbook of the National Society for the Study of Education. Part II.* Chicago: University of Chicago Press.

Clements, S. D., & Peters, J. E. (1963) Minimal brain dysfunction in the school-age child. *Archives of General Psychiatry, 6,* 185–197.

Corah, N. L., Anthony, E. J., Painter, P., Stern, J. A., & Thurston, D. (1965) Effects of perinatal anoxia after seven years. *Psychological Monographs, 79,* Whole No. 596.

Critchley, M. (1966) Is developmental dyslexia the expression of minor cerebral damage? *Clinical Proceedings, 23*(8), 213–222.

Critchley, M. (1970) *The dyslexic child.* London: Heinemann.

Cruickshank, W. M. (Ed.) (1966) *The teacher of brain-injured children.* Syracuse, N.Y.: Syracuse University Press.

Cruickshank, W. M. (1967) *The brain-injured child in home, school, and community.* Syracuse, N.Y.: Syracuse University Press.

Cruickshank, W. M. (1971) *Psychology of exceptional children and youth.* Englewood Cliffs, N.J.: Prentice-Hall.

de la Cruz, F. F., Fox, B. H., & Roberts, R. H. (Eds.) (1973) *Minimal brain dysfunction. Annals of the New York Academy of Sciences, 205.*

Denbigh, K. (1979) *Neurological impairment and educational achievement: A follow-up of learning disabled children.* Unpublished M.A. thesis, University of Victoria.

Denckla, M. B. (1977) *Minimal brain dysfunction and dyslexia: Beyond diagnosis by exclusion.* In: M. E. Blaw, I. Rapin & M. Kinsbourne (Eds.) *Topics in child neurology.* New York: Spectrum.

Denhoff, E. (1973) The natural life history of children with minimal brain dysfunction. *Annals of the New York Academy of Sciences, 205,* 188–205.

Denhoff, E., Siqueland, M. L., Komich, M. P., & Hainsworth, P. K. (1968) Developmental and predictive characteristics of items from the Meeting Street School Screening Test. *Developmental Medicine and Child Neurology, 10,* 220–232.

Deutsch, C. P., & Schumer, F. (1970) *Brain-damaged children: A modality-oriented exploration of performance.* New York: Brunner/Mazel.

Doehring, D. G. (1968) *Patterns of impairment in specific reading disabilities.* Bloomington: Indiana University Press.

Dykman, R. A., Peters, J. E., & Ackerman, P. T. (1973) Experimental approaches to the study of minimal brain dysfunction: A follow-up study. *Annals of the New York Academy of Sciences, 205,* 93–107.

Flach, J., & Malmros, R. (1972) A long-term follow-up study of children with severe head injury. *Scandinavian Journal of Rehabilitative Medicine, A*(1), 9–15.

Friedman, R., Dale, E. P., & Wagner, J. H. (1973) A long-term comparison of two treatment regimes for minimal brain dysfunction: Drug therapy versus combined therapy. *Clinical Pediatrics, 12,* 666–671.

Gaddes, W. H. (1968) A neuropsychological approach to learning disorders. *Journal of Learning Disabilities, 1,* 523–534.

Gaddes, W. H. (1976) Prevalence estimates and the need for definition of learning disabilities. In R. M. Knights & D. L. Bakker (Eds.), *The neuropsychology of learning disorders: Theoretical approaches.* Baltimore: University Park Press.

Gaddes, W. H. (1980) *Learning disabilities and brain function: A neuropsychological approach.* New York: Springer.

Gottesman, R. L. (1979) Followup of learning disabled children. *Learning Disability Quarterly, 2,* 60–69.

Gottesman, R. L., Belmont, I., & Kaminer, R. (1975) Admission and follow-up status of reading disabled children referred to a medical clinic. *Journal of Learning Disabilities, 8,* 642–650.

Graham, F. K., Ernhart, C. B., Craft, M., & Berman, P. W. (1963) Brain injury in the preschool child: Some developmental considerations, I. Performance of normal children. *Psychological Monographs, 77,* Whole No. 573.

Graham, F. K., Ernhart, C. B., Thurston, D., & Craft, M. (1962) Development three years after perinatal anoxia and other potentially damaging newborn experiences. *Psychological Monographs, 76,* 522.

Hallahan, D. P., & Cruickshank, W. M. (Eds.) (1973) *Psycho-educational foundations of learning disabilities.* Englewood Cliffs, N.J.: Prentice-Hall.

Hardy, M. I. (1968) *Clinical followup study of disabled readers.* Unpublished doctoral dissertation, University of Toronto.

Hechtman, L., Weiss, G., Finklestein, J., Werner, A., & Benn, R. (1976) Hyperactives as young adults: Preliminary report. *Canadian Medical Association Journal, 115,* 625–630.

Helper, M. M. (1980) Follow-up of children with minimal brain dysfunctions: Outcomes and predictors. In H. E. Rie & E. D. Rie (Eds.), *Handbook of minimal brain dysfunctions: A critical review.* New York: Wiley.

Herjanic, B. M., & Penick, E. C. (1972) Adult outcomes of disabled child readers. *Journal of Special Education, 6,* 397–410.

Hermann, K. (1959) *Reading disability.* Springfield, Ill.: Charles C Thomas.

Hern, A. (1979) *Health and behavioural adjustment in later life for learning handicapped children with and without neurological impairment.* Unpublished M.A. thesis, University of Victoria.

Hern, A., & Spreen, O. (1982) Health adjustment in learning handicapped children: Results of a followup study. *Developmental Medicine and Child Neurology.*

Hertzig, M. E., & Birch, H. G. (1968) Neurological organization in psychiatrically disturbed adolescents: A comparative consideration of sex differences. *Archives of General Psychiatry, 19,* 528–538.

Hertzig, M. E., Bortner, M., & Birch, H. G. (1969) Neurological findings in children educationally designated as brain damaged. *American Journal of Orthopsychiatry, 39,* 437–446.

Hinton, G. G., & Knights, R. M. (1971) Children with learning problems: Academic history, academic prediction, and adjustment three years after assessment. *Exceptional Children, 37,* 513–519.

Howden, M. E. (1967) *A nineteen-year follow-up of good, average and poor readers in the fifth and sixth grades.* Unpublished doctoral dissertation, University of Oregon.

Huessy, H. R., Metoyer, M., & Towsend, M. (1973) Eight–ten year follow-up of children treated in rural Vermont for behavioral disorder. *American Journal of Orthopsychiatry, 43,* 233–238.

Huessy, H. R., Metoyer, M., & Townsend, M. (1974) Eight–ten year follow-up of 84 children treated for behavioral disorder in rural Vermont. *Acta Paedopsychiatrica, 40,* 230–235.

Johnson, D., & Myklebust, H. (1967) *Learning disabilities: Educational principles and practices.* New York: Grune & Stratton.

Johnson, E. L., & Neumann, C. (1975) Multidisciplinary evaluation of learning and behavior problems in children: A follow-up study of 40 cases. *Journal of the American Osteopathic Association, 74,* 168–174.

Jones, F. H. (1973) A four-year follow-up of vulnerable adolescents: The continuity and interrelationship of measures of social competence and psychopathology from adolescence to early adulthood. *Dissertation Abstracts International, 33*(8-B), 3942–3943.

Kagan, J., & Moss, H. (1962) *Birth to maturity: A study in psychological development.* New York: Wiley.

Kalverboer, A. D., Touwen, B. C., & Prechtl, H. F. (1973) Follow-up of infants at risk of minor brain dysfunction. *Annals of the New York Academy of Sciences, 205,* 173–187.

Kaspar, J. C., Millichap, J. G., Backus, R., Child, D., & Schulman, J. L. (1971) Study of the relationship between neurological evidence of brain damage in children and activity and distractability. *Journal of Consulting and Clinical Psychology, 36,* 329–337.

Kaste, C. M. (1972) A ten-year followup of children diagnosed in a child guidance clinic as having cerebral dysfunction. *Dissertation Abstracts International, 33*(4-B), 1797–1798.

Kinsbourne, M. (1973) Minimal brain dysfunction as a neurodevelopmental lag. *Annals of the New York Academy of Sciences, 205,* 268–273.

Klasen, E. (1972) *The syndrome of specific dyslexia.* Baltimore: University Park Press.

Kleinpeter, U., & Goellnitz, G. (1976) Achievement and adaptation disorders in brain-damaged children. *International Journal of Mental Health, 4*(4), 19–35.

Koppitz, E. M. (1971) *Children with learning disabilities: A five year follow-up study.* New York: Grune & Stratton.

Laufer, M. W. (1971) Long-term management and some follow-up findings on the use of drugs with minimal cerebral syndrome. *Journal of Learning Disabilities, 4,* 518–522.

Lenneberg, E. H. (1967) *Biological foundations of language.* New York: Wiley.

Levine, M. D., Brooks, R., & Shonkoff, J. (1980) *A pediatric approach to learning disorders.* New York: Wiley.

Levinson, H. N. (1980) *A solution to the riddle dyslexia.* New York: Springer.

Lucas, A., Rodin, E. A., & Simon, C. B. (1965) Neurological assessment of children with early school problems. *Developmental Medicine and Child Neurology, 7,* 145–156.

Mendelson, W., Johnson, N., & Stewart, M. (1971) Hyperactive children as teenagers: A follow-up study. *Journal of Nervous and Mental Diseases, 153,* 272–279.

Menkes, M. M., Rowe, J. S., & Menkes, J. H. (1967) A twenty-five year follow-up study on the hyperkinetic child with minimal brain dysfunction. *Pediatrics, 39,* 393–399.

Minde, K., Lewin, D., Weiss, G., Lavigueur, H., Douglas, V., & Sykes, E. (1971) The hyperactive child in elementary school: A five-year, controlled follow-up. *Exceptional Children, 38,* 215–221.

Minde, K. G., Weiss, G., & Mendelson, N. (1972) A five-year follow-up study on the hyperkinetic child with minimal brain dysfunction. *Journal of the American Academy of Child Psychiatry, 11,* 595–610.

Minskoff, J. G. (1973) Differential approaches to prevalence estimates of learning disabilities. *Annals of the New York Academy of Sciences, 205,* 139–145.

Muehl, S., & Forell, E. R. (1973–1974) A followup study of disabled readers: Variables related to high school reading performance. *Reading Research Quarterly, 9*(1), 110–123.

Muehl, S., Knott, J., & Benton, A. (1965) EEG abnormality and psychological test performance in reading disability. *Cortex, 1,* 434–440.

Myklebust, H. R., Boshes, B., Olson, D. A., & Cole, C. H. (1969) *Minimal brain damage in children—Final report.* Washington, D.C.: Department of Health, Education, and Welfare.

Page-El, E., & Grossman, H. J. (1973) Neurologic appraisal in learning disorders. *Pediatric Clinics of North America, 20,* 599–605.

Pasamanick, B., & Knobloch, H. (1960) Brain damage and reproductive casualty. *American Journal of Orthopsychiatry, 30,* 298–305.

Peter, B. M., & Spreen, O. (1979) Behavior rating and personal adjustment scales of neurologically and learning handicapped children during adolescence and early adulthood: Results of a follow-up study. *Journal of Clinical Neuropsychology, 1,* 75–92.

Peters, J. E., Romine, J. S., & Dykman, R. A. (1975) A special neurological examination of children with learning disabilities. *Developmental Medicine and Child Neurology, 17,* 63–78.

Pirozzolo, F. J. (1979) *The neuropsychology of developmental reading disorders.* New York: Praeger.

Poremba, C. D. (1975) Learning disabilities, youth and delinquency: Programs for intervention. In H. R. Myklebust (Ed.), *Progress in learning disabilities* (Vol. 3). New York: Grune & Stratton.

Preston, R., & Yarington, D. J. (1967) Status of fifty retarded readers eight years after reading clinic diagnosis. *Journal of Reading, 11,* 122–129.

Rawson, M. (1968) *Developmental language disability: Adult accomplishment of dyslexic boys.* Baltimore: Johns Hopkins University Press.

Rie, H. E., & Rie, E. D. (Eds.) (1980) *Handbook of minimal brain dysfunction.* New York: Wiley.

Rie, E. D., Rie, H. E., Stewart, S., & Rettemnier, S. C. (1978) An analysis of neurological soft signs in children with learning problems. *Brain and Language, 6,* 32–46.

Robinson, H. M., & Smith, H. K. (1962) Reading clinic clients—Ten years after. *Elementary School Journal, 63,* 22–27.

Roesler, H. D. (1971) Mental development of minimal brain-damaged children. *Acta Paedopsychiatrica, 38,* 71–78.

Roesler, H. D., & Kurth, I. (1975) Motorik, Intelligenz, Schulleistung. In G. Goellnitz & H. D. Roesler (Eds.), *Untersuchungen zur Entwicklung hirngeschaedigter Kinder.* Berlin: VEB.

Rosenthal, I. (1963) Reliability of retrospective reports of adolescence. *Journal of Consulting and Clinical Psychology, 27,* 189–198.

Rourke, B. P. (1975) Brain–behavior relationships in children with learning disabilities: A research program. *American Psychologist, 30,* 911–920.

Rourke, B. P. (1977) Neuropsychological research in reading retardation: A review. In A. L. Benton & D. Pearl (Eds.), *Dyslexia: An appraisal of current knowledge*. New York: Oxford University Press.

Rourke, B. P. (1978) Reading, spelling, arithmetic disabilities: A neuropsychological perspective. In H. R. Myklebust (Ed.), *Progress in learning disabilities* (Vol. 4). New York: Grune & Stratton.

Rubin, R., & Balow, B. (1971) Learning and behavior disorders: A longitudinal study. *Exceptional Children, 38,* 293–299.

Rutter, M., Graham, P., & Yule, W. (1970) *A neuropsychiatric study in childhood. Clinics in developmental medicine No. 35–36*. Philadelphia: J. B. Lippincott.

Rutter, M., Tizard, J., & Whitmore, K. (Eds.) (1970) *Education, health, and behavior*. London: Longman.

Schain, R. J. (1972) *Neurology of childhood learning disorders*. Baltimore: Williams and Wilkins.

Schmitt, B. C. (1975) The minimal brain dysfunction myth. *American Journal of Diseases of Children, 129,* 1313–1318.

Segal, S. S. (1968) *Research relevant to the education of children with learning handicaps.* London: Advisory and Information Centre, College of Special Education.

Silver, A. A., & Hagin, R. A. (1963) Specific reading disability: A twelve year follow-up study. *American Journal of Orthopsychiatry, 33,* 338–339.

Silver, A. A., & Hagin, R. A. (1964) Specific reading disability: Follow-up studies. *American Journal of Orthopsychiatry, 34,* 95–102.

Silverman, L. J., & Metz, A. S. (1973) Number of pupils with specific learning disabilities in local public schools in the United States, spring 1970. *Annals of the New York Academy of Sciences, 205,* 146–157.

Solomons, G., Holden, R. H., & Denhoff, E. (1963) The changing picture of cerebral dysfunction. *Pediatrics, 63,* 113–130.

Spreen, O. (1978) *Learning disabled children growing up.* Final report to Canada Health and Welfare, Monograph, University of Victoria.

Spreen, O. (1981) The relationship between learning disability, neurological impairment and delinquency: Results of a follow-up study. *Journal of Nervous and Mental Diseases, 169,* 791–799.

Spreen, O., & Lawriw, I. (1980) *Neuropsychological test results as predictors of outcome of learning handicap in late adolescence and early adult years.* Paper presented at the meeting of the International Neuropsychological Society, San Francisco, 1980.

Stine, O. C., Saratsiotis, J. B., & Mosser, R. S. (1975) Relationship between neurological findings and classroom behavior. *American Journal of Diseases of Children, 129,* 1036–1040.

Tarnopol, L., & Tarnopol, M. (Eds.) (1977) *Brain function and reading disabilities*. Baltimore: University Park Press.

Trites, R., & Fiedorowicz, C. (1976) Follow-up study of children with specific (or primary) reading disability. In R. Knights & D. J. Bakker (Eds.), *The neuropsychology of learning disorders: Theoretical approaches*. Baltimore: University Park Press.

Vacc, N. A. (1972) Spontaneous improvement in the social positions of emotionally disturbed children in regular classes. *Psychological Reports, 31,* 639–645.

Weiss, G., Minde, K., Werry, J. S., Douglas, V., & Nemeth, E. (1971) Studies on the hyperactive child, VIII: Five-year follow-up. *Archives of General Psychiatry, 24,* 409–414.

Wender, P. H. (1973) Minimal brain dysfunction in children: Diagnosis and management. Symposium on Habilitation of the Handicapped Child. *Pediatric Clinics of North America, 20,* 187–202.

Wepman, J. M., & Morency, A. S. (1971) *School achievement as related to speech and perceptual handicaps: Final report.* Chicago: Chicago University Press.

Werry, J. S., Minde, K., Guzman, A., Weiss, G., Dogan, K., & Hoy, E. (1972) Studies on the hyperactive child, VII: Neurological status compared with neurotic and normal children. *American Journal of Orthopsychiatry, 42,* 441–451.

Subject Index

A

Ability to define words, 161, 167
Ablation, 316
Abstractness, 349, 352, 360
Abstract reasoning, 32, 399
Abstract words, 8, 9, 15, 155, 312, 335
Academic problems, 397–400
Academic tests, *see* specific tests
Acalculia, 309, 310, 326
Accent patterns, 380
Achievement criteria, 396
Acoustic stimulus, 14
Acquired illiteracy, 309
Acquired reading disorders, 281–291
Acting-out behavior, 392, 403, 488
Added words, 27
Adolescents, 389–408
  academic problems of, 397–400
Adult illiterates, 206
Adult outcome, 473–498
Adults, 386
Aggression, 400, 453, 455, 456, 458
Agnosia, 325, 326, 342, 358, 359
Agnosic alexia, 101, 324, 343, 346
Agrammatic errors, 15, 27, 43, 47, 317, 332,
  344, 349, 352
Akinesia of speech, 333
Alexia, 6, 8, 12, 14–16, 38, 58–59, 79–80,
  81, 101, 124–125, 241–253, 281–291
  agnosic, 101, 324, 343, 346, 362
  aphasic, 313, 324, 328–334, 343, 346, 362
  congenital, 411
  evaluation of, 306
  frontal, 310
  global, 307
  information–processing model, 282–283
  literal, 305–306, 307, 311, 335, 344, 346,
    347, 352, 358, 362–363

neuroanatomical model, 282–283
nonaphasic, 324–328
parietal, 343
phonemic, 139
phonological, 353, 358
primary, 124, 138, 324
psycholinguistic model, 282
pure, 306, 307–309, 310, 342–343, 362
secondary, 124, 139
sentence, 346, 347, 362
subangular, 309
subcortical, 324
symbolic, 101
syntactic, 332
tertiary, 124–125, 139
third, 310–311, 332
verbal, 305, 307, 336, 344, 345, 346–347,
  362–363
with agraphia, 306, 309–310, 326, 331,
  332, 336, 342–344, 362
without agraphia, 306, 307–309, 324–326,
  332, 344–345, 358, 362
Alpha activity, 222, 223, 237, 240–241
  asymmetrical, 240–241
  brain growth and, 295
Alphabetic script, 40–45, 48, 53–56, 155
Ambidexterity, 39–40, 415
Amerind, 330–331
Amnesia, 325
Amnestic aphasia, 321
Amphetamines, 404, 453, 455
Anagram tiles, 324
Analog matching, 15, 30
Analytical reading, 356, 363
Analytic–sequential process, 449–452
Analytic skills, 206
Anatomical studies, 216–218, 313, 341,
  342–345

PERSPECTIVES IN
NEUROLINGUISTICS, NEUROPSYCHOLOGY, AND
PSYCHOLINGUISTICS: A Series of Monographs and Treatises

Harry A. Whitaker, Series Editor
DEPARTMENT OF HEARING AND SPEECH SCIENCES
UNIVERSITY OF MARYLAND
COLLEGE PARK, MARYLAND 20742

HAIGANOOSH WHITAKER and HARRY A. WHITAKER (Eds.).
Studies in Neurolinguistics, Volumes 1, 2, 3, and 4

NORMAN J. LASS (Ed.). Contemporary Issues in Experimental Phonetics

JASON W. BROWN. Mind, Brain, and Consciousness: The Neuropsychology of Cognition

SIDNEY J. SEGALOWITZ and FREDERIC A. GRUBER (Eds.). Language Development and Neurological Theory

SUSAN CURTISS. Genie: A Psycholinguistic Study of a Modern-Day "Wild Child"

JOHN MACNAMARA (Ed.). Language Learning and Thought

I. M. SCHLESINGER and LILA NAMIR (Eds.). Sign Language of the Deaf: Psychological, Linguistic, and Sociological Perspectives

WILLIAM C. RITCHIE (Ed.). Second Language Acquisition Research: Issues and Implications

PATRICIA SIPLE (Ed.). Understanding Language through Sign Language Research

MARTIN L. ALBERT and LORAINE K. OBLER. The Bilingual Brain: Neuropsychological and Neurolinguistic Aspects of Bilingualism

TALMY GIVÓN. On Understanding Grammar

CHARLES J. FILLMORE, DANIEL KEMPLER, and WILLIAM S-Y. WANG (Eds.). Individual Differences in Language Ability and Language Behavior

JEANNINE HERRON (Ed.). Neuropsychology of Left-Handedness

FRANÇOIS BOLLER and MAUREEN DENNIS (Eds.). Auditory Comprehension: Clinical and Experimental Studies with the Token Test

R. W. RIEBER (Ed.). Language Development and Aphasia in Children: New Essays and a Translation of "Kindersprache und Aphasie" by Emil Fröschels

GRACE H. YENI-KOMSHIAN, JAMES F. KAVANAGH, and CHARLES A. FERGUSON (Eds.). Child Phonology, Volume 1: Production and Volume 2: Perception